CORRESPONDENCE

OF

ROBERT DUDLEY, EARL OF LEYCESTER,

DURING HIS GOVERNMENT

OF

THE LOW COUNTRIES,

IN THE YEARS 1585 AND 1586.

EDITED BY

JOHN BRUCE, F.S.A. TREASURER OF THE CAMDEN SOCIETY.

PRINTED FOR THE CAMDEN SOCIETY,

M.DCCCXLIV.

Reprinted with the permission of the Royal Historical Society
AMS PRESS
NEW YORK • LONDON

First AMS EDITION published 1968
Manufactured in the United States of America

Series No. I, 27

AMS PRESS, INC.
NEW YORK, N.Y. 10003

COUNCIL

OF

THE CAMDEN SOCIETY,

FOR THE YEAR 1843-4.

President,
THE RIGHT HON. LORD BRAYBROOKE, F.S.A.

THOMAS AMYOT, ESQ. F.R.S. Treas., S.A. *Director.*
C. FREDERICK BARNWELL, ESQ. M.A., F.R.S., F.S.A.
THE REV. PHILIP BLISS, D.C.L., F.S.A.
JOHN BRUCE, ESQ. F.S.A. *Treasurer.*
JOHN PAYNE COLLIER, ESQ. F.S.A.
C. PURTON COOPER, ESQ. Q.C., D.C.L., F.R.S., F.S.A.
T. CROFTON CROKER, ESQ. F.S.A., M.R.I.A.
SIR HENRY ELLIS, K.H., F.R.S., Sec. S.A.
THE REV. JOSEPH HUNTER, F.S.A.
SIR FREDERICK MADDEN, K.H., F.R.S., F.S.A.
THE REV. LANCELOT SHARPE, M.A., F.S.A.
THOMAS STAPLETON, ESQ. F.S.A.
WILLIAM J. THOMS, ESQ. F.S.A., *Secretary.*
ALBERT WAY, ESQ. M.A., DIR. S.A.
THOMAS WRIGHT, ESQ. M.A., F.S.A.

The COUNCIL of the CAMDEN SOCIETY desire it to be understood that they are not answerable for any opinions or observations that may appear in the Society's publications; the Editors of the several Works being alone responsible for the same.

INTRODUCTION.

In the year 1840 Frederic Ouvry esquire kindly placed at the disposal of the Camden Society a MS. volume which had been found amongst certain old papers preserved in the office of a solicitor in the city of London. Besides a treatise upon another subject, Mr. Ouvry's volume contains a transcript of a collection of letters of Robert Dudley earl of Leycester, written between the 3rd of April and the 25th of October 1586, during his first mission to the Low Countries as lieutenant-general of the forces sent by queen Elizabeth to the aid of the united provinces in their great contest against Spain.

In the course of inquiries instituted by the council of the Camden Society, it appeared that the originals of these letters were not known to be in existence, but that there were preserved in the national collection at the British Museum certain other letters written by and to the earl of Leycester during that same mission to the Low Countries, which tended to complete the correspondence of which the letters contained in Mr. Ouvry's volume formed a part.

Such being the case, it was proposed that a selection from those letters in the British Museum should be published together with those in Mr. Ouvry's volume, in such manner as to present, as nearly as possible, a complete view of the correspondence between the earl and the English government during the mission alluded to. This proposal was agreed to by Mr. Ouvry and the

ii INTRODUCTION.

Council of the Camden Society, and is carried into effect in the present volume.

Mr. Ouvry's MS. is a folio volume containing 74 leaves. It commences with the earl of Leycester's letters, which are entitled, " Letters from the earle of Leycester to the lords of the councell, Mr. secretarie Walsingham, and others, &c. 1586." They are copied book-wise, in a hand-writing of the beginning of the seventeenth century, and extend from fol. 1 to fol. 62, both inclusive. The remainder of the volume is occupied with a narrative entitled, " A relation written by sir Daniell Dunne knight, doctor of the civill lawe, of the whole prosecution of the nullitie between the earle of Essex and his then wife the lady Frauncis Howard." This is written in a hand of a little later date.

The transcript of the earl's letters was all made by one scribe, and, from occasional corrections in the hand of an older person, may be concluded to have been examined.

The transcriber was not a practised hand, which especially appears from his mistakes in the copying of numerals. Obvious blunders in his transcript prove, also, that he was not acquainted with the names of the persons and places in the Low Countries mentioned by the earl. In some instances he endeavoured to supply the place of a word which he was unable to decypher by a poor attempt at a *fac-simile*, which has frequently increased the difficulty.

It was thought, at first, that the transcript was a book kept by the earl for the entry of his letters before they were despatched, which seemed to be rendered the more probable by the circumstance that in no single instance has the transcriber copied the signature to a letter. But besides the inference deducible from the mistakes in the transcript and especially from those in the names of places in the neighbourhood of which the letters were written, an entry on fol. 14 proves that at any event one of the letters was copied after it had passed through the hands of the person to whom it was addressed. At the place referred to (see page 255) there ends a long letter from the earl to Walsyngham, and immediately afterwards there follows, as if it had been a postscript to the letter, an abstract of its contents, which the transcriber no doubt found written on the back of it. From a comparison of one item in this abstract—" meaneth to send over so much as I have prested," with the parallel passage in the letter, —" I will speedely send over to you for that *you* have prested,"—it is clear that the abstract was made by Walsyngham, and, if so, of course after the letter reached its destination, and that it must have been copied afterwards. If that was the case with one of the letters, it was probably so with all of them.

Within the left-hand board of the binding of Mr. Ouvry's volume is written the name " H. Powle," which a comparison of hand-writing proves to be the autograph of Henry Powle of Shottesbrooke, in the county of Berks, speaker of the house of commons and master of the rolls in the reign of William III. Mr. Powle was an antiquary of some eminence, very learned in precedents and parliament-journals,[a] and a great collector of MSS. principally those relating to English history. Upon his death, in January 1692, his collections were added to those of lord-chancellor Somers, and when his noble library was divided between sir Joseph Jekyll, then master of the rolls, and sir Philip Yorke, afterwards lord-chancellor Hardwicke, portions of Mr. Powle's collections were assigned to each of them. In 1739, shortly after the death of sir Joseph Jekyll, his MSS. were sold by auction, and certain lots which originally formed part of Mr. Powle's collection were purchased by Mr. Umfreville, and are now in the Lansdowne Collection in the British Museum. It is probable that Mr. Ouvry's volume was sold at sir Joseph Jekyll's sale, but to whom does not appear. Some entries on its blank leaves show it to have been in the possession of one " G. Eld," in the year 1776, but who he was, or in what manner it came to the place where Mr. Ouvry found it, is quite unknown. What is known, however, is sufficient to establish the genuineness of the volume.

[a] Burnet's Own Time, ii. 82, ed. 1823, 8vo. Oxon.

Mr. speaker Powle's autograph carries it back to about 100 years after the letters were written, and the hand-writing reduces that period to about from 30 to 50 years.

If the original letters should hereafter be discovered, which is very likely to be the case now that attention is drawn to them, there will probably appear to be some slight inaccuracies in the present publication, arising out of the incompetency of the transcriber, and the circumstance that he generally omitted the stops, which no doubt exist in the originals, and often made no distinction between the end and the beginning of sentences. I have consequently been obliged to insert such stops, and, occasionally, to make such division into sentences, as I have thought to be in accordance with the sense.

The other letters inserted in the present publication are principally derived from four volumes of MSS. in the British Museum, the Harleian MS. No. 285, and the Cottonian MSS. Galba, C. VIII. IX. and X.

The first of these is a singularly valuable collection of letters relating to the affairs of the Low Countries, principally written by the earl of Leycester to secretary Walsyngham. Of these letters some precede and others follow those contained in Mr. Ouvry's volume. They are all originals, in the best preservation. The present volume contains forty-six letters derived from this important MS.

The Cottonian MSS. Galba, C. VIII. IX. and X. contain part of a great body of diplomatic correspondence between England and the Low Countries, arranged under the titles of Galba, B. C. D. and E. I. This invaluable collection extends over a period of nearly three hundred years, from the reign of Edward III. to that of James I., and is a vast treasury of knowledge upon all subjects connected with the affairs of the Low Countries. From this source are derived seventy-six letters printed in the present work.

Sixteen other letters have been selected from miscellaneous volumes in the national collection.

INTRODUCTION.

Having explained the origin of the present volume, and the sources whence it has been compiled, I might now leave it to receive the small share of notice which falls to the lot of collections of this description, but, valuable as such collections are to the writer and to the student of history, they are pretty nearly of all books the most unreadable, and I hope, therefore, I shall do what will neither be unacceptable to the members of the Camden Society, nor useless to the reader who consults this volume with a view to any specific inquiry, if, before I dismiss the subject, I give a general notion of the historical bearing of the documents which are here printed.

There were circumstances connected with the war of independence in the Low Countries which occasioned it to be regarded with peculiar interest in England. The oppressions of the duke of Alva, the executions of counts Egmont and Horn, the cruelties of the inquisition, and the fortitude and endurance of the besieged citizens of Haerlem and Leyden, excited feelings of abhorrence against the oppressors, and of commiseration for the oppressed, wherever they were heard of; but in England, the people felt that, in the issue of that tremendous contest, they had something of a personal concern. The principal and ultimate object sought to be attained in the Low Countries by Philip II. was the suppression of a form of christian doctrine which was dearly prized, and was then dominant, in England; but only a few years had elapsed since that same sovereign was king-consort of England, and then multitudes of Englishmen, and amongst them some of the most venerable men in the country, had been driven into exile or consigned to the fagot for the maintenance of that very form of doctrine, and its continued preservation in England depended, under Providence, upon the life of the queen, and her ability to withstand the power which could be brought against her by the oppressor of the united provinces. Recollection of the past and dread of the future in religious matters were at the bottom of all the great political questions of the reign of Elizabeth. The men of that day had witnessed the practical effects of the ascendancy of Roman principles, and feared nothing so much as a return to them. Hence the question of the succession was one of such great anxiety during the life of Mary queen of Scots, hence the long-standing popular hatred against Spain, and hence the peculiar interest felt in the success of the Low Countries in the contest in which they were engaged.

Nor was it a mere dread of a possible, a distant, or a contingent danger by which the minds of English protestants were excited. The contest was one in actual progress, although not exhibited in the form of warfare. It was want of power, and not of will, which prevented the execution of the papal bull by which Elizabeth was declared to be excommunicated and deposed, and her subjects to be absolved from their allegiance. Before the issuing of that bull, Mary had acted in its spirit; she had treated Elizabeth as virtually a usurper by assuming the title of queen of England, and, although it became politically necessary to lay aside that pretension, Mary did so by secretly transferring her claim before she openly renounced it. When her misfortunes as queen of Scots deprived her of direct political power, the eyes and hopes of the English adherents of Rome were turned towards Spain, and it was declared for years before the sailing of the armada, to be the intention of Philip to invade England and drive the heretical usurper from the throne. To hasten the coming of that day, and to keep alive in the minds of the people the expectation of the re-ascendancy of Rome, were objects of the bands of seminary priests and jesuits by whose plottings the government of Elizabeth was disturbed. The contest in the Low Countries was the greatest, if not the only, obstacle in the way of Philip's meditated expedition, for, great as was the power of Spain, it seemed insufficient to maintain at one time a crusade against protestantism in England as well as in the Netherlands; and hence it was, that not merely an abstract community of religious opinion, but a practical regard to the safety of the queen, to the peace of the country, and to the preservation of protestantism, pointed out to Elizabeth's government, that it was policy, if not duty, to keep alive the cause of liberty in the Low Countries.

These considerations were rendered greatly more cogent by the assassination of the prince of Orange. At first that atrocity seemed to be a death-blow to the patriot cause; but, like all similar acts, which are as impolitic as they are wicked, it ultimately increased the popular feeling of which the prince was but the impersonation, and being considered as a consequence of Philip's infamous offer of a large reward to any one who would bring the prince to him, "dead or alive," it aggravated the political hostility by an augmented personal dislike of the Spanish monarch.

Elizabeth had before given assistance to the patriot cause; she was now counselled by her ministers to do so more openly. They advised her to decline the offered sovereignty of the Low Countries, but to send over a considerable body of auxiliary forces, and to place them under the command of some eminent person, who should not merely direct the military operations, but should also assist the states-general with his counsel, and put them in the way of correcting many errors of government into which they had fallen.

It was with great difficulty that the queen was brought to adopt this advice. As a support of subjects against their sovereign, it was a precedent which she disliked. She spoke hardly of the councillors who favoured the interference, even although overborne by their weight and authority. Their high mightinesses the states-general, a many-headed government which had fallen into disrepute amongst its own subjects, formed a theme for her contemptuous ridicule. She doubted whether a contest which was subject to the controul of such persons could ever be successfully conducted. She distrusted the policy of sending away her best soldiers at a time of anticipated invasion, and, with a very customary and characteristic caution, she feared that in the end "the whole burthen of the charges" would light upon her, or that, after years of struggle and expenditure, she should be forced to abandon the cause " in respect of charges."

As soon as a consent was "wrung" from her by her patient ministers, the proposed military aid was despatched under the command of general Norris, and a declaration was published in many languages,[a] in which it was announced to the world that the causes " moving the queen to give aid to the defence of the people afflicted and oppressed in the Low Countries, were not any desire of aggrandizing either herself or her subjects, but to aid the natural people of those countries to defend their towns from sacking and desolation, and thereby to procure them safety, to the honour of God, whom they desire to serve sincerely as Christian people, according to his word, and to enjoy their ancient liberties; to free herself from invading neighbours; and to ensure a continuance of the old-standing intercourse of friendship and merchandise betwixt her people and the inhabitants of those countries."

In the selection of " the person of eminence" to be sent over as lieutenant-general of the queen's forces, and adviser of the states-general, I have not found that there was any doubt. Leycester's previous interference in the affairs of the Low Countries, and his position in this country, as a leader of the low-church party and an acknowledged favourite of the queen, rendered him peculiarly acceptable to the people whom it was desired to succour, whilst his fondness for magnificent display, and the circumstance that, although powerful in the government, he held no office which made his personal attendance at court indispensable, rendered his acceptance of the honourable dignity agreeable to himself and not inconvenient to his colleagues.

The present correspondence opens in September 1585, when the queen's intention to appoint the earl had been notified to the commissioners of the Low Countries, who were waiting in London

[a] There are in the British Museum copies printed in English, Latin, French, and Italian.

to arrange the terms upon which her majesty's assistance was to be granted, and Leycester was in the full bustle of preparations for departure, summoning his friends to accompany him (p. 5), and purchasing armour and provisions (p. 6). Of a sudden, some previously unconsidered difficulty occurred to the mind of the queen, and she ordered the earl to suspend his preparations (p. 4). He received the mandate in bed, at one o'clock in the morning, and immediately returned two letters to Walsyngham, through whom the order had been transmitted, one evidently intended to be shown to the queen, all submission and respect (letter II.), the other designed for the eye of the secretary alone, full of disappointment and annoyance, a genuine expression of the feelings of a jaded courtier, " weary," as he says, " of life and all." (letter III.)

The hinderance, whatever it was, was soon removed, and the earl's preparations were resumed, his friend Walsyngham warning him of the difficulty which would be sure to arise with the queen, if his requests " should minister matter of charge." (p. 9.) The earl protested that he had no such design, that he sought nothing by his journey but to do service to her majesty and the realm, and had no desire but to go properly accompanied. With that view he obtained permission to levy 500 of his own tenants and servants to attend upon his person (letter V.).

The documents which follow, numbered VI. VII. and VIII. contain the heads of the earl's instructions, the advice given him by the commissioners of the states-general, and his own paper of memoranda as to the points to which his attention should be directed. These papers prove with what different intentions the queen despatched the earl, and the earl himself went upon this important mission. In his instructions it is obvious that he was sent with an express disavowal on the part of the queen of any intention to govern the Low Countries, either directly or through the medium of the earl. Both had been offered to her, and both had been refused. " She would not take so much upon her as to command them in such absolute sort;" but, she told the states-general, that unless she found them ready to listen to the advice to be given to them by her lieutenant-general for the remedying of the disorders in their government, and the more speedy attainment of a peace, she should esteem her favours unworthily bestowed. The advice of the commissioners and the earl's own private minute proceed upon an entirely different basis. The administration of the government by the earl was clearly anticipated by the commissioners, and an authority as large as that of the prince of Orange or any previous governor was considered necessary by the earl.

Even after every thing had been settled, the queen delayed to dismiss the earl, either, as he suspected, from a mistrust of his discretion in pecuniary matters (p. 21), or, as is more likely, from some suspicion of his real intentions in reference to the assumption of the government of the Low Countries. At length all difficulties were overcome, and on the 4th of December 1585, having taken leave of the queen, and gratified the citizens of London with a review of a body of 600 horse, the earl set off to Harwich, the place of his intended embarkation, and was received by the corporate towns on his road with honours only paid to the most distinguished visitors. His farewell letter to Lord Burghley, written on the road (p. 21), and the reply of the veteran statesman (p. 29), are of importance, and will be read with interest. They emphatically express the deep sense which the writers entertained of the importance of the earl's mission. The earl reiterates the most earnest entreaties for Burghley's assistance, and adjures him to maintain the cause in spite of the queen's occasional mislike. Burghley, with a solemnity which cannot be doubted, pronounces himself an accursed person in the sight of God, if he omitted to advance a cause which tended to his glory, to the safety of the queen, and the preservation of the realm.

In the appendix (No. 1.) will be found a journal of the earl's voyage, written by the distinguished seaman who had the charge of the accompanying fleet. Even in this narrative are found traces of that hasty, uncertain, and impetuous temper, which so often marred the success of the earl's best designs. He had omitted to give notice of the port at which he designed to disembark, and was "greatly offended" with the admiral because he had not provided a sufficient number of pilots to carry all the fleet to any place he might appoint. Upon a meeting of such pilots as could be procured, the earl was advised that the Brill, the place where he declared it was his "will and purpose" to land, was not a suitable harbour for his fleet. Leycester dismissed them with a peremptory declaration that to the Brill he would go. The submissive pilots professed their willingness to do their best, but within a few hours the earl changed his mind, and agreed to adopt the advice which he had before despised (pp. 461, 462).

On Friday the 10th December, Leycester's fleet, consisting in the whole of nearly a hundred sail, neared the low land of Flushing, and shortly after noon he disembarked with a very gallant and noble body of attendants (p. 464). His accomplished nephew sir Philip Sydney was there to welcome him, and upon his removal on the following day to Middleburg, the chief persons of Zealand assembled around him, and amongst them the widow of the prince of Orange and his illustrious son Maurice, then a boy of about eighteen. At Flushing began a course of rejoicing and feasting which marked Leycester's course for a considerable time. Bonfires, fireworks, acted pageants, and all the grotesque accompaniments of civic rejoicing, awaited him at every town. The triumphal pomp of his reception at the Hague was celebrated in a series of engravings. The people of Rotterdam availed themselves of this joyful occasion to erect the well-known statue of their townsman Erasmus. The inhabitants of Amsterdam sent forth to welcome him a shoal of monsters of the deep, "whales and others of great hugeness," who seized upon the ship in which he sailed, and towed it in safety to the shore. The cities and towns emulated each other in the warmth of his welcome, the burghers formed themselves into a body-guard for him, and the streets resounded as he passed with cries of "God save queen Elizabeth!" uttered as heartily "as if the queen herself had been in Cheapside." (p. 31.)

The earl's correspondence during this period of public gratification has little reference to the main objects of his mission. It seems rather designed to interest the queen on behalf of the people of the Netherlands, by setting before her the exuberance of their gratitude, and the strength of their trust in her powerful support. All sorts of people, from the highest to the lowest, assured themselves, he declared, that, having the queen's good countenance, they should beat all the Spaniards out of their country (p. 30). " Never was there a people," he exclaims, "in the jollity that these be. I would be content to lose a limb that her majesty did see these countries and towns as I have; she would then think a whole subsidy well spent but only to have the good assurance and commandment of a few of these towns. I think there be not the like places again for England to be found." The earl is constant in this story (pp. 29, 46), but the queen's deep-seated prejudices could never be removed, and his representations worked not " that good effect that were to be wished," (p. 35.) which Walsyngham attributed to the unpleasantness of " all things that minister matter of charges." (ibid.)

Other countries regarded the queen's interference with admiration. It was a throwing down the gauntlet to the king of Spain, which in a female sovereign seemed an act of heroism. The protestant princes of Germany were loud in her praise (pp. 35, 48); even out of Italy there came kindly messages (p. 35); and the king of Sweden declared, with astonishment, that Elizabeth had taken the crown from her head and suspended it upon the uncertain chances of the war.

For some time after the arrival of the earl the forces of the Dutch and English were dispersed in winter quarters, but the enemy still kept the field with 4000 foot and 1500 horse, scouring the country, now here now there, and putting in danger the unprotected frontier towns (p. 64). The states agreed to form a camp in order to bridle these incursions; and the earl, in anticipation of an active compaign, solicited permission to levy a body of the " Irish idle men." He also entreated the queen to advance a portion of the stipulated payment for her troops, and to send over sir William Pelham, an experienced soldier whose services he desired to use. But all these things were interrupted by an incident which turned the thoughts of men, both at home and abroad, into another channel.

In the earl's letter of the 14th of January, 1586, (p. 57.) he describes himself as taken by surprise, on new year's day, by a visit paid to him by a solemn deputation from the states-general, headed by the chancellor and accompanied by heralds, who came to offer him the absolute government of the united provinces. Through Mr. Davison he replied to the deputies in French, that this was a matter not provided for by the contract between the queen and the states; that he had already more laid upon him than so weak shoulders were able to bear; that the queen had sent him only to serve them, which he had promised to do faithfully and honestly, and that he wished it rather to be in the way already agreed upon than in that now proposed.

This answer only stimulated them to further entreaties. The people of all classes supplicated him to yield to the general wish; and finally, with the advice and concurrence of Davison, sir Philip Sydney, and the other Englishmen there present, who thought it a proceeding likely to advantage the public service, the earl accepted the offered authority. On the 25th of January he was solemnly installed, taking an oath to preserve their religion and maintain their ancient rights and privileges, whilst the members of the states-general, and other persons in authority, bound themselves by an oath of fidelity to him. On the same day, which was the 6th Feb. N. S., a public placard, or proclamation, certified to the people the consummation of this important proceeding, and that the authority given to the earl over and above that vested in him by her majesty, was that of " the highest and supreme commandment and absolute authority above and in all matters of warfare," with the administration and use of policy and justice over the united provinces, " to execute and administrate the same, with such power and authority as have had in times past all the other governors of the Low Countries before him...also with power to collect profits and receive and administrate all contributions towards the maintenance of the war." In conformity with this authority all persons were admonished to acknowledge " his foresaid excellency," as governor and captain general, and to " honour, respect, and obey him as they ought to do."

When the earl determined to accept the proffered authority, he also resolved to send Mr. Davison home to explain to the queen " upon what necessity" he had acted. This intention was announced on the 14th January (p. 63) during a long-continued easterly wind, which would have brought Davison to England in a few days, but for some reason which does not appear, his despatch from the Hague was delayed until the 5th of February. (p. 94.) He was detained at the Brill " five or six days" (p. 117) by stormy weather, and did not arrive in London until the 13th of February. Four weeks had then elapsed since Leycester first announced to Burghley his intention to accept the government. During that period his few letters had been principally occupied with other matters, contenting himself with general and rather flippant allusions to the acceptance of the government, and the reasons to be yielded " when Mr. Davison comes." In the mean time the act of assumption had been formally concluded, and the principal persons in the country, both Englishmen and others, had taken the oath of fidelity to the new governor.

Leycester must have known little of the temper and disposition of Elizabeth, or must have presumed upon the possession of far more authority over her mind than he really had, if he thought she could be thus treated with impunity. The first whisper of the earl's intended acceptance of the government aroused her indignation. To do so was to contradict not only his instructions and her verbal command, but also her published declaration, in which she had protested that she sought not to obtain any authority over the people of the Low Countries, whom she still recognised as subjects of the king of Spain, but merely designed to assist them in maintaining their ancient privileges against his oppression, and the exercise of their faith against the tyranny of Rome. " Such an act," she declared, " would make her infamous;" and she determined to prevent the acceptance of the obnoxious authority, or, if it were too late to do that, to compel the earl to lay it down. Burghley, Walsyngham, and Hatton, strove in vain to mitigate the fury of their mistress. They argued that the action was both honourable and profitable; honourable, that a servant of hers should command such a people, and profitable, as placing all their resources at her controul. Such arguments admitted the justice of the queen's complaints, and were consequently altogether ineffectual to appease her anger. And although the earl did not write to her, which was another cause of complaint against him, persons about the court received glowing narratives of his proceedings in the Low Countries, and reported them to the queen, not always with the best feeling towards the absent governor. One circumstance which thus came to her ears especially displeased her. She was told that the countess of Leycester was about to go over to the earl with a train of ladies, and such rich " coaches, litters, and side-saddles," as should make a court which should surpass her own. (page 112.) This information stirred the impatient queen to " extreme choler and dislike of all the earl's proceedings;" and she declared " with great oaths" that she would have "no more courts under her obeysance than her own, and that she would revoke the earl with all speed." (ibid.) The earl's friends denied the report most vehemently, perhaps with more vehemence than truth,* and succeeded in pacifying the queen

* It seems clear, from a passage in a letter of sir Philip Sydney's, dated 24th March, 1586, (Harl. MS. 287, fol. 1.) that the countess certainly at one time designed to join the earl in the Low Countries. Sir Philip Sidney disapproved of her intention, and wished that " some way might be taken to stay my lady," as he terms her, " in England."

upon that point; but still the retention of Davison, and the earl's omission to write to her, with the constant arrival of messengers bearing letters from him to persons about her court, offended her majesty more and more. Perhaps her anger was never so much excited.

The first rumour of this state of things in London reached the earl on the 7th February, two days only after Davison had been despatched. "A flying tale," as he expresses it, was then told him, that her majesty disliked his assumption of the title of "excellency." He immediately wrote to Walsyngham upon the subject, most injudiciously defending that assumption by alleging, that, if he had delighted in titles, he might have taken a higher one, which Mr. Davison could tell them had been offered to him (p. 94).

On the following day the character of the coming storm was made more apparent to him by the receipt of a joint letter from the treasurer, the chamberlain, the vice-chamberlain, and secretary Walsyngham, written by the queen's command, and in which the earl was informed that her majesty greatly misliked his acceptance of the government, and would "disavow wholly that which was done therein." (p. 96.) This letter was written in London on the 25th January, the very day when Leycester's glory attained its summit, in the acceptance of the government at the Hague. Never did bubble burst more suddenly. The earl instantly perceived that he had gone too far, that he had raised a spirit against which it was impossible for him to contend, and in two letters, one to the lords who had written to him (p. 95), and the other a private letter to Walsyngham (p. 99), with most commendable pliancy submitted himself to her majesty's pleasure, but with an evident hope that the reasons to be assigned by Davison would work a change in her opinion. To aid those reasons, he indulged, also, in some little rhetorical flourishes, by which we must presume that Elizabeth was occasionally weak enough to be moved, for they are common to all letters designed for her eye.

Leycester's friends at court, and indeed all the members of the government, and especially Burghley and Hatton, made most strenuous exertions on his behalf, but his own folly in detaining Davison had ruined everything. Such defence as they could make the queen would not hear (p. 104), and all that Burghley could do was to beseech her " to keep one ear" for the reasons to be rendered by Davison (p. 113), whilst Hatton and Walsyngham studied day by day how to delay her meditated purposes in the hope of Davison's arrival. (ibid.)

On the 7th of February further delay was found to be unattainable, and instructions in conformity with the queen's angry views were begun to be prepared for sir Thomas Heneage, whom she determined to send off immediately into the Low Countries. Burghley, the only person who on such an occasion possessed any influence over the queen, was at this time absent from the court, and was not expected to return until the 13th. It was hoped that he might be able to procure some modification of her fiery instructions, and every possible artifice to gain time was resorted to by Hatton and Walsyngham. On the 10th the instructions were completed (p. 105), and on the same day the queen wrote that celebrated letter to the earl which stands pre-eminent amongst her majesty's specimens of royal objurgation (p. 110.) Still Davison had not arrived, nor had Burghley returned, and Hatton and Walsyngham, to gain a few days' longer delay, went the length of altering a letter written by Leycester to Hatton, blotting out some things which they thought would be offensive, and mending some other parts as they thought best (p. 113). In that shape they shewed or read it to the queen, and by that or some other manœuvre succeeded in still further delaying the departure of Heneage. Early on Sunday the 13th February, Davison arrived. Thunderstruck at the tidings which awaited him, this unhappy minister, whose hard fortune it was to be made the scape-goat in the only two transactions of great moment in which he was engaged, immediately presented himself at the court. He was doubtful whether the queen would admit him into her presence, but as soon as she was informed of his arrival, she "retired into her withdrawing chamber," whither Davison was immediately ushered. The scene which followed is related by him in letter XLIII. p. 118, although with less particularity than could have been desired. He was so anxious to detail his own speech, that, in comparison with it, he esteemed "the bitter and hard terms" used by the queen, and "the old griefs" into which she "oftentimes digressed," to be unworthy of notice. It is clear, however, from his own statements, that Davison, like the ministers at home, altogether failed in answering the queen. He proved, as they had done, that it was politic and expedient for the earl to accept the government, but her objection was, that it impeached her honour, and she added, in aggravation of the earl's conduct, that he had taken the authority without consulting her, "as if her consent had been nothing worth" (p. 118), and in a way which shewed that "he respected more his own greatness than her honour or service."

Davison tendered the earl's letter, of which he was the bearer, but in her anger the queen refused to receive it, and, soon after Davison had left her, she ordered Heneage to depart with his memorable instructions and letter, the substance of which was, that the earl was to resign his authority with the same publicity with which he had received it.

Alarmed for the consequences of this determination, Davison again sought an interview, and so far prevailed that the queen received the earl's letter, opened and began to read it, and then put it into her pocket, "to read," says Davison, "as I think at more leisure." (p. 122.) Its contents we know not, but the same evening she stayed Heneage until he heard her further pleasure.

The next day Burghley returned, and "laboured very earnestly," but in vain, to procure the revocation of her angry message. All that he could obtain was an authority to Heneage to withhold a letter which the queen had written to the states if he thought its delivery would be prejudicial to the public cause, and a withdrawal of that portion of his instructions which imposed upon the earl the disgrace of a public resignation.

Heneage being long detained by contrary winds, (p. 152,) did not reach Flushing until the 3rd of March, when he immediately intimated to the earl, that he had been sent, "both most suddenly and unlooked for," to deliver to him her majesty's pleasure. (p. 149.) He was an old friend of Leycester's, and the two courtiers proceeded very amicably to concoct, out of the discretion given to Heneage by his second instructions, such a case as would justify them in neutralising as much as possible the queen's displeasure. Leycester, also, strove to divert the storm from himself to Davison. He wrote to the lords of the council (p. 162), to Walsyngham (p. 165), and to Davison himself (p. 168), bitterly complaining of the insufficient way in which Davison had defended his conduct, and urging that he himself was earnest to acquaint her majesty before he accepted the office, but that Davison and others, presuming upon the urgency of the case, persuaded him against his will to take the authority at once, and that Davison undertook to satisfy her majesty. Davison's comments upon this mean-spirited accusation are a complete answer (p. 168). He intimates that the earl needed very little entreaty to induce him to accept the honour, and asserts that he concealed from those who persuaded him to do so the all-important fact, that the queen had commanded him to the contrary. They thought that they were merely dealing with a case in which the earl doubted whether the queen would approve; the earl knew that the queen had already considered the question and expressed a most authoritative adverse opinion. Leycester's best friends at court saw the fallacy of his subterfuge (p. 206), but, between the queen and the earl, Davison was obliged to absent himself from court for a considerable period, and was recalled only to fall into greater trouble.

The earl's next messenger to the queen was sir Thomas Sherley, whose letter, No. LXII. in the present volume, (p. 171,) will take its place amongst the best extant accounts of Elizabeth's mode of dealing in state affairs. It presents also the reasons of her displeasure with Leycester in a more tangible form than the similar letter from Davison, No. XLIII. p. 117. It is impossible to read this letter of sir Thomas Sherley without feeling admiration for the great qualities of the sovereign whom it portrays. Her acute perception of those moral consequences from Leycester's act which the practised politicians around her treated with too much disregard, her ready way of disentangling the sophistical webs in which the clever and unscrupulous advocate endeavoured to inclose her, her firmness in adhering to opinions which, although opposed by all her ordinary advisers, were clearly right, and the spirited way in which she defended her own views, offer incontestable proofs of her fitness for the high office in which she was placed. Two of her brief and forcible sentences contain the pith of the whole question between her and Leycester, and as long as they remain will justify her opposition to his vainglorious attempt at self-aggrandisement. "It is sufficient to make me infamous to all princes, having protested the contrary in a book which is translated into divers and sundry languages;" this was one point: " I may not endure that any man should alter my commission and the authority that I gave him, upon his own fancies and without me;" this was the other.

Whilst this question remained open there was the greatest difficulty in engaging the queen in any other business relating to the Low Countries. Men and money were wanted, but she was immovable until she heard from sir Thomas Heneage. Confusion and danger necessarily ensued, which renewed and increased the queen's desire for peace, and induced her to listen to proposals made by various merchants who offered to open negotiations with the prince of Parma (p. 231). They turned out to be but indiscrete negotiators. Their employment became known, and did infinite harm by giving rise to jealousies and suspicions in the minds of the people of the Low Countries (p. 247).

INTRODUCTION.

The report of sir Thomas Heneage's proceedings was brought by Mr. Vavasour, whose account of his reception (letter LXXII.) is printed at p. 195. He does not state the contents of his despatches, but it is evident from other letters that the alterations which Burghley procured in Heneage's instructions were taken advantage of to defeat the queen's intention. Heneage set before her that he found that great danger was likely to result to the public cause from compelling the earl to resign, and that he therefore thought it best to delay acting upon his commission until he received further instructions. The ministers at home determined to take advantage of this representation in order, if possible, to procure Heneage's recall, and, accordingly, Burghley, in the presence of Walsyngham, startled his royal mistress by a very solemn tender of his resignation unless she would consent to change her course of policy towards the earl. The experienced statesman expressed himself in language which the queen deemed to be presumptuous. His "round speech" amazed her, but after several other interviews and some vacillation she consented " to do anything she might with her honour." Burghley proposed that she should consent that the earl should continue in his government " until the state of the matter might be better considered by her," which she at first agreed to. A little reflection seems to have shewn her that such a consent was in effect a ratification of that very authority which she had so vehemently opposed, and she sought to modify her acquiescence in a way which brought on fresh arguments, and ultimately terminated in her agreeing that the earl should continue in his office " until the council of state could devise some such qualification of his title and authority as might remove her objection without peril to the public welfare." Heneage was also directed to communicate to the states, in reference to the underhand negotiations for peace, that in any treaty between the queen and Spain, she would have no less care for their safety than for her own. Two letters of lord Burghley's (LXXIII. p. 196, and LXXV. p. 204,) contain the particulars of these transactions related in his usual copious manner. There are other letters also upon the same subject from Walsyngham to the earl (p. 205), and from the queen to Leycester (p. 209).

This change in the queen's mind was received by Leycester and Heneage as if it had amounted to an absolute confirmation of the earl's authority, leaving the question of qualification to be considered by the council of state at some future time, and Heneage, after communicating the queen's pleasure to the states-general in such manner as was the least disagreeable to the earl, and making in her name such promises in reference to the negotiations for peace as were likely to be most pleasing to the people of the Low Countries, prepared to take his departure for England.

But they were reckoning without their host. The queen was anxiously waiting to hear what was done by the council of state, (p. 233,) and, when she found that Heneage was returning without effecting any qualification whatever, all her former angry feelings were re-excited. She summoned Burghley and Walsyngham to her presence, and insisted upon their sending letters to Heneage prohibiting his return until he had executed her former commands. Burghley argued against doing so, he contended that nothing had been done contrary to her majesty's direction, he begged her to await the return of Heneage who was already on the road, he predicated all kinds of evil if she persisted, but in vain; "she grew so passionate in the matter as she forbade him to argue any more." (p. 240.) The official letter written on this occasion is printed at p. 241, and was accompanied by the one that follows it, No. LXXXIX. p. 243, which was written by the queen herself to sir Thomas Heneage. This is another of those singular letters which, like that to Leycester, before commented upon, and others which are well known, give us such a vivid perception of the character of this extraordinary woman. "Do that you are bidden," she says to Heneage, "and leave your considerations for your own affairs; for in some things you had clear commandment, which you did not, and in other none, and did. . . . . Think you I will be bound by your speech to make no peace for mine own matters without their consent? It is enough that I injure not their country nor themselves in making peace for them without their consent. I am assured of your dutiful thoughts, but I am utterly at squares with this childish dealing." These terse and forcible sentences may indicate qualities which in a woman are not amiable, and which may have made Elizabeth a very disagreeable person within the narrow circle of her court, but they indicate also powers of understanding and moral qualities, which, in a state of society like that in which Elizabeth lived, and in a government like that of which she was the head, fitted her to be a great and popular sovereign.

These fresh instructions reached Heneage at Flushing, where he was detained by illness on his route homewards. Leycester professed the greatest readiness to obey her majesty's commands. All Holland and Zealand, he protested, should not make him keep the obnoxious authority one hour after Heneage's arrival, and nothing would better content him than to leave not only the title but all authority of government. (p. 262.)

Heneage's illness gave Leycester's friends at home an opportunity of still further trying their influence over the queen on his behalf. Burghley laboured to procure from her a permission for Leycester to continue for the present in his authority, and that Heneage, "being sick," might return home; but no inducement could prevail upon her to forego a public manifestation of her dislike to the earl's government. Insisting upon that, she yielded thus far, that Heneage should confer with the council of state in what manner, without damage to the state, the earl might resign the title and authority of absolute governor, having granted to him in his character of her majesty's lieutenant-general the direction of the martial affairs of the Low Countries. (p. 267.) After conference upon this point Heneage was to return home and report to her majesty the resolution of the council of state.

With these new instructions Heneage returned to Arnheim to hold the directed conference (p. 280). Leycester's letters are silent as to the result, but it appears in a letter from the council of state to the queen, printed in the appendix. (p. 473.) After the most humble acknowledgment of the blame-worthy precipitation with which they had originally granted the authority, they set before her the difficulty and peril of revoking it in the existing position of their affairs, and entreat her not to insist upon their doing so, until, their affairs being more settled and the circumstances of the whole business fully discussed, they might, with greater security, confer with her majesty, and determine what might be most honourable to her and most conducive to the welfare of their commonwealth and religion.

Here this matter ended. Incidents of a more stirring character fully occupied the attention of the council of state and the queen during the few months which intervened between the date of the letter of the council of state and the period when the correspondence in this volume closes. Heneage returned to London, and was favourably received (p. 307), and Leycester retained his bubble dignity. By the successive comparatively trifling alterations and modifications to which the queen was induced to yield by the practised statesmen about her, there is no doubt that she was driven from her first position; but, in effect, she was as successful as if Leycester had been instantly deposed. She had made her displeasure known, and, in doing so, had far more than vindicated herself from any suspicion of collusion. No sooner was the state of her feelings whispered in the Low Countries than the council began to watch with jealousy every exercise of the authority they had bestowed. Neither Leycester's prudence nor his temper was fitted to withstand a hostile scrutiny. Bickerings ensued on both sides; he began " to set the better leg afore" with them, and to handle " my masters," as he termed them, " somewhat plainly and roughly too." Crouch as he might to the queen, he was unwilling to be " over-boarded by churls and tinkers " (p. 312); but even that he was obliged to submit to. He soon found that it was " a monstrous government where so many heads do rule" (p. 367);

that "her majesty was wont most rightly to hit them off" (ibid.); and that, although willing enough to promise allowances and contributions, they reduced the amount by a variety of deductions, and delayed the payment in such way as to make the sum received of little avail (p. 426). At one time he took "a little conceit" to absent himself from their deliberations (p. 378); a political expedient which has seldom answered, nor did it in that instance. He returned, but it was, as he says, to use flattery to men who ought to have sought him (p. 393). Soon his greatest anxiety was to be recalled. "Would God I were rid of this place!" (p. 392) became the burthen of his letters, and when at length he was enabled to announce to the council of state that he was about to leave them, they mortified his vanity, and convinced him of his unpopularity, by using "but slender entreaty" to him to stay. "My credit hath been cracked," he truly remarked, "ever since her majesty sent sir Thomas Heneage hither." (p. 424.)

The dispute with his royal mistress considerably distracted the attention of the earl from the more active duty of his government, that of protecting his subjects against the incursions of the Spanish troops under the command of the prince of Parma. When the earl landed in Holland the Spaniards possessed the whole of Flanders and Brabant, with the exception of some few fortified towns. The Waal was the general boundary between the opposing parties; but the states, and their ally the deposed elector of Cologne, possessed Grave, Venlo, Rhineberg, Ostend, and some other places on the south of that river, whilst the Spaniards held Doesburg, Zutphen, and other places on the north. When Antwerp fell, in the autumn of 1585, it was anticipated that the prince of Parma would immediately advance into the northern provinces, but the early approach of winter, and the gallant defence of Grave, prevented his doing so. Some inroads were made by the Spaniards into Friesland during a frost which occurred in February 1586 (p. 86), but the first considerable exploit of the campaign was the capture of Werle in Westphalia, by Schenck, an indefatigable soldier then in the service of the states (p. 139). The curious stratagem by which this achievement was effected will be found detailed in a paper printed in the appendix (p. 475). Shenck captured the town but not the castle, and being consequently unable to maintain his conquest, gained nothing ultimately by his daring exploit but the destruction of a place in the possession of the enemy. In a few days after the town was taken, a considerable force advanced to attack the intruder, when, finding himself between two enemies, he sallied forth, defeated the advancing army to their great loss, and fought his way in safety to Nuys (p. 167).

As the spring advanced, attention became fixed upon the movements of the prince of Parma. Rumours of various kinds were soon afloat as to his intentions, and several points of attack were successively suggested. In the meantime the earl determined to make an attempt to relieve Grave, the siege of which began to be pressed. A body of Dutch and English troops, commanded by Hohenlohe and Norris, undertook the perilous duty, and accomplished it under circumstances which I have related in a note at p. 225. The relief was effectual. It seemed to place this important town in a state of security (ibid.), and, being the first blow of the campaign, inspired the defenders of the Low Countries with confidence, and, as the earl believed, " appalled" the Spaniards. Advantages of various kinds were sanguinely anticipated from it. The earl even seemed to fancy that the prince was about to retreat in despair into Flanders, whither he talked of following him " at an inch." (p. 245.) He had not yet learned to know his enemy.

The prince, having sent out bodies of troops in various directions, whence arose the contradictory rumours respecting his intended movements, suddenly drew his forces together, and whilst the earl was holding a St. George's day festival at Utrecht (pp. 235, 238), and reviewing the troops which he dreamt of leading into Flanders (p. 251), tidings were brought to him that the prince was in full march towards Grave.

On the 3d of May, the earl was fully apprised of the prince's design. " God send him no better speed than his predecessors had!" was his ejaculation, but he made no mention of any intention to use the human means of prevention at his command. This was written at Amersfort, where he had mustered his troops. Three days afterwards he was still at the same place, but talked of " going" to the succour of Grave, which the prince, he says, was coming to batter with eighteen cannons (p. 258). On the 8th the earl had advanced to Arnheim, but was quite uncertain as to the movements of the enemy (p. 262). On the day following he wrote that Grave had been actually attacked (p. 265), and that he himself was proceeding, not thither, but towards Nimeguen, in order to divert the prince from his design. Three weeks were spent in the expedition to Nimeguen, and the capture of a few forts of little value was its only result; but, in the meantime, the prince gathered his men around Grave without any attempt at interruption, and, in the end, after a furious battery of three hours and a half, and a feigned assault, the timid and inexperienced governor, baron Hemart, rather precipitately capitulated (p. 284, and see note) upon honourable terms.

A panic fear ran through the country, when this disastrous event became known (pp. 287, 291). Grave was the key of the northern provinces. It gave the prince the command of the Waal, and the power of marching forward when he pleased. All the advantages of Leycester's first success were lost at once, and the ridiculous exaltation which ensued upon that petty triumph, was succeeded by a depression not less unwarrantable. The anger of Leycester against the governor was unbounded. He not only subjected him to a public trial for treason against the states, of which there does not seem to have been any proof, but with revengeful enmity sent the unhappy man to the scaffold, in opposition to the advice of all the principal persons of the country. This sacrifice terrified the people rather than inspired them with courage,[*] and if the prince had advanced at once, it seems likely

[*] The circumstances of Hemart's trial and execution are related at pp. 308, 309.

that his success would have been considerable. Caution, and the entreaties of the elector of Cologne, made him determine rather to follow up his success by clearing the country in his rear, and he first directed his march to Venlo. No effort was made for its relief, except a daring but very inadequate attempt of Schenck and Williams, related at p. 319; indeed the prince had scarcely commenced the siege when the inhabitants, actuated by fear, seized the gates and let in his forces (p. 322).

The general terror was now at its height, and, as is usual amongst incompetent men in a time of trouble, dissension and mutual recrimination took the place of action. Leycester's letters are mere complaints of every thing and every body. At home and in the Low Countries, the queen, the council of state, sir John Norris, count Hohenlohe, prince Maurice, the treasurer, the auditor, everybody, was out of favour with him.

The sinking courage of the people was for a while arrested by the surprise and capture of Axel, by prince Maurice and sir Philip Sydney; an heroic action, the particulars of which are related by the earl at p. 337. The place was important, and the mode of securing it highly creditable to those concerned; but its capture had no effect upon the movements of the prince of Parma, who, still bent upon clearing the country in his possession of all the enemy's garrisons, had now set himself down before Nuys. The earl, apparently abandoning all hope of arresting the prince's progress, scattered his men about in the fortified towns which were in no danger (p. 350), and trusted in the strength of Nuys, and the inspiriting character of its historical recollections, for its defence. The result may be anticipated. It followed the fate of Grave and Venlo, but with horrors from which they escaped, and which, even in that cruel war, were not common. It was sacked and utterly destroyed (p. 369).

The prince, still pursuing his design of clearing the country northward, now advanced from Nuys to Berck, or Rhineberg, which was occupied by a strong garrison of English and Dutch troops, commanded by Schenck. From this time an obvious change took place in the conduct and policy of the earl. Influenced by the better counsels of sir William Pelham, who had now joined the army in the character of marshal of the host (p. 352), compelled to silence his paltry bickerings and complaints by a letter from the queen, who set them all down to jealousy and other unworthy motives (p. 384), inspirited by supplies of money both from the queen and the states, and urged by strong necessity, he once more determined to gather together the troops scattered about the country, and proceed to the field, in the hope of saving Berck. " We are driven to the last refuge," he remarked, " to try it by force, or all our towns will be gone."

The muster of the troops took place on the 28th August. The earl inspected his army with great ceremony, and every thing seemed to indicate an immediate advance to drive the prince from the siege of Berck, which Schenck was prolonging with unparalleled activity and valour. But a council of war, held after the assembly of the troops, determined that which might just as well have been discovered before, that the earl's force was insufficient for a direct attack upon the prince; and that it was consequently better to endeavour to compel him to raise the siege of Berck by suddenly marching upon Doesburg, an important fortified town to the northward of the Waal, in the possession of the Spaniards (p. 400). This determination was prosecuted with unwonted steadiness and vigour, and the earl was rewarded by the surrender of the place on the 2nd September (p. 406). He then advanced to the siege of Zutphen, and of two forts situate on the opposite bank of the river.

This policy was successful. The prince, tired out by the unceasing activity of Schenck, and alarmed for the safety of his garrison towns in Guelderland, relinquished the siege of Berck and marched to their succour. The memorable contest in which sir Philip Sydney was wounded took place on the 22nd September, upon an attempt made by the prince to throw a supply of provisions into Zutphen. Being repulsed, he withdrew his troops, and shortly afterwards retired into winter quarters. Leycester kept the field for a few weeks longer, during which time the forts opposite to Zutphen were taken by the extraordinary bravery of sir Edward Stanley (p. 428); and Deventer was garrisoned by a proceeding neither less extraordinary nor less courageous on the part of sir William Pelham. The narrative of this last exploit written by Archer, which is printed in the appendix (p. 478), will be found well worthy of attention.

Here ended the military exploits of a campaign which neither added to the stability of the Low Countries nor conferred any glory upon Leycester. It was not devoid of brilliant actions, and, except an accusation which the earl brings ostensibly against the English troops, but really against sir John Norris, and which is not therefore much to be depended upon (p. 244), there is nothing in the present volume which indicates any want of valour in the newly levied forces which were under the earl's command. Whenever engaged with the enemy they were successful; but the inactivity which prevailed at head quarters, and the extraordinary policy of throwing the troops into towns not in danger, instead of leading them to the succour of places actually invested, are altogether unaccountable. The poor fellows suffered many varieties of hardship. Leycester's disputes, first with the queen and afterwards with the states, interposed great difficulties in the way of procuring supplies, and reduced " the old ragged rogues," who had been in the service for several months, into such miserable plight for want of clothing, that when the raw recruits, just landed from England, came to see them, they ran away by hundreds (p. 388). Leycester hanged "divers of" these runagates, and desired good watch to be kept at Dover and at Sandwich for those who returned to England without his passport (p. 338), but even the fear of hanging could not retain men who were actually famishing. They joined the service with " the gladdest minds," (p. 347) but " tasting of want," " the poor starved wretches," (p. 260) endeavoured to find their way home again (p. 389), or went over to the enemy (pp. 365-389). At one time five hundred ran away in two days, of whom two hundred were brought back from the sea-side (p. 338). At another time four hundred deserters were taken and some executed "for example," but "not many," adds the earl, "for that in conscience they suffer overmuch." (p. 365.) At the close of the campaign their miseries still continued unredressed, for, in a letter from sir William Pelham to Leycester, which is not printed in the present collection, but which is dated the 15th October 1586 "at the camp before Zutphen;" the gallant lord-marshall thus describes the condition of his troops : " To say rightly, such are their miseries as I know not how to turn me to satisfy them, for some wanting wherewith to feed them, others almost naked, many falling daily sick, and all in general barefoot wanting hose or shoes, do by hundreds flock about me if I stir abroad amongst them, crying for relief of these extremities." [a]

The conduct of one portion of his recruits drew from the earl an observation the accuracy of which has been confirmed by the experience of military men in all ages. After stating to Walsyngham the grief of his heart to see "your youths in England how clean they be marred and spoiled for ever being able to serve her majesty and the realm," the earl proceeds thus: "I am ashamed to think, much more to speak, of the young men that have come over. Believe me, you will all repent the cockney kind of bringing up at this day of young men. They be gone from hence with shame enough, and too many that I will warrant shall make as many frays with bludgeons and bucklers as any in London shall do : but such shall never have credit with me again. Our simplest men in shew have been our best men, and your gallant 'bludd and ruffin men' the worst of all others." (p. 228.)

Besides containing a narrative of the important events of which I have given an outline, the present collection presents many of those brief but vivid glimpses of the minds and morals of promi-

[a] Cotton. MS. Galba, C. x. fol. 65.

nent persons, and of the general state of society, those living exhibitions of men and manners, which constitute the chief value and the great charm of original letters. Of the character of Elizabeth herself a more valuable exhibition can scarcely exist. At all times she took a great share in the actual business of government; but in reference to the transactions in the Low Countries, whether on account of her feeling of interest in whatever related to Leycester, as some persons may insinuate, or on account of the importance of those transactions in her estimation, as I incline to think, she retained "the whole direction of the causes of that country to herself," and would " by no means .. endure" that they " should be subject to any debate in council otherwise than as she herself should direct." (p. 237.) This circumstance obviously gives the present work an unusual degree of importance. We here see this celebrated sovereign practising the art of government, not through the dim and often deceptive medium of official forms, but, being herself, from the commencement of the book to its conclusion, the moving spring, the real and actual governor. We hear that in her anger against Leycester for accepting the government she gave way in a most unseemly manner to " great oaths" (p. 112), and "bitter and hard terms" (p. 118), and " great threatening words" (p. 151), and "most bitter words" (p. 172), and "stormy speeches" (p. 199), forms of language too common in those days amongst all classes, and in which her father's daughter must have found it rather difficult not to indulge, but the book contains many better things relating to her than these, and no one who would penetrate into her character, or find out the secret of her extraordinary popularity, can do better than study the evidences which are here presented of the working of her mind in its calmer moments.

But these evidences must be regarded with a proper appreciation of the characters of the several persons from whom the letters proceeded. There is a great difference, for example, between the statements of Walsyngham and Burghley. The former writes to Leycester with the freedom which might be expected to be found in a correspondence between two members of the government united by relationship and by a community of opinion and purpose both in politics and religion; but his style is hard, his nature suspicious, his judgments severe and consequently often mistaken. He is apt to refer all the queen's decisions to her little-understood feeling of parsimony, and even insinuates that her mind was failing, when the defect was probably merely a momentary one in his own temper (p. 279). Burghley's letters are quite of a different character. The absence of the same entire confidence is supplied by a great increase of courtesy expressed with something of the verbosity of age. There is a manly plainness in all his statements, whether of facts or opinions; but all that he says of the queen is tempered by a courtier-like respect and deference, and even when he obviously thinks her wrong he strives to make the best of her opinion, and writes with due consideration for her station and her sex. Between the two writers it is not difficult to form an accurate estimate of her conduct, and indeed in this respect we have advantages which they themselves did not possess. For example, they both in the first instance attributed her opposition to Leycester's acceptance of the government to underhand advice, and wrote under that impression. Walsyngham, in his blunt way, exclaims, " Surely there is some treachery amongst ourselves, for I cannot think that she would do this of her own head" (p. 240), whilst Burghley, less positively, remarks that she acted " as one that had been by some adverse counsel seduced." (p. 198.) This notion throws a tinge over several of their letters, and historical writers, building upon those letters alone, might draw very positive and yet very erroneous conclusions, since it is clear from the result that both Walsyngham and Burghley were mistaken. Sir Walter Ralegh, who was suspected to be the queen's private adviser, took measures to vindicate himself (pp. 193, 207); the queen herself assured Leycester " upon her honour," that in the time of her displeasure Ralegh dealt earnestly on his behalf (p. 207). Ultimately Walsyngham admitted his mistake, and wrote to Leycester that he was persuaded that the opposition proceeded from the queen alone, and was not prompted by any person whatever (pp. 269, 279).

In like manner Elizabeth regulated every step that was taken. All Leycester's requests were submitted to her, and we find her determining, directing, controlling every thing, with characteristic decision, combined with forethought, watchful care for the welfare of her people, attention to popular opinion, correct appreciation of the character of her agents, and unquestionable energy of mind. I would not be misunderstood to assert that she was always as right as I think she was in the dispute respecting Leycester's absolute governorship. The very contrary is my opinion; but even in her mistakes there were generally mixed up some of the elements of greatness, and we often stand in need of the clearer light of the present age to enable us to discover her errors. [a]

In such an introduction as the present it is obviously impossible, even if it were desirable, to dwell upon a point of this kind, but I will select a few evidences of the interference I have asserted. At one time Leycester wanted money; the queen was consulted, she refused to allow it to be remitted until she had received an account of the expenditure of the sums which had been sent

[a] One very striking proof of the enlarged and liberal character of the queen's political views occurs in reference to Leycester's proceedings in the Low Countries, although the authority for it does not appear in the present correspondence. Her majesty complained to the earl that he had greatly discouraged the papists, "being good patriots," and "having no less interest in the cause than the protestants themselves," and that by his exclusive conduct in reference to that portion of his subjects, and his new impositions and exactions generally, he had lost much of his popularity. The earl answered, that he had used the papists indifferently as the rest, but that he found them nothing different from those at home, "for both desire change, both love the pope above all things, and no longer hide it than severe laws keep them under." The authority for this will be found in Dr. Birch's note of a letter of Leycester's, dated the 26th June, 1586, contained in the Addit. MS. 4105. If the Camden Society are not weary of the subject I shall hope at a future time to be permitted to publish the original authority with other letters relating to the conclusion of the earl's career as an absolute governor.

already. Again, men were wanted; she consented that they might be enlisted, but limited the number to one or two thousand, because her subjects began to murmur at the employment of so many people of this realm in defence of others at a time when this country was threatened with invasion. For the same reason she objected to sending experienced military men out of the island. She directed the earl to make arrangements for a supply of additional sailors for the English navy in case the Spanish fleet should sail for England. She not only held personal interviews, as we have seen, with Davison, Sherley, Vavasour, and other messengers from the earl, but instructed those who were sent to him with a business-like precision, which Burghley thus describes in the instance of Wilkes when he went over in July 1586:

"After long debate had before her majesty, it was thought most necessary to send one specially from her majesty unto your lordship, having named two or three, but, in the end, her majesty made choice of Mr. Wilkes, the bearer of these my letters, who is instructed not only by some writings as memorials delivered unto him, but also by long speeches of her majesty herself, which she hath recorded in her own tables, and, nevertheless, caused him to put the same more at length in writing, so that he cometh very well informed of her majesty's mind, and appointed, also, to be informed by your lordship of many necessary things for satisfaction of her majesty. And, besides this, he hath letters from her majesty for assurance of her constant persisting in this common action." (p. 360.)

With her own hand she wrote letters containing practical directions, and official letters and instructions were prepared in pursuance of her verbal directions, and probably often in her very language, of which letter LXXVII, p. 208, is a clear instance. When a communication was to be made from the queen to the council of state in the Low Countries, and Leycester's secretary, who was then in England, had been selected by Burghley and Walsyngham as the bearer of it, "her majesty misliked that Mr. Aty should, being your secretary, impart her pleasure to the states in things that might concern yourself" (p. 313), and "suddenly commanded sir Thomas Cecill to be the messenger." Many instances occur of her refusal to adopt the advice of her ordinary ministers. "I have advised her majesty," says Lord Burghley, "to permit my lord of Leycester to continue in the government of those countries wherein God hath lately prospered him, and that you [sir Thomas Heneage] being sick, might return without following that hazardous course that is appointed to you; but her majesty will neither allow of the one or the other, but she saith you shall go back and do that she hath commanded you." One instance more of the nature of her personal interference will suffice. When the early approach of winter suspended military movements, the meeting of the English parliament, and the uneasiness of Leycester's position in his government, determined him to "hie him home," at once, "leaving all things as well as he could." (p. 446.) Without waiting for the queen's permission, with his usual impetuosity, he immediately announced his determination to the states-general (p. 443), stopped the sailing of some of the queen's ships which chanced to be at Middleburgh (p. 444), in order that he might return with them, and entered into a negotiation with the English merchants to make an advance of money. (p. 439.) Shortly afterwards the queen's reply to his application for permission reached him. Her majesty was willing that he should return, but not until a proper arrangement had been made as to how the government should be carried on during his absence "without harm to the public cause, and how her own army, consisting of her people, might also be ruled and directed." (p. 449.) Two days after notice of this determination had been sent to the earl, the queen was apprised of his proceedings at Middleburgh, and that he was expected to sail from thence on the following Friday. (p. 455.) She instantly despatched another messenger with a letter written by her secretary, in which, after referring to "a few lines of her own hand," and the reasons which made her conclude that it was "neither for the earl's honour nor the surety of the cause" that he should leave his government before the arrival of his successor, the secretary continues, " she hath commanded me again to iterate her former order unto you by this bearer, for your continuance on that side till you hear further from her in this behalf." (p. 455.) The earl was too wise to disobey.

The letters of Walsyngham are shrewd, full of facts and business details, and occasionally contain excellent advice and important private information. Like all men who have a genius for plotting or for unravelling plots, he writes about his proceedings in a dark mysterious way, of which the passages in his letters relating to the discovery of Babington's conspiracy, and especially those in letter CXXVIII, p. 340, are examples. Walsyngham wished his correspondent "to make a heretick" of that letter as soon as he had read it (p. 342), but the earl contented himself with running his pen through the more important sentences. I fear they bear a construction not over favourable to the English government, but I must content myself with merely directing attention to them. In the course of Walsyngham's secret inquiries we find that he occasionally stumbled upon information as to little underhand dealings of the queen and other members of the government, which they endeavoured to conceal from his inquisitive eyes. (pp. 223, 231.) He complains of the queen that she trusted too much to fortune, and anxiously wishes that "she did build and depend upon God." (p. 276.) His own practice makes one fear that, in public affairs, his confidence was reposed in a Machiavelian subtlety of which very discreditable persons were the instruments.

Lord Burghley's letters are altogether of a higher order. They partake of the wordy character of the compositions of all cautious men; but abound in information upon practical political subjects, expressed with something of the tone of authority which is natural to "old experience." His lectures upon coin and currency (pp. 41, 356, 357), upon the value of sea-ports to Spain (pp. 39, 40, 359), and upon the removal of the woollen staple (pp. 157, 160, 398), will be read with interest. One regrets to find him advising Leycester to flood the enemy's country in order to destroy their harvests (p. 315); and to read such a sentence as this, "the matter would be evil spoken of, to erect up a coinage in a foreign country of our current money; but, if the gain might be sure, the profit would answer the speech." (p. 153.)

But by far the most important letters in the present volume are those of lord Leycester. In them we not only find the details of the incidents of his government and campaign, but they are the most ably written, and the fullest of information upon every point for which we refer to compositions of this kind. The style in which he wrote is often the simplest, the freest, the most colloquial that can be conceived, and at every turn we find some phrase which we meet with only in the Elizabethan dramatists, or in the compositions of authors who have professedly written in the language of the people. As we read we feel compelled to remember that the earl was an eminent patron of the drama, and that even Shakspere himself was in all probability one of "lord Leycester's players." That his lordship picked up phrases in the same school of language as the dramatist is evident from the following brief quotations. "I am loth to have squares with him now." (p. 12.) "This fellow . . . . took it in such snuff as he came proudly to the states and offered his letters." (p. 47.) "They so shook him up, and with such terms, naming her majesty in scorn, as they took it, as they hurled him his letters and bid him content himself." (ibid.) "It shall go hard but I will win the young count and get the knave about him removed." (p. 74.) "The count Hollock . . . in a great rage . . . sware by no beggars that he would drive his priest in the haven before his face." (ibid.) "He hath some matter a-brewing that will be worth 'God-a-mercy!'" (p. 75.) "I have no cause to have played the fool." (p. 17.) "I am threatened to be used as the prince of Orange was, but I am at a point for that." (p. 141.) "I am sorry to trouble you with the discomfortable dealings of our treasurer here; I assure you it passeth." (p. 264.) "He playeth the knave with me, that being my servant and saying he would follow me, but never came. He is a tall fellow and a good soldier." (p. 304.) "I have now at a pinch helped them, when all their own power and forces are not able to stand them in stead." (p. 312.) "The state of causes here I have written to her majesty at length. They stand uppon tickle terms." (p. 322.) "It is reason they do allow me ... yet it is no reason for me to stand hucking with them for myself." (p. 323.) "Suddenly made a pay to his footmen ... and since to his horsemen: a part he never play before now." (p. 331.) "Fourteen towns moe ... had been gone at a clap." (p. 349.) "I will be master while I remain here, will they nill they." (p. 380.) "Trusting in papists and knaves for the nonce." (p. 389.) "As for the states, I warrant you they see day at a little hole." (p. 217.) Such extracts might be multiplied, but I have quoted enough.

Nor is it only for the use of popular phrases that the earl's letters are conspicuous; they abound in passages of forcible, manly, energetic writing. Where, in the prose writers of that day, can we find any thing more simple and effective than the following explanation addressed to the lords of the council?

"If your lordships will know the cause of so sudden defection of these towns, I must pray you to consider withall, that not only these towns but the whole provinces are in the same wavering estate; yea, the principal men also, and those that have most especial cause to repose themselves upon her majesty, that, to tell you the truth, I know not where I set a sure foot, nor with whom of these countries I may confidently confer of these matters. And requiring of the cause, both by myself and with others of judgment, I find it is not corruption from the prince, for he hath little to give; not desire of the Spanish government, for even the papists abhor it; not mislike of being under her majesty, or her officers, for they desire nothing more than that it will please her majesty to take the sovereignty of them; but, indeed, the cause cannot be imagined to be any other than a deep impression in the wiser sort, and such as look most into the doing of things, that her majesty careth not heartily for them; and then being left or weakly assisted by her they must fall, for which they had rather provide in time than by delay to expect the war one after another in their own doors. This conceipt took beginning two or three months since, but now bringeth forth its effects, and wanteth not politick heads to nourish it on, which even then laid their plots that they now follow. And yet, my lords, though the case be very dangerous, and such as for duty's sake and for my own discharge I thus lay plainly and truly open to you, I do not make it desperate, but do accept it easily recoverable if remedy be used in time. But the remedy must be according to the nature of the disease, which, growing of the mistrust of her majesty's effectual dealing for them, must be cured not with a shew but by a plain demonstration of the contrary by deed, and presently, the means whereof your lordships can better consider of than it shall boot or be fitt for me to prescribe. For my own part, what a man without money, countenance, or any other sufficient means, in case so broken and tottering every way, may do, I promise to endeavour to do to the best of my power." (p. 350.)

In the narration of events the earl writes with ease and considerable descriptive power. Witness his account of the wounding of sir William Pelham and of sir Roger Williams in the trenches before Doesburg (pp. 401, 407). The latter was the same person, whose narrative of Actions in the Low Countries was published under the editorship of sir John Haywarde, and who is elsewhere described by the earl as " worth his weight in gold, no more valiant than wise, and of judgment to govern his doings." (p. 430.) With all this he had some little spice of foppery or heedlessness, and often running in and out of a trench " with a great plume of feathers in his gilt morion " became so conspicuous that many shots were fired at him, and it was a marvel he escaped with only "a blow thorough the arm." See also the account of Edward Stanley's exploits at Zutphen (p. 428).

Equally skilful is the earl's delineation of character. With a few words he hits off the men around him better than many historians have accomplished by laboured description. The following contain his first impressions of the celebrated count Hohenlohe, or Hollock as he was more frequently termed; "The count Hollock [is] surely a wise, gallant, gentleman, and a right soldier, and very well esteemed with many of the captains and soldiers; he hath only one fault, which is, drinking, but good hope that he will amend it." (p. 61.) "He is a plain gentleman . . . a right Almayn in manner and fashion, free of his purse and his drink." (p. 74.) "A very noble soldier." (p. 75.)

Prince Maurice, then a lad of eighteen, to whom Leycester left the task of establishing the freedom of the Low Countries, is delineated not less clearly, although, perhaps from some little feeling of jealousy, not quite so fairly. "He hath a sullen, deep wit, and shrewd counsellors of his father's about him." (p. 71.) "He hath a solemn, sly wit; but in truth if any be to be doubted toward the king of Spain it is he and his counsellors." (p. 74.) "He stands upon making and marring as he meets with good counsel." (p. 374.)

Truchses the elector of Cologne deposed for protestantism is the subject of several descriptive passages in letters CXXXVI and CXXXVII. He found an asylum in the united provinces, but was deprived of all his means of support by a law-suit with the count de Meurs and the successes of the prince of Parma. In his destitution, not having "a groat to live on" (p. 378), "his heart almost broken through want" (p. 374), he submitted to play the undignified and not over honest part of an intelligencer between the count Hohenlohe, who wholly imparted "his secret heart" to him, and the earl of Leycester. The earl repaid him with money "and other helps," and pictured his hard case to the queen in the vain hope of procuring him a pension. "He is a gentleman she would like as well as any man I have seen come to her being a stranger. His wisdom, his behaviour, his languages, his person and all will like her well, and as great affection he beareth her as any man, not her own subject, can do. . . . He begins to fall toward a palsy, and yet he is but a young man." (pp. 373, 374.)

Some of the most striking passages of this kind relate to sir John Norris and Paul Buys. They are too long to quote, but can be found through the index, and at once lead to an important question in connection with these letters, What light do they throw upon that great mystery of the reign of Elizabeth, the character of Leycester himself? My own impression is that it is an unfavourable one. They place his intellectual power beyond a doubt, but with equal clearness they exhibit moral qualities which sufficiently account for the fear and hatred in which he was held by so many of his contemporaries, and which if they had been conjoined with greater power would have made him a most formidable tyrant. The commencement of his inglorious government was a mere vanity fair, and its progress was distinguished by unstatesmanlike neglect of his instructions (pp. 109, 437), and a succession of disputes, conducted on his part, except in the instance of that with the queen, with a feeling of rancorous hatred which it is painful to conceive possible. To fall out of favour with Leycester was to become the object of his unsparing abuse, and, if in his power, of vindictive persecution. Paul Buys, who in the first instance was the earl's chief adviser (p. 386), shortly afterwards became in his estimation "a devil, an atheist, and the only bolsterer of papists and ill men," and of "late used a detestable practice against me, in respect of religion and to please the papists. But give me countenance," continues the earl, "*his head shall pay, perhaps, for it* and other villainous parts towards her majesty, *which shall be justified when my authority shall serve*." (p. 303.) "If her majesty mean to stand with this cause *I will warrant him hanged*, and one or two of his fellows, but *you must not tell your shirt of this yet*." (p. 291.) This man was subjected by the earl to a persecution which excited a great outcry throughout the states, and which would have gone hard with its victim but for the interference of the queen. (p. 436).

Notwithstanding the eminent services of sir John Norris in the relief of Grave, services which the earl is compelled to admit although he strives to lessen them by insinuations, sir John soon fell into disfavour (p. 306). The earl found himself eclipsed by Norris's military talents, and nothing could exceed his anxiety to get rid of him. Amongst many accusatory passages there is one in which the earl makes his tenacious hatred of the earl of Sussex, who had then been dead nearly three years, a vehicle for more effectively conveying to Walsyngham a notion of the bad qualities of sir John Norris. "John" he says, "is right the late earl of Sussex' son; he will so dissemble, so crouch, and so cunningly carry his doings as no man living would imagine that there were half the malice or vindictive mind that doth plainly his deeds prove to be." (p. 301.) In this letter the earl earnestly begs and entreats, over and over again, that Norris should be recalled, and in a subsequent letter, after describing him as " a most subtle dangerous man, not having a true word in his mouth" (p. 379), the earl begs Walsyngham to deal with Norris's father, but especially with his mother, to procure his return. (p. 379.) But the queen knew Norris's value and would not listen to the request. In her reply she attributed Leycester's mislike of Norris to some private feeling, whereupon the earl with his accustomed pliancy suddenly discovered that no man was more careful or forwarder in all services than the person he had so recently maligned, that no doubt he was an able man, and he declared that he should want no encouragement (p. 385).

The earl's mean-spirited accusation of Davison, and his vindictive execution of Hemart have been noticed already. From the first tidings of the surrender of Grave he seems to have determined upon the death of that unhappy man. " I will not complain any further, and yet *I will never depart hence till, by the goodness of*

xliv   INTRODUCTION.

God, I be satisfied some way for this villain's treachery done, how desirous soever I am to come home." (p. 285.) He seems at one time to have meditated some violent attempt to extort supplies from the states; "*If we have force,*" he remarks, "*we will have money.*" (p. 303.) The same lawless spirit was manifested on many other occasions. When apprised that one Cæsar an Italian was coming over to him, and, as was suspected, "for some mischief," he writes, " by his description it should be a surgeon, for there were two Italians, both surgeons, and both their names Cæsars, and be both of Rome, and very villains, yet found they great favour of me in England. If it be either of them, as he saith this man confessed he served me, it were not amiss he and his companion were stayed there, or else, if they desire earnestly to come over to me, give me warning and write your letters by them to me and then *I will handle them well enough here.*" (p. 409.)

Perfectly in character with all this were the earl's repeated entreaties for the speedy, even if irregular, execution of Mary queen of Scots (pp. 431,* 447); and many other similar circumstances will occur to the reader of the volume. They manifest a violent, ill-regulated temper, an unprincipled recklessness as to means, a harsh revengeful spirit which might be hurried by circumstances into the commission of the very worst of those crimes which have been popularly attributed to Leycester. Elizabeth declared that "there lacked a Northumberland in his place." (p. 388.) If the earl did not possess the bold and commanding temper of his father, it is to be feared that he too certainly inherited both his subtlety and his meanness.

It is a delight to turn from the character of the earl to that of his illustrious nephew sir Philip Sydney. The present volume

* This letter reveals to us that in 1569, during the rebellion in the North, the great seal was put to a warrant for the execution of Mary queen of Scots. The dispersion of the rebels probably rendered it unnecessary to act upon the warrant, and the fact of its existence remained unknown to historical writers until the discovery of Mr. Ouvry's volume.

contains a brief account by the earl of the capture of Axel, one of those achievements in the accomplishment of which Sydney gave such glorious promise for his future life (p. 337). The closing pages possess a melancholy interest from the details of the contest in which he was wounded (p. 413), his long sufferings which gave rise to fallacious hopes of his recovery (pp. 415, 421, 429), his death (pp. 442, 445), and, finally, the miscarriage of his wife, brought on by her attendance upon him after his wound (pp. 446, 480), and the manner in which his affairs were embroiled, and his honorable intentions as to the payment of his debts defeated by the strict rules of law. It is but justice to Walsyngham, especially after my former observations upon his letters, to direct attention to his conduct in reference to Sydney's debts. Walsyngham's letters, CLXVIII. and CLXX., prove that, apart from his official duties, he had a kind and generous heart.

The facts here published relating to Sydney not only add to the materials for his biography, but rectify errors into which writers upon that subject have fallen. The same remark may be extended to all the subjects treated of in the following correspondence; indeed, the mistakes of our most distinguished historians in reference to the circumstances of Leycester's conduct in the Low Countries, and especially in reference to his acceptance and retention of the government, are not a little extraordinary. It was thought desirable that I should point out some of the more glaring of those mistakes, and I made some progress in an attempt to do so, but I found the task so distasteful and invidious that I soon abandoned it, and now only recur to the subject as a notice to future inquirers.

In closing this introduction, which has extended to a length I never anticipated, I must remark that I alone am responsible for whatever it contains. The Council of the Camden Society have permitted me, subject to their usual regulations, to prefix such observations as in my judgment are likely to render the book more useful; but their desire to add to the utility of the book ought not to make them responsible for the correctness of my opinions or the accuracy of my statements.

JOHN BRUCE.

York Crescent, Clifton,
    28*th Feb.* 1844.

TABLE

OF

DOCUMENTS PRINTED IN THIS VOLUME.

                                      Page

ARCHER, HENRY.
   Letter to SIR THOMAS HENEAGE, dated 23rd October, 1586 478

BAKER, CHRISTOPHER.
   Letter to the EARL OF LEYCESTER, dated 22d October, 1586 444

BOROUGH, STEPHEN.
   Journal of THE EARL OF LEYCESTER'S PASSAGE from England to the Low Countries in December, 1585 461

BURGHLEY, LORD.
   Letter to SIR THOMAS HENEAGE, dated 13th May, 1586.... 266
   Letters to THE EARL OF LEYCESTER,
      dated 6th December, 1585 24
          26th   ,,   ,, ... 38
          27th   ,,   ,, ... 44
          12th January, 1585-6.... 50
          17th   ,,   ,, ... 66
          7th February, ,, ... 103
          6th March   ,, ... 152
          The same date 154
          31st March, 1586 196
          1st April   ,, ... 204
          8th June   ,, ... 293
          10th ,,   ,, ... 296
          The same date 306
          20th June   ,, ... 313
          21st July   ,, ... 354

                                      Page

Letters to THE EARL OF LEYCESTER,
    dated 18th August, 1586 396
        15th September, 1586.... 411
        1st October   ,, ... 420
        4th November ,, ... 449

BURGHLEY, LORD, AND SECRETARY WALSYNGHAM.
   Letters to THE EARL OF LEYCESTER, dated 21st June, 1586 316
        28th October, 1586...... 447

CLERK, BARTHOLOMEW.
   Letter to THE EARL OF LEYCESTER, dated 22nd October 1586 441

DAVISON, WILLIAM.
   Letters to THE EARL OF LEYCESTER, dated 17th February, 1585-6.................... 117
      28th February, 1585-6 .. 142
      2nd July, 1586 331
      4th November, 1586.... 451
      6th   ,,   ,, ... 454
   Comments on a letter of the earl of Leycester, dated 10th March, 1585-6 168

DUDDELEY, THOMAS.
   Letter to THE EARL OF LEYCESTER, dated 11th February, 1585-6 111

TABLE OF DOCUMENTS.

	Page
ELIZABETH, QUEEN OF ENGLAND.	
Letters to SIR THOMAS HENEAGE, dated 27th April, 1586	241
The same date	243
Letters to THE EARL OF LEYCESTER, dated 10th February, 1585-6	110
1st April, 1586	209
Letters to THE STATES GENERAL AND COUNCIL OF STATE OF THE LOW COUNTRIES, dated — November, 1585	20
13 February, 1585-6	468
— April, 1586	469
HENEAGE, SIR THOMAS.	
His INSTRUCTIONS when sent into the Low Countries, dated 10th February, 1585-6	105
Letters to THE EARL OF LEYCESTER, dated 3rd March, 1585-6..	149
15th October, 1586.	437
HOHENLOHE, COUNT.	
Letter to SIR EDWARD NORRIS, n. d.	474
LEYCESTER, EARL OF.	
His INSTRUCTIONS when sent into the Low Countries, dated December, 1585	12
His MINUTE OF WHAT THINGS HE OUGHT TO CONSIDER, N. D.	19
Letters to LORD BURGHLEY, dated 5th December, 1585	21
17th ,, ,,	28
14th January, 1585-6	57
7th February, ,,	90
29th September, 1586	418
Letters to THE LORDS OF THE COUNCIL, dated 1st March, 1585-6	145
9th March, 1585-6	163
27th ,, ,,	189
23rd April, 1586	233
15th July, 1586	349

	Page
Letters to Mr. DAVISON, n.d. February, 1585-6	80
10th March, 1585-6	168
Letter to THE CORPORATION OF LONDON, dated 3rd February, 1585-6	83
Letter to THE LORD TREASURER, THE LORD CHAMBERLAIN, THE VICE-CHAMBERLAIN, and MR. SECRETARY WALSYNGHAM, dated 8th February, 1585-6	95
Letters to MR. SECRETARY WALSYNGHAM, dated 27th September, 1585	5
The same date	7
n. d. about 28th September, 1585	10
n. d. about December, 1585	21
dated 15th December 1585	25
26th ,, ,,	29
31st ,, ,,	46
3rd January, 1585-6	49
15th ,, ,,	64
22nd ,, ,,	67
31st ,, ,,	76
1st February ,,	83
3rd ,, ,,	86
4th ,, ,,	87
6th ,, ,,	89
7th ,, ,,	92
8th ,, ,,	99
14th ,, ,,	114
15th ,, ,,	116
18th ,, ,,	126
21st ,, ,,	128
22nd ,, ,,	131
24th ,, ,,	134
26th ,, ,,	137
27th ,, ,,	139
1st March, 1585-6	147
3rd ,, ,,	148
9th ,, ,,	165
17th ,, ,,	177

TABLE OF DOCUMENTS.

xlix

	Page
Letters to Mr. Secretary Walsyngham,	
n. d. March or April, 1585-6	202
3rd April, 1586	211
5th ,, ,,	214
The same date	219
16th ,, ,,	225
24th ,, ,,	235
28th ,, ,,	244
30th ,, ,,	249
1st May ,,	255
3rd ,, ,,	256
6th ,, ,,	258
8th ,, ,,	261
9th ,, ,,	264
17th ,, ,,	271
23rd ,, ,,	276
25th ,, ,,	280
29th ,, ,,	282
31st ,, ,,	284
6th June ,,	287
7th ,, ,,	290
10th ,, ,,	297
18th ,, ,,	309
26th June, 1586	321
27th ,, ,,	326
1st July, ,,	330
8th ,, ,,	337
11th ,, ,,	345
15th ,, ,,	348
27th ,, ,,	362
29th ,, ,,	365
30th ,, ,,	375
7th August, 1586	383
The same date	384
8th ,, ,,	390
10th ,, ,,	394
31st ,, ,,	399
4th September, 1586	405
12th ,, ,,	410
27th ,, ,,	413
28th ,, ,,	415
29th ,, ,,	419

LEYC. CORR.

	Page
Letters to Mr. Secretary Walsyngham,	
dated 2nd October, 1586	421
6th ,, ,,	427
10th ,, ,,	431
25th ,, ,,	445
22nd December, ,,	480
23rd ,, ,,	481
Low Countries, Commissioners of the.	
Their advice to the Earl of Leycester, n.d. November, 1585	15
——————, Council of State of the.	
Letters to Queen Elizabeth, dated 18th March, 1585-6	468
1st May, 1586	469
11th June ,,	472
Merchant-Adventurers of England, Company of.	
Letter to the Earl of Leycester, dated 18th October, 1586	439
Norris, Sir Edward.	
Letters to count Hohenlohe, n.d. November, 1586	474
Another	ib.
Ralegh, Sir Walter.	
Letter to the Earl of Leycester, dated 29th March, 1586	193
Schenck, Sir Martin.	
Narrative of his capture of Werle, and of Leycester's reception at Amsterdam, March, 1585-6	475
Sherley, Sir Thomas.	
Letters to the Earl of Leycester, dated 7th March, 1585-6	159
14th ,, ,,	171
21st ,, ,,	180
Sydney, Sir Philip.	
Questions and legal opinions,	

h

TABLE OF DOCUMENTS.

	Page
touching the execution of his will, November, 1586	481

VAVASOUR, THOMAS.
  Letter to THE EARL OF LEYCESTER,
    dated 31st March, 1586 194

WALSYNGHAM, MR. SECRETARY.
  Letters to THE EARL OF LEYCESTER,
    dated 26th September, 1585.... 4
      27th ,, ,, .. 8
      n.d. December, 1585 34
      20th March, 1585-6 178
      21st ,, ,, ... 184
      The same date 185
      24th March, 1585-6 186
      28th March, 1586 190
      1st April ,, ... 205
      11th ,, ,, ... 221
      21st ,, ,, ... 229
      25th ,, ,, ... 236
      The same date 239
      14th May ,, ... 269
      20th ,, ,, ... 272
      The same date 275
      23rd ,, ,, ... 278

Letters to THE EARL OF LEYCESTER,
  dated 26th May, 1586 281
    3rd June ,, ... 286
    22nd ,, ,, ... 318
    24th ,, ,, ... 318
    30th ,, ,, ... 327
    The same date 329
    8th July, 1586 336
    9th ,, ,, ... 340
    11th ,, ,, ... 342
    20th ,, ,, ... 353
    30th ,, ,, ... 382
    15th August ,, ... 395
    2nd September ,, ... 403
    n.d. ,, ,, ... 404
    5th November ,, ... 453
    6th ,, ,, ... 457

WARWYKE, AMBROSE EARL OF.
  Letter to THE EARL OF LEYCESTER,
    dated 6th March, 1585-6 150

WYLKES, THOMAS.
  His INSTRUCTIONS when sent into
    the Low Countries, October,
    1586 432

CORRESPONDENCE

OF

ROBERT EARL OF LEYCESTER,

A.D. 1585 AND 1586.

THE assassination of the prince of Orange on the 10th July, 1584, reduced the defenders of protestantism in the Low Countries almost to despair. Deprived of their only leader, exhausted by a long continued war, opposed to the power of Spain, then the greatest empire in the world, and that power directed by the consummate military skill of the prince of Parma, the states general regarded the further prosecution of their unequal contest with despondency, and looked anxiously around for some helper in their distress, some potentate at once powerful enough and zealous enough to come to their aid. Their first application was made to France; but, tempting as the notion of the annexation of the Netherlands has always been to the holders of the crown of that kingdom, and inclined as Henry III. was to adopt any course of policy which had a tendency to reduce the power of Spain, he felt that, in the unsettled state of his own kingdom, he dared not undertake the defence of protestant interests abroad. Upon his refusal, the sovereignty was tendered to queen Elizabeth, who received the offer with complacency, and referred it to the consideration of her council.

In the mean time, the prince of Parma urged the war with vigour, and, after some considerable successes, advanced to the siege of Antwerp, the richest and most populous city in the revolted provinces, and the one which had exercised the greatest influence over their proceedings. The fate of the contest seemed to hang upon the determination of this memorable siege, and, with the instances of heroic perseverance and long-continued submission to privations exhibited by the citizens of Haerlem and Leyden still fresh in men's minds, it was confidently anticipated that, if it were possible, still nobler achievements would crown the defence of this most important city.

Whilst this momentous siege was still pending, Elizabeth and her advisers deliberated as to the course which she ought to adopt. Of her willingness to assist the protestants in the Low Countries no one could entertain a doubt; she had already done so when their affairs were in a more promising condition, and now her own safety, and the preservation of her dominions from invasion, were in some degree dependent upon the occupation which the continuance of this contest afforded to the forces of Spain. On the other hand, Elizabeth entertained high notions of the indefeasible nature of the royal authority, and was not without fear that the precedent of interference which she was establishing might be urged against herself, on behalf of her own Roman catholic subjects. Her deliberations, and those of her advisers, were long and anxious, and, in the end, she decided upon the adoption of a middle course. The sovereignty was absolutely refused, but military assistance was determined to be given, and, with a view to fill that great void which had been occasioned by the murder of the illustrious prince of Orange, it was resolved that the English auxiliary troops should be placed under the command of " a person of quality and esteem," one well inclined to the protestant faith, and who was not merely to be the lieutenant-general of the queen's troops, but also a member of the council of state, and, with the council, to have power to redress certain abuses, and to have regard to whatever concerned the preservation of the common weal of the United Provinces.

The selection of a proper person to fill so important an office, and the completion of the arrangements to which he was a party, occasioned considerable delay, and, in the mean time, the want of military assistance, and the necessities of Antwerp, daily became more urgent. The stipulated auxiliary force of 4000 foot and 400 horse was raised immediately after the conclusion of the treaty, and was placed under the command of sir John Norris, a soldier of established reputation,[a] but before he could pass out of England, the event which this armament was primarily designed to prevent had taken place. After some hard fighting, and many wonderful exhibitions of the science of the military engineers on both sides, St. Aldegonde, the governor of Antwerp, a nobleman long distinguished for his zeal for the protestant cause, was compelled by popular clamour to enter into treaty with the besiegers. The prince of Parma offered most favourable terms of accommodation, and ultimately the city was yielded, upon payment, by the citizens, of a fine of 400,000 guilders, the Spaniards releasing all prisoners and granting a general amnesty. The joy of the Spaniards at this result, and the depression of the inhabitants of the United Provinces, were alike unbounded, and, if the prince of Parma had been able to follow up his success by an immediate invasion of the northern provinces, the consequences might have been most disastrous. But time was allowed to escape unimproved; the protestant inhabitants of Antwerp removed into Holland, and carried with them the commerce of which Antwerp had been the centre; Elizabeth agreed to increase her auxiliary forces to 5000 infantry and 1000 horse,[b] and, as successive bodies of English troops landed at the ports of Holland, and proceeded to the stations assigned to them, the hopes of the people revived, and

[a] The treaty was concluded on the 10th August, 1585, (Dumont, corps diplomatique, v. 454. General collection of treaties, 8vo. 1732, vol. ii. p. 85,) and sir John Norris was appointed two days afterwards. (Murdin's state papers, 783.)
[b] Galba, C. viii. fo. 134.

all eyes were turned with eager anticipation towards the lieutenant-general whom the English queen was about to send to their assistance.

It soon transpired that Elizabeth designed that high office for the earl of Leycester. The treaty by which she agreed to increase the number of her auxiliaries was dated on the 2nd September, 1585, and before the end of that month it will appear by the following letters that she had communicated her pleasure to the earl. It is just after that communication had been made that the following correspondence opens, and this brief notice of the political position of the Low Countries has been prefixed, in order that the real historical value of the letters to which we now proceed may be more clearly understood.

LETTER I.

MR. SECRETARY WALSYNGHAM TO THE EARL OF LEYCESTER.

26TH SEPTEMBER, 1585. COTTON. MS. GALBA, C. VIII. FOL. 168. ORIG.

The queen desires the earl to forbear his preparations for the Low Countries until he speaks with her.

My verry good lord, her majestie sent me woorde by M^r Da*** that I shoold speak unto your lordship that her plesure is you forbeare to proceed in your preparatyons untyll you speake with her. How this commethe abowt I know not. The matter is to be kept secreat. Thes chaynges here may woorke somme sooche chaynges in the Lowe Contrye as[a] may prove irreparable. God give her majestye an othur mynde and resolution then in proceadyng otherwyse yt wyll woorke bothe hers and best

[a] is *in MS.*

affected subiects ruine. And so I most humbly take my leave. At the courte, the 26. September, 1585.

Your lordships to command,
Fra: Walsyngham.

Addressed.
To the right honourable
  my verie good lord
  the earle of Leycester.

LETTER II.

THE EARL OF LEYCESTER TO MR. SECRETARY WALSYNGHAM.

27th September, 1585.   harl. ms. 285. fol. 135.   orig.

Answer to the last letter—statement of the earl's preparations —his submission to the queen's will.

Sir,
I have this night, at j a clok, received your letter, which doth signyfie that her majesties pleasure ys, I shuld stey my preperations untyll I doe speake with her. I wyll lett you knowe how farr I have gonne, and than I shall obey hir majesties comandment, being knowen from you, for stey of the rest, and to undoe of that ys donn, as hir wyll shalbe.

First; uppon hir first order geven, both from hir self and also confirmyd further by your letters by hir majesties comandment, I dyspached, betwene Thursday night and yesternight iiij a cloke, above ij^c lettres to my servaunts, and sondry my frends, to prepare themselves, according to the order I had my self, with all the spede the could possible, to serve hir majestie, under me, in the Low Countreys. I am sure ther be a c of these alredy delyvered, and the rest wylbe before I can revoke them; having apointed the xviij. and xx. of the next month for ther repayr hether with all ther furnyture. I have since, and before I cam my self to the Tower, taken upp both armours and stele saddelles, as many as must cost me a good pece of money. I have sett in hand sondry furnytures also for my self. I have taken upp ij or iij vessells to carry away presently certen provissions, as bear and other necessaryes, which must be ther before me.

And, lastly, that I am most sorry for, the states that were at court[a] cam hether to me this morning by ix a cloke, and spent ij owres with me, touching my dyspach, in so much as they werr reddy to knele to me for to make what hast for my none aryvall on the other syde that I could possibly, yea by all perswasions pressing me that I wold not stey tyll my full preparations werr made, and my companyes, but to be knowen once to be aryved at Mydelborow, or Flushing, with such as may sonest be reddy, for by that meanes I shuld be the cause of stey of greter matters than wold be wyshed thorow longer delay, for, they sayd, yt was very long alredy. They offerd me with all, that many things shuld be ther made reddy to receave me, even so sone as yf I went within vj days I shuld be prepared for. I did, hereuppon, tell them what streyt comandment I had received from hir majestie to hast me over, and what good wyll they shuld now fynd in me to performe the same. We agreed that I shuld send som servant of myne to have ther lettres over to se all things made ther reddy for me, yf I shuld followe within 14 or 15 days; I dyd so, and sent D. Doyly, whome ye know, who hath ther lettres, and, except my messenger find him, he ys gonn this morning tyde before iij a cloke; yet have I, uppon the sight of your lettre, sent one to seke him and to stey him. This farr alredy have I proceded. I told the states, also, that I steyd hereabout tyll I shuld prepare for my owne speedyer dyspach.

Whereuppon this sudden change doth groe, M^r secretary, I

[a] Certain commissioners who were sent by the states general of the Low Countries into England to supplicate the assistance of Elizabeth. Their authority is printed in the Fœdera, xv. 798.

can not imagin, nether wyll I meddell withall, but must obey her majesties pleasure yf she have determyned any alteration, which I desyer to hear from you, for yf I com to the court yt must more easyly breake out, as yt wyll notwithstanding, and I can but greve at the myserable estate of the pore aflycted; as for my owne, hit must be as the potters vessell, &c.

For that I know this forenoon some of the estates wyll com ageyn to me about this cause, I wylbe absent somwhear tyll after none, by which tyme I wyll hope to receive further dyrectyon from you, which God grant to be best for her majesties own servyce and hir realme, by whose wysdom and government we are all lyke ether to stand or faule. Thus in much hast, praing you to excuse the imperfectyon of yt, being scrybled in my bed this Monday morning almost ij a clok.

Your assured frend,
R. LEYCESTER.

Addressed.
To the right honourable
  Mr secretary Walsingham,
    hast, hast,
      hast.

LETTER III.

THE EARL OF LEYCESTER TO MR. SECRETARY WALSYNGHAM.

27TH SEPTEMBER, 1585. HARL. MS. 285, FOL. 146. ORIG.

Private letter sent with the one preceding—surprise at the alteration in the queen's mind—if the matter alters he cannot come to court, or look upon any man—urges him to let him hear again speedily, to send sir Philip Sidney to him, and to learn, if possible, the cause of the change.

This ys one of the strangest dealings in the world. I find yf any lytle stey be longer, the alteration on the other syde wylbe past remedy. They ar so importunatt uppon me as I was feyn to promys them to be reddy my self to goe within xv days. I have don as I have wrytten, both in dyspach of my lettres and taking upp of the other necessaryes, which comes to no smale som, and now, was I in my money matters, and have my frends abrode for yt![a] What must be thought of such an alteration! For my parte, I am wery of lyfe and all. I pray you let me hear with spede. I will goe this morning to Wansted, to se som horses I have ther, where I wyll tary tyll iij a clok, and than retorn hether ageyn, and, yf the matter alter, I can have no hart to com at court, or look uppon any man, for yt wylbe thought some myslyking in me doth stey the matter. Send Philip[b] to me, and God kepe you, and, yf you can possible, lern out the cause of this change.

Your assured,
R. L.

LETTER IV.

MR. SECRETARY WALSYNGHAM TO THE EARL OF LEYCESTER.

27TH SEPTEMBER, 1585. HARL. MS. 285. FOL. 133. ORIG.

Will acquaint the queen what comfort the earl received from her gracious communication to him touching his employment in the Low Countries—the council are willing to further the service, but in any matter of expence there will be difficulty with the queen—proposed removal of the queen of Scots to Chartley—the earl's presence greatly desired in the Low Countries.

My verry good lord, I wyll not fayle to acquaynt her majestye with the great compforte your lordship tooke thorrough her

---

[a] This obscure sentence is printed as it stands in the original.
[b] Sir Philip Sidney.

grateowse dealyng towardes you, at sooche time as she dyd delyver her plesure unto you towching the imployment of you in the Lowe Contryes.[a]

My lords have semed to be verry wyllyng to further any thinge your lordship shall require for the advauncement of the servyce. But yf your lordships requests shall mynister matter of charge, thowghe yt be for publycke servyce, the impedyment wyll be fownde in her majestye, with whom I have had verry sharpe conflyctes abowt the Scottyshe causes, and all for charges.

I wyll excuse your lordships absence in respecte of the necessytye of your being at London for the better expedytyon of your preparatyons. Sir Amyas Paulet proceaded forther in the preparatyons at Chartley then I lookd for. I wyll doe what I can to staye the intended remove thither, but I feare neyther ser Wat. Ashetons howse, nor Gyffordes, wyll be founde so apt.[b] I wyll cause a sayll to be made of the felling of the quenes woodes, and of the used of hir stuffe.

I fynde by the comyssyoners that they desyre greatly your presence on the other syde the seae, for that they dowbt, in respect of the present confusyon of governement, and the practyces in hand to drawe them to gyve eare to the prince of Parma, ther may faule owt somme dayngerowse alteratyon in thos contryes.

I knowe your lordship wyll make what speed you may, and yf your good wyll myght have taken place, the daynger they feare by delaye had ben avoyded.

I wyll doe my best indevor to see your lordship somme tyme to morrowe, or next daye, at your howse in London, and so, in the

---

[a] It would seem that between the writing of letters II. and III. and this letter, the earl of Leycester had an interview with the queen, and that the suspension of his preparations had been withdrawn.

[b] At the date of this letter Mary queen of Scots was confined at Tutbury castle, in the custody of sir Amyas Paulet; but upon the interference of M. de Mauvissiere, the French ambassador, a promise had been given, that she should be removed to a more healthy and commodious place. She was removed to Chartley in January 1586.

meane tyme, I most humbly take my leave. At the courte the xxvij[th] of September, 1585.

Your lordships to command,
Fra: Walsyngham.

I woold be glad to undarstande
  whether your lordship hathe had
  sir Thomas Cicell[a] in remembraunce.
    Addressed.
To the right honorable my
  very good lord the earle
  of Leycester.

LETTER V.

THE EARL OF LEYCESTER TO MR. SECRETARY WALSYNGHAM.

N. D. HARL. MS. 285. FO. 147. ORIG.

Answer to the last letter. He will not increase her majesty's charges—hopes he may have five or six hundred of his own tenants, whom he will reckon as good as a thousand others—requests Walsingham to protect a poor man whom lord Hunsdon threatened to send to prison.

Sir, I doe not meane to make any request that shall encreace any neu chardge, albeyt hir majesty, I trust, shalbe well provided to have hir own chardges saved in the end.[b] You know what my sutes ar lyke to be, only to se me go accompanyd with such suffy-

---

[a] The eldest son of lord Burghley. He served in the Low Countries during Leycester's government as governor of Brill. Fœdera, xv. 802.

[b] It was stipulated in the treaty between the queen and the Low Countries, that she should advance the pay and other charges of her troops, and that the sum thus expended should be repaid within five years after the conclusion of peace. The town of Flushing, the castle of Rammekins in Walcheren, and the town of Brill, were delivered into the queen's hands as security for the repayment of her advances.

cyent persones as shalbe requysytt in so weighty a servyce as this ys. And herein, good Mr. secretary, stand fast to me in dede; for I wyll seke nothing, by my jorney, in this world, but to doe servyce to hir majestie and this realme, and nothing I am in sure hope wyll hinder yt but letting me from such able persons as I shall desyer. I gave my nephew Philip this morning som notes to conferr with you about.

I hope, sir, I may have that I made you acquantyd with v or vj c of my owne tenauntes, whom I wyll make as good reconing of a[s] of 1000 of any that ar yet gonn over, and no way to encreace hir majesties chardges,[a] and whan I shall speak with you, which I much desier, I wyll further satysfye you.

Sir, my lord of Hunsdon[b] hath sent his comandment, uppon his sonn Hobbyes[c] informacion, for a bayly of Hersam,[d] who had a book concerning ther own lybertyes and myne also, delyvered them by a stuard of myne only for a tyme to pleasure them, and now they have retornyd the booke ageyn to my offycer, and my lord, he sends, wyll comytt him for yt, but I trust that justyce[e] wyll not be, for I must rather inform hir majesty; and this being the truth of the cause, I pray you, sir, help to kepe the pore man from prison, as I know yf you send to my lord that the party hath opened the cause to you, I know he wyll forbear him. I am

[a] Power was given to Leicester to raise five hundred men " of his tenants and servants" to attend his person during the time of his absence in the Low Countries. The letters patent for that purpose, dated the 2nd October, 1585, are printed in the Fœdera, xv. 799. Leicester's commission as lieutenant-general, dated the 22nd October, 1585, is also printed in the same work, xv. 799.

[b] William Carey, lord Hunsdon, queen Elizabeth's cousin; being, not her sister's son as is stated by mistake in Dugdale's Baronage, ii. 397, but the son of William Carey and Mary Boleyn, sister to queen Elizabeth's mother.

[c] Margaret, second daughter of lord Hunsdon, was married to Sir Edward Hoby, knight. Dugd. Bar. ii. 398.

[d] This word is doubtful in the MS.

[e] i. e. punishment, vindictive return.

loth to have squares[a] with him now. God kepe you, and so I rest your assured,

R. LEYCESTER.

Addressed.
To my honorable
  good frend Mr.
  secretary Walsingham.

LETTER VI.

THE EARL OF LEYCESTER'S INSTRUCTIONS.

DECEMBER 1585. MS. COTT. GALBA, C. VIII. FO. 119, b. AND FO. 215.[b]

Abstracts of the earle of Leicesters instruccions, appointed by her majestie to be her lieftenaunt-generall of her forces in the Low Contreys.

To have care that her majesties subjectes serving under his lordship maie be well governed, and to use all good meanes to redresse the confused government of those countreys, and that some better forme might be established amongst them.

Touchinge the good ruling of her majesties subjectes, his lordship is directed to bend his course, during his charg there, rather to make a defensive then an offensyve warr, and not in any sort to hazard a battaile without great advantage.

To establish martiall discipline, and see those severlie ponished shall not duelie observe such orderes as shalbe made, and the insolencies of the soldiers against the common people to be reformed.

That the captaines be not suffred to lett their bandes decay, but see that their number be full, and check rolles to be kept of euerie band.

---

[a] "To have squares," is to have a disagreement or contention.
[b] This paper has been divided and misplaced by the binder of the volume in which it occurs.

That his lordship uppon his arrivall doe cause an exact view to be made of all the English forces, and to have speciall care to paie the bandes by the head, and by generall paymentes to the captaines.

That the abuses of captaines, and their under officeres, be narrowlie looked into and severelie ponished.

That of the bandes under her majesties paie such as shalbe found weake and decaied to be cashed,[a] and with the nomberes remayninge to suplie the defects of thother bandes, or elles those bandes to be renforced by other her majesties subiectes serving in those countreys.

To see that the garrisons of the cautionarie townes[b] maie be duelie paid euerie moneth, aswell for avoiding discontentments as for their better maynetenaunce, in respect that they paie accise which the soldieres of the camp paie not.

To have care that the cautionarie townes maie be suplied with greater forces, such as the governores shall require, in case they shall dowbte of anie revolt, or perceive that the enimye shall draw his force that waie.

For the second part, touching the reformacion of their government, to deale with the states that, for avoidinge the confusion which soe manie councelles doe breed, they wold make choice of a lesse number of wise, discreete, and well affected persons, to whom the directions of matters of policie maie be comitted, and for cutting of the tediousnes and delaies in matters of councell, to move them that the deputies of the severall provinces maie have authoritie to consult and conclude, and cutt of the often references to the particular states.

To appoint some well chosen persones to collect the contributions made towardes the maynetenaunce of the warres, and to see them dulie ymploied and yssued for the publique service.

[a] i. e. quashed, cashiered.
[b] Flushing, Rammekins, and Brill; vide p. 10, note b.

That the abuses of the officeres of the receipt maie be reformed, and they to be charged with their deceiptes, and theruppon to require to understand how the ymposicions and taxacions have ben expended.

To cause a view to be taken of the cautionarie townes, in what state they stand, and that there maie be magazines appointed for them, with a sufficient proporcion of municion and victuall to be kept in redines there att the charges of the states.

To appoint in euerie of the cautionarie townes certaine well chosen persones to compound such differences as maie happen to grow betweene the garrisons and the townesmen, to thend they maie be kept in good union and agrement, and remove such as they shall understand to be evill affected.

His lordship to enforme himself of all the forces both of horse and foote entertained by the states both by sea and land, where they are placed, how they be paid, and what meanes they have to contynue and defraie those charges.

To advise in what sort the abuses in raisinge and abatinge the value of money maie be reformed, and the coynes reduced to one certaine value, to thend the soldieres maie receive and paie their money att one rate.

To restraine the transporting of victualls to the enimie, and to see the offendores that waie seuerelie ponished.

To deale with the states that the Dunkirkes maie be better looked unto, and the passadges unto that countrey cleered.

That the nobilitie of that countrey in the states entertainement, especiall the prince of Orenges children,[a] maie by his lordship be ymploied into places of creditt and honorablie respected.

---

[a] William prince of Orange left issue four sons and eight daughters. His eldest son Philip William was at this time, and for many years afterwards, a prisoner in Spain; Maurice succeeded his father as stadtholder, and ultimately established the independence of his country: Henry Frederic succeeded Maurice. Of his daughters it will be sufficient to remark that Mary was married to count Hohenlohe; Louisa Juliana was mar-

To recommend unto the states the estate of Truxes, archbisshopp of Collen.[a]

To lett the states understand, that, where by their commissioneres they made offer unto her majestie, first, of the soueraintie of those countreyes, which for sundrie respects she did not accept, secondlie, unto her protection, offring to be absolutelie gouerned by such as her majestie wold appoint and send ouer to be her lieftenaunt. That her majestie, although she would not take soe much uppon her as to comaund them in such absolute sort, yet unlesse they should shew themselves forward to use the advise of her majestie to be delivered unto them by her lieftenaunte, to work amongst them a faire unitie and concurrence for their owne defence, in liberall taxacions and good husbanding of their contribucions, for the more speedie atteyninge of a peace, her majestie wold think her favours unworthelye bestowed upon them.

To offer all his lordships travaile, care, and endevour, to understand their estates, and to geve them advice, from tyme to tyme, in that which maie be for the suretie of their estate and her majesties honour.

LETTER VII.

ADVICE OF THE COMMISSIONERS OF THE LOW COUNTRIES TO THE EARL OF LEYCESTER.

A.D. 1585. MS. HARL. 285. FO. 137. ORIG.

The commissioners of the Lowe Countryes advise.

To serve his excellence, accordinge to his desire, by waye of advys, for better directyon of the affaires of the Low Countryes,

ried to Frederic IV., elector palatine; Elizabeth was married to Henry de la Tour, duke de Bouillon, and was the mother of the great Turenne; Catharine was married to Lewis, count de Hanau; Charlotte Brabantina to Claude, duke de la Tremouille, and was mother of the celebrated Charlotte countess of Derby.

[a] Gebhard Truchsés, archbishop of Cologne, elected in 1577, but deposed by the

the deputes of the sayd countryes remayned[a] here thinke, under correctyon, most convenient that his excellence first arryve in Zealande, makinge his resydence at Middlebourghe, and there to keepe his court till such tyme that, uppon the assuraunces of the townes and forteresses mentyoned in the treatye, shall deu contentment be gyven unto her majeste.

To which end, and for to proceade to the fulfillinge of the other pointes of the foresayd treatye, to hale,[b] first, ample commyssyon from the states generall of all the provinces to him, authorytye sufficient as her majeste hath don, yt may please his excellence presentlye to advertyse the states of the united provinces of his arryvall there, and desire of them a generall assemblye at Middlebourghe aforesayde, or at least to send anye of there especyall commyssyoners wyth full power and authorytye for the better proceadinge and effectuatinge of the foresayd poyncts.

That yt allso please his excellence to cause, with the first,[c] a college or councell of estate to be established, for to serve and assyst his excellence dewtefullye in all thinges, whereto yt shalbe good to putt her majeste in mynde to nomynate and appoint twoe in the sayd councell, accordinge unto the treatye, yf such be her majestes pleasure.[d]

And, forasmuch as at this present the service of her majeste, and preservation of the unyted Lowe Countryes, with that which dependeth thereof, princypallye consysteth in the admynystration and conducte of the martyall affaires and warres, aswell offensive as defensive, by sea and lande, and that in the same countryes,

pope in 1583, on account of his adoption of the opinions of the reformers. He sought protection in Holland. L'art de verifier les dates, xv. 283.

[a] Several of the commissioners from the states general had returned home.
[b] i. e. to procure by solicitation.
[c] i. e. in the first place.
[d] The queen appointed Bartholomew Clerk, LL.D. and Henry, afterwards sir Henry, Killegrew, to be members of the council of state in addition to the earl of Leicester. Clerk and Killigrew, who were both distinguished men at that period, had been employed before in foreign embassies. Galba, C. viii. fol. 116; Strype's Life of Parker, ii. 183; Annals, i. part ii. 268.

by fault of authorytye, comaundement, and dew order, is fownde greate confusyon, fraude, negligence, and dysobedience, to greate advauntadge of the enemye and noe lesse harme, losse and daunger of the foresayd countryes in severall respectes, that, therefore, yt please his excellence, as before, to hale authorytye, with the first, to declare him selfe unto all and everye unto whome yt shall appertaine, chiefe head and gouvernour generall, accordinge to the chardge and comyssyon of her majeste.

And forthwith to take information of the nomber, quallytye, and circumstaunces of the souldiers in generall, as allso of the commaunders, captaines, and officers of the same in particular, with all other officers and commyssyoners of warre and martyall affaires, namelye, vyctualls, admunytyon, and others thereon dependinge, whereof must be delivered unto his excellence a generall declaratyon aswell of the footemen and horsemen as the commaunders and officers of the same, wyth their names, surnames, and wages.

To th'end that thereuppon order maye be gyven for the intertaynementes of those that are most meete and fytt for the service of her majeste and the countryes, and chaunged or dyscharged all needelesse and unable persons; for the more proffitt of her majeste and conservation of the countries, wythout respect of anye person whosoever; causinge the foresayd souldyers to be kept under their aunciants[a] at a competent nomber, and the aunciants to be placed under certayne good colonells, prouydinge the same with sufficient officers, which actuallye doe their dewtyes and dyschardge themselves honestlye, to th'end that the better government and martyall dyscipline maye be kept amonge souldiers, and the better service had at their handes.

Lykewyse, to take such regard uppon the reveus, mosteringes and paymentes, that her majeste nor the states aforesayd be on the one syde not defrauded, nor the commone souldiers on the other

---

[a] *i. e.* ensigns.

deceaved of their dew and competent wages, by the captaines or others.

The like maye be done with the shippes and marryners of warre, and of the rigginge of the same, by sea and uppon the ryvers.

His excellence shall allso please sufficientlye to enquire of all sortes of artillerye, weapons, and other prouyson of admunytyon, especyallye of those that are ordayned for the commone service of the countrye, and might be employed in the commone cause, whereby his excellence and the countryes maye at all tymes knowe whereuppon to trust in tyme of necessytye.

Allso, that yt please the same to holde a vigilant eye uppon the state of all the townes and forteresses, especyallye uppon the borderes, or them that are before others in anye daunger or attempt of the enemye, to th'end that the same townes, forteresses, or borderes, maye be repayred and strenghthened in tyme with good and needeful garnyson, victualls, and other necessaryes, to the better resistaunce of th' enemye, and, as neare as ys possible, actuallye to cause the same to be provyded against all surpryses, and soddayne sieges, and, before all other, such places which in winter season and in frost hardelye maye be succoured wyth men or provysyon.

There needeth, likewyse, greate regarde uppon all manner of contributyons graunted for the better maintenaunce of the warres, whereby the same maye well and dewlye be handeled, receaued, and payd, and that in the same all possible egalitye maye be kept betweene the foresayd provinces, and not to see the money employde otherwyse then to the martial affaires, where unto they are appropriated and destinated by the estates.

And to the end that in the provinces aforesayd, betweene the inhabitaunts and citizens in the townes and villages, good order, and rest and concorde maye be kept, to the encrease of God's honor and maintenaunce of the commone wealthe, yt maye please his excellence to have in singular commendatyons the churches and the reformed evangelyke religion, and by all dew meanes to advaunce, confirme, and to cause the same to encrease so muche as ys possyble, not admyttinge or sufferinge anye of contrarye or papystycall religyon to anye offices or chardge of importaunce.

That yt likewyse please his excellence to see, within the sayd countryes, good justice and pollitique gouvernement to be administred and mainteyned, restoringe and establishinge, wheare neade doth require, the lawfull authorytye of magistrates and officers respectivelye, so well in townes as without, and lykewyse to provyde uppon all other necessarye matters with advyce of the councell of estate which shalbe ordeyned to assyst his excellence in all occurrences, for the better service of the commone wealthe, accordinge unto the lawes, priviledges, and lawdable customes of the aforesayd countryes, provinces, and townes respectivelye.

LETTER VIII.

THE EARL OF LEYCESTER'S MINUTE OF WHAT THINGS HE OUGHT TO CONSIDER TOUCHING THE GOVERNMENT AND CONDITION OF THE LOW COUNTRIES.

A.D. 1585. MS. HARL. NO. 285. FOL. 144. ORIG. IN THE EARL'S HANDWRITING.

What thinges ar most necessary to understand touching the estate of these Low Countreys.

First, to be satysfied how they have byn gouerned since the death of the late prince of Orange.[a]

[a] After the death of the prince of Orange, the government of the Low Countries was carried on by a council of state, created for a period which expired in the autumn of 1585. Previous to its expiry, Walsyngham intimated to Davison, the English ambassador in the Netherlands, that, as the queen could not immediately send over the nobleman whose advice the states general were to use in the settlement of their government, she wished them to renew the authority of the council of state. In opposition to this advice, the states gave the government provisionally into the hands of Prince Maurice, alleging a previous understanding upon the subject, and directing their deputies in London to acquaint her majesty that "the counte Maurice should respect my lord of Leister as a generall, and be under his conduct." MS. Cotton. Galba. C. VIII. fo. 115, b.

What councellors and officers they have had, and have.

What there authorytye was.

What forces they have had, and have, in their pay, for defence of the countreys in all places.

What certeyn meanes they have to mainteyn the same, and how they be collectyd.

What the countres be indebtyd synce the princes death, and what order ther ys taken for them, and all other ther debtes.

What gouernment ys requysytt to be apointyd to him that shalbe ther gouernor.

First, that he have as much authorytye as the prince of Orange had, or any other gouernor or captain generall hath had heretofore.

That ther be as much allowance by the states for the seid gouernor as the prince had, with all offices aportenaunt.

That the generall contributions and collectyons for the expence of the warr be apoyntyd at his dispocytyon.

That ther be a certeyn nomber of the best sort of persons apointyd for councellors of estate.

LETTER IX.

QUEEN ELIZABETH TO THE STATES GENERAL OF THE LOW COUNTRIES.

NOVEMBER 1585. COTTON MS. GALBA, C. VIII. FO. 115, b. CONTEMPORARY MINUTE.[a]

The queen's affection for the Low Countries, and her regard for the earl of Leycester.

Her affection towards them to be seene in sending the earl of Leister, a personage whom she did make more accompt of then anie of her subiects; him she appointed to be generall of her forces there, to assist them in their affaires.

[a] A copy of the letter itself has not been found.

LETTER X.

THE EARL OF LEYCESTER TO MR. SECRETARY WALSYNGHAM.

DECEMBER 1585. COTTON MS. GALBA, C. VIII. FO. 118. CONTEMPORARY MINUTE.[a]

The earl presses for the completion of the arrangements for supplying him with money, — offers the queen the security of his own lands against misapplication of her advances.

Wondereth and complaineth that the queen will not seale his booke of assurance. He can nor will not goe without monie. Her majestie meaneth he would deceive her. If she putteth anie mistrust in him, he offereth her to sell his land unto her for 30,000 or 26,000^{li}. which is either 30 or 26 yeare purchase, and the same at such rate as her own officers shall saie themselves it is well worth 60,000^{li}. besides the wood, which is worth 5,000^{li}, so that her majestie shall gaine by him 40,000^{li}.

LETTER XI.

THE EARL OF LEYCESTER TO LORD BURGHLEY.

5TH DECEMBER 1585. HARL. MS. 6993. FO. 119. ORIG.

A letter of farewell on the earl's departure towards the Low Countries, most earnestly entreating the lord treasurer to have the cause of the United Provinces at his heart, and not to allow the earl to be thwarted by want of supplies.

My very good lord, I am sorry I could not take my leave of you before my departure,[b] but I hard, which I am sorry for, that

---

[a] A copy of the letter itself has not been found.

[b] " December 4th.—The earl of Leicester having taken leave of her majesty, and caused six hundred horse to pass muster in London, departed thence for Harwich, in

your lordships paines encreaced after my going from the court, and dyd lett your intended coming to London; but, seing that oportunyty taken away, I have thought yt my parte to byd your lordship fare well by these fewe lynes, whearin I shall wyshe your lordship perfect health, and many yeres to serve hir majesty, comending you for the same to the mightye protectyon of the Lord.

My good lord, I may not, having this occasion, be unmyndfull of these thinges also, which I did think at my leave taking to have remembred to your lordship, albeyt I know the care you always have of hir majesties good servyces. Your lordship can not but remember the cause for which hit hath pleased hir majesty to send me into the Low Countreyes. Hit was not only by your lordship, but by the hole nombre of councellors agreed uppon, how mete and necessary hit was for hir highnes to yeld ayd and assistance for the relyfe of those aflicted countreys, her neghbours and most auncyent frendes: hit hath grown synce to nerer termes and resolucyons, aswell by hir majesties own wordes of comfort to them, as by contractes sett down betwen hir and them, by hir majesties comyssioners apointed for the purpose. I trust, my good lord, now that I have taken this voyage uppon me to serve hir majestie as she hath commanded, your lordship will be myndfull of me, poore man, but of the cause comytted now to my delinge chifely.

Albeyt I have no mystrust but in so great absence, and such a servyce, I might greatly relye uppon your partyculer good wyll and regard of my self, but in this case I desier no respect nor regard of me, but of the cause, which I besech you, my lord, I may at this farewell recomend to your wysdome and great care. Hit cannott be but whatsoever lack shall happen to me in this servyce, but the want must turn to hir majestie; and, as ther can

---

order to cross the sea to Zealand." MS. journal of Leycester's proceedings in the library of the college of arms, printed in Retrospec. Rev. i. 277. 2nd series.

no good, or honor, fall to this actyon, but yt must be wholy to the prayse and honour of hir majestie, so whatsoever disgrace or dyshonor shall happen (growing for lacke of our good maintenaunce) but yt wyll redownde to hir majestie also. Hir majestie, I se, my Lord, often tymes doth fall into myslyke of this cause, and sondrye opinions yt may brede in hir with all, but I trust in the Lord, seing hir highnes hath thus farr resolvyd and groen also to this farr executyon as she hath, and that myne and other mennes pore lyves and substances ar adventured for hir sake, and by hir comaundement, that she wyll fortefie and mainteyn hir owen actyon to the full performance of that she hath agreed on. Than shall ther be no dowbt, but assured hope, of all good success, to the glorye of God and perpetuall honour to hir majestie.

My good lord, you may conceave my meaning without more wordes used to you, and the rather for that I desiered Mr. secretary to imparte a lettre to yow I wrote to him. I besech your lordship have this cause even to your hart, as yt doth appear yow have donn by consentynge to the adventure of your eldeth sonne in this servyce; for this I must say to you, yf hir majesty fayle with such suplye and maintenance as shalbe fytt, all she hath donn hetherto wylbe utterly lost and cast away, and wee hir pore subiectes no better than abiectes. And, good my Lord, for my last, have me only thus farr in your care, that in these thinges which hir Majesty and yow all have agreed and confirmed for me to doe, that I be not made a metamorphocys, that I shall not know what to doe.

And so the Lord have you in his keping, preserve hir majestie for ever, and send me good spede in this servyce. In som hast this 5th of December, on my way to the sey syde;

by your lordships assured frend,

R. LEYCESTER.

My lord, no man feleth comfort but they that have cause of

grefe, and no men have so much nede of relyfe and comfort as those that goe in these dowbtfull servyces. I pray you, my lord, help us to be kept in comfort, for we wyll hazard our lyves for yt.

Addressed.
To the right honourable
my very good lord, the
lord Burley, lord treasurer
of England.

LETTER XII.

LORD BURGHLEY TO THE EARL OF LEYCESTER.

6TH DECEMBER 1585. COTTON. MS. GALBA, C. VIII. FOL. 220. ORIG.

Reply to the last letter. Lord Burghley will promote the earl's proceedings as if he were his kinsman—would deserve to be an accursed person if he did not strive to advance the cause—had dealt earnestly with the queen to favour the earl.

My very good lord, I have receaved your courtess ** letter, wherein your lordship doth commend to me your honorable ca** that your state and service now in hand doth require, whereof truly, my lord, I do assure yow, no less a portion of my care and travell for many respects to the furtherance of your own honor than if I war a most neare kynsman in bloode; and for the avancement of the action, if I should not with all the powers of my hart contynually both wish and work avancement therunto, I war to be an accursed person in the sight of God; consideryng the endes of this action tend to the glory of God, to the savety of the queens person, to the preservation of this realme in a perpetuall quietnes, wherin for my particular interest, both for my self and my posterite, I have as much interest as any of my degree. And this I pray yow, my lord, mak a perfect accompt of me and for my doyngs. I referr the report to Mr. secretary, who hath this afternoone hard me, in most ernest sort, dell with hir majesty to favor and maynteane you and your action, as the only meanes at this tyme to bryng hir to savety.

From my couch in my chamber, not yet hable to rise from it. God send your lordship a spedy good passadg.[a] This vi. of December, 1585.

Your lordships
assured as any,
W. BURGHLEY.

LETTER XIII.

THE EARL OF LEYCESTER TO MR. SECRETARY WALSYNGHAM.

15TH DECEMBER 1585. HARL. MS. NO. 285. FO. 167. ORIG.

The earl wishes to have the treaty between the queen and the Low Countries sent to him—requests explanations of the allowances made to himself and the commissioners—and to be informed how the queen accepts his proceedings—wishes some Irish recruits to be sent to him—and two leases to be granted to him—St. Aldegonde's treachery—desires sir William Pelham may be sent to him.

Sir, I have not the contract which passed betwene hir majesty and the states, which you promysed me I shuld have, and of necessyty I must nedes have yt sent to me, and, yf yt may be, the

---

[a] The earl sailed from Harwich on the 8th December, and on the 10th arrived at Flushing. On the 11th he again embarked, and proceeded to Middleburgh, where he was received with great honour, and remained until the 17th. Stowe's Annals, 710, and Retros. Review, i. 277. 2nd ser.

very oryginall ys best, whearatt ther handes be; you may cause the coppye to be exemplyfied yf ye lyst.

I have also perused the rates for the armye, which you sent me by Lloyd my secretarye, wherein you sett down my rate as generall without my ordynary company, as a gard, phisytyon, chaplen, clerkes, drom, fyfe, and such lyke, as other lyvetenauntes had, and as you dyd delyver me before, at the beginning; for all other great offycers, as marshall and such lyke, you told me yt must be alowed by this countrey chardges; which I meane to deale accordingly, &c.

You sett doun all Mr. Kyllegrew and Mr. D. Clerk lx^s a pece *per dyem*, which ys more than the governors of Flushing and Bryall have, and, as I remember, you told me that their allowance shuld be xl^s a pece. I pray you lett me be answered of these iij matters with as much spede as may be.

My laste is, to hear from you as ofte as may be, and to take ordre for your ordynary passenger[a] on that syde, and to lett me hear how hir majesty acceptes of my doinges and wrytinges.

The longer the winde doth holde our shipps the more occasion I shall howerly have to wryte. The greatest of all ys, first, to pray you to gett hir majestys favor that I may have vj^c. or a 1000 of your Iresh idell men, such as be not only in her majestyes pay but very mete to be out of that countrey. The cause of my desier to have them ys, for that they be hard, and wyll abyde more pains than our men, tyll they have byn well trayned with hardnes as they have byn. My desier only ys, that hir majesty wryte a letter to my lord deputye to gyve such leave to come as he shall not imploye ther, and to further the beror that ys sent thether in all reasonable sort for his conveying and transportacion of them, without any chardge to hir majesty. Herein ye shall [do] hir majesty very great servyce, for I assure you ther be many dedd of

---

[a] The word *passenger* is used here in the sense in which it occurs in a document printed in the Rutland Papers, p. 71, namely, as a vessel for the conveyance of passengers, a passage boat.

our souldyeres, and the enymye hath contynevall intellygence from us, only they think I have brought a mervelous suply, by the nomber of vesselles that cam over with me, and the rest that went into Holland, thinking my company ther and her ys not under iiij^m at least. Ther be tyckettes also sent from London hether which no dowbtes past to the enymye quykly, and wyll doe no hurt, setting done the names of such as com with me, wherein there ys ij^c. names of my none gentlemen sett down, and they, hearing I have so many gentlemen in my company, imagyn they are not without servauntes, and so owr nomber must be great; which opinion hath doon no harm, but yet yt wyll not long hold, and therfore, I pray you Mr. secretary, ether gett me this suply or elles 6 or 700 at the least out of England, to fill up our bandes, elsewyse you wyll be sorry to hear of the want and dyshonor that ys lyke to follow.

Ther ys an other matter which I wold gladly be asuered of; I wrote yt in an other lettre, touching the allowance of the souldyer, at what rate he shalbe payd, whether after viij^d the day stirling, or after Flemysh money, which maketh much adoe here.

For our selues here, also, I trust you wyll remember, you ther may hereafter have cause to fele that we doe, and shall doe; therefore doe as you wold be done unto.

Ther ys a pore matter of my none I left with you, Mr. secretary, which ys, a byll for ij leases, an ordinary matter, and I wyll pay for them; but my chefe care ys, there ys a statute of forfeture uppon yt of iij.^m ℔., or ij^m. ℔. at least, yf yt be not gotten before Crystmas day and delyvered to the party. I dyd once tell you of yt, as also comandyd Tho. Dudley to inform you therof; I pray you, sir, doe me the favor to dyspach yt, or yf hir majesty think you styll to partyall toward me, I pray you desier and besech certeyn to do yt; yt standeth me so much uppon me as I tell you.

I wrote somwhat of sir Aldagond to you in putting his case; but this ys certeyn, I have the coppy of his very letters sent hether to practyce the peace not ij days before I cam, and this day one hath told me, that loves him well, that he hates our countreymen unrecouerably. I am sorry for yt. So the Lord kepe you this Wenysday the xv. of December.

Your loving frend,
R. LEYCESTER.

I pray you, sir, lett me know whether I shall have sir Wylliam Pellam,[a] or no; for I hear he sayth he dowbteth now whan.

LETTER XIV.

THE EARL OF LEYCESTER TO LORD BURGHLEY.

17TH DECEMBER 1585. LANSDOWNE MS. NO. 45. ART. 39. ORIG.

The earl requests the lord treasurer's interference on behalf of certain merchants of Middleburgh, one of whose ships bound to Havre de Grace had been captured by English cruisers.

My very good lord, the love and affection that I finde in this people of Middelbourch to my souveraigne, and the good will and desier they shewe to do me honour for her majesties sake, do the rather persuad me to recommend unto your good lordship a cause of certain merchantes of this towne, towchinge a ship of Vlussingue that was loaden with oyles and cottens, and bond for New Haven, but mett by the way, in their course, by three Englishe shippes, and by them taken, and carried into England. This was donn within these fifteene dayes; but because the marchantes have one their that doth follow and solicite the cause, and will wayte upon your lordship to impart the particulars hereof unto you, I will not troble you therwithall. I hartely praye your good lordship to

---

[a] Sir William Pelham was an experienced soldier of this period, who will be frequently mentioned hereafter. He was at this time in disgrace with the queen.

shewe them your good favour for the releasing of their shippe, and recovering of their goods, and the rather at my earnest request unto your lordship, for which you shall allwaies find me very thankefull in all I maye. I am now here amongst them, where I wold be very glad to requite their good wille, and to contynewe their affection, by accomplishing their reasonable requestes, and therfore once againe I am bold to put your lordship in mynd of my request. Thus leaving your good lordship to God, who send you as well and as good health as to my self, I end. At Middelbourgh, this xvijth of December 1585.

Your lordships ever assured frend,
R. LEYCESTER.

Addressed.
To the right honorable
my very good lord, the lord
Burghley, lord high
treasurer of England.

LETTER XV.

THE EARL OF LEYCESTER TO MR. SECRETARY WALSYNGHAM.

26TH DECEMBER 1585.   HARL. MS. NO. 285. FO. 171.   ORIG.

Gratitude of the people of the Low Countries to queen Elizabeth for her assistance,—the earl recommends a suit of the bailiff of Dort, whose son was a prisoner with the enemy,—also wishes letters of thanks to be sent to Dort, Rotterdam, and Delft, for their cordial reception of him,—narrates the manner of his reception at Delft,—desires a pursuivant to be sent to him, Segar having made excuses,—effects of the earl's coming upon the German states,—complains of want of assistance,—insufficiency of Dr. Clark,—notices of Ruddykirke, Walke, and Paul Buys,—intreats for St. Aldegonde.

Mr. secretary, albeyt I wrote lately to you from Dordrick, having thes convenyent messengeres, who doth meane to goe presently into Englande, I wold [not] lett them pass without letting you know where I am,[a] and how greatly hir majesty ys in all places reverenced and honored, of all sortes of people, from hiest to the lowest, assuring themselves alredy, now they have hir majestyes good countenance, to beatt all the Spanyards out of their countrey ageyn. Never was ther people I think in that jollyty that these be. I could be content to loose a lymme that hir majesty dyd se these contreys and towens as I have; she wold than think a hole subsedye well spent, but only to have the good assurance and commandment of a few of these townes. I think ther be not the lyke places agayn for England to be founde. I am now going to the Hage, whear I shall have matter to wryte to hir majesty shortly. In the meane tyme I meane not to trowble hir majesty with any lettre, having written from Dort also unto hir.

Thys sute I am to recomend unto you most ernestly. Ther ys a gentleman, one Jacob Muys Van Holy, who ys one of the ablest men in all these partes to serve hir majesty, both for his credytt and wysedome. He hath a sonne prisoner with the enymye, and very yll used. He besought me, yf ther were any Spanyard taken among our seamen, as he heareth ther ys, he wold be a proude man to have him, or any, to redeme his sonne,[b] for they wyll not sett him at any ransom, for the hate to his father; who in dede hath, by his credytt, donn notable service in this cause, and no man better able at this day to serve her majesty. I assure you, in my opinion, hit were a good tern to bestow Seburo uppon him, and yt ys my sute; I know it shall doe more good with all than xx^m crowns in money. He ys chefe bayly of Dordryght, where they have ij^m and iiij^c able sol-

[a] The earl sailed from Middleburg for Dort on the 17th December, but owing to calms, a thick fog, and contrary winds, he was five days on the voyage. Retros. Rev. i. 277. 2d ser. His arrival is dated on the 22d December in the journal printed in the Retrospective Review, but by Stowe, more accurately, on the 21st. Annales, p. 713.

[b] The earl has added in the margin, "Yf Steuen be not redemed this may redeme him also."

dyers of the very townes men as ever I saw in any place, and the kindest people; beside there ys belonging above ij^m maryners to this town alone. I assure you yf such a parte might com to him uppon the sudden, with a letter of thankes to the hole towne besides, for ther honorable usage of me, hir majesties lyvetenant here, you shall wynn her more frends withall thorow all this countrey than a c Spanyardes be worth.

I must besech hir majesty, also, that ther may be partyculer letters wrytten of thankes to those towns who have so honorably and chargeably receaved me in hir majesty's name, as Dordryght, Rotradame, and this towne Delf,[a] which ar all iij notable fair towns, and all trafyquers with England. Flushing and Mydelborow had letters, which makes me the bolder to crave these. The worst of these towns presented me with xv^c shott [b] and armed men, at the least, and dyd conduct me from town to town with vj and vij^c shott.

This town ys an other London almost for bewty and fairnes, and have used me most honorably, as these berors can tell you; with the greatest shewes that ever I sawe. The mett me along the ryver as I cam, v^c shott ij myles of; at my landing ther was not so few as xv^c shott more, standing in a row from my landing tyll I cam to my lodging, which was nere a long myle; by the way, in the great merkett place, they had sett a squadron, at the leaste of viij^c or a 1000 pikes, all armyd, which was a mervellous fayr sight, and tall able personages as ever I saw. Ther was such a noyse, both here, at Rotradame, and Dordryght, in crying, "God save queen Elisabeth," as yf she had ben in Chepesyde, with the most harty countenances that ever I sawe; and therfore, whatsoever hath byn sayd to hir majesty, I beleave she never bestowed hir favor uppon

---

[a] The earl proceeded from Dort to Rotterdam on the 23d December, and on the 24th to Delft. The ceremonies and rejoicings at his reception into these and other chief towns, may be read in Stowe's Annales, and in the Life of Robert Earl of Leicester, 8vo. Lond. 1726.

[b] *Shott* were soldiers armed with firelocks.

more thankfull people than these countryes of Holland; for the states dare not but be queen Elyzabethes, for, by the lyving God, yf ther shuld fall but the least unkindness, thorow ther default, the people wold kyll them, for these towns woll take no dyrectyon but from the queen of England, I assure you; and yf hir majesty had not taken them at this nede, but forsaken them, she had lost them for ever and ever, and now hath she them, yf she wyll kepe them, as the cyttysens of London, in all love and affectyon.

All our horses, that have byn uppon the water at London and here above xxvj days, ar as well aryved as yf they had never byn travelled, and not so fayr when they wer shipt as they be now.

Lastly, sir, I besech send me a pursevant; he that I apointed, and desyered to goe, made sute a day before I cam away to tarry at [home,] with xx excuses, his name ys Segar. I prey you, sir, lett some one, and an able boddy, be apointed with spede. Yf you call for clarencius[a] he wyll name some fytt man to you. I have great nede of such a one. Yf he have French, or Duch, or Latyn, yt shall suffyce.

I perceave not only these people here dowbtyd of hir majesty dealing thus with the king of Spayn, but the princes of Germany also, of whome one yesterday hath told me, that they know alredy of my coming, and so mervell at yt as he thinkes her majesty shall fynd them in an other tune than ever she found them yet; shortly I shall hear more, and, uppon this, yf the matter of Segaro werr satysfyed touching Cassamere, she wold shortly dyrect them all. I speak yt not for any respect for my self (God ys judge), but you wyll not beleave what a reputacion this dealing in the Low Countreys hath alredy gotten hir.

I have most cause to complayn, that was sent out as I was, and yet stand, without help, or assistance, of such persons as I hoped for. I hear nothing of Sir William Pellam, nor Mr. Kylligrew,

---

[a] Cooke was clarencieux at this time. It would seem that Segar, then portcullis, ultimately went to Leycester. Stowe's Annales, 717.

and, for my parte, yf I lak them one weke longer, I had as leave the taryed styll, for now am I at the worst, even at the first; for now wyll all the busynes be: yt were to much pytty to lose so great good thinges for lack of some help at the first. Yf yt were not for Mr. Davison[a] I shold be very farr to seke, God knows.

I find no great stuffe in my lytle colleage,[b] nothing that I looked for. Yt ys a pytty you have no more of his profession able men to serve. This man hath good wyll, and a pretty skollers wytt; but he ys to lytle for these bygg felloues, as heavy as hir majesty thinks them to be. I wold she had but one or ij such as the worst of half skore here be.

I find Ruddykyrke a very grave, wyse, honest man; now, in the fayth, he confesseth, he was almost out of belefe of hir majesties goodnes. Walke dealeth most honestly and painfully. Paule Buys I find greatly envyed and myslyked; but he must nedes be had, albyt all devyces ar used to putt him out from being a councellor.

Now a few wordes for St. Aldegonde.[c] I wyll besech hir majesty to stay hir judgement tyll I wryte next. Yf the man be as he now semeth, hit were petty to loose him, for he is in dede mervelously frended. Hir majesty wyll think, I know, I am easily pacyfied, or ledd, in such a matter, but I trust so to deall as she shall gyve me thankes. He hath made my nephew[d] and Mr. Davison deall with me; he hath sent his sonn, also, to me, to gyve him to me, but I forbare, tyll I had good advyce in dede, to send one to him, which was Gilpyn, and doe looke every oure to

---

[a] William Davison, afterwards so well known in connection with the execution of Mary queen of Scots, was sent into the Low Countries on a special embassy from Elizabeth, in August 1585. Murdin's State Papers, 783.

[b] Dr. Bartholomew Clerk; the profession alluded to was that of the civil law.

[c] Elizabeth and the states general were greatly, but very unjustly, displeased with St. Aldegonde on account of his surrender of Antwerp. Watson's Philip the Second, 407, edit. 1839.

[d] Sir Philip Sidney.

hear from him agayn. Once yf he doe offer servyce yt ys sure inough, for he ys esteemed that way above all the men in this countrey, for his word yf he gyve yt. His most enymyes here procure me to wynne him, for sure just matter for his lyfe ther ys none. He wold fayn come into Englond; so farr he ys com alredy, and doth extoll hir majesty for this work of hirs to heaven, and confesseth, tyll now, an angell could not make him beleave yt. Well, I hope you shall hear that wyll not myslyke you hearin. Fare you well, this Sonday morning, at Delph.

Your assured,
R. LEYCESTER.

I never herd out of Englond yet synce I cam away.
   Addressed.
To my honourable good frend
sir Francis Walsingham,
knight, her majesties principall
secretarie.

LETTER XVI.

MR. SECRETARY WALSYNGHAM TO THE EARL OF LEYCESTER.

DECEMBER, 1585. HARL. MS. 285, FOL. 152. ORIG. DRAFT.

Answer to the last letter—the queen's dislike of all things that occasion expence—desirableness of contribution by the states—increase of reputation to the queen in Germany and Italy, arising from her interference in the affairs of the Low Countries—the unpopularity of that interference in England—son of the bailiff of Dort—the queen and lord treasurer dislike St. Aldegonde—Leycester's complaint of want of assistance—the queen's displeasure against sir William Pelham—Killegrew detained by adverse winds—allowances—letters of thanks.

My verie good lord, your letters sent by Mr. Henrie Astell and your servante Underhill, I have receaved, by the which I am verie gladd to understand that your lordship hath ben so honourably used in those places where you nowe are, and that they stand so greatlie devoted towardes her majestie as by all owtward shewe dothe manyfestly appeare, which ought to move her majestie to like the better of the actyon, and to countenance the same in such sorte as maie both encourage your lordship and increase the love and goodwill towardes her, of those well affected people. But, as farre as I can learne by such of my frendes as are acquainted with our court proceadinges, it wourketh not that good effect that were to be wished, so unpleasant are all thinges that mynister matter of charges. I praie God frame an other minde in her majestie, as well for her owne honour and safetie, as for the encouragement of such as are emploied in publicke service.

I am verie gladd that the promised contribution by the states carrieth likelyhood of perfourmance, which stoppeth the mouthes and practises of those that sought to wourke an other conceipt in her majestie, by bearinge her in hand that she was abused, and that the burthen of the charges would light uppon her, or at least that she should in the ende be forced, in respecte of charges, to geve over the cause. I would to God their meanes might have ben found such as some parte of her owne charges might have ben diminished, whereby she might have ben the rather encouraged to have put on a resolution to have proceded constantlie in the maintenance of the cause.

As your lordship heareth out of Germanie that this enterprise of her majesties hath greatlie encreased her reputation in those partes, so do we here the like out of Italie, and I thincke that, if they might stand assured that her majestie would throughlie prosecute the cause, they might be drawne in some sorte both to yeald supporte and to kyndell some fyer ther; so necessarie do they find it that the king of Spaynes greatnes should be abated in respect of their owne perryll.

I perceave by your lordships letters that if you had not come at that tyme you did, there would have fallen out some dangerouse alteration in that countrie, and therefore all honest and well affected subiectes here have cause to thancke God that you arrived there so seasonablie as you did; for, houesoever we mislike of the enterprise here, all England should have smarted if the same had not ben taken in hand.

If the princes of Germanie could be drawne to congratulate your lordships repayre into those partes, as your lordship is put in hope they will doe, it will greatlie countenance the cause.

Touchinge your lordships request to have Sebur gewen in exchange for the bayliffe of Dortrechtes sonne, I will doe my uttermost endevor to bringe the same to effecte, wherein I hope there wilbe found no great difficulty, for that his releasement, beinge a man of no great capacitie thoughe otherwise malliciouslie affected, can wourke no great preiudice to this estate.

This daye, I understood by Mr. vice-chamberlaine,[a] who came to vissitt me, that her majesties mislikes towardes St. Aldegonde contynuethe, and that she taketh offence that he was not restrained of his libertie by your lordships order. I did acquainte him with the letter he wrote unto your lordship, which carryinge a true picture of an afflicted mynde, cannot but move an honest harte, weyinge the rare partes the gentleman is endued withall, but to pittie his distressed estate, and to procure him releif and comforte, which Mr. vice-chamberlaine hath promised on his parte to perfourme. I thought good to send St. Aldegondes letter unto the lord threasurer, who heretofor hathe carryed a harde conceipt of the gentleman, hopinge that the viewe of his letter will breed in his lordship some remorse towards him. I have also praied his lordship, if he see cause, to acquainte her majestie with the said letter.

Sorie I am that your lordship should have that iust cause you

[a] Sir Christopher Hatton was at this time vice-chamberlain of the queen's household.

have to complaine of lacke of assistance. There falleth out daylie, as I am informed, newe discoverie of abuses touchinge the office of the ordenance, as that there should be a hundred brasse peeces missinge, which doth so much agravatt her majesties displeasure against sir William Pelham, in that he did neglect, with that care that appertained, to oversea the inferiour officers, as she can hardely endure anie man to deale for him. Yett, notwithstandinge, my lord threasurer hathe of late sent the gentleman woordd, that he is nowe in some hoape that her majestie wilbe content to extend some grace towardes him, whereby he maie be sent unto your lordship, who canne never come to late, in respecte of the contynuall use your lordship shall have of his advice and assistance, so longe as you shalbe emploied in those countries in a martyall coorse.

Touchinge a coppye of the originall contracte that your lordship writeth of, I am assured the same was delyvered either to Mr. Atye, or to Mr. Fludde; in the meane tyme, until the same maie be found, your lordship maie use a coppie I delyvered to Mr. Killegrewe, who hathe been long at the seae syde for a wynde.

The allowance gewen to doctour Clarcke and Mr. Killegrewe is mistaken by the writer, for that it ought to be onlie 40*s. per diem.* And, as touchinge your lordships allowance as generall, it is true that the enterteinement due to all such necessarie attendantes all other generalls have had, was omitted. Your lordship therefore shall do well to write a joynte letter to the lord threasurer and to me, to move the rest of the counsell to geive warrant to the threasurer for the paiement thereof.

The letters of thanckes your lordship desireth unto the townes of Dortrecth, Rotterdam, and Delft, I will not faile to procure: as also that ther maie be provided a passage boate for the transportation of letters.

LETTER XVII.

LORD BURGHLEY TO THE EARL OF LEYCESTER.

26TH DECEMBER, 1585.   COTTON MS. GALBA, C. VIII. FOL. 235.   ORIG.

Continuance of adverse winds—relief of Sluys and Ostend—importance of sea-ports to the Spaniards—export of provisions from Kent—loss upon the exchange of English money— reformation of the mints in the Low Countries—preparations of the king of Spain for the invasion of England, and the queen's anxiety to make ready a fleet to withstand the Spaniards — her majesty's desire that the earl should ascertain what assistance she can procure from the Low Countries.

My very good lord, sence the retorn of Mr. Gorge from your lordship, who cam the next daye after his shippyng, we have not hard from your lordship, nether I thynk hath your lordship hard from hence; the lack of both hath bene in default of passages. And now, as soone as any shippyng cold be made redy, which, though I wryte these letters this Mo[nday] being the 26. yet, untill Wednesday, the officers of the admyralte say, the shippyng cannot be redy, and if it than shall be, I d[oubt] of nothyng but want of wynd to bryng over to your lordship a gret nombre of your good frendes and servantes, and amongst them my son,[a] who hath bene hable and redy these x dayes, if he cold have gotten shippyng, which he cold not get untill your shippes retorned.

By Mr. Gorge and others I receaved two letters from you, the on of the xjth the other of the xiijth, both wrytten at Midelburg. By the former, your lordship signefyeth your saff arryvall, and the perswasion that your coming hath wrought in that nation of hir majesty's mynd to help them, wherof they war in doubt afor. By the second, your lordship wryteth in what state Sluse and

---

[a] Sir Thomas Cecil.

Ostend ar, and how much yow fynd above your formar opynion the importance of those ij places ar for the service ageynst the enemy, and therfor your lordship hath entred into consideration how to releve ther wantes; wherin, in my opynion, I think your lordship hath no on thyng, now at your first coming, mor nedefull for avoyding of that danger, which, if it shuld happen, will not be remedyed without gret charges and hazard. For I have allweise thought, that ther was nothyng more nedefull for the kyng of Spayn than to have mo and better places on Flanders syde than he yet hath for shippyng, as well to send ayde of men, mony, and victells, from Spayne, or from France by frendshipp, as to kepe shippes of warr to offend all passengers betwixt England and Zelland or Holland; as, by experience, the possessyng of Dunkyrk haven hath served, with a few beggarly vessells, to have done gret dammage by sea, presyng of men, shippes, merchandise, and victells; and suerly, my lord, if Sluse shuld be lost, the Spanyards might incress ther strength by sea with shippyng hable to overmach both Flussyngars and a good nombre of our shippes, for if the haven shuld be thers, they might kepe as well j^c sayle as x., and what cost will a kyng of Spayn spare, to be a master on the sea, wher he now is commanded? But I am to long herin, although I might wryte much more; but I know and perceave by your lordships own wrytyng, yow look depely into this matter, which in dede can not be to spedely looked unto, that both these places he victelled, manned, and ther weaknes also spedely strengthened, and, in my opinion, the states ought, at this tyme, more largly to contribut to this chardg than to a doosen of other towns in any part of Holland, and therfor, good my lord, as you have begon to take care hereof, so procure the states to yeld monny plentifully, to pay a sufficient nombre there whylest the imperfections of the places may be reenforced, and than the

---

[a] In the margin there is written by Lord Burghley, "The Flushyngars valiantly [pre]ssed ij vessels [of] Dunkyrk within [si]ght of the town."

nombers may be the fewar afterward. I wold to God that your lordship cold procure such a releff, as ether of those ij towns might have but j^c horsmen, who, joynyng togither, might ether spoyle the country, or might cause the ennemy bryng a great force to that frontyer, wherby ther own nombres shuld also dammag ther own towns, as Bruges, Newport, &c. by reason of ther lack of victells.

Mr. Wylford wrote a letter to Partridg of Kent, to help send hym some victells, and therwith he sent a letter of your lordship to the commissioners of Kent, and so I have procured letters from the counsell to the commissioners, to authorise on Mr. Avyer to send it over, with bond to have it saffly sent, wherof Mr. Brown your lordships servant is by me made[a] prive.

Your said servant also required my warrant for sendyng of ce[rtain] victell uppon your lordships letters wrytten to hym, and I was v[ery] willyng so to have doone of myn own authorite, but I am otherwise directed by a warrant signed by hir majesty afor your lordship departed, wherof, it is sayd, that your lordship was prive; but it bredeth, in [my] opinion, some hyndrance with the circumstances; for, first, it is by the warrant apoynted, that your lordship must, first, by your letters to me, signefy what quantite yow require, and than ther must be an other letter procured from four of the counsell to me, also, for allowance therof, and than am I authorised to gyve warrant to the portes, but yet with condition that bondes must be put into the chequer for the retorn of trew certificat from that syde. With all these circumstances I am circumscribed more than in former tymes hath bene thought necessary, but I fynd no lack in that I am so directed, but sometyme ther will be required more spede than this manner doth prescribe. Of this Mr. Brown is now prive, and yet I have ventured to gyve hym warrant, havyng also gotten a letter from the counsell, for such a proportion as he required, which was, for j^m quarters of

---

[a] made made, *in MS.*

wheat, as much malt, j^c ton of beare, xl bulloks, vj oxen, j^c shepe, vj barrells of tallow candells, a hoy with wood and cole. And he sayth, he will wryte to your lordship to have yow hereafter to signefy your mynd in particular wrytyng to me, for such thynges as yow shall have nede, wherin I wish your lordship caused accompt to be made of the charges of our prises, with charges of transportation, with the lyk kyndes there to be had, for I here report that manny thynges ar to be had ther with easyer prices, and, of those thynges, I doot not but your lordship will forbeare to require any provision from hence, which will also be good for our country, wher, by collor of these provisions, prises will ryse without reason.

I heare also, my lord, that there is gret gayne made of our coyn, both of gold and silvar ther, to the loss of our countrymen uttryng the same for that country monnyes, and the gayn sought by merchants both of that country and of England, by choppyng and changyng therof under the trew vallew; for, in truth, our monny, both gold and silver, is worth in eschange above xxxiiij^s. the pownd, and yet the marchant holdeth the eschange but at xxxiij^s. iiij^d, and therfor, my lord, yow may do a good dede to cause some honnest skillfull men to make a trew assaye of the monnyes of that countrye, and rate both our gold and silver at the same price, and to cause our people to be well instructed at what prices they ought to utter our monnyes for the monnyes of those con[tryes]. In this matter, I thynk a servant of alderman Martyns, that went over with the tresorer, can inform your lordship, or any of your counsell ther, what order war to be taken.

And I wish, also, that your lordship wold deale with the counsell of the states for reformation of ther myntes, which, being many in nombre, serve only by fraude to gayne to them that ar the officers of the myntes, and to the decept of the people.

Your lordship, also, is to be advertised, which I do by hir majesties direction, that she understandeth very certenly, that the king of Spayn maketh all the provision that he can possible, to mak a mighty navy for a great army to come by sea, to annoy hir majesty, and, for the furniture therof, beside his own shippes and gallyes, both of Spayne and Itally, in Millan, Naples, and Sicilly, he is promised ayd of men and gallyes from the pope and the dukes of Savoy and Florence, and, some report, from the Venetians, but therof I dout, so as, in conclusion, it is here found most necessary that hir majesty shall also make preparation of all the strength that she can mak by sea, and, for that purpooss, it is here resolved, that hir own shippes shall be removed to Portesmouth in March next, and a gret nombre of hir subjectes shippes shall also be made redy to come, ether to Portesmouth, or to Plymmouth, or to other places in our west partes, as, by further intelligence of the king of Spayns preparations, shall be requeset. And for this purpooss hir majesty thynketh it most nedefull that your lordship shuld presently procure some persons of understandyng, such as here is named, Mr. Nicholas Gorge, to repayre to the portes of Holland and Zelland, ether with the pryvety of the states or without it, as your lordship shall thynk best, and to attayn to a certen knolledg of the nombre of shippes provisable for warre, as to be about ij^c tons or vij or viij^{xx}, and of ther furnitur, and what nombre of marrynors ar also in every port, and whyther any nombre of marrynors might be had to be hyred, to help to supply our lack that may happen in the queen's navy, wherof we have cause to dowt, because of the gret nombre absent with Sir Francis Drak,[a] and abrod with our merchantes shippes being adventurers, and after that your lordship shall have understandyng hereof, than hir majesty wold have your lordship to impart to the states, or to ther counsell, how and in what sort hir majesty looketh to be this sommer, and that very tymly in the

[a] Sir Francis Drake sailed on the 14th September 1585, with a fleet of twenty vessels of various kinds carrying 2300 soldiers and sailors. They took their course to the West Indies, captured St. Jago, St. Domingo, and Carthagena, and returned to Plymouth on the 27th July 1586, bringing 240 captured cannon and about 60,000l. in prize-money. Vide Camden's Annals, anno 1585; Stowe's Chronicle, 709.

spryng, assayled by a gret army of the king of Spayns, and how nedefull it is, that all meanes possible be used to have a navy hable to withstand the same, and specially to impeach the comming of this Spanish navy towardes those Low Countryes, for which purpoos, as hir majesty will spare no chardg to arm hir own navy to the seas, and hir subjectes also, which must prove an unknowen chardg, so wold she have your lordship to exhort them, accordyng to the necessite of this tyme, to put in order spedely as gret a navy as maye [a] be by them fully furnished, to be redy to come to the narrow seas by the end of March, or the midd of Aprill, if by the king of Spaynes hasty preparations hir majesty shall be therto so spedely provoked. And though, by an article of the treaty, they ar bound hereunto in a certain quantite, as by the article wherof I send your lordship a copy, (I know not whyther you have the same,) yet the tyme requiring all help possible, to match with so puissant army as the king prepareth, your lordship may with reason soll[icit] them to a farder proportion, if it may be. And hir majesty is desyrous to be advertised hereof with such spede as your lordship may procure.

Thus, my lord, consideryng Mr. Aty maketh hast to depart, and I am as yet not so hable to wryte as I have bene, I pray your lordship that I may mak an end, with my assurance to your lordship that, in any thyng that in my power lyeth to plesure you and furder your service, I will be as redy as any frend that is here behynd yow. And to conclud, I hartely thank your lordship for the trust you have committed to me joyntly with my lord chancellor for your office of the forrest,[b] but we must have some directions from your lordship what to do, or els we shall not know what to doo.

I nede not wryte to yow of our common news here, because so

[a] they maye be *in MS.*
[b] The earl of Leycester was justice in eyre of the forests south of Trent. Amongst the Burghley papers is an account of the fee deer due to the chancellor and treasurer as the earl's deputies. Lansd. MS. 47. art. 1.

many come over at this tyme fully fornished with such matters. From Grenwich, the 26th of December, 1585.

Your lordships to be commanded,
W. Burghley.

Addressed.
To the right honorable my very good
lord the erle of Lecester, lord
[lieutenant of] the queens majestys forces
[in the] Low Countres of Holland, Zelland,
&c. and of hir majesty's prive counsell in England.

LETTER XVIII.

LORD BURGHLEY TO THE EARL OF LEYCESTER.

27th december, 1585.   cotton ms. galba c. viii. fol. 239.   orig.

Letter sent by sir Thomas Cecill, whom lord Burghley recommends to the earl's protection—the queen's anger with sir William Pelham and her hard usage of him—advice to the earl to search out the intention of certain works in progress at Antwerp.

My very good lord, whan I wrote my letters on Sonday, which I do send by Mr. Aty, I wrote the same in hast, as I am forced by multitude of causes to do allweis, but the rather because Mr. Aty told me, that he wold come for them as yesterday, and depart, which, fyndyng hym not to come, as I thynk by some necessary lett, and havyng my sonn here redy to pass towardes his shippyng, I have thought good to wryte a few thynges by hym.

First, I am so assured, and my sonn also, of your lordships honorable good will towardes hym, more than in common sort, as I forbeare to wryte any more, but, breffly, to recommend hym to your protection, and to wish [him] Godes grace to do as well as I am sure your lordship will wish hym.

My lord, now Mr. secretary being absent, I am occasioned to deale with hir majesty in manny thynges, and suerly I am gretly discoraged with lack of hir resolutions. For Mr. Pelham, I have delt ernestly with hir majesty to dismiss hym with hir favor to come thyther to your lordship, but hir majesty refuseth ether to pardon hym, wherof he hath most nede, or to stall [a] his dett, which he also requireth, yea to take as much of his land as resonably may satisfy his dett, so as he may, with the rest, live and pay his other dettes, but hir majesty peremptorely commandeth me to chardg hym to depart, and to hope uppon hir favor at his retorne. Herwith he is so discontented as he offreth rather to go to the Tower: in this hard terme his cause resteth. Hir majesty sayth, he nede be at no chardg ther, for he shall bot as a privat man attend on your lordship. I saye, I thynk your lordship meaneth to mak hym marshall. She sayth, that therin she will not deale, for she will charg hym with no service, but only to attend on yow. In these termes is this poore gentleman; and yet I will continew, with all importunite I can, to obteyne hir majestys more favorable opinion of hym, because I know how nedefull his service is to your lordship.

Good my lord, serche the intention of the works in Antwerp by the carpynters that work uppon shipps, in secret sort. I feare ther is ment to mak some multitude of flatt botes to bryng people into the flatt seas, to attempt Tergooss and Zyrecksea. Uppon the purpose of the ennemy your lordship is to provyde some conterwork to withstand such enterprises. I have hard that ther ar manny papistes in Tergooss.

And thus, the tyde callyng my sonn awey, maketh me and my letter in hast. At Grenwych, 27 December, 1585.

Your lordships at command,
W. BURGHLEY.

---

[a] *i. e.* to forbear for a time.

LETTER XIX.

THE EARL OF LEYCESTER TO MR. SECRETARY WALSYNGHAM.

31ST DECEMBER, 1585. HARL. MS. NO. 285. FOL. 160. ORIG.

The earl's reception at the Hague—treatment of a French ambassador—deliberations of the states general in reference to the settlement of their government and the power to be given to the English queen—her popularity in the Low Countries—news out of Germany—treatment of the king of Navarre.

Mr. Secretary, I cam hether to the Hay, uppon Monday last,[a] whear I was very honorably receaved, all the states being assembled together for that purpose, to make as much shew as they could devyse of their good wylles to hir majesty, as in many orations, pagentes, and such lyke, was expressyd, besyde the people with great joye cryed, " God save the quene, God save the quene," in every place of the stretes as I passed.

The next day all the hole states generall cam to me, and ther openly ageyn ther chauncelor Leonius (some call him Longonius) made a longe oratyon in thankes and prayses to the quenes majesty for hir great clemency, bounty, and goodnes, shewyd to these pore aflycted countreys; attrybuting all their good and happines, under God, to hir majesty only. As sone as he had donn than cam comyssioners from partyculer provinces, as from Utrycht, Geldars, and Fresland, besides sondry spetyall towens, as Ansterdam, Leydon, Auchuson, and others, all which must nedes use ther gratulacion, with oratyons, as the other dede, and much to the same effect all with thankes and prayse to hir majesty.

[a] Leycester removed from Delft to the Hague on the 27th December 1585, not on the 28th, as is stated in the journal published in the Retrospective Review, i. 277, 2nd series. The ceremonies of his reception are largely dwelt upon by Stowe and Holinshed, and form the subject of a series of twelve engravings published with the title of " Delineatio pompæ triumphalis quâ Robertus Dudlæus comes Leicestrensis Hagæ Comitis fuit receptus."

At all this cerymony-doing was ther a French secretary, sent hether v or vj [days] before with lettres from the king. He sayd yt was about merchantes matters, but in dede contrary, only to have impeched, yf he could, this bynding themselves to hir majesty as they doe. But the states gave him no audyence all the while, alleaging they were occupied about the servyce of the quene of Englond, which they wold dyspach before all princes in the world. This fellow, being present at all this solemne dealing with me, tooke yt in such snuffe[a] as he cam prowdly to the states, and offred his letters, saing: "Now I trust you have donn all your sacrafyces to the quene of Englond, and may yeld me some leysure to rede my masters letters." They so shooke him upp, and with such termes, naming hir majesty in skorn, as they tooke yt, as they hurld him his letters, and bidd him content himself, they wold first dischardge all the least dewtyes whatsoever to hir majesty before they wold hear him. So they have every day synce sett about the contract with hir majesty, spetyally how to gyve me answere for hir full satysfaction touching ther abyllytye to maynteyn ther warrs, whearin I hear credybly hir majesty shalbe well satysfied, and further then any of us looked for. And both roundlye and frankley they goe to worke, that ye shall se they wyll doe indede more than ever they promysed, considering her majestes denyall [of] the souerauntye and name of protector. For they meane, and must doe yt, for the hole people wyll have yt, that hir majesty shall have in hir handes the hole bestowing aswell of ther money and contrybucions as of ther men of warr; and the desire no longer hir good favour to them than they shall deall in all sincerytye with hir. Wherein yt apperes that all the comyssioners have wonderfully sett fourth her majesty to them all here, and Paull Buys hath donn his parte thorowly, so hath Walk also. And all thinges alredy [are carried on] with the most unyversall obedyence of hir majestys name that ever I sawe. And

[a] To take in snuff, is to be angry, to express resentment by contemptuous motion of the nostrils.

flatly yt apperes now, they wyll no other authorytye but under hir majesty, nor that their treasure nor lyves shalbe at the dysposing of any but hir majesty, which, yf you saw that we se here, ye would wonder at [what] these people doe, and ar able to doe, and yf God had not moved hir majesty to send when she dyd, the prince of Parma had byn by this tyme in the best and greatest tounes they have; but ye shall hear others in this and not me.

And as I wrote before how hir majestyes dealinges here ar alredy blowen into Germany, so this day the elector[a] brought me letters agayn newly com there, whereby they wryte most honorably of hir majesty, and the duke of Sax geues much better eye than he did, synce his wyfes death, and lyke to marry ageyn with the hows of Hanalt,[b] a great protestant and a great howse. He hath sent to speak with Seiguro, and very lyke to joyn with the other princes, who ar agreed, not only to send a messenger to the French king, but to lett him know, that they will com to the ayd of the king of Navare, who ys most iniuriously delt withall by the practyce of the pope and king of Spayn. The ellector vowede to me that they have donn more in these causes within this xx dayes, synce they understood of her majesties resolucyon agaynst the king of Spayn, aswell by Sir Francis Drakes going into the Indyes as her sending into these countreys, than they have don this x yeres, or wold have don this twelmonths yet. God send hir majesty to think of his mercyfull dealinges accordingly. The king of Denmark also hath joyned and encouraged greatly these princes. Hit ys told me by the elector that dyvers of them meane to send hether to me, to congratulate hir majestyes gracious doings toward this countrey.

I have no other nues tyll these states have fully ended ther consultacions, which wylbe to morrow, as I hear, and wholy, without contradyctyon, to be at the devotyon and dispocyon of hir

---

[a] *i.e.* the elector of Cologne. See p. 15, note [a].

[b] Anne, daughter of Christiern III. king of Denmark, and wife of the duke of Saxe, died 1st October, 1585. On the 3rd January, 1586, he married Agnes Hedwig, daughter of Joachim Ernest, prince of Anhalt.

majesty absolutly. Of this ye shall hear as sone as I shall know ther further answere. Two of our men of warr of Flushing hath taken ij Dunkirk men; one sonk and drouned all the souldyers and maryners. Thus fare ye well, sir, this last of December.

Your assured frend,
R. Leycester.

Hit ys sayd that the princes ar resolvyd to entreate Cassymere to be generall, and shall have xxv^m men levyed by the princes to goe with him into France.

LETTER XX.

THE EARL OF LEYCESTER TO MR. SECRETARY WALSYNGHAM.
3rd January 1585-6. Harl. MS. 285. fo. 174. orig.

The earl forwards letters omitted on a former occasion—he wishes the secretary to exercise his discretion as to shewing St. Aldegonde's letter to the queen—the earl is at Leyden.

Good Mr. secretarie. I had forgotten in my former letters to send unto you theis letters which I therein mencioned, which I presently send unto you herinclosed; and so committ you to the blessed tuicion of the Almightie. From Leyden, this iij. of Januarie, 1585.

Your assured loving frend,
R. Leycester.

I leave yt to your self whether you think yt good hir majesty se St. Aldagondys letter or no. I cam hether to Leydon whilst the states ar fynyshing all thinges ageinst my retorn, which wylbe to morrow: this ys a goodly town and very strong, and most loving people. Cassimers letter ys not here.

Addressed.
To the right honourable
  my very good frend, sir
  Francis Walsingham, knight,
  principall secretary to her majesty.

LETTER XXI.

LORD BURGHLEY TO THE EARL OF LEYCESTER.

12TH JANUARY 1585-6.   COTTON. MS. GALBA, C. IX. FOL. 15.   ORIG.

Interruption of communication with the Low Countries by contrary winds—delay of Sir Thomas Cecill and his great expences—reference to former letters—the queen has agreed to advance money towards an army to be conducted by don Casimir into France to the assistance of the king of Navarre—state of affairs in Scotland—doubts respecting the threatened Spanish armada—proposal to stay a convoy of provisions intended for the Spanish army, with the queen's special directions to the earl of Leycester upon the subject—sir William Pelham's difficulties with the queen and his creditors—the queen consents that lord Grey should join the earl—lord Burghley's illness—sir Thomas Cecill's horses taken by the Spaniards.

My very good lord, though ther ar manny difficulties both for your lordship ther, and for us here, to concurr to the furderaunce of this noble necessary service under your chardg, yet ther is no on thyng that more annoyeth the expedition than the advers wyndes, that somtyme kepeth us from understandyng of your procedynges, not many dayes but manny wekes; but, that most greveth us, the contrariete also of the wyndes stayeth us from sendyng to your lordship, not only of letters but of men, horse, victells, and monny. Amongst which evill accidentes my son, Thomas Cecill, feleth at this tyme the burden and greff therof, as he shuld have bene less damnefyed with an agew of on or two monthes. As soone as he had recovered his evill fate he went towardes the sea syde, the secound day after Christmas daye, shipped about lx horses and ij^c foote men, besyde lx other servantes and followers, about the tyme your lordships secretary, Mr. Aty, went also as I thynk with some monny of your lordships. Henry Killigrew, also, and William Knolls and sir Thomas Parrot went anon after. All these have lyne at Margat in Kent ever sence, to this 12. of January, for any thyng that I can heir to the contrary, savyng they have bene on to the seas three or four sondry tymes, and put back, ether with chang of wyndes or lack of wyndes, and, at this present, we have had these five or six dayes constant esterly wyndes with frostes, so as I feare a longer contynuance of the impedimentes, but hereof ther is no remedy. Whan God shall please to send them passadg, your lordship shall of ther own report here more particularetyes of ther incommodytes.

My son feleth very gret charges herby, for, as he wryteth hyther, victellis ar dearer wher he lyeth than at London, and, as he thynketh, at the Brill. He kepeth at his chardg, with his horses, his band of footemen being ij hundredth, and with his howshold servantes, and dyvers gentillmen that accompany hym, above iij^c mouthes. If your lordship be not good lord to hym for allowance, ether for wages or for charges of this transportation, or rather, I may saye, of this retardation by occasion of the lack of wyndes, he shall mak a shipwrack of his jornaye; but I wryte not this to move your lordship to do more than I knowe you will of your self consider what is mete, and what you may doo.

Now, my lord, I will leave this long preface, and come to some matters in my former letters. Whan Mr. Aty went from hence I wrote,[a] that hir majesty was desyroos to have your lordship to deale with the states to put ther navy in order to joyne with hirs, which shall be at Portesmouth in March next. Hir majesty also wold that your lordship shuld procure knolledg of the state of ther shippes mete for warr in every of the portes, and what nombre of marryners might be spared from thence, if the navy of England shuld have nede therof, which we dowte of, because of a gret nombre gon with Sir Francis Drake, from whom, sence he departed from the cost of Spayn, we never hard word, nether do we

[a] See p. 42.

look to here afor March. In lik sort, to your lordship to have inquisition made in Antwerp to what purpooss the vessels war made by a nombre of shipwryghtes that lately cam out of Itally, from Janua. These thynges I do repete to your lordship, not knowyng how my formar letters may come to your handes.

Now the rest that shall follow ar of thynges not mentioned before. The queens majesty hath yelded to procure a some of monny to be on hir part redy at Frankforth, towardes the levy of an army that, we hope, don Cassymyr will conduct into France, for the releff of the king of Navarr and Christes flock ther persequuted;[a] hereof monsieur de Grytry, that cam from Germanny afor your lordship departed, will inform your lordship.

In Scotland, to outward apparance, all thynges procede well. The kyng hath kept a parlement at Lythquoo, wher the lords that war bannished ar restored to ther states, and ar by the kyng cleared of the crymes imputed. He hath sent a gentleman of his chamber, named Kyth,[b] therof to advertise her majesty, and to offer all frendship that he can to his power yeld to hir majesty; he desyreth to have the leag that was begon to be fynished. Arrayn, now called but James Stuard, lyveth on the west seas, hoveryng ther, from whom the kyng requireth his jewells, which he, at his fleyng away, took out of Edenburgh castell, but he will not delyver them without a pardon to come back, which is denyed, but with condition that he will appeare to justyce, which he as yet declyneth. Mr. Randolf is to go to the Scottish kyng, and so the treaty, as I thynk, shall go forward. Tyme must trye these thynges, for we fynd that the French kyng hath sent, by sea, a baron of France, the son in law of Pynartes, a man of gret lyvyng but of lytle understandyng, and therfor he hath a shrewd instrument with hym, called Courselles, whom your lordship did, I

---

[a] The party of the league had taken arms against the king of Navarre, with a view to his exclusion from the succession to the crown of France.

[b] Sir William Keith. See a narrative of these transactions in Tytler's History of Scotland, VIII. 276. Randolph arrived in Edinburgh on the 26th February 1586.

thynke, know here with Malvesyn, a notable servitor to the Scottish quene and the house of Guise, and, addyng to this, that we understand how Lyddyngton, the secretary in Scotland, and Robert Melvyn, who both remayn in good creditt with the kyng, ar devoted to the kinges mother and to France, we may dout of the eventes.

Sence the puttyng of our shippes in order ageynst March, it was ment to have sent this next month ten shippes of warr, wherof five of hir majesty's and five marchantes, to have lyne uppon the cost of Spayn, to have impeached the coming togither from sondry portes of ther victells and shippyng, and also to have discovered the truth of the reportes of the gret preparations of a Spanish navy and army, accompted for iij^c sayle of shippes and gallyes and nere to iij^{xx} thousand men, by meanes of the helps out of Itally, from the pope, the duke of Florence, duke of Savoye, from Naples and Sicilly; but, lately, advertisement is come out of Italy, that ther is no such preparation made there, nether of men nor shippes, but whyther we be duly advertised I am yet in dout. Nevertheless, I did never thynk it lykly that any such nombres, ether of men or shippes, cold be sett forth by the king of Spayn as was reported, specially for want of victells for such a nomber; but hir majesty, uppon this advertisementes, stayeth the sending forth of the sayd ten shippes, but yet both they, and all the rest of the navy, contynew ther equippage to be in Portesmouth afor the end of March.

Now, my lord, I will resort to a speciall matter, whereof hir majesty hath sent me chardg to wryte sence I began this letter. A gentleman of the duk of Bullyon,[a] whom your lordship knoweth, named de Sevilly, cam two dayes past to hir majesty from the duk, to inform hir of a gret preparation of grayn and other victell provyded in Louvayn and Champayny, for to be sent down by the ryver of Maze to the Lowe Countreys, for the prince

[a] Robert de la Marck, duke of Bouillon from 1574 to 1588. After the battle of Coutras he commanded the army of the king of Navarre against the league.

of Parma's army, which mass of victell is to come by the dukes castell of Sedan, under his bridg; and though he have good will to stay it, yet he dar not so doo, for feare of offence to be intended ageynst hym, but if he cold devise how to by it of the owners, with collor to serve both for his own provisions to store his own castells and houses, and to distribut amongst his neighbours that do want, he sayth he wold aventur the staye with that collor, and though the vallew may be, as it is thought, above j^c thousand crowns, yet his desyre is to borrow but forty, or thirty, or, I thynk, twenty thousand crowns, towardes that purpos. And herin hir majesty hath gret lykyng to have this stayd, as a matter of very gret moment, as your lordship hath gret cause so to thynk by the want of victells presently in Flaunders and Br[abant], but hir Majesty, fyndyng hir charges otherwise so great, she doth not yeld to this loone, but hath thought of some other meanes, as hereafter followeth.

First, she wold have your lordship to impart this matter, as you shall thynk mete, to the states ther, in secret sort, for which purpos the gentillman Sevilly offreth to come to your lordship, as he sayth he also ment to have doone, as sent from the duk his master, and hir majesty thynketh this intention to stay this provision of such a moment to weaken the adversaryes forces, as, in very truth, a power of men ageynst them hyred with j^c thowsand crowns cold not so much annoy the adversaryes, and, if the states might yeld to the loone of the some of xxx thousand crowns to this purpooss, hir majesty wold thynk very well of them, the consideration wherof hir majesty hath willed me, in hir name, to be left to your lordship.

And besyde this meane, as if it shold not take place, hir majesty hath also commanded me to instruct our ambassador in France to understand the duke of Bullions mynd, whyther he shall not lyk that the French kyng be moved from hir majesty, very ernestly, ether to impeach this great convoye, consideryng the great derth of victells in France, or consideryng how hir majesty hath bene hertofore animated to enter into this action, to save the Low Countreys from the conquest of the Spanyardes, and to impeach the king of Spayns gretnes; and, therfor, to move hym, in honor, to prohibitt the frequent convoy of victells out of France, or els that he will not mislyk if the duke of Bullion can stey this convoye. And in these two sortes, hir majesty hath thought to devise meanes to stay this convoy, but whyther the same will be stayd I do dout, and yet, truly, I know not how the adversary might receave a greter blow, without drawyng of any weapon.

Wher your lordship hath had gret desyre to have had sir William Pellham, and also my lord Graye, your lordship shall understand that I have done my uttermost for Mr. Pellham, but hir majestes offence appeareth such towardes hym as she wold in no wise yeld ether to acquit hym of his dett, or to stall it as he desyred, and so he, alledgyng his dishabillite to passe for want of furnytur, though he confessed to me, and some others, that he had receaved v^{cl} of your lordship towardes his furnytur, which he had layd out, and so was indetted to your lordship; but his gretest impedyment was, that he did ow to other persons about v^{Ml} which he cold not pay, as he had a desyre, by sellyng of some landes, but that no man wold by of hym whylest he was in hir majesties dett; and in this sort his stey remayned xv or xvj dayes, notwithstandyng that I never cessed, I thynk, any iij whole dayes together, without movyng and intreatyng of hir majesty to shew hym favor, in remittyng part and stallyng the rest, but I cold not obteyn my request, and yet she willed that he shuld be commanded to depart; whereto he answered, that, as a privat soldier, he wold go, so commanded, but to tak any chardg, he was so unhable, as he offred hymself to be ether a prisoner or a banished man. In this sorte the poore gentillman being afflicted, he fell sodaynly and daungeriosely sick, whereof I informed hir majesty, and thereby to have pitte of hym. Wheruppon hir majesty yelded only to have his dett stalled, without remission of any part, addyng that he shuld not go over to your lordship, but that the lord Gray shuld come to yow, whose case I also reported for his dett to hir majesty, but therunto she hath yelded to remytt hym a part, and to stall the some that he borrowed whan he went into Ireland,[a] which was ij^{M1}. Hereof I have even this daye wrytten to Mr. secretary, to advertise my lord Graye.

My lord, all this letter I have bene forced to wryte in my bed, which I have kept these two dayes, not, as your lordship hath knowen, for payne of my gout, but in dede havyng seven dayes past rubbed of a good deale of skyn uppon my shyn, I did neglect the healyng of it whan I shuld, and so am I now forced to kepe my bed without any hose, or without any salve, hopyng within two dayes more to have it whole; and, therefore, I pray your lordship to accept my scriblyng in a rude sort in good part, and, doutyng of passadg, I mynd to dooble[b] this letter, and to send it by some others. From the court at Grenwych, 12. January, 1585.

Your lordships most assured,
W. Burghley.

After I had wrytten this letter thus farr, I have hard of the takyng of a hoye of Holland, wherin are taken ten or twelve horses of my sons. God send better luck for his own passadg.

My lord, we heare dayly that the Hollanders carry vyctells to Calliss under pretence of cockettes[c] to come to England. I assure your lordship ther can be no more care taken than is to stey carryadg out of England.

W. Burghley.

---

[a] Arthur lord Grey of Wilton went to Ireland as lord deputy in 1580.

[b] *i. e.* to make a duplicate of it.

[c] A cocket was a certificate that goods had paid duty, which was granted by the authorities at custom-houses to merchants, and without which no taxable commodities could be exported. The name is thought to be a corruption of "*quo quietus,*" words which occurred in the Latin form of the document.

LETTER XXII.

THE EARL OF LEYCESTER TO LORD BURGHLEY.

14TH JANUARY, 1585-6.   HARL. MS. 285. FOL. 176.   ORIG.

The earl reports conferences with the deputies of the states general, in which he was offered the absolute government of the Low Countries—the chancellor's address to him—his answer through Mr. Davison—the earl's expectations of success in the contest with Spain—devotion of the soldiers to the queen—characters of count Hohenlohe, count William of Nassau, and count Maurice—representations made by the states to the earl to induce him to accept the government — intended mission of Mr. Davison to England, to state more fully the reasons why the earl should comply with their request.

Mr. secretarie, I know yow think long to hear of some certein proceeding here, which, for my parte, I doe as greatly hasten, assuring yow, that, since I came to the Hage, I have not ceassed calling upon the states for their resolution, which they will in no wise make other then that I must be absolute governour, both of warre and peace, over all their provinces.

As upon new yeers day in the morning they came all to me, and brought with them a heralt and trumpettes, meaning as soone as they had delyvered their speech, which D. Leoninus had to make for them, which was to offer to me, with many good woordes for her majesties sake, the absolute governement of the whole provinces, and to proclaime the same immediatly. I was skarce readie, when one brought me woord of their being all in my great chamber, desyring to speake with me. Not knowing or thinking it had ben for any such matter, I made haste to goe to them, and so did, having the best of my company there with me. As soone as I came to them, by and by Leoninus began an oration to me, and, even as he began, one told me in mine eare, that they were come to offer this matter, and had brought heralt and all, &c. I was so bold presently to interrupt the chauncelour, telling him, that I heard he had some matter rather to deale more privately in, than so openly, and therfore prayed him and the rest, to come in with me to my chamber, where they should have a more convenient place. He turned abowt and said, " Yow hear my lord desyers us to withdraw with him into his chamber," and so they all went with me into my bedchamber, and I called such of the best of my companie as I thought meetest for v or vj, wherof Mr. Davison and Mr. Dr. Clerk were ij.

And there the chauncelour began again, and proceeded with his matter, which was, indeed, after a long discourse of her majesties goodnes, of the love of the country to her, of the trust they had in her above all the world, of the necessity they had for safetie of their state and countreys, albeit her majestie would not take the soveraigntie upon her, which they yet desyred might be, to choose some person of honour and creditt to be their governour. And as there was no prince in the world whom they ought obedience and duety unto, but to her majestie, so seing the creditt and trust it pleased her to putt me in here alredie, and the favour, creditt, and I cannot tell what, so many good woordes they used of me, they tooke knowledge of that I had long had at her majesties handes, with manie yeers contynuaunce in her service, as appeered, they said, both now by her own commendation by lettres, as also to their commissioners in England, that had reported the same of her own mouthe: they did not know any person whom they could desyre so much to take this office in hand as my self, and, therfore, with one whole consent they did there beseech me, even for the love her majestie bare them, and for the help of so afflicted a countrey, that was ever a faithfull frend to the crowne of England, that I would take the place and name of absolute governour, and generall of all their forces and souldiers, with their whole revenues, taxes, composicions, and all manner of benefittes that they have, or may have, to be putt freely and absolutely into my handes, disposicion and order, with so ample woords and termes as here were too long to recite, seing I will shortly send you the whole by Mr. Davison.

As soone as he had ended I aunswered by Mr. Davison, whom I required to delyver it in French, as they all speak only French, that, as this was a matter unlooked for, being further then had past in the contract with her most excellent majestie heretofore, so was I presently very farre unprovided to give them aunswer to this matter, albeit, in her majesties behaulf, greatly to thank them for their ernest goodwills and great affeccion borne to her majestie; and very true it was they did all acknowledge, that her highnes had shewed herself a most loving princesse and neighbour to them, as did well appeer to their embassadors in England, that what she did was only for the good will she bare to this afflicted countrey, and for no private respect or commoditie to her self. I did also give them most hartie thankes for myself, that did conceive so well of me, being but a straunger to them, that they would hazard so great a matter upon me, as all their state, both well and ill dooing, should depend therupon. But as her majesties gracious favour towardes me ledd them to this conceite of my abilitie, farre more then was in me to deale in any such cause, so I prayed them not to take it in ill parte, that I desyred at their handes, to proceed with them in thoes cawses which I had to doe in her majesties behaulf with them, and give me time, or els some of them to come unto me, to hear what I had to delyver unto them touching the contract alredy past betwixt her majestie and them, wherin I thought they should finde I had more alredy layed upon me, than so weake shoulders were able to bear, and well to goe thorow withall. That her majestie had sent me only to serve them, and so I promised I would, both faithfully and honestly, even as her majestie had commaunded and willed me to doe. So they returned, after Mr. Davison had made this aunswer for me, not leaving, at their departure, to insist upon their former request very ernestly.

The next morning they appointed v or vj to come to me, which were of the chief of them, and, leaving the former matter, as not to speak of it at all, I delt with them upon certain pointes and questions, such as her majestie had willed me principally to remember; as, first, to know what their forces were, who were their chief governours, and had charge of townes and fortes, what meanes they had to contynue and mainteyne their forces, how their people and garrisons were paied, what debtes they were in to their souldiers. Theis, and sundry other, which are sett downe for her majestie, ye shall receive : leying before them what a mighty enemy they had against them, it behooved them to shew good force and good means to withstand such an enemy. To theis thinges, and all other questions, I think their wilbe good satisfaction given to her majestie, to cawse her think their state not so hard as hath ben doubted, nor for her majestie to repent her cost or charge adventured for them. I doe assure myself it will proove the best expences that ever shee bestowed in her life, and the best repayed againe to her coffers, if God overthrow not the world.

I did never see greater probability in my life of assured good successe, and protest unto you, I like the matter xx tymes better then I did in England, and so I beleeve any man here of judgement doth the like. And yet is it nowe at the verie woorst, as well for the decaie of our men, as for the season of this time, which is such as we cannot, till the wether break, send by water or land almost to any place. I could not hear owt of Zeland but by long seas, all the ryvers be ycie and frozen, but not to bear any horse or cariage.

Th'enemy hath attempted sundry places, but repulsed at all, and I dare presume thus much for her majesties name only, that if her comfort had not come, yow had heard of many a revolt er this daie, and the poor garrison-men, the straungers chiefly, suffer presently the greatest miserie in the world for all thinges, and yet send good comfort daily hither to me, that for the queen of Englandes sake they will suffer more yet. The queen of England they would serve as their mistris, and under me as her minister here, with a better will then ever they served under the prince of Orange; yet they loved him well, but they never hoped of the libertie of this countrey till now.

It is assured me the states are verie well able to perfourme their charge, and with great ease. The count Hollock[a] [is] surely a wise, gallant gentleman, and a right souldier, and verie well esteemed with many of the capteins and souldiers; he hath only one fault, which is, drinking, but good hope that he will amend it. Some make me believe I shalbe able to doe much with him, and I meane to doe my best, for I see no man that knowes all theis countreys, and the people of all sortes, like him, and this fault overthrowes all. Here is another little fellow, as litle as may be, but one of the gravest and wisest young men that ever I spake withall; it is the count Guilialme of Nassau,[b] he governes Frizeland; I would every province had such another. He had noe lettre from her majestie yet, nor his father, but that makes not so great matter as for this young gentleman. Her majestie may doe well also to contynue some kindenes from time to tyme with this howse of Nassau, especially to shew to take care for the count Maurice, who hath ben greatly laboured to have harkened to a composition, I can tell you, and I see him much discontented with the states for certein. He hath a sullen, deep witt, and shrewd counsellours of his fathers abowt him, now that they see the hope of Holland and Zeland taken awaie, which was the marke was wholy by the father shotte at, and almost hitt, as I am sure you have heard. The young gentleman is yet to be wonne only to her majestie, I perceive, of his owne inclination. The howse is merveilous poor, and litle regarded

[a] *i. e.* Count Philip of Hohenlohe, who married Mary of Nassau, one of the daughters of the late prince of Orange. When the states elected prince Maurice, then only eighteen years of age, to succeed his father as stadtholder, count Hohenlohe was appointed his lieutenant or deputy.

[b] William Lewis, stadtholder of Friesland, brother of Ernest Casimir, count of Nassau Dietz, and son of John brother of William prince of Orange.

by the states hitherto, and if they gett any thing it is like to be by her majestie, which I wishe should be altogether, and she maie easily doe for him to wynne him sure; I will undertake it.

Well, now I will returne a litle backe again, to tell you what followed since my former conference with the states. They went to their fellowes and told them what had passed; they aunswered me again, and brought me an act sett downe in writing by them all, that I should be pryvie to all their state, as well for their forces as their means, and that I should see very flatly that they abused not her majestie, neither with the offer of sovereigntie, nor yet with the state of their abilitie to mainteine their cawse, but better then ever they told her of, and referred to me what I thought of the strength and force of theis countreys. " Well, now we will say, and make your lordship know," say they, " the people bearing the love wee see they doe to her majestie, if she had taken the sovereignty over us, she should have had monethly 300,000 florens, certeinly payed to her purse, which is 30,000[li] sterling, every moneth, beside the customes of merchauntes, and Flaunders if it might be recovered, which did yeeld as much and more alone; and her majestie should doe more good, and defend th'enemy farr easilyer, with 100,000 than we shall with 200,000, for the obedience and reverence to her majestie would be as great as in England, and that we doe is even with feare and force among them, which bringeth such confusion as there is no remedie, but either your lordship must take the whole governement upon you, at our humble suite, and at the request of all the rest, or els all wilbe yet lost;" confessing that confusion of officers hath undoon their governement, and not to be recovered but by som one to take it that is so backt as I should be by the countenaunce of her majestie, whom the people only trust and love, for unto no other will they committ that which they will to her majestie, or one of hirs; and so doe they flatly conclude the matter upon me.

All the lords here have ben in like sort with me, and all the captens, and governors, and magistrates of townes, pressing me most earnestly, if I love her majestie, if I love the good of England, and theis countryes, to take it, and that forthwith, bycawse the souldiers be unpayed, and no man will contribute any longer but to her majesties minister, and to him all places doe promis, and have sent their procuratours, as they told me alredy, to bind themselves and all their townes for the payment of ij^c m. florens monethly, beside the admiraltie to be discharged by their customes, as it is alredy. They will also make their oath to me, and all officers, to returne presently to paie all sommes to me. Thus it standeth presently, as either all must be hazarded and lost, or els I must take it, which, as farre as I can see, and all here with me, as the case enforceth it, must needes be best for her majesties service everie waie.

The reasons Mr. Davison shall delyver you, who hath seen how I have proceeded, and upon what necessitie either this waie must be taken, or els all overthrowne. It is doon for the best, and if so her majestie accept of it, all wilbe to the best. I have had none other scope herein, nor shall have, but her majesties service above all worldly respectes, and well knowne to the wisest here with me, how desperately both the lords and capteins were and are bent, if I should not take this upon me, to have left and given over the whole service of theis states, which had made an easie conquest for th'enemie, but a most dangerous for her majestie. Thus referring the full declaration of our doinges here to Mr. Davison, who shall shortly be with you, doe take my leave, and commytt you to the Lords protectyon. At Leyden, this xiiij. of January.

Your assured frend,
R. Leycester.

LETTER XXIII.

THE EARL OF LEYCESTER TO MR. SECRETARY WALSYNGHAM.

15TH JANUARY 1585-6.   HARL. MS. NO. 285. FO. 180.   ORIG.

The earl earnestly entreats a remittance of money—the enemy are active, and have put several important towns in danger—they are now upon " Zeland syde"—the states have agreed to form a camp to restrain the incursions of the enemy—an important enterprise in hand—if the queen continues favourable to the cause, the earl will be able to ease her charges—Mr. Davison coming over.

Mr. secretary, as you shall shortly hear of our hole procedinges by Mr. Davyson, so must I entreat you most ernestly, even as the well doing of my poore servyce here may be tendred, but spetyally for the honor and servyce of hir majestie, that you wyll be meanes that ther may be a good quantytye of money sent over, as ther ys behind of the hole some her majestie dyd sett done, as I take yt, above lxx^{m}li. So you wyll procure, as much as in [you] may lye, that the most parte may be sent over. Hit shalbe the worst, and the most, she shalbe charged with, but, at the beginning, xx^{m}li. shall stand in more stead than xl^{m}li. iiij monthys hence, and I am well perswaded, as you shall se at Mr. Davysons coming, that they here have good meanes to maynteyn ther warrs, and when we make reconing at home of a defencyble warr, hit must be so defencyble, as we must be able to have always vj or vij^m men, horse and footemen, to frunt the enymye, who, all this hard wether, hath gon from place to place with iiij^m footemen and xv^c horse, and at this day he kepes the fyld, and hath putt in danger iij or iiij townes of great importance, as Brabee, Wenloe, Vianna, and Bomeley, as also now he ys come uppon Zeland syde, and wyll doe what he can to Lylle and Lyskinshook, whear ther hath byn much decay of soldyers, but ther ys doing all that ys possible for defence, for otherwyse we ar no way able to resist them, which they know, and doth make them presume the more at this tyme. But the states have agreed, and doe find ther ys no remedy, but we must erect a camp to brydell this lyberty of the enymye, or ells he wyll kepe a warr this xx yere, and make us all wery, and, this way being taken, I warrant ye we wyll shortly wery him as well, and yet never hazard any battell, which he wyll be as loth to come to as we.

I am in hope of an enterpryse to tak place shortly which ye wylbe gladd to hear of. God send yt to fall out as I looke for, and that ye may provyde us spedyly with a good some of money, being all one to hir majestye, and I wyll undertake she shall com to no furder chardge whatsoever. I wyll help to ease hir, before the end, of a good parte of this, yf she doe but contynew hir favour and good countenaunce to this cause only, as I trust she wyll, or elles she knoweth not the lacke she wyll fynd of the frendshipp of these countreys. As, uppon my honour and truth to you, they were almost utterly gonn yf I had not aryved when I dyd.

Thus, referring ye for the rest to Mr. Davyson at his coming, I wyll take my leave, protestyng my hole care and endeavour his to doe hir majestie acceptable servyce, or elles God not to lett me lyve, yf otherwyse yt shuld be. In much hast this xv. of Januery,

Your assured frend,
R. LEYCESTER.

Addressed.
To my very honorable good frend
sir Francis Walsingham knight,
principall secretarye to her majesty.

LETTER XXIV.

LORD BURGHLEY TO THE EARL OF LEYCESTER.

17TH JANUARY, 1585-6. COTTON. MS. GALBA, C. IX. FOL. 24. ORIG.

Lord Burghley re-states his inquiries respecting the amount of assistance which the states can give towards repelling the armada—also as to the works carrying on secretly in the churches of Antwerp—Ortell's proposals as to trade between the Low Countries and France—news from Lisbon.

My very good lord, as matters do rise so I am bold to wryte unto yow, and yet I se so many misaventures in savety of arryvall of lettres, as I se it necessary to repete thynges in second lettres, wherewith your lordship may be trooblod by readyng, but I had rather, so woole your lordship, than leave it undoone.

In my former lettres I have shewed yow that hir majesty wold have your lordship to cause inquisition to be made of the nombre and power of the shippes of warr in Holland and Zelland, and with what nombre they wold be content, uppon ther charges, to serve this yere with hir majesties navy agaynst the king of Spaynes power, which hath bene reported greater than I can beleev, but hir majesty is resolved to have hir navy redy at Portesmouth before the end of March. Hir majesty, also, wold gladly have your lordship discover to what purpooss the Itallien carpyntors do work, as it is sayd, very secretly in chirches, in Antwerp, about shippes or gallyes.

Of late Ortell, that remayneth here agent for the states, propounded certain questions uppon the trade to be used by the shippars of Holland and Zelland; the articles I do send herewith to your lordship, with an answer by us here gyven, under your lordships advise, uppon conference with the states. We fynd here, that, under collor of any trade with merchants to any part of Pycardy, the enemy is succored. Nevertheless, as your lordship shall ther fynd the states conformable, we here will prescribe that same order to be kept. Truly, my lord, it is most necessary that all kind of victells, or matters for shippyng, be utterly forbydden.

We have advertisementes from Lyshborn by sondry come from thence, that all English men ar at liberty ther, and that the preparation is as yett not grett, only all manner of great hulkes ar stayd. And so I end from any farther trooblyng of your lordship. 17. January, at Grenwych.

Your lordships most
assuredly,
W. Burghley.

Addressed.
To the right honorable my
very good lord, the erle of
Lecester, lieutenant generall
for all hir majesties forces in
the Low Contreys.

LETTER XXV.

THE EARL OF LEYCESTER TO MR. SECRETARY WALSYNGHAM.

22nd January, 1585-6.   harl. ms. 285, fo. 182.   orig.

The earl is dissatisfied with the treasurer of the army— entreats that money may be remitted—knows the difficulty of obtaining it from the queen, but offers reasons why she should send it — the devotion of the people to her majesty, and their determination that the earl should be their absolute governor—Mr. Davison's services —proceedings of the prince of Parma upon hearing of the arrival of the earl—rumours spread by the prince that the earl had merely come to bring about a peace—arguments in favour of carrying on the war in the offensive—the earl wishes for more troops—notices of the characters and designs of Villers, count Maurice, St. Alde-

yonde, Mallory, Meddykirk, Paul Buys, count Hohenloe—enterprises in meditation—the earl wishes lord North to be appointed to some office or else recalled—Dr. Barth. Clerk is of little use.

Mr. secretary, I can wryte nothing to ye touching the state of the tresure or tresorer. I wyll not blame him yet, nor excuse him, but I dowbt he hath a conning under-tresorer. This vj wekes can I gett no reckoning, nor the awdytor any bookes from them, tyl this last weke. Our money goeth very low, and I beleive ye will not be best pleased with the former expences, and yet am I forst to dysburs much of this money for relyfe of the souldyers not payd, and, as I wrote of late to you, so doe I now also to my lord tresorer by Mr. Davyson, to besech ye both, yf ye wyll have any hope of good of our servyce here, to gett us a good pece, or rather the hole somme, of that ys behind of hir majestys allowance. Yf hit be not well ordered and husbanded, lett the blame light hevyly uppon me.

My thinkes I hear your answere alredy, that no man knoweth better than I the dyffycultye to gett money from hir majesty, and so I must satysfye myself. But, as I confes yt ys hard to procure great sommes from hir majesty, so must I lett you know, and more now than whan I was partaker of those dyffycultyes ther with you, that yf hir majesty doe not deall now gratyously and princely with these people, and consider how infynyttly hit doth import her highness to bring these causes to a good end, whan yt ys in such forwardnes as they be, and that yt ys only the expence of a lytle money, and no more than she hath alreddy contractyd and agreed with them for, and for which she hath such a pawen as she may assure hirself, by them alone, to have all hir charges ageyn, yf the worst fall owt that can be. And here I say to ye Mr. secretary, and I speak yt in the presence of God, I am veryly perswaded, yf hir majesty had not donn this she hath donn, these hole countreys had byn gonn by this day; and, se the good providence of God! yf I had not come when I dyd, the wynd turned the next daye, and hath so contyneued ever synce, that, this being the xlij day since my aryvall, I never hard word from Englonde; I trust, therfore, whan yt comes yt shalbe good. But, if I had steyd tyll this day, all hope had byn gone of hir majesty, and all the practyces of the enymye had byn sett afoote, for I founde them very well onward at my aryvall; yet, I testyfye a truth, as sone as hir majestys favour hether was sene and known, I thinke from the beginning of these trowbles the people were never hotter ageinst the enemye than at this day, nor better devotyd to hir; in so much as she may now dyspose of all, and dyrect all, that otherwyse had lost all, both countryes and credytt, yea, with a mortall hate for ever to our natyon; and yf the case be thus for hir majesty, for Gods sake lett hir comfort all here, and lett hir be sure the enymye was never so dowbtfull, nor so perplexed, as he ys at this day; for he stoode in great hope, before my coming, to have had certen places delyvered unto him of great importance, and I think hit was so promysed to him in dede, but as sone as the souldyers hard of hir majesty taking the cause in hand, and that I was com, they setled themselves wholy this way, and so doe contyneue, and have resisted the enymyes attemptes most faythfully; yet have they not byn payd a long while, nether wold have trusted the states but for hir majesty, takyng my word only that they shalbe payd; and so they shalbe forthwith, I have wroght so for them. Nether wold they wyllingly trust the states touching hir majesty, but that I must have the absolute government, and the recept of their reveneues, or elles they wold not be pacyfyed, nor trust to their paymentes more; which suerly hath byn yll handled, for they have meanes and meanes ageyn to meyntayn all these charges, but their careless imploying of yt hath hindred all; but this requyres a hole wekes informacion of Mr. Davison, who hath donn hir majesty notable servyce here, and doe pray ye, and as ever ye tender the success of this servyce, retorn him hither, with the more credytt the better, for without him I confes myself quyte maymed. His credytt ys mervelous great here that ever I sawe of any stranger in any countrey, in my lyfe, and he lyves lyke a gentleman and chargeably every way. And my nephew Sydney, I assure ye, ys notably estemed, and I think within a few months shalbe able to doe hir majesty here other manner of servyce than may well be looked for.

The prince of Parma, uppon my aryvall, and hearing of the dysposicion of these countreys wholy bent to shew their good trust of hir majesty, by comytting all chardge and confydence to me, being hir servaunt and subiect, he assembled the counsell, the presydent &c. ther opened the matter, shewing the great dyffycultyes happened unto them unlooked for, for yt was a matter assured them that the queen of England wold never attempt any thing, ether here or elleswhere, but he saw now yt was otherwyse, and that she had sent Drake to the Indyes, and the erll of Leycester into the Lowe Countreys, alleaging all he could do. The president answered him: " Now sir," quod he, " ye may se what yt was for the king our master to forsake the councell was geven him, and the offer the people made of these countreys to have had a peace, and whether yt had byn better to [have] accepted that, or elles to consume his treasure and people in vayn; for yt was never other lyke whan all such meanes as the queen of England made accompt of was taken away, as the prince of Orange that was at hir devotyon, and Monsieur who was in stryct league with hir, but she wold rather defend and kepe these countreys hir frendes, then suffer our master to enioye them, being afreyd of his greatnes to be so nere hir as these countreys shuld be, except there were better love betwene them than ther ys. But refusing that peace his people offred him to have had religyon fre, was the cause of all these warrs, and losse now of thes countreys, which than he had byn sure of, yea, and, after a while, to be sure also to have putt down the herytykes and protestantes, as he might have used the matter; but now," saythe [he], " yt ys to late for councell, the queen of Englond ys not so easy to be removyd, being received as she ys among them, nether doe I ever looke now for so good an end ageyn."

Synce that, ther cam within these ij daies one from Antwerp, beside here ar sondry letters from thence of yt, (which ys donn of purpose to bring this people in dowbt of hir majestys dealing for them,) that there was a howse in Antwerp, the Englysh howse, preparing for me; that she made but a shew of warr, her intentyon ys only to make a peace, and that I had instructyons to prepare the myndes of the states to conformetye, and to be reconcyled to the king. I assure ye a pestylent practyce yt ys, and no one thing under heaven so lykely to cutt my throte, but yt doth agre well with a tale that was wrytten also from Bruxelles to the cont de Hollock here. That the prince of Parma, hearing of my aryvall, chaft very much, and semed greatly to be deceaved that hir majesty wold send as she hath donn, "but," sayth he, "ther ys no remedye but one; we must gyve out brutes that the queen of England hath offerd talk of peace, which wyll brede presently jelosye in the states heads, and some devyces we must have to make devyssion among them, to breake this resolucyon to lett the government be at the queen of Englands dyspocytion." This letter cam to him, which he shewyd me, above iij wekes agoe, and, as the cont sayd, from a very credyble place; so that he presumeth styll of the umore[a] of Englond. But God defend hir majesty shuld loose the honor, credytt, and saftye, she ys in so good way to obteyn, and lett me have shamfull death and utter reproch, yf hir majesty goe princely and couragiously forward, yf ever she receive the lyke porcyon of all these as she shall doe by this actyon here. And I assure you yf ye saw these places, with the dysposicion of the people, as I doe, ye wold think, even for hir majestys own safty sake, but for her own tyme only, beside the respect of Englond, that more money than yet she hath leyd out to be most happely spent yf ther were no gage or hope to have yt payd ageyn.

[a] *i. e.* humour.

Lett me retorn, therfore, once ageyn, to pray ye, and entreat ye, to stand ernestly for the spedye sending away of money; and to send yt by dryblettes causeth yt to be consumed to lytle purpose, and no honour or credytt, nor yet relyfe in dede of the soldyer. Touching this I have wrytten in a scedule enclosed, which I pray ye break after ye have redd yt.

And touching the opinion of a defensyve warr, I know ye wyll now chang yt, for ther ys no wey to overthrow this state but that. Experience doth teach yt, for the enymye goeth where he wyll, he makyth skours now in every place; as, ferst, in Flanders, about Ostend and Sluce, he hath made so many, as no man can sturr out to anoye the enymye any way, nether can they be taken with all the garasons ther. He hath byn synce about Grave, a place of great importance for us, not farr from Bolduke[a] in Brabant; he hath attemptyd yt iiij or v tymes this frost, but myshing[b] of yt, he hath buylt iij or iiij forts about yt, that no vyttell can com to yt. He hath donn the lyke at Venlou, and ys presently in doing ther, and hath ther iij[m] men and a 1000 hors; all the garasons we have ther ys not able to deale with him. So from this place he wyll to some other, but yf he follow these ij so strongly as he may doe, I se no way we ar able to mach him yet in the fild to relyve them, and, lett him alone, he wyll surely have them. Therfore ther ys no remedye for us but to make a camp, which wylbe, with those we have alredy, without any great chardg donn, whereby we may be masters of the fild, for he dares not draw his garasons fourth of his great towens, so shall we relyve the places thus beseged, and recover the skonces and fortes he hath buylt to anoye us. Besides he doth spoyll all countreys that ar most frutefull and help us most, by his contynewall incursions, which is a great matter I se here, to loose the servyce of the bours,[c] and yt ys also a dyscouraging warr to this people that ar dayly charged with taxes and contrybucions, to se an endles warr,

---

[a] *i. e.* Bois le Duc.   [b] *i. e.* missing.   [c] boors.

as they caule yt when yt ys altogether defensyve, and so yt ys in dede; and we ar sure the enymy ys more ferfull to adventure than we ar, for yf we loose, we have styll strong townes able to defend, yf he loose, he hath no townes to hold him, for all he hath ys alredy by the force of his garasons.

I have sent to ye, sir, also, for leave that sondry gentlemen may have leave to take upp som men in Englond, without any peny charge ether to hir majesty or the countrey, and our enymyes ar the bolder for that they know the decaye of our soldyers. I wold be gladde, also, to have leave for v^c of my none servantes more, not in Wales alone, but of my other tenantes, where I shall think mete; for I tooke but $iiij^c$ of the v^c hir majesty dyd graunt, and I wyll not gyve those $iiij^c$ for the best v^c & l. that I se or can hear of here, nether shall ther any man have charge, by my good wyll, but such as shall have good cause to care for his men. I think xv^c wyll skant well furnyshe all the bandes decayd here, and I wold ernestly desier ij^m more, such as wyll wyllingly com. Ye have people to many, and ye nede not fear any attempt to Englond in assaling yt by force, as long as hir majesty hath these countreys, I warant ye; therfore help us yf ye wyll styll be quyett. And yf I may be able to wander a while with ij^m horse, and 4 or 5000 footemen, about Easter ye shall hear, without any meting withall, all those skonces shalbe caught, our own places putt in good sewrty, and the enymye as well spoyled. And I pray ye, for these things, beleave us pore men that serve, and have best cause to know what course in reason ys best.

When Mr. Davyson comes he shall tell ye at lardge of some partyculer thinges ye wold have lytle beleved, but I know them to be most true. That Vyliers ys a most vyle trayterous knave, and doth abuse a young nobleman here extremely, the conte Morys; for all his religion he ys a more ernest perswader secretly to have him yeld to a reconcylliacion than St. Allagonde was, and hath an instrument about the young gentleman, one that pleasyth his affectyons, that ys a very dangerous man. The young man hath a solem, slye wytt; but, in troth, yf any be to be dowbtyd toward the king of Spain, yt ys he and his counsellers, for they have byn altogether so farr French, and so farr in myslyke with Englond, as they cannot almost hide yt, and this umore ys styll kindled by this prest, and some say yet St. Allegonde, but I doe not beleve yt, for that he hath geven his word for yt to me. The other shall not tarry ten dayes nether in Holland nor Zeland; he ys greatly hated here of all sortes. And yt shall goe hard but I wyll wynn the young conte, and gett the knave about him removed, whose name ys Mallorey, one the prince himself dowbtyd of before his deth.

Old Medykyrk was farr gonn ageinst hir majesty, and our natyon also, and so farr dowbtyd, as now, at the nomynacion of councellors, I named him for one, thinking he had good credytt among the states, and I found them all ageinst him, and made request to me to leave him out, which I mervelled at, and doe plainly chardge him with his yll mynd to hir majesty. Paule Buys, I lern, certenly was putt from his offyce in Holland only for standing agenst the French, and preferring Englond alweys, and indede he passeth them all for skyll and judgement.

The cont Hollock deserveth great countenaunce at hir majestys handes, for he ys a plaine gentleman, and one that always delt flatly with the prince for the French, even tyll his death; and was also so reddy and had best power to delyver both Flushing and the Bryll into hir majestys handes, and yt ys most true that he was greatly pressed to stand agenst yt, and the yong count was not wyllyng to have yt rendred, only by Vyllyers meanes, and the cont Hollock perceving told the cont Morrys, in a great rage, that yf he tooke any other course than the queen of England, and swear by no beggers he would drouen his prest in the haven before his face, and turne himself and his mother-in-law out of there howse there, and thereuppon went with Mr. Davyson to the delyvery of yt. This man must be cheryshed; he ys sound and faythfull, and hath indede all the chife holdes in his handes, and at his comandment. Ye shall doe well to procure him a letter of thankes, taking knoledge in generall of his good wyll to hir majesty. He ys a right Almayn in manner and fashion, fre of his purse and of his drynk, yet doe I wysh him hir majestyes pencyoner before any prince in Germany, for he loves hir, and able to serve hir, and doth desyer to be knowen hir servant. He hath byn sought and labored by his nerest kinsfolkes and best frendes in Germany, to have left the states, and to have the king of Spaines pencyon, and very great reward, but he wold not. A cheyn of ij^c li. wold be well bestowd uppon him in the meane tyme; and uppon his further desart, which I think wylbe shortly, I trust hir majesty wyll accept of his offer to be hir servaunt during his lyfe, being in dede a very noble soldyer. He hath some matters a-brewing which he hopeth well of; for my parte I have an other, brought to me by Mr. Davyson, which yf yt fall out as I verylye looke for yt, that wylbe worth 'God a mercye!' and nerer home, and of exceding great consequence for hir majesty and this cause, and or xx days ye shall hear of yt, I trust in God.

Ther ys another matter and I must trowble you withall, and full fayn I wold have yt redressed; hit ys my lord North. Hir majesty hath comaunded him hether in my company; he doth certenly doe me all the honor he can devyse, and he hath not the best boddy for such a place, spetyally he having no chardge, nor any allowance in the world, and surely his expences cannott be lytle, albeyt his grefe must be more to have no countenance at all but his own estate, and a man of his yeres and long servyce.[a] He doth take yt hir majesty doth place him for some respect of myne, which wyll gender an inward grudge to me at length. I am not the cause of yt. He ys a wyse gentleman, and for any nede I se I shall have of Mr. Bartholomew Clerk, I assure ye I had farr rather have my lord Northes councell and assistance; and for lawe here ys one, the other lytle Clerk, who ys much beyond Bartho-

[a] Roger, the second lord North, succeeded to the title on the death of his father in 1564, and died in 1600, Camden describes him as "vir vivido ingenio, animo consilioque par." Annales, sub anno 1600.

lomew in all lerninges of lawe, as hath well appered here alredy. Yf at Mr. Davysons coming ye can, ether with honour and allowance kepe my lord here, or elles in some good sort by hir majesty cauled for home, rather than to attend here without any charge or countenaunce, I wold gladly wysh yt. That in the mean tyme yt wyll lyke ye to wryte to my lord how carefull and myndfull I have byn of him, shall doe me a great pleassur. And thus having bin long, as I cannott others [a] chuse having so much to imparte to you, I wyll byd ye farewell, longing styll to hear from ye. At the Hage, this xxij. of January.

Your assured frend,
R. LEYCESTER.

Bycause I se how the wynd kepes back all hearing from ye, being xlij days synce I hard from England, sir, Grant Herns hath a man that doth bring dayly fishe from this cost, and when no shipp goeth out he wyll shift ageinst the wynd, and he comes very safely. I pray ye bear with the faultes of my letter, hit ys so long I cannott peruse yt.

I am afrayd ye will compare me shortly to Wylliam Herll.[b]

Addressed.
To Mr. secretary
Walsingham.

LETTER XXVI.

THE EARL OF LEYCESTER TO MR. SECRETARY WALSYNGHAM.

31ST JANUARY 1585-6. HARL. MS. 285. FO. 190. ORIG.

Mr. Davison is returning home to explain the earl's proceedings—the earl begs Mr. Davison may be allowed to rejoin him—great value

[a] So in MS.
[b] Herle was at this time occasionally employed in public affairs. Many of his letters are in existence which are generally extremely long, and are written in a very illegible hand. See Cotton MS. Titus, B. VII. fo. 44.

of his services—sir William Pelham no longer expected—lord Grey would be very serviceable, especially if any mischance befel the earl—entreats that money may be sent—refers to Mr. Davison for matters of state—exploit of Schenck—the earl's care for Ostend—the queen may procure any number of seamen in the Low Countries—begs that the merchants of those countries may be better treated in England.

Mr. secretary, Mr. Davyson doth now retorn home, which I coulde hardly have yelded unto but only to have hir majesty fully answered and satysfyed touching all our proceedinges here synce my aryvall,[a] and noe man able to doe yt but himself, praing ye, good Mr. secretary, yf hir majesty wyll shew me any favour, that thys may be one, to have Mr. Davyson retorn ageyn to me, who I assure you ys the most sufficient man to serve hir majesty that I know of all our nation; for he knoweth all partes of these countreyes, and all persones of any accompt, with all ther umores, and hath great credytt among them all here. And the better servyce shall he be able to doe yf yt may please hir majesty to gyve him such countenaunce as may encrease his credytt here, for here hath byn many brutes and reportes of hir good intentyon toward him, and he wyll deserve any goodnes she shall bestow uppon him, whatsoever yt be.

[a] The principal object of Davison's mission was to reconcile the queen to Leycester's assumption of the government of the Low Countries; an important step, for the taking of which his recent letters were evidently designed to prepare his friends at home. On Tuesday the 25th of January the earl was installed at the Hague in a very solemn manner, in the presence of count Maurice and the other principal persons, both natives and Englishmen, then in the Low Countries. The ceremonies may be seen in Holinshed, iv. 647, and in Stow's Annals, 715. The placard or grant by which the states-general appointed Leycester to be supreme and absolute governor over all the United Provinces, with like authority to that exercised by governors in the time of Charles V. is printed in the General Collection of Treaties, (8vo. 1732,) ii. 89, and in Holinshed, iv. 648. A copy of the oath taken by the earl to his new subjects is in the Cotton MS. Galba, C. x. fol. 345.

As for sir Wylliam Pellam, I look not for him; I se his delayes be such. When I departyd thence he promysed me faythfully that he wold follow me, what end soever he had, and theruppon he had v^{c}li. prest,[a] but I se his joynders and reioynders doth seke all delay, and spetyally that I saw in his letter to hir majesty of late wrytten, wherein he asketh ageyn a new suply of hir majesty, to sett him furth; a matter I know, of old, what yt wyll doe. Therfore, sir, yf you find this diffyculty styll, lett me no longer expect his uncerteinty. My lord Grey for many respectes I wold be gladd of, but I can as lytle hope of him, and except I might have one of them by the end of this month, I shall after not much nede any of them, and therfore I thought good to signyfye thus much unto ye; and the only cause I wysh for my lord Grey, yf God call me, ther might be such a one reddy here to command as he ys: but lett me know, I beseche ye, with spede, what to trust unto.

Now, sir, to my old sute, and more than tyme that yt were grantyd, or rather here, which ys, for money; for I told ye, before my coming, ther was no more payd than wold serve the end of this month of February next, and you all there made a stryckt reckoning how farr all your money wold strech, not accompting the horsmen, nor sondry other charges leid out by all your warrants to the tresorer before yt cam over, and yf we had the full of that was delyvered for the armye, without these paymentes, yet had yt payd no further than the end of February. And I pray ye remember what I wrote touching the tresorer and his deputye; I doe send over the audytor to you, who I take to be an honest man, he wyll tell ye as much as I wrote, for I had yt of him. But yf yt wyll please hir majesty to send over the hole some behind for the yere, yf I make yt not strech as farr as possibly yt may, and to serve the torn for this yere, lett yt lye uppon me and all that I have to answer yt. But yt shalbe otherwyse

[a] *i. e.* imprested, ready money advanced on account.

handled than this was. Ther ys to to much pryvatt gayn soght, more than ever I wold have beleavyd, and all leyd uppon hir majesty, for hir proffytt, they say.

Touching any procedinges here for the matters of this state, I leave to Mr. Davyson to declare to you. I trust very shortly to send ye some good nues of some enterprise uppon our enymyes, who of late, in the frost, went into Freseland, and ther overthrew iij or iiij^c of conte Wylliams soldyers, and tooke sondry boores prisoners. Synce that, Schenk[a] hath mett twyce with them; at the first, he overthrew a cornett of Italians, and tooke xl horse and men prisoners; the second tyme, being this last weke, he overthrew v^c of the bravest soldyers they had, and kyld iij^c in the place, and took a captain and xv prisoners. I doe not hear of any man that dealeth so lustyly with the enymye as he doth. I wyll cherysh him accordingly, and wyll shortly be at Utryck and vyssett those places. Albeyt I hope ye shall here some nues from me ye look not for or I com thether.

I assure ye Wylford[b] ys to busye in advertysinge of that place at Ostend; hit ys in good case, and yet have I taken order for to better yt: he ys not to have credytt to all hys wrytinges. The soldyers ther of late have taken uppon the river vj boates, loden with corn and other vyttelles coming from Dunkirk and Calles.

My lord thesorer wrote to me to know, what nombre of shipps and maryners here be to be had, yf nede werr. I have wrytten to my lord, here be many more than hir majesty shall nede to beat

[a] Martin Schenck, whose indefatigable exertions, first on the side of the Spaniards and afterwards on that of the United Provinces, are the theme of general admiration amongst the writers of the time, was a native of Guelderland and nobly born. Conceiving himself to be neglected by the prince of Parma he quitted the service of Spain in 1585, and distinguished himself on the other side by some most gallant achievements. Meteren and Strada, writers of opposite parties, unite in their praises of his bravery and skill.

[b] Thomas Wylford was an intelligencer in the employ of the English government. See Cott. MS. Galba, C. viii. fo. 209.

the king of Spain and all his frendes. Uppon small warning ye shall not want inough to serve hir majesty, I warrant ye. I pray ye make more of the merchantes of these countrey people ther; they begyn a lytle to complayn of some hard dealing, but I have satysfied these for this tyme. Ye wyll find these people are worthe the cheryshing. So farewell, good Mr. secretary, in much hast, this last of Januery.

Your assured frend,
R. LEYCESTER.

I will have care to do for captain Veall, your servant.

Addressed.

To my honourable good frende sir Fraunces Walsingham knight, principall secretarye to the queenes majestie.

LETTER XXVII.

THE EARL OF LEYCESTER TO MR. DAVISON.

FEBRUARY 1585–6. COTTON. MS. GALBA C. IX. FO. 68. ORIG.

Reasons which Mr. Davison, on his return to England, is to urge in explanation of the earl's acceptance of the absolute government of the Low Countries.

Remembrances for Mr. Davison.

First, how all the states here in every place, from my first aryvall, receaved me as well for there generall and governour as for hir majesties, pressing me very ernestly at my coming to the Hage, to take uppon me the same absolute goverment of all these provinces unyted; nevertheless I deferred yt by as many meanes as I could, tyll I was fully informyd by the knoledge and meanes which Mr. Davison had gotten of ther estate and abyllytye, whereby beinge fully satysfied, hit was thought best service for hir majestye any way to accept ther ernest offer.

The causes which moved me to accept this place werr these. By hir majesties apointement, I was hir generall of all hir forces in these countreys, and by a contract, lykewyse generall of their armye, and ther first counsellor. The confusion that was amonge the states-generall bredd many dysorders almost uncurable amonge them, as the discontentation of the captens, governors and soldyers, in all places becom desperatt for lack of pay, the yll imploying of ther treasure, whereby all matters most necessary for the warrs and defence of the countrey was utterly neglectyd, the unyversall hate and myslyke which both these and all the people had conceaved ageinst them, being such as, yf hir majesty had not sent when she dyd, ether they must have chosen some one governor, to have taken this charge in hande to remedy there confusions, or elles have reconcyled themselves to the enyme, for avoyding the further ruyn and hazard of themselves. And yf they had had any other governor then myself, hit ys most certen hir majesty could not have these countreys so fully at her commandment as now she ys lyke to have. Nether might she convenyently have kept, ether an armye, or any nobleman here, to be hir generall, but must have byn at the directyon and dysposytion of that governor. Besides, how the contractes and agrementes could be so well kept, ether for paymentes or otherwyse, that ys betwene hir majesty and these countreys, ys as dowbtful, or rather owt of dowbt. Beside yt had byn by that meanes also very dangerous that a peace might have byn procured and concluded with the enymye without hir majesties consent or prevety, hir people and captens, and towns delyvered for hir seurty, in great danger to be all lost. The enymye offeryng any revenge to any hir majesties domynions she might be depryved also of such helps and succors as these countreys may well asist hir now withall, the governor being at hir majestie comandment, with all other services lykewyse. But, the governor being at hir majesties dysposytyon and dyrectyon, these wantes aforeseyd ar provyded for and suplyed; hir people ar to be in all sewrty and to be well treatyd; hir contractes and agrementes ar always to be well observyd and kept to hir majesties most advantage. He also, having the placyng and disposing of these garysons, the paymentes and other condycyons toward hir majesty ar most lyke to be better kept. No treaty or peace to be made or delt in but by hir majesty. No attempt can be made by the enymye ageinst hir majesties domynyons, but she may dyspose and have all such succors as shalbe nedefull for hir. The last, and chefe, ys, that hir majesty having hir one servant, whome she may comaunde, to be ther governor and comaunder, she ys sure to comande them as absolutly as he hath his authorytye from them to comand other under his charge. So for this first parte, these ar reasons that perswaded the acceptance of this goverment, seing of necessyty this state dyd require one, and hir majesty having so nerely placed me therein before, and being so farr interressed in these countreys as she ys alredy.

For the secound, which was the reconcylliacion to the enymye, hit nedeth no argument; he ys sensles that conceaveth not that yf the king of Spain had these countreys at his comandment, lett hir majesty have the best peace that ever was or can be made, and wee shall find, as the world now standeth, that he wyll force the queen of England and Englond to be at his dysposytion. What with Spain for the west and what with these countreys for the est, England shall traffyqe no furder any of these ways than he shall gyve leave, without every voyage shall aske the charge of a whole navye to pass withall.

LETTER XXVIII.
THE EARL OF LEYCESTER TO MR. SECRETARY WALSYNGHAM.
1ST FEBRUARY 1585-6. HARL. MS. 285, FO. 190. ORIG.

If the queen intends the earl to remain in the Low Countries, he wishes to have the assistance of Mr. Daniel Rogers.

Mr. secretorye, amongest my manye letters unto you of other matters, I have forgotten one. I would gladly have Daniell Rogers[a] here, for some good services which I thincke he is fitt for. Yf you fynde that her majestie meane to continue me in service here, I hartely pray you that Daniell Rogers may be sent to me. And so, with my right harty commendacions, I bid you farewell. From the Haghe, the first of February, 1585.

Your very loving frende,
R. LEYCESTER.

Addressed.
To my honorable good frende sir Fraunces
   Walsingham knight, principall secretory
   to the quenes majestie.

LETTER XXIX.
THE EARL OF LEYCESTER TO THE LORD MAYOR AND ALDERMEN OF LONDON.
3RD FEBRUARY 1585-6. HARL. MS. 6993, ART. 66. COPY.

The earl informs the citizens of his success in his service—the kind disposition of the people of the Low Countries—recruits

---

[a] Daniel Rogers was a man of considerable celebrity both as a literary man and a statesman during the reign of Elizabeth. He was employed on several foreign embassies in which he acquitted himself to the satisfaction of the government. He was also one of Camden's intimate friends, and assisted him in the composition of his Britannia. Many of his papers remain in MS. in our public libraries. He died on the 11th February, 1590, and was buried at Sunbury, in Middlesex.

wanted—the devotion of the people to the queen had led them to appoint the earl their absolute governor—benefits to England from this arrangement—the enemy had entered Friesland, but had been repulsed with loss.

My lord and loving frends, as I ame for many curtesies much beholding unto you, so cann I nat forgett, in most hartie and friendlie sorte, to salute you; and for that I perswade myself you will not bee unwilling to heare of thestate of thynges here, and of our proceding in them, I will make bold to report somewhat therof unto yow.

And for the people, I must nedes saie, I never came among any so kynde and so loving towards hir majestie, and our cuntry of England, in my lyf; great afflictions have they suffred, and almost at the poynt not onely of discouragment but of utter dispaire of hir majesties favour, till at my aryvall they perceaved hir goodnes towardes theim; whereupon, although they had many workers to have drawne theim to a reconciliation with the king of Spayne, with faire promisses made them, yet, as soone as they founde hir majesty to thinke upon them, they have taken new spirits, and as forward myndes as ever I sawe, to defend hir cause, and will committ cuntry, goodes, lyf, and all, into hir majesties handes, and to no prince els in the world. And most ashamed and angry are they that ever they were ledd to seeke frendship with Fraunce, and are perswaded hir majestie was never well dealt withall on their behalf, for they beleve nowe, that shee hath had ever this good mynde towardes theim to releive them, and most joyfull are they uppon hope of contynnewaunce of this amitie with hir majestie and the realme, and so hartned be they now in hir majesties favour (next God) as thei seeme to make no accompt at all of the mallice and force of the enemie. And I doubt not, that after our bandes here that are decayed be filled agayne with some supplie of more men, without further charg to hir majestie or the realme, but yow shall heare of good successe of our service ere it be longe. For myn owne parte, as I had very good will to the cause before my comminge, (in respect of the dutifull love to the queenes majestie, my sovereigne, and my cuntry,) so, since I have sene the cuntry and people, I have tenn tymes better lyking to proceede in it. And I must saie, as they have geven me grate encouragment thereunto, so have they geven iust cause to move hir majestie to thinke, that they both trust hir and love hir, for I being sent hither but as hir minister and officer, they have, even for hir sake, made me their governour and generall absolut, with the whole commaunding, not onely of all their provinces, their townes, and men of warre, in all places, but lykewise have geven me power and authoritie to dispose of all their revenewes, compositions, impostes, customes, and what ells that yeld them money, theyre receivours, mynt-masters, with all other officers, at my appoyntment and disposition. A very great shewe of trust and love in hir majestie, that do so absolutlie committ so greate a charg to one of hir subiects and servauntes, as a mere straunger every waye to them and theire cuntry; whereby it playnlie appeareth, that thei hide not their devotion they beare to hir majestie, that by this meanes make themselves at the commaundement of no prince, but hir majestie onelie. And surely so long as these cuntries maie be held in their ernest good will, I warraunt yow in England maie sleepe quietly for any greate harme yow shall take, eyther by sea or by land, as no doubt yow shall daylie fynde it more and more. God graunt good successe to my hartes entent. From the Hagh, the 3. of Februarie, 1585.

Your very frend,
ROBT. LEICESTER.[a]

In the tyme of the little froste the enemy entred into Freesland and gave a little overthrowe to a fewe soldiers, and some of the

---

[a] So in the MS. which professes to be a copy, but the earl's signature was invariably " R. Leycester."

boores of the cuntrey, but they have well payde for it since. A full reveng hath beene had, both of some of theire horsemen and some of their best footemen.

Addressed.
To the lord maior of the citie of
London and thaldermen his brethern.

LETTER XXX.
THE EARL OF LEYCESTER TO MR. SECRETARY WALSYNGHAM.
3RD FEBRUARY 1585-6. HARL. MS. 285, FO. 192. ORIG.

The earl has written to the lord treasurer for 1000 *pioneers, in the levy of which he requests Walsyngham to give his aid—he wants* 100 *of them to be miners, respecting whom he has written to sir Walter Raleigh—the remainder to be single men and of able bodies—they are wanted by May—the treasure is all gone.*

Mr. secretory, I have written to my lord treasourour for his healpe to procure that I may have one thousand pioners out of Englande, men very necessary for the service here, and not to be well had in these partes. Whereof one hundred I would have to be myners, and have written to Sir Walter Rawleighe to healpe procure them out of his jurisdiction in Cornwall and Devon. For the other nyne hundred, I hartely pray you to conferre with my lord treasourour, and to put to your healpe that they may be had out of dyvers shyres in Englande, here and there, where you shall thincke they may be best taken. There was abuse in the levye of those that were sent before, many of them being househoulders, and maryed men, and of bodye not fit for this service. I pray you lett there be care had in these, that they may be single men and of apt bodyes. And I woulde be gladde to heare from you with speade, whether they be to be had or not, that I may cause mony to be readye at London for them. And yf they be to be had, yf the taking of them up may be gone in hande with in the meane tyme it shalbe well, for I would have them here abowt the ende of Aprill, and not before. And so with my right harty commendacions, I bid you farewell. From the Haghe in Hollande, the 3d. of February, 1585.

Your very loving frende,
R. LEYCESTER.

Yf I may have these pioners, I desier to have them in a redynes agenst the mydst of May.

I besech ye lett me hear oftener from you.

I must lett ye know all our tresure ys gonne, and have leyd out iij or iiij^m li. beside my expences, only for the causes and service here. And how the tresure hath byn payd out lett the awdytor tell ye, and yet he ys not able to tell ye all, but before I cam, all was gonn, and many debts owing, and the soldyers reddy to sterte, yet yt was thought that ther had byn inough here tyll the end of Decembre, of the first money; nether cam ther, as I now I find, over with the treasurer above 14,000 li. of the xx^m., and he had but warant of me for 2,000 or therabout, whereof xvij^c li. was for our shipping, yet he sayth he broght but 14,000 with him.

Addressed.
To my honourable good frende sir Fraunces
    Walsingham knight, principall secre-
    torye to the queenes majestie.

LETTER XXXI.

THE EARL OF LEYCESTER TO MR. SECRETARY WALSYNGHAM.

4TH FEBRUARY 1585-6. HARL. MS. 285, FO. 194. ORIG.

The earl begs earnestly for a supply of money with all speed— uncertainty of communication between England and the Low

Countries—sir John Norris going to Utrecht—The prince of Parma circulates delusive reports of an ambassador coming from England to treat for peace.

Good Mr. secretary, even as ye love the furtherance of this servyce, send us money with all spede, for, as you shall understand by Mr. Davyson, all our treasure ys gonn, and ye may se, by experyence, how dowbtfull the wyndes ar to pass at your wyll. I pray you also that you wyll obteyn lycence that we may have men, and the captens I have sent over may be dyspached only with hir majestys authorytye for the leavy of them.

Mr. Norrys [a] doth this day departe hence to Utrycht, whether also I send all my horsmen. Yf we may have money and men from Englond only to abyde the first brunt this sommer, I trust you shall hear of great servyce to the honour and quyett of hir majesty.

The prince of Parma gyves yt out styll, and hath sent ageyn to Antwerp, to provyde for hir majesties embassador, ether to com thether or to Brusselles, only to make shew of yt, to brede busses [b] in these mens heddes here. The preparacion at Antwerp for shipping ys not as ye have hard, for certen, nether his forces to be feared, spetyally yf we may once gett before hand with our men this spring. Here ys a man that doth offer to cure your decease uppon loss of his lyffe. Fare ye well; in much hast, this 4. of February.

Yours assured,
R. LEYCESTER.

Addressed.
To my honourable good frende
  Mr. secretory Walsingham.

---

[a] Sir John Norris is said to have "left for Utrycht" on the 5th February. Retrosp. Rev. i. 280. 2nd series. The enemy was at this time engaged in besieging Grave, a place which was almost the only barrier between him and the northern provinces, and Norris was sent to its relief.   [b] *i. e.* Buzzes, idle fancies.

LETTER XXXII.

THE EARL OF LEYCESTER TO MR. SECRETARY WALSYNGHAM.
6TH FEBRUARY, 1585-6. HARL. MS. 285, FO. 198. ORIG.

The earl, on the return of M. de Sevilly, explains the reasons why the states declined the offer of the duke de Bouillon mentioned in letter XXI.—*services of the Low Country shipping.*

Mr. secretory, this bearer, monsieur Civile, retourneth well inoughe, I thincke, satisfyed with the dealinges here. Yet do not the estates thincke good to goe throughe with the matter offred by him on the duke his master his behaulfe,[a] partly because they do not take it to be of so great importaunce as the duke thincketh, and more specially because mony at this present groweth skant with them, being to satisfye me for my allowaunce monethly, and to paye their ould debtes, (which I covenanted they shoulde do before I would take the gouvernment on me,) and having some other payementes to make; so that, by their former desordre and confusion in all thinges, a litle money is nowe at the first more unto them then a great deal wilbe hereafter, when they have overpassed these paymentes, and thinges shalbe settled in good ordre. I have a meaning also to do the duke ere longe some pleasure an other waye, which I hope shalbe well to his lyking. And so, with my right harty commendacions, I bid you farewell. From the Haghe, in Hollande, the vjth of February 1585.

Your very loving frende,
R. LEYCESTER.

I have partly remembred my lord tresorer of a matter wherein I have at large wrytten to my lord admyrall, wherein both you there and we here may be better servyd, and hir majesty farr less charged. I pray you further yt to my lord admyrall, who I know wylbe very reddy therto.

---

[a] This was the proposal to intercept a convoy of provisions intended for the Spaniards mentioned at page 53. The bearer of this letter is there termed de Sevilly.

And for those portes here, I can assure you they have doun great servyce, both in taking and burning of sondry of the Dunkerkers, as also in reskewing dyvers shipps taken by the enymye, both Englysh and Flemysh, and ij of the best and greatest were cast away uppon the Goodwyns lately, with all ther men and artyllery, save 4 or 5 maryners; iij small barkes on your side wold ease all, as ther ys also on this side as many and moe sett out, but ther ys more trust x tymes to ours to kepe Dunkirk, than these here, for they mete with many frendes whom they lett slypp.

Addressed.
To my honourable good frende sir Francis Walsingham knight, principall secretory to the queenes majestie.

LETTER XXXIII.

THE EARL OF LEYCESTER TO LORD BURGHLEY.
7TH FEBRUARY 1585-6. LANSD. MS. 46, ART. 62. ORIG.

The earl recommends to lord Burghley the case of certain Low Country merchants, whose ship had been seized by English cruisers, and explains the artifices by means of which trade was carried on between the Low Countries and Spain.

My lord, there are two marchaunts of this countree, the one of Middlebourge, called Mr. Jehan Cooman, bourgmaster of that towne, the other, Jehan Berrhee, eschevin and senatour of Amsterdam, who have a shipp with merchaundise taken coming from St. Lucars in Spayne, by certeine shipps of warre of England in October last, under pretence that they were the goods of the king of Spaynes subjects, because there was found in the shipp a bill of lading making mention that the goodes appertayned to a marchaunt of Anwerp, which indeade was done to thintent that the goodes should not be confiscat in Spayne; for that, since the taking of Anwerp, all Anwerp-men are free from arrestes in Spayne, and this manner of lading in other mens names is used here, and allowed by an order of the estates, to thintent thereby the goods and monie of this countreemen arrested in Spayne and Portugall maie be gotten thence, and that those that are here against the king maie have some kynd of trade thither.

Theise two marchaunts are verie honest men, of good religion, devoted to her majestie, and have suffred verie much for theis countrees service. He in Anwerp, though he dwell in Anwerp, and be therefore taken as reconcyled to the king of Spayne, yet is he an honest man accompted, and doth no hurt but great good to the cause. Theire humble suite to me is, to be meane to your lordship that the said goodes, being a 100 pypes of oyle and 19 balles [a] of cotton, maie either be delivered to themselves upon good caution and assuraunce, or at least sequestred till sentence be geven, doubting greatlie least yf their adversaries, who are John Bird, Jo. Wattes, and John Stokes, should gett the possession of them, they would distract them at meane pryces, and dryve of thise men with long processe; which request seemeth to me verie reasonable. I doe earnestlie praye your lordship to cause good consideracion to be had of it, the rather the men being so well affected. And so, with my right hartie commendacions, I comitt your lordship to thallmightie. From the Hage in Holland, the 7th of February 1585.

Your lordships loving frende,
R. LEYCESTER.

Addressed.

To the right honourable my very good lord, the
  lord Burghley, lord highe treasourour of Englande,
  knight of thordre, one of the lords of her majesties privie
  counsaile, and master of her highnes wardes and liveryes.

---

[a] *i. e.* bales.

LETTER XXXIV.

THE EARL OF LEYCESTER TO MR. SECRETARY WALSYNGHAM.

7TH FEBRUARY 1785-6.   HARL. MS. 285, FO. 200.   ORIG.

Receipt of a letter from England—loss of sir Thomas Cecill's horses—proposal of the duke de Bouillon—the earl regrets that the queen will not let him have the Irish soldiers he requested—he is afraid that the rumours of the queen's desire for peace will prove true—strongly urges the impolicy of any present treaty for peace — the enemy have information of the queen's speeches against the advisers of the military assistance given to the Low Countries—their personal enmity against the earl, and his consequent danger—he will adhere to the course at the risk of his life —has heard rumour that the queen dislikes his assumption of the title of "excellency"—that title has been given him ever since he was created an earl—he has refused a higher title—has sent over the auditor with the accompts.

This vij. of February I receive your letter, with a pece of lead in yt[a] lyke a patern of a booke; I know not what yt meanes, nether have ye wrytten any word of yt.

The master of the hoye that lost Sir Thomas Cecylles hors,[b] I have putt him in prison, and great presumtyons ar ageinst him, which shalbe tryed to the uttermost, for such felloes have doon much harme, but no more than your great recourse to Calles now of your merchauntes doe, which ys so notable as wyll cause all here to runne at lyberty yf ye hold yt on, for all thinges doth pass to Calles.   I besech ye consider of yt.

[a] The lead was probably inclosed to ensure the sinking of the letter, in case the messenger were taken at sea and threw the pacquet overboard, which was not at all an uncommon occurrence.   See Cotton. MS. Galba, C. viii. fo. 206.
[b] See p. 55.

For the duke of Bullyns matter I wrote somwhat to ye of yt, but ther ys no aparaunce in dede that yt can be trew that so much vyttell can come to that place. I beleave ther ys some other matter in yt.

I am sorry hir majestie wyll not suffer the Ireshe soldyers to come hether;[a] hir majestie shuld not have byn at a peny charge for them; ther servyce in Ireland wyll not doe hir that servyce that ther want here wyll hinder hir in a hier degre.

I fear the brutes the prince of Parma doth gyve out wyll prove trew, which ys, that hir majesty lookes rather for a peace than to goe any further into any warr, and making no questyon at all, whan he doth se the worst we can doe, but to have what peace he wyll at hir handes, at all tymes. What hurt yt doth, ye wyll, I fear, se to sone, for yf [it] be once setledd in these mens heddes, I warant ye they wold provyde for themselves, yf they had ther forces in ther handes, well inough; yt ys the thing hir majestie nedeth least desier, and sonest wylbe offred hir, yf she hold fast a lytle for the warr; otherwyse, farewell all these countreys, and ye shall never have peace but a shamfull one. And yf that shalbe thought mete, yf I bring not an offer, and a seking to hir for peace, or half the rest of hir money be spent, lett me loose hir favour and my credytt with hir majestie. But to make shew of your parte to desier a peace, and procede not in manyfest actyon of warr first, and with that ernest shew indede which apperteynes to so weighty a cause, look for no peace for England, whosoever elles can have yt: and be not deceaved, for I know yt, and doe fear the sequell of yt.

The enymye doth as asuredly know what conferences have byn about sir Jo. Smyth's imbassage, and how ernest hir majesty ys for peace, how hardly she hath spoken ageinst the councellors of this enterprise of the Low Countreys, as any ye that ar at home; and by devyces ys brought hether, to corrupt men of best

[a] See p. 26.

credytt. But finding by my preparatyon to the contrary, and my sending for men into England, doth hold them all here back from any thought yet that waye, wherein someway I know I endanger myself at the enymyes handes, for his practyces to my none hurt, for he ys perswaded that I am a great hinderar to peace, and much of this here donn leyd uppon me. Beside, he hath intelligences partyculer out of Englond of me, whereby yt may the rather provoke him to seke my ryddance. But I am resolvyd of the protectyon of the Almighty ageinst all devylls and his enymyes, and that he wyll defend all that constantly trust in him. I have no interest, God doth know, in desier of warr; but the state of our prince and countrey requyring that ys done to be for there safty, I think this lyfe well imployd for there servyce, and xx tymes shall I be more wylling to be imployed in an honorable and good peace for them, which may be, I think, yf hir majesty take the way and follow yt.

Some flyng tale hath byn told me here, that hir majesty shuld myslyke with the name of "excellencye." Suerly I know the great encreace hit hath geven me, but that I had the same at all straungeres handes that ever cam into England, synce I was made by hir majesty an erll, and abrode where she hath sent me. Yf I had delighted, or wold have received tytles, I refused a tytle hyer than excellency, as Mr. Davyson, yf you ask him, wyll tell ye; and that I my none self refused most ernestly that, and, yf I might have donn yt, this also, but I have had this both wrytten and spoken to me whan I used but the place of hir majesties master of hir horse, and both then and now asmuch to hir majesties honor as any advauncement to me, as one that desyreth no name but my none name, longer than I may serve hir majesty to hir honour and good lyking.

I have sent the audytor over [a] with the accomptes here, and, yf hir majesty wyll looke for my good servyce, there must be hast of

---

[a] Davison and the auditor left the Hague for England, by the way of Brill, on the 5th February, 1586. Retrosp. Rev. i. 280. 2nd series.

money hether, for here ys none left, and we have now above viij^c horse to pay.

So, in som hast, I comytt ye to God; at the Hage, this vij. of February.

Your assured frend,
R. LEYCESTER.

Addressed.
To Mr. secretary Walsingham.

LETTER XXXV.

THE EARL OF LEYCESTER TO THE LORD TREASURER, THE LORD CHAMBERLAIN, THE VICE CHAMBERLAIN, AND MR. SECRETARY WALSYNGHAM.

8TH FEBRUARY 1585-6. HARL. MS. 285. FO. 205. ORIG.

The earl has received notice of the queen's great dislike of his acceptance of the government of the Low Countries—the queen gave little favour to the earl before his going, but he hoped she would not have condemned him until she had heard his reasons, which he protests were not his own glory but her advantage—beseeches that the reasons to be stated by Mr. Davison may be examined— if they are not deemed sufficient he will submit to the queen's pleasure— begs that some nobleman may be sent out to supply his place—the appointment was unanticipated—and has been a cause of great loss to him—will retire to some corner of the world and languish out the rest of his days—will await her majesty's pleasure—begs the mediation of their lordships on his behalf.

My very good lords, I have to my great discomfourt receyved from you [a] her majesties great mislyke of my acceptaunce of this

---

[a] It appears from an indorsement upon this letter that the communication here referred to was written on the 25th January 1585-6.

gouvernment, and that she will by no meanes avowe, but rather disavowe wholy, that which is done therein. I was somewayes a very unfortunat man, I must confesse, that founde scant of her majesties wonted favour towardes me before my going to take so great and weightye a charge as this in hande, not being ignorant of the infinite hazardes that I must put my own poore estate unto, bothe lyfe and all. Neverthelesse, the Lord God doth knowe, unto whose mercye I do appeale, the very aboundaunce of my faithfull harty love, borne even to the preservation of her sacred person, and the care of her prosperous raigne over our poore endaungered countrye, was only cause thereof. But, my lords, thus muche hope had I allwayes notwithstanding, in the great goodnes of her majestie, that in so weightye a cause as this is, her majestie would, before she had condemned me so farre, have hearde what reasons have moved me to do this I have done, above her commission or commaundement. And I doubt not but her majestie and you all shall well fynde, that I have adventured more to do her majestie acceptable service thereby, then to do my selfe eyther honour or good. And as your lordships have had good experience heretofore of the uncertaintyes of these passages; so was I here xliij dayes before I did once heare worde out of Englande.

And, for this matter, to satisfye eyther her majestie or your lordships as it ought to do, must stand upon sondry reasons which necessitye brought fourthe at this tyme to cause me to accept of this gouvernment, which I had delivered to Mr. Davison to declare bothe to her and to your lordships, I do moste humbly beseche your good lordships to examine all those reasons but indifferently. Yf they seame to your wisdomes other then suche as might well move a true and a faythfull carefull man to her majestie to do as I have done, I do desire for my mistaking offense to beare the burden of it, which can be no greater then that which her majestie hathe allreadye decreed, to disavowe me with all displeasure and disgrace; a matter of as great reproche and griefe as ever can happen to any man. And according to her will, which I perceyve is ment by her majestie, I wilbe readye (seeing it is not otherwise to be presently used) to obey her pleasure, yf it were presently to give it, without any more adoe, over agayne to them. But respecting what hinderaunce it may be to her majesties service at this tyme, and to the whole cause, I trust I shall not offende your lordships, nor her majestie, to give this simple advise, that it may pleas her to send somme nobleman with all speade whome it shall lyke her to supply my place, according to her first meaning, and to revoke me, which I will humbly obey, and take it as a matter from God, who can and will correct the wayes of synners, protesting in his presence, and by the beliefe I have in Chryste, that I have done nothing in this matter, but, to my iudgement, of suche consequence for her majesties service, besides the furderaunce of the cause here, as, yf lyfe, lande and goodes had lyne upon it, I must have adventured it as for an acceptable service. And yet when I sett my foote on lande I no more imagined of any suche matter to be offred me, or more then was by her majesty and the estates contracted, then I thought to be king of Spayne; nor till I came to this town xij dayes after: and yet was there some were affinitye with this by that contracted betwene her and the estates.

I have no cause to have played the foole thus farre for myselfe; first, to have her majesties displeasure, which no kyngedome in the worlde culd make me willingly to deserve; next, to undoe myselfe in my later dayes; to consume all that should have kept me all my lyfe, in one haulfe-yeare. And so muche gayne have I heare by it as I have lyved and spent only of my own since I came, without ever having pennye or groate from them, neyther shall gett so muche by them all here, yf I had served them this xij monethes, as I have spent since I sawe her majestie and your lordships laste. But I must thancke God of all, and am most hartely grieved at her majesties heavy displeasure. I neyther desire to lyve, nor to see my country, with it. For yf I have not done her majesty good service at this tyme, I shall never hope to do her any, but will withdrawe me into some out-corner of the worlde, where I will languishe out the rest of my fewe, to many, dayes, prayng ever for her majesties longe and prosperous lyfe, and with this only comforte to lyve an exile, that this disgrace hathe happened for no other cause but for my mere regarde of her majesties estate, being driven to this choyse, eyther to put myselfe into her handes for doing that which was moste probably best for her service, or elles loose her that advantage which, at that present lett slippe, was not possibly to be gotten for her agayne.

I doubt not but ere this Mr. Davison hathe presented to her majestie my own letter, and acquaynted all your lordships with suche reasons as have moved me to deale as I have done, who was dispatched hence fower dayes before I receyved your lordships letters, leaving me in opinion yf her majestie had not thus conceaved of it as she nowe dothe, that I would have thought my service had deserved more thanckes. I shall nowe attend her majesties furder pleasure, not daring wryte to herselfe being thus offended, but will humbly desire your lordships good constructions of my doinges to hir highnes, yf you shall fynde the consideration worthie, with your honourable and frendly meanes in my behaulfe, being a man absent, but moste faythfull and loyall to my moste dread soveraigne mistres, and so wilbe to my lyves ende, and to my power humbly thanckefull to your lordships all, for the good favour you shall shewe herein towardes me. And so will pray unto God to keape you all in his feare with longe lyfe. From the Haghe, the 8th of Februarye, 1585.[a]

Addressed,

To the right honourable my very good lords the lord highe treasourour of Englande and the lord chamberlayne, and my very good frendes Mr. vice-chamberlaine and Mr. secretory Walsingham, and to every of them.

[a] The following memorandum is written on the back of this letter in the handwriting

LETTER XXXVI.

THE EARL OF LEYCESTER TO MR. SECRETARY WALSYNGHAM.

8TH FEBRUARY 1585–6.   HARL. MS. 285, FO. 202.   ORIG.

Letter sent at the same time as the last—the earl is wounded to the heart—if some other man had rendered the services he has performed, they would have been better accepted—the queen would not have condemned any other man unheard—refers to the queen's opinions before he left England—the authority given him by the queen's treaty with the Low Countries necessarily led to his appointment—regrets his employment on this service—as her majesty's favour is withdrawn, he craves leave to retire to some obscure corner of the earth, where he will end his days in prayer for her majesty.

Mr. secretary, being lothe to trouble my lords with to longe a letter, maketh me thus bould to use some addition to you, being not only grieved but wounded to the harte. For it is more then death unto me, that her majestie should be thus ready to interpret allwayes hardly of my service, specially before it might pleas her to understande my reasons for that I do. For my own parte, I am perswaded hitherto there could not any better service be done unto her majestie in these partes, and yf some other man had done it, yt coulde not be but it had bene muche better accepted : at the least I thinke she would never have so condemned any [other] man before she had heard him. And, undre her highnes pardon and favour, I dare referre the judgement of this matter, when it shalbe duely examined and hearde, to her majesties own selfe, or to my worst enemyes, wheresoever they be, muche rather to any or to all her privye counsayle. All her majestie can laye to my charge

of Lord Burghley : "Nota. This letter is not signed by my lord." The letter, it may be added, is sealed with the earl's seal, and is in the handwriting of his secretary. The next letter, which was no doubt despatched at the same time, was also unsigned.

ys going a little furder then she gave me commission for. Yf the matter be well considered, the steppe forwarde is not so great, yf my authoritye contracted before betwene her majestie and the states be well perused, and I thancke God there is no treachourye nor falshoode in this I am blamed for. The Lord graunt her majestie paciently to consider by this my doing wherein she is any waye damnefyed, or furdur engaged to the estates then she was before.

Her majestie I do remember well indeade, and so may you, howe before all my lords she seamed to mislyke that I should take any other charge then as her generall, or to make any othe to them here, any manner of waye. I tould her majestie lykewyse, in the same presence, it was then to no purpose for me to goe into these countryes; for yf it were but to be her generall only of v^m. men, Mr. Norrise had that charge alreadye, and better able to discharge it then I. I did lykewise put her bothe in remembrance of her contract with the states, which had allowed me farre more authoritye then that, and of the dealing of my lord treasourour and of yourselfe also with them abowt a furder enterteignment for me, as in respect I should be their officer as well as her majesties, in which I referre myselfe to both your reportes, being then present. For they alwayes aunswered me, there was no doubt but they would deale with me as well as ever they did with the prince of Orange. But her majestie indead then would not heare of it, thoughe I made petition to be discharged of the journey. Yet, afterwards, in speaking with her, I founde her very well content I should receyve any thinge from their handes whatsoever, so it mought not proceade from herselfe, but of themselves. I did desire you, sir, at that tyme, to move her majestie most earnestly for my stay at home, telling you howe much I should undoe myself, and do her majestie no service, going after that manner. And, yf I be not forgeatfull, it seamed then to you lykewise, that her majestie was willing inoughe that I should receyve suche charge and enterteignment as, of themselves, the estates would lay upon me and give me: but I will not stande greatly hereupon.

But, admitt me to be even acccording as her majestie did contract with the estates, ys it not there agreed I should be the generall of their warres and armyes, as well as of her majesties? Was I not there placed as chiefe counsailour of the estate amonge them, and two nominated also by her majestie to assist me? I suppose in this place it was not ment, neyther for me nor them, as counsailours for the warres only, for then I am sure there should have bene named more famous captaines to assist me. Besides, I am there authorized to deale in monye matters, and myntes, with such lyke, which are mere civile causes. Yf, then, it be so that this authoritye was given me before, by her majesties and the estates contract, and that they would, partly for the honour borne to hir majestie, and partly for that they would have the worlde knowe they relye wholy upon her, make choyse of me, so farre interessed allreadye amonge them, and give me a tytle and place which some other must have had, as shall playnly appeare to her majestie by Mr. Davison, and that hir majesty is neyther furder charged therby, nor by any means drawen into any furder action or bonde, then she was before, and that of necessitye some one must have had the place, I woulde fayne knowe, yf any other had had it but one wholye hir majesties, whether she had not bene disappointed of every parte of that she looked for: specially for a good peace for herselfe and Englande? And whether the sure payement of her waged souldiors by them, or the strengthe of all the garrisons placed by them, or the navye and mariners of these countreyes, had bene, without this authoritye to one of hers, at hir majesties commaundement or no? Yf then, by taking this place upon me, hir majestie being thereby no waye to be charged, ·eyther by the king of Spayne or otherwise, since it was the estates own election, and a matter merly done by themselves, to offre these great advauntages to one of her own, methinckes it should not receyve so harde a construction, seing by the placing of me, the only benefite and greatest honour dothe growe to hir majesties selfe every waye.

For my own particular, I knowe it had bene farre better another had had it then I. But for hir majestie, yf hir gracious good opinion were not prejudiced allready against me in this matter, bothe hirself and all others must thincke it is muche better for hir service in the handes of one of hir own, then of any other whosoever. But yet I am nowe sory that ever I was employed in this service. For yf any man of a great nomber elles had brought suche a matter to passe for hir, I am sure he should have had, instead of displeasure, many thanckes. But suche is nowe my wretched case, as for my faythfull, true and loving harte to hir majestie and my countrye, I have utterly undone myselfe; for favour, I have disgrace; and for rewarde, utter spoyle and ruyne. I could have taken warning of this before, yf I would have doubted so muche of hir majesties goodnes, or have cared more for my quyet and ease at home then for hir service abroade. And I am not so riche but I might bothe well have spared my charge, and saved the labour of so daungerous a journey.

But, to conclude, yf to make hir majestie to have the whole commaundement of all these provinces, of their forces by sea and lande, of their townes and of their treasure, with knowledge of all the secrettes of their estate, yea and to have brought her what peace she woulde, besides divers wayes and meanes lykely to have eased a great parte of her charges, only by taking upon me the name of gouvernour, is so eveill taken as it hathe deserved dishonour, discredite, disfavour, with all grefes that may be laide upon a man, I must receyve it as deserved of God and not of my quene, whome I have reverenced with all humilitye, and whome I have loved with all fydelitye. Hit shall ende thus, that as I fynde myselfe moste deapely wounded, and seeing hir majesties good favour and good opinion drawen from me, that she conceyveth I have or do belyke seake rather my own glorye then her true service, not forgetting that some suche wordes were used of me when

I made suyte to her majesty to have a fewe lords over with me, I do humbly beseche her majestie by you, for I know my wryting to hirselfe having these conceipts of me shall but trouble her, to graunt me leave, as soone as she shall appoint one here to supplye my place for her better service, which I desire with all speade, and the sooner the better, to go lyve in somme obscure corner of the earthe, where I will ende these grievous dayes in true prayer to God for her. And, as the Lord doth knowe, when she thought me any way touched with vayne glorye, I had no cause of vayne glorye to boste of. Yf I may glorye in any thinge, it must be, I see, in the crosses of this worlde, whiche allmightye God strengthen me unto. And so, thincking every daye a yeare till I may receave ordre and dispatche of this place, I bid you hartily farewell. From the Haghe in Hollande, the 8th of February 1585.

Your loving frende.[a]

Addressed
To my honourable good frende sir Fraunces Walsingham, knight, principall secretorye to the queenes majestie.

LETTER XXXVII.[b]

LORD BURGHLEY TO THE EARL OF LEYCESTER.

7TH FEBRUARY, 1585-6. COTTON MS. GALBA C. IX. FOL. 71. ORIG.

Lord Burghley acknowledges the receipt of the earl's letter of the 29th January—long continuance of adverse winds—the queen so discontented with the earl's acceptance of the government that she will not hear any speech in defence thereof—Lord Burghley will continue to move her to alter her opinions. This letter sent by Hor. Pallavicino.

My very good lord, Your last letters come to my hands war by your lordship written at the Hage the 29. of Janvary, by which I

[a] See note page 99.
[b] A mistake of the transcriber has occasioned this letter to be a little misplaced. It should have preceded the letters numbered xxxv. and xxxvi. The mistake is of

was glad to perceave [you] had receaved my letters sent by Mr. Atye[a] and my son;[b] which war made old letters by the contrary wynd, which of late hath bene so constant to hang long in on cost, as ether your lordship there have cause, or we heare, to wish it; for it holdeth strongly ether west, which pleseth vs to send, but not to heare; or els in the est, which discontenteth ether of vs in contrary manner.

By your lordships letters I fynd manny thyngs of my letters answered, and so I shall be hable to satisfye hir majesty; but, to be playn with your lordship, in a few words, I, and other your lordships poore frends, find hir majesty so discontent with your acceptation of the government ther, befor you had advertised and had hir majestys opinion, that, althovgh I, for my own part, judg this action both honorable and profitable, yet hir majesty will not endure to heare any speche in defence therof. Nevertheless, I hope a small tyme shall alter this hard concept in hir majesty, whereunto I have allredy and shall not desist to oppose myself, with good and sound reasons to move hir majesty to alter her hard opinion.

But, to end this wrytyng, I could not but to accompany this gentilman, Horatio Palavicino,[c] with my letter, whom, for his

little consequence, as the present letter could not have reached the earl of Leycester until long after those two letters were written.

[a] Letter xvii.   [b] Letter xviii.

[c] Horatio, afterwards sir Horatio Pallavicino, was a well-known commercial and political agent of the government of Elizabeth. He came into England from Italy about the middle of the sixteenth century, and becoming a convert to Protestantism settled here, having lands and a residence at Babraham, in Cambridgeshire, where he died on the 6th of July, 1600. Many stories are told to his discredit, especially one respecting his misapplication of certain papal treasure, which, being in his hands upon his conversion to Protestantism, he is said to have applied to his own uses, and by the loan of a portion of it to Elizabeth, to have laid the foundation of his connection with the government and of an immense fortune. Whether it be true or not that " he robbed the pope to lend the queen," he certainly did good service at the time of the armada, to oppose which he fitted out and commanded a ship of war. His portrait was amongst those of the principal persons engaged in the defeat of the armada given in the tapestry destroyed at the burning of the late house of lords.

wisdom and all other good quallites, I nede not to commend to your lordship, being so well knowen and approved to your lordship as he is. From my house in Westminster, 7. February 1585.
Your lordships assuredly at command,
W. BURGHLEY.

LETTER XXXVIII.

INSTRUCTIONS OF SIR THOMAS HENEAGE SENT BY THE QUEEN TO THE EARL OF LEYCESTER.

10TH FEBRUARY 1585-6. COTTON. MS. GALBA, C. VIII. FOL. 24. A CONTEMPORARY COPY.

To inform the earl how highly the queen is offended at his acceptance of the government of the Low Countries, as being contrary to her commands and his instructions, and the more so because he had accepted such office without acquainting her beforehand, and had delayed sending Davison to her with his reasons for doing so— that his acceptance of that office impeached her honour as being contrary to her published protestation, and that the world would not believe that it was done without her concurrence—that he is publickly to resign his authority—sir Thomas Heneage is to inform the states that the queen thinks herself wronged by their inducing her officer to contemn her commands, and by offering to her minister an authority which she had refused.

Instructions for sir Thomas Heneadge.

Youe shall lett the earle understande, how highly, uppon just cause, we are offended with his last late acceptacion of the government of those provinces, beinge done contrary to our comaundement delivered unto him, both by ourselfe in speche, and by particular letters from certaine of our counsaile written unto him in that behalfe by our expresse direction, which wee do repute to be a verie great and strange contempt, least looked for at his handes, beinge he is a creature of our owne; wherwith we have so much the greater cause to be offended, for that he hath not had that regarde that became him, to have, at the least, by his letters acquainted us with the causes that moved him so contemptuously to breake our said comandement, nor used that diligence that apperteyned in sendinge our servante Davison unto us with instructions how to answer the said contempt, which hath greatly aggrevated the faulte, though for our owne parte we cannot imagine that any thinge can be alledged by him to excuse so manifest a contempt, at the least to make yt appeare that there was any such necessitye in the matter, as we doubt not that wilbe greatly prevented, but that thacceptacion might have bene stayed untill our pleasure had bene first knowen.

You shall let him understande, that we howld our honour greatly touched by the said acceptacion of that government, and least as we may not with our honor endure, [f]or that it caryeth a manifest apparance of repugnancy to our protestacion set out in print, by the which we declare, that our only intent in sending him over into those partes was to direct and govourne thenglish troopes that we had granted to the states for their ayde, and to assiste them with his advice and counsell for the better orderinge both of their civill and marshall causes, as is contayned in the late contracte past betwene us and their commissioners that weare here,[a] so as the world may justly thereby conceave.

You shall say unto him, that men of judgment will conceave another course taken by him; that the declaration published by us was but to abuse the world, for that they cannot in reason perswade themselves that a creature of our owne, havinge for that purpose given him expresse comandement, uppon paine of his allegiance, to procede, all delayes and excuses layd apart, to the present demission thereof, consideringe the great obeydience that, even from the beginninge of our raigne, hath bene generally yelded us by our subjectes, would ever have presumed to have accepted

[a] him, *in MS.*

of the said governement contrary to our comaundement, without some secret assent of ours, or at least they will thinke that there is not now that reverent regarde caryed to our comandement as [hereto]for hath been, and as in due coorse of obedience ought to be.

For the removinge of which hard conceite that the world may justlye take, uppon consideration either of the said abuse or contempt, you shall let him understande, that our expresse pleasure and comandement is, uppon paine of his allegancie, that, all delayes and excuses sett apart, without attendinge any further assembly of the states then suche as shalbe provided present with him at the time of youre[a] accesse there, or in some other convenient place, he shall make an open and publycke resignation in the place where he accepted the same [b] absolute governement, as a thinge done without our privitie and consent, contrary to the contract passed betweene us and ther[c] comissioners, lettyng them notwithstandinge understande, that this direction of ours given unto the said earle for the demission of his absolute aucthority proceadethe not of any decay or alteration of our owne good-will and favor towardes them, whos welldoinge we doe no les tender then our owne naturall subjectes, as yt hath manifestly appeared unto them by our former actions, havinge for their sakes apposed ourselves to one of the mightiest prynces of Europe, assuringe them therefor, that we doe meane the continuance of the same towardes them, and our intent is, that the said earle should howld that forme of goverment both lykely to towch us greatly in honnor. We see, you maie tell him, no other way but the said election must be revoked with some suche solemnytie as the same was published, and the states and people let understande, that our meaninge is not he shall hould or exercise any other sorte of goverment, duringe the time of his aboade there, than as is expressed in the said contracte, which we doe purpose inviolably to observe according to our promise, not doubtinge but that thassistance they shall receave that way wilbe as effectuall for their safetye

[a] theare, *in MS.* [b] same the, *in MS.* [c] her, *in MS.*

and benefit, or rather more, for some causes best knowen to our self, as thoother coorse.

After the delivery of which messuage to thearle, we thincke meete, to thend the states, or suche as shall assiste the erle at the time of your arrival, may knowe the cause that moveth us to dislyke of the said acceptance, and to have the same revoked, that you shall advertise yourselfe to them and let them understand, that we fynde yt[a] strange that a nobleman, a minister [of] ours, sent thether to execute and holde suche a course of governement as was contayned in the said contract, should, without our assent, be pressed to assent to accept of more large and absolute authoritye over the said countries then was accorded on by vertue of the said contract, espetially seeing that ourselfe beinge oftentimes pressed by their comissioners to accept of thabsolute government did alwayes refuse the same, and therefore by this manner of proceedinge we hould ourselfe two sondrye wayes wronged by them, greatly to our dishonnor: thone by provokinge a minister of ours to comit so notorious a contempt against us, thother in that they shew themselves to have a very slender and a weake conceipte of our judgment, by pressinge a minister of ours to accept of that which wee refused, as thoughe our longe experience in governement had not yet taught us to discover what were fitt for us to doe in matters of our state. And though we cannot thinke but that this offer of thers[b] proceded of the great good-will they beare us, and so consequently acknowledge the same with all thankfullnes, yet maie it minister cause of suspicion to suche as are apt to judge the worst of thinges best-meant, that the said offer, under color of good-will to us, was made by some, thoughe not by the generalitye, of a malitious purpose, supposinge the same would have bene refused, and that theire would thereby have followed a change and alienacion of the heartes of the common sorte, when they shall see a playne refusall of an offer that contayned so evident and manifest a staied argument of their goodwill and devocion towardes us.

[a] yet, *in MS.*   [b] thes, *in MS.*

You shall further let them understand, that, forasmuch as we conceave that the said acceptacion hath greatly wounded our honor, for the causes above specified, we have resolved to have the said earles aucthoritye revoked, requiringe them therefore in our name to see the same executed out of hand.

And, to thend they may not enter into any hard or jelious conceite uppon knowledge of this our purpose, you shall, on our behalfe, assure them, that the promised assistaunce, accordinge to the contentes of the[a] contract, shalbe faithfully performed, and that the said earle, duringe his abode there, shall second and assiste them with his best advice and councell accordingly, as is above expressed, and is also at large conteyned in our owne letters directed to them.

Youe shall also lett the said earle understand, that whereas by his instructions he hath spetyall directyon, uppon his first aryvall, to enforme himselfe of the particular state of their forces there, both by sea and land, as also of their meanes and hability to maintayne the same, and of the likelyhood of their contynuance of the said meanes, we fynde it very strange, that, in all this tyme of his abode there, we heare yet nothing thereof, consideringe how often he hath otherwise written hether since his aryvall there, and that he cannot be ignorant how muche it importeth us to have knowledge of thes thinges, which maketh the fault of his slacknes therein so much the greater.

And whereas, in the late governement in those contryes, thear hath bene great abuse comytted, as well in the collection of the contributions as in the distribution of the same, which hathe breade no less[b] offence and mislyke in the people then hinderance in the publycke service, you shall, in our name, chardge[c] bothe the earle and suche as by the states are appoynted to assyste him, to have an espetyall care the said abuses [be] redressed, and the offenders punished; for the better performance whereof yt shal be necessary, that the earle doe presse the states to graunte him extraordenary power and aucthority, in their name, aswell to displace such

---

[a] this, *in MS.*   [b] litle, *in MS.*   [c] shewinge, *in MS.*

officers as shalbe founde to have comitted the said abuses, as to take chardge of the destribucion of the said contribucions, which we knowe may be well ynoughe performed without carreynge the title of an absolute governor.

LETTER XXXIX.

THE QUEEN TO THE EARL OF LEYCESTER.

10TH FEBRUARY 1585-6. COTTON. MS. GALBA, C. VIII. FOL. 29, b. A DRAFT IN THE HAND-WRITING OF MR. SECRETARY WALSYNGHAM.

Reproving him for his acceptance of the government of the Low Countries, and directing him to obey her commands intimated through sir Thomas Heneage.

To my lord of Leycester from the queen by sir Thomas Henage.

Howe contemptuously we conceave ourselfe to have been used by you, you shall by this bearer understand, whome we have expressly sent unto you to charge you withall. We could never have imagined, had we not seen it fall owt in experience, that a man raysed uppe by ourselfe, and extraordinarily favored by us above anie other subiect of this land, would have in so contemptible a sort broken our commandment, in a cawse that so greatly toucheth us in honor; whereof, although you have shewed yourselfe to make but little accompt, in most undutifull a sort, you may not therefor thinck that wee have so litle care of the reparation thereof as we mynd to passe so great a wronge in sylence unredressed: and, therfor, our expresse pleasure and commandment is, that, all delayes and excuses layd apart, you doe presently, uppon the dutie of your allegiance, obey and fullfill whatsoever the bearer hereof shall direct you to doe in our name: wherof fayle you not, as you will answer the contrarye at your uttermost perill.

LETTER XL.

MR. THOMAS DUDDELEY TO THE EARL OF LEYCESTER.

11TH FEBRUARY 1585-6. COTTON MS. GALBA C. IX. FO. 79. ORIG.

The queen's discontent at the non-receipt of any letter from the earl and at the delay in the arrival of Davison—rumour that the countess of Leycester was about to go over to the Low Countries, and that a court was to be kept there—the queen's extreme anger on hearing this rumour, and her remark thereon—endeavours of the earl's friends to delay the departure of sir Thomas Heneage and moderate the tone of his instructions—determination to alter a letter recently written by the earl to sir Christopher Hatton and shew it to the queen in order to pacify her—the earl is advised to write to the queen and to send her a present of some rare thing—how rumours are brought to the queen by the women about her—lord North discontented.

I have long forborne to write vnto your excellencie of the great dyslykes hir majestie hath conceyved of your honours doyngs there, towching thacceptacyon of the absolute government of those contries, hoping, long before this time, your excellencie would have sent awaie Mr. Davison to have satysfied hir majestie towching your hole proceedinges in those causes, as yt pleased your excellencie to wryte unto me, in your last letter, dated the 10th of Januarie, you wold doo. But, forasmuche as neyther Mr. Davison ys as yet come, neyther hathe your honour hytherto written to hir majesties selfe of those cawses, which hir majestie takyth in so yll part as all your honourable frends heare haue muche adoo to satysfie hir majestie in, and to staie her frome suche proceedinges to the overthrow of your lordships doynges ther, as wold not onlye brede your great dyscontentment, but also be the vtter ruyen of that service and countries, and withall to aggravate hir highnes dislikes of that actyon.

It was told hir majestie that my ladie was prepared presentlye to come over to your excellencie, with suche a trayne of ladies and gentylwomen, and such ryche coches, lytters, and syde-saddles, as hir majestie had none suche, and that ther should be suche a courte of ladies, as shuld farre passe hir majesties court heare.

This informacyon (thowghe most falce) dyd not a lytle sturre hir majestie to extreme collour and dyslike of all your doynges there, sayng, with great othes, she would haue no more courtes under hir obeysance but hir owen, and wold revoke you frome thence with all spede. This Mr. vice-chamberleyn fyrst told me in great secrette, and afterwards Mr. secretary, and last of all my lord treasurer. Vnto them all I answeryd, that the informacyon was most falce in euery degree, and that ther was no such preparacyon mayd by my ladie, nor anye intencyon in hir to goe over, neyther had your lordship anye intencyon to send for hir, so farre as I knewe. This beyng told hir majestie by my lord treasurer, and Mr. vice-chamberleyn also, thowghe not bothe at one tyme, dyd greatlye pacifie hir stomach; and trewlie I doo knowe, by verey good meanes, that my lord treasurer delte most honourablie and frendlye for your lordship to hir majestie, both to satisfy hir highnes in this report, as in thother great accyon, and so hathe Mr. vice-chamberlain donne also. But the long stay of Mr. Davysons commyng, and your honours forbearing to write to hir majestie all this while, notwithstanding so many messingers as commythe frome thence, dothe greatlye offend hir, more and more, and in verey truthe makythe all your frends heare at ther wyttes ende, what to answere or saye in your behalfe.

Hir majestye hath, these ten or twelve daies, devysed and bene in hand with manye courses how and in what manner to overthrowe that which your honour, to your infynyte fame and hir majesties greatest savetie and service, that euer any subiecte dyd to there soveraygne, hathe most gravelye and polytykelye begunne, and hathe set downe many plattes for that purpose, which I hope your excellency ys not ygnorant in. And trulie the lord treasurer hathe alwaies besowght hir majestie to kepe one eare for your answere to hir dyslykes, and to suspend hir judgment tyll Mr. Davyson come, or that your honour dyd write vnto hir majestie. The lord treasurer having bene frome the courte thes eight daies, hir majestie hath, four daies agone, purposed to send sir Thomas Hennege vnto you, with what commissyon I knowe not; but Mr. vice-chamberlen and Mr. secretorie verey honourablie bothe delaie his dyspatche by all the meanes they can, and hopyth to put it ofe tyll Sondaie nexte, at which time the lord treasurer wylbe at the courte, and then, by his helpe, they hope to qualifie some part of hir majesties intencyons; looking before that tyme that Mr. Davyson will aryve and satysfie all furies.

Mr. vice-chamberlen hath of late told me of the letter your honour wrote vnto him, which he acquaynted Mr. secretorie withall, and tooke his oppynyone whether to shewe yt to hir majestie or no, but fynding hir majestie in such hard tearmes for your lordships not wryting to hirselfe, they thowght yt better then to conceale it; but yesterdaie, fynding hir majestie styll dyscontentyd and hastnyng them to send awaie sir Thomas Hennege to your lordship, they conferred of the letter agayne, and blotting out some thinges which they thowght wold be offencyve, and mending some other partes as they thowght best, Mr. vice-chamberlen resolved yesterdaie in the afternone (I beyng with him) to shewe yt to hir majestie, hoping yt wilbe some satysfaccyon to hir majestie in some poyntes vntyll further matter doo comme. All this they doo to put ofe sir Thomas Henneges dyspatche, and yet, yf he doo come, I hope he shall bryng no evyll newes, for I am sure hir majestie could not have sent anye gentylman of this courte that lovythe you more dearlye, and would be more lothe to come with anye vnpleasant message unto you. Mr. vice-chamberlen thinkythe that your honours owen letters to hir majestie will do more good, and better satysfie hir majestie in all thinges, than all that they can doo or saie; and wysheth withall, that you wold bestowe some two or three hundred crownes in some rare thing for a token to hir majestie.

There be divers of that syde which wrytythe to ther frends here at the courte of suche thinges as fallethe out ther, and so commythe to hir majesties knowlege by the women, which breadythe some offence, and were better they wrote more wyselye, or not at all. The lord North seamyth to be a malecontent, and hath so wryten to hir majestie, and also to my lord of Warwick, and, as yt ys sayd heare, commythe awaie very shortlye. Thus your excellencie seythe how your honourable frends of the cowncell doth mayke me acquaynted with some of thos secrettes that concernythe your honour, which I thowght yt my diwtie to aduertyse you, hoping your excellencie wyll take it in good parte, and so prayng thalmightye to blesse all your doynges, and send you most proseperous success in all your attemptes. Leycester howse, this xjth of Februarye, 1585.

Your honours humble servant,
Tho. Duddeley.

LETTER XLI.

THE EARL OF LEYCESTER TO MR. SECRETARY WALSYNGHAM.

14TH FEBRUARY 1585-6. HARL. MS. 285, FO. 207. ORIG.

Letter sent by sir Robert Jarmine, recommending him to the favour of secretary Walsyngham—reference to a former letter on behalf of Mons. de Meux, whose son had been taken by the Spaniards.

Mr. secretory, this gentleman, sir Robert Jarmine,[a] hathe in my knowledge causes of great weight which force him at this tyme to come over. He myndeth to retourne hither within a moneth or therabowtes, and for that tyme he may be best spared hence. I

---

[a] Sir Robert Jermyn, of Rushbrook, in the county of Suffolk, father of sir Thomas Jermyn, comptroller of the household to Charles I., and grandfather of the well-known Henry lord Jermyn, Earl of St. Alban's, and K.G.

have founde him to be very wise and stowt, and most willing and ready to this service, and he hathe come hither as well appointed as any that hathe commen over. I very hartely pray you to accompt of him as of one specially recommended to you from me, and yf he shall neade your favour in his causes, that you will the rather affourd it him for my sake: I wilbe behoulden to you for it. And so with my right harty commendacions I committ you to the Allmightye. From the Haghe in Hollande, the xiiijth of February, 1585.

Your very loving frende,
R. Leycester.

I nede not commend this gentleman to ye, but assuredly he ys gretly to be estemed. I besech further him yf he shall nede your favour.

I did wryte very ernestly to ye,[a] and I think to my lord tresurer also, touching a request one munsieur de Meux made unto me at Dort; he ys the hye-bayly[b] ther, a very honest, religious, constant, stout gentleman, one that hath gonn thorow all these troubles with great constancy. His only sonn ys taken by the enymye; they wyll not release him, nor sett him at any ransome, for the fathers sake. He desyred Saburo, by whose meanes he hoped to redeme him. The gentleman ys worthy of a greater favour, and able to serve hir majesty many ways in this countrey; he thinkes some lack in me that he receaves no answere or comfort all thys while. I pray ye, sir, favour him further, and ye shall do hir majesty a good service in yt, and yet I dout not to get some other in Dunkirk also with him.[c]

Addressed.
To my honourable good frende sir Francis
    Walsingham knight, principall secretorye
    to the queenes majestie.

---

[a] Letter xv. p. 39.   [b] *i. e.* the high-bailiff.
[c] The postscript is in the earl's own handwriting; the letter in his secretary's.

LETTER XLII.

THE EARL OF LEYCESTER TO MR. SECRETARY WALSYNGHAM.

15TH FEBRUARY, 1585-6. HARL. MS. 285, FO. 209. ORIG.

Letter sent by a messenger who was the bearer of letters from lord Willoughby— the earl advises that the contents of those should be kept from the queen until she had fully determined upon the course to be adopted as to the Low Countries after hearing Mr. Davison—want of a man of judgment in martial affairs.

Mr. secretorye, I opened the packett which this bearer comming from my lord Willoughbye will deliver you, because there was a letter in it for me. By that letter I fynde but doubtfull aunsweres from the king of Denmarcke,[a] and therefore do thincke it not amisse yf you staye the imparting to her majestie of the contents of these letters, untill her pleasure shalbe fully knowen touching the matters of these countryes, nowe after the arrivall of Mr. Davison. Yf she go throughly on with these causes, she shall not need to make doubt of having frendes inowe. So, with my harty commendacions, I bid you fare well. From the Haghe the xvth of February, 1585.

Your very loving frende,

R. LEYCESTER.

If sir William Pellham be not hastened hither, or some suche man of judgement in martiall affayres, we shall hardly do that good I wishe for here.

Addressed.

To my honourable good frende sir Francis Walsingham knight, principall secretorye to the queenes majestie.

[a] Lord Willoughby had been sent to solicit the king of Denmark to give his assistance to the United Provinces in their war against Spain.

LETTER XLIII.

MR. DAVISON TO THE EARL OF LEYCESTER.
17TH FEBRUARY 1585-6.   COTTON. MS. GALBA C. IX. FOL. 82.

Davison reports the circumstances of his voyage, arrival in London, and discovery of the extreme anger of the queen against the earl for his assumption of the government, and against himself and sir Philip Sydney as his advisers—his first interview with the queen —her objections, and Davison's reply—his second interview, when she received the earl's letter to her, which at the first interview she refused, and now merely broke the seal and put it in her pocket —Davison's further explanations—sir Thomas Heneage stayed— Davison's interview with the lord treasurer, who obtained from the queen some modifications of Heneage's instructions—Davison's third interview—sir Thomas Heneage on his way to the earl— the earl advised to write more frequently to the queen, and not to seek permission to return—the earl's supply of money stopped by the queen's anger—sir William Pelham still anxious to join the earl.

My singuler good lord, after my departure from your lordship I was detayned at the Briell some 5 or 6 dayes by the wind and weather. The Fryday following I put to the seas, and, by God's goodnes, had so happy a passag as the next morning, by x or xi of the clock, we ankered at the Recolvers within Margate, and the same night, about mydnight, came to Gravesende, and from thence ymediatly, with the tyde, hither, wheare I arrived the next morning early. Within an hower after I sent to Mr. secretary, to signify so much unto hym, and to know his pleasure wheare I might wayte on hym befor my access to the queen, that I might the better understand in what termes they stood in court, and accomodat my course therafter. He returned me answer, that your lordships long detayning me theare had wounded the whole cause, that he thought her majesty would not speak with me, and yet wished me to come fourthwith to the court, least her majesty, knowing of myne arryvall before I presented myself, might thearat take occasion to encrease the offence.

The same afternoone I repayred unto him, finding him utterly discomforted with her majestys hard opinion and course against the cause. He let me understand how haynously she took your acceptacion of the gouvernment, how she had resolved to dispatch sir Thomas Henneage to commaund you to resigne it upp, and to protest her disallowaunce therof to the states. That she had threatened sir Phillip Sydney and myself as principall actours and perswaders therof, for which it seemes we owe our thankes to some with your lordship. I was amased at his discourse, as a thing farr from that I looked for, and let him see, as clerely as I could, what reasons and necessity had drawen, both the states to press your lordships acceptaunce of the gouernement, and yourself at length to yeld unto yt, assuring him that, if her majesty took the course she pretended, not only yourself should be therby most unhappely and unworthely disgraced, but the cause withall utterly overthrowen, with the perpetuall stayne of her honour and detriment of her estate. Within a while after he went upp to her majesty, and myself, in the meane tyme, to Mr. vice-chamberlain, whither one of the groomes of her privy chamber came for me.

I found her majesty above, retyred into her withdrawing chamber, which I tooke for some advantage. She began in most bitter and hard termes, first against your lordship for taking that charge upon you, not only without warraunt but (that which she urged greatly) against her express commaundment, delivered unto you sondry tymes, as she said, both by her owne mouth and confirmed by her counsell, as a thing done in contempt of her, as if either her consent had bene nothing woorth, or the thing no way concerned her, agreaving your fault herin by all the circumstaunces she might. And, for my particuler, found herself no les offended, in that I had not openly opposed myself against it, wherin I had, as she pretended, greatly deceaved her opinion and trust she had reposed in me.

To all which before I tooke uppon me to make any aunswer, I

humbly beseecht her majesty, first, to retayn that gracious opinion of my poore duty as to thinke, that no particular respect whatsoever could cary me to deale otherwise with her then became an honest and dutifull servaunt, resolved faithfully and truly to report unto her the true causes and circumstaunces of your lordships proceadinges in this behalf; and next, that it wold please her to lend me a patient and favourable eare, which obteyned, I doubted not but that her highnes would conceave more equally both of your person and proceading then she presently appeared to do. And here fell to discourse unto her the estate of the country before your lordships coming, the generall discomfort and discouragement conceaved uppon the length and newes of your stay, the doubtfull termes wherein you found thinges at your arryvall, not only some townes of singuler importaunce but some whole provinces inclyning to a peace with thenemy, as despayring of any sound or good fruict to grow of her majesties cold begynnyng; the generall hatred and contempt of their governement, taxed with corruption, partiality, and confusion; the continuall proffit and advantage thenemy made thereof, with the infinit hurt and perrille of their estate by no meanes able to subsist or stand long, if it were not the more tymely and discreately refourmed. That to help this and save themselves, they found no way either so safe or so proffitable as [a] to set some person of wisdome and authority at the helme of ther estate. That amongst themselves there was none qualified for so great a charge. The lord Maurice being a child, poore, and of litle respect amongst them, the elector, the countes of Hohenloe and Nuenar,[b] strangers, and incapable of the burden. That theis consideracions had moved the estates by their deputies to insist so earnestly and peremptorily uppon that point with her majestie, beseeching her to vouchsafe some principall person of hers to take the charg, as the thing without which all the rest of her goodnes, benevolence, and favor was to litle purpose. That themselves

[a] as as, *in MS.*

[b] Adolphus count of Nienar, in the archbishopric of Cologne, better known by his other title of the count of Meurs.

(howsoever the woordes of the contract appeared not in full and plaine termes to express so much) did and had alwaies taken it as a matter graunted, and theruppon not only intended the same to your lordship long before your comming, but plainely disposed all their doinges to that end, leaving their estate in manner without all forme of governement (as your lordship found yt) tyll your arryvall, and, therefore, did the more importunatly press your lordship to accept therof. Wherin, though you had under one pretext or other longe forborne and delayed to satisfie them, neither flattly refusing yt for the dangers sake, nor willing to accept therof till her majesties pleasure had bene knowen, and yourself in the meane tyme thoroghly informed of their estate, fynding yourself at the length weryed with ther importunityes, moved with their reasons, and compelled with necessity, unles you would have lyved theare as an eye-witnes of the dismembring and division of the whole country, not otherwise to be contynued and kept together then by a reposed hope in her majesties found favour, which had not only bene called in question but utterly dispayred of by your refusall, you thought it better to take the course ye did, carieng with itself encrease both of honour, proffit, and suerty to her majesty, and good to the cause, then, by refusing therof, to have utterly hazarded the one and overthrowen the other; the necessary consequence of which I proved unto her by a nomber of plaine and particuler circumstaunces.

Against which, albeyt she could in truth reply litle, yet could I not leave her much satisfied, at this first meeting, with any thing I could alleag in your behaulf, but, persisting still in her offence, brak many tymes fourth into her former complaintes; one while accusing you of contempt, another while of respecting more your particuler greatnes then either her honour or service, and oftentymes digressing into old greeves which were to long and tedious to wryte. And, bycause she had often and vehemently charged myself to have forgotten my duty, in that I had not disswaded or opposed myself against your fact, being theare as her ambassador, and knowing, as she pretended, her pleasure and meaning, I let her see that I never deemed so meanely either of her owne favour towardes your lordship in the sending of you, or of your owne iudgement in coming over so meanely authorised and backe[d], as to take the commandement of the reliques of Mr. Norris his worne and decayed troupes, as a charg very unfitting to a person of your quality, and utterly disagreing to the necessity of the tyme and state wheare you were; letting her see the dishonour and perrille must of necessity have growen, if either the action had bene longer suspended, or any other course taken to establishe their governement then by your lordship, both commaunder, soldier, and subject refusing all other meanes, and protesting rather to ronne headlong to the Spaniard then to fall againe into ther former disorders and confusions: and herewithall tooke occasion to remember unto her, that being at the most part of the conferences the last yere betwene my lords her majesties commissioners and ther deputes, I had heard some one of my lords, if not her majesties self, answer the deputees to that point, that, albeyt her highnes, for her owne part, intended not to take any further authority then was agreed uppon, yet would she not restrayne them to give what authority and commaundement they should find expedient and necessary for ther estate, to him that should by her majesty be sent over to take the charg of her owne, a thing which (I told her) had bene confirmed unto me by some of ther commissioners since ther returne home: adding withall, for my further iustificacion, that I never receyved lyne, either from herself or any counsellour she had, tending to any such charge or commaundement, without which, I might have bene accused of madnes to have disswaded an action in myne owne poor opinion so necessary and expedient for her honour, suerty, and greatenes. Protesting unto her majesty, that, if I were yet theare, and myne opinion demaunded, I could not tell what other advise to give your lordship then that you had taken, especially having no contrary direction or commaundement from her highnes. And thus, after long and vehement debate, for the first night departed, leaving her, as I thought, much qualified, though in many pointes unsatisfied.

The next morning, notwithstanding, sir Thomas Henneage was dispatched in great heate, which so soone as I understood of I repayred againe unto her, and, so much was I perplexed, with teares besought her to be better advised, laying before her the dishonorable, shamefull, and dangerous effectes of so unseasonable and unhappy a messag, and humbly craving at her handes, that, howsoever shee stood hardly perswaded of your lordships dealing, in conscience, as I told her, without cause, she would yet forbeare to take a course so violent, not only to the utter disgrace and dishonor of one she had heretofore so highly estemed, and now specially deserved better measure at her handes, but also to the utter ruyn of the cause, loss of her best neighbours, and discomfort of her good subiectes, with her owne dishonour and undoing; and here she fell againe into her former invectives, aggreeving your fault the more in that all the tyme this matter was on foote yow had never vouchsafed to impart it with her, which I excused with all the art I had, and at this tyme tooke occasion to presse her majesty to receive your lordships lettre, which the day before she utterly refused. And now, after she had opened and begonne to peruse, putt upp into her pocquett, to read, as I think, at more leysure. At length, having againe, by many insinuacions, prepared her to lend me a more patient and willing eare then she had vouchsafed me the day before, I renewed unto her my former dayes discourse in excuse of your lordships action, which, if she did respect either honour, suerty, or proffitt, she would rather esteme a service of singuler desert, then any wayes worthy of her discountenance, letting her plainely to understand, that there was no meane course to be taken, either for them or for your lordship, without a willfull hazard of all; that their miseryes grew especially from the lack of order and authority, and therfore dryven to seeke their cure from the contraryes; that the fact, besides, did proceed from a singuler affection, confidence, and devotion to her majestie, and therefore worthy her gracious construction. That in your lordships behaulf I could not, in my poor iudgement, conceave what might justly offend her, for, if she would be pleased to consider the necessity, as well of her particuler service as of the estate of those poor countries, left desperat if your lordship had refused them, she should fynd you had no other remedy; if her honour, what greater might be done her by a subject then, without encrease of her charg, to bynd unto her the devocion and hartes of so strong, rich, and populous countries, whose good or ill neighbourhod might of all others most proffitt or annoy her; if her suerty, what might be greater then to have the disposicion of that whole estate, so as she might give the law to the one syde and other, and either lengthen or shorten the warr at her own appetite; and here, urged her majesties scope and end in this action, which, if tending to the releif and delivery of her poor neighbors, ther was no other way; if to abate the greatnes of a suspected and dangerous neighbour, ther could be no greater or more happy opportunity offered her; if to a peace, a thing (I told her) comonly feared and suspected, what other way had she to make a peace, either good for the poore countries or safe and honorable for her self; with a thowsand other thinges to lyke effect. Against all which she had litle els to replye then her alleaged complaintes of the forme and manner of your proceading, confessing that if you had taken the same thing in substance, " which," said she, " the contract offered you," without the title, she would have bene, for her owne part, better satisfied, and her doinges, if she should allow of yours, the better justified. Wherto when I had replyed, that it was not to be thought that thenemy might be more offended, or her case more empayred, by the name then by the thing itself, she began to break of, letting me first understand how litle she looked for so peremptory, and, as she termed, partiall dealing at my handes, of whom she had conceaved better opinion, and towardes whom she had intended more good then now she found me woorthy of; for the which, after I had given her majesty my most humble and dutifull thankes, taking herself to witnes how farr of I had bene ever from affecting or seeking any such grace at her handes, I concluded with this humble sute unto her highnes, that she would be pleased, in recompence of all my travaills, to vouchsafe me her favorable leave to retyre myself home to bestow the rest of my dayes in prayer for her, whome, in all appearance, salvation itself was not able to save, if she contynewed the course she was in, and therfor esteemed hym happiest that should have least interest in her publique service. And thus ended my secound dayes audience, which, howsoever she disguised the matter, wrought thus much effect, that the same night late she gave order to stay sir Thomas Henneage till he heard her further pleasure.

The next morning early I repayred to my lord treasurer, whome I mette uppon the way and followed downe to the courte, wheare I acquainted him with the whole course and reasons of your lordships proceading, leaving him as little as I could unsatisfied in any particuler and necessary circumstaunce. From me he went upp directly to the queen, and, as I certenly understand, laboured very earnestly, first, to revoke sir Thomas, which failing of, he insisted uppon the qualificacion of his messag, whereof grew her majesties secound lettres to Mr. Henneage, to inhibit the delivery of the first lettres addressed to the states, if he found it might hurt the common service, and that, howsoever she rested offended with yourself, he should forbeare your publique and open disgrace.

The same afternoone my lord treasurer procured my therd audience, before whome I confirmed my former discourse, which I found her majesty to conceave somewhat better, and the same night obteyned leave to retyre myself home for some few dayes. Since, I heare sir Thomas Henneage is in Kent, awayting the shyp, intending to go forward if the tyme yeld not some new occasion of his stay, which I have the better hope of, bycause I find the heate of her majesties offence towardes your lordship to abate every day somewhat, and herself disposed both to hear and speak more temperatly of you, and, when all is done, if thinges be well caryed theare, will, I trust, deale more graciously both with yourself and the cause then she hath of late seemed affected, which your lordship may help somewhat by a more dilligent enterteigning her with your wise letters and messages, your slacknes wherein hitherto appeares to have bredd a great part of this unkindenes. And albeyt some of your frendes, discouraged with her majesties proceadings in your behalf, do happily perswade you to seeke to withdraw yourself thence, and to gett leave for your returne as soone as you might, yet dare I not, under your lordships correction, second their opinion, notwithstanding I know it proceades on their partes of an honorable affection to yourself, and dispaire of our sound dealing here, bycause I see no other fruict can grow of that course then utter [un]doing the cause, dishonour to her majesty, and discredit to yourself: whereas, on the contrary, the tyme may woork some better effect in her majesties disposicion towardes both yourself and your service. The trafficque of peace goeth on underhand, as I am advertised; but whether to use it as a secound string to our bowe, if the first should faile, or of any settled inclinacion thereunto, I cannot affirme; howsoever it be, I have not let to tell her majesty that the difficulties, for any thing I can observe, wilbe infinitly great to make any safe or honnorable peace, either for them or herself, without an honnorable warr, which every man heer apprehends not.

Your lordships supply of men and mony hath bene cooled and hindered by the other accident of offence taken at your proceadinges, and yet lyve I in good hope that her majesty will go thorogh with her promis, and give order for your satisfieng, when this storme is a litle more overblowen. I have herin dealt exceeding earnestly both with herself and my lord treasurer, letting them see how greatly it importeth her honour and service, and have here his faithfull promis to hold good hand to the furtheraunce thereof.

Of sir William Pelhams comming over I wote not what hope to give your lordship; he is now at his house in the country afflicted both in body and mynd. I have once or twice allready heard from him, and find the gentleman exceedingly troubled with the strang and hard measure he hath receyved, ynough to break the hart of any gentleman in the world of his sort and deserving, that were not armyd with his vertue and constancy, but, amongst all his other woes, he doth protest to me there is no one that greves him more, then, by the malice of his ennemyes and unhappines of his fortune, to be kept and detayned here from the person and cause he so much affectith, as I think your lordship shall at more length perceave by his owne lettres.

For all other matters leaving your lordship to the report of such as be better infourmed then myself, and craving your pardon for so long and tedious a discourse, I will here conclude, with my most humble prayers to God to bless your honnorable laboures with happy and honnorable success. At my poore house in London this xvijth of February, 1585.

Your lordships ever bounden and assured to
do you humble service,
W. Davison.

Addressed,
To his excellencie my singuler goode lorde.

LETTER XLIV.

THE EARL OF LEYCESTER TO MR. SECRETARY WALSYNGHAM.

18TH FEBRUARY 1585-6.   HARL. MS. 285, FO. 211.   ORIG.

Proposal on behalf of the people of the Low Countries that a mart for the sale of English cloth should be established at some town in Holland or Zealand—the like for English wool—advantages anticipated from such a commercial arrangement—money wanted—Sir William Pelham.

Mr. secretary, these men here doe very ernestly press me to be a sutor to hir majesty, that hit will please her to consider of the traffyq of hir marchauntes for clothes, whether these tounes in Holland and Zeland may not be thought convenyent places for the utterance of ther clothes, as they hope all yt wyll; and, yf yt so be found good, than wold they be sutors to have them com hether, offring all manner of good usage, and in what place or places so ever the merchantes wyll lyke best they shalbe provyded for to ther contentacions, without tax, or talliage, or any manner of charges uppon ther merchandyzes. For my none parte I have somewhat travelled to understand what vent they may have, and I find plainly, yf you hold your hand from lycenses, and forbid going to any other places eastward from Hamboro hetherward, and to the Haunces but only some suche number of clothes as heretofore ye have allowed them, that here wylbe a notable mart for them.

Amsterdame, or Enchuson (a place I lyke best for some causes), or Rotradame, any of these iij, wylbe very apt places, and, with Mydelborow in Zeland, ye shall not only be sure our clothes shall have spedy utterance but greatly content these people, and I am perswaded yf all other places be well examyned ye wyll fynd this the surest every way. For alredy our clothes goe away apace from Mydelborow, but yf the hole trade come hether, all the east partes wyll seke hether, and here ys no fear of any arestes or exactyons, except we offer them to to much wrong. I pray ye, sir, consider of yt, and with some spede, for that the king of Denmark hath promysed to deall for the Stedes,[a] and ye had nede take hede of them, the king of Spain hath a great hand over them, spetyally of the Count de Embden, who, I can assure you, ys wholy at his comaundment; his letters hath byn taken.

These men, also, doe offer some place, or places, for your woll of England, and wyll deall with nether French nor Spanyesh woolles yf hir majesty wyll, and ye may utter here a great quantyty to those that make sayes, and bayes, and other wollen workes, which shall only spend our Englysh wooll: and I wyll warrant your merchantes never found such markettes for ther clothes as they shall doe here, yf they wyll not skatter to other places. Thys being a matter of great weight I thought to wryte yt to ye, and that I may hear from ye as sone as may be, at least that hit be

[a] The people of Stade in the duchy of Bremen.

not forgotten to these folkes, howsoever ye deall with the lord lyvetenant here. God preserve and kepe hir majesty from all evyll, and with longest and happiest yeres to rayne. From the Hage, this xviij. of February.

Your assured frend,
R. LEYCESTER.

Hit is thought, that yf our woolles cam over hether into Holland, that yt wold draw a great nomber out of Flaunders hether that occupie wollen occupacions from the parte of the enemye. For God's sake remember money, with all possible spede; and sir Wylliam Pellam.

Addressed,
To my honourable good frende sir Fraunces Walsingham, knight, principall secretorye to the queenes majestie.

LETTER XLV.

THE EARL OF LEYCESTER TO MR. SECRETARY WALSYNGHAM.

21 FEBRUARY, 1585-6.   HARL. MS. 285, FOL. 214.   ORIG.

The return of lord Willoughby from Denmark, and his favourable report of the disposition of the king, who offers to send 2000 horse to Leycester's aid—interference of the German princes on behalf of the king of Navarre—the count d'Emden and his brother count John—Hamburgh favourable to Spain—the states general well inclined and liberal—Paul Buys a villain—Ortell wholly his.

This Monday, the xxj. of February, after I had dyspatched my other letters to ye, my lord Wyllowby aryved here very well, and doth tell me how very well affected he hath left the king of Denmarke toward hir majesty, that, for hir owen service, he wyll mak warr uppon any prince, and ys content, uppon any least word from me, to lett ij^m of the best horsmen in all his countrey to com to me, and they may better com that way, I find, than any way out of Jermanye, to serve this countrey, spetyally in East Fresland and Gelderland.

I perceave, also, that the princes of Germany ar mervellosly gladd of hir majesties dealing with the king of Spayn. The duke of Sax ys becom a new man synce his mariage,[a] and hath sent very playn messages to the emperour; he hath lykewyse agreed with sondry princes to send to the French king, and to perswade him to leave his prosecuting the king of Navare and the protestantes; yf not, they protest not only to stey all succors for him out of Germany, but to ayd and asyst the sayd king of Navare, with all the force they may.

I fynd yt plainly, yf her majesty send any man of countenance now to them, and to com this way, though yt werr but boddeleye, I dare warrant ye shall find them in an other manner of tune then ever they werr yet, synce hir majesties tyme.

The ellector of Culloyn received letters ij days [ago] to the same effect, touching the princes of Germanyes devotyon, as also of the duke of Sax August.

The count of Emden ys stark naught, and the king of Spains for lyfe, only I wyshe hir majesty to send some one to his brother, count John, whos hart ys almost kyld synce he was in England, and languysheth in great mallincholly, finding so small comfort ther, as he sayth, yf hir majesty had geven him any good comfort, his brother shuld never have don any thing but what she wold. He is so decayd and out of comfort, as yt ys thought his brother wyll shortly gett the Nort, and another place next the sea called Gryte, of good importance, but the other called Denord ys able to doe very great servyce agenst the enymye now, yf yt werr at hir majesties dewtye, but ther must be no tyme lost in yt.

Hamborow ys a villanous town, and wholy the king of Spaynes;

[a] See page 48, note b.

my lord Wyllouby was in great danger to be taken in their territorye. But, yf yt please hir majesty to bestow hir merchants in other places, I beleive veryly more to their proffytt but far more for ther surety, which, yf yt may be, I besech ye give me but a spedy incling.

We ar here in good forwardnes as well for sea as land; ye shall hear shortly that our contrybutions wylbe very much encreased, spetyally yf her majesties countenance contynew. I have wonne them to dyvers very large pointes alredy, for they se I only serve hir majesty and ther cause, and do venture both my lyfe and my lyving for them, and I assure ye I find great favour with them, spetyally with the honest councellors and the comon people.

Paule Buys ys a very vyllayn, a dissembler, an athest, and a practyser to make himself rych and great, and no boddy elles; but ye shall see I wyll doe well inough with him, and that shortly. He ys the most hated man generally that ever I knew in any state: but kepe this, I pray ye, to yourself. Ortell ys holy his, and he hath alredye newes of hir majesties myslyke of me, and I warrant ye he hath taken advantage of yt, and yet wyll not seme to me to know any thing; but I am here every way to hard for him. He wold seme altogether to be for Englond, and in troth he doth skorn us.

Hir majestie never had such a waye unto the world to daunt hir enymys as she hath now. I pray God she may take the offers of hir parliament in tyme: she wyll find herself happy. And, in hast, fare ye well, the shypp steying this beror.

Your most assured,
R. LEYCESTER.

To my honourable good frend sir Frauncis Walsingham,
    knight, her majesties principall secretarie.

LETTER XLVI.

THE EARL OF LEYCESTER TO MR. SECRETARY WALSYNGHAM.

22ND FEBRUARY 1585-6.   HARL. MS. 285, FOL. 215.   ORIG.

Although uncertain whether he shall continue in his service, the earl has made preparation for the levy of an army, the opinion being in favour of an offensive war—40 ships and 25 smaller craft in preparation, and 4000 horse—the earl's politic mode of procuring the concurrence of the states in these levies—advantages to her majesty from this service—she should send to the German princes, especially to the duke of Saxe—bad effects of Pallavicino's delay—pay for the soldiers wanted—count Hohenlohe.

I must nedes trowble ye as oft as occasion may serve, albeyt I can hear nothing from you, whether I shall contynew in my servyce or be cashed, and being loth to loose tyme whilst I am hear, I have alredy proceded with these men for the leavy of an army, as the only way in dede to help and save all; for, whatsoever discourse men may make to you ther, I find by all the wysest and best experymented men here, that if we stand but uppon a defensyve warr, all wyll be lost, as all was almost quyte gonne when I cam hether, as I wrote unto you, and chifely for that men were out of hope to resyst the enymye in the fyld, but he had way to doe what he lysted in all places; he was able both to besiege towens and to anoye all places where he lysted, and no man to make hedd with force ageinst him, every man looking but to his singell charge, in this towen and that towen, and none to commaunde or dyrect for the hole: and ye shall se now, that a meane comander shalbe able to doe more than was donn this good while.

We have alredy, concluded and in making reddy, almost xl good shippes and good cromsters, beside xxv smaler vesselles to runne upp and down the ryvers, well furnyshed; so that, for the sea, we wyll provyde well inough.

For the land hit ys almost concluded, also, that we shall leavye iiij^m horse, the most reyters, beside those we have alredy, for yf we may mach the enymye with horse, I dowbt not for the rest; yet he hath iij^m. Spanyardes aryved a month agoe, and I hear he ys preparing men in Germany..

Much adoe have I had with these men to bring them to consider of this matter, for they imagyn ther places inpregnyble, and doe not remember how the people groe wery of ther contynewall burden, and standing only uppon defence. They contynewally lost towens, cyttyes, and almost ij hole provynces, Flanders and Brabant, all which, yf they had had but vj^m men in the fyld, they had saved; but I may boldly say it, for I am well informyd of yt, they were both carelesly and neglegently lost, and assuredly many more had byn gonn but for hir majesties comfort and countenance, and yet wylbe, yf we shall doe but as others have donn. Wherefore I have byn very round, and the rounder, to be playn with ye, that I wold rather torn myself out of service for such a cause than to be torned owt otherwyse, as perhapps ye among ye ther have resolyd. And my dealing hath taken such good success, as now they procede very willingly in all thinges that I move to them for ther defence, and every man wylling to contrybute, and to enlardge their contrybutyons, now they hope somwhat shall be donn for ther money, as, God wylling, ther shall, yf I tarry by yt; praing ye, ageyn and ageyn, to send away sir Wylliam Pellam. They here have hard so much of him as almost they beleave in him.

Hir majesty must think that this servyce standes hir more uppon than all hir debtes, yf they be a C^m li., and the prosperity therof must bring hir, not only safetye to hir state and person, but the saving of many a C^m li. hereafter. Besyde, sir, yf my poore advyce may be hard, as I have wrytten yt to ye and my lord tresorer heretofore, hir [majesty] shuld send with all spede into Germany to the princes, to encourage them, spetyally a gentleman of some quallyty to the duke of Sax, to congratulatt his mariag with the howse of Hawnalt, who is the ablest and noblest gentleman in all Germany and a great prince; and, beside that he wyll take himself bound to hir majesty, the old duke wyll take it most kindly, for he loveth his yong wyffe so well as whosoever sendes to him therabout he useth all the thankfullnes in the world to him. He hath sent of late a stout messag to the emperour, and hath refused to gyve any audyence or access to the French kinges comyssary. Seguro hath ben greatly enterteyned at his handes, and loged in his own howse.

Yf Palavasyn com not away ye marr all.[a] Gyttory ys almost madd, having wrytten into Germany of hir majesties gracyous dealing in their cause, and that Pallavasyn and he were both on the way; now Gyttory lyeth styll at Harlem, and almost desperatt, yet doe I comfort him by messages, to lett him know that I myselfe have not hard this month from England. God send them better whan they com next.

The king of Denmark doth marvellously love hir majesty, as my lord Wyllowby telles me; he hath sent me very kind messages by my lord, and doth offer to let me have ij^m of his best horsmen, and best captens to lead them; and lykewise to send his own sonne, yf I think yt good, and that it may any way advance hir majesties servyce.

Thus ye may se how greatly hir majesty may further both hir own good servyce and the servyce of all christendome, yf hit shall please hir. And bycause she hath alwayes harped uppon a peace, lett all wyse men judge whether ther be any way in the world for hir majesty to have a good peace but this way; yea, and the more show of princes good wylles that she may procure, the better and surer must yt be for hir. Well, I can doe no more but open my pore conceattes, and pray to God to dyrect hir majesties hart to doe that which may be most for his glorye and best for hirselfe and realme, and so commytt you to his safe protectyon. At the

[a] See page 104.

Hage, from whence I goe toward Utrycht uppon Saturday next; this xxij. of February.

Your assured frend,
R. LEYCESTER.

I besech ye, Mr. secretary, lett not the pore soldyers be forgotten, and the rather for that we shall goe very shortly to the fyld; at the least to have a flying camp of iij or 4000 men, to doe very necessary and nedefull servyce.

The count Hollock ys a most wylling and obedient servant, and surely wyll doe well, and begyns to leave his drynking. Hir majesty is much beholden to the elector Truxy, and he ys able to doe great servyce; he ys very pore but very wyse.

Addressed,
To my honourable good frend Mr. secretarye Walsingham.

LETTER XLVII.

THE EARL OF LEYCESTER TO MR. SECRETARY WALSYNGHAM.

24TH FEBRUARY 1585-6. HARL. MS. 285, FO. 217. ORIG.

The states have doubled the earl's allowance—payment of the troops to the 10th February—fortification of Lillo and Liefkenshoeck—anticipated breach between France and Spain—report of the muster-master as to the state of the English troops—he is a very useful officer—satisfaction of the people with the earl's preparations—sir William Pelham much needed—as Ireland is not likely to be troubled by the Spaniards, the earl would give one of his fingers to have sir Richard Bingham for four months—the count d'Embden—money, money!

The messenger which had my last letters was returnyd back by whether ageyn, which causeth me to make my letters as freshe to ye as may be, styll; and, touching the encrease of allowance to our former rate sett down, which was ij^{cm} florins by the month; fynding yt very skant to descharge that which this sommer servyces shall require, I have procured at the states handes, and with best wyll at the countreyes handes, to gyve for iiij monthes ij^{cm} florins more, with which I trust ther wylbe good servyce donn, and I have not byn idell nor neglygent in cauling uppon these men for this matter, and other very nedefull, though I find many of them slak inough in furthering those thinges that be nedefull for themselves. I cannott blame the countreys to myslyke with them as they have donn. Well, I hope now the gretest matter ys past, this money being so redyly agreed unto at length; and whosoever shall suplye the place for hir majesty here, shall find a good preparation.

I have, lykewyse, mustered all our men, and to be payd untyll the xij. of February, but not our horsemen. I stey tyll I com to Utryght, which shalbe within viij days after this, yf wether wyll suffer me. I have changed many garisons upon some smale suspition, but, I thank God, I find all men wylling to serve for hir majesties sake, and I trust no place at this day to be feared, where any garyson ys. I am about to make Lylle and Lyfskynhose somwhat stronger; places of great importance. I have lerned to be of a good nature synce I cam hether, for I hope to sett the French king and the king of Spain together by the eares, as well as they love, or this day month, and cost hir majesty never a grote. I trust ye shall very shortly hear of som towns of importance to be had into our handes.

I find by the muster-master that the bandes be wonderfully decayed, though many sleyttes were used, as he saith, to deceave him, and wyll save hir majesty a good deall, I think; he ys not yet retornyd, but a very wyse stout fellow he ys, and very carefull to serve thorouly hir majesty. I am gladd I named him to yt. I wold he had byn here at the beginning;[a] but yf I tarry here I

---

[a] Thomas Dygges was the muster-master referred to. His report of the state of the English troops here alluded to is in the Cotton MS. Galba c. viii. fo. 37.

wyll be sure we wyll have men for our money. Hetherto I was not able to use the servyce of v^c. Englyshe soldyers beside the garrysons of Flushing and Bryll, which places I styrr not. Ther are ij lytle places which I meane to gett the government of, and shalbe no charge to hir majesty, and yet of as great importance as any of the other almost.

These men be mervellously pleasyd with me that they perceave I prepare forces for the fyld, for yt ys the only way to brydell and overthrow the enymy, and to putt in hart these people, who care not what they gyve so they know they have men in the fyld to defend them, spetyally in the somer tyme. Wherefore, Mr. secretary, yf hir majesty wyll looke for honour and good servyce, send away Mr. Pellam; we have no such man to govern the armye of all the men they have here, nor any comparable to those I have brought alredy. They have very few that ar any thing able. I wold I had the ij Italians that Pallavasyn promysed me; but, seing I trust the Spanish shall have no cause to trowble Irland, I wold, yf I shuld tarry here, gyve one of my fingers to have Mr. Bingam[a] here but iiij months. I dyd think ther had byn both more and better choyce of captens than I can find here, and therfore ther ys the more nede of such as he ys, for surely I am in very good opinion of happy success, I find all men so willing to this servyce. I besech ye, yf ye find hir majesty well disposyd, remember Bingam, but first dispatch away sir William Pellam, whose abode one month now may hinder us greatly here.

There ys an other matter concerning Emden of very great importance; I have wrytten alredy thereabout to ye; he ys a very enymye to this countrey, and fast to the king of Spayn, and doth chifely vyttell the enymye; yf he were not, we shuld get Groyning in xx days, and all that part of Freseland the enymye now holdeth.

[a] Sir Richard Byngham was a celebrated soldier of the reign of Elizabeth. He was of an ancient family in Dorsetshire, and a man "eminent both for spirit and martial knowledge, but of a very small stature." See Camden's Annals, sub anno 1598; Thoms's Anec. and Trad. p. 18.

Thus, having scrybled in much hast, I comytt you to the Lord. At the Hag this xxiiij. of February.

Your assured frend,
R. LEYCESTER.

I pray you remember that I may receive answere to the partes of my letters, for I have no coppy of my requestes. Forget not money, money; and I wyll never press for any more than hir majesty hath promysed these countreys alredy for this yere.

Addressed,
To my honourable good frend Mr. secretary Walsingham.

LETTER XLVIII.

THE EARL OF LEYCESTER TO MR. SECRETARY WALSINGHAM.

26TH FEBRUARY 1585-6. HARL. MS. 285, FOL. 219. ORIG.

The earl reports an interview between himself and one of the council of the Low Countries, respecting a report that the queen was endeavouring to bring about a peace with Spain by indirect means—Pallavicino not yet arrived.

Mr. secretary, yesterday being the xxv.[a] of February, I wrote unto you. This day, having occasion of a messenger going over, I thought good to lett you knowe, that there came one of this councell to me, and in verye honest sort told me, that I could not forgett what brutes the prince of Parma had geven out touching hir majestyes disposytion for to have peace with the king of Spain. " I have received," sayth he, " now a lettre from a frend of myne in London, who dothe wryte, that a Spanish marchant, one Lewis de Pace, was gonn into Spain with all hast, uppon a sudden, a month agon, and thought to be not without the knowledge of some councellor, and that some secretly devyned, that hit was to pro-

[a] xxvj. *in MS.*

cure some spech of peace, but," sayth he, " I wyll not beleave yt, for yf hir majesty had had that minde, I am suer she wold never have gon thus farr with us here, nether can all the Paces in England or Spain cause the king of Spain to speake or seke a pece so sone as this course she doth take with him. And we trust that hir majesty wyll never doe herself so much dyshonour, nor us that have comytted ourselves unto hir so much wronge, as to take any such course whereby that king shall receive so great encouragement, to hir owen harme and ours; for," quod he, " hir majesty knoweth not the pryde of the Spaniard, yf he be any way sought unto, how inderectly soever. I doe not beleave it, nether wyll I speake of yt, but to tell your lordship of yt, to know yf ye have hard any such thing."

I told him, uppon my truth, no, (no more dyd I in dede) nor I could not beleave yt whosoever shuld wryte yt, bycause I knew hir majesty had meanes inowe offred hir to have herkened to a peace or this, yf she had lysted; and he and the rest here might assure themselves she wyll never deall or herken to peace but their parte wylbe in yt as well as for hirself. " Seurly," sayth he, " I wyll beleave so, for hir majesty hath bounde us by treaty and contract that we shall no waye speake of peace without her pryvytye fyrst, which, God wylling, wylbe truly observed. For now ys yt in her majesties power both to save us, next unto God, or to undoe us for ever." I dyd all I could to putt any such conceatt out of hys head, for I wold be as loth to have yt in myne owen, knowing how utterly hit wold both overthrow hir majesty and thes countreys also; and how easily hir highnes ys like at all tymes, whansoever she wyll, to have a peace at that kinges hand. Nevertheless I could not be quyett but to advertyse you hereof, trusting that ther wylbe no such matter in hand but you wyll gyve your frend som knoledge wherby to govern himself the better, and I wold be sorry my credytt werr so yll, seing I dyd putt hir majesty in a better hope, and wyll perform yt, when any good cause shalbe, than by such a meane to bring hir to a peace. And so having donn all my arrand for this tyme, I wyll byd you farewell this xxvj. of February.

Your assured frend,
R. Leycester.

Yf Pallavasyn come not, Gyttery wyll home to his master, and com into England as he goeth, and so to his master. He wyll not into Germany. He ys wonderfully greved, but I satysfie him all I can, with the lacke of wynd to com out of England.

Addressed,
To my very honorable good frend sir Francis Walsingham, knight, principall secretary [to] her majesty.

LETTER XLIX.

THE EARL OF LEYCESTER TO MR. SECRETARY WALSYNGHAM.

27TH FEBRUARY 1585-6.   HARL. MS. 285.   FO. 221.   ORIG.

Schenck has taken Werle in Westphalia—and, upon information privately given to the earl, the count de Meurs has put down a conspiracy to deliver up Deventer to the enemy—the earl is waiting for the queen's pleasure—prosperous state of affairs—good disposition of the count de Meurs and colonel Schenck—the number and zeal of the protestants is on the increase—religious condition of the country.

This day, being the xxvij. of February, having wrytten yesterday another letter unto you, I have received intelligence from Gelderland. Coronell Shenkes hath ageyn donn a notable pece of servyce. He hath taken a towen and castle of great importance for impeching the enemye in those partes, a place we have bynn busye about this good while to gett, and now by his dyllygence and dyscrete handling brought to effect. Hit ys a town in Westfalia, the principall town of all that provynce, called Werle, belonging to the byshop of Colloyn, but in the enymyes handes, and dyd us here great dyspleasure. This good fortune, God be thankyd, ys now com to us.

Beside, the count de Meurs hath donn a notable pece of servyce very lately uppon a lettre I wrote unto him, beinge discovered unto me from a man of Deventer that was one of their councell and of the religyon, a place of mervellous importance to this state, who opened a full conspyracye of certen magystrates of that town to delyver yt upp to the enymye, and had sworne a company among themselves for the purpose. The honest mans letter I sent to the count, who presently without delaye repayred thether, at whose coming they wold not lett him entre but with vj persons, for indede they wold never yet receive garyson into the towen, albeyt they held for this state always, and beside they had comytted the party that wrote to me to pryson before the countes coming, for that he semed to refuse to joyn with the rest, being one of the chefe of the towen, in this conspyracye. And the count hath so well behaved himself, as he hath overthrowen all this practyce, and hath changed all the magystrates, to the great lykyng of all the towen and the full assurance of the same as at any tyme before, which, God wylling, shall [be] better assured or long, uppon this occasion. I trust ye shall hear of other manner of places taken or long.

Myself had byn at Utrycht or now, but expecting styll hir majesties pleasure from England, which tyll this day I hear nothing; and yt ys most requysytt that I repayr into those partes about Utrycht, for, tyll the houer of hir majesties pleasure knowen, I wyll not neglect the servyce of this aflycted countrey, which God, I trust, wyll prosper, yf not by me, yet by som other that hir majesty shall apoint more fytt. For very fezeable yt ys at this present, yf God putt into hir majesties hart to procede in geving hir good countenance to them. I dare undertake this v yeres they werr not in so good towardnes of well doing as synce they tasted of her majestys good favour, which God Almighty styll contynew her in toward them.

I am thretned to be used as the prince of Orang was, but I am at a point for that, and yet, yf yt be founde that hir majesty wyll go thorow with all how many soever shalbe so delt withall, they wyll leave those practyces. I besech you procure a gracious lettre, first to the count de Meurs, and next to coronell Shenkes, who hath notably deservyd synce my coming; he hath now donn iij exployttes uppon the enymye synce I cam to the Hagu, and he desyers nothing more than to have her majestye know his good hart toward hir. The count de Meurs, whome som call Newener, ys lykwyse very greatly affected to hir majesty, and he ys the best protestant that I here of in all these partes, and doth most earnestly deall in causes of relygyon. And those at Utrycht begynne excedingly to encreace in relygyon, who werr lately the worst of all these provinces. Even synce my coming they have shewed great frutes of yt; and so hath some other places, also, that lyved newtraly before. The mynesters begynn to be bolder than then they durst be before hir majesties authoryty was here, for fewe did care for relygyon in dede, and they have prospered accordingly, but only the meaner sort, and God be thanked they be manny, and the work of God doth appeare in them, by ther trade of lyfe from all others. The mynysters be not many lernyd, but those that be ar very honest and dylligent, and I am perswaded, within vj months, you shuld heare that these provynces wylbe equall with any countrey for religyon, they doe so dayly encreace.

Thus, for this tyme, meaning to goe to morrow toward Amsterdam and so to Utrycht, I wyll byd you farewell; in much hast, trusting shortly to send you more as good newes as this. At the Hag, this xxvij. of February.

Your most assured,
R. LEYCESTER.

I pray you bear with my scrybling; this berer can informe ye of all our state here. I wold hir majesty had many such, and so able men, and of lyke good wyll.

Addressed,
To the right honorable my very good frend sir Francis
    Walsingham, knight, principall secretary to her majesty.

LETTER L.

MR. DAVISON TO THE EARL OF LEYCESTER.

28TH FEBRUARY, 1585-6.   COTTON. MS. GALBA C. VIII. FOL. 46. ORIG.

The storm at court on Davison's arrival has blown over—sir Thomas Heneage is thought to have embarked on the 27th February—good offices done by the lord treasurer—the queen is in reasonable good terms, but will not seem satisfied—all the earl's friends complain of his not writing to the queen—advice how to proceed with sir Thomas Heneage—lady Leycester greatly troubled with the tempestuous news from court.

My singuler good lorde, yesterday I receyved your lordships letter of   [a], and even nowe another of the xth of this present. By them both I see how much your lordship longeth to heare how thinges have succeaded with me since my return, wherein, bycause I have written at some length in my letters of the x[vijth], comytted for suerty sake to this bearer, one of the captaines that wafted [me] over, though detayned here ever since by the contrarety of wynd and weather, I shall not neade in theis to make any new or long rehersell.

Since my second and therd dayes audience, the stormes I mett withall at myn arryvall have overblowen and abated dayly; sir Thomas Henneage, notwithstanding, continueth his journey, and, as we think, is yesterday embarqued. He intendeth to go by Flushing, wheare I wish he might not fayle of sir Philip Sydney.

[a] The MS. burnt.

Since the qualificacion of his message, I do not heare of any change, neither hath her majesty or himself imparted any thing therof to Mr. secretary. The most I have learned therof hath bene from my lord treasurer, who, I can assure your lordship, hath herein done good offices, though he have not bene able to do all that he wished.

On Satterday last, uppon some newes out of France, wherein it seemes they grow jealous of your lordships interest in that government, her majesty fell into some newe heate, which lasted not long. This day, I was myself at the court, and found her in reasonable good termes, though she will not yet seeme satisfied to me, either with the matter or manner of your proceading, notwithstanding all the labour I have taken in that behaulfe: howsoever it be, I am jealous of the success of things theare uppon the bruites delivered abroad, especially when they shalbe confirmed by sir Thomas his arryvall, if he cary not himself very temperatly and discreetly, which I have the better hope of, as well for the common opinions had of his judgement, as for the love he beares both to your person and the cause. It shall not be amyse, in my poore opinion, that, in your next letters to my lord treasurer, your lordship take knowledg, as from myself, of his good offices done in your behalf; in the meane tyme I do not forgett to labour him all that I may. I had no speach with him this day, by reason both himself and divers others of the councell were o[ccupied] together in hearing the old difference between my lord presedent of the north and my lord Mountjoy. Mr. vice-chamberlain protesteth, that he hath, and will, deal honorably with you, and, for any thing I heare, hath perfourmed yt. Mr. secretary hath bene behind hand to no one of the rest in an honest and honorable defence of your doings, but thopinion of his partiality to your lordship hath somewhat prejudged his credit with her [majestie]. Both he and the rest of your good frendes do fynd a great lack in your lordship seldom enterteyning her majestie with your owne letters, and think it a speciall helping cause to all the offence and myslyke here against you, which I find to be true, and wish your lordship would labor to refourme.

Though I dare not take uppon me to give advise to your lordship how to proceade with sir Thomas Henneage, yet, would I wish, under your correction, in case he have order to proceade in the delivery of any other letters then to yourselfe, that they were retayned till, uppon the information of your lordship and others, [he] had signified the danger and inconvenience therof to her majestie, and receyved her full pleasure; bycause, in the mean tyme, I hope thinges may be wroght here as you wish them, so your lordship forgett not to amend your noted fault in her majesties behaulf; for, in particular, I find not her majesty altogether so sharp as some men look, though her favor [hath] outwardly cooled in respect both of this action and of our plaine proceading with her here in defence thereof. In your supply of men, &c. there is nothing yet resolved, though her majesty promised to determyn something this day.

I am sorry your lordship hath cause to myslyke the partie I recommended you, not without some forewarnings of his particular wantes, which your lordship will in your wisdom either help or beare with. The man I know is able to do you very good service, but his long use to gouverne alone doth make him somewhat incompatible fellowship.

I have not seen my lady theis x or xij dayes; to morrow I hope, God willing, to do my duty towardes her. I found her greatly troubled with tempestuous newes she receaved from court, but somewhat comforted when she understood how I had proceaded with her majestie. It hath been assured unto me by some great ones, that it was putt into her majesties head that your lordship had sent for her, and that she made her preparacion for the journey, which added to a nomber of other thinges, cast in by such as affect neither your lordship nor the cause, did not a litle encrease the heat of her majesties offence against you. But theis passions overblowen, I hope her majesty will have a gracious regard both towardes yourself and the cause, as she hath not let sometymes to protest since my returne, knowing how much it importeth her in honor, suerty, and necessety, which recommending to the blessing of God, and your lordship to his gracious protection, I do here most humbly take my leave. At my poore house in London, this last of February, 1585.

    Your lordships ever bounden,
      and devoted to do you humble [service,]
              W. DAVISON.

LETTER LI.

THE EARL OF LEYCESTER TO THE LORDS OF THE COUNCIL.

1ST MARCH 1585-6. HARL. MS. 285. FO. 278. ORIG.

The earl, upon the representation of the merchants at Middleburgh, requests their lordships to interfere with the queen for an enlargement of the privileges of the company of merchant-adventurers.

My very good lords, I remember, a while ere my cominge over, upon certayne requestes and articles delivered over to the councell-boarde by the governor of the marchaunts-adventurers for enlargment in some respect of theire priviledges, theire booke was committed to the view of her majesties solliciter and attorney, whose aunswere and advice thereupon had, fyndinge the sute reasonable and allowable, I movyd her majestie, in the marchauntes behalfe, in hope to have obteyned that desyred; but, ere her highnes pleasure knowne thereof, I departed thince towards these contries, leavinge yt unresolved. Now, forsomuch as the marchaunts of Myddleborowe have made earnest sute unto me, declaringe how diverslye there trade is hyndered, and they endomaged, by thindirect and coullorable dealings of interlopers and disorderlye bretheren of theire societie, contrary to the trewe meaninge and construction of the priviledges by her majesties charter geven them; which they could not remedye, unlesse by the favor of her majestie they might be assisted to bare a hande and hynder sutch disorderous courses; consideringe theire demaund founded on reason, and knowinge the sarvice duringe theire beinge a corporation doun to their prince and contrie, also theire willing readines to continew in the lyke, thought good to recomend theire cause unto your lordships, most earnestlie desyringe [you] to be so favorable unto them as to deale so effectuallye with her majestie that theire longinge and wished desyre may take effect, [a] and your lordshipps shall not only, in my opinion, do a good deed, but also bynd them to do their indebvor by all meanes to be most readye allwayes at commaundment. Wherwith, expecting some good aunswere from you, I ende, and comytt your lordships to the tuition of thalmightie. From Harlem, this first March, 1586.

Your lordshippes to commaunde,
R. LEYCESTER.

Addressed,
To the moste honorable my very good lordes
the lordes of her majesties most honorable privy councell.

---

[a] The company of merchant-adventurers first termed merchants of St. Thomas à Becket, was one of those commercial corporations for which England has long been celebrated. Less ancient than the merchants of the staple, the adventurers eventually superseded them, by procuring chartered privileges through which they were enabled to trade with greater advantage than their less-favoured rivals. The application to which this and the following letter refer was successful. The queen confirmed all the previous privileges of the merchant-adventurers, and gave them the same right of trading to Germany, in exclusion of all persons except merchants of the staple, which they had before possessed in reference to the Low Countries.

LETTER LII.

THE EARL OF LEYCESTER TO MR. SECRETARY WALSYNGHAM.

1ST MARCH 1585-6. HARL. MS. 285, FOL. 280, ORIG.

The earl, on the application of the merchant-adventurers, requests Walsyngham to use his interest to procure an enlargement of their privileges.

Mr. secretarye, I wryte presentlye to my lords of her majesties counsell, in the behalfe and for the furderinge of the marchaunt-adventurers sute, touchinge the inlargment of theire priviledges. The cause is to you sufficientlie knowne, and of yourself recommended, for the good-will you bare them, and yett, thinkinge that my commendation may stand them in some steed unto you, I was willinge, at theire sute, by a fewe written lynes to desyre, that, the rather at this my request, you will stand theire honorable freend in preferringe theire booke and petition, and speake so effectually with fytt oportunitie, that her highnes graunt may the sooner passe. And, besydes the good which you shall doe unto them, which I am sure they will indebvor themselves by sarvice to desarve, I shall also take yt very freendlye, and wilbe as willinge to pleasure any at your desyre in the lyke or otherwyse. Wherewith I ende, and commytt your honour to the tuition of the Almightie. From Harlem this first March, 1586.

Your lovinge assuryd freend,
R. LEYCESTER.

Addressed,
To my honorable freend sir Frauncys Walsingham, knight, her majesties chief secretarye.

LETTER LIII.

THE EARL OF LEYCESTER TO MR. SECRETARY WALSYNGHAM.

3RD MARCH, 1585-6. HARL. MS. 285. FOL. 223. ORIG.

The earl has received intelligence that one Hyman has been sent by the prince of Parma into England upon a secret service, which the earl insinuates is to assassinate the queen.

I have received intelligence this day, from a very honest man that hath remayned in Bruges tyll now he ys retyred to Myddelborow, that ther ys a man, called Hyman, somtyme pencyonar of Bruges, and was the dealer for the Fleminges in London v or vj yeres agoe. Thys Hyman ys now sent by the prince of Parma, into England, to some servyce of his, and hath undertaken somwhat. He was once an offycer of the councell of state here among them, and did than great servyce for the king of Spain, for which he ys much esteemed. And this man that hath dyscovered this ys one that redd with his eyes the offer this Heman made to the prince for his servyce in England, and therin used wordes which did shew that matters of great secresye had passed from him when he was in England. You shall do well to enquire for him, and yf he be ther, you may be bold to clapp him upp. I understand credybly, that the Prince fedes himself in great jolytye that hir majesty doth rather myslyke than allowe of our [a] doinges here, which, yf yt be trewe, lett hir be sure hir own suete self shall first smart, and, as I hear, he doth now provyde accordingly. Fare you well, in all hast, at Harlem, this 3. of March.

Your assured,
R. LEYCESTER.

Addressed,
To my honourable good frend sir Francis Walsingham, knight, her majesties principall secretarie.

[a] her, in *MS.*

LETTER LIV.

SIR THOMAS HENEAGE TO THE EARL OF LEYCESTER.

3RD MARCH, 1585-6. COTTON. MS. TITUS, B. VII. FOL. 86. ORIG.

Announcing his arrival at Flushing on a special message from her majesty to the earl, and requesting that a lodging may be appointed for himself and his company near the earl.

It may please your lordship, both most sodenly and most unlooked for, I have been appoynted by her majesty to coomme into these contryes to delyver her majesties pleasure to your lordship, etc., and now, desyrous to be lodged near your lordship I have sent by this bearer my servant hearwith, humbly to beseech your lordship, that, by your harbynger, I may be appoynted some convenyent place for myself and my servantes; my company in all ys not above xviij^{ten} persons. As soone as I can I mean to be with your lordship, being desyrous, now I am coommen, not to be long from your lordship, having tarryed for passage at Marget a fortnyght, and lyen on the sea 2 nyghtes.

All the newes I can send your lordship at this tyme that will best please you ys, that her majesty the xxviijth of this last moneth was in very good helthe, which the Lord Jesus long contynew, with all good to your lordship. From Flysshing this iijrd of Marche, 1585.

Your lordships most assured at comandment
in all I may ever,
T. HENEAGE.

Addressed,
To the right honorable the erle of Lecester,
her majesties lieutenant generall in the Lowe Contries.

LETTER LV.

THE EARL OF WARWYKE TO THE EARL OF LEYCESTER.

6TH MARCH, 1585-6.   COTTON MS. GALBA, C. IX. FOL. 113, ORIG.

Congratulations on Leycester's successes, a continuation of which would make England the only flourishing realm of christendom— Warwyke scorns the notion of Englishmen becoming slaves to Spain, the vilest nation in the world, and thereby losing the true religion—the queen's rage rather increases—Leycester is advised to make the best assurance he can for himself, and not to trust to her oath, or to the friendship of others—he was never so honoured amongst good people as now—if the queen persists in revoking him, Warwyke, if in his situation, would go to the farthest part of christendom rather than return to England—Warwyke will take such part as Leycester does.

My dear brother, I have receaved your letter by syr Thomas Sherley,[a] whereby I doe perceave some good exployte hath byn donne off late, for the which I am nott a lyttell glad, and I pray God make us thanckfull here, both for thatt and for all thinges els, the which our good God hath made you the instrument, for the saftye of our contrey. Yf all thinges prosper as you have begonne, there is no dowtt but ytt wyll make Englande the only florysshinge relam of crystendom, since yt liethe in her majestyes hande to be a most stronge prince, and by this meanes to bryddell the radge of all enemyes she hath, and wyll nott acceptt of ytt. What shall we thincke, butt this nobell contrey of ours to be ruynated for ever, yea and to become slaves to the vyallest natyone of the worlde, besydes oure soules greff, the whytch passeth all the rest, and that is, the true religioune of Jesus Christ to be taken from us; and what is ytt that we have nott desserved for our unthanckfullnes, therfore lett us make evyn wyth God,

---

[a] Sir Thomas Sherley was sent into England by Leycester, to urge forward the desired supplies of men and money. His proceedings will be found detailed in his own letters inserted hereafter.

and loke for our payment pressently. Yt may be, that these gallauntes, and others lykewyse, for lacke off care in tyme, shall curse the tyme that ever they werr borne.

Well, our mystrys extreme radge dothe encrease rather then any way dymynishe, and givethe out great threatninge wordes against you, therefore make the best assuraunce you can for yourselff, and trust not her awthe, for that her malyce is great and unquenchabell, in the wyssest off their opynyons here, and, as for other fryndshipp, as far as I can learne, is as dowtfull as the other; wherefore, my good brother, repose your wholl trust in God, and he wyll deffende you in despytt of all your enemyes, and lett this be a greate comfortt to you, and so ytt is likewyse to myselff and all your assured friendes, and that ys, you warr never so honored and loved in your lyff amongest all good peopell as you ar att this daye, only for dealinge so nobly and wysely in this actione as you have done, so that, whatsoever comethe of ytt, you have done your part. I prayse God from my hartt for ytt. Once againe, have great care of yourselff, I meane for your saftye, and yff she wyll nedes rovoke you, to the overthrowinge of the cause, yff I werr as you, yff I cold not be assured there, I wold goe to the furdest partt of crystendom rather than ever come into Englande againe. I pray you make me no sotche straunger as you have done, butt deall franckly with me, for that thatt towcheth you towcheth me lykewyse. I have sentt you dyvers letters of importaunce and as ytt never had answer off them. Take hede whome you trust, for that you have some fallss boyes abowt you. Lett me have your best advyce what is best for me to doe. for that I meane to take sotche partt as you doe. God bless you, and prosper you in all your doinges. In hast, this pressent 6. day of Marche.

Your faithfull brother,
A. WARWYKE.

Make motch of this powre jentellman Rychard Candyss for that he is most assured to you.

LETTER LVI.

LORD BURGHLEY TO THE EARL OF LEYCESTER.

6TH MARCH, 1585-6. COTTON. MS. GALBA C. IX. FOL. 115. ORIG.

The queen's disinclination to have any speech of the business of the Low Countries since the departure of sir Thomas Heneage—Burghley's continued but unavailing applications to her—answers to the earl's letters to be sent in another paper written by Burghley's 'man,' himself being disabled from writing by an accident—the queen disinclined to a proposal for gaining thirty or forty thousand pounds by a foreign coinage of rose-nobles.

My very good lord, I shuld be ashamed greatly for not oftenar wrytyng to your lordship of late, having receaved so manny from yow, but that I have an excuse more sufficient than I lyke of, which also this beror can inform yow of.

Since Mr. Hennadg was sent from hence, who tarryed very long at the sea-cost, for want of convenient wynd, hir majesty wold never be content to have to any speeche of the state of thinges nedefull to be knowen for your chardg. I have not desisted to move hir to gyve eare, but she contynued hir offence as in no sort I cold attayn to any answer mete to be given to your lordship. And now of late having had a myshap by a fall, wherby I have bene and still am to kepe my bed, I have at sondry tymes wrytten to hir majesty. I have also sent my mynd by Mr. vice-chamberlen, who hath ernestly vsed my name to hir majesty, specially to send monny and men to supply the broken bandes, but no answer to purpooss can be had, and yet I mynd not so to cess, but, being pushed thereto with conscience and with care of hir honor, yea, of her savety, I will still sollicit hir majesty, hopyng that God will move hir to harken to necessary motions, pryncipally for hirself.

Now, my good lord, though I can gyve yow no answer to many thynges, for lack of her majesties good disposition, yet I will remembre the matters conteaned in your lordships lettres, and wryte somewhat therof, in another paper her included,[a] with my mans hand, because, in very truth, the payne of my broosed forad dishableth my hand to wryte as I wold.

My lord, I imparted to hir majesty the secret offer made to yow for to yield to hir majesty the gayn of xxx or xl^m pounds by the yere, for the permission to coyne the ross-nobles ther, but hir majesty wold not be tempted therwith; and suerly, my lord, I marvell how such a gayn can be made therof, for though for a reasonable porcion to be coyned there, at the first uttrance the same might be uttred for great gayn, yet when ther should be any plenty, the gredynes of them will be stayd, and the trew vallewe wold be knowen, and the estymation would abate.

It wold be knowen to what quantitie he wold monthely or quarterly coyne, and if it should be taken in hand, and within a few months quayle for want of uttrance, the matter wold be evil spoken of, to erect up a coynadg in a forrayn country of our currant monny; but if the gayne might be suer, the proffit wold answer the speeche. As I may heare more from your lordship, so will I procede herin.

And so I tak my leave of your lordship, praying yow to take in good part my devyding of my lettre, by wryting part with myn own hand and part with my servantes.

From the court at Greenwych, the 6th of March, 1585.

Your lordships allways assured,

W. BURGHLEY.

---

[a] includ, *in MS.*

LETTER LVII.

LORD BURGHLEY TO THE EARL OF LEYCESTER.

6TH MARCH 1585-6.   COTTON MS. GALBA C. IX. FOL. 116.

Answer written by Burghley by the hand of his secretary to various points in the earl's correspondence—hire of foreign sailors—the lord-admiral refuses to have them—return of Mr. Davison unlikely—auditor's accounts—increase of allowance by the states—arrangements for coinage of rose-nobles—levy of troops for the earl—count d'Embden—purchase of armour—Seburo—considerations respecting the merchant-adventurers and the proposed removal of the staple into Holland—skill of the people of the Low Countries in making a profit of coinage—sir William Pelham—— Killigrew—arrival of sir Thomas Shirley.

An awnsweare of divers matters mentioned in sondrie lettres of the erle of Leicesters.

LETTRES SENT BY MR. DAVISON, 1° FEB.

I have informed hir majestie, that his lordship is assured that theire maye be shippes and mariners enough to be hired to serve hir majestie uppon reasonable warning, whearein is required to be understood, what nombres of shipps of warre may be had to joine in consort with hir majesties shippes uppon the seas, and wheather it be not ment the same shall be at the charg of the states, otherwise hir majesty hath noe meaning to increase hir charge; and though, at the first, it was thowght meete, for supplie of our lacke of mariners, to hire sum from thence for the navie of Englande, yet nowe, my lord-admirall and the officers doe resolutelie awnsweare, theie will never have anie mariners, being strangers, to be matched with the Englishe. As for the request that M^r. Davison might retorne, I find noe likelood to geve your lordship anye hope thereof.

The awditor Hunt hath shewed a forme of an accompt of the treasurer for the expence of the treasure delivered to him, which commeth to lij^{m} ^{li}, with v^{m} ^{li} delivered to M^{r}. John Norris at the beginning. In this accompt theare [are] sondrie thinges dowbtfull, spetiall for manie paimentes made by the treasurer withowt anie warrant either from M^{r}. Norris or from your lordship. Theare is, also, noe good reckoning made by the treasurer of the v^{m} ^{li} first delivered to M^{r}. Norris, whie the same is not repaid by the states; neither of such monie as he hath laide owt for the pioners serving the states; other particular dowbtes theare be whereof M^{r}. secretarie hath made a colleccion, which shall be, either by Hunt the awditor or sum other, sent over thither to be awnsweared; but that which I waie more of than all this is, that I find certainelie, uppon the vewe of this accompt, that the treasurer had not sufficient for a monethes paie before the end of Januarie, so as he lacketh both for Februarie and for this present moneth of Marche, for which purpose it is more than good time the treasure weare on the waie thither.

I have informed hir majestie of the 200,000 florins accorded to be monethlie paid by the states, to be clearelie expended, besides discharge of their former debtes, and the charges of the sea; thes thinges weare mentioned in the former lettre.

LETTRES OF 2. FEBRUARY.

A matter concerning coinage shall be awnswered in a lettre of mine owne handes, yet your lordship shall understand what bargaine hath been made heare before the threasurers departure, with him and alderman Martin, that is, that hir majesty should be awnsweared for the coinage of everie pownd, vizt. of gold in rozenobles, the summ of xxx^{s}, wheare before theare ware paid for the coinage but vj^{s}. so as nowe the encrease is xxiiij^{s}., which by reckoning cometh in tale to x^{d}. for every xx^{s}., that before was but ij^{d}.; thus much for matters of the second lettre.

LETTRES OF THE 3D. FEBRUARY.

Concerninge the levienge and sending of 1000 pioners, of [whom] one hundred to be miners, bicause I thinke it weare verie necessarie for your service theare, I have furthered it the best of my power, but howe it proceadeth your lordship shall understand from M^r. secretarye.

That which your lordship writeth of the comte of Embdens affection to Spaigne I am sorie to thinke it to trewe, although since your lordships departure from hence the comte sent spetiall lettres to hir majestie, with grevous complaintes against the Hollanders by spoilinge of his people with their shippes in the river of Emps, requiringe hir majestie to write hir lettres to the states in Holland to reforme the abuses of their shippes and men of warre, with an offer to showe his good will to the cawse which hir majestie had taken in hand for them, and, for this purpose, hir majestie wrote hir lettres unto him of cumfort to procure the redresse, and lettres to them of Holland to performe the same; at which time, also, theare weare lettres written to your lordship to [take] sum meanes to compound the same controversie betwixt them, [all] which lettres as I thinke Ortellius had to send into Holland; what was done thearebie I knowe not, but yet, within a few daies, Ortell reported, that all thinges weare well compounded betwixt [the states] of Holland and the comte, and so I thought thei had been, untill nowe that I doe otherwise understand from your lordship, as likewise sir Thomas Shurlee reporteth the same.

LETTRES OF 12. FEBRUARY.

I find that our merchant-men doe greatlie misuse themselves in enhaunsing up the prices of armour theare, and, according to your advise, I wishe the provision that is to be made for hir majestie might be made from thence with your assistaunce.

Your lordship writeth to have one Seburo, a Spaniard that is a presonar heare, to be delivered in exchange for the sonne of the bailir of Dort, whearein what to awnsweare your lordship at this time I knowe not, for that theare hath been great motion made to procure for him the deliverie of Stephen le Sire, which I thinke M^r. secretarie hath furthered. And if he might free them both [it] weare noe ill bargaine for England, for that Seburo is a man of small valeue to do either good or hurt, onelie his kin[sman] the governour of Dunkirke doth desire him for frendshipp.

LETTRES OF 15. FEBRUARY.

Your lordship moveth to have our merchantes to trade into Holland with theare cloathes, and also with theire woolles, which thing hath been moved unto them heretofore, and theie of the staple for wooll have alledged, that theie have noe hope to have anie great vent for theire woolle, considering theie have had good quantetye of theire woolles lieng long at Middleborough, for the which, theie saie, thei never could have vent but to their great losse: and I moved them to change their staple to Brill, according to the request of the towne of Brill sent hither the last sommer by M^r. Davison, but I could not at that time induce them to loke thereof. Nevertheles, I will assaie them nowe uppon your lordships newe motion, with the offer of the Hollanders that theie will leave draping of the Spanish woolles and occupiours, whearebie I thinke, in truthe, our woolle maie have good utterance. For the merchaunte-adventurers, I will also deale with them for theire trade thither, with theire cloathes, considering neither Hamborough nor Embden are fitt places for them as the worlde shapeth, but I feare the greatest lett will be, that theire will be noe safe passag for theire cloathes to be carried upp into Germanie by the river of the Rhein, speteallie considering the towne of Newmeggen is in the enemies hand, and the convoies of such against the streame will be subject to dangers in divers places, being waited for by the enemie: but if our merchantes could be content to keape theire martes in thes Lowe Countries, withowt seeking to conveie them upp into Germanie themselves, it is likelie that both

Italians and Germaines would com into thos cuntries and buie them at the first hand themselves, and by meanes of safe conductes would make theire passages free. By this your lettre, also, your lordship doth confirme your opinion of the comte Embden to be Spanishe.

LETTRE OF THE 18. OF FEBRUARY.

I was glad to perceive that your lordship hath obtained a grawnt of 100,000 florins more for fowre monethes, and yet I am gladde to understand, by report of sir Thomas Shurleie, that yt should be 200,000, so as then your lordship shall have by the moneth xl$^{m\ li}$. sterling, which surelie is a great yeld, and an argument of the liking of your government. I am glad, also, that you have obtained the erecting of the howse of finances, whearein I dowbt not but you have men of sufficient conning for the guiding thereof: but I feare theire subteltie, for theire be noe people can better skill to make a gaine of coinage than thos Lowe Countriemen.

In that your lordship is so desirous to have sir William Pelham theare, I thinke you have great reason, for, in truthe, I knowe noe one man borne in England of more sufficiencie than he is, but the lett of his not comming I thinke this bearer can fullie informe yowe, which, for my part, I have sowght to remedie in all that I can, as well for the releef of the gentleman himself, as for the proffit of the service that might growe by his being with you.

I am glad that yowe have the use of my brother Killegrewe, who, as he is of great experience, so I knowe he doth of verie, meere affection towardes your lordship serve theare at this time, which otherwise noe reward could provoke him, such desire I knowe he hath to live privatelie and unoccupied.[a]

My good lord, in this sort hytherto have I eased myn own hand to releve my evill forhed. And now, since sir Thomas Shyr-

---

[a] Up to this place this paper was written by a secretary. The remainder is in the hand-writing of Lord Burghley himself.

leys coming, which was on Fryday at night, I must leave to hym to send yow report of his actions. Hopyng, that, within some few dayes, he shall have more matter to wryte of than that he hath. And so I end at this tyme, overcom with feare of sham that I may have to wryte but on lettre, to so manny as I have receaved from your lordship, and manny of them of your hand: but the fault is not lack of good will to wryte oftenar, if oftenar I might have a subject of matter. I dout not but by M^r. secretory your lordship doth understand of the proceadynges both forward and syde-wey in Scotland, of which variete truly the cheff cause cometh from hence. God amend it, whan it shall please hym to thynk us worthy of better. From the court at Grenwych the 6. of March, 1585.

Your lordships assuredly,
as anye,
W. BURGHLEY.

LETTER LVIII.

SIR THOMAS SHERLEY TO THE EARL OF LEYCESTER.

7TH MARCH 1585-6. COTTON MS. GALBA C. IX. FO. 120. ORIG.

The queen's humour of mislike still continues—she refuses to see Sherley or receive Leycester's letters sent by him—commands him to deliver his messages to Hatton and Burghley—Lewis de Pace—count d'Embden and the merchant-adventurers—objections to payments made by Leycester's orders—sir Thomas Cecill—urged to write frequently to the queen and the body of the council.

May yt please your good lordship, bycawse by this tyme your lordship hath receaved her majestyes disposytyon by sir Thomas

Hennage, I forbeare to trubble your lordship wyth longe dyscoorce of those stormes, espetyallye fyndynge Mr. Candysshe allso so well instructed therin, who canne, allso, very well enforme your lordship of the good affectyon of the lords of the councell in this case, and of soome noe good offyces donne from thence, as yt is heare thowght, towardes your lordship.

I fynd, that the quene contyneweth near in the same humore of myslyke of your lordships acceptance of the government ther, that shee was in when sir Thomas Heneage went hence, and hath hytherunto refused to speake with me, or to receave your lordships letters, thowghe Mr. vyce-chamberlayne hath most nobly and carefully solycyted her hyghnesse therin.

Uppon saterdaye in the afternoone, shee dyd commaund me by Mr. vyce-chamberlayne, that I shold delyver suche matter as I had to saye unto my lord-tresewrer and hym, whyche I dyd, and therin I labored most to sett forthe unto them the necessytye of your lordships acceptaunce of that government, and then proceedyd to treat for men and monney, and concequently to all the rest of my instructyons. My lord-tresewrer put all my proceedynges wyth them into artycles, and delyvered yt unto Mr. vyce-chamberlayne to relate unto the quene, for his selfe is lame, and cold nott goe unto her. Wheruppon she sayd, she wold as yesterdaye speake wyth my lord-tresewror, but that is nott yeat donne.

I spake only unto Mr. secretory towchynge Lewes de Pace, who doth assure me that ther is noe dowght of that matter: so as, by his advyce, I forbeare to saye anny thynge therof unto my lord-tresewror.

My lord-tresewror myslyketh not that her majestye shold wryte unto the earle of Emden, but sayth, that to remove the coorce of marchantes from thence to Holland and Zelland were nott good, bycawse ther is noe good meanes to convaye marchantdyce from thence to Collen and those partes, except your lordship were possessed of Newmegyn and the rest uppon the ryver. Ther shall present order be taken for somme shyppes and pynnyces to chastyce the Dunkerkers.

In the accomptes of the quenes tresewror yt is myslyked, that your lordship hath made full allowaunce of paye unto every captayne, allthowghe they wanted somme of them more then the halfe of theyre men, as yt is sayde heare. I wysshe your lordship, ether by a letter unto my lord-tresowror or by somme other meanes, to make somme answer therunto. I had noe instructyon or acquayntaunce howe to answere yt. Mr. secretory doth wysshe, that your lordship had taken order for the paye or imprest at Brylle, equally with other places, and that you wold, allso, use kynesse unto sir Thomas Ceycell, for he doth assure me, that my lord-tresewror doth deale very dyrectly and honerably towards your lordship and that whole cawse.

Fynally, all your frendes doe wysshe your lordship to wryte more often unto her majestye, and that, at all tymes when ther is cawse, you wold please to dyrect one large letter unto the boddy of the councell, as unto pryvate frendes. A present letter is allso wysshed from your lordship unto her majestye uppon the message of sir Thomas Hennage, and then, yf ther be cawse, and[a] your lordship please to send me anny addytyon unto my instructyons, I wyll contynewe suche faythfull care therin as beccometh me towardes your lordship. And I dowght nott, in the end, but all wyll be well, and her majestye will be reduced by reason to allowe well of that whyche your lordship hath donne.

I deale only with my lord-tresewror, Mr. vice-chamberlayne, Mr. secretorye, and my lord Buckehurst. I doe assure your lordship I fynd them all very honnorably affected in this cawse, and carefull to doe in yt accordynglye. I am, and ever will be, at your lordships servyce, and I doe for ever wysshe your lordship all happynesse. At coort this 7. of March, 1585.

Your good lordships ever most
assured at commaund,
THOMAS SHERLEY.

[a] that, *in MS.*

LETTER LIX.

THE EARL OF LEYCESTER TO THE LORDS OF THE COUNCIL.

9TH MARCH, 1585-6. HARL. MS. 285, FOL. 228. ORIG.

The earl thanks them for their mediation with the queen—will not excuse his acceptance of the government without first acquainting her majesty—he was earnest to consult her, but yielded to the persuasions of Davison and others—denies with imprecations the accusation of having acted contemptuously—complains of Davison's answers to the queen—desires to be recalled, and to serve her majesty with his prayers.

My verye singuler good lords, I am to render most hartye and humble thankes unto you, for that, I am informyd, hit hath pleaside you to be meanes to hir most excellent majesty, to quallyfye hir hard conceatt agenst my pore servyce donne here.

I wyll not excuse myself of a great fault, that I dyd not first aquaint her highness before I dyd accept this office, and to receave hir good pleasure therin, but what I may alleage for myself I trust Mr. Davison hath delyvered, or elles hath he greatly both deceaved me and broken promys with me. How ernest I was, not only to aquaint hir majesty, but, imedyatly, upon the first mocion made here by the states, to send him over to hir majesty with my letters and his report of the whole state of these matters, I dowbt not but he wyll truly affyrme for me, yea, and how farr ageinst my wyll it was, notwithstanding any reasons delyvered me, that he and others persisted in, to have me accept first of this place. Albeyt, I must confes, all that he dyd, presuming the exstremytye of the cace to be such as he thought himself fully hable to satysfie hir majesty, as a matter either than to be taken without all delaye or to fall utterlye to the ground, and his knowledge therof I know to be farr beyond myne, having byn contynewally beaten[a] here among them, long before my coming, and most carefull was he to bring all to the best pass for hir servyce. Uppon which exstremytye of the cace, as yt was, and being perswaded that Mr. Davyson might better have satysfyed hir majestie than I perceave he can, caused me, nether arrogantly nor contemptuouslye, but even merely and faythfully, to doe hir majesty the best servyce. And as I say not thys to worke any blame to Mr. Davyson, whose most sincere honest minde toward hir servyce I must acknowledge, so yet may I not leave so greatt a conceatt remayne in hir majestyes minde of my undewtyfullnes, whan I did not only remember my dewty as I have told you, but dyd urge the performance therof as I have wrytten. But my yelding was my none fault, whatsoever his perswasions, or any others, might be, seing the reasons be no more acceptyd of hir majesty than they be; but farr from a contemptuous hart, or elles God pluck out both hart and bowelles, with utter shame.

And finding hit thus hardly to light uppon me, which I thought should have wonne a more favorable constructyon, the doing having wholye tended to the advauncement of hir majesties most honorable servyce, as all men here hath and doth see, I doe most humbly besech your good lordships, to contynew your good favors towards me, and to wey whereuppon hir majesties offence hath groen, only uppon presuming to much of hir good opinion of my fidellytye toward hir, and partly by Mr. Davisons over-great slacknes to have answered soner and better for me, as he promysed he wold. And being greatly dyscouraged, albeyt I could allege for the cause and place very much to satysfie your lordships for my honest servyce therby to hir majesty, yet wyll I not seme to travell ageinst the groundes of hir majestyes so depe conceatt, but leave yt to God and your lordships most frendly medyation to conceave, that I am hir most loyall faythfull bondman, and had never ether contemptuous or unworthy thought of hir sacred majesty, but as becam so bounded a servant and subject as I am, and

[a] *i. e.* stationed as upon a beat.

ever wylbe to hir, lett hir use me as shall please hir. And, yf withowt offence and with hir favour, hit ys not only the leaving of this place I shall humbly desier, but to serve hir majesty where elles soever by my humble and dayly prayer, which shall never ceas for hir most happie preservacion and long contynewance, finding myself very unfytt and unable to wade in so weighty a cause as this ys, which ought to have much more comfort than I shall ether find or desarve. Thus, beseching God to bless and govern all your councelles to his glorye and hir majestyes best servyce, I humbly take my leave. At Harlem this ix. of March, 1585.

      Your lordships most assured
        pore frend,
         R. LEYCESTER.

As far as I can perceave, hir majesty doth think, that by this place I tooke I have engaged hir in some further sort than she was before, but your lordships shall find, I did both forsee that, and ther ys no such cause to think yt; for yt ys most certen, ther ys no more donn on hir majestyes parte than hir owne contract doth bynd hir, only she hath hir own servant to comaund here, wheare some one other must, which wold, I think, more have myslyked hir.

Addressed,
To the right honourable my very good lords, the lords
 of her majesties moste honourable privye counsaile.

LETTER LX.

THE EARL OF LEYCESTER TO MR. SECRETARY WALSYNGHAM.

9TH MARCH, 1585-6.   HARL. MS. 285, FO. 225. ORIG.

The earl complains of the imperfection of Davison's explanations to the queen—protests that he accepted the government only upon his earnest persuasions and his promise to discharge him to the queen—hopes the cause will take no harm—Heneage proceeds warily—the earl has advanced above £11,000—miserable state of the soldiers—the earl anxious to be rid of his "heavy high calling," and be at his poor cottage again—Schenck's exploits.

Mr. secretary, I thank you for your letters, though you can send me no comfort; I trust God wyll not leave those that meane truly, and trust in him. Hir majesty doth deall hardly to beleave so yll of me. Hyt is true that I faulted, bycause I dyd not advertyse hir majesty first or I shuld take such an authorytye uppon me, but she doth not consider what comodyttyes she hath withall, and hirself no way engaged for yt, either one way or other, as Mr. Davison myght have better declaryd yt, yf yt had pleasd him. And I must thank him only for my blame, and so he wyll confess to you, for, I protest before God, no necessyty here could have made me leave hir majesty unacquantyd with the cause before I wold have acceptyd of yt, but only his so ernest pressing me, with his faythfull assured promys to dischardge me, howsoever hir majesty shuld take yt. For you all se ther, she had no other cause to be offended but this, and, by the Lord, he was the only cause, albeyt yt ys no suffycyent allegacion, being as I am.

And as for the importance of the cause I did adventure, so considering the importance of hindering the cause thorow the dyspleasure that doth fall uppon me, hit had byn an honest part yet to have lett hir majesty know how ernest I was, and how resolute, to acquaint hir with the cause or I would have taken the place; and hit could not have had any blame almost, doing yt, as he did indeede, for hir great servyce, and assuredly all had byn lost yf I had not than acceptyd of yt as I dyd, and, accepting yt as I dyd, with my former resolucyon and myndfullnes to advertyse hir, he had, I think, saved all to have told hir, as he promysed me. But now yt ys leyd uppon me, God send the cause to take no harm, my grefe must be the less; though yt toucheth me as nere as doth hir majesties so hard dyspleasure, yet have I no way, I thank God, tyed hir majesty to any inconvenyence by my acceptance. How farr Mr. Henneages comyssion shall deface me here I know not; he ys wary to observe hys comyssyon, and I content withall. I know the tyme wylbe hir majesty wyll be sorry for yt. In the meane tyme I am to to wery of the high dygnyty, I wold any that could serve hir majesty werr placed in yt and I to sytt down with all my losses.

I assure you, uppon my fidelity, I have spent and leyd out for hir majesty's servyce above 11,000^{li} sterling alredy, in these iij months. I thought yt wold have served me v months longer here. I tell you truly my howse alone hath cost me a 1000^{li} a month, and some month more. I have also payd hetherto v^c and l. men; of my owne purse these, and furnyshed them of my none chardges. And for the horsmen, I am sure all these countreys enymyes, or other, have not such vj^c. horse as I have. I receavyd but for iiij^c. as you know, and I have payd, both for the other ij^c. and, synce I cam hether, a c. and l. more; so that I have above iij^c. and l. that myself hath raysed, above the iiij^c. hir majesty payd for at London. And all this ys lyke to light uppon me, instead of better happ. I am sure ther hath not a gentleman past hence, ether of my none or otherwyse, but the least hath had x^{li}. some xx^{li}., some xxx^{li}., and the most xx. Well, so I might have gott any more money for my land that ys left, I wold as well have spent more, for ther be many here have spent much.

But, sir, whatsoever become of me, gyve me leave to speake for the pore soldyeres. Yf they be not better mainteyned, being in this strang countrey, ther wyll nether be good service donn, nor be without great dishonour to hir majesty, and the less she shall send at once the more unproffytable for hir, and she shall find yt so, and xx^{mli}. to send now, I doe assure you yt ys all dew alredy, and you se what lettes you have by the wynd. Ther was no soldyer yet able to buy himselfe a pair of hose, and yt ys to to great shame to se how they goe, and hit kills ther hartes to shew themselves among men. Well, you se the wantes, and hit ys one cause that wyll gladde me to be rydd of this hevy high cauling, and wyshe me at my pore cottage ageyn, yf any I shall find. But, lett hir majesty pay them well, and apoint such a man as sir William Pellam to govern them, and she never wann more honour than these men here wyll doe, I am perswaded.

For newes, I wrote you of late that Shenkes had taken a town and castle in Westfalia called Werl. Synce that, the enymyes of that countrey gathered together, both the gentlemen and ablest men, and offred a kind of siege of the towne, but Shenkes issewed out and sett uppon them, slewe that [there] ley ded in the fild 2500 persons; he toke a great nomber prisoners, among which wer 25 of very good cauling, and the ij chife captens beside. Surely this ys a noble fellow, having done this he fecht in all ther vyttells, and vytteled the towen and castell, and left a good garison, and putt himself now safe into Nuse, which we doubtyd to be besiged shortly. Ostend ys thought wylbe beseged, but I fear yt not.

Thus, having spent my paper and all my news, I betake you to God, &c. At Harlem 9. March.

Your assured frend,
R. Leycester.

Addressed,
  To my honorable good frend sir Francis Walsingham,
    knight, principall secretary to her majesty.

LETTER LXI.

THE EARL OF LEYCESTER TO MR. DAVISON, WITH HIS COMMENTS IN REPLY WRITTEN IN THE MARGIN.

10TH MARCH, 1585-6. HARL. MS. 285. FOL. 230. ORIG.

The earl complains, that he having unwillingly accepted the government, upon Davison's persuasion, and his promise to satisfy the queen, Davison had procured him displeasure by not stating those facts—Davison answers, in the margin, by insinuating that the earl was not unwilling, and that the queen's anger proceeded upon the ground of her having expressly commanded the earl not to accept such an authority, which command the earl never mentioned to Davison and the others who advised him to the contrary.

Denyed.	Hit hath not greved me a lytle, that, by *your meanes*,[a] I have fallen into hir majesty's so depe displeasure, but that you, also, have
I appeale to the testimony of others.	*so carelesly dyscharged your parte*, in the dew declaracion of all thinges as they stoode in troth. Knowing most assuredly, that, *yf you had* delyvered to hir majesty indede
The contrary appeares.	the troth of my dealing, *hir highnes could* never have conceavyd, as I perceave she doth. For, by the letters, and message I
He was dispatched the same night I arrived.	have received by *Mr. Hennage*, nether doth
Let sir Philip Sidney and others witnes.	hir majesty know, *how hardly* I was drawen to accept this place before I had acquainted hir, wherein no man living knew so much as yourself to have satysfied hir, as you faythfully tooke uppon you and promysed
I did my best to satisfie her majestie, wherin I appeale to	you wold, in such sort as you wold not only

[a] The words printed in Italics were underscored in the original by Davison. They indicate the points to which his marginal observations principally apply.

gyve hir majesty full satisfaction, *but wold procure me many great thankes.* Nether ys hir majesty informyd rightly what authorytye I have received; for yf you had don that certenly as yt was, she wold not be offended as she ys, for, as *you dyd chifely perswade me* to take this chardge uppon me, so yet did I not deall so vainlye as yt semes hir highnes conceaves, as though I was so gladd of the place I did not care how I engaged hir majesty, contrary to hir wyll and pleasure, by my acceptance of the place, of which no man knew better how to dyscharge me of that than yourself, who can remember, *how many treatyes* you and others had with the states before I agreed, for all *yours and their perswasions to take* yt soner; and nothing dyd I seke more, as both the doctors Clerkes can also tell, than to have hir majesty clere from conclusions in this matter every way, and so dyd you all assure me, elles had I never taken yt as I dyd; which, when I found hir majesty no wey bound nor tyed by my doing, and by the acceptance of this place I might so greatly, as I have indede, advaunced hir servyce, (yf yt be so considered) and withall help this countrey from the present imenent danger yt stoode in, made me more wylling to doe as I have done, and to adventure, uppon *that assurance you gave me to satysfie hir majesty,* but *I se not that you have done any thing.* Spetyally, I, aquainting you with all

her owne conscience, and testimony of others.
This had beene a woorke of supererogacion, more then I was fitt to undertake.

As truly and particulerly as himself or any man theare could have done.

His ende in coming over, with some other circumstances, may decide this question.

For the clearing of some scruples depending on that charge, not for the thing itself.

All this while theare was no note of any contrary commaundement.

All this makes nothing to the purpose against me.

As far fourth as I was able; as much as any privat frend he hath.

LEYC. CORR.

my comyssions and instructyons before, *and dyd not hide from you the dowbt* I had of hir majestyes yll taking yt, except you dyd thorowly make her know indede, both my care to please hir majesty before all thinges in the world, and the cause of hir servyce, chifely without engaging hir any way, caused me *yeld to your perswasions here.* Therfore I conclude, *charging you with your conscience how you* doe deall now with me; seeing you *chifely broght me into yt,* and to suffre me to rest mysjuged of by hir majesty, which could no wey *have byn heavy to you though you had told the uttermost of your own doing,* as you faythfully promysed me you wold, and, rather than hir majesty shuld mysconceave of me, you wold lett hir know *the hole troth* in dede; for that *I dyd very unwillingly come to the matter,* dowbting that to fall out that ys com to pas, more *thorow lack of* good and substancyall making hir majesty trewly understand the cace, than for any offence in reason comytted, and all thus lost; and *falls out by your negligent carelesnes, whereof I many hundred tymes told you of, that you wold* both marr the goodnes of the matter and brede me hir majesties dyspleasure. But, *housoever yt fall out, she shall know all* my reasons, and Mr. Hennege, I trust wyll [declare] his knowledge, and than referr all to God and hir majesty. Thus fare you well, and, accept your *embassages have better success,* I shall have no great cause to

Sidenotes:

A doubt bewrayed, I confess, but no commandement to the contrary.

Standing with her majestyes honour and service, not against her express commaundement.

As a man honestly affected to the cause, and more to himself then this dealing meriteth.

Absolutely denyed.

Though it were les then yow make it, yet is it heavier than many men would beare for your sake.

It is done.

Herof let the world judge.

Non causa pro causâ.

You might doubt it, but if you had uttred so much, you shold have employed some other in the journey, which I had no reason to affect much, preseing well ynough how thankles it wold be.

So let it be; so the endes of truth and justice be kept.

comend them. In som haste at Harlem, this x. of March, 1585.

Your loving frend,
R. Leycester.

Addressed,
To my cousyn Davyson
esquire.

LETTER LXII.

SIR THOMAS SHERLEY TO THE EARL OF LEYCESTER.

14TH MARCH, 1585-6. COTTON. MS. GALBA C. IX. FO. 128. ORIG.

Sherley reports that he had had an interview with the queen, in which she used most bitter words against the earl—Sherley's reply—the queen insists that Leycester's proceeding was sufficient to make her infamous to all princes—Sherley praised the policy of Drake's expedition, and pointed out that it was more offensive to Spain than the course taken by the earl—the queen replied that Drake would not care if she disavowed him—Sherley suggested that neither would Leycester care for her disavowal of his government if she still retained her favour towards him—Sherley's stratagems to induce the queen to receive Leycester's letter but in vain—he reports a subsequent interview, in which he worked upon her regard for Leycester, by representing that he was ill, and soliciting permission for a medical man to go over to him, which the queen granted—difficulties as to procuring men and money—feelings of the queen's advisers towards Leycester— Hatton has at length induced her to receive Leycester's letter—Sherley's anticipations.

May yt please your good lordship, after eight dayes I spake with her majestye, beynge browght unto her by Mr. vice-chamberlayne, into the pryvy chamber, when she used most bytter wordes agaynst your lordship for your receavynge that government, affirmynge, that shee dyd expressly forbyd yt unto your lordship, in the presence and hearynge of dyvers of her councell. I aleged the necessytye of yt, and your lordships intent to doe all for the best for her majestyes servyce; and I told her, how those countreyes dyd expect you as a governor at your fyrst landynge, and that the states durst doe noe other but to satysfye the people allso with that oppynion; whose myslyke of theyr present government was such and so great, as the name of states was growen odyose amongest them, and that the states, dowgthynge the furyose rage of the people, conferred the authorytye uppon your lordship wyth insessaunt sewt unto you to receave yt, notwythstandyng, your lordship dyd deney yt untill you sawe playnely bothe confusyon and reuyne of that countreye, yf your lordship shold refuse yt: and, of the other syde, when you had seene into theyre estates, your lordship found great proffyt and commodytye like to come unto her majestye by your acceptaunce of yt. And that, by this meanes, her majestye shold have the commandment bothe of theyr monney, shippes, and townes; that they of themselves henceforeward cold doe nothynge to prejudyce her hyghnesse; howe her owne people in those partes were lyke to be in so muche the better assuraunce to be well used; howe her hyghnesse myght have garrysones of Inglysshe in as manny of theyr townes as pleased her, wythowght any more charge then she is now at; how noe peace canne, at any tyme hereafter, be made wyth Spayne, but throwghe her, and by her. I put her majestye allso into remembraunce, that, if anny of another natyon had bene chosen, it myght have wrowght great dawnger, besydes the indygnytye that her levytenaunt-gennerall shold, of necessytye, be under hym that so shold have bene elected; fynally, that this ys a stopp to any other that may affect the place of government ther. But all my speeche was in vayne; for shee persysted, sayinge, that your lordships procedyng was suffycyent to make her infamose to all prynces, havynge protested the contrary in a booke which is translated into dyvers and soondrye languages ; and that your lordship, beynge her servaunt, owght nott, in your dewtye towardes her, to have entred into that coorce, wythowght her knowlege and good allowaunce.

Then, to draw her into soome better consyderatyon of your doynges, I told her majestye, that the world had conceaved a hyghe jugement of her great wysdome and provydence, whyche shee shewed in assaylyng the kynge of Spayne at one tyme both in the Lowe Countreys and allso by sir Frauncis Drake; I dyd assure myselfe, that the same jugement of hers whyche, at the fyrst, dyd cawse her so to take it in hand, dyd lykewyse contynewe a certayne knowlege in her majestye, that one of these actyons must needes stand muche the better by the other; and that, yf sir Frauncis dyd prosper, then all was well; and thowghe he shold nott prosper, yeat this hold that your lordship had taken for her uppon the Low Countreyes wold allwayes assure her of an honnerable peace, yf yt shold at anny tyme stand so wyth her majestyes pleasewre. I besowght her hyghnesse, allso, to remember, that, to the kynge of Spayne, this government of your lordship made noe greater matter then to be her majestyes levytenaunt-gennerall ther, but that the vyage of sir Frauncis was of muche more offence unto hym then this. To that shee sayd, shee cold very well answere for sir Frauncis, " but, yf nede be," sayde shee, " the gentleman careth nott yf I shold dysavowe him." " Even so," sayd I, " standeth my lord, yf your dysavowynge of hym may allso stand wyth your hyghnesse favour towardes hym."

Then I told her majestye, that, yf this brute of her myslyke of your lordships awthorytye theyre shold comme unto the eares of those people, beynge a natyon both suddayne and suspytyose, and havynge heretofore benne used unto stratagem, I feared that yt myght worke somme straunge notyon in them, consyderynge that, at this tyme, ther is an encrease of taxatyon raysed uppon them, the bestowynge wherof perhapes they knowe nott of, nether were lyke to judge the best of yt; and that your lordship gyvynge upp of that government shold leave them alltogyther wythowght government, and in worce case then ever they were in before, for nowe the awthorytye of [the] states was dyssolved, and your lordships government is nowe the only thynge that holdeth them togythers; I dyd, therfore, beseche her hyghnesse to consyder well of yt, and that, yf there wer anny pryvate [cause] for whyche shee tooke greefe agaynst your lordship, yeat that shee wold please to have regard unto the pupplyke cawse, and to have care of her owne saffetye, whyche, in manny wyse menes oppynions, stoode muche uppon the good mayntenaunce and upholdynge of this matter. Shee wold nott beleve me in the dyssolvynge of the awthorytye of [the] states, but sayd, shee knewe well inowghe, that the states dyd remayne states styll, and sayd, shee ment nott to doe harme unto the cawse, but only to reforme that whyche your lordship had donne beyond your warraunt from her. And so shee leaft me. And this is the effect of all that passed then, but your letter in no wyse her majestye wold then receave, thowghe I dyd often beseche yt; and in dyvers thynges that she asked of me I semed more ignoraunt then I was, and told her, that I thowght your lordship had wrytten therof, bycawse I wold have herr to receave your letter, but yt would nott be.

Uppon Frydaye last, as her majestye walked in the garden, I thowght to tast her affectyon unto your lordship by an nother meanes, and stepped unto her and sayd, that your lordship beynge in dowght of fallynge into a dyssese that Goodrowse[a] dyd once cure you of, your lordship was now an humble sewtor unto her highnesse, that yt wold please her to spare Goodrowse, and to gyve hym leave to comme unto your lordship for soome tyme. I assure your lordship yt moved her much, and shee answered me, that with all her hart you shold have hym, and that shee was sorry that your lordship had that need of hym. I told her that shee

[a] Goodrowse was a physician in the confidence of the earl of Leycester, and a legatee under his will. Sydney Papers, i. 75.

was a very gratyose prynce, that pleased nott to suffer your lordship to perryshe in your health, thowghe otherwysse shee tooke offence agaynst you, wherunto shee answered me, " You knowe my mynd. I may nott endewre that my man shold alter my commyssyon, and the awthorytye that I gave hym, uppon his owne fancyes, and wythowght me ;" and therwithall shee called an other unto her, dowghtynge, as I thynke, that by degrees I wold agayne have treatyd wyth her abowt the other matters, whyche indeede I had donne, espetyally to delyver your lordships letter.

Thus I have trubbled your lordship longe, and I have told you all and every part of the speeche that I have yeat had wyth her majestye, savynge soome speeche of my lady your wyffe, not materyall to wryte of. I have ever synce, and styll wyll, attend uppon Mr. vyce-chamberlayne, to knowe her hyghnesse pleasewre abowt men and monny, but, by reason of cold that shee hath taken, her majestye keepeth her chamber thes three dayes, and is very unapt to be dealt wyth in these matters, as Mr. vyce-chamberlayne tellyth me. My lord-tresewror is allso lame, so as he cannot goe to her, and wythowght hym I perceave shee wyll conclude nothynge, but, as farr as I canne gather from anny of them, your lordship is lyke to have but a verie poore supply of monney at this tyme, she talketh of x. thowsand, but, yf yt comme to xx. thowsand, yt wyll be all, I beleve. To be playne with your lordship, I feare shee groweth weerye of the charge, and wyll very hardly be browght to deale throwghly in the actyon.

Uppon Saterdaye last, her majestye commaunded Mr. vice-chamberlayne to conferr with my lord-tresewror and Mr. secretory, abowt monney to be sent thyther, but they concluded nott. I fynd them all very well dysposed in this matter, but Mr. vyce-chamberlayne is the man that dealeth most, or rather only, with her majestye therin ; for shee wyll hardly endewre Mr. secretorye to speake unto her therin, as he telleth me. And trewly, my lord, as Mr. secretarye ys a noble, good and trew friend unto you, so doth Mr. vyce-chamberlayne shewe hym selfe an honnerable, trew and faythfull gentleman towardes you, and doth carefully, and most lyke a good frend, for your lordship. Yeasterdaye he told me that her majestye was now perswaded by hym to receave your lordships letter, whyche I then delyvered unto hym. He hath, allso, moved the quene for Goodrowse to comme unto you, and shee hath confyrmed her promyse made unto me for him; so as ther is no dowght of his commynge unto your lordship.

I have herin declared unto your lordship thynges just as they stand. Your lordship is exceedynge wysse. You knowe the quene and her nature best of anny man. You knowe all men heare. Your lordship canne juge the sequell by this that you see; only this I must tell your lordship, I perceave, that feares and dowghtes from thence, are lyke to worke better effectes heare, then comfortes and assuraunce. I thynke yt my part to send your lordship this as yt ys, rather then to be sylent. I wyll wayght for better, and your lordship shall have a messenger from me as often as anny thynge ys worthy the wrytynge. And when thynges be ether effected or resolved, I wyll wayghte uppon your lordship myselfe by the grace of God, and take my part in your fortunne in that servyce. I wyll nott goe hence, nor forbeare anny solycytatyon of frendes, or travayle of my owne, to doe your lordship servyce. I beseche your lordship to pardon my longe lynes. I suppose you canne be contented to heare these matters at large, therfore I am bold to use yt so. And so I doe most humbly commytt your good lordship to God. At coort this xiiij. of March, 1585.

Your good lordships most assured,
ever at commaund,
THOMAS SHERLEY.

My lady your wyffe is well, but had now noe cawse to wryte. I wayghtid uppon her yesterday to know her pleasewre.

LETTER LXIII.

THE EARL OF LEYCESTER TO MR. SECRETARY WALSYNGHAM.

17TH MARCH 1585-6. HARL. MS. 285, FO. 232. ORIG.

The earl complains that Anto. Poyntz, whom he had employed to go into the enemy's camp, had been sent by Walsingham into Spain.

Mr. secretorye, touching Pointes, of whome you wryte, I am sory he is sent any other waye. I delivered him an hundred poundes, and he promised me to have gone into the enemyes campe. And so, with my harty commendacions, fare you well. From Amsterdame the xvij. of Marche.

Your very loving frende,
R. LEYCESTER.

I am forst to use a secretary,[a] but yet, perhapps, you wyll not very plainly understand whome I meane; hit ys Anto. Poyntz, whome I sent over to gyve you knoledge how I had imployed him to the enymyes camp, a matter of most nede for me, and I mervelled that I never hard from [him,] and within these iiij. days, my nephew Phillip told me he received a letter from him that you had sent him into Spayn, whereof I am hartyly sorry, having greatly dysapointyd me, having not one to suply that place nowe, and a great tyme lost, also, that you dyd not at the first gyve me knoledge of yt.

Addressed,
To my honourable good frende Mr. secretory Walsingham.

---

[a] The letter is in the handwriting of the earl's secretary, the postscript in that of the earl himself.

LETTER LXIV.

MR. SECRETARY WALSYNGHAM TO THE EARL OF LEYCESTER.

20TH MARCH 1585-6. COTTON. MS. GALBA, C. VIII. FOL. 63. ORIG.

All speed is being used in procuring the money resolved by the queen to be sent to the earl—her majesty cannot be induced to resolve as to the levy of men—she is disposed to allow certain discharged ' bands' in Ireland to be transported thither—the earl is advised to take advantage in part of the offer of the master of Gray—disposition of the French king towards the king of Navarre.

My verry good lord, theire is [all con]venient speed used in the prepa[ration] and putting in a ready[ness] the money resolved on by her majestye to bee sent over, which I am sorrye fawleth not owt in proportyon large as the necessytie of the servyce requirethe, so that your lordship, contrarye to your own lyking, shall be forced to stand uppon a defencyve warre: yt wyll be verry discompfortable to the people of thos contryes, espetyally when they shall see there townes lost, which your lordship for lacke of hennowghe assistance, shall not be able to prevent.

Suche gentlemen as your lordship appoynted to levye men ar tyred with long attendaunce here, for that her majestye cannot be drawn to resolve therin. Her awnswer is, that shee wyll see an accompt of thos allreadye sent over, before she yeld her assent to the sending over of any more. I shewed un[to] her highness the hard estate the towne of Grave stands in, which coold not be releeved withowt an encrease of forces, which moved your lordship to presse my lords of the cownsell here to take some care for the speedye dyspatche of the gentlemen. I dyd also shew unto her, that the losse of that towne woold woorke some changing in the peoples hartes, when they should see themselves subject to lyke misfortune as they were before her majestye tooke uppon her to protect them. But nothing that can be alleaged can drawe her majestye to yeld to any thing that tendeth to the furtheraunce of the servyce there, otherwyse then led by mere necessytye.

I fynde her dysposed to lyke that certeyn cashed bandes in Ierland, uppon dowbt that otherwyse they wyll put her to some charge here, shall be transported into the Lowe Countreys, so yt may be don withowt her burden. I have caused Mr. Davison [to] sette downe with what charge the same may be performed, which I wyll send unto your lordship.

Seing her majestye is no better dysposed to send over her owne subiectes, I thinke your lordship, in case you resolve to contynewe your servyce there, shall doe well to take part of the master of Grayes offer, whoe, as my cosyn Randollph[a] sendethe me woord, sendethe an expresse gentleman unto your lordship to knowe your lordships resolutyon therin. I fynde the gentlemen that your lordship hath appoynted to make the levye are lothe to take upon them that charge with the allowance of xx^s. the man, and herof your lordship shall doe well, in case her majestie may be drawen to assent that any levyes shall be made here, to move the states to increase the somme.

By the inclosed copy of sir Edward Staffordes[b] letter your lordship shall see, howe resolutely the king ther is bent to prosecute the warre, with the uttermost of his power, agaynst thos of the relygyon.

Ther hath ben certeyn offers made unto her majestye, and by her rejected, and yet of no great charge, that carryed great proba-

---

[a] It has been noticed already (p. 52.) that the well known sir Thomas Randolph, whom Walsyngham here styles his cousin, was sent upon an embassy to Scotland in February 1585-6. The master of Gray had just entered upon public life, and was in great favour with the young king James VI.

[b] Sir Edward Stafford was at this time ambassador at the court of France.

bylytie to have withstoode both Godes and her enemyes. I praye God, the lacke of fealing and compassion of others myseryes, doe not drawe uppon us hys heavye hande; to whos protection I commyt your lordship, most humbly takyng my leave. At the coorte, 20. Marche, 1585.

Your lordships to commaunde,
FRA. WALSYNGHAM.

LETTER LXV.

SIR THOMAS SHERLEY TO THE EARL OF LEYCESTER.
21ST MARCH 1585-6. COTTON. MS. GALBA, C. IX. FOL. 136. ORIG.

The queen has signed a warrant for £24,000, to be sent to the earl, and consents that he shall have 1000 men out of Ireland—she will not consent to any Englishmen being sent, but it is hoped she will allow the going of volunteers—directions solicited as to payments for clothing, arming, and transporting—the earl urged to write to the council on these matters not merely to his friends—lady Warwick will send a company—sir Thomas Cecill has leave to return home—letters from the earl and sir Thomas Heneage anxiously looked for—the queen has forborne to speak openly against the earl since Sherley's interview with her.

May yt please your good lordship, her majestye sygned a warraunt yeasterday, for fowre and twentye thowsand poounds to be presently sent unto your lordship, and her majestye is pleased that your lordship shall have one thowsand men, and perhapes more, owt of Ireland. Yt ys required, that your lordship shold take order in London for monney for transportatyon and other neccessaryes for them, and that your lordship allso wold appoynt some suche as pleaseth you, for the levyinge and convayinge of them from thence. Amonge whom, if your lordships pleasewre be to imploye * * * Chester, he is well acquaynted in that coountrye, and I heare wyll otherwysse nott be provyded of a band, for I dowght muche that he wyll procure none hence; and yf, by your lordships favor, he may be imployed to hys good amonges these Irysshe, I shall very well provyde myselfe otherwyse of an offycer in my regyment, yf I have anny.

Her hyghnesse wyll nott yeat consent to send anny men from hence by commyssyon, but only to mayntayne the contract; nether doth throwghlye agree to suffer voluntaryes to passe thyther, neverthelesse your lordships frendes doe hope that shee wyll be wonne to alowe of the goynge of voluntaryes, and that ther shall be allso letters into sheeres from the lords of the coouncell for the ferderaunce of yt. But very hard yt wyll be, certaynely, to levye manny voluntaryes, the jorney standeth so slawndered heare, and men stand in dowght of good usage, and espetyally of paye ther; suche vyle brutes have bene raysed heare. Yt wyll, allso, be very chargeable to rayse bandes in that sort, for yt is heare consyder- ed that suche as wyll in that manner make anny, he shall be enforced to imploye dyvers in the pursewt of yt. And as yt wyll be charge- able to gather men togythers, so is yt impossyble to procure anny great noomber at one tyme, or wythin few dayes; so as dyvers must rest uppon the charge of the capetayne, whyles others be in gatherynge. And to everye small companye ther must soome one offycer be imployed, for yf monney shall be delyvered unto suche soldyars owne handes for prest and conduct, they wyll sewrely rune awaye, bycawse ther is noe suche lawes to meete wyth them as is for men prest by commyssyon. Yt ys, therfore, wysshed by Mr. secretorye, and trewly, in my poore oppynion, yt is most neccessarye, that your lordship wold please to wryte hyther, what allowaunce of monney shall be made by the states for the levye of suche men, for cootynge and for transeportatyon of them, and allso for armynge of them, bycause soomme per- hapes wyll arme heare. Yt is thowght heare, that xx^s. for every man is over lyttell to make cootes and for conduct monney, and that under xxx^s. yt cannott be donne, besydes the armynge of them, for whyche, lykewysse, yt is wysshed ther shold be a suffycyent allowaunce, for the better encoragement of suche as shall take yt in hand, and the avoydynge of the oppynion that is heare had of the beggerye of these warres. And then somme order from your lordship for monney to be had heare for that purpose.

Agayne I must put your lordship in remembrance, that, in this and such lyke, yt ys looked for, that your lordship shold wryte one letter unto the boddy of the councell, as well as to pryvate frendes, for I have benne so sayd unto by soome of your lordships frendes, that, in these cases, they are to deale for your lordship as councellors, and nott as pryvate frendes; that pryvate letters be nott taken knowlege of in councell. Yt ys hoped by your lordships frendes, that, uppon your next letters unto her majestye, shee wyll stand better qualyfyed towardes you, and consequently better affected to the generall cawse. Mr. vycechamberlayne most honnerably persysteth and contyneweth his frendly coorce towardes your lordship, and I fynd myselfe very wellcome unto[a] hym, whensoever I attend hym in your lordships servyce. Mr. secretorye, lykewysse, as a trewe and noble frend, fayleth in nothynge that he can doe for your lordship and the cawse, but, as I wrote unto your lordship in my last, hys speeches in these matters be nothynge gratyose unto her hyghnesse.

Uppon knowlege of your lordships mynd I wyll streche my credytt and my frendes to levye men for you. And I trust your lordship wyll be well pleased, that suche gentlemen as shall be wyllynge and able to brynge men, shall have your lordships countenaunce and good favour to be captaynes over suche as they shall brynge, for that waye indeede I intend to proceede, that, in such a sheere as I thynke myselfe to have frendes and meanes to levye men, I wyll in that sheere choose owt a gentleman that inhabyteth and is frended ther, and I wyll joyne my creddytt wyth his, and make

---

[a] unto unto, *in MS.*

hym capetayne of suche as in that sheere may be had ; wherin, yf your lordship please to leave yt to my poore dyscressyon, I wyll doe you the best servyce that I canne. My lady of Warwyke [a] wyll send your lordship one companye of her procurement, under the conduct of a kyseman of hers, one Mr. Mawryce Dennys; shee allso desyreth to understand of the allowaunce.

Sir Thomas Cecyll hath leave of her majestye to retorne to Ingland for the recovery of his health. Mr. secretory told me this evenynge, that he sawe a letter of his very honestly and well wrytten unto her majestye, towchynge your lordship in those matters nowe standynge so hardly in her fancye, wherunto shee gave good allowaunce. Mr. secretorye dothe wysshe that your lordship wold use hym with all kynesse. Mr. Ward is this daye come hyther, he speaketh of capetayne Vavyster his comynge wyth letters from your lordship and sir Thomas Hennage, for whyche wee longe, but he is nott yeat landed, for anny thynge that is yeat knowne heare.

Yf your lordship doe not bestowe the regyment of the Irysshe uppon sir Wylliam Stanley, then is theyr here sir Henry Harryngton whome I fynd desyrose to serve your lordship, yf yt please you to imploye hym. Soe I doe, wyth my daylye prayers for your lordship, and my most humble dewtye unto you, commytt your good lordship to God. At coort this xxj. of Marche, 1585.

I beleve veryly that her majestye wyll uppon your lordships letter be browght to better [mind], but, untyll then, wythowght dowght she wyll be all one as shee nowe is; therfore I wold to Chryst your letters were come. When the world doth amend your lordship shall know immedyatly. She forbeareth anny evill speeche of your lordship openly, ever synce I spake wyth her hyghnesse.

Your good lordships most faythfully
ever at commaund,
THOMAS SHERLEY.

---

[a] Anne countess of Warwick, third wife of Leycester's brother Ambrose earl of Warwick, and daughter of Francis earl of Bedford.

LETTER LXVI.

MR. SECRETARY WALSYNGHAM TO THE EARL OF LEYCESTER.

21ST MARCH, 1585-6. COTTON. MS. GALBA, C. VIII. FOL. 65. ORIG.

Walsyngham transmits to Leycester an application made by the Duke de Nevers for a license for his subjects to procure salt from Holland and Zealand.

My very good lord, thincloased hath of late [been] written unto me by the duke of Nevers, conteyning a r[equest], as your lordship may perceave by the same, that, by my means, the subjectes of his dutchy may obteyne licence to be served of salte for their owne necessarye use out of the countryes of Holland and Zelland, with sufficient ca[ution] that the sayd salte shall by no meanes come into the [hands] of thenemy. The nobleman is one to whom I [was] greatly behoulding in the tyme of my imployement [in] Fraunce, for the which I would be glad to shew [my] self thanckfull towardes him with any service I [can] do him, which moveth me earnestly to pray your lordship, that, uppon consideracion of the said request, and communicating of the same to the states, yt may please you to returne an aunswer unto me, whether yt [can] be graunted or no, to thend I may accordinglye satisfye the duke, according to his expectacion and myne owne promise. And so I humbly take my leave. At Grenwich the xxj[th] of March.

Your lordships to commaunde,
FRA. WALSYNGHAM.

LETTER LXVII.

MR. SECRETARY WALSYNGHAM TO THE EARL OF LEYCESTER.

21ST MARCH, 1585-6.   COTTON MS.   GALBA, C. IX. FOL. 135, ORIG.

Walsyngham, having understood from sir Thomas Sherley that the Irish troops are to be commanded by sir William Stanley, recommends Mr. Dautrye as his lieutenant-colonel to proceed with the levies in the absence of sir William—proposed allowances—captain Tiry sent to London by the master of Gray for an answer to his offer to levy four or five thousand Scots.

My very good lord, there are einowe here who [having] knowledg that hir majesty is intent that there shalbe a [levy] made in Ireland for the states, have offered ther services [to] take that chardg uppon them, nevertheless understanding [from] sir Thomas Shirley that your lordship meant the sayd chardg unto sir [William] Stanley, I have theruppon geven all others their answer. And, because your lordship, as I suppose, cannot well spare sir William Stanley himself from thence, to come and make the sayd leavye [in] Ireland, I have thought good to move you in the behalfe of Mr. Dautry, who offireth his service in that imployement. He may, withall, have the chardg of lieutenant-coronell [for sir] William Stanley of thes Irish troopes. The gentleman [is] one that loveth sir William Stanley well, who I heare [doth] also make verye good accompt of him. I have conferred with him about the chardges of the leavy, his demaund is [three] pound a man, and myn offer but fifty shillinges, he sayeth, [that] part therof may be defalked out of their enterteynment, [and] he telleth me, that two thousand maie well be had out [of the] countrie where he is to make the leavy, by meanes of [sir] Henry Harringtons credit, who is hable to make up [two] thowsand.

Yt may please your lordship to returne aunswer of [the] states disposicion, whether they can be content to be servid with [that] country people, and how many they are willing to enterteyne; [and] what chardges they shall yeld to allowe for the leavyeng of them.

The master of Gray hath lately sent one captain Tiry hether, [to] sollicit your lordships aunswer to thoffer he hath hertofor made to [find] fower or fyve thowsand Scottes to the service of the states under your lordship, with direction ether to stay here or to passe [over to] your lordship for this purpose, as I should advise him. And, for I am uncerten how your lordship may be resolvid touching your continuance or discontinuance in that service, uppon occasion of the late accident that hath fallen out, I have therfor directid the party to stay untill I may heare from your lordship, wherof I pray your lordship to [be] myndfull, for the better satisfaction of the master. And so I now humbly take my leave. At Grenwich this xxjth of March.

Your lordships to commaunde,
FRA. WALSYNGHAM.

LETTER LXVIII.

MR. SECRETARY WALSYNGHAM TO THE EARL OF LEYCESTER.

24TH MARCH, 1585-6. COTTON. MS. GALBA, C. IX. FOL. 137. ORIG.

Hyman, mentioned in the earl's letter of 3rd March, has been stayed at Calais—the queen delays her determination as to the levies until she hears from sir Thomas Heneage—Randolph's success in Scotland—the Spanish preparations will prove nothing this year— rumours of successes of sir Francis Drake—overtures for peace.

Your lordships of the 3. of this [present] sent by your servant Wyllyam, I have receyved, by the [which] you desyre that an eye be [given] unto Iman; yt may please your lordship to understand, that Iman, abowt a two monthes past, was at Callas, and sent over for a save-conduct, which being denied unto him, he stayed his commyng into this realme.

I doe daylye sollycyt her majesty for the lycensyng of sooche gentlemen as were recommended by your lordship to make ther levyes of [such] nombers as were by you appoynted, but she delayethe her resolucyon therin untyll she heare from sir Thomas Henneage, whos letteres are not yet come to this coort, thowghe, as I understande, master Vavaser, to whom they were commytted, was dyspatched from thence the 10th of this present. Mr. Warde, whoe was dyspatched thence about that tyme, arryved the xxth. He imbarked at the Brill, and Mr. Vavaser went to Flusshing, wharby he lost the benefyt of the wynde.

By letters of 17. of Marche owt of Scotlande, we heare, that the king there dothe yelde all satysfactyon unto her majestyes mynister, Mr. Randolphe, and contrarye measure unto the Frenche kinges mynister, which he takethe in extreme yll parte. I wyll send your lordship the coppie of soche letteres as we have receavyd from Mr. Randolphe, whoe receyvethe at the kinges handes far better usage then he looked for. I praye God this opportunytye be not lost, as others before have ben. I fynde a greater cowldenes then the state of the present time requyrethe.

The Spanishe preparatyons, as they reporte that came from Lysbon the xth. of this present, wyll prove nothing this yeare, and I hope lesse the next, yf yt be trewe that is wrytten also from the Spanishe coorte to an Englyshman in Andelesya. The substaunce [is], that sir Francis Drake hath 6000 Semironets [a] repayred unto him, whoe have chosen and crowned him king, and that he hathe great store of them sure. I doe not desyre to be awthor of thes news for that methinkes they are [too] good to be [b] trewe.

---

[a] i. e. Cimarrones, Symerons, or Maroons, negroes who had escaped from slavery and established themselves in freedom on the isthmus of Darien. On his first voyage Drake received much assistance from them. See Camden's annals, sub anno, 1580.

[b] my, *in MS.*

Somewhat I am induced to belyve them for that Don Antonio de Cas * * * , late imbassator for the cardynall-king of Portugall, hathe [made], by letters dyrected unto my[self], some overture for a peace, wherein he desyrethe to be imployed, for that he fyndeth the king of Spayne, as he saith, desyerowse thereof. I [would] to God her majestye woold put on a good cowntenaunce for only fowre monethes, and I dowbt not but Spayne woold seake peace greatly to her majestyes honor and advantage. But God for owre synnes sake wyll not suffer us to doe that which myght owre most good. And so I most humbly take my leave. At the coorte the 24th. of Marche, 1585.

Your lordships to command,
FRA. WALSYNGHAM.

Addressed,

To the right honourable my verie good lord the erle of Leycester, lord lieutenant-generall of her majestyes forces in the Lowe Countries.

LETTER LXIX.

THE EARL OF LEYCESTER TO THE LORDS OF THE COUNCIL.

27TH MARCH, 1585-6. HARL. MS. 285. FOL. 234. ORIG.

Sir Thomas Heneage abstained from proceeding in his commission to the states, and wished the earl to continue in his government until he again received instructions from the queen, whereupon the earl had gone to Amsterdam, and thence to Utrecht, and was then engaged in the relief of Grave, which was besieged by the enemy—want of money for the soldiers.

My verie good lords, althoughe I doe expect her majesties good pleasure daily for my revocacion hence, yet will I no waie, in the meane time, neglect my duety to my service in the charge committed by her highnes to me, nor leave your good lordships unadvertised what hath past since my last letters, which as I remember was from Harlem upon the arryvall of sir Thomas Heneage, before whoes coming I had determined this journey to Utrecht, and was onward so farre in my waie.

And, for that sir Thomas Heneage would not proceed with any resolucion here with the states touching his commission, till he had received againe hir majesties pleasure, nor yet thought good I should staie my journey, bycause it was of verie great consequence, and the assembly of all our souldiers that maie be spared owt of garrison, as well horse as foot, appointed here by a certein daie, I did follow the former determinacion accordingly, the rather being commaunded by her majestie to take my direccion from sir Thomas Heneage, who in any wise wished me to proceed on, till I should hear again from her majestie. So I went to Amsterdam, and there remained iiij or v dayes, and from thence hither to Utrecht, where I am taking order for the present service now to be sett foorth, which is for the releef of a town called Grave, a place of verie great importaunce. We have other places to deale in like sort with, as also to doe what I can to drawe thenemies forces owt of Brabant and Flanders hitherward, which it is like they will, for the defense of such fortes as they have left garded, and by which indeed they doe besiege Grave, albeit they have layed no battry to it, for there be five skonces that they built abowt it before I arryved here: yet have I by stelth intelligence from thence, and, upon some good oportunitie, have cawsed it to be both vitteiled and 300 men putt into it, notwithstanding their skonces: and now I hope it shalbe fully releeved. I have sent the horsemen alredie onward, being 1500, very strong. The footmen are also marching to the randevous, and wilbe there too morrow night, all of them, being dryven to separate them for a time, and, till the service of Grave be past, our horsemen lie at a village called Nycark, and our footmen at Amaron.

Now am I most ernestly to recommend to your good lordships

the nedefull estate of the capteins and souldiers here. I have ben driven to borrow for their relief and for this journey, to helpe them, 4000^{li}. of the merchantes of Middleburghe, and what I have disbursed of mine own purse is not unknown here, I thinke, to all men. I would the full estate of the disbursing of her majesties treasure heretofore were certeinly knowne to your lordships. I wishe it for sundrie respectes, but it will requier a very skillfull man to examine it. Her majesty cannot loose by it &c., and yt wold be a very good satysfactyon to me. And thus, prainge to the almighty God to preserve all your good lordships, do take my leave. At Utrycht, this 27. of March.

Your good lordships always
to comaunde,
R. LEYCESTER.

Addressed,
To the right honourable my verie good lords, the lords of her majesties most honourable pryvie councell.

LETTER LXX.

MR. SECRETARY WALSYNGHAM TO THE EARL OF LEYCESTER.

28TH MARCH, 1586.   COTTON. MS. GALBA, C. VIII. FOL. 66. ORIG.

Receipt of the earl's letters of the 9th and 20th March—Mr. Vavasour, the bearer of the former, being a person very agreeable to the queen, had wrought in her a better conceit towards the earl—the queen unwell with a cold—the treasure to depart on the morrow—more money not to be looked for unless sir Francis Drake's successes work favourably on the queen—" the sparing humor" on the increase—treasurer's accounts to be investigated—sir T. Cecill to return to the Brill—sir P. Sydney out of favour—Burghley dissatisfied with the earl's treatment of his son—Walsyngham weary of his place.

Your lordships of the ix[th] of [this present] and of the xx[th], the one sent [by] Mr. Vavisor, the other by * * * , I have receyved.

The choyce of Mr. Vavasor, [who is] a person very agreable unto her majestye, hathe wrowght in [her] a better conceipt towardes your lordship then any other sent from the[nce]. Besydes, the gentleman hath performed the charge commytted unto hym by your lordship in so goode sorte as owre stormes begin [a] to caulme, so as I hope I shall have cause to chaynge my style, which heretofore hath ben verry dyscompfortable unto your lordship. Her majestye hathe not yet read the letters browght by Mr. Vavisor, being trobled with an exstreeme cowld and defluxion into her eyes, so as she cannot indure to reade any thing.

The treasure departs hence to morrowe, but no increase of the somme, nor non doe I looke for, howesoever the stormes be overblowen. Yf the inconvenience lykely to insue therbye be not helped thorrowghe sir Francis Drakes good successe, which is a matter accydentall, I feare your lordship shall receave very scarce measure from hence, for you wyll not beleve how the sparing humor doth increase uppon us.

The audytor retornethe with the threasure, whoe is dyrected, with sooche assystaunce as your lordship shall thinke meate to yeld unto him, to examyn strycktly the imparfect items of the threasorers accompt, who, yf he shall not yeld good satysfactyon, as I thinke he can in no sorte performe, then is yt meant that he shall no longer supplye the place.

Ther are letters wrytten unto hym, that he shall make no dysbursementes but as he shall be dyrected by your lordship, and, yf he shall doe contrary wyse, he can no way be dyscharged, for that withowt your lordships warrant he owght to make no payement.

[a] being, *in MS.*

Towching the governement of the Bryll, which your lordship wyssheth unto the lord Northe, I fynde her [majesty] most resolute that sir Thomas [Cycell] after the recoverye of his [health] shall returne thither. I think she coold lyke better of the removing of sir Philip Sydney [towards] whom she hathe put on a very hard conceypt. The lord thresorer dothe some-[what] complayne that there hathe ben better contentement yelded to other garrysons then that of [the] Bryll, which I fynde he taketh unkyndely. Of late her majestye shewed me a letter wrytten from sir Thomas Cycell, to as goode purpose in defence of your lordships acceptinge of the governement as any other I have seene wrytten by any thence.

The opynion of my partyalytie conytnewethe noryshed by factyon, which makethe me weerye of the place I serve in, and to wysshe myself emongst the trewe harted Swy * * . And so in hast I most humbly take my leave. At the coorte this xxviijth of Marche, 1585.

Your lordships to commaunde,
FRA. WALSYNGHAM.

The inclosed towching Ryngowt cam from a person of good credyt, and therfor your lordship shall doe well to have an eye to his doinges.

Addressed,

To the right honourable my verie good lorde the earle of Leicester, lord lieutenaunt-generall of her majesties forces in the Lowe Countries.

LETTER LXXI.

SIR WALTER RALEGH TO THE EARL OF LEYCESTER.

29TH MARCH 1586. HARL. MS. 6994. ART. 2. ORIG.

In reply to the earl's request for pioneers, to which the queen consented, but which had since been stayed—Ralegh reported at court to be opposed to the earl, which he strongly denies, and hopes the earl will not let any "poeticall scribe" make him doubt of Ralegh's sincerity—the queen is reconciled to the earl, and calls him again her "sweet Robyn."

My very goode lorde, yow wrate unto me,[a] in your laste letters, for pioners to be sent over, wheruppon I moved her majestye and found her very willing, insomich as order was geven for a cummishion; but since, the matter is stayd, I know not for what cause. Also, according as your lordshipe desired, I spake for on Jukes for the office of backhowse, and the matter well liked.

In ought elce your lordshipe shall fynde me most asured to my poure to performe all offices of love, honor, and service towards yow. But I have byn of late very pestilent reported in this place, to be rather a drawer-bake then a fartherer of the action wher yow govern. Your lordshipe doth well understand my affection towards Spayn, and how I have consumed the best part of my fortune, hating the tirannus prosperety[b] of that estate, and it were now strang and monsterous, that I should becum an enemy to my countrey and conscience. But all that I have desired att your lordshipes hands is, that yow will evermore deal directly with mee in all matters of suspect dublenes, and so ever esteme mee as yow shall find me deserving good or bad. In the meane tyme, I humbly beseich yow lett no poeticall scrib worke your lordshipe by any device to doubt that I am a hollo or could sarvant to the action; or a mean wellwiller and follower

[a] See Letter XXX. p. 86.   [b] sprosperety, *in MS.*

of your own, and yeven so I humble take my leve, wishing yow all honor and prosperety. From the court, the xxix. of March, 1586.

Your lordships to do yow service,
W. RALEGH.

The queen is in very good tearms with yow, and, thanks be to God, well pacified, and yow are agayne her "sweet Robyn."

LETTER LXXII.

MR. THOMAS VAVASOUR TO THE EARL OF LEYCESTER.

31ST MARCH, 1586. COTTON. MS. GALBA, C. IX. FO. 153. ORIG.

Vavasour reports his arrival at court, his interview with the queen and delivery of the earl's letters—her majesty's desire for peace—remark respecting lord North.

May yt please your excellency, after I had bene longe stayed at Flushing, by the contraryete of the wynd, I aryved at court, wher, making my first repayre to Mr. secretarye, as to hym whom I did think most assured to your excellency and best affected to this action in truth, although other make noe lesse shewe of forwardnes than he doth, who sent unto hir majesty that I had letters from your excellency, I was presently sent for, being something discouraged as well by ser Thomas his usage, who was ther fowr or five dayes ere he could deliver your letters, as also by Mr. secretarye, who towld me how yll her majesty was affected to the dispatch of any thing. I presented your letters, and delivered the message yt pleased your excellency to commytt unto me, in as good sort and as effectually as my wytt and duety to your excellency, or my affection to the cause, could teach or instruct me; wherin, if the effect hathe not fallne out according to your expectation, I canne be but sory with the rest who wish all forwardnes to the action and all happy contentment to your excellencye.

For the perticulerytes of my proceedings, for that it were long to wryte, I have committed them to ser Thomas Sherly, who hath followed your excellencyes business with noe lesse care then becometh an honourable and honest gentleman. Onely this, if under correction I may be so bould, I thought good to advertise your excellency, yf you know yt not alredye, that I gather by hir majesty that an indifferent peace wyll not be refused, whereof you are onely used for an instrument; for talking with hir majesty of the necessity to put men into feald, to the which I fond hir eares altogether stopped, especially blaming the chardges, " and what," quoth she, " yf a peace should come in the meane tyme?" I answered, yf she ment a convenyent peace, yt was the readyest way; for yet the king had no reason to feare hir, but dayly to looke when hir owne slacknes should give hir an overthrowe, beside they were souldgers, and were not to be moved with shadowes.

Pardon me, I humbly besech your excellency, yf I have been overbould to wryte unto yow, and excuse me yf I have not performed yt with effect, which my desires were to have done, assuring your excellency I wilbe as redy to serve yow in any thing I may heare, yf my fortune be to stay, as forward to serve yow there if my happe shal be to retorne, beseching you to contynue me in your grace, and accept of this my first service not according to the effect but after my care and desire to serve yow in all things, humbly thanking your excellency for the favour yow did me in commending me to hir majesty with the which hirself did acquaynt me, and humbly taking my leave wishing your excellency all prosperity ther and myselfe some meanes to serve you heare; not forgetting that one question, which perchance may import yow to know was demanded me, which was, how you used and esteamed my lord North. I answered, so well as yt was impossible to use any better. Answer was made me, and by great persons, " I pray God he deserve yt." What ther meaning was, I know not; your excellency may best gather.

Thus I humbly, with all reverence, once agayne commytt you to

God, who send your excellency your hartes desire in all things, and happy successe in your pryvate affayres. From the court, this last of March.

Your excellencies most assured to be commanded,
Tho. Vavasour.

Addressed,

To the right honorable and his singular good lord thearle of Leicester, leavetenaunt-generall of hir majestyes forces in the Low Contryes.

LETTER LXXIII.

LORD BURGHLEY TO THE EARL OF LEYCESTER.

31 MARCH 1586. COTTON. MS. GALBA, C. IX. FO. 149. ORIG.

After conference with Mr. Vavasour, Burghley, in the presence of Walsyngham, protested to the queen against her conduct to Leycester, and tendered his own resignation if such a course were to be persisted in, whereupon her majesty became calmer and more ready to qualify her displeasure—that she afterwards relented " as one by some adverse councell seduced"—that Burghley and Walsyngham then very boldly remonstrated with her and procured a favourable answer, although not to their liking—on the unexpected receipt of a letter from the earl they again saw her, and after a strong appeal agreed that the earl should continue in his office until the matter were farther considered—her farther relenting towards the earl upon receipt of letters from him—Burghley advises him to 'throw over his shoulders' what is past—more money not to be expected—Drake is said to have captured seven rich ships—trade between Hamburgh and Spain—Champigny's negociations—return of sir Thomas Cecill—unprotected state of the Brill.

My very good lord, although of late many crossees or stormes have happened to trooble your lordships mynd, to the hyndrance of the commen utillite of the servyce of God and of hir majesty in that countrye, yet sence your conscience doth testefy and warrant your doynges to have bene ment for the furderance of the weale therof, and the successes also, exceptyng the thwartes from hence, do make good proffe that your actions do prosper, I wish your lordship to contynew your disposition, and to comfort yourself with your own integrite, which God will not have oppressed, though he may exercise your patience, and prove the fortitude of your mynd to contynew well-doyng and suffer reprooff for a time. Thus much for a small preface, and now to the matter.

I dout not but this bearor shall come with some better satisfaction, both for yourself and for the cause, than the enemyes therof have looked for. Suerly unto [a] Mr. Vavasor cam, we here that ment well both to yourself and the cause found dayly litle comfort, and yet suerly your frendes here did not omitt any opportunite. But, uppon such conference as I had with hym, of the doutfull state of that country, I, in presence of Mr. secretory, used some boldnes with hir majesty, and protested to hir as a counsellor, that for discharg both of my conscience and of my oth of hir counsellor, I cold not forbeare to lett her know, that this couers that she held ageynst your lordship was lyk to endaunger hir in honor, suerty, and profitt; and that, if she contynued the same, I prayed hir majesty that I might be discharged of the place I held, and both afor God and man, be fre from the shame and perill that I sawe cold not be avoided. I used boldly such bold language in this matter as I found hir dowtfull whyther to chardg me with presumption, which partly she did, or with some astonishment of my round speche, which truly was no other than my conscience did move me, even *in amaritudine animæ*. And then hir majesty began to be more calm than befor, and, as I conceaved, redyar to quallefy hir displesur and hir opinion. And so, finding sir Thomas Shyrley redy to wryte, about three dayes past, I willed hym to advertise your lordship, that I douted not

[a] For until; into, *in MS.*

but that matters wold not contynew in that evill state wherin they were; and so, as he can tell yow, he did wryte, but stayd the sendyng therof on daye, in which tyme, to my great greff, lookyng for some good resolution, I and Mr. secretary found hir gon backward, as on that had bene by some adverse counsell seduced, to thynk that all shuld do well in those countryes though your lordship war displaced; and so he with greff stayd his wrytyng.

But yet, I did not thus leave the matter, and so, yesterday, Mr. secretary and I aventured very boldly to declare our censures of perill to come, which no councell nor action shuld recover, and hereuppon, we obteyned a favorable answer, though not to our full lykyng, but yet such as she commanded to put in wrytyng, and so we war therin occupyed. And then, unlooked for, cam a letter of your lordship to Mr. vice-chamberlen, wherewith he made hir majesty acqueynted, and she told hym, that she had declared hir resolution to Mr. secretary and me, and so willed hym to come to my chamber, and so he did, and there we fyndyng some new occasion to seek a better resolution of hir majesty, we all three went to hir majesty, and there I told hir very playnly, that I did see that if she used not spede to content the states and the people of those countryes, she wold not only lose them, but hir honor in the world, and she shuld fynd certenly as gret daunger from those countryes, as she had looked for comfort. Herewith she was greatly troobled, and so being thereto moved, she assented to do any thyng that she might with hir honour.

In fyne, we moved hir to assent that your lordship shuld contynew your office for some tyme, untill the state of the matter might be better consydered by hir, and so letters were appointed to be spedely wrytten, both to your lordship and the counsell of the states, and that Mr. Shyrley might be sent awey with all spede. And whan the letters war redy wrytten, came Poyntes from Mr. Hennadg, with letters from your lordship to me, includyng a letter to hir majesty, which I spedely delyvered with such good speches as in honesty becam me for your excuse. She red your letter, and, in very truth, I found hir princely hart touched with favorable interpretation of your actions, affyrming them only offensyve to hir in that she was not made prive, not now mislykyng that you had the authorite. Suerly I had cause, and so I did, commend hir pryncely nature, in this sort, of allowing both of yow for your good intention and excusing yow of any spott of evill meaning. And having hir majesty in this sort calmed, though it was not possible to mak your lordship amendes, yet I thought good to hasten hir resolution, which your lordship must now tak to come from a favourable good mistress, for so truly she doth profess, and yow must stryve with your natur to throw over your sholders that which is past. Thus your lordship seeth I have bene somewhat long, to shew you the course to bryng this honest gentleman, sir Thomas Shyrley to this messadg, who suerly hath very honestly behaved hymself for your lordship, and truly so hath Mr. vice-chamberlen, and Mr. secretory, and bydden many stormy speches. And now I will write no more hereof, but of some other particular advises, the consideration whereof I leave to your lordship as leisure may serve yow.

My lord, untill the state of the queenes army by muster book, and hir monthly charges, may appear more cleare, here will be no further meanes for any more monney. At this present ther is paid 24,000*l.* and that, added to hir majestyes former chardg of 52,000*l.* maketh 76,000*l.* which some hir majesty doth often repeat with gret offence.

My lord, I am very glad to see a disposytion of sendyng some shippes from thence to impeach the Spanish king towards his Indyes. It is a matter that many yers past I did project to the princes of Oranges ministers to have been attempted. We here that sir Francis Drake is a fearfull man to the king, and that the king cold have been content that sir Francis had taken the last yers flete, so as he had not gone forward to his Indies. We here that he hath taken seven rych shippes on the coast of the Indyes. I wish they war saf in the Thamiss.

We ar here troubled to understand, that from Hamborg, and Dansk, Lubeck, &c., there ar a gret nombre of hulkes laden for Spayn, and do meane to pass about Scotland and Irland, as some of them did this last yere, which they do attempt to avoyd all steyss in our narrow seas. I wold to God your flete, now intended from these countryes, cold mak a good prize of them, for so shuld the king of Spain be unhable to defend his seas, or to offend any other.

My lord, wher yow wryte to me of that yow heare of Champygnyes arantes, I will tell yow what I know thereof, and what els is knowen to any other, I cannot wryt of. There is an Itallion merchant in Antwerp that pretendeth acqueyntance with Champigny, and he hath wrytten hither to another merchant to know, whyther hir majesty can be content to come to peace with the king of Spayn. The answer is made, that, by the publication published, it is to be sene wherfor hir majesty hath sent hir forces into the Low Countreys, and, if the king of Spayn shall satisfye hir majesty in honor, accordyng to hir protestation, by restoryng to these countryes liberty and peace, and remove all men of warr from thence, and restore to hir own subjectes ther losses, she can be content to heare any honorable offer from the king, and otherwise, she myndeth to persist in defence of hir neighbors, and recovery of hir subjectes losses. This answer is made by wordes only, but not from hir majesty, and whyther Champigny will any farther procede I know not, but suer I am, he hath no cause to make any avant hereof, and I trust ther nede shall mak them sooner yeld than any cause to come of this answer.

It may be that ther are other lyke motions made to hir majesty, but I thynk suerly hir majesty myndeth not to show any yelding, for, God be thanked, she hath no cause but to expect the yelding to come from the king of Spayn and his mynisters.

And, wher your lordship wryteth, that the comming of my son from the Bryll in this tyme may brede some dowt in mens concepts, suerly, my lord, sir Thomas Shyrley can tell yow, that, uppon his report of his sickness, with daunger not to recover without changyng the ayre to come into England, the queens majesty hearyng therof, without any motion of me, commanded Mr. secretory to send hym hir licenss, with all possible spede, and, as I understand from hymself, he is much discomforted with the noysomes of the place, wher the water is not only brakkish, but, being heated on the fyre it stynketh. He also fyndeth the town in a manner utterly unfurnished of ordonnance, and without powder and bollets, so as, in very truth, it was as good out of hir majestyes handes, by reason of the chardg, as to have it only in a name. But how this should be remedyed I know not, for hir majesty will not yeld to any more chardg, and I see the states unwillyng to paye that which they ow; and by a clause in the treaty, they ar bound to furnish both the towns of Flushyng and Brill uppon your lordships demand, as hir majestyes governor-generall, and, if there be any hope furder, it must procede from your lordship as governor of the provynces with the counsell of the state. I thynk sir Philip Sidney hath also some want of ordonnance, but nothyng lyk to that of the Brill, wher ther ar not above seven peces, few ynough for one bullwark, but the daunger is not to be feared as long as your lordship shall prosper in your government. My son, also, brought thyther two hundred footmen and fifty horss, but he never cold get penny for them, nor on penny to that garrison sence he had the chardg; and yet it may be that hath had some help of late, for the tresorer did wryte that your lordship gave hym order to help them with some monny. I am now in dowt to wryte any furder for troublyng of your lordship, knowing how infinitt your occupations be to wryte and to reade, besides contynuall actions.

By such letters as shall come from hir majesty you shall fynd as much comfort from hir majesty as you have receaved discomfort, though ther be gret differencees in the effect, for the former I know hath depely wounded your hart, and these cannot sodenly synk so low as the wond is, but your lordship must add to this your own fortitud of mynd. And so I most hartely wish yow to be strengthened by Godes speciale grace.

Your lordships most assuredly,
W. Burghley.

31. Martii, 1586.

LETTER LXXIV.

THE EARL OF LEYCESTER TO MR. SECRETARY WALSYNGHAM.

MARCH OR APRIL, 1586. HARL. MS. 285. FOL. 157. ORIG.

The earl has received intelligence of an intended attempt to be made to assassinate the queen by two foreign jesuits, young men who are about to visit England as merchants—he advises that the queen should for safety pass the summer at Woodstock or Farnham.

Sir, I have mett with dyvers letters and inteligences that the pope hath greatly labored some desperatt persons to doe vyolence to hir majesty. The prince of Parma of late dyd use very brode speches, saying, that he dyd not fear the Englyssh ayd, yt wold not contynew many wekes, meaning hir majesties lyfe. I wold not putt yt into my letters for yt wold [fear] hir majesty I know, albeyt I doe not mystrust yt, yf you hold a good course at home. God hath and wyll defend hir, I dowbt not, but gett hir from London into som countrey well affected for this somer, and the soner the better. Woodstock wer a good place, and a holsome, or to Farnam, for yt ys hard for any suspected persons to com so farr but som or other wyll gyve knoledge; and, as I hear, hit ys ment now to use some straunger, and, under collor of merchants, to make sute at the court, and an Italian that cam iiij days past from Antwerp told me, that a dere frend of his declared to him, that ther wer two jesuyttes of Bruges, one a Walloun, and the other of those partes lykewyse, had undertaken a great enterprise in Englond, and did say they had pretences inow to com to the court. I am promysed they shalbe dyscrybed to me, but you must banyshe your popish Low Countreymen that suckes all honye ther and be lazy drones and worse, and lett good wach be leyd among the merchantes for such ij fellowes. They be yong men, and seme as merchantes, but very lewd and wyked. I besech you, for Godes sake, lett no respect of comodyus lying about London cause hir saftye to be neglected, and albeyt she is in all places in the handes of God, yet yt ys good to advoyd the most lykliest places for harme. Ther be few careful about hir. And you kepe hir tyll Mychelmas, by the grace of God, all ys past for those thinges.

Yf hir majestie meane to use my servyce, I trust you will send som boddy, that yt may appere here to men that you sett a lytle more store by me than hetherto ther ys cause for them to think, for ther was never yet so much as a letter wrytten to any person here of any thankes for those curtesies I had received before you hard any thing of this place. And, how yll soever hir majestie may conceave of me, yet these men have deservyd great thankes for there good wyll to hir, as ever any people could doe. And these many letters you must remember; first, to the states generall, than to the councell of estate, and one to the councell and towen of Utryght. I wold fayn have more but I fear yt wyll hinder the rest. The rest may be hereafter.[a]

---

[a] This letter was evidently left imperfect by the earl; it was probably inclosed in another letter. I judge from its contents that it was addressed to Walsyngham, and that it was written about the end of March or the beginning of April 1586, certainly before the earl received the letters from England dated on the first of the latter month. The earl's advice respecting the queen's residence at Woodstock or Farnham during the summer was not followed.

LETTER LXXV.

LORD BURGHLEY TO THE EARL OF LEYCESTER.

1ST APRIL 1586. COTTON. MS. GALBA, C. IX. FO. 163. ORIG.

A farther change in the queen's resolution—an interview thereon between her majesty and Burghley and Walsyngham, when she agreed to abide by her former determination—arrival of sir Thomas Cecill—state of the garrison at the Brill.

My very good lord, aftir that I had yesterday wrytten my letter unto yow, being perswaded that sir Thomas Shyrley shuld tak his leave that morning, as hir majesty promised over night, whan she also agreed uppon certen letters redy to be signed, as they war joyntly by Mr. secretory [and] me devised to content hir, I went to London, and comyng back this morning, I found by Mr. secretory a chaung of the former nightes resolution alltogither very absurd and perilloose.

And so this morning, at sermon tyme, we cam to hir majesty, and, for myn own part, I told hir majesty, that I marvelled she should so chaung to the worss, but, after manny argumentes, she yelded [to] alter ageyn to hir formar resolution, as by the letters sent both to yourself, to sir Thomas Hennadg, and to the counsell of [the] states, may particularly appeare, which, though all be [not] as I wold, yet it is as neare therto as hir majesty [can] be brought unto; for wher hir majesty, by hir alteration yesterdaye, wold have yow assembled the generall states, and [upon] ther advise to have gyven you a quallefyed power, without any other title than as hir lieutenant, I found that both peri[lous] and absurd, and therfor did draw to this form, that yow [should] contynew in your office untill the counsell of states cold devise how to quallefy this matter. And, for that I presume that [they] cannot in any congruete, nor, with the good quietnes of ther state, devise any such, I rest satisfyed in opinion [that] the country shall contynew in your government, for the m[ost] benefitt of the country itself.

My son[a] is at Gravessend, but not hable to com to the court; I am sorry of the cause of his comming. He sendeth me word, that, for want of monny, he hath left a lamentable company of his soldiers at Bryll, and he hath disbursed of his own so much, as he cam home with v^{li}. The tresor is redy to be imbarked this evening. From Grenwich, primo Aprilis, 1586.

Your lordships most assured,
W. BURGHLEY.

Addressed,

To the right honorable my very good lord, the erle of Leicester, lieutenant and governor-general of her majesties forces in the Low Contryes.

LETTER LXXVI.

MR. SECRETARY WALSINGHAM TO THE EARL OF LEYCESTER.

1ST APRIL 1586. COTTON. MS. GALBA. C. IX. FOL. 157. ORIG.

Walsyngham never knew her majesty better affected towards the earl—she has assented to the levy of volunteers, but is very unwilling to supply treasure—sir Thomas Heneage's friendly conduct towards the earl—Davison's grief on account of the earl's disfavour—Ralegh wished to justify himself against rumours that he had fomented the discord between the queen and the earl—the queen assures the earl 'upon her honour' that it was not so—advice to the earl touching the qualification of his authority which the queen desires—the master of Gray—complaint of the lord-admiral respecting commissions granted by the earl—Poyntz sent into Spain at his own request.

My very good lord, I pray [that] the compfort you now re-

[a] lord, *in MS.*

ceyve come [not] to late bothe for your selve and [the] cause. I never knewe her [majesty] better affected towardes you [than] she seemethe to be nowe, [and], for that she dothe now testefye [the] same unto you by her letter wrytten with her owne hand, I shall not need to dwell uppon that matter. I pray [that] this favor may be accompag[ned] with effectes by well farth[ering] of the cause.

She h[ath] alreadye assented to the [levy] of voluntaryes, but [still] she wyll be fownde strayte [in the] supplye of threasure. [Your] lordship shall doe well by your letters to herselve to lay [before] her the dysproffyt she [receiveth] by sending over threasure [in such] scant measure as ther [can be] no full paye made. The * * that regardethe more his pu[rse than] his dutye lykethe better of [credit] then of thorroughe paymentes.

I may not forget to tell you, that sir Thomas Henneage hath dealt towardes your lordship [like a] most honest faythefull gentleman, having left nothing undon, by letters and message, that might woorke your good towardes her majestye, whom, next after God, I doe assure your lordship I thinke you have cause to esteem to be a pryncypall instrument in the recovarye of her favor, in that compfortable measure you now receyve the same. This I wryte uppon verry goode grownde, to the ende your lordship may use the gentleman with that thankefulnes that apperteynethe, and as he worthely deservathe.

Poore Mr. Davyson dothe take yt verry grevowsely that your lordship shoolde conceyve so hardly of him as you doe, whoe I doe beleve, by the great protestatyons he hathe made unto me, hathe acquyted himselve honestly towardes your lordship. I fynde the conceapt of your lordships dysfavor hath greatly dejected him. At sooche time as he [arrived] her majestye was so incensed agaynst your lordship as all the argumentes and orators in the world could not have wrought any satysfactyon; and yt [may] be ther hathe ben some [yll] reporte made unto your lordship of the poore gentleman from [hence.]

At the tyme of her majestye [sig]ning of the dyspatche she let me understand, that Rawley, hearing of some [rumours] geven owt here in coorte [that] he had ben an yll inst[rument] towardes her agaynst [your] lordship, dyd humbly desyre [to] have ben sent awaye w[ith this] dyspatche, to the ende [he might] have justefyed himselfe towardes your lordship, in case [any] sooche synister [information] had ben gyven unto you agaynst him: which her [wish] was that I shoold signe[fy unto] your lordship, and to assure you, [upon] her honor, that the gentleman hathe don good offices [for you], and that, in the tyme of hir dyspleasure, he dealt as earnestly for you as any other in this world that professythe most good wyll towardes your lordship. This I wryte by her majesties commaundment, and therfor I praye your lordship to take knowledge therof, in suche sorte as you shall thinke good.

Touching the qualyficatyon her majesty so greatly affectethe, I woold to God yt could be brought to passe accordingly as she desyrethe, but I feare sooche a motyon at this present may breed in the peoples heades there somme unnecessary jealowsye; espetyally for that yt can not be don withowt an assembly of the states generall. For her majesties contentement yt shall be well don for the counsell of estate to sett downe sooche reasons as may shew the inconveniences lykely to insue uppon sooche a motyon, and to delyver them unto sir Tho. Henneage at the tyme of his departure from thence. And I dowbt not but [your] lordship wyll in tyme doe yo[ur] indeavor to brynge this to [pass] which her majesty desyrethe, [and that] you wyll by your next [letters] put her in compforte [thereof], yf your lordship shall see [any] lykelyhode to perfor[m the same].

Ther are dyvers here [frequently] with me to know what [allow]aunce will be gyven for [the] levye of voluntaryes, wherein I woold be glad to know from your lordship [how] to answer.

The gentleman that the [master of Gray] sent unto you meanethe to repayre [unto] you owt of hande [for] your full resolutyon towching his masters [offer].

208   LEYCESTER CORRESPONDENCE.

The lord-admyrall com[plaineth] that the commyssions your [lordship] grawntethe to her majesty[es sub]jects which hawnt those [countries] dothe woorke somme [prejudice] to his jurysdyctyon. He [would] be lothe any waye to offend your lordship, and wyll be [ready], for the savyng of his ryght, to grawnte hys commyssyon to any that your lordship shall recommend unto him.

Towchyng the party that is gon to Spayne,[a] whom your lordship wysshed rather to have ben imployed emongest the malcontentes, yt grewe of himselfe, uppon a conceypt that, being recommended by the kyng of Spayn unto the prince of Parma, he shall be the better able to serve your lordships torne.

And so, prayeing your lordship to exscuse thes scrybled lynes, wrytten with bothe a tyred head and hande, I most humbly take my leave. At the coort, the fyrst day of Aprill, 1586.

Your lordships to commaund,

Fra. Walsyngham.

Addressed,

To the right honorable my very good lord thearle of Leicester, lieutenant-generall of her majestyes forces in the Lowe Countreys.

LETTER LXXVII.

THE QUEEN TO THE EARL OF LEYCESTER.

1st April, 1586.   cotton ms. galba, c. ix. fol. 167.   a contemporary copy.

The queen and the earl are both grieved, he at her displeasure, she that a creature of her own, one that had always received an extraordinary portion of her favour, should give the world cause to think she is had in contempt by him—the earl is to confer with sir T. Heneage and others as to the relinquishment of his title of

[a] Ant. Poyntz, see page 177.

absolute governor, retaining the same authority, but only as the lieutenant-general of the queen's forces—if it is thought that this change will be attended with present peril the queen will, if it be absolutely necessary, tolerate the continuance of his government for a time.

By the Quene.

Right trusty and right welbelovid cousin and counseler, we grete you well. It is alwayes thought, in the opinion of the woorld, a hard bargayn when both parties ar leasers, and so doth fall out in the case betwene us twoo. You, as we heare, ar greatly grieved, in respect of the great displeasur you find we have conceved against you, and we no less grieved, that a subject of ours, of that qualite that you ar, a creature of our own, and one that hath alwayes receved an extraordinary portion of our favour above all our subjectes, even from the begynning of our reign, shuld deale so carlesly, we will not saye contemtuously, as to geve the woorld just cause to think, that we ar had in contempt by him that ought moost to respect and reverence us, from whom we could never have looked to receve any such measure, which, we do asseure you, hath wrought as great grief in us as any one thing that ever happenid unto us.

We ar persuaded that you, that have so long knowen us, cannot think, that ever we could have ben drawen to have taken so hard a course herin, had we not ben provoked by an extraordinary cause. But for that your grievid and woundid mynd hath more nede of comfort then reproof, whom we ar persuaded, though the act in respect of the contempt canne no waye be excused, had no other meaning and intent then to advaunce our service; we think mete to forbeare to dwell upon a matter wherin we ourselves do fynd so litle comfort, assuring you that whosoever professeth to love you best taketh not more comfort of your well doing, or discomfort of your evill doing, then ourself.

Now to cum to the breach itself, which we woold be glad to

repayr in such sort as may be for our honnor without the perill and danger of that countrey, we do think mete, that you shall, upon conference with sir Thomas Henneage, and such others whose advise you shall think mete to be used therin, think of sum waye how the point concerning the absolut title may be qualified, in such sort as the authoritie may, notwithstanding, remayne (which we think moost nedefull to contynue, for the redres of the abuses, and avoyding of confusion, that, otherwise, is likely to ensue) which, as we conceave, may be parformid, if the states may be induced to yeld that authoritie unto you carying the title of lieutenant-general of our forces, that they do now yeld unto you under the title of an absolut governor.

And, for that we ar persuaded that you may be best able, knowing the dispositions of all sortes of people there, as well of the inferiours as the superiors, to judg what is fitt to be don to bring such a qualificacion as we desire to passe, we think mete, that the whole of proceding should be referred to the good consideracion and extraordinary care of you and sir Thomas Henneage, and such others whose advise you shall use in this matter. For we must needes confes it is a thing that we doe greatly desier and affect, and therefor, we do looke that you should use all the best endevor that possibly you maye, to bring the same presently to passe. And yet, notwithstanding, if by conference with sir Thomas Henneage and others whose advise you shall like to use therin, you shall fynd, that any such mocion for the present may woork any peril of consequence to that state, then do we think mete it be forborn, and ar content to yeld that the gouvernement shalbe continud as it now doth, under you, for a tyme, until we shall heare from youe, how the said qualificacion we so greatly desier, touching the title, may be brought to passe without breding any alteracion in those countrees; for our meaning is not that the absolut gouvernement shall contynue, though we can be content, if necessite shall so requier, to tollerate the same for a tyme, and so we think mete the counsel of state be geven to understand, for that they may be the rather drawen thereby to devise sum way to yeld us contentement in this our desier.

And wheras, by our letter directed to our servant sir Thomas Henneage, we have appointed that the aunswer to the request of the counsel of estat there conteyned in their letters directed unto us for the stay of the revocacion of your authoritie, shuld be delivred by him unto the counsel of state there, according to such resolution as shuld be taken betwene you; which, if it shall fall out to be such as you shall think meet that our assent be yelded for the contynuance of your gouvernement as it nowe standeth for a tyme, then woold we have the sayd sir Thomas, in the delivery therof, let the said counsel of state understand, how we ar drawen for the love we beare towardes them, and the care we have that nothing shuld procede from us that might any waye work their peril, to leave all respectes unto our own honnour, hoping that the consyderacyon therof will drawe them the rather to devise sum waye how to satisfie us in the point of qualificacion, as also to be more redy from tyme to tyme to cary that respect and regard to you, our minister, during the tyme of your imployement there, as may be both for our honnour, your comfort, and the particulier benifit of themselves.

Geven under our signet at our manour of Grenewich the [first] day of [April] in the xxviijth yere of our reigne.

LETTER LXXVIII.

THE EARL OF LEYCESTER TO MR. SECRETARY WALSYNGHAM.

3RD APRIL, 1586. OUVRY MS. FO. I. A COPY.

The earl sends an act passed in the Low Countries for the stay of all traffic with Spain—executions for carrying victuals to the enemy—false rumour that the earl had granted licenses to export provisions—siege of Grave—apprehension of John Jentile, a poisoner—the earl warned of persons hired to poison him.

Mr. secretary, I doe send you an act that is past here touching the stay of all traffique with Spayne, which is determined here to be kept very strictly, and how you doe hold your determinacons there I knowe not, but, at my coming away, you were then all of that mind also. They heare, that [is], the councellours, are very forward and willing to doe all thinges that may annoy the kinge of Spayne, and there is verie strait order taken for conveyance of vittell. There was executed * *[a] about vj weekes past for carying of vittell to the enemie; there be iiij more ready for it againe, and yesterday I heard there was certain vessells stayd at the Bryll, and the merchant withall whoe frayted them [b], being of Rotradame, how[c] rich or great soeuer he be, he is like to hange for it.

Here was a practice used to haue made me to loose many good willes, giving it out that I had granted manie licences for carying of vittell out of the countrey, and greatly was it beleeued, and good cause was there, for in troth I was much pressed here by sondrye councellers to haue granted many licences to passe out of North Holland, but I vtterelie refused it, and will doe, by the grace of God; yet these councellers would fayne have perswaded manie countreymen here to find it necessarye, by which they imagined I had agreed therevnto. And as I trust to hold my hand safe ynough if I tarry here, soe I hope her majestie, and you all there, will consider, that the enemie is vtterlie vndone if he be a little longer restrayned from victuayles, which, I beseech you, remember. And beware that such pretty devises as Tomsons intyce you not to break it. I doe assure you, you neuer hard people so rayle as the Flushingers did against you and my lord-admirall, thinking that you in England had giuen licence to releeue the enemie, as by your pasport and letters they might, but I sent to them and have satisfied them, I doubt not.

[a] A blank in the MS. [b] then, *in MS*. [c] who, *in MS*.

I looke euery hower to heare somethinge to be done touching Graue, or taking some necessary pece for vs. Yf God would put into her majestyes heart to goe princlie forward in this cause, I would suffer death if the enemye were not soe weakened this sommer as he should not recover it agayne this three yeares, but it must not thus be handled as now it is, for we are in a good way to overthrowe all.

Here is apprehended yesterdaie one John Jentile; he had the coppy of a letter about him written to you; he pretended his arand to the princes of Pynoy,[a] as hired to poyson her by her husband; he seemes to be a very villayne; he hath such store of false dyce, and so many severall poysons, as noe doubt we will find somwhat from him. He brake the matter to the princes, and shee sent presently to me, and I sent Mr. Killigrew and one other of the councell to examine him. He confesseth to haue bine in England.

I haue more warning from the prince of Parma's court, and from Antwerpe, and out of Germany, that there was some hired to poyson me, but I am at a point for all these matters. Her majestyes displeasure, and the feare of the ruyn of this noble cause, is all my care and feare; for all other perills I rest vppon the providence of God. Thus, having written of late to you, [I] doe bid you farewell, praying you to lett me heare sometimes of your advises, as also answere to such things as concerne[b] this countrey causes when I writte. In hast, at Vtrycht, this 3. of Aprill.

Your assured freynd.

I meane to goe visit our campe within ij or iij dayes at furthest. This berer repayres home having his health very ill here.

Yf the style of the act I send you shall offend, I pray you make a coppy as you shall thinke good.

[a] So in the MS., but it appears afterwards that it was the princess Symeye, who is also mentioned by Stowe as having been at Utrecht on the 23d April 1586. See Stowe's Annales, p. 717.

[b] corcerne, in MS.

LETTER LXXIX.

THE EARL OF LEYCESTER TO MR. SECRETARY WALSYNGHAM.

5TH APRIL, 1586.   OUVRY MS. FO. 2.   A COPY.

The earl complains of practices out of England to discredit him, which are believed in consequence of the want of letters to him from the council and the queen—he relates what had been represented respecting him to merchants of Amsterdam, who had sent to the English merchants at Middleburgh to search out the truth —diminution in the affection of the States General towards the earl—danger of a mutiny occasioned by reports to his prejudice —communication made to the earl by the countess of Nienar— apprehension of captain Carsey, charged with a design to betray Ostend to the enemy—count Hohenlohe has taken a fort near Grave—Norris sent to join him.

Mr. secretory, as I wrote in my last letters to you, soe haue I cause more and more to call vppon you, if you doe wish anie good to this cause. I protest, before the Lord, I doe not dissemble with you, nor vse these vehement speeches for anie indirect furtherance, but it is to be [a] well knowen to all sorts here, what hazard is of the whole matter, vppon this her majestyes late displeasure. Some by-practises out of England, and not only vsed here into this countrey very diligently of late but imediatly vppon my arrivall, [have] written to Loveyne, and to Antwerpe, as I thinke I did advertise you. Theie haue giuen assurance to marchants of great creditt in Amsterdame, but I cannot haue them yet confesse from whome, that her majesty had not this longe while anie liking of me; that I was in noe creditt with the councell of England, as might well appere by her majesty and their

---

[a] "to be well knowen," *in MS.* but perhaps the earl wrote "to to well knowen."

sending to me; that she had refused to send anie more men over, nor anie more moneie then shall pay only vntil this time; that my estimacion in England was nothinge, and that I had consumed all my living, and now a bankerout, and, if I had taried but two monethes longer in England, I had gone with a man and a boye; that the queens majestie did wish her men at home againe, and that her meaning was never that I should haue anie other authoritye or government here then Mr. Norrys had; and that she did not care for the loosinge of me, nor anie that is now with me, but rather glad that she had such a cause to be ridd of me, when she sent me hether, and without anie meaning that the states should call me to anie place of government, as doth well appeare by that that she cannot abide that there was name of "excellency" vsed to me; and that her majestie will not heare of me, much lesse either herself or her councell write or send to me. And the party enquire, whether I did ever since I came shew to the states, or the councell, her majestys hand to myself, or whether she did ever write thanks or comendacions to them, either for me or of me, which is a matter, I must confesse, hath both astonyed me and marvelled at by nombers here. Insomuch as these men, vppon such particuler lessons and informacions, haue not lett to make inquisition, yea some gone as farr as Midleborow to their friends of the English marchants, to learne what degree I was of in England, and what abilitye, what fauor with her majestie, why I would leave Ingland if I had bine a man of so great qualitye as was here reported, why I should be here thus longe and to heare noe word from the queenes majesty, nor noe more Englishmen to follow me, as was looked for, and spoken of, before my cominge; whether I had anie lands in England, or office but master of the horse, with manie such like questions. In the end, playnly telling his freind, that theie were advertised to looke to themselves, for theie should never find anie help or good by me; that the quenes majestie would doe nothinge in respect of me; and that theie should find all but a shew of mine owne, for neither men and mony more then is come shall come, and that she had forbidden all men coming over, specially noblemen and gentlemen, as I had procured at first some to grant to come, but her majesty would not suffer it; and that she harkened for a peace, which, "if this had bine so," quod he, "we are well handled," and spake his mind very frankly, saying, in the end, that if her majestie had sent a disgraced man to abuse them, or to entertayne them, whilst she wrought a peace, when theie, being offered a peace at my cominge over, vppon confidence of her majestyes goodnes quite brooke of with the instrumentes that dealt for it, yt wil be remembered to the end of the world, and we never abide the name of England againe. But the marchant did deale verie wiselye with the party, and did satisfye him thorowlie, as he thought. But yet, he sayd, such matter was more comonlie written of late out of England into euery towne of Holland, then anie other newes, and you may ghesse what fruit it will bringe forth.

I doe faithfully assure you, I haue some cause greatly to doubt the affeccion of the states-generall, and some bussing[a] there is amongst them, whatsoever it be; God torne it to good. Theie begunne to deale very stranglye within these few dayes; yet I sett the best countenance I can of the matter. I maie feare her majestyes countenance may come to late; if it doe, I am like enough to beare a shrewd parte, but all as please God. I shalbe able to say more by my next; but this I must say, a straunge course was like to haue followed, even amonge our owne, by some ill dealinge; whosoever was the doer, I hast to find it out. But a common mutiny in all places was like to haue ben, and the culler, only that my lord of Leicester had abused the quenes majestie, and that she would send noe more monie; he had spent all for his owne private causes. I am sure I haue not had hetherto iijC^{li} of her majestyes, and I haue disbursed among her souldiers here vC^{li} of my monie; and, before the Lord I speake it, I am sure

[a] Buzzing, see p. 88.

some of these good townes had bine gone ere this, but for my monie. As for the states, I warrant you theie see day at a little hole. Theie will wayt vppon her majestyes pleasure and example at any tuch. Perhapps if a wiser man had bine in my place thinges had bine ill enough, and God doth knowe what a forward and a ioyfull countreie here was within this month; God send her majestie to recover it soe againe, and to take care of it, on the condition she sent me after sir Francis Drake to the Indies, my service heere being no more acceptable.

I must lett you knowe, and I hope to catch the man or to morrow night, the countes of Newenor[a] told me yesterday, whoe is a marvellous wise and well-spoken gentlewoman and a grave, that an English merchant that doth haunt Antwerpe sayd to a gentleman, a seruant of hers, within these iij or iiij days, that theie must looke for noe good heere by me, for he and all England knewe the quene[s] majestie loued me not, and had refused both to send men and money, and he told his freindes here so at the first; yet, in respect of the povertie of her souldiours, she will send a pencion for them, but to maintaine noe further warres here, and that he should heare of another matter shortlie, meaning [there]by peace, "and," saith he, "I wyshed men at the first, after Antwerpe was taken, to take hold of the offer made to these countreys; and warne your master," quod he by the count de Newenour, "that he looke to himself in time, and be not ledd with the shewes of the earle of Leicester, for the queene cannot abid him;" and withall fell into infinit prayses of the prince of Parma, what a man he was, and the kinge of Spayne wold haue these countreys in despite of all men again. That the prince of Parma was to reward both noblemen and others at his masters hands; as for my lord of Leicester, he may commend what he will, but theie shall fare the worse that he shall commend. The other replied, as my lady told me, very honestly, telling the man[b] what her majesties

---

[a] Wife of Adolphus count of Meurs and Nienar; see pp. 119, 141.
[b] men, *in MS.*

forces and greatnes might doe, and had done already, making such a full quiett in all these provinces as she had done, and that men here tooke my lord to be of anie other manner of calling then he reported, and of better credit with her majestie. "Well!" sayth this companion, "doe but marke and enquire what graces she hath shewed him this iiij monethes that he hath bine here, and tell me when you see me next what you find of my wordes." You maie see, sir, what I am subiect vnto, and what advantage men take vppon princes wordes and doinges. I assure [you] it makes me wery of my life, for I see theie say trew in manie of their speeches, how little soeuer I ioy to heare of it, but I trust to haue this companion furthwith, but it will little help the matter. I beseech God to make her majestie doe one thinge or other, for her owne best service, either to disgrace me cleane, or discredit these lewd bruits and devices.

I haue this day apprehended captain Carsey, whoe is discouered vnto me by a partie that dealt with him on the other side, to haue sold Ostend, and must haue 30,000*l.* for his parte; he was one of the captens there. The matter had bine better deferred x daies longer, as was agreed betwene thother and me, to haue taken him with an act to confirme the accusacion, but some inclying was giuen to the governour of Ostend, and knowen to iij or iiij, and coming hether with letters sent of purpose by the governour, I did take him, and haue him very close, and I am made beleeue he is like to confesse the matter, but true it is in my opinion. He doth wonderfully lament and weepe, but doth not[a] yet confesse anie thinge. It was but this morning I took him.

I receaued a letter yesterday that the cont Hollocke hath taken the greatest fort that kept vs from Grave by force, and, because the knaves within raild at her majestie, he wrott to me he would hang them all. I trust Mr. Norris be with him, for I sent him to meet him nere that fort, with as manie English companies as we

[a] doth yet, *in MS.*

might spare here. I hope the next wilbe of the relife of Grave, for the messinger left them going to the skale of an other fort nerer Grave. After this, if God send good speed, you shall here of other maner of maters of greater consequence. But why doe I say so till I heare of men and monie, and knowe what I shall doe myself? God keepe you. At Vtrycht, this 5. of Aprill.

Your assured.

LETTER LXXX.

THE EARL OF LEYCESTER TO MR. SECRETARY WALSYNGHAM.

5TH APRIL, 1586. OUVRY MS. FO. 4^b. A COPY.

The earl acknowledges the receipt of Walsyngham's letters of the 20th and 21st March—sir William Stanley is gone into England in order to proceed to Ireland to conduct the Irish levies—50s. a man is too much—the earl would like to bargain with the master of Gray for 2000 Scots—wishes the application of the duke de Nevers to be declined—regrets her majesty will not authorise a levy of men in England—hopes of relieving Grave—the earl at his wit's end for want of letters from the council.

Mr. secretory, this vth of Aprill I received your three letters, one of the 20th of March,[a] and two of the one and twentith of the same;[b] in answere whereof, touching the Irishmen, sir William Stanley[c] I hope by this time is arrived in England, to departe from thence into Ireland, and soe to bring the men with him with all speed, for soe the case requireth here, being soe

---

[a] See p. 178.   [b] See pp. 184, 185.

[c] by this time I hope, *in MS*. Sir William Stanley was the same person who was afterwards seduced into the treasonable surrender of Deventer to the Spaniards. See Camden's Annals sub anno 1587.

scanted out of England as we are; for his lieutenant, I haue left it to himself to take some man of good service. I doe thinke he is bent^a vppon Haultree, and I pray you presse him not for anie captaynes or officers except they be fitt men indeed, for that we haue to many young and vnskilfull captaynes and officers here already, and doe every day see and feele the want that groweth to the service by them; and for the offer you haue made of 50*s.* for a man, I am sorry you haue made it soe great, and doubt not but he will bringe them much better cheape.

Touchinge the master of Gray, I haue receiued two or three letters and messages of the self same offer from himself, and haue sent agayne my answere to him, being willing to haue two thousands Scottes, of whome indeed I would be glad, and am not much willinge to haue anie moe then that nomber, and for theis I must knowe what he will also.

For the salt for the duke of Neverrs, I pray you, if you can possibly, excuse it in some good sort, for ye will not beleeue what a doe here is for carying of victuall; a matter we knowe will cutt the enemyes throat if we can hold it, but every man is soe for his particuler as all [orders] ar broken almost, yet we dayly hange poore men for it, and, aboue all things, salt is the cheife want they haue, and your marchant Tompson dealt not well with you; iijC^{li} worth of salt that he would haue caried to Dunkirk, besides other victualls and provision of municion in his shipp.

The Flushingers are quit out of patience with you and my lord-admirall for the license, and it is not to be tould why it was; I devised the next best excuse that might be for it. There is nothinge here so odious as licenses for victuals, and forced we shalbe now to restrayne all places, Fraunce, &c. I am sorry her majestie cannot be pleased to grant levye to be made of men for this seruice, being indeed her one most speciall service; for my owne parte, I shall beare the want of this, as of all other things,

---

^a spent, *in MS.*

the best I may. But if anie come, either prest or voluntary, I hope convenient order shalbe taken here for the reasonable satisfaccion of their charges.

Yesternight I haue newes come from the count Hollock, that he hath taken [the] forte, which [a] was one of the enemies cheife sconces about Grave, and that theie are in good hope to doe some good presentlie to the towne. And so, with my right hearty commendacions, I comitt you to the Almightye. At Vtricht, the 5. of Aprill, 1586, *stilo Angliæ*.

Your loving frend.

I pray God you doe not deferre matters so longe as you loose all here; for my parte I am so at my wittes end, as I knowe not what to say. I thanke God I neuer receaued lettre from my lordes of the councell but two, and one I durst not for shame shew, it was by her majestyes commandement in the bitterest sort; the other was to send William Herll to Vindon. I never yet receaued instruccion, advice, nor order, from you there, whereby either to direct myself or to satisfye these I liue here withall. God send some of you better comfort when you shalbe in service so far of. It[b] is strange a generall, a councellor, a true man, for soe will I be in despite of all malice, shall neuer receaue more in iiij monthes.

LETTER LXXXI.

MR. SECRETARY WALSYNGHAM TO THE EARL OF LEYCESTER.

11TH APRIL 1586. COTTON. MS. GALBA, C. IX. FO. 172. ORIG.

Mutiny of Utrecht—censure of Norris—Walsyngham will endeavour to procure sir W. Pelham to be sent over—difficulty of the levies

---

[a] Taken forte was was, *in MS.*   [b] In, *in MS.*

—master of Gray's offer—weakness of Spain—eagerness of the queen for a peace—Salesberye shall be arrested on his return to England—deaths of gaol-fever in Devonshire.

My very good lord, as I have alwaies thowght, sythence your lordships first entrie into the charge you now howld, the assystance of sir William Pelham most necessarye for your lordship, so have I just cause, wayghing the late mutiny happened at Utreck by a bande perteyning unto coronel Norryce, to thinke the removing of the one as necessarye as the placyng of the other. I see some reason to dowbt that the grownde of the seyd coronells caryag of himself towardes your lordship grew by practyce from hence. The nurishing of factyon at home and abroade is thowght here the best coorse of pollecye, but the myschefe yt wyll breed I feare wyll prove irreparable.

I fynde, as your lordship wrytethe, that the partyes that doe chefely possesse the coronell are but bad instrumentes, thowghe I must neades confes that I have ben a chefe preferrer of somme of them unto him. I woold to God that with his valewe and courage he carryed the mynde and reputation of a relygyowse sowldyer. The chefe exsperyence and nuryture that he hathe receyved in the warre hathe ben in thos contryes where neyther dyscyplin-mylytarye nor relygyon carryed any swaye, and therefor yt hathe tawght him nothing elles but a kynde of a lycensyowse and corrupt governement, sooche as being weyed eyther in pollecye or relygyon can never prosper. I wyll, therfor, doe my best indeavor, as well in respect of the cause as for the honor and love I professe to bare unto your lordship, to procure the speedye sending over of sir William Pealham, hoping that, nowe your lordship standeth in verry gratyowse termes with her majestye, she wyll be pleased, for your sake and her owne servyce, to send him over.

I feare your lordship shall be greatly dysapoynted in the leavye of the voluntarye men, bothe in respect that many of the partyes appoynted by your lordship to make the seyd levyes have no abylytye nor meanes to furnishe them, as also for that there are verry harde brutes geven owt here of evyll usage of sowldyers there, and of the great pauwryll and exstremytye they endure. Yf your lordship coold fynde the meanes to furnishe the master of Graye with an imprest of 2000^{li}, to be sent hether, he myght be able to bryng over with him 3000 footmen and 200 lyght horse. I am of opynion that your lordship shoold be more readyly served from that, than owt of this realme. Besydes the imployment of that natyon in thos cuntryes (the same being with the good allowaunce of the king) cannot but greatly further and grace the cause, for, as I am informed, the brute thereof, as also that there shoold be an offre made of certeyn reysters to be sent by the king of Denmarke to serve under your lordship, doth verry greatly troble the prince of Parma. The provysyons of money promysed him owt of Spayn faule not owt accordyng to his expectatyon.

The enterpryse of sir Francis Drake layethe open the present weakenes of the king of Spayn, for of late he hathe sollycyted the pope and the dukes of Florence and Savoye for a loane of 500,000 Δ,[a] but cannot obteyne neyther the whole nor parte of the sayd somme. The Genuoyse merchauntes that were wont to furnishe him with money in tyme of necessytye, for that they feare a revolt of the Indians, begyn to drawe backe.

The repayre of thos of Bomel and Deventrye unto your lordship, to offer themselves ther servyce and obedyence unto her majestye, dothe shewe most manyfestly, that yf the cause myght have ben thorrowghly countenaunced, the most part of the provynces now possessed by the enemye woold have revolted er this. But we heare are so greadye of a peace, in respect of the charges of the warres, as in the procuring thereof we neyther weyghe honor nor savetie. Somewhat here is a dealing under hande, wherin ther is great care taken that I shoold not be made acquaynted withall.

I wyll not fayle, according to your lordships request, to take order for the apprehensyon of Salesberye immedyatly uppon his

[a] Ducats.

returne hether. I have alwaye held a dowbtfull opynion of him, having received somme informatyons ageynst him that gave just cause of suspytyon. According as your lordship desyerethe I have an espetyall care of sooche letters as your lordship desyerethe to have pryvat to myselve, and therfor am perswaded that parte of the adverticement your lordship maketh mentyon of, taken owt of somme letter of yours sent hyther, was, I dare assure your lordship, owt of non of thos sent unto me, and therfor I praye your lordship caul to mynde to whom you dyd wryte to lyke effect. For the proceadings in Fraunce and Scotlande I refer your lordship unto the inclosed coppyes, and so I most humbly take my leave.

At the coorte, the xj[th] of Aprell, 1586.

Your lordships to commaund,

Fra. Walsyngham.

Sir Art. Basset, and Sir Jhon Chichester, and thre justices more in Devonshire, are dead thorrowghe the infectyon of the gaole. Baron Flowerdewe, one of the justyces of that cyrcute, is also dead.[a] The takyng awaye of well affected men in this corrupt tyme shewethe that God is angrye with us.[b]

LETTER LXXXII.

THE EARL OF LEYCESTER TO MR. SECRETARY WALSYNGHAM.

16th April, 1586.   Ouvry MS. fo. 5 b.   a copy.

Sir William Russell, the bearer, returns to seek permission to raise a band of horse—the relief of Grave has been effected to the great joy of the people—the queen is considered the Messias of the country—sir Thomas Heneage's mission—the earl complains of want of

[a] In Holinshed's chronicle (iv. 868) there is a full narrative of this sad event written by Hooker *alias* Vowell of Exeter. The infection was carried from Exeter throughout the county, and occasioned an immense number of deaths. Hooker's account contains a frightful picture of the condition of the gaol.

[b] Some passages in this letter which are defective in the original have been supplied from an original draft in Harl. MS. 285, fol. 149.

countenance at home—recent want of money—the earl has raised 4000l.—Shenck has been with the earl, who presented him with a gold chain as from the queen—the earl is astonished that the queen does not summon a parliament, the people desiring it and offering an aid—" cockney kind of bringing up" of the young Englishmen complained of—the French ambassador is " a very naughtie man towards her majestye"—Nixhus, a mischievous fellow.

Mr. secretorye, I haue written to her majestie how things have passed here, God be thanked, greatlie to her honour and her poore soldiours here. I haue thought good to send this berer, sir William Russell,[a] as well to informe her majestie more particulerly, as also to desire you in his behalf to deale with her majestie for him, that he rayse there a band of horsmen, for I assure you horse are growen here very scarce, not that the bred is decayed, but that there is such continuall vse of them as theie are not so soone able to serue but theie are bought vpp. This gentlemen is worthy to be cherished, for he is a rare man both of courage and government; it were pitty but he should be encouraged in this service, where he is like to learne that knowledge which three yeres perhaps in other places wold not yeld to him. In few words, there canot be to much good said of him.

Touching our present affaires, God hath blessed vs with a most comfortable beginning. I wrote of late what hath happened vppon our attempt for the relife of Grave. We first tooke the myll sconce, after Battenbourg castell, and now, God be highly thanked, we haue done that we can, which is, that Grave is relived thorowly already, with 28 hoyes loden with as much as can serve them every way.[b] This good successe, with the great losse the

---

[a] Afterwards deputy of Ireland, and created in the 1st James I. lord Russell of Thornhaw.

[b] From its situation, Grave was a place of great moment, being, after the loss of Antwerp, one of the few fortified towns which restrained the Spaniards from advancing into the northern provinces. The success of the endeavour to relieve it fully justified

Spaniards had for losse of his men, which was noe lesse then you have heard, hath so comforted all these countreies as you will not beleeue what ioy theie make. Her majestie is taken for the only Messias of these countries.[a] God grant theie be estemed as theie be worth, howsoeuer theie maie be disgraced thorow ill handlinge of some men here.

Sir Thomas Heneage hath vsed himself here exceedingly well, and I must humbly thanke her majestie to allow some liberty in her limitacion, otherwise, I assure you, I had bine noe able man to haue served here, as I should doe. Well! God send me her fauour, and I will leaue nothing vndone fitt for a faithfull servant to doe for her. Albeit, I must say, that this c yeres there was never man soe weakly assisted as I haue bine, from my first day til this. I haue bene one of you ere now, but none of you as I haue beine and am here. I would God some of you had felt that half that I haue these iiij monethes. I never had good word, good coun-

---

therefore the exultation of Leycester and the people. The garrison, which consisted of " about eight hundred Dutch and Netherlande souldiours," under the command of baron Hemart, had been besieged ever since December, and their communication with the army of the states cut off by a series of forts erected by the Spaniards on the banks of the Maes. To accomplish its relief it was necessary to take possession of those forts, which was very skilfully managed by the troops under Hohenlohe and Norris, after some sharp fighting, in which the English auxiliaries distinguished themselves, Norris and sir John Burroughes being wounded, and " six or seauen score " of " our men " slain, whilst the Spaniards are said to have lost five hundred men killed, and about two hundred wounded, who were taken prisoners. " After this fight the count Hollocke battered and tooke Battenbourge castle, and the forte de Guanden, and the strong house of Empell, and then his victual being come he victualed Grave by water twise, went himselfe into it, supplied the garrison with newe men, and left it furnished with all prouisions sufficient, by acknowledgement of Hemart the captain himself, for nine monethes." I quote these particulars from the scarce tract entitled, " A briefe report of the militarie services done in the Lowe Countries by the erle of Leicester: written by one that serued in good place there, in a letter to a friend of his. Imprinted at London, by Arnold Hatfield, for Gregorie Seton, 1587 ; " with the loan of a copy of which for the purposes of this publication I have been favoured by Bolton Corney, Esq.

[a] these countrey, *in MS.*

sell, nor anie help at all, from England, since I came hether, which was the xth of December, and this is the xvjth of Aprill. I pray God send others more comfort then I haue had.

I haue written humbly to her majestie that we maie not fall into our former lackes hereafter agayne as heretofore, from January, we haue felt. I protest before the Lord, there hath not bine one penny of her majestyes here since January, and to be sure that we should haue no creditt for anie more, our treasurer went his way, by collour to make pay at Flushinge and ells where, but they were neglected, and I heare forgotten, for neither there nor here could a penny be gotten, till I did writt myself to the merchants at Midleborow. But only from January till this time, my money and my credite releeued the poore men. And if I had not borrowed this last somme of 4000^{li} it had been vnpossible this service had taken place, for there was not a groate to be had to sett them forward but that I did provide for them; noe not one groat. I thanke God Almighty for it that so good successe is followed.

Here hath bine corinell Shenke with me, I assure you a worthy gentilman, and hath done notable service here since my coming: he protesteth to serve noe creature but her majesty. Sir Thomas Heneage told me her majestie meant to send him a present by him; I haue deliuered him a chain as brought by sir Thomas from her majestie; yf you shall heare it is thought to much, whatsoeuer shalbe soe thought, I wold beare the rest, rather then anie mislike should happen.

Mr. secretary, I marvell that all this time is lost at home, that her majesty doth not call her parliament; and, albeit she doth not meane to send anie more then she hath agreed vnto, yet doth not her majestie knowe what need of monie she shall haue in this [a] troublesome world? What harme is it to have iij or iiij cM^{li} lying by her? Hir countreie and people is rich, and, if God should putt her to anie need, monye is not so easily gottin. I find by

---

[a] these, *in MS.*

these men here, what it is for a prince to be before hand. Such a prince shall doe more with a cm^{li} then others shall doe with a million. When parliaments be called vppon suddens we have sene what effect they worke; but too loose such opportunityes, as now that her majestie is sought and sued to to call a parliament, and offers infinitly made [a] of her good subiects to assist and help her, and with as good thanks to take their offer as to refuse it, I am sorry to heare and see it.

As also, to the greif of my heart to see your youthes in England, how cleane theie be marred and spoiled for ever being able to serue her majesty and the realme. I am ashamed to thinke, much more to speake, of the younge men that haue come over. Beleeue me you will all repent the cockney kind of bringing vp at this day of young men. Theie be gone from hence with shame enough, and to manie that I will warrant will make as many frayes with bludgeons and bucklers as anie in London shall doe; but such shall never haue creditt with me againe. Our simplest men in shew haue bine our best men, and your gallant bludd and ruffin men the worst of all others. I pray you esteme them there accordingly, except I commend them to you, and yet no one [b] hath iust cause to complayne to my knowledge.

Well, sir, to retorne to this gentleman, I praie you helpe that he maie haue allowance to make c horse ther, according to her majestyes contract, which was, to furnish this armye with 1000 horse, and there is not one horse made since I came, but onlie fifty by sir Thomas Cecill, and the company of my nephew Sidney, which I thinke is fiftye or lx. more. I assure you the tresorer is a negligent man; but I thinke it be others fault, for the money hath bine a-land this xv dayes and yet he comes not withall.

God send sir William Pelham over shortlye. Sir Thomas

---

[a] need, *in MS.*

[b] *not*, in the MS. which I take to be a mistake of the transcriber. Probably the earl wrote " no j."

Heneage will departe here shortly. Thus with my heartie commendacions, I bidd you farwell. [In] hast, this xvj. of Aprill.

Your assured frend.

I pray you remember that you put vs not to wind and weather anie more for moneye. He gets her majestie nothing, and puts her whole service in hazard. And I beseech helpe to speed this gentilman with some money for his horsmen, that he maie retorne with them in tyme.

One thinge more of greatest weight I had almost forgott. Your French embassador there is a verie naughty man towards her majestie, and doth dangerous offices. He doth writ to many places of her majestyes mislike of this countrey causes; he assureth alteracion or it be longe, and vaunts of his credit there amonge you, and how gladly you vse him to further your peace. Wold God you would vse such men ther as other princes vse evell instruments. You must take heed of Nixhus, he is discouered to be a mischeiuous fellow.

LETTER LXXXIII.

MR. SECRETARY WALSYNGHAM TO THE EARL OF LEYCESTER.

21ST APRIL, 1586. COTTON. MS. GALBA, C. IX. FOL. 179. ORIG.

Joy of the queen upon the earl's restoration to favour—her concurrence in the levy of troops for the Low Countries—allowances—negociations for peace—Grafini—Champigny—message from the queen to the council of the states—Kersey's treachery—Walsyngham advises the earl to take the lead in negotiating for a peace, the queen being determined to bring one about—punishment of Weldon for libelling the earl—the queen longs to hear what is done upon the last direction to sir Thomas Heneage.

My verry good lord, [I am glad to perceive the] great chaynge in your lordships letters, the one wrytten the vth the other the vij[th] of this present, the fyrst full of dyspayre in respect of the harde coorse helde here, the other full of compfort uppon the receypt of her majesties gratyous letters, and the happye success in the late conflyckt with the ennemye. I doe assure your lordship I think her majesty tooke as muche joye uppon the viewe of your letter, in seing you restored to your former compforte grownded uppon her favor, as she dyd [in] the overthrowghe of the enemye.

Her highness is now pleased that [a] comyssyon be gyven for the levy of the 300 men in northe . . wherin before she made great dyffycultye. She hathe also commanded that all dylygence be used in the sending over of the voluntarye men. I dowbt greatly for lacke of money the captain wyll not be able to levye them, and yf your lordship, besydes the imprest of the 1000[li] I caused sir William Stanley to be furnyshed withall, doe not also gyve order for a supplye of 500[li] to be sent unto him, he shall never be able to brynge them of Irelande. He cannot get them to be transported under xx[s] the man.

I am earnestly desyred by Mr. Edward Dyer to move your lordship that his brother Andrewe, thorrowe your good favor, may be allowed after xx[s] the man for sooche nombers as he shall bryng over. The states have offered unto him, by Mr. Ortell, only xiij[s] iiij[d] the man, wheras in verry deede they cannot be sett owt in that good sorte yt were fytt under xxx[s] the man; and yt were muche better to have an armye compounded of 10,000 well furnished men, then 15,000 in sooche slender sorte as heretofore they have been sent from hence. I doe heare, by somme come from thence, that the harde allowance now made for the levyes intended hathe growen owt of coronell Norryce advyce, whoe notwithstanding, as he himself towld me, hathe ben allowed by the states heretofore for all manner of charges after the rate of . . . the man, which is verry skant.

To the ende your lordship may see what instrumentes are used in owre medyatyon of peace, I sende you the coppyes of certeyn letters by good happ come to my handes. I have let her majesty understande howe dangerowse and dyshonorable yt is for her to have sooche base and yll affected mynisters used therin. Norryce, the controwlers man, is bothe a notable papist and hathe served Mounsyer heretofore as a spye. Yf eyther your lordship or myselfe shoold use sooche instrumentes I knowe we shoold beare no small reproche: but yt is the good happ of hollow and dowbtfull men to be best thowght of. But, to returne to the desyred peace, your lordship shall understand that Grafini, sometymes Spinolas servaunt, having ben of late at Antwerp is nowe returned, whoe reportethe that the prince of Parma, understanding that he was to returne into England, sent for him, and, after long speeche had of the awntyent amytye betwen the howse of Burgundye and this crowne, the great myschefe that bothe contryes were lyke to indure by the coorse nowe held, and of the great good wyll he bare unto her majestye, he prayed him to let eyther her majestye or somme of her cownsell understande, that, althowghe he myght be thowghte more inclyned rather to contynewe the warres then to affect peace, yet no man woold be more wyllyng then himselve to be a medyator therof, and, for that purpose, yf he myght understand that her majestye wold lyke therof, he woold send somme well chosen instrumentes unto her to make some sooche overture in that behalf as she shoold have cause to lyke of. He dyd, for the incoragement of Grafyni, assure him that the king shoold bestowe some honorable rewarde on him, so as he coold bryng the same to passe that some myght be sent over with her majestyes good lykyng. He dyd, also, let him understande that Champigny tooke uppon him [too much] in the matter, and that he had intellygence with some person of qualytye within this realme [of] the same, but that he dyd not lyke that he shoold be a dealer therin, but woold rather imploy a contryman of his owne. This myche have I receyved from her majestye towching Grafyinis proceeding, wherwith her plesure was I shoold acquaynt your lordship, whoe doth think meet that you shoold, yf you shall see no cause to the contrarye, acquaynt the cownsell of the state there, that certeyn overtures for peace are dayly made unto her, but that she meanethe not to proceade therein without ther good lyking and privyty, being perswaded that ther can be no peace made profitable or suer for her that shall [not] also stande with ther savetye, [and] that she dothe acknowledge [hers] to be so lynked with thers as [nothing] can faule owt to ther prejudyce but she must be partaker of theire harme. Her pleasure ys, that you shall not acquaynt them with the partycularyties of the overture, but woold have you deale with them in generall termes, usyng the matter in sooche sorte as they may not enter into any jealouse conceypt of any alyenation of her good meaning towards them.

I am glad that Kerseys trechery was dyscovered in tyme; I praye God ther be no more of that crewe as lewdly dysposed as he. I feare the lyttle hope that owre martyall men have of rewarde wyll drawe somme of them to fayle in their dutye, and therfore yt wyll behove your lordship to have a watchefull eye of the looser sorte of the capteyns. But, to returne ageyn to the peace, seing her majesty is so inclyned unto yt, and is fownde altogether unapt to prosecute the warres, I cannot but wyshe your lordship to be a pryncypall dealer therin, as well in respect of your own honor as that I hope yt wyll be performed with bothe honorable and profytable condytyons: wheras I dowbt, yf yt passe to others hands, yt wyll not be so carefully dealt in.

I cannot but let your lordship understande that the lord-chamberlyn hathe dealt verry honorably and frenly towards your lordship of late, in causyng Weldon, sometyme pensyoner,[a] to be punished for delyvering, as he is charged thowghe by him denyed, lewd speeches of your lordship. I fynde that bothe the lord-admirall and he doe take yt verry kyndly that your lordship dothe wryte so at large unto them, as you have of late don.

[a] Probably this was an ancestor of sir Anthony Weldon, the author of " The court and character of king James." See Thorpe's Reg. Roff. p. 1005.

Her majestye dothe longe to heare what is don uppon the last dyrectyon geven to sir Thomas Henneage. I praye God owre nyce dealyng therin doe not more [a] harme, in respect of the lewde brutes geven owt there, then may afterwarde be well repayred.

I cannot but put your lordship in mynd to returne your speedy awnswer to the master of Graye, towching the imprest I last wrote of, for the levye. I wyll seeke to satysfye the duke of Nevers towching the salt, in sooche sorte as he shall notwithstanding thinke himselve behowlding unto your lordship.

The Flusshingers have dealt hardely bothe with the lord-admyrall and me; wee shall be forced, for the relefe of Thomson, to take some other waye of redresse. Eyther her majestye must increase her garyson in that towne, or elles ther must be somme devyce to imploye thos rude barbarouse maryners in some longe vyage. And so, fearing I have over-tyred your lordship with thes scrybled lines, I most humbly take my leave. At the coorte, the xxj[th] of Aprill, 1586.

Your lordships to commaunde,
Fra: Walsyngham.

LETTER LXXXIV.

THE EARL OF LEYCESTER TO THE LORDS OF THE COUNCIL.

23rd april, 1586.   ouvry ms. fo. 7 b.   a copy.

Letter sent about the time of sir Thomas Heneage's meditated return, having faithfully discharged the service committed to him—further exploits of count Hohenlohe—sir John Norris has recovered from his wound—the prince of Parma is on his way to the siege of Grave.

My very good lords, because sir Thomas Henneage is a very sufficient gentleman, well knowen vnto your lordships, and tho-

[a] Moche, *in MS.*

rowly instructed in all matters here, I shall not need to trouble your lordships at this time with anie longe discourse. Although his cominge hether at the first brought me noe great comfort, yet her majestys gratious dealinge with me sithens hath very well incouraged me. He hath taken very great pains since his coming hither, and very well and faithfullie discharged the service commited to him; wherefore, because I will not anie way hinder his sufficiencye, I referre all to his declaracion. And soe committ your lordships to the gratious gouernment of the Almightye. From Utrecht, this xxiijth of Aprill, 1586.

Your lordships to comand.

Since sir Thomas Henneage departed yesterdaie morning, I haue heard from the count Hollocke, whoe after he had fullie vittelled and furnished Grave, wherin he hath done notable good service, he went toward Bolduke, and hath taken two fortes held by the enemie and did vs much displeasure, the one called Knoles skonce and thother Embell, and is now reterid with his companies to refresh them. Sir John Norris is now cleane whole of his hurt, and for that I am enformed for certen that the prince of Perma is on the way toward Grave, to defend the succour if he can, but shall come to late, and, lest he attempt some other place, I will cause him to be waited on with all the litle force we haue at an ynch, and though our forces are not able for him, yet I hope to keep him from doing anie great harme. I trust after your lordships shall heare of our estate here by sir Thomas Henneage, that you will favorably consider of it, even as it is most requisit.

LETTER LXXXV.

THE EARL OF LEYCESTER TO MR. SECRETARY WALSYNGHAM.

24TH APRIL, 1586. OUVRY MS. FOL. 8. A COPY.

The prince of Parma has advanced from Brussels to Bergen op Zoom on his way to Grave—his recent losses turn out to be greater than was supposed—insufficiency of the money brought by the treasurer and anticipations of coming difficulties on that account.

Good Mr. secretarie, I am so extreamly overtoiled with busines that I am inforced to vse a secretary in writinge to you at this time; but the greatest matters sir Thomas Heneage and this berer are so well instructed in, as I shall have the lesse need to write of them myself. I receiued aduertisment this day, that the prince of Perma hath gathered his forces togither, and is come from Bruxelles nere to Berges, pretending to goe to Grave himself in person, and not to trust other men anie longer; wherevpon I haue sent to take order with those that we haue at Graue, and then, if he doe come thither, he shall come to late, for the towne is both sufficiently vittelled and manned allready. I heare say he is 4,000 stronge of horsmen, and we are not aboue 1500 horse here in all, for we want of her majesties number 200 yet; I would her majesty had graunted forth comissions in time that we might haue had more men here, for some of them that went ouer for men, without comission, haue alreadie brought over their nombers, which are but few, but if we had had some 3 or 4000 men more here at this present, we might haue bine able to haue shewed our faces in some abler sort to him. Yet, with theis few that we haue, we meane he shall not be vnattended. The losse he had in this late conflict was full as great as I wrote vnto you, for we haue lately intercepted diuers of their lettres, some this daye, whereby we perceaue the overthrow was not lesse, but rather greater, then we thought, and that of his best capteins and men of name. Thus with my hearty comendacions, for this time I committ you to God. From Utrecht, this xxiiijth of Aprill.

Your assured frend.

I pray you giue credit to this berer, he can informe you of all things. By that time Mr. treasorer came hether to me he brought but 8000^{li} with him, nor hath anie more, and yet hath payed but only Flushing, Brill, and Ostend, and our horsmen are 800, and nere v^m footmen vnder her majesties pay beside, and some ij moneths, and some 3, behind; what case we shalbe in iudge you, and how we can tarry in the feild. For my none parte, I take God to record, at this instant I have not ij^c.^{li} in my purse, neither doe fynd anie care of men, and yet doe I neither spare paine, travell, nor chardge, here.

LETTER LXXXVI.

MR. SECRETARY WALSYNGHAM TO THE EARL OF LEYCESTER.

25TH APRIL, 1586. COTTON. MS. GALBA. C. IX. FOL. 191. ORIG.

The queen's reception of letters brought by sir W. Russell—her desire for peace— the excuse of the lords of the council for writing to the earl so seldom—cost of the transport of troops from Ireland— designs of the enemy—the earl advised to avoid a battle —sir W. Pelham about to be sent over.

My very good lord, the news browght by sir William Russell was verry welcom vnto her majestye, yet dyd she not greatly lyke to be pressed for the supplye of horsemen agreable with the contract; she styll harpethe after peace, bothe in respect of charges, as of some dowbt she hathe that somewhat wyll be attempted ageynst her own person, and, therfor, seing she dothe so greatly thirst after yt, I cannot, as I wrote vnto you in my former, but wyshe your lordship to be a chefe dealer therin; yt were a grete wronge, consydering the brunte and burden of warres your lordship susteynethe, that peace shoold be made withowt you. Yt were not amysse that your lordship tooke somme apt occasyon, by your owne letters unto her majestye, to let her understand no les.

I have let my lords here understande, how unkyndly your lordship takethe yt that you heare so seldom from them, and that sythence your charge there you never receyved any letter of advyce from them. They awnswer, as yt is trothe, that, her majestye reteyning the whole dyrectyon of the causes of that contrye to herself and sooche advyce as she receyvethe underhand, they knowe not what to wryte or to advyce. She can by no meanes, as I have heretofore wrytten unto your lordship, indure that the causes of that contrye shoold be subiect to any debate in cownsell, otherwyse than as she herself shall dyrect, and therfor men forbear to doe that which otherwyse they woold.

I sende your lordship sooche thinges as were yesterdaye propounded to ther lordships in cownsell, with theire resolutyons taken thereuppon. Mr. Dawtrye tellethe me, who attendethe here by sir William Stanleys appoyntment, your lordships resolutyon towching a further supplye of money besydes the 1000^{li} alreadye delyvered unto sir William Stanley, that they cannot be conveyed owt of Ireland under xl^s. the man. The only transportatyon will cost a 1000^{li}. Yf your lordship cannot drawe the states to yeld that allowance, then were yt meet sir William Stanley were speedyly made acquaynted withall, to the end he may forbeare further proceading.

I learne by letters owt of Flawnders, that the enemye meanethe to sende all his forces towardes Guelderlande, in hope to drawe you to a fyght, which I hope your lordship wyll geve order that the same shall be avoyded, unles yt shall be uppon a mervaylowse advawntage. Yf an overthrowghe shoold happen yt woold put in hazarde the whole cause, for we are not armed here with that constancy that shoold endure sooche a revers without dysmay.

My lords mean shortly to sende sir William Pelham unto you with there best advyce in this wayghtye poynte. I thinke yf your lordship dyd convert some of your soldyeres into pyoners, you should have great use of them, bothe for defence and to bryng you to fyght uppon advauntage.

And so, having for the present no other thinge to imparte unto your lordship, I most humbly take my leave. At the coorte, the xxvth of Aprill, 1586.

Your lordships to commaunde,
FRA: WALSYNGHAM.

Ther hathe fawlen owt no electyon this S^t. Georges feast.[a]

Addressed,

To the right honourable my verie good [lord] the earle of Leycester, lord lieutenaunt-generall of her majesties forces in the Lowe Countries.

---

[a] Although Saint George's day passed over undistinguished in the court of Elizabeth, it had been far otherwise in the earl's court at Utrecht. Segar the herald communicated to Stowe a narrative of the earl's princely doings upon that occasion, which the chronicler has inserted in his Annals, (p. 717,) and which, but for its length, we should like to quote entire. The earl proceeded " to the cathedrall church called the Dome " with a very royal retinue all mounted, and comprising, amongst many others, "6 knights, 4 barons, with the counsell of estats, the earl of Essex accompanied by the bishop of Cullen prince elector, and the prince of Portugale rode by himselfe; next proceeded the captaine of the guard, the treasurer and controller of the houshold, bearing their white staues; after whom followed two gentlemen ushers, and Portclose herault in a rich coat of the armes of England: then came my lord most princelike, invested in his robes of the order, guarded by the principal burghers of the towne, which offered themselves to that seruice, besides his owne guard, which were a fifty halbarders in scarlet cloakes, guarded with purple and white veluet. Hee being thus honourably brought unto the church, after due reverence done unto the queenes maiesties state, which was erected on the right hand, he tooke his own stall on the left, by certaine degrees lower: then began prayers and a sermon made by master Knewstubs, my lords chaplaine, after which my lord proceeded to the offering, first for her maiestie and then for himselfe, the which he performed with such decorum and princely behauiour that all generally spake most honorably of him." He returned in procession to his court, a large house which formerly belonged to the knights of Rhodes, and

LETTER LXXXVII.

MR. SECRETARY WALSYNGHAM TO THE EARL OF LEYCESTER.

26TH APRIL, 1586.   COTTON. MS. GALBA, C. IX. FOL. 193.   ORIG.

Walsyngham announces a sudden change in the queen's mind adverse to the continuance of the earl's authority as supreme governor—Burghley's remarks to her, whereupon the queen grew " so passionate as she forbad him to argue any more "—Walsyngham suspects treachery at home and harm done by letters from the Low Countries—a safe-conduct sent to Champigny to come over and treat for peace.

My verry good lord, howe this unlooked for alteratyon happenethe at this tyme, when the goodnes of God, thorrowghe the most happye coorse and successe thinges take there, owght to have led her majestye to have proceaded most resolutely in the cause, I knowe not, nor can by no meanes imagen how the same shoold be wrowght. Ther was only cauled unto the resolutyon the lord thresorer and I. He moved her to staye the resolutyon untyll sir Thomas Henneages returne; he shewed her that ther was nothing don contrarye to her dyrectyon; he protested unto her, that, yf she dyd goo forwarde with the resolutyon, yt woold utterly over-

in which was " a very great hall richly hung with tapistrie." Here, in the presence of a splendid assembly, he knighted Martin Schenck; after which "the ushers marshalled the feast," which was " most princelike and abundant," and was adorned with many rare and magnificent devices, baked meats in the shapes of lions, dragons, leopards, and such like, and "peacocks, swans, pheasants, turkie-cocks, and others in their naturall feathers spread as in their greatest pride." The feast was succeeded by dancing, vaulting, tumbling, and " the forces of Hercules," which last " gave great delight to the strangers, for they had not seene it before." The supper was as plentiful as the dinner, and was succeeded by jousts and feats of arms, and the day's amusements were closed by a sumptuous banquet of " sugar meates for the men-at-armes and the ladies." Leycester does not make any mention of this splendid festivity in his letters to his friends in England.

throwghe the cause. She grewe so passyonat in the matter as she forbad him to argue any more. Suerly there is somme trecherye amongest owreselves, for I cannot thinke that she woold doe this of her [a] owne heade. I conceyve also, that ther are bad offyces don from thence by secreat letters sent hether, by the which they doe advertyce that the states shall not be able to yeld the contrybutyons promysed, so as the burden of the warres wyll lyght on her majestye. She is the rather confyrmed in this opinion, for that your lordship dyd sygnefye unto her, that the contrybutyons came verry slowly in. Now hereuppon I gather, that her majestye, dowbtyng that a greater charge wyll be cast uppon her then she shall be able to beare, wherby she shall be forced to abandon the actyon, she conceyveth yt may be don with lesse dyshonor, being an assyster, then when her mynister shall carrye the tytle of absolute governor. I conjecture also, yt may growe upon a hope of a peace; for that, as I am secreatly informed, ther is a save-conduct sent over unto Champigny, eyther for himselfe or some other, that shall secreatly repayre into this realme. Sorrye I am, that your lordship shoold be so yll handeled as not to be made acquaynted with the proceadinges here, having ingaged yourselve so far as you have don for her majestyes servyce. I looked that her majestye woold have wrytten letters of thankes, bothe unto your lordship and others there of good desert, bothe strayngers and her own subiectes, but we are more apt to wownde then to compfort. God geve your lordship pacyence to beare thes crosses, to whos protectyon I commyt you, most humbly takyng my leave. At the coorte, the xxvj[th] of Aprell, 1586.

Your lordships to commaund,
Fra: Walsyngham.

Addressed,
To the right honourable my verie good lorde the earle of Leycester, lord lieutenant-generall of her majesties forces in the Lowe Countries.

[a] Owr, *in MS.*

LETTER LXXXVIII.

THE QUEEN TO SIR THOMAS HENEAGE.

27TH APRIL, 1586.   COTTON MS. GALBA, C. IX. FOL. 197.   COPY IN THE HAND-
WRITING OF SIR THOMAS HENEAGE.[a]

The queen's dissatisfaction that nothing has been done towards the qualification of Leycester's title of absolute governor—Heneage is commanded, wheresoever this letter should find him, to return to Leycester, and with him to confer with the counsell of estate how the said title might be qualified, and the power be given to Leycester not as governor of the country, but as the queen's lieutenant-general—the queen complains of Heneage's delay in the delivery of her letters to the states—and also that he had assured the states that she would make no peace with Spain without their privity and assent.

Trusty and welbeloved, we grete you well. Upon perusall of your late letters, and of the coppy of the speach in oure name unto the states, we fynd yt very strange, that in that matter that doth so greatly touch us in honor, and the contynuance of the title of absolute governor, there is nothing yet done for the qualification thereof, for any thing we have yet receaved from you. For we did looke, accordingly as we directed, that there would have bene some resolution taken in that behalfe, between the counsel of estate, oure cosin of Leycester, and you. Which being not performed, falleth out farr contrary to oure expectation, and the regard we looked you would have both had to oure honor and contentment, being a thing by us so much affected. And therfore owre pleasure ys, wheresoever thies oure letters shall fynde you, you shall with all convenient spede retorne to oure

[a] The MS. is entitled, " Copye of her majesties letter."

cosin of Leycester, and to ioyne with him in conferenee, and with the counsell of estate there, howe the said qualification in poynct of title may be performed accordyngly as we desyer, and yet the autority reserved unto oure cosin the earle under the title of oure lieutenant-generall, which we see no cause to dowbt but that the same will worke as good effect for the avoyding of the confusion of governement ther, as the other title of absolute governor.

We are further to lett you understand, that we have cause greatly to mislike of too poynts in your proceding there. The one, that there was stay made in the delivery of our letters unto the states, for the doing wherof we gave no speciall direction, nether to oure cosin of Leycester nor unto you, nor yet do see any cause to allow therof for any thing conteyned in your letters. The other ys, the assurance geven by your speach unto the states, that we would make no peace with the king of Spaine without their privitie and assent, wherin we ether thinke that you have farr exceded your commision, or els oure secretary had greatly mistaken our direction geven unto him in that behalfe; for that oure meaning was, that they should only have ben assured, that, in any treaty that might fall out betwen us and Spaine, we would have no les care of their safetie then of oure own. And wheras, by your letters unto us, you do lett us understand, that you receaved a short answer from the counsell of estate to the poynts by you propounded, we mervaile greatly why you forbare to send the same unto us, importing us so much as yt doth to have some spedy resolution in the said poynt of qualification, wherin we do assure you we shall receave no satisfaction untill the same be performed as we desyer. And therfore oure meaning ys not that you shall retorn unto us before the same be accomplished; and, in the mean tyme, we do looke to heare often from you touching your proceading therin. Geven under our signet at oure manor of Grenwich, the xxvijth day of Aprill, 1586, in the xxviijth year of our reign.

LETTER LXXXIX.

THE QUEEN TO SIR THOMAS HENEAGE.

27TH APRIL, 1586. COTTON. MS. GALBA, C. IX. FOL. 197b. A COPY MADE BY SIR THOMAS HENEAGE.

This letter was written to sir Thomas Heneage by the queen with her own hand and sent at the same time as the last—she reminds him that a man who has faulted will not willingly retreat—she orders him to do what he is bidden, and leave his consideration for his own affairs—she will not be bound not to make peace by his speech to the states—it is enough if she does not injure their country—she dislikes his childish dealing.

What flegmaticall reasons so ever were made you, how happeneth yt that you will not remember, that when a man hath faulted and commetted by abettars therto, that nether the one nor the other will willingly make their own retrait. Jesus, what availeth witt when yt failes the ownar at greatest nede? Do that you are bidden, and leve your considerations for your owne affayres; for in some things you had cleare commandement, which you did not, and in other none, and did, yea, to the use of those speaches from me that might oblige me to more than I was bounde, or mynde ever to yelde. We princes be wary enough of our bargaines, thinke you I will be bounde by your speach to make no peace for myne own matters without their consent? It is enough that I iniure not their countre, nor themselves, in making peace for them, without their consent. I am assured of your dewtifull thoughts, but I am utterly at squares with this childish dealing.[a]

---

[a] Sir Thomas Heneage has written under the copy from which we have printed, "Thys above ys the copie of her majesties lettre wrytten with her own hand to me."

LETTER XC.

THE EARL OF LEYCESTER TO MR. SECRETARY WALSYNGHAM.

28TH APRIL, 1586. OUVRY MS. FOL. 8 b. A COPY.

The earl has received many of Walsyngham's letters at one time—further successes of count Hohenlohe—misbehaviour of English soldiers at Grave—Hohenlohe's great services and merit—the prince of Parma has returned to Brussels, but still intends to proceed towards Grave—desertions from the Spaniards—Graffyn—negociation for a peace—the earl's advice as to the proper course to be taken to procure a peace, and as to who are proper persons to be negotiators.

Mr. secretary, I haue receiued the xxvijth of Aprill manie letters from you at one time. Theie will require some time to answere them all, which I will doe. In the meane time, I haue thought good to lett you knowe, that, besides the ij fortes which the count Hollock hath taken since the vitellinge of Grave, the one called Knoles sconce and the other Embell, this morning I have receaued assured intelligence by coronell Shenkes, whose lieutenant brought him the word and was present at the fact, that, on Tuesdaie last, certen of his horsmen issued out of Venloe and mett with v^c of the enemye belonging to Mastrickt, and charged them and overthrew them, kild fiftye, tooke a c prisoners, with their ainsigne, which doth shew that God doth blesse this action of her majesties clearly. Both the count Hollocke and this Shenke are two notable servantes, and, next God, wee must thanke the count Hollocke in all trueth for the victorye at Grave; for he did not only most valiantly in his owne person, but very wisely and souldierlike governe the matter, when, in secret be it spoken to you, and as sir Thomas Heneage can tell you, v^c Englishmen of our oldest Flemish trayning ran flatly and shamfully away. And how farr this count hath saved some mens credites I know most assuredly, and soe can sir Thomas Heneage tell you, if he will; but I doubt he will not, for he was at the place, and indeed had the salutacion of enemyes cannon, and he had the truth of all, but not fitt to be knowen to many. But the count Hollock, of all men, hath deserved most iust commendacion, whome I pray God her majesty maie in some honorable sort remember; for he hath giuen over service of the states, and will serve none but her majestie, and soe declared long since to them, and keeps his promise faithfullie. He is both a valiant man and a wis man, and the painfullest that ever I knewe. I beseech you be meane to her majestie to remember him. If he had her picture in a tablett, which might be worth ij^{cli}, would content him as much as 1000^{li} in money. He hath, for hir majestyes sake, greatly left his drinkinge, and amonge the souldiers greatly beloued.

The enemie, we heare, was a daies iourney outward toward Grave, as I wrote to you, with all his forces, and xv canons. He heard then of his losse at Grave, which so appauld him as he retorned back to Bruxells, but with intent, as wee heare, againe to come into those parts presently. The losse of the number of Spaniards were certenly more then I wrote, and soe confirmed to him, which, with the losse of so many his best captaines, and as yet we hear it still confirmed that don John de Aquilaue,[a] thair cheif leader and master of camp,[b] was slayne; if it be trew, as we knowe not the contrarie, and all lettres from Antwerpe and Bruxells confirme it, he hath lost his cheiftest capten and greatest souldier he had.

This overthrow hath drawen them from Newes, and as I am perswaded will rayse the rest from Grave, except the princes coller presse him to seeke revenge, whereof I haue noe great feare, speciallye yf he continue collerick, for be you assured we will giue him litle advantage, and yett will we waitt vppon his pleasure at an inch, whersoeuer he goe; yea, perchance, if God send vs

---

[a] Aquitave, *in MS.*   [b] The word is illegible in the *MS.*

money, which is our whole want, either bring him, or led him, into Flanders, and if moneie faill nott here shalbe noe doubt of it; yet are we many fewer then he, both for horse and foote.

There is at this hower a notable capten of the Albaneses gone from the enemye, and doth offer to serve me vnder her majestie, and to drawe ij^{ca} of the best Albeneses that doth serve him to serve here and furthwith. Theie be the best men he hath.

You gave a pasport to one Aug. Graffyn to goe to Antwerpe of late, he had letters to me to giue him leave alsoe, but he speed soe well as he neuer sent me my letters till he had done all his busines, and returned with a great masse of merchandizes, and then he sent me my letters and a dish of plumes, which I will boldly say to you, by the liuing God, is all that ever I had since I came into these countreys. This man I vnderstand ys great with the prince of Parma, and receaued great favors for the dispach of his merchandises, and the rather as it is secretly and assuredly giuen me to vnderstand from my intelligencer, for that he hath vndertaken to sett abroch the peace betwene her majestie and the kinge of Spayne, a matter for my parte I doe not mislike, soe that it be not mard in the handlinge. For, as it is not vnfitt for princes to heare anie offers that may be made, soe is it most necessary to make their best bargaine that anie way maie be procured, but I beseech you lett these advantages be considered that her majestie now hath, and to assure her, she may bringe the kinge of Spaine to anie peace if it be princly and well handled, but if you relent one iotte all is overthrowen. I meane not, that you should not entertayne and heare, in some sort, to these offers made, but not to shewe to haue to great a desire to it, as in troth it is here geuen out, to to much to the disadvantage of her majestyes service. What sending, what practising there is, on every side, some in Spayne, some in the Low Countreys, from some of yourselues in England, it is a world to heare. But, for my none parte, both before I came hether and since my coming, I take God to record, I haue and doe wish a good and a sure peace

^a ij^{cli}, *in MS.*

for her majesty, and haue taken no other waye here amonge these councellors then such as I maie alway turne to that course, being ripe and ready for her majestie and them; but I haue ever said that, and doe still say it, that doe you all you can, with all the instruments you can haue, and, except a necessitye drive it, you shall never haue a good peace with Spayne, and your best waie and meane must be to force them in this sort by a hard warre. Whereby, if it shall please her majestie to back me princly, and to shew a care indeed to settle these countreys in good securitye, I will adventure my hedd of it, that her majestie shall haue what peace she will. And it shall not grow by a merchants brokerage, but from the verie states of Heynalt, Flaunders, and Artoys themselues, wherevpppon there maie be good ground taken indeed to worke uppon, which otherwise thother is dellitorye and equall, and he that seeks maie leaue vppon anie advantage, as he likes best. And I haue not doubt but to bringe such a manner of dealing to passe, soe that you by paultring dealing, by beggerly instruments, be cutt of; which at all times maie be vsed, if God should send our case harder than it is. And beside, when it is sought by men of creditt, whoe are interessed in the cause, you are like to obteine better conditions then when it shall growe by a broker; beside the honor is as much worth almost as the matter. I can assure you, by all faith and trueth, that the brutes of your treatinge vnderhande hath done more harme to the cause here then anie one thinge in the world, ioyned with the mislike geven out by lewd fellowes, that her majestie had noe care what became of these countreys, and that she sought but for a peace for herself, and till sir Thomas Henneage last assurance geuen to the councell here thereof, I knew theie all feared it, almost to their vtter greife, but now it stands well, and theie well perswaded, wherein sir Thomas Henneage hath done her majestie exceeding great service, in satissfyng these men in many things.

To conclude, if her majestie doe wish a peace, as I beleeue she doth, this is the only way to cause the enemie to seeke hir, which neuer beleeue me if he doe not. So that there, as I saied before, [be] geuen the enemy noe hope of by and vnderhand dealinge, and that her majestie doe deale playnly and franklye with these people, as sometimes in sending some men of creditt to visitt them, and to see their estate, to comfort them, and me also, as her servant amonge them; and having such a one here, I could call him sometimes [a] to breake that with them which were meete, and yet not soe fitt for myselfe to doe. Hit is but iij monethes dealinge to bring what her majestie will to passe, and with great honor; beside, I doe [believe] this last conflict hath marvellously appaulled the Spaniards, and theie doe daylie run away by good nombers. Well, I pray you let vs lack noe moneie. If I liue till August, yf I take not order, if her majestie will haue a peace, that she shall likewise haue all her money in verie short time, lett me be blamed. Thus, having bine longer then I meant, I will take my leaue. In som hast this 28. of Aprill.

Your assured frend.

LETTER XCI.

THE EARL OF LEYCESTER TO MR. SECRETARY WALSYNGHAM.

30TH APRIL, 1586.   OUVRY MS. FO. 11.   A COPY.

The earl has received Walsyngham's letter of the 21st April, which was the first letter of comfort he had received since he left England—laments his late hard condition—will send money for the troops to be raised in England and Ireland—has acquainted some of the council with the proposals for peace made to the queen—by using her advantage her majesty may have offers far more

---

[a] to sometimes to, *in MS.*

advantageous—dejection of the prince of Parma—exploits of count Hohenlohe and Shenck—the earl has knighted the latter and Norris—anticipated desertions from the Spaniards—the earl would creep on his hands and knees to procure a good peace—rumour of interference of the king of Denmark to stay trade with Spain—it will turn out that Jentile designed to poison the earl.

Mr. secretary, I did writt ij dayes past to you at some lenght, and in that letter by chaunce haue answered some thinges that your last letter of the xxj[th] of Aprill[a] doth require, which letter I receaued this last of Aprill; but one thinge I must cheifly remember and thanke you for, which is, that I neuer receaued letter, or word, of comfort from you, since I came over, but by this letter. I would be sorrie my enemie, much lesse my freind, should suffer such a time as I did, almost foure monethes together; but the blessednes of England I see hath made manie forgett the miseries of others. God grant me his grace to strengthen me in this service, and that he will send her majestie victorie over all her enemyes; and that poore men, whoe doe hazard there life, honor, and liveing, maie be better remembred then I haue bine. But now that her majesties good favor is promised me, and is the onlye worldlie thinge I begge of God, I doe greatlie quiet myself, and doe protest, even before the majestie of the eternall judge, that I haue sought nothinge in this service of mine, but, first, the glory of God, and, next, the saftye and service of her majestie, for which respect He doth knowe, and I doe feele, I haue lost the sweet comfort of her majesties presence, my most gratious soueraigne, the safe protection of my happy countrey, the contented life among my deere and loveinge freinds, and the libertye with all comfort in a most blessed state. What I purchase here, in-

[a] See p. 229.

steed of all theis, lett my companies and beholders witnes. But if x times worse were possible to be felt, and maie doe my gratious mistress but half the service I desire, with enioying her favor, all would be pleasure, ioy, and comfort; for I knowe, if God be pleased, this accion must needs turne to her majesties great securitie, or ells was I vnhappy to enter into it. Well, sir, I thanke you now, at last, that I receaued some lines of comfort from you; as that her majestie is my good ladye, that she will assist me in her service here, with licensinge of voluntary men to come over, in favoring sir Wylliam Stanleys fechinge men out of Ireland, in imparting to me the offers for peace.

For the voluntaries, I trust noe way to chardge her majestie, but shall all be borne here, and shortlie to send moneie over; there are v or vj^c come already, whoe had prestes out of my owne purse.

For sir William Stanley, also, I will speedily send over to you for that you haue prested, as also to send him a further prest, wishing of God that it had pleased her majestie to haue sent, or yet to send, sir William Pelham over. I knowe, I say I knowe it, that all the debt he oweth had bine saved another way if he had bine here, beside the great service to the whole cause, as you shall find in a tickett, &c.[a]

Touching the matter of peace, I haue, I thinke, said in my other letter as much as I now can say. And I doe most humbly beseech her majestie to consider well of it. I perceaue that I heard here is true, and confirmed by your letter, soe that there is dealing for peace as well by Grefyne as others, which intelligences being so knowen caused me to take that course which I perceaue her majestie doth will me, which is, to let the councellers vnderstand of the meanes which are offered her majestie, as, in very troth, I haue done but to the wisest sort of them, alwaies to

---

[a] Either some paper was inclosed or there is some error in the MS.

prevent the hearing of it; for theie be very subtill, and as suspicious people as ever I delt withall, which made me to vse some speech of this matter to them; how greatly her majestie is sought for peace, and how carefull I knowe she wilbe to doe anie thing to their hurt. And theie beleeue she is soe, for I tell you theie knowe it, and I am sorry I haue not heard sooner, for I haue often writen what I haue heard of this matter, that I might haue authority to say somethinge, as, I thanke God, I did it sondry times of myself, to avoid the iealousye. And I knowe it hath done great good, and sir Thomas Henneage declaracion thereof, also, did exceeding much good, and confirmed in good time, and fully, that I had said before to them.

But to the peace, what I thinke I referre you to my other letter, protesting, before God, I desire nothing more in this world then a good and sure peace for her majestye, being I knowe most agreable to her best liking, whome, next God, I would in all dewtifull service most please, and, beside, I am most perswaded that all good Christians ought to seeke and preferre. My onlie advice doth tend to haue her majestie haue as sure peace as in reason may be gotten. And I doe verilie thinke, as matters stand here, if her majestie will vse her advantage, she shall bringe the kinge, and specially this prince of Perma, to seeke it in other sort then by waie of merchantes. I can assure you he was never soe deiected, nor soe mallancholy, since he came into these countreys, as he is at this daye, nor so far owt of courage. I protest vnto you, I would gage my life and creditt, if I were supplied as were but reasonable, I would haue Antwerpe towne and Burges or midd June. This last overthrow is greater then you there can imagin, with the vitelling of Grave, being a towne of greatest importance of all the places we hould in theis provinces, for Brabant, Gelders, Vtryckt, and Over Isell, being the very passage into all those places, saving into Gelders the enemie maie goe another way, but far worse and more discomodious, and the prince made as sure accompt of it as ever he did of anie skonce that he tooke in hand. His men doe marvellously beginn to mutinie; manie run away, specially Spaniards.

I thinke I wrot to you, how Shenks lieutenant very latlie again hath overthrowen, nere Mustryckt, aboue v^c footmen, whereof onlie 1 are kild, and a c with their cheif ainsynes taken and brought awaie,[a] with losse of five or sixe at most; he himself was, and is, here with me, about a service presentlye to be done, in building a fort whereby we will choke vpp Newmeagen, and stopp all vittells that waie to the enemie.

The count Hollocke is here also, a most noble gentleman, and, to deale plainlie, geuing every man his right, he was the cheife cause, vnder God, of our days victorye, wherein, beside his valiant behaviour, he delt as like a good souldier as ever I heard of, and afterwards, for the vitellinge the towen, in his person he did most desperatlye adventure it, and went into it himself, where he past a 1000 shott of muskett and caliver, and a c shott of cannon and great ordinance; surelye he is to be honored and cherished. Shenks is a worthy fellow. I made ij knights as theie shuld be, one having a bloodye wound, thother not whole of a shott thorow his thigh at the overthrow at Werll, where he slew almost iij^m men of the enemies, which was Shenke, thother Mr. John Norris, whoe was but newly hurt, and is as valiant a gentleman as ever liued, and he giues this commendacion to the count Hollock that I tell you for that dayes service, whome, before his face, he saw kill a Spaniard with his pistell, when thother was ready to throst his pike thorow him; these two knights deserved it well.

I am likewise in assured hope to drawe awaie from the enemie furthwith ij^c of his best Albanesines, whoe be his cheif

---

[a] Stowe, writing upon the authority of H. Archer, who was present in the Low Countries, describes this incident as follows: " The 26 of Aprill, the lieutenant of sir Martin Skinke, his master being with my lords excellencie, knowing of a company of footmen Spaniards, hee with certaine of his horse layd themselves in ambush, set upon them, killed thirty of them, and tooke 81, and caried them to their garrison." Annales, p. 718,

horsmen. I haue spoken this daie with the capten, whoe is secretlie stollen hether to me, being within a dayes iourney or litle more of their troupes, being not farr of Grave; he is as manlike a gentleman as euer I looked vppon, and Shenks tels me, the onlie leader among them. He asketh me nothing till he brings his bandes to me. I assure you there cannot be a thinge will frett the prince more at the heart. This man doth tell me for all troth, vppon his owne knowlege, that there is three hundred Italians and Spaniards of his best cauallery gone to the duke of Guise against his will, and that he hath written to the duke against them, but he keeps them, and hath done this moneth. This capten was in hight of the fraye at Grave, but the waters kept all the horsmen off; he doth assure me that there was not so few as vj^c Spaniards kild, and the verie flowre of all their campe, but don John de Aquilau is alive, whoe we thought was kild; soe that for peace, you maie see whether it be not like that it wilbe sought in better sort at her majesties hands then by merchants. I am borne in hand of all, the lords and cheif gentlemen of Heynalt, Arteyes, and Flaunders will seeke it, and presse the prince for it, and there is one that will giue me knowlege verie shortlie thereof, and, if I be not abused, the prince and kinge both will dailie, as longe as theie can, to entertain, talke of peace, and to discourage these countreys thereby, before theie will either harken indeed to a peace, or to treat of anie. And, vnder corection be it spoken, if these men here conceave once her majestie to be in hand with a peace, theie are gone without once looking back, and will make their men, and overthrow her majesties, or lett me suffer for it. God I take to record, vppon that I haue conceaued, and what you haue written, of her majesties disposition, I would creepe vppon the ground as farr as my hands and knees would bere me, to haue a good peace for her majestie, but my care is to haue a peace indeed, and not a shew of it to devid her freinds and her insonder; they loaue her not that wish that kind of weake dealing. Yf all the Spanish faction in England procure her majestie a peace fitt for hir, in any respect, lett me be hanged for it. Nay I thinke, if you or I should shew to haue so much creditt that waie as some doe as I heare of in England, I doubt whether we should be thought worthy to be hanged or noe; but I haue not to doe with other mens doings, God preserve her majestie, and send her trew faithfull councellors. And the best waie for a good peace, I thinke still, is to bring it by a good sharp warr; and if I had monie, noe more but that her majestie hath promised to imploye here for this yeare, if her majestie be not sought and sought againe, as she should be, lett me beare the blame. But, soe long as pedlers and merchantes be seking and paultringe in so weighty a cause, the enemy will make his profitt of it, or, if it were knowen that I did but advise thus much, the enemy would be in the greatest prid in the world, and hold out to the vttermost houre, whereas now, hard handling must doe the feate, without conceat of hasty or easy beleeuing. Thus, I pray you beare with my tedious writinge, and lett me certenly knowe her majesties will and pleasure therein indeed, for what her will is must be obeyed, and, after I knowe it, I will deall accordingly, by the grace of God, to the vttermost of all my witt.

I receaue even now a lettre from Amsterdam, by which it is written, that the kinge of Denmark hath stayed in the Sound a great number of shipps, and will suffer none to passe except he promise, or put in bands, not to goe either to Spaine or to Portugall; if it be true, as I doe verilie hope it is, hit is a verie happy matter for her majestie.

I thinke it will fall out plainely that [John][a] Jentile which I wrote to you of, that came to the princes of Symeye,[b] seming to discouer that he was hired to poison her from her husband, came onlie to doe it to me; all circumstances of his speeches leanes to it. He was not yet put to anie torture, but he shalbe, his tales

[a] A blank is left in the MS.   [b] See page 213.

be so full of contrarietyes and doubtes as he beginnes now to wish himself dead, and craves mercye. He confesseth now his meaning was to serve me, and he doubteth there be others that haue comission for the matter, though he hath not; but all is one for him or anie other, my God hath chardge of me, and will not suffer their malice to take place. Yf it should, welcome be his blessed will, hit is for a good cause and soe I am at a point, and yet will I be as carefull as I may be. Thus God haue you in his good keeping. From Vtrickt this last of Aprill.

Your assured fieind.[a]

LETTER XCII.

THE EARL OF LEYCESTER TO MR. SECRETARY WALSYNGHAM.

1ST MAY, 1586. OUVRY MS. FO. 14 b. A COPY.

The earl has reason to distrust the information lately given to him respecting Ralph Salisbury, and therefore wishes that his former letter may not do him any prejudice.

Albeit I wrote of late vnto you what informacion I had giuen

---

[a] There follows this letter in Mr. Ouvry's MS. the following abstract of its contents:

"Meaneth to send over so much as I haue already prestid to sir William Stanley, with some further increase.

"Wisheth that her majestie had sent sir William Pelham over, whose service might haue bine to great purpose.

"Hath acquainted some of the counsell with the ouertures of a peace made to her majestie, thereby to take all occacions of iealousy and suspicion from them.

"Her majestie, by prosecuting the action roundly, maie haue many advantagable offers of a peace made vnto her.

"The prince of Parma greatlie deiected in mind.

"Grave a place of very great importance, which barreth thenemie from an easye passage into all those parts.

me against Raph Salsbury,[a] yet have I noe good proofe of it, for the partie doth giue me no satisfacion that accused him. He came to me hether to offer service, and first to retorne into England about his earnest busines, which I haue licensed him to doe, and I pray lett not my former letters doe him preiudice, except you shall heare further from me, or knowe, by some good meanes, anie iust cause against him. Thus, having written at large to you in another letter at this time, as also ij daies past another by a man of Edmund Cares, I committ you to the Lord, meaning to writ to her majestie within two daies by an expresse messenger. At Vtrickt, this first of May.

Your assured frend.

I wold God you would help me to Boddyby, or such a one as he is, that hath good language; none of the Da.[b] I like.

LETTER XCIII.
THE EARL OF LEYCESTER TO MR. SECRETARY WALSYNGHAM.
3RD MAY, 1586. OUVRY MS. FO. 15. A COPY.

The earl requests that money may be advanced to the persons employed to levy men—sir William Stanley shall have more than 30s. a man for the men from Ireland—the prince of Parma has advanced to the siege of Grave—the treasurer disliked—sir William Pelham longed for.

Good Mr. secretary, lett me intreat you, for that I hope moneie

---

" The kinge of Spain and prince of Perma will entertaine a longe time the speech of a peace before theie enter into it, onlie to discourage the states.

" Yf the states have anie incling that her majestie beginneth to hearken to a peace it will overthrow the cause.

" To knowe her majesties disposicion touching the matter of the peace."

[a] See p. 223.
[b] Perhaps this should be " Du." for Dutch.

wilbe sent shortly to vs, that you will cause some prestes to be deliuered to such as I shall write vnto you for, to be paid there, for the leavye of voluntaries. And I shall, without all faile or delay, pay that moneie here againe to the treasorer vppon your letter, though it come to a 1000 or 1500li. I shall hardly make it over so sone, and it [a] shalbe all one, to be parcell of other sommes that you send, to haue it answered here. I beseech lett it be done for me.

Sir William Stanley shall haue aboue xxxs.; if I can, hit [b] shalbe xls. for euery man he brings out of Ireland, and if you help him with vc li, beside that you haue imprestid him, hit shalbe also paid here as you shall appointe.

The prince of Parma is come to Grave to ley the cannon to it. God send him noe better speed then his predecessors had.

I like not the proceeding of the treasorer here; the auditor, but for me, had come back againe. I am sorry for it, but it is to badd, and without helpe.

I will take the best order I can to impech our enemyes. I lack fitt instrumentes. Sir William Pelham will neuer come. I am well assisted, both for warr and peace, God help me. And soe God be with you. In hast, hauing written lately at large. At Amersfort this 3. of May.

Your assured frend.

I praie you, sir, further this noblemans suit for men, and lett him receiue ijc [1] for prest.

[a] he, *in MS*.   [b] hit it shalbe *in MS*.

LETTER XCIV.

THE EARL OF LEYCESTER TO MR. SECRETARY WALSYNGHAM.

6TH MAY, 1586.   OUVRY MS. FO. 15 b.   A COPY.

The prince of Parma has advanced in person to the siege of Grave—the earl will obey her majesty's command, and will take it more than thankfully to be revoked—arrival of men from England—embassy from Denmark into England—bad management of the money transmitted to pay the army.

Mr. secretary, I could not answere your letter which came by the pursevant before this, for that I haue bine two dayes busie at the musters,[a] and giuing order for the paiment of soldiours, which falleth out soe short as hit is pitty to see it; but I am going now into the feild with such forces as I am able to make. The cheifest cause, to withstand the prince of Permas enterprises in these parts, coming, as I am credibly aduertised, in person, with xviij cannons to batter Grave, which if he doe, I trust to prevent his intention. Some other causes there be of great necessitye to settell these partes, and I see, except I goe myself with these companies, this campe will hardly be mainteined or kept together. There is some emulacion amonge the commandours, and captens over-hard to their souldiors, and, by my will, there shalbe noe advantage giuen the enemye throwe our disorder. I will take the more paine myself among them, by the grace of God.

For the matter your pursevant brought, I haue answered in a letter by Aty to her majestie. I will not faill to obey her comandement very precisely. And, for my owne parte, I was at the point at the first time sir Thomas Henneage came, and offered most

[a] Stowe says, upon the authority of Archer, "The 4. of May his excellencie did view all his horsemen, being in number about 13 or 14 hundred, by Newkirke, on a great heath betweene Newkirke and Amerford." Annales, p. 718.

reddily to satisfye her majesties comandement, but much more now I trust her majestie is not offended with me, and I care not how sone I be deliuered of this burthen, speciallie since I find it noe way acceptable to hir majestie, the service of this countrey, for, I thanke God, I haue neither done her majestie anie dishonour here, nor haue had anie ill successe for her service, yet haue I had as little thankes, and as great blame, as he that had lost a countrey or a battell. Well! for the obseruing of her majesties pleasure for this last commandement, albeit we had very good warrant for it, hit shalbe done, as soone as sir Thomas Henneage comes. And if I maie find anie grace to be honestly revoked, I will take it more thankfullie then some men that should receave x^m ^{li} for a reward.

I trust in this voyage, if God lett me liue, to settell all these partes thorowly for a good while. I will then retorne to Hage except I heare of anie sege, either of Berges or Ostend. Of Ostend I cannot thinke; Berges is more like, and yet if he take it not in 2 dayes, which I thinke he shall never, without treason bringe aboue ij^c men in it, I will warrant we will reliue it well enough.

There be allready viij or ix^c men come over, and the states will entertaine them all, and the rest that come, and I am in good hope the meanes will rise verie great for the maintenance of all theire charges here, yf her majestie will goe thorow with this matter. I would God my lord Gray, or some other noblemen, were here to supply this place, not doubting but theie should farr better accomplish this service then I can, and their service farr better accepted then mine is. Hit sufficeth me that my conscience doth witnes with me that I doe serue her majestie as in the presence of the Almightie; I pray God send me but her majesties reasonable fauor for it.

I am sorry I had not knowledge enough to send you worde of the great embassage the kinge of Denmark doth send to her majestie, which, as it is reported, is the greatest that euer went out of the east countreys;[a] his expectacion is great of her majesties forwardnes in their causes. I praie God he maie receaue that comfort I wish. He hath again made offer to me of his ij^m royters, and I beseech you, sir, lett it be acknowledged there to his embassador.

I am here perplexed in my soule for the vntowardly dealing for our money. I assure you here is not a full moneth to pay the soldiours at this time, and there is none paid but Brill, Ostend, and Flushing. I doe protest to you, if I were as well encouraged to serve as ever I was, I would not deale anie more with her majesties servants here, hauing such disbursers of the monie. I doe assure you it is enough to ouerthrow all our whole service here, and there is noe speaking nor warning, theie presume either vppon chaunge or favour, or som what, for never man hath dealt soe playnely nor soe rigorously as I haue done, but theie care not one pennie for it; theie say theie must and will answere it. You shall doe well, whosoeuer haue the chardge here, to direct the treasor to his chardge vntoucht or vnbroken vpp, and thin the treasorer to make his reconing, and to receaue out, that which is due to be paid, and that which remaines to be locked vpp vnder ij keys; for my parte if anie come before my departure, surely I will neither make pay nor warrant if he delivered any penny before yt come to me. The auditor is both simple and fearefull, and, except you appoint another comission, I dare vndertake her majestie shall loose xx^m mark, at least, in this already past. What a thinge is this, Mr. secretary, that the poore stervid wreches that have susteined penury this iiij monethes almost full, shall haue but one moneths pay, and not that, now to goe to the feild. Withall, by your leaue, I must say it againe, you did her majestie and your-

[a] Henry Ramelius, the ambassador alluded to, arrived in London on the 8th May. He was lodged in Crosby place, and remained in England until the 30th May. (Stowe's Annales, p. 720). Holinshed, with the precision which renders the narratives of our chroniclers so valuable, describes his person and entertainment (Chron. IV. 894); Camden explains the nature of his business and the answer he received from the queen. (Annales sub anno 1586.)

self wronge, when you appointed such officers, so vnited, as you did, specially being interessed as theie were. For my parte, I trust I shall stay noe time here; yf I should, I would never agree to haue this man deall with the money agein, I will command noe souldiours * * *ᵃ and, as the souldiers hath noe pay but for a moneth, soe is there no officer in the feild paid anie thinge but myself. It is verie late, yet I wish there were care in time.

As for peace, I am at a point. My care was for hir majestie and the realme, and I wilbe hanged when she shall haue a good peace but as I wrote to you, and therefor there needes noe hast, matters going as theie doe; but I am noe fitt councellor in this. God speed it well, and keep you alwaies. At Hamersford this 6. of May.

Your assured freind.

LETTER XCV.

THE EARL OF LEYCESTER TO MR. SECRETARY WALSYNGHAM.

8th MAY, 1586. OUVRY MS. FOL. 17. A COPY.

The earl is with the army ready to withstand the prince of Parma, who makes great preparations, the object of which is uncertain— the earl will, in obedience to her majesty, resign his title of absolute governor within an hour of the arrival of sir Thomas Heneage, who is detained by illness at Flushing—the earl craves to be recalled—warns the queen of the perilous consequences of underhand dealing for peace.

Sir, when I receaued her majesties letter I was at Amersford, as I doubt not but my servaunt Aty hath or this made knowen vnto you, as well to muster and put our men there in readines, as for

---

ᵃ A word in the MS. that is illegible.

myself to goe into these parts where now I am, to withstand the pretence of the enemie, whoe was once removed from Bruxells one dayes iourney, and then retired agayne, and yet after went to Antwerpe, which is the last newes I haue of him. Great preparacion he makes, some say to continue his enterprice at Grave, some saie to beseige Berges op Some; whether of both he shall attempt I am ready to releue them, and if he doe nether, then doe I hope to sett these parts freer and in better securitie then theie were these vij yeres, for I trust to clere the Reyne, and to stopp him from anie releif, either to his campe at Grave or for Newmegine; of these things you shall heare more verie shortly.

Now, touching the satisfing of her majesties pleasure for the title of absolute gouernor, which title is not soe, though absolute gouernment is granted, indeed, with the title of gouernor of all the prouinces united, an office that, if I could haue bine ridd of without the hazard of all the rest, I told you longe agoe I was most vnwillinge to take it, and most ready to be quitt of it, and with a lesse caution then her majesties mislike; but to satisfie that, as my deuty is, all Holland and Zeland with all their appurtenaunces shall not make me keep it one howre longer then I heare of Mr. Henneages arrivall, whoe, as I heare, was ill at Flushinge, but I looke for him within vj or vij dayes. In the meane time, being provided and appointed for this jorney, I thought it good to proceed in it, for that it concernes noe peace of the other matter of title, for I execute now only the authorityte of her majesties lieutenant, and lieutenant for these countreys according to the contract. And, I pray you, lett her majestie, and all my lords, knowe, that, yf she maie be soe pleased, there was never thing that better contented myself then to leaue, not only title but all authoritye of gouernment withall. And what service her majestie shall comand me I will not faile to obey her. I am not ceremonious for reputacion, soe longe as I doe nothing reprochfull to my prince, myself, or my cuntrey, for I am to serve her majestie here vnder God, and, soe farr as my poore abilitye, and my decaied yeres will suffer me, I wilbe as hit shall please her majestie to direct me, trusting in God it will please her to haue consideracion of me, and to remember she said I should staie here but a while. And I am perswaded, for this short time, all thinges here are in as good estate as theie were this xij yeres. And her majestie may doe what she will for the stay of this gouernment, soe she deall not vnderhand with anie peace, as I see noe cause why she should, for then I beleeue she shall loose all these countreys, and never the nerer of the kinge of Spaines freindshipp; for, if theie may gett anie prince in the world of anie countenaunce, theie will rather take him, and offer that to him, then make anie hard peace with Spayne, to yeild him anie footinge here, or gouernment for his ministers of Spayne, by their good wills. And, truelie, I am thorowly perswaded that a good warr, held but this sommer, shall drive him cleane to forsake the countrey, or to be content to be receaued there lord onlie, without anie gouernor appointed by him to rule over them, but such a one as theie shall like of. There is noe way to ouerthrow this but ther certen knowledge that her majestie is desirous of a peace with him, as dailie brutes come hether to them, both from Antwerpe and London. This might worke a perillous end, both to them here and to her majestie there, for, without a necessity, indeed, to make the kinge to harken willingly to a peace with both, and to ioine so together as he must take anie reason offered to him, lett it be a peace disiunctive, and I warrant both will repent it. And, therefore, I perceaue these men should growe desperate, if her majestie deall weakly or carelesly for them. I would you knewe how eselie her majestie might goe forward with these causes here now. This xx yeres theie were not at this point. But what haue I to doe, but only to wish a good peace, or to crave a speedy retorne home. I am wery, indeed I am wery, Mr. secretary, but neither of paines nor travele; my ill happ that can please her majestie noe better hath quite discouraged me. God graunt me her gratious favor, with a speedy revocacion, but neuer to torne her princlie mind from helping these poore oppressed people. Farr you well, this 8th of May, at Arnham.

Your assured freind.

Oh, that her majestie knew how easie a mach now she hath with the kinge of Spayne, and what millions of afflicted people she hath reliued in these countreys. This sommer, this sommer I say, would make an end, to her immortall glorie.

LETTER XCVI.

THE EARL OF LEYCESTER TO MR. SECRETARY WALSYNGHAM.

9TH MAY, 1586.   OUVRY MS. FOL. 18 b.   A COPY.

The earl complains of the conduct of the treasurer of the army—unsuccessful attempt by the Spaniards to take possession of a suburb of Grave—the earl is in the field ready to succour any place the prince of Parma may attack—the earl designs to stop all carriage by water between Nimeguen and the enemy.

I am sorry to trouble you with the discomfortable dealings of of our treasurer here; I assure you it passeth, and our auditor a foole in comparison to mete with there subtelties. I saw this day an abstract. I see there is yet due to souldiers aboue x^m.[li] when all this monie almost shalbe paid that cam last. This cornel Norris doth mach the late earle of Sussex, of all men that euer I haue sene, for such matters, and sett countenaunce withall vppon them. I trust you will provide for my speedye cominge home; but, if I tarrie, either lett an other dispencer of the monie be appointed, or lett it be deliuered into my custodye, that their be noe paiments made before a perfect reckoning cast vpp; for, if it goe on with the rest as with this past, I will warrant a full third parte lost from her majestie and the souldiers now. I haue so often spoken I haue done, for I will not beare anie burthen at the souldiers and captens hands, for all the treasure in this countrey. And howsoeuer the matter is, the treasurer hath some back hope, and little doth care what fault I find.

This day I heard for certen, that, vpon the new supplie of men I caused to be sett into Grave, which was 350 with 4 or 5 very good captens, the enemye attemptinge to take and spoyle a subvrbe to Grave,[a] being about 1000 Spaniards, theie haue lost dead in the place 400, all Spaniards, such as they lost before for gallant fellowes, soe that there is a good abatment of them of late. We heare the prince doth meane to follow that seige still, but now I little feare that place, for this 350 fresh lusty souldiers having vittels, store, and munition, is a good assurance ; beside, the place is stronge, and well fortified, and hath more with these last, beside burgers, which are stout and willing fellowes and well trained. Their is 1000 able souldiers, and the burgers stronge 800. And I am now here, provided to rescue anie place the prince shall attempt. I am v^m. footmen and 1500 hors.[b] This day I haue sent most of my horsemen into the Betowe[c] toward Newmeagin. I sent Shenks two daies since with 1000 footmen

---

[a] "The base towne of Grave." Stowe's Annales, p. 718. The prince of Parma had on this occasion a very narrow escape. Having advanced to view the town, preparatory to the attack, a cannoneer aimed at him and "tooke away the hinder part of his horse." *Ibid.*

[b] The earl's movements are thus related in the "Briefe Report." "The earl of Leycester hearing of the princes preparations towards Grave, being as yet unreadie and destitute of all meanes to furnish a campe sufficient to meete with him on equall ground in fielde, yet to the entent to be neere at hand with the forces he had, and to waite such advantages as occasion might offer, with a small campe of about three thousand foote and one thousand horse, he passed in person the river of Rhyne at Arnham in Gelderland, into the province of the Bettowe, with intent from thence to passe the river of Wale also, and so to approch to Grave itselfe." Briefe Report, sig. B 2.

[c] "The Bettowe is a province in Gelderland, lying between the rivers of Rhyne and Wale, verie fertile, and then whollie held by the enimie, or at least infested by him with his fortes of Luytesforte and Berckshoofe and the two castles of Alon and Bemell." Briefe Report, sig. B 2.

to take a peice of ground called Mellin, where I haue appointed a fort to be made, which shall stopp all cariage by watter betwene Newmeagin and their campe at Grave. It maie be that I will putt that towne in hazard, at the least I will [leave] them noe places to hinder vs vppon the Reyne betwene Newes and this towne. Yf the enemie attempt Burges vp Some, as a brute there is, I will sone relieve it, by the grace of God, and yet there is both good store of men and victells in it, neither doe I greatlie mistrust anie place now that I am in the feild, that, either by watter or land, I can recover anie place, nether doe I thinke that the prince can well tell what yet to doe. God send me good successe this iorney, and well to acquit me of this countrey, and some happier man to stepp into it. Soe God be with you, and to morow I will lodge toward Newmeagin, with my companie altogether, from whence you shall heare as occasion will serve. In some hast at Arnham, this ix. of May, without money or ware.[a]

Your assured freind.

Yf you send not speedlye a nimbler fellow then this auditor there will neuer fault appere.

LETTER XCVII.
LORD BURGHLEY TO SIR THOMAS HENEAGE.
13TH MAY, 1586. COTTON MS. GALBA, C. IX. FOL. 225. ORIG.[b]

Lord Burghley has advised the queen to permit lord Leycester to continue in the government of the Low Countries, and that Heneage might return, but she will not agree to the one or the other—

[a] wart, *in MS.*
[b] This letter is not signed, but it was written by the hand of lord Burghley's secretary, and is, I think, the original. In the catalogue it is erroneously stated to be a letter from sir Thomas Heneage to lord Burghley.

Heneage is to confer with the earl and the council as to his relinquishment of the title—after such conference the queen wishes Heneage to return home and report the result to her—Burghley has had more difficulty in this matter than in any other since he was a counsellor.

Good Mr. threasurer,[a] although theare is heare matter mines [tiring?] plentifullie to write uppon concerning the subiect of your charge, yet, bicause the same conteineth noe such resolucion as both I have advised and wished, I doe forbeare to enlarge the discours thereof by particulers, and breefelie doe concurr with Mr. vice-chamberlaine, whoe nowe writeth to youe such an imperfect resolucion as hir majesty hath delivered unto him, nothing agreable to our advises.

Uppon manie urgent and poignant cawses, as I maie so terme them, I have advised hir majesty to permitt my lord of Leicester to continue in the gouverment of thos cuntries, wherein God hath latelie prospered him, and that you, being sick, might retorne without following that hazardous course that is appointed to you: but hir majestie will neither allowe of the one nor of the other, but she saith, that you shall goe backe, and doe that she hath commaunded you, which she is content to interpret in this sort, that though she still misliketh that my lord of Leicester hath accepted the title of governor-generall of thos provinces, yet she meanethe not that he should presentlie or hastelie leave it, bicause of the inconveniences that might happen to the publique cawse by want of gouverment; and yet hir mind is, that you should conferre with his lordship and the counsell theare, yea, you should also further the same, that it might be devised there by authoritie of the states, howe my lord might forbeare the title and absolute authoritie of the gouvernor of thos provinces, and yet, remaining with the title and authoritie of her majesties lieutenant-

---

[a] Sir Thomas Heneage was treasurer of the queen's chamber.

generall, to have, by the graunt of the estates, authoritye according to the articles of the mutuall treatie with the counsell of the states, to order, governe, reforme, and direct the martiall affaires in like sort as his lordship nowe maie doe, by the comission of the states whearebie he is made theire governour-generall; and this is that hir majestie desyreth, and wisheth to be done, and, to that ende, would have by your meanes conference had betwixt my lord and the counsell, howe this maie be brought to passe, and thowgh, if it can be so compassed, it cannot by anie likelood be browght to passe without sum length of tyme, and manie circumstances and difficulties, yet hir majesty willeth you to retorne, with the report of such conclusion as shall fall owt uppon this conference betwixt my lord, yourself, and the counsell of the states: and further, also, hir majestie plainely saith, that she would not have my lord to leave this authoritie untill she shall, uppon your retorne, understand howe, and in what manner, this devise shall be thowght faisible to be done, withowt anie evident danger of the common cawse. In this sort you see howe I take hir majesties wordes and mind, and so also I thinke you shall perceive the like, or equivallent, from Mr. vice-chamberlaine and Mr. secretarie, for with noe other would hir majestie deale in this cawse, as I could understand.

This matter hath been more cumbersome and more severe to me and others that hath at sundrie times delt therin with hir majesty, than any whatsoever since I was a counselor; the will of God be, to bring it to some better resolucion, both for his owne glorie and for the quiet and weale of hir majestie and hir estate, to which ende I se my praiers must be hereafter accommodated to God rather then advise as a counselor to hir majestie, and yet I mind not to leave either of them as God will geve me grace. I praie you praie my lord to excuse me for my short writing, and my lord North for my not writing, for truelie I am at this time overtoiled. 13° Maij 1586.

LETTER XCVIII.

MR. SECRETARY WALSYNGHAM TO THE EARL OF LEYCESTER.

14TH MAY, 1586. COTTON. MS. GALBA, C. IX. FOL. 236.   ORIG.

The queen is resolute in her determination to have the question of Leycester's title submitted to the council of state—she has been fully warned of the danger—this strange proceeding groweth of her majesty's own self.

My verry good lord, I had hoped that your letters sent by Mr. Atye woold have drawen her majestye to have revoked sir Thomas Henneage, and to have stayed the motyon for the qualyficatyon of the tytle, in respect of the alteratyon that the same is lykely to woorke there. But nothing that can be sayd can woorke any staye here, so resolutely is her majesty bent to have the matter propounded to the counsell of state ther; whoe, I doe assure myself, wyll be greatly perplexed with the motyon, and, as I take yt, they have no awthorytye to treate uppon yt, but must refer the consyderation therof unto an assembly of the states, which wyll woorke sooche a busse in the peoples heades, and mynister to the evyl-affected there sooche a plotte to woorke on, as to mans judgement may perryll the whole cause. Ther hathe ben as muche sayd towching the daynger as myght be alleaged. And truly, my good lord, I am now perswaded that thys straynge proceading growethe from her majestye selve. I have prayed this gentleman, who is honest, to acquaynt your lordship with my opinion herin; and so I most humbly take my leave. At the coorte, the xiijth. of Maye, 1586.

Your lordships to commaund,
FRA: WALSYNGHAM.

By the coppye of Mr. Randolphes letter your lordship may see the present state of Scoteland.

LETTER XCIX.

THE EARL OF LEYCESTER TO MR. SECRETARY WALSYNGHAM.

17TH MAY, 1586.   OUVRY MS. FOL. 19 b.   A COPY.

Proceedings of the army—Schenck has erected a fort at the junction of the Rhine and Waal—attempt to divert the prince of Parma from Grave by a movement towards Nimeguen—surrender of a fortified place to Leycester—want of pioneers—and of money— the earl has borrowed 5000l. of the merchants.

Mr. secretory, I sent my companies as I wrote vnto you of late, some to make a fort nere Tolhowse, in a little iland [a] where the rivers of Reyne and Wale do [b] devide, for which matter I appointed coronell Shenks, whoe hath performed it most notably. He had xv[c] men with him, and in xiiij dayes he hath brought the fort to that perfecion as he feareth not the enemie with all his forces; to morrow I goe to se it. I sent the rest of my forces hether to Newmegyn, as well to divert the prince of Parma from his seige at Grave as to sett this ryver clere and free hereabout from all impediments, as, a few forts being taken, it wilbe. And, if the states had kept promise with me, I had had the fort there or this time, but it will not be many dayes or you will heare of it. I haue bine here these ij dayes, and pervsed all our trenches and skonces our men haue made to anoy the other, and this day haue giuen some new order, I hope, for the speedier getting of this fort. We have taken ij or iij castles and vnhappy places against vs here, whereof one yelded yesterday to myself; [c] hit had not past 35

---

[a] " Called Grauenswest." Briefe Report, sig. B 2.   [b] to, *in MS.*

[c] These places are termed Luytesforte and Berckshoofe in the " Briefe Report," and in the attack of them it is said that Leycester himself ordered " the batteries at some of them, and without respect of trauel or danger," put " his owne hand to the trenches and other workes to be made for the approches." Sig. B 2. The capture of these places cleared the province of Bettowe of the enemy.

men in yt, but it was very stronge and well vitelled, and a very large deepe water about it. They only desired life, which I was willing to yeild them, albeit they abode x shott of such ordinance as we had, which was very simple, for our cannons and good ordinance were not come, neither was this castle the worse for our battery, yet theie yeilded it at length only for life.

I will se our busines here sett in some forwardnes and then write againe. We are lost for lack of pioners; we have not had ij^c pioners all this yere, and, at this present, not j^c, and not decaied by death but many stolen home, and many taken secretly into bands, but I beseech you help vs to v or vj^c pioners. You will say, we maie haue them here; I assure you, not possible, for all such as should be pioners be of these countreys, Gelders, Vtrict, and such soylls of husbandry, theie [a] all are as newtralls, and dwelling out of anie towne takes himself so and pay tribute to both sides, therefore there is not a pioner to be had here. I beseech you remember it, and the states will and shall pay for it. All thinges goeth soe well here as I trust you may shortlie help me home ageyne.

Of our want of moneye I haue sent so often as I am weary. I haue borrowed against we remove hence v^m.^{li} of our merchants, which I will pray you may be answered, as the last was, vppon our paiment there. Well, sir, my encouragment is soe great, as, with her majesties lawfull favor, I desire home, with all my losses. God keepe you for euer. In some hast this xvij. of May.

Your assured freind.

I send her majestie a lettre, and doe send it by the way of Midelborowe.

[a] but theie, *in MS.*

LETTER C.

MR. SECRETARY WALSYNGHAM TO THE EARL OF LEYCESTER.

20TH MAY, 1586. COTTON. MS. GALBA, D. I. FOL. 11. ORIG.

The queen has written to the earl complaining of his acquainting the council of state with the offers made her for a peace, although Walsyngham declares that she commanded him to direct the earl to do so—she will not allow the levy of any more volunteers, it being said that the subjects of this realm complain of so many Englishmen being employed in the defence of others, to the weakening of their own country—Walsyngham will endeavour to procure the earl's recall—the queen gives good ear to the complaints against the treasurer, but will not appoint another—sir Valentine Brown—sir Thomas Shirley—the queen will not send more money until she has an account of the treasure last sent.

My verry good lord, her majestye hathe made me acquaynted with the letter she wrytethe with her owne hande unto your lordship, and where she chargethe your lordship with the acquaynting the cownsell of state there with the overture of peace made unto her by the prince of Parma as a faulte, herin your lordship is wronged: for the fault is myne, yf any were commytted, but, in verry trothe, she gave me commaundment to dyrect you to acquaynt them withall, thowghe nowe she dothe denye yt. I have receyved within thes fewe dayes many of thes harde measures.

Her majestie dothe, also, revoke her resolutyon towching the sendyng over of voluntary men in sooch nomberes as doe nowe goe; she saythe, she was content that a 1000 or 2000 shoold be permytted to goe, but no greater nombers. Sooch as are alreadye levyed shall, notwithstanding, be permytted to passe, but the rest are ordred to be stayed. This chayng as I learne growethe uppon a malytyouse informatyon, that the subiectes of this realme shoold murmore greatly at the imployement of so many pcople of this realme in defence of others, to the weakening of the seyd realme; wheras, contrarywyse, all men of judgement, lookyng into the persons that are imployed, being for the moste parte loose men and having nothing to take to, or into the present dearthe, doe thinke her majestie happye to have so apt an occasyon to imploye them in so necessary a servyce. So lyttle love is carryed to the contynewaunce of this actyon as the weakest argument that may be used wyll suffyce to woorke an hinderaunce to the cause. I wyll, therfor, doe my best indevor to procure your lordships revocatyon.

The thre last letters your lordship sent unto me, by Browne the messenger, I thowght good, for sundrye causes, to shewe them unto her majestye, but espetyally to the end she myght see the yll husbandrye used by the thresorer, and how necessary yt was, both for her proffyt and her servyce, to have another substytuted in his place. I fownde her disposed to geve good eare thereunto, and thereuppon I moved her for the sendyng of sir Valentyn Browne, for that your lordship fownde the audytor nowe imployed there verry weake, but coold not drawe her to any resolutyon. For, fyrst, towching sir Valentyn Browne, she alleaged two impedymentes; the one, that she was necessarily to use his present servyce in Ireland abowt the peoplyng of Monster. The other, that yt woold be a matter of great charg to have two audytors imployed there at one tyme. For the fyrst, yt is trewe that he cannot be well spared, being, as he is, best acquaynted with the plott for the peopling of Monster; towching the charge, I shewed how that the benefyt she shoold reape therby woold verry largely requyt the charge. The audytors here be so softspryted men as I dowbt there wyll not any one be fownde owt emongest them more suffytyent then he that is now imployed. I fynde her majestyes dysposytyon to be sooche, as rather than she wyll entre into an extraordynarye charge of an hundrethe pownd she can be content to be deceyved of 5000 li. I suppose when the thresorer shall be dysplaced your lordship wyll make choyse of sir Thomas Shurley, whoe, I doe assure your lordship, is a most constant affected gentleman unto you, and deservethe an extraordinary good usage at your lordships handes.

This daye the lord-thresorer and I dealt with her majestie for the sendyng over of money, in sooche a proportyon as ther may be a thorrowghe paye made, which we shewed her woold proffyt her at the least thre thowsand pownd; but we coold no waye prevayle, she styll standethe uppon the returne of the accompt of the threasure last sent. Your lordship therfore shall doe well to hasten the sending over of the same. The next threasure that shall be sent over shall be chested under two lockes, as your lordship advysed, to the ende you may be assured to see the imployement thereof.

I doe rejoyce greatly, notwithstanding the dyscowntenancyng of your lordship every waye, that God dothe blesse your care and travayle with most happye successe, which suerly faulethe owt so myche the better for that your lordship hathe cause to ascrybe the same to the goodnes of Almyghtie God, to whos protectyon I commyt your lordship. At the coorte, the xx[th] of Maye, 1586.

Your lordships to command,
Fra: Walsyngham.

Addressed,
To the right honorable my
  verie good lord the earle of Leycester.

LETTER CI.

MR. SECRETARY WALSYNGHAM TO THE EARL OF LEYCESTER.

20TH MAY, 1586.   COTTON MS. GALBA. C. IX. FOL. 241.   ORIG.

Walsyngham has advised the master of Gray to desist from his levies for the Low Countries on account of the uncertainty of Leycester's continuance there—the queen's dangerous policy towards Scotland—difficulty of preserving peace with that country—the queen presumes too much upon her good fortune—distress in Flanders and Brabant.

My verry good lord, fyndinge the uncerteyn coorse helde [here] towchyng thos cuntrye causes, [and] that her majestye dothe rather [wish] to weaken then strengthen your awthorytye there, I [have] dyswaded the master of Graye from his further proceading [in] his preparatyon for thos cuntryes, lettyng him playnly understand howe greatly your servyce is crossed, wherby your lordship shall not be able to perform that good usage, both towards himselve and sooche troopes as he shoold bryng with him, as you desyre, for lacke of cowntenaunce and awthorytye ; [and,] for his better satysfactyon therein, I have sent unto my cosyn Randolphe one of your last letters, by the which your lordship desyreth to be revoked, wherby he may see that ther is no cause whye your lordship shoold incorage him to imbarque himselve in the servyce, seing you mynde yourselve to geve it over. I have desyred sir Philip Sydney to put your lordship in mynde to wryte somme letter of thankes to the master of Graye, and to assure him of your good affectyon towards him.

How hazardowsly her majestye dealethe in causes of Scotland your lordship may perceyve both by Mr. Randolphe and the coppye of the kinges owne letter unto hir majestye. The master of Graye dothe assure me, that she never had so weake a partye in Scotland as she hathe nowe. I fynde yt a verry harde matter to conserve the amytye of that contrye in the coorse now held heare, and what daynger may growe by the losse thereof, a verry mean-wytted man may see. She greatly presumethe [on] fortune, which is but a [very] weake foundatyon to buylde uppon. I woold she dyd buyld and depend uppon God, and then all good men shoold have les cause to feare any chaynge of her former good happ.

The myserye growethe so great in Flaunders and Brabant, as, yf the Dunkerkers might be restrayned, yt woold owt of hande woorke a great chaynge there. I hope the G * *[a] wyll doe more good in one monethe, then the shyppes set owt by her majestye hathe don all this year. Ther is daylye carryed owt of Holland and Zelland both merchandyce and vyctualls to Calles, which dothe greatly offende oure merchauntes here that are restrayned. I wishe to God ther coold be some coorse taken to prevent this mischefe of transportyng of vyctualles. And so I most humbly take my leave. At the corte the xx[th] of Maye, 1586.

Your lordships to commande,

FRA: WALSYNGHAM.

Addressed,

To the right honorable my [very good] lord the earl of Leycester, lord [lieutenant-gene]rall of hir majesties forces in the Low Countryes.

LETTER CII.

THE EARL OF LEYCESTER TO MR. SECRETARY WALSYNGHAM.

23RD MAY, 1586. OUVRY MS. FO. 20. A COPY.

The earl, not having been able to procure the treasurer's accounts of the expenditure of the money transmitted from England, has

---

[a] The word is gone in the original, and it is not easy to guess what it may have been. Walsyngham evidently alludes to the distress occasioned to the enemy, and the provinces in his possession, by the prohibition of the export of provisions thither from the united provinces and from England.

sent him and the auditor over to the lords of the council—various complaints of negligency, insufficiency, and mismanagement against them both.

Mr. secretary, I perceaue there wilbe noe monie sent hether before the accompt be sent over. I haue done what I can to cause the treasorer and auditor to make it vpp. Theie promised me fiue weekes agoe to end it within fiue dayes. This day I called for it, and found them as far as at the first day theie tooke it in hand, soe that I cannot see theie will end it befor Michelmas as theie proceed. I haue, therefore, thought good to send them both over to my lords, and lett them end them there, for in the meane time the souldiers shalbe in great extremitye, for of all the money that last came there was but a moneths pay, save to Brill, Flushing, and, till March, Ostend. The treasorer deliuers bookes one day, and fetcheth them away another day, and till this day noe perfect booke geuen the auditour, as he told the treasorer before me this day; besid, you shall see a badd manner of reconing, and find Mr. Norrys, his nephew, is gotten well aforehand for their paiments, and all the Norryses. Ther is a bad fellow, the vnder-treasorer, one Mr. Norrys fauoreth of all men, whoe is cause of all this; beside the treasorer hath delt coningly with me, which I tooke him with the manner,[a] foysting into my warrant, made for the bandes in her majesties pay, iij or iiij captens at the states pay, and only to make his disbursmentes for the states great, when it will fall out that neither the monie is paid for the one nor for thother; a fowle practice and a lewd. This berer shall tell you of it, and other foule things sett downe into his other accompt, which I wrote to you of then, and desired Mr. Davison should be called to declare yt, whoe was previe to it, and opened it to me, and the auditour also, whoe, if he did not revell [b] it, is worthy to lye by

---

[a] "We commonly use to say, when we find one doing of an unlawful act, that we took him with the maynour or manner." Les termes de la ley, p. 439. edit. 1721.
[b] rebell, *in MS.*

the heeles, for he knew it, and hath it in his booke sett downe. For my parte, if I should remaine here I will noe more deall with him, and doe pray that these reconings be delt substancially in, for it wilbe thought I am the ill husband.

As for such prestes as I haue made warant for, such as I speake of before excepted, I will take order for such as the states must pay, to pay it againe, as to such as capten Read, and sir William Stanley, &c. and yet haue I prested out of my none prest v$^{m\,li}$.[a] amonge both sortes, and surely Mr. Davyson dealinge here so far as he did in these first reconings, and to giue informacion of them before the auditor to me here, did not well, that he did not, at least secretly, acquaint you or my lord-treasorer with it; but, betwene the auditor and the muster-maker, you will easilie find the faults, which some of them be open, and very grossly sett downe, but others you shall haue enough to doe with all. Thus, in hast, I comitt you to the Lord, being much troubled with busines, this 23. of May.

Your assured.

LETTER CIII.

MR. SECRETARY WALSYNGHAM TO THE EARL OF LEYCESTER.

23RD MAY, 1586. COTTON. MS. GALBA, C. IX. FO. 245. ORIG.

Walsyngham believes that the opposition to Leycester proceeds entirely from the queen's own disposition, and is not fomented underhand by ' some great personage'—departure of the Danish ambassador—his master not willing to interfere agaynst Spain or France—the Germans cold.

My verry good lord, sythence I last wrote unto your lordship there is nothing come to my knowledge worthye to be imparted

---

[a] It is " vv$^{m\,li}$" in the copy, which may be a mistake for " xv$^{m\,li}$," but I rather think, from the appearance of the MS. that the first " v " is altogether surplusage.

unto your lordship, and yet, having so convenient a messenger, I woold not suffer him to passe without a fewe lynes. There is no man here dealethe more honorably and faythefully towardes your lordship then this bearers master, and yet, as he tould me secreatly yesternight, he hathe ben informed that there are some that seeke malytyowsely to [persuade] your lordship to conceyve otherwyse of him. But he reposethe that confydence in your sownd conceypt of him as yt dothe not greatly troble him.

I begyn now to put on an opinion that the only thwartes your lordship receyvethe growethe owt of her majestyes owne dysposytyon, whom I doe fynde dayly more and more unapt to imbrase any matter of weyght. And, wheras I dyd by Mr. Barker let your lordship to understande, that I thowght you were crossed under-hand by some great personage, I doe nowe quyte him of yt, and am perswaded that he dealethe honestly in the cause.

The imbassator of Denmarke departythe hence within a daye or two. He hath ben honorably used.[a] I doe not fynde by him that his master is greatly inclyned to doe any thing that may offend Spayne, or to attempt any thing in favor of the king of Navar. By late letters from Palavicino her majestye is advertysed, that thinges goe cowldly forwarde in Germany. By former letters from him we were in better hope. The wyne is so weake this yeare as yt dothe not revyve ther spirytes.

The king of Navar is drawen towardes Rochell. And so I most humbly take my leave. At the coorte, the xxiijth of Maye, 1586.

Your lordships to commaund,
FRA: WALSYNGHAM.

---

[a] " The said Ramelius, during the time of his tariance, had attendance doone him conueuient for his person, both by water and land: the queenes maiesties barges and seruants imploied about him to and from London, the court then being at Greenewich; whither alwaies when he came, the nobilitie of England failed in no point of courtesie that might be shewed. Which he seemed (as he could no lesse) verie acceptablie to take." Holinshed, iv. 894.

LETTER CIV.

THE EARL OF LEYCESTER TO MR. SECRETARY WALSYNGHAM.

25TH MAY, 1586. OUVRY MS. FO. 24. A COPY.

Leycester having come to Arnheim to meet sir Thomas Heneage, count Hohenlohe had proceeded to attack Berckshoofe, the garrison of which had desired to capitulate upon conditions which the earl refused—tidings just received of a furious assault upon Grave, in which the Spaniards had been repulsed with great loss.

Having written to hir majestie of our doings before Newmegyn, and that I had giuen order to the count of Hollock, my lieutenant, to goe to with the canon to Berkshoofe, nerer to this towne then the other fort was, for that I came myself hether vppon sir Thomas Henneage letters to meet him here at Arnham, I thinke it not good to trouble her again with the successe of the rest, but to desire you to lett her majestie knowe, that, after theie had suffered 8 or 10 shott of the cannon, they offered parley, which the [a] count sent to me, and I did retorne him word agein, that I would haue no condicion at all yeilded, for that theie did suffer the cannon, but either simply to yeild or ells [b] to prosecute the battery.

Herevppon I haue receaued word again, theie simplie yeilded, either to be hanged or to be saved, as I will. I doubt some must hange, for example. I heard, also, even now, that the enemie attempted Grave [on] Monday with all furie, from midnight till 8 a clock yesterday morning, beginning both their battery with such an assayly as hath not bine heard of, noe breach being made, but, at the instance of the shott of xv canons, twice or thrice attempted a kind of assault withall, with all the shott he had; at which attempt he was not onlie repulsed, but the messinger reportith,

---

[a] theie, *in MS.*   [b] ell, *in MS.*

that he lost v or vj^c men at it, which cannot be soe few, being so longe a fight, and in such furie, and to continew fiue howres after day, and I am perswaded I shall heare of a farr greater losse to him.

The Albanese I wrote of wilbe with me within ij or three dayes with the company, &c.

Thus, hoping you will help me hence, and that God will send noe worse successe to this cause hereafter; meaning, whilst I doe stay, to loose noe opportunity, I comitt you to the Lord, in much hast, this xxvth of May.

Your assured freind.

LETTER CV.

MR. SECRETARY WALSYNGHAM TO THE EARL OF LEYCESTER.

26TH MAY, 1586. COTTON. MS. GALBA, C. IX. FOL. 251. ORIG.

Walsyngham sends the earl letters lately received from the master of Gray—he has answered them advising the master to desist from his levies on account of the queen's change of mind in reference to Leycester's authority—Burghley and Walsyngham had urged upon the queen the necessity of the earl's governorship, with a view to the master of Gray's employment, but in vain.

My verry good lord, I send your lordship her enclosed such letters as I have lately receavid from the master of Gray. In aunswer wherof, fynding hir majesty so couldly disposed still towardes that action, I have thought good to acquaint him directly with the change of her majesties resolution towching the continuaunce of your authoritye, being a matter not secreat but oppen and common, which I do tell him proceadeth thorough the practise of ill instrumentes here, that favour the Spanish proceedinges, and seeke to crosse your lordship, letting him withall understand, that your authoritye be[ing] by such meanes so weakened as you shall not nowe be hable to yeld him that satisfaction and good enterteynement for himself and his company that aperteyne, you have just cause not to encourage him to come over to the service, least, yf he should fynd any want, yt [might] geve him occasion to blame your lordship, and breede in his company a mislyke of him that had brought them to so [bad] a bargayn. This aunswir in effect I have made to the master, to whom my lord thresurer hath also written to lyke purpose. His lordship and I have dealt earnestly with her majesty about the matter of the masters imployement, letting her understand how necessary yt weare that hould weare taken of his offer, in respect of thimbarking of the king his master into the action, which, we tould hir majesty, could not be don, unles yt might pleas hir to mayntayne your lordships authoritye in the title of governement geven you there, but she conceaveth still that the matter might well enough be performid by vertue of your authority of generall only. And so I humbly take my leave of your lordship. At Grenwich, the xxvjth of May, 1586.

Your lordships to commaund,
Fra: Walsyngham.

LETTER CVI.

THE EARL OF LEYCESTER TO MR. SECRETARY WALSYNGHAM.

29th May, 1586. Ouvry MS. fol. 21 b. a copy.

The bearer, Mr. Darcy, offers to levy 500 horse if the queen will give him some little pecuniary help—the queen's number of cavalry stipulated to be furnished by the treaty is not complete—inconveniences resulting therefrom—effects of the treating for peace upon the enemy—queen's mislike of the earl's communicat-

ing thereon with the council of the states—the earl regrets that they know what they know, and he too.

Mr. secretary, this gentleman, Mr. Darcy, is, as you wrote, verie willing to serve, and doth offer to bring, within vj weeks, c light horse, whereof we haue great need; he doth only desire to haue some helpe of monie, yf but a parte, not the half of the allowance; and her majesty hath not performed her nombers of 1000 horse yet, my onlie vj^c horsse and Mr. Norris is all we haue. Two or iij gentlemen here haue made vpp, some xx some xxx, but not able to rayse a band, and, till her majesties band be performed, I cannot prese these men to levye anie of our nacion, which theie would willinglie doe but theie call dayly for her majesties band to be full, which I can doe noe more but advertise. But I see the goodnes and offers of God is despised, what hope then is to be had? Well, I recommend this gentleman vnto you. If he may be releeued with a little,[a] and assured promise of the rest, I knowe he will goe thorow with his offer. I can say noe more but your dealing there hath made the enemy prowd, and giues out manie threatenings to this countrey, as though theie shall shortly be left, and turnd to thir handling, which God defend! Thus, praying to God to direct her majestie with his spiritt of wisdom, I take leaue, lettinge you knowe, for the matter her majestie wrote in mislike, to imparte to these councellors the dealinge for peace, I am sorry theie know that they doe knowe, and I both; I trust it is more then her majesty knoweth, or ells the case is harder with you then I tooke it. In some hast, this xxix. of May.

Your assured poore frend.

[a] letter, *in MS.*

LETTER CVII.

THE EARL OE LEYCESTER TO MR. SECRETARY WALSYNGHAM.

31st may, 1586. ouvry ms. fol. 22. a copy.

Loss of Grave by surrender, after a battery of three hours and a feigned assault—however desirous to come home, the earl will never return without satisfaction for this villainous treachery—pioneers wanted—the soldiers are ragged and torn, but it is a folly to ask for money.

Good Mr. secretary, I will pray you give creditt to this gentleman for all matters here; he knoweth them better then I. He hath bine as carefull a man as euer I saw to satisfie her majestie, and surely he hath exceedlye well behaued himself here.

I trust the traiterous losse of Grave [a] shall not gether anie ill opinion of vs here; for my parte I haue a clere conscience. I haue iij times bine only the help and releif of it, beside my none coming in person now to giue all assistance to it. The circumstance sir Thomas Heneage can tell you as much as I; but, to be shorte, being the best fortified place thorowlye of all theis pro-

---

[a] The loss of Grave came like a thunderbolt upon the defenders of the Low Countries, whose career, from the time of Leycester's arrival up to that moment, had been one of uninterrupted success. It is clear that the prince of Parma out-generaled them. Whilst Leycester, Hohenlohe, and Schenck were scattered about the country, each occupied upon a separate object of comparatively trifling importance, the prince suddenly drew his forces together and came down upon Grave with an overwhelming power. The soldiers, animated by the presence of their general, and the example of his personal courage, attacked with a fury which entirely confounded the young and inexperienced Hemart. There can be little doubt that the prince would have taken the place at whatever sacrifice, but Hemart's courage failed him before the moment of extremity arrived, and, forgetting the boastful letters which he had written to Leycester, up to that very day, in a sudden fit of despair he offered terms of surrender, which the prince was delighted to accept. See Briefe Report, sig. B 2. Strada, vol. ii. lib. vii.

vinces, none like it, being full-manned, vitelled, and stored with all manner of artillery and municion, having but iij howres battery layd to it, and a shew of an assalt vppon Thursdaie last in the morning, gaue it vpp at afternoone. What hath corrupted them there I know not, but what hath altered nombers here lett this gentleman vppon his deuty and fidelitye declare. I will not complayne anie further, and yet will I neuer departe hence till, by the goodnes of God, I be satisfied some way for this villaines trechery done, how desirous soeuer I am to come home. But of anie cause that waie lett me referre you, also, to this honest gentleman, not for parciallity I desire at his hands, but I see he is a man of conscience, and loues her majestie truelie and most faithfullie. God send neuer generall out of the realme soe little comfort as I haue had all this whole time of my being here, till within theis iiij dayes. What harme it doth me it is not to be cared for, but what is donn to the cause is already easilie found. I wrote most earnestlie to you for some pioners. Once againe I beseech you, lett vs haue either 1000 or 600. All charges shalbe allowed here, and with all the hast that maie be, and with Mr. Rawleys 100 myners,[b] whoe writes to me are ready to come.

Hit is follie to speake for moneie, though our men be ragged and torne, and like rogues; pitty to see them. Specially those of hir majesties pay be wors. I haue sent you all our officers for reconinge, and you knowe our care. Would God some of you were heare to see it, then would you speedily help vs. Thus, with my heartie commendacions, I bidd you farr well. In hast, this last of May.

    Your assured freind.

[a] myoners, *in MS.*

LETTER CVIII.

MR. SECRETARY WALSYNGHAM TO THE EARL OF LEYCESTER.
3RD JUNE, 1586. COTTON. MS. GALBA, C. IX. FOL. 254. ORIG.[a]

Walsyngham apprises the earl that it is the purpose of the prince of Parma to attack Sluys—refers to a communication from sir William Pelham as to the importance of the sea-port towns.

My verry good [lord, I think] good by the opportunyte of this gentleman to let your [lordship] understande, that I am advartysed that the prince of Parma is determyned to attempt somewhat agaynst Sluse, which maketh me to doubt that he hathe some intellygence within that towne. He meanethe to commit the executyon of the matter unto the count of Egmonde,[b] governor of Flaunders, and unto La Mota,[c] in whom [he] reposethe his chefest trust. I am greatly affrayde, unless ther shall be some Englishmen placed there, that that towne wyll be lost. By [sir] William Pelham your [lordship] shall understande howe greatly yt importethe her majestye to kepe the porte townes owt [of] the Spaniards handes. And so I most humbly take my leave. At the Barnealmes, 3. June, 1586.

Your lordships to command,
FRA: WALSYNGHAM.

This gentleman hathe verry well acquited sooche favor as yt hathe pleased your lordship to shewe him. He was verry desyrowse to have levyed a bande of footemen, but could not performe yt for lacke of meanes.

[a] This letter is not mentioned in the catalogue of the Cottonian MSS.

[b] Son of Philip count of Egmont, whose execution in 1568 was one of the many scandalous atrocities perpetrated by the duke of Alva. The son here mentioned was not restrained by his father's fate from taking the side of the Spaniards. In 1580 he was taken prisoner by the Dutch, who offered him, together with the baron de Selles, in exchange for La Noue, but Philip declined to accede to the exchange until 1585. During his imprisonment Egmont suffered under a melancholy which affected his reason, but was restored to health by the affectionate attention of a beloved sister who was permitted to share his confinement.

[c] " Valentinus Pardiæus Mottæ dominus," Strada, vol. ii. lib. i. La Motte was actively and successfully engaged in the siege of Sluys which took place in 1587.

LETTER CIX.

THE EARL OF LEYCESTER TO MR. SECRETARY WALSYNGHAM.

6TH JUNE, 1586.   OUVRY MS. FOL. 22 b.   A COPY.

Some captains as much to blame for the surrender of Grave as baron Hemart—effect of the surrender upon the neighbouring towns— little damage done by the Spaniards before the surrender—presumptions of treachery against the governor—harm done by the agents employed by the queen to treat for peace—Davy Hamilton, late a jesuit, gone into England on some secret matter—the earl is set by his friends in England " in the forlorn hope."

Sir, I haue written out myne eies already, but this berer, your old servant, I must needs write by, whoe hath delt honestly and painfully, having bin at Antwerp and Bruxells, and learnid manie thinges whereof he will informe you; and retorne him againe, I pray you, with speed.

Of the lewd villaines giving vpp of Grave, with all the declaracions of the souldiers and some captens against him, finding some captens as deepe as himself in fault, and shall pay with him.[a]

This towne[b] was terrible at the first, for that[c] the villainous and traiterous manner of giuing it vpp did amaze many other weaker places, for theie knew Grave so fortified, and soe stronge, as noe man doubted but that the prince should take the greatest foyle in the world there; and seing it so sone taken, with a shew of only force, could not blame weaker places to feare; but, in all troth, there was neither sufficient breach made for anie assault,

---

[a] This sentence is printed as it stands in the MS. The meaning seems to be, that finding, upon investigation of the circumstances of the surrender of Grave, that some captains were equally in fault with the governor, the earl determined that they should suffer with him.

[b] Bomell, whither Leycester repaired after the surrender of Grave. Briefe Report, sig. B 2.

[c] that by the, *in MS.*

nor anie assault geuen, but a more shewe made onlie to discouer the brech, where there was the capten kild that gaue the attempt, and a souldier seeing him well-apparrelled lying in the ditch, went out, downe the brech, to spoile him, which he did, and the place was soe stepe that the rest within were fayne to help him vpp with their pikes, and to drawe him by the hand with much adoe in againe; yet the governor would needes render it. Noe cause in the earth for women to have left it! And one of the captens hath sett it downe, and another souldier also, that, vppon their liues, the battery did them soe little hurt as that place of the towne was as stronge as any other parte of it when they lett the enemye in. And whatsoeuer bruts are spread, there cam none in at [a] the brech but such as the gouernor caused to be helpt vpp, some with ladders and some with pikes, and that the prince and others there captens came in at the gate, which did argue there was noe brech saltable or passable, for if it had bine, they would for glorye sake, and for the more feare to others, haue entred all there. And one that came thence this last night doth assure me, the [b] Spaniards hath made noe alteracion at all at that place, and is as defensible as anie other parte not at all touched.

One presumption against the gouernor of some trechery in him is this, that a Spanish capten, one Martino, was taken in October last, and, being a prisoner in Grave, he practised with a capten Wallen there, and did corrupt him, and some of his officers. The matter was discouered as I wrote longe since to you, by a little tickett written by count Manxfyeld to a clarke of the count Hollockes band, which was brought to my hands, and did aduertise both Hemert, the governor of Grave, of it, as also apprehended the clark, whereuppon execution was done of many there, and of the clarke here. This Spaniard, Martino, notwithstanding, found such favor after with Hemert as he gaue him libertie, as is told me now, and made him goe to feasts with him, and to go frelie

---

[a] all, *in MS.*   [b] they, *in MS.*

round about the towne. And, without either making me previe, or the count Hollock, a litle before the prince came before the towne, he licenced the Spaniard to goe his waie vppon hostage, which was but a collor. This matter he answereth very slenderly, as he doth all the rest,[a] but this doth argue some practice, or dealing, with the prince, deliuering him soe lately before, and now to giue vpp the towne so suddenlye, in the worst manner, from vs, that could be; for I had rather farr, that he had manifestly traterously geuen it vpp, and sett open the gates, then to doe it with a shewe of such terror to these people as he did it; but notwithstanding, albeit at the first it amazed manie, it is now well knowen, and men resolved, as appears by many good letters I have alreadye receaued from manie townes, crying for justice against the governor and captens, and promisinge to liue and dye in defence still of this cause. Only the trouble and greif is, the feare of her majesties leaveing them, wherein the enemy hath fully playd his parte, in practisinge with many townes to make them knowe her majestie will not maintaine their cause, that she is sorry for that she hath don.

Divers particularities I haue written to Atye,[b] to whome I praie you call [for] them, which I assure you be most trewe, beside that your man Charles can tell you. Among others this late coming into Antwerpe of August, Grafino and Andreas de Lope, who make noe secret talke of it, but doe imparte to the merchants flatly, that the peace betweene her majestie and [the] king is agreed on. Graffyn is at the campe with the prince, having ij English geldings to present him, and a brace of greyhounds. These newes being certen, as theie be, for I haue them brought me also by an Englishman from thence purposely, you maie imagine what care

---

[a] After the surrender of Grave, Hemart, the governor, repaired to Bomell, where he was immediately placed under arrest and conveyed to Utrecht for trial. Briefe Report, sig. B 2.

[b] Atye, who was one of Leycester's secretaries, was sent to England about this time. See a letter of lord Burghley's dated 20th June 1586 and printed hereafter.

it will cast these people in; specially hit will appere what an alienacion it will worke in the wiser and higher sort here, perhapps cause you haue but a badd peace, and that is it the prince seeks to make with you, and perhaps some care not much for, soe it beare the name of a peace. Well, I am noe fitt councellor!

Sir, you shall also vnderstand, that this merchant brought me worde, both from a zelous man in Antwerpe, and from Pigott, that there is one Dauy Hammilton gon into England, latelie a Jesuit, a mischeiuous fellow, in the company of an Englishman, and doth goe like a merchant, a square thicke fellow, with a redd beard; he is imployed by Cosmo, the princes cheife secretary, and being knowen to be soe ill a man, makes them carefull to haue advertised that serch be made for him, for he hath some great mater in hand.

For myself, I will write noe more. I thinke you all mene me a forlorne man, as you sett me in the forlorne hope. Gods will be done, and to his great mercy I commend you, and vs all. In much hast, this 6th of June.

Your assured freind.

LETTER CX.

THE EARL OF LEYCESTER TO MR. SECRETARY WALSYNGHAM.

7TH JUNE, 1586. OUVRY MS. FOL. 24 b. A COPY.

Complaints of the conduct of the agents for treating of a peace—consequences of the loss of Grave—villainy of Paul Buys—preparations for further levies—master of Gray.

This dealing vnderhand, and yet most openlie, for peace, doth marr all; yt dishonoreth her majestie, hit overthroweth all here. Yt is to much to appoint such instruments as must lay so open all our councels; for, vppon my dutie to her majestie, the doings for this peace is as particulerlie knowen here, as with them that hath the managing thereof.

This matter of Grave was fearfull at the first, onlie by the manner of it, that it appeared the enemy had with his great force and violent batteryes gotten it, which being trew, all the townes-gates in this countrey might be sett open to him, for there is noe more such places for strength. But theie found it otherwise, that very trechery and villanie hath betrayd it and delivered it. There is noe way to remedye this but her majesties countenance towards this countrey, and some speciall wise person to be sent, with all possible speed, hether, to comfort them, wherein you shall see better successe then you can imagin. Yf that be not done, then all is lost, and xx millions will never bringe such a countrey wholie at her majesties devocion agayne.

Here be some very villaines, among whom Paul Buis [a] is the greatest and most traytor to his countrey, but to her majestie, and to me, her minister, a most vnthankfull man. Yf her majestie meane to stand with this cause I will warrant him hanged, and one or two of his fellowes, but you must not tell your shirt of this yet.

Lett her majestie never feare that anie further charge shalbe cast vppon [her], than she hath contracted, and, if I doe not see all our English paid by these men, and as manie other strangers as I shall entertaine, lett her majestie both disauow me and banish me.

And, now, for manie respects I like to haue the master [of] Gray come over; from whome, as God will, I haue this day receauved a messinger of purpose, from him, of the continuance of his old desire. And I meane to send over to you verie shortlie money to imprest him. I haue, also, given comission to levye ij$^\text{M}$ royters, and hartilie angry that I had not the kinge of Denmarks offer takin, and yet, as I see practises in hand, it falleth out well

---

[a] Paul Buys was one of the commissioners deputed by the united provinces in 1585 to supplicate the assistance of Elizabeth. He was the deputy for the state of Utrecht, and is described in the instrument of authorization as a doctor of laws. Fœd. xv. 793.

enough otherwise.[a]   And when I haue the supply of the Scotts, with the ij^M royters, and our English master sir William Stanley, which aboue all other I desire, I doubt not, if her majestie leaue vs not, but to haue all things better then ever it was. Though I myself am discouraged, yet the cause doth encourage me, knowinge it to be not onlie for the service of God, but for my prince and countrey. And feare you not, if I doe bringe all these states about to better devotion, and good dewtye to, then ever theie were yet, lett her majestie thinke she hath bredd me to the least purpose that euer she did anie man, and I wilbe ashamed of my soe longe bringing vpp yf I doe her not this service I speake of.

The master [of] Gray wilbe readye to passe his men in xx days. I will not lay out a peny of her majesties to him, nor anie man; lett her onlie giue present stout countenance to [the] cause, and send with all speed a man of wisdome and creditt to deall with these men, if what she will haue be not done, lett it light vppon me. But, my masters, your instruments must a litle be touched, for theie haue deeply touched her majesties honor, and worthy to be hanged though theie were instruments appointed for such a matter, for this is a worse battery a good deall then that at Grave, and will peirce deep, and make another manner of brech, how light soeuer you make at home of it. Now is the time, if it be not almost to late.

I pray you lett me heare from you by Coks. I will send more. Use this as it maie doe good, for God doth know, I deale simply as the cause provoketh, and litle doe I looke vppon my none case; to God I remitt that.   In hast, this 7th of June.

Your assured.

I pray you be good to this your old servant; he hath spent well xv xx[b] in hazard for this service.

[a] Otherwise out, *in MS.*

[b] A word in the MS. which is illegible. The copyist did not understand what he was copying, and, as in many similar instances, made a very poor attempt to represent it in fac-simile.

LETTER CXI.

LORD BURGHLEY TO THE EARL OF LEYCESTER.

8TH JUNE, 1586. COTTON MS. GALBA, C. IX. FOL. 256. ORIG.

The queen disposed to allow greatly of the earl's service, although she had been " sowre"—confusion in the treasurer's accounts—treaty with the merchant-adventurers to pay money to the earl in the Low Countries so as to save the expence and risk of carriage—the earl is advised to establish the rates at which English money shall pass—and is apprised that the lords of the council, of the want of whose countenance he complains, have more to say in their defence than is convenient, as it would remove the fault from them to (as is insinuated) the queen—the earl is advised now the queen is pleased to turn his griefs into comfort, and to endeavour to abridge her charges—complaint of the merchants respecting the interference of the Dutch in their traffic with Emden—lease to the earl of the fines upon alienations objected to by the queen, with Burghley's reply.

My very good lord, the soddayn comming to me this afternoone of ser Nicholas Gorge, with declaration of hir majesties meaning to send hym with spede to your lordship, forceth me to scrible a a few lynes, though I have cause to wryte very manny. What hir majesty wryteth I know not, but I hope very comfortably, for so I lately found hir majesty disposed to allow greatly of your service, howsoever she had bene in manny thinges sowre, if I may so term it. At this presence, uppon the comming of the tresorer and the auditor, hir majesty hath shewed some mislykyng of hir charges ther, and evill content to heare how more than nedefull it is to send monny thyther. As yet we cannot by any accompt fynd what is dew, ether now or till any tyme past, though in apparance for the footemen the paye is full till the xj. of Aprill, but how farr the horsemen ar behynd we cannot conjectur, for lack of any certenty at what tym ther pay begann, and the mo dowtes ar therin, because it is not known how the rest besyde your lordships own nombres, did enter; but of these thynges, and manny more, Mr. Aty is partly informed, and shall be of manny mo.

But now at this present, by hir majesties commandment, I am treatyng with the merchantes-adventurors, to make payement of a mass of monny ther, and to receave the lyk quantite here, therby to avoyd the carriadg of tresor in monny out of the realm, and yesterday I found them redyar than this daye, uppon the news by them receaved of the loss of Grave. Besyde this, I fynd it very hard to mak any bargayn with them, except the certenty of the valews of our monnyes and of the currant monnyes ther might be knowen and stablesshed certenly, and therin, truly, my lord, your lordship shall do an honorable act to publish a certenty in those countreys, wherin it is sayd ther is great abuse, not only to the monnyes of England, but of manny other countreys.

To be short in this poynt, my lord, I fynd, that, if our aungell might be rated at 16^s. 8^d., and our shyllyng at xx^d., the eschang wold be at $xxxiij^s$. $iiij^d$. Flemmish for our pownd, and in very truth this is the trew vallew of our monnyes and no more, havyng respect that the floryn or gildern ther is currant but for ij^s., and, if your lordship shall stablish this matter for our monnyes, I dout not but our merchantes shall be brought to mak over monthly v^m. sterlyng, wherby both transportation of our monnyes shall be stayd, and the chardges of carriadg, both by land and sea, shall be saved.

This daye I perceave your lordship hath procured from our merchantes v^m., wherof I am glad, and I wish it had bene x^m., and, though the v^m. be not payable befor the end of this month, yet, my lord, I hope to have warrant to paye it to our merchantes by Fryday next.

Your lordship hath no few causes of greff, as partly appeareth by your lordships late letters sent by Mr. Barber to Mr. vichamberlen, Mr. secretary, and myself, and, in truth, I cannot blame your lordship, ether in thynkyng or wrytyng hardly of your state, considering the small comfort from hence, notwithstandyng your good desertes ther, and the good successes of your service ther; but yet, my good lord, we here have more to saye in our defence and purgation than is convenient for us to say truly, by removyng the fault from ourselves, and so I hope your lordships own ministers here can declare and express unto your lordship, for, otherwise, truly, for my own part, if I war not cleare of all fault, I might lyve with a conscience tormented. Wherfor, my good lord, howsoever your lordship feleth cause of much greff, yet condemn not your frendes here, that ar not hable to remedy such accidentes as ar out of ther power. Good my lord, now that hir majesty is disposed to allow of your honorable servyces, torn your greves into comfort, and, in on word, ther is no way so redy to contynew hir majesties good lykyng therof as to help to abridg hir extraordinary chardges, the natur wherof, truly, doth make here gret changes with hir majesty.

I will leave now this humor, and end with the other matter of our merchantes. They complayn grevoossly of the Hollanders shippes of war, that kepeth the ryver of Embden in such sort as they can have no trade to Embden, the lett wherof empeacheth ther trade so as they are less [a] hable to help you with monny; and, truly, my lord, if yow can help that, and by placard stablish the rates of our monnyes ther, yow shall not want ther help with monnyes from hence, the carryeng wherof thyther, is here very evill spoken of, and gretly mislyked of hir majesty, and, as it is here comenly reported, by the over-vallewyng of our gold ther, it is stollen over thyther, and partly chested up ther, or molten and converted into bass gold, and of this here is very lowd speche by persons malcontent.

Mr. Dudley can wryte to your lordship in what case your lord-

[a] so as ther less, *in MS.*

ships leass is for the matter of the alienations and fynes for wryttes of covenant. Hir majesty hath bene by some lewd busy persons very hardly informed of the great gayn made therof, which being by me affirmed to be untrew, she answereth, that your servantes hath gayned more than your lordship, and I have answered, that, in truth, the principall dealer therin, which is Mr. Thomas Dudley, is of that honesty that I durst shewe for hym that he gayneth nothyng wherof your lordship may [not] allweise be prive.

To end; my lord, I pray your lordship to advertise hir majesty, as soone as yow may, what yow thynk of the mocion that my sonn hath made for the chang of his chardges of Brill for Harlyngham, for, uppon that answer made, he will depart hence within 3 dayes. And so I take my leave, meaning to wryte of manny mo thynges hereafter. 8. Junii, 1586.

Your lordships at command,
W. BURGHLEY.

LETTER CXII.

LORD BURGHLEY TO THE EARL OF LEYCESTER.

10TH JUNE, 1586. COTTON. MS. GALBA, C. IX. FOL. 260. ORIG.

Some English merchants have complained to lord Burghley of certain silver coins stamped at Amsterdam in imitation of the queen's silver testern, but which, not being of the value of 12 pence, will occasion loss to English persons taking it—lord Burghley requests the earl to rectify this fraud.

My good lord, after that I had inclosed my letters herwith sent, ther cam to me some of our marchantes shewyng to me certen coynes of silver stamped at Amsterdam, alltogither in form answerable to hir majestyes testern of silver, both for hir majestyes person, and hir armes, only it had a privet mark by the mynt-master of a litle splayd egle. It is thought that this kynd of coyne shall be a grete fraude to our English people, who receavyng it for xij^d. sterlyng, shall lose therby if they send it into England, or els the subjectes of England receavyng the same in pay here, shall also suffer detriment. I thynk your lordship shall do very honorably to look into these indignytes, for, in very truth, this realme hath hertofor suffred gret losses by the lyk imitation of our coynes, embassyng the same in substance, and yet gyvyng a resemblance such as may a long tyme deceave vulgar people.[a] I wish therfor that your lordship shuld, in this time of your government ther, to cause some regard to be had.

Mr. secretary hath promised to send for Palmer to come over to your lordship, and I movyng hym within these 3 dayes, he semed very loth to take the jorney, but he sayd, that he cold instruct Mr. Aty as perfectly to the purpooss [b] as hymself shuld do if he cam. How Mr. Aty shall understand the same I know not. From my house in Westminster, the 10. of June, 1586.

Your lordships most assured,
W. BURGHLEY.

Addressed,
To the right honorable, and my verie good lord, the erle of Leicester, lieutenant-generall of hir majesties forces in the Lowe Cuntries.

LETTER CXIII.

THE EARL OF LEYCESTER TO MR. SECRETARY WALSYNGHAM.

10TH JUNE, 1586. OUVRY MS. FO. 25 b. A COPY.

Mr. John Norris favourably mentioned—details of the treasurer's

[a] Lord Leycester has written against this passage in the margin of the letter, "M^d. that I wrote for Palmer of the mint and had no answer."
[b] Lord Leycester has written against this passage, "not possible."

alleged misconduct—the earl wishes to have the rest of the money agreed by the queen to be advanced for the year paid at once—proceedings against Hemert—great complaints against sir John Norris—he is " right the late earl of Sussex sonne"—Norris's anxiety to save Hemert, and the reasons he assigned—the earl entreats that if he is to remain Norris may be recalled—would have him sent to Ireland—examination and escape of Hemert's " woman"—growth of a general selfishness—the earl has agreed with the master of Gray for two or three thousand men, and is levying all the cavalry he can—" if we have force we will have money"—intrigues of Paul Buys—" his head shall pay, perhaps, for it"—the earl requests the queen to countenance him by sending " a sufficient man . . . with favourable words"—other persons to be sent over—the people begin to take heart again notwithstanding the plotting of Paul Buys—earnest appeal to Walsyngham to procure the recal of Norris.

I pray you breake or burne this.

I thinke Mr. John Norris will doe service here. He is best acquainted with all the parts of this countrey that I knowe anie man. He tooke some vnkindnes, but all is well now, and I doe find him willing to doe all service.

I would I had geuen you 1000^{li} that you had not tied me to the choyce of this tresorer; you and I both shalbe sorry for it, specially for some respects. I see there wilbe noe assurance to keep money from disbursinge. Mr. Da:[a] shall tell you, or can tell you, more. I dare not advise to haue the treasure committed to anie of his, no, not himself. I can assure you, of the former money deliuered, all was payd or I came, longe. Many souldiers vnpaid, the mony laid out, noe defalkacions at all brought in, nor like to come, that I see. The money I brought was fayne to pay of that the other should haue done; a good deall. Yf anie cer-

---

[a] Either Mr. Dawtrye, see p. 237, or Mr. Darcy, see p. 283.

tificate be made to my lord-tresorer, or yourself, I am not privye to it; noe more is the auditor. There is noe allowance demanded one way, but paiment is made, and, if great chance had not bine, ij^m ^{li}. had bine payd also, without either my warrant or knowledge, for levying a horse-band, which you knowe was not to be allowed out of this monie, yet, but for me, had it bine; vppon a bare word and surmise, it had bine deliuered. I assure you the dealing [is] so great [b] and disorderlye for her majesties comoditie and service, as I haue vtter mislikinge, and, if you send monye hereafter, either make it by exchange, or send it in siluer and coine, expressly the soldier to be paid therwith, whatsoeuer sophisticall declaracion may be made, except her majesties gaine be marvellous great. I pray you let no man perswade you to keepe from the poore souldier his gaine, which is this, he shall for his English viij^d in silver haue more meate, and every thinge ells, then for x pennyworth of this coine. The treasorer saith, he must make profitt for her majestie of the gold; of the siluer, he, or his deputie, hath it. Truely the dishonor is great to be laid to her majestie, for to get, in vij or 8000^{li}, 4 or 500^{li}. If all her monie had bine turnid into the great dowble rose-nobles, the gaine had bine great indeed to her majestie, and some quantitie of siluer withall would doe well, but your angell gets noe gaine here, nor our siluer to be exchanged here, to her majestie, then were it pittye that the siluer, and the angell, should not be paid to the poore souldier. For his naughty monie he receaues, he can haue but naughty and dere ware for it. Beside here is a new exaction vsed vppon the souldier, he payeth the c penny, which, though it seeme little, ys ij^M marke a yere to the treasorer; but I do not thinke you meane anie new exactions vppon the souldier. What with that, and the paying for their armour, although the countrey hath paid in England for them, theie haue paid manie a bodie into the grave for hunger and cold, and yet her majestie hath not a pennie answered. Judge you, then, what dealinge there is. I pray you appoint a substanciall

[a] Perhaps it was *gross* in the original. It is *great* in our MS.

discreet person to bringe the moneie, and to take note here of the states of our paiments. The auditor here is an honest true man I suppose. He told me, that the c peny of euery souldier, with the gaine of the siluer and monie as he deliuereth it, beside her majesties dew, comes to more then all my rents of land in England, a good deale; but his honest gaines I am not against, but his careles paiments, of which, if I should complayne, he were vndone. But I haue spoken enough, and yet helpes not, nor anie help wilbe. He presumes so much of freindshipp, and soe ready to pleasure his freinds, trusting withall to the coming of his deputye, which will deceaue him. I pray you consider of this, and to move [a] Mr. Da. to tell you what he knowes of this matter.

If you help vs now with the rest of the monie, or at lest with 50,000^{li}, her majestie shall not be called vpon for so manie monethes againe, and it will stand vs here in a c$^{M\,li}$ at another time, and I will deliuer her majestie at the end of this yere 30,000^{li} into her cofers, if not 40,000,[b] soe she shall saue so much of her 120,000^{li}; and, if these warrs shall continue anie longer then a yere, as I hope theie will not, her majestie shall not be charged with anie more, and yet, perhaps, deliuer her as much against the next yere.

Since my other letter by your man Charles the matter of Hemert was proceeded in; and this was the course, by the advice of all men. The count Hollock, being my lieutenent, was chief in comission, and other the next best offycers of the feild, besides all the collonells, were called also to it. And, albeit both he and others seemed the most vehement in the world before to haue iustice done vppon him, yet, when it came in triall, there was as many cavillacions found as could be, and the count himself wrought as farr as the best to delay the iustice, but, as I was and am credibly informed, none hath secretly more wrought it then sir John Norris, who, in all troth, because I would

[a] The word in the original which is here printed "to move," is very doubtful. It looks like "comerce."
[b] 14,000*l*. in the MS.

not like of his vncles[a] doings and his, and haue bine bitter to him in these matters, doth not farther at all my service, na, I will not now tell you how it hath bine, and is, hindred onlie by him. I assure you, vppon my fidelitie, I cannot heare that he can brooke either capten, gentleman, or souldier, that came over with me. Mutines haue bine offered by some vnder him, and the fowlest spoyles that may be, and yet, except I should devide our army and companies, I see noe helpe, vnlesse I should be quite deliuered of him. His brother Edward [ys] as ill as he, but John ys right the late earle of Sussex[b] sonne; he will soe dissemble, so croch, and soe cunninglie cary his doings, as noe man living would imagine that there were half the malice or vendicatiue mind that doth plainely his deeds prove to be. And, for this matter of Hemert, knowing that by the examinacion of some captens, yea, of some that sett their hands to Hemerts agrement, of divers lieutenents, and of all the souldiers almost, hit fell out flatly that there was noe cause in the earth why he should giue vpp the towne, as the proofes shall all be brought to you, but both traiterouslie and villainously deliuered it, yet Mr. Norris soe cuningly carieth himself, one while in respect of the gentlemans blood, fearing offence that way to the people, which is very ridiculous, and another while, which is lesse honest, but to his freinds it is very trew and good proofe for it, he shames not to say, he loued his aunt, and for her sake he will neuer sett his hand to the death of soe nere a man of hir blood.

Beside this, I must deall plainly with you, since the losse of Grave, I protest before God, he is as coye and as straunge to giue anie councell, or anie advice, as if he were a mere stranger to

[a] The treasurer was uncle to sir John Norris. See page 277.

[b] This and a similar passage at p. 264 are singular outbreaks of the old hatred between Leycester and Sussex. The latter nobleman died just three years before the date of this letter; but it is evident that his rival still retained that enmity towards him and his which prompted Sussex upon his death-bed to warn his friends " to beware of the gipsy," as he termed Leycester on account of the darkness of his complexion. Dugdale's Bar. ii. 287.

vs; wherefore, before I enter further into Hemerts matter, I pray you, if you thinke I shall tarry here, if it be but ij monethes, lett me haue better assistance, for he doth contemne all our souldiers here, both old Reade, sir William Stanley, Roger Williams, coronells Morgan, Edrington, Wilford, and all but ij or iij ruffians that be brought vpp, being his owne servants, and some of them his boyes within this vij yeres, be the only servants of the world, and, in very troth, such men as be the most riotous and disordered persons of this campe, and not one man that ioynes with him but yonge Burrow. Our service hath bine vndone for lack of Pellam, or my Lord Gray. Norris is borne in hand he is like to be generall againe here, after I be gon; but I can tell you thus much, doe you there appoint him what you will, there is none here, I meane of the states, will accept him. As for our Englishmen, I warant for anie more then his owne bands that will tarrie with him. If there had bine anie possible way to haue wonn him, I would not haue troubled you in this sort, with this matter; but, beleeue me, there is noe hope, he is soe subtle, and soe extreamly geven to factionne. I beseech you get him hence, and send him to Ireland againe, you haue cause enough soe to doe; for my parte I will not serve with him, for, whatsoeuer I haue to doe, I meane not to vse him anie otherwise, but will[a] send him to some place to gouerne till I heare further.

Now to Hemert. He was yesterday so freinded by the count Hollock and others of that countrey, for that I see theie will not haue losse of townes punished, and, as I tell you, by Mr. Norris vnderhand, as the proceeding is put of for ij dayes, the pretence openlie very good, but the intent indeed starke naught, and to deliuer him from iustice. But, before he be so, I will cary him to all the townes in Holland, for, since I was borne, I never heard man so cryed out on, and manie letters, which I send you, haue I receaued from all places, to haue severe iustice executed. His woman, whoe [is] thought to be his perswader, and so was it in-

[a] will and send, *in MS.*

formed me, I caused to be committed and examined, and the next day stolen away, which doth argue there was some guiltines, or why should she steall awaye, being a gentlewoman of a very good house? But, what signe all this is, I leaue to you to iudge, that such a matter could be so fauored. But there is a feare of some side[a] that a chaung wilbe, and theie beginn in all places to thinke vppon this brute of peace, and what dainger I am like to be in you maie consider. I feare everie man will speedlie seeke for himself, and noe waie to help other, the cause, and vs her majesties subiects here, but a stronge force to comand here, with all speed. I haue thought good to call the master [of] Gray with ij or iij^m. I am leveing all the horses I can beside here. The master of Grey hath a gentleman now with me, latly arrived, with his offers still to me, whome I will retorne hastelie ageine. If we haue force we will haue monie, both for them and all the rest. And, beside, I doubt not but to recompence Grave or I haue done, and the way for all this is, if you can procure her majesties countenaunce but till Michaelmas, that, by her good dealinge indeed, this countrey may be releiued, and myself haue creditt according as you shall thinke the cause worthy.

Paule Buys is a very knave, even to her majestie. Remember, in my other letter I wrate for some person of creditt to be sent hether to this purpose, and to her majestie also, I pray you forgett it not, it importeth all. I am this day taking a new order for Hemert, which I trust shall take place, and I beleeue, er it be longe, if my credit stand and be countenanced by her majestie, you shall heare Mr. P. B. shall follow. He is a devill, an atheist, and the onlie boulsterer of all papists and ill men, and of late vsed a most daingerous and detestable practice against me, in respect of religion, and to please the papists. But, giue me countenance, his head shall pay, perhapps, for it and other villanous parts towards her majestie, which shalbe iustified when my authority shall serve. The whole countrey, save his colleages, detest him.

[a] So in the MS. but perhaps the earl wrote ' sign.'

Now is the time, or never, to help this countrey, and only a sufficient man sent with favorable words from her majestie, to encourage these men, will doe it. Lett me alone for forces, and all things ells, save the monie her majestie hath promised, to sett these countreys in better state then theie were at anie time since I came; but speedye comfort must come, and another man in Mr. Norris place. Yet, if Pellam come, yea, I wish him the man, or my lord Grey, to bringe her majesties good favor and pleasure, it is yet time to doe great good. As also to send Rowland York away, whome I haue written for. I would I had Bryan Fitzwilliams here, and Edward Barkley. I will provide place or good entertainment for them, to their liking, and, if there be anie good souldiers there that haue servid here, I pray you procure them hether with all speed, iij or 4 of them. And there is a man of mine, muster-master in the west countrey, called Huddy, I pray you lett him not serve there. He playeth the knave with me, that, being my seruant, and saying he would follow me, but never came. He is a tall fellow, and a good souldier, but I will not seeme to call for him, but rather to be offended with him, and, for his ill dealing at this time, [desire] you and others my lords to displace him, and shall doe well to reprehend him sharplie, and send him to service.

And, where her majestie doubteth that I will either bringe the charge vppon her, or vppon myself as her minister, if I doe either of them I will haue no trust or creditt but vtter displeasure rather. If her majestie[a] supply this necessitie with her fauor, as I haue tould you, I shalbe better able to proceed in this service then ever I was heretofore, for heretofore I haue neither had favor, countenance, creditt, nor supply, from hir majestie, and by that meanes almost as little here otherwise. The people beginn to gett hart againe, and seeke, by letters from all places, to encourage me, and acknowledge the villany of there owne countreymen. Theie de-

[a] The MS. stands thus "displeasure nether of her majesties supply." There is clearly some mistake. In the text I have ventured upon a conjectural emendation.

sire now in all places to haue English garrisons, and where Mr. Paul Buys had secretly practised, to haue made these people to mislike of the coming of our nacion over in such nombers as theie did lately, theie all aske for more, and wish that all their souldiers were English and theie would double their reuenew. And the states now offer me verie larglie to gather and levie men, both horsse and foote, and I hope to gether them soe as I will leaue but a little releif in all the enemies cheif countreis er longe. But I beseech you remember to send me those captens I writt [for,] with all hast, and if you geue them prest of the treasure there, it shalbe allowed againe; for, lett men say what theie will, giue me a good tresorer, and haue away Mr. Norris, and, if you find fault with lack of makinge these men to answere all charges dew by them, lett me pay it with my bodie and life, for, if God lett me liue v weeks, I am already sure of the meanes, and but for the contempt that some places of Holland, and these not past ij, and one in Zeland, Midleborrow, haue vsed by the practise of the former partye,[a] all had bine had or this day. For, as soone as he found her majesties favor declined both from them and me, he lost noe time to sett it fourth, secretly, in many places; but, I thanke God, his creditt is not so generallie good as that he hath overthrowen all hope, though mischeuously he hath shaken mens minds, but, with one messinger of credit, her majestie maie help and salue all. And if your peace proceed without this manner of dealinge, God help vs all, and cheifly her majestie.

I haue imparted to Coxe, Mr. vice-chamberlens secretary, some matter concerninge this, both to tell his master and you. I pray you giue creditt to yt, and consider weightily of it, and, lastly, I most earnistly entreat you, even as you first tooke the cause and her majesties service here, and next as you beare good-will to me, and wish me good successe, that you ridd me of Mr. Norris. You have good cullor to doe it to haue him to Ireland. I had rather

[a] Paul Buys.

be without the others that I would haue, than to haue him remaine anie longer. Yt is trew he adventured his lief at Grave, but how you shall better one day knowe, and yet he is a very hardy gentleman. Yf you can revoke him for the cause of Ireland, I desire not anie way his hinderance, or harme, and, for that, I thinke you may doe it, his office there is great and honorable. Beside, beleeue me never yf you thinke to make him a seruant gratfull to these countreis. I knowe hit will neuer be. His creditt is wholy gonn, and hath bine longe, and I speed the worse for him.

I am sending with all speed to Cassamir.[a] I heare nothing of that preparacion, but some would make me doubt Palavicino, that he dealeth not sincerely but hath an intrest.[b] Thus, having trobled you longe, and praying you not to find yourself trobled with dew consideracion of the matter, I bid you farewell. Hast, at Gorkom, 10th of June.

Your most assured.

LETTER CXIV.

LORD BURGHLEY TO THE EARL OF LEYCESTER.

10TH JUNE, 1586. COTTON. MS. GALBA, C. IX. FOL. 267. ORIG.

Sir Thomas Heneage arrived at court the preceding night, and, according to a general report, the queen is very well contented with him and his message—treaty with the merchants for the payment of 30,000l. in the Low Countries, so as to avoid the carriage of money in specie—difficulties alleged by the merchants—Burghley wishes the earl could make the Rhine free.

My very good lord, though I wrote late on Wednesday at night to your lordship, uppon Mr. Nicolas Gorge comming to me with

[a] Cassamore, *in MS.*   [b] See page 104.

signification that he was to depart erly in the next morning, and therfor I wrote more hastely, yet now, being lykwise moved by Mr. Unton, the beror hereof, to know if I would have any thyng to your lordship, who is also moved to tak shipp this evening, with commodite of a western wynd, I am also occasioned to wryte in lyk hast, and yet, as the tyme falleth out, if I had mor leasur, I shuld not wryte of such matters as war mete, because I am here at Westminster, being Fryday, and have hard that sir Thomas Hennadg cam to hir majesty yesternight, and that, in a generall report, I here that hir majesty is very well contented with hym and his messadg; for which cawse, untill I shall be at the court, which I mynd to be to morrow at nyght, I am unfurnished what to wryte of such matters as his retorn shall minister cause, so as, untill that tyme, I cannot so conveniently wryte to your lordship as Mr. Hennadg and others at the court may doe.

But yet, my lord, I have thought good to lett you know, that I had, by hir majestyes commandment, on Teusday last, treated with our marchantes-adventurers to mak payment ther, on that syde, of the some of xxx^m ^{li}. wherby to stey the carriadg out of monny in specie, and, about the same tyme, I did also deale with some marchantes straungers to the same effect, that, if they cold mak payment ther of some good somes of monny, I wold repay the lyk here, and herof I was in good hope to have spedd, by the manner of ther answers, so as our monnyes, namely our aungell and xij^d. might be ther stablished at ther just valleus in certenty, namly, the aungell at xvj^s. viij^d. and our xij^d. at xx^d., and so ratably other monnyes, wherof I gave them hope, uppon report made, that your lordship was purposed to publish a placard ther for the lyk purpooss. And to comfort our merchantes, I did also promiss payment of the v^m ^{li}. presently, that was last payd ther by your lordships request, though the same was not payable befor the last of this month; but yesterday, both our own and the straungers cam to me, with declaration, that, by this mishapp of Grave, they both, but specially the straungers, cold not possibly perform that which I required of them; and so I was perplexed, and yet I so pressed our marchantes-adventurors as I told them, if they wold not now strayn ther credittes to pay ther $xx^{m\ li}$. within xiiij dayes, I wold procure from hir majesty a licenss for the straungers to carry out clothes undressed, wherby I hoped both to vent our clothes, which is a thyng very nedefull in this tyme, and to obteyne my request for payment of monny. By this threatning of them they have bene styrred to mete togither, and do offer to send awey this night a post to provide $xx^{m\ li}$. to be ther within xiiij dayes, if it be possible, and, for certenty, they offer, that monthly they will be hable to paye $x^{m\ li}$. Thus your lordship seeth how uncerten thynges pass here, but knowyng how great nede ther is to have monny ther, rather than ther shuld be want any long tyme, I will press hir majesty that monny may be sent in specie, wherof your lordship shall shortly here.

Our marchantes do alledg another gret difficulte, in that ther shippes can not have fre passadg to Embden by reason of the Hollanders shippes in that ryver, wherof I have gyven them hope that your lordship had delt therin betwixt the cont of Embden and the Hollanders, and so I hope your lordship hath doone some good therin, for so indede our marchantes shuld be more hable to pay you monny from thence than at Midleburgh.

I wish your lordship that good success that yow cold mak the ryver of the Rhen free, as by your late takyng of the sconce in the duke of Cleves contrey, I hope a gret furderance.

And so now, prayeng your lordship to accept this my hasty kynd of wrytyng in good part, I wish you success of all your honorable actions.

Your lordships most assuredly,
W. BURGHLEY.

10 Junii, 1586.

Addressed,

To the right honorable my very good lord, the erle of Leicester, lieutenant-generall of hir majesties forces in the Lowe Cuntries.

LETTER CXV.

THE EARL OF LEYCESTER TO MR. SECRETARY WALSYNGHAM.

18TH JUNE, 1586. OUVRY MS. FOL. 30. A COPY.

Proceedings against Hemart—manner of his trial and condemnation —executed that day with two others—arguments used to intimidate the earl from executing him—conduct of sir John Norris— establishment of a chamber of finances—conduct of Paul Buys— request that Ortell, who is Buys's intelligencer, may be sent out of England into the Low Countries—Buys's slanders—the earl has been obliged " to sett the better legg afore" towards the council of state—he will not be " overborded by theis churles and tinkers"—nobody shall remove him from his authority but the queen.

Sir, this berer can well informe you of all our present state, speciallie of the proceedinge with the vngratious Hemert, governor of Grave; against whome there was many manifest parts of his trecherous dealinge leyd, both by confession of captens, lieutenents, souldiers, and the very minister of the towne. Manie freinds he had, and I was made to feare proceeding with him, for that he was of a good howse, well allied, and of great freindshipp; that there was none proceeded against in all the prince of Orange his time, nor he durst not, albeit divers townes were ill geuen vpp and lost in his time, but, notwithstandinge, knowing the vilenes of the act, and the necessity of such an example, for that indeed there is noe more made in giuing vpp a towne then to forsake a mans howse, and how earnist the people are to see some example for loss of their townes and fortresses, I haue proceeded soe farr as by all the lords that be rulers here present, as count Hollocke, and Newynor, with many coronells and officers of the feild, I had him tried and condemned, and this day, he and two other captens, the one called Dubaud, and the other Robuckom, were executed here, publickly, loosing their heads, for that theie were all gentlemen and captens.[a] He confest his fault, I meane Hemert, and to be worthy to dye, but would not confesse the treason, or practice to giue it vpp, which most manifestly apperes by all his whole doings ever since he was last releeued, when the overthrow of the Spaniards warre. And to haue holpen this man, I doe assure you, you will not beleeue except you had sene it, how many devices one of our owne companie, Mr. Norris, vsed; which, aboue all other things, doth argue a notable matter in that man, but, I trust you will find meanes to retorne him to his owne charge, for he is neither for this countrey nor for our souldiers liking. I assure you I will hope of noe good if he remain here, and yet I am loth to harm him, therefore lett him be revoked for Ireland.

I haue latly altered the fynancs, and brought now to a chamber, and haue setled officers and all; yet some spurne at it, and theie that first cheifly sett me on for it, which is Paul Buis, a most lewd man as ever liued, and a most hated man to all sorts here. He is about some matter, whatsoeuer it be. He hates the queen and vs all. I shall knowe it, I am sure. Yf there fall out good matter, he shall be removed from his place, and perhaps committed further. Yf you knewe what I haue done for him here, you would thinke him the most vngratefull wretch that liues. He hath blased the queenes majestie secretlye of late, from place to place, to sondry capitall ringleaders, as, after I get sure knowledge, I will not lett slipp. He bidds them not trust her, she deceaues all

---

[a] The Briefe Report mentions "what difficultie the matter was thought to do this execution, the party being a baron, of a barons liuing, and great by birth and alliance in those parts; his excellencie, a stranger; the estate in broken termes; and the example there scant seene before. But the fact fell out so plaine, that his excellencie would not be intreated but that iustice should proceed: the iudges could not but condemn him, and the people though sorye for the man yet much reioiced to see the iustice done." Sig. B. 2. Neither that writer, nor, I believe, any other English author, mentions the execution of the two others, but Strada says that "una cum duobus centurionibus, capite plecti jussit Leicestrius." II. lib. 7.

the world with hir words, she performes nothinge she promiseth, she hath vsed them only for her owne turne, and to sett them further into danger, whilst she might make her owen peace with Spayne, and delivered them particularities to bite vppon. That she cared not a strawe for me, nor what became of me. (By the way, least I forgett yt, send away Ortell. He is his intelligencer, and I haue written twice for him and he comes not. Use my name and send him waye, without anie ill words, but that I haue great want here of him.) That I was mistaken, for I was not the man in such favor as they thought, nor as I must stand them in stead. And askid of them, what one grace or speciall fauor had they received since I came over? Or what strength haue I brought, but a few horsmen? It was neither horsman nor footman theie so greatly wantid, but a man of speciall fauor with her majestie, and such a one as she would haue countenanced in his gouernment here, which she hath not done, nor liked I should haue so great authority, as appeared by her own letters which she sent both to the states and the councell, but the states letter was held back by my sute, and they faine to dull the matter for me to her majestie by thir lettres, and yet she would not be satisfied, but retornid Heneage in great collor againe. That she had denied her monie and her men to come over. Thus vyly hath this knave secretlie wrought, saying, that I was a puritan, and had almost made a great broyle in England for religion, and that her majestie was gladd to be ridd of me, and to send me hether. But, since the people doth see our nombers come over so fast, and be doubtfull that he[a] speaks of practice and malice, for even so did he deall with the prince of Orange when he saw him growe to great, as except he rule all he will adventure to overthrow all, theie beginn to mutter owt thes matters against him, and thinke he would haue another change, not being pleased with this, for that he hath not his will; and I will tell you whie that I did not

[a] the, *in MS.*

take all such councellors as he did name vnto me at the first, which, if I had, I had left out all the best protestants, and haue taken in none but papists of his comendacion, but good patriotes he cald them, and yet doth not remember, as Dauison can tell you, all against them heare I tooke him in, being spoken against by all the states, and his owne provinces most of all; but, having a naughty, ambicious, covetous mind, there is nothing can content him but to governe all. I thinke he was workinge, at least till now he seeth the peoples hearts to her majestie, to make an alteracion, whatsoeuer that was; some thinke St. Allagend[a] busy ageine. I shall knowe more within ij dayes, but [for] once Zeland is worst out of order of all the rest. Paul Buis doth flatly fauor all the worst papists, and vtterlie mislike all honest protestants, either ministers or councellors; but, if her majesties fauor hold, and that you send with speed, as I wrote to you to procure, a wise discreet person to come over from her majestie to the states, and that you coniure Ortell a little, and to tell him her majesties disposicion to be increaced rather then diminished toward this countrey, you shall see I will course[b] Mr. Paul Buis he was not soe this xx yere.

I haue been faine of late, thorow his meanes, to sett the better legg afore, to handle some of my masters somwhat plainelie, and roughlye to, for theie thought I would droupe, but I will rather be overthrowne by her majesties doings then overborded by theis churles and tinkers. Theie find I will beare noe badd dealinges at their hands, and theie see, I knowe, I am better able to deall then heretofore I was with them, and theie find I haue care of them, and that I haue now at a pinch helpt them, when all their owne power and forces are not able to stand them in steed. And, whatsoeuer become of me, you shall heare I will keep my reputacion here amonge them, or dye for it; and, if her majestie remove me not, all theie heare cannot, from the authority I haue,

---

[a] St. Aldegonde, see p. 3.
[b] This word is doubtful in the MS. It has been altered and left very indistinct.

(which if I had now wanted, her majestie had found what it had bine, even for her owne service,) no more shall all this world make me keepe it an houre if her majestie shall not both like it and comand me to it.

Thus, not knowing what I haue scribled, I will end with manie thanks for your good freindshipps, and to pray you to hast sir William Pellam, or ells all is mard, I can assure you, and I would God her majestie would, for countenaunce sake, lett some noblemen and young gentlemen come over for a moneth or ij, to see some service, which a moneth hence wilbe somwhat warme, and worth the sight. God keepe you ever. Hast, this xviijth of June.

Your assured freind.

LETTER CXVI.

LORD BURGHLEY TO THE EARL OF LEYCESTER.

20TH JUNE, 1586. GALBA, C. IX. FOL. 274. ORIG.

The queen objected to the employment of the earl's secretary, Mr. Atye, as her messenger to the council of the states, and has appointed sir Thomas Cecill—the queen is well-affected to the cause, but she wishes the risk of a battle to be avoided, and dislikes all extraordinary charges—letter from sir Edward Stafford—the earl advised to destroy the harvests in the enemy's country—Scottish affairs—colonization of Munster.

My very good lord, tymes do alter matters in all places, and therefor this forenoone, when Mr. secretary and I had taken care for makyng some instructions for Mr. Aty, wherof some part tended to declare som thynges beside hir letters to the counsell of the states from hir majesty, and some part to yourself, hir majesty mislyked that Mr. Aty shuld, being your secretary, impart hir pleasure to the states in thynges that might concern yourself, and therefor soddenly she gave Mr. secretory order to command my sonn,[a] who was redy to take shippyng towards Holland, to stey and to be informed of those matters that concern the speches to the counsell of the states, and that he shuld be directed with those to your lordship, and as your lordship shuld thynk mete upon perusal of them, so to direct hym in hir majesties name to utter the same; and this was the very cause that Mr. Aty was not employed therin.

I se still hir majesties disposition very resolute to continue hir first purpooss for the defence of that action, and therin she is with good cause fully perswaded of your lordships honorable mynd to prosequut the same to hir honor and surety, but allweiss I fynd two obstacles in hir majesty. On is, she is very carefull, as a good naturall prynce, although in such a case as this somewhat too scrupulooss, to have hir people adventured in fightes. The other is, she will not have any more expended on hir part, [than] that she hath yielded unto, mislyking all extraordinary charges. And therefor she still calleth on us to wryte ernestly to your lordship, that yow shuld now, hauyng that generall authorite which yow haue with hir good lyking, press and command that the commen collections of that countrey shuld answer all manner of charges, to the disburdening of hir majesty, otherwise than to the sums assented unto. And so hir majesty doth often repeat that your lordship hath wrytten hyther that yow wold so doo.

By a letter which this daye Mr. secretary hath gyven my sonn, sent out of France from sir Edward Stafford, to be showed unto your lordship, yow may see how dilligent the enemyes and their partyners ar to disperss news for ther advantages, not regardyng how they mint lyes with truthes. That which in that letter is most marquable for your lordship is that of Utryct, which I doot but your lordship will regard.

[a] Sir Thomas Cecill.

I know no better waye to impeache these excursions of the prince of Parma, with his nombre of soldiers, wherwith he semeth that he will kepe the feld, than by all pollycy to distress his victell, which enterprise must now be taken in hand afor harvest. For suerly, my lord, I understand all the countreys in Flanders and Artoiss ar well taken with corn, and lyk to yield great plenty to serve all the wynter and spryng followyng. Surely, if the ennemy did not thus avance hymself towards you ther in Holland by the waye of Braband, wherby I see your lordship is forced to kepe your strengthes there also, to defend your frontier townes, as Bommell, Nuiss, Gorcum, and such lyk, your lordship might, with a small band of horsmen to be leyd at Sluse and Ostend, compell the towns of Bruges and Gant to revolt, for I know suerly the people ther are bent so to doo for want.

I doubt not but Mr. secretary advertiseth your lordship of the state of Scotland, where Mr. Randolf fyndeth none better nor more constantly disposed to kepe good amyty with hir majesty than the kyng hymself. The lords that war here bannished ar, as the Scottes termeth it, somewhat drye, which I impute to fearfullness. Of them all, the master of Glames is most cold, joyning himself stryctly with the secretory ageynst the master of Gray and Archebold Dowglass, which twoo men remayn constant to the quenes majesties frendshipp.

Out of Spain we here that the kyngs navy, so long prepared to have followed sir Francis Drak, ar newly stayd, and all other preparations out of Italy.

In Irland all thynges are quiet, and a nombre of gentilmen of Somersett, Devon, Dorcett, Cheshyre, and Lancashyre, are making themselves to go to Monster, to plant two or three thousand people, mere English, there this yere,[a] and it is pretended by them

---

[a] Stowe records the names of the "honorable and worshipfull gentlemen" who made the attempt to colonize Munster, and "wherof some went into the said countrie, others according to order taken sent their people, amongst which were sir Christopher Hatton, sir Walter Rawly, sir Wil. Courtney, sir Richard Mollineux, sir George

to plant about twenty thousand people, English, within a few yers.

And thus, my good lord, I beseeche God prosper you, for his honor, to govern those countryes as your noble hart can desyre, and I beseeche your lordship to contynew my sonn in your favor, as he desyreth.

From the court at Grenewych, ready to pass to London, the the [a] of June, 1586.

Your lordships assuredly to my power,

W. BURGHLEY.

Addressed,

To the right honorable my very good lord the erle of Leycester [lieutenant-generall] for hir majesty in Holland, &c.
20 Junii, 1586.

LETTER CXVII.

LORD BURGHLEY AND MR. SECRETARY WALSYNGHAM TO THE EARL OF LEYCESTER.

21ST JUNE, 1586. COTTON. MS. GALBA, C. IX. FOL. 272. ORIG.

The writers recommend to the earl to procure some compensation for the bearer Richard Tomson, a sea-faring man, whose cargo had been seized and partly destroyed at Flushing, upon suspicion that it was intended for the relief of the Spaniards.

After our right hartie commendacions to your lordship, the bearer hereof, Richard Tomson [b], hath a longe tyme beene a sutor

---

Bourcher, sir Edward Fitton, sir Valentine Browne, sir Walter Luson, John Popham her majesties attorney-generall, and other." (Annales, p. 718.) It was at this time that Spenser the poet obtained his grant of the castle of Kilcolman.

[a] A blank in the original.
[b] See pages 220 and 233.

unto us for some recompence of his losse sustained by those of Flushinge, and we have beene desierous to releive the poore [man by] some convenient course, in takinge satisfaction upon such Netherlanders as goe daylie and usuallie to Callis, and other portes adjoyninge, with comodities no lesse helpfull to the enimie than those which were transported by himself. But since, havinge considered the inconveniences that may ensue by such our graunt sundrie waies, we have thought good to remitt the said Tomson to your lordship, prayinge that yt may please you to extend your favour towardes him, eyther by way of entreatie or commaundement to those of Zealand, and, allthough he cannot have full restitution of all such goodes as he loste, by reason a great parte thereof was consumed and wasted by such as tooke the same, that yet he may have redelivered unto him, by your lordships direction, so much as was taken from him, with licence to embarke the same for any forreine country not inhibited. And, if yt may stand with your good likinge, in consideration of his hindrance, to permitt him to transporte from Holland some quantetie of graine, fishe, and cheese, for this realme, your lordship shall releive this poore man greatlie. We have thought good to write the more earnestlie unto your Lordship in the behalf of this man, for that he attempted the action by our consentes and permission, for some service pretended, and not of contempte, for we doe conteinue our restraynt of trafique for thos countryes without violation, allthough we understand, that the shippes of Holland and Zealand doe passe daylie to Callis, with commodities not a little helpefull to the countryes of Flaunders and Arthois. And thus we bid your lordship most hartelie farewell. From the courte, at Greenwich, this xxjth. of June, 1586.

 Your lordships verie lovinge frendes,
    W. BURGHLEY. FRA: WALSYNGHAM.

Addressed,
 To the right honorable our verie good lord the erle of
  Leicester, lieutenant-generall of hir majesties
   forces in the Lowe Countries.

LETTER CXVIII.

MR. SECRETARY WALSYNGHAM TO THE EARL OF LEYCESTER.

22ND JUNE, 1586.   COTTON MS. TITUS, B. VII. FO. 81.   ORIG.

Recommending his servant, the water-bailiff of Flushing, to the earl's favourable consideration.

My verry good lord, I am to recommend unto your honorable favor this bearer, my servaunt, that by your lordships good meanes he may enioye lyke benefyt of his offyce of water-bayly in Flusshing, as the water-baylye in Bryll dothe presently enioye. I hope he wyll deserve any favor yt shall please you to bestowe on him, and I shall thinke myselve greatly bownde unto you for the same. And so I most humbly take my leave. At the coorte, the xxijth of June, 1586.

Your lordships to command,
FRA: WALSYNGHAM.

Addressed,
To the right honourable my verie good lord the earle of Leycester, lord lieutenant-general of her majesties forces in the Lowe Countries.

LETTER CXIX.

MR. SECRETARY WALSYNGHAM TO THE EARL OF LEYCESTER.

24TH JUNE, 1586.   COTTON. MS. GALBA, C. IX. FOL. 246.   ORIG.

Arrival of Grafigna and Bodenham from the prince of Parma as messengers in relation to a peace—Grafigna's report of an attack made by Schenck and Roger Williams upon the Spanish camp—

the prince intends to attack the earl—the prince in his letters to the queen treats the subject of peace as if it had been sought at his hands by the queen, which she takes most offensively—the prince says that he has no commission to treat, but if her majesty desires a peace, upon knowledge of the terms she proposes, he will be ready to further it.

My very good lord, yt may please your lordship to hould me excused yf I use the hand of annother in writing unto you, being [at] this present meself overburthened with other busynes. The cause of this my dispatch is to acquainte your lordship with the late comming of Augustin Grafigna and Bodenham from the prince of Parma with some overture of a peace, though but in generall termes, having only yet delyvered, that, yf the king of Spayne can lyke to have a peace, the prince, for his part, who hath now receaved honner enough in that countrye, will very willingly undertake to becom an instrument and dealer in yt, for which purpose he meaneth to send over hether some personage of quality yf the matter go forward, but to other particularityes they descend not. And whether the prince have any commission or authorite from the king to treate appeareth not. Bodenham seemeth to have some further directions, and a letter for her majestyes self, theffect whereof your lordship shalbe made acquainted withall so soone as yt is knowen.

Grafigna telleth me, that he was lodged in Cosmos lodging when Skinck and Roger Williams gave the camisado to the campe,[a] and,

[a] After the capture of Grave it was at once suspected that the prince of Parma would turn his course towards Venlo, a town in the government of Schenck, who was himself engaged elsewhere. It was occupied by a garrison of seven hundred Dutch soldiers, but Schenck was desirous of himself getting into it, and he and Roger Williams, a well-known, brave, and experienced Welshman, the very prototype of Fluellen, determined to make the attempt. But the prince was not a general whom it was likely to take by surprise. All the passages were found to be occupied by the enemy with overpowering force, and Schenck and Williams became convinced that their design was impracticable; but, in the mere madness of a reckless bravery,

by that meanes, was prevye that the disorder and confusion was so great as there appeared no smaule lykelyhood, that, yf they had ben followed by their horsemen, the whole campe might have ben overthrowen; and yet that there weare not so many slayne as was otherwyse reported, the whole number being not above three or fower score, and of our people betwin thirty and forty taken and slayne, which happened for that, by reason of their longe taryeing, they gave the prince tyme to pursue them with his horsemen. They gave our men the prayse to have guided thenterprise with no lesse skill and good discretion then yt was hazardously undertaken. He telleth me, that, to shunne the danger of Berges up Zome, he was constrayned to returne by Mastrich, Liege, and thos quarters, where he understood that the people had violently resistid the carriadg of the intended provisions of vittalls to the campe, in respect of their owne want and necessitye; by meanes wherof the prince cannot long continue before Venloo. He understood that the merquis of Pescara, who was looked for with 1500 horse and 3000 footmen, bringeth now with him but an hundreth and fyfty horse and eight hundreth footemen. The prince of Parma, as he telleth me, was informed, that your lordship should have 18,000 fotmen and 3,000 horse, wheruppon, calling his captens to counsell, yt was, at the first, advised to go from Ventloo and hazard the battell with your lordship, and in thend resolved to leave some strength before Venloo, and yet go forward with their purpose to

they determined to make a sudden midnight attack upon the prince's camp, in the forlorn hope that "they might possibly breake through the gardes." The daring attempt was made, and the passage in the text informs us with what success. The Briefe Report, which states the circumstances rather more particularly, says, that they "slue many, euen neere to the princes owne lodging. But directing themselves towardes the towne, and finding the turnpikes shut, and garded with strong watch of muskeyteires, and the campe nowe all up in armes, and the day drawing on, they turned their course towards Wachtendoucke, a towne of the estates, seauen or eight miles of, where themselues and manie of their companie entred, and saued themselues from the whole cauallarie of the enimie, now pursuing them. Some thirtie or fortie of their company were slaine and taken." Sig. B. 2.

bid your lordship battell; wherof I have thought good to geve your lordship speedy knowledge. And so I most humbly take my leave. At Greenwich, the xxiiijth of Juin, 1586.

Your lordships to commaund,
FRA: WALSYNGHAM.

The prince of Parma, in his letter to her majestye, which I have seene, doth use the matter in sooche sortt as thowghe sooche as have ben dealors in this peace had sowght the same at his hands in her majesties name, which is taken most offensyvely agaynst both the prince and the mynisters; for her highnes protestythe, that she naver gave any sooche commyssyon. The prince protestethe, that he hathe not any comyssyon, neyther generally nor perticularly, to deale in the matter, and yet, yf her majestye shall be dysposed to have the seyd peace proceaded in, uppon knowledg in what sorte she wyll have the same performed, he wyll be ready to further so good a worke. Your lordship may see what effectes are wrowght by sooche weake mynisters. They that have ben the imployers of them are ashamed of the matter. I praye your lordship that this advertycement towching the contents of the prynces letter may not be made publycke.

LETTER CXX.

THE EARL OF LEYCESTER TO MR. SECRETARY WALSYNGHAM.

26TH JUNE, 1586.   OUVRY MS. FOL. 31 b.   A COPY.

The earl wishes 2,000l. to be sent to the master of Gray—capture of Venlo by the prince of Parma through the treachery of the burghers—great complaints of want of assistance and of proper allowances, and of general neglect on the part of the government in England—treasure not arrived—mismanagement and dishonesty of the treasurer—frauds upon the soldiers—leases desired by the earl.

Mr. secretary, I thanke you for your remembrance to stay ij^{m} ^{li}. for the master [of] Grey. I pray you procure it to be sent to Mr. Randoll,[a] or to some in his place, if he be come away. I haue written the like of this by Hekerstone; if he take the way of England, I beseech you to hast awaie the monie as soone as may be, and to write that I looke for his owne presence, ells I should be to sorry.

The state of causes here I haue written to her majestie at length. Theie stand vppon tickell termes,[b] and but for my late come forces, I thinke all had bine gon, speciallie all these parts without Holland. There is a generall conceit of her majesties leaving this countrey, which hath done all this harme. I haue done, and doe, what I can, to satisfy men, and I thinke I haue done some good. Venloe I heard had suffred an assalt, but I now knowe the whole troth. There was neuer brech made saltable, nor anie assault offered. The burgers onlie armed themselues, and opened a gate, and lett in viij^{c} Spaniards, and iij^{c} horse, and some souldiers were slaine, the rest let goe.[c] This place, Grave, and sundrey other

---

[a] Sir Thomas Randolph, see pp. 52 and 179. He was often called Randall.

[b] The word here in the original is "townes," but that seems clearly to be a mistake for "termes." "To stand on tickle terms" was a common phrase for "to stand insecurely." An instance in proof of this occurs in the "Briefe Report," sig. B. 2., in reference to Leycester's proceedings immediately after the surrender of Grave: " Understanding also that almost all the townes nere aboute, as Bomell, Arnham, Amersfort, Deuenter, and the rest of Guelders and Ouerissell, stoode in tickle tearmes, likely to yeelde if the enimie came neere them." Another example of the use of the same phrase was adduced by Steevens from " The True Tragedy of Marius and Scilla, " in illustration of Meas. for Meas. Act. i. sc. iii. where Shakspere has, " Thy head stands so tickle on thy shoulders, that a milk maid, if she be in love, may sigh it off." Malone's Shakespeare, ed. Boswell, ix. 26.

[c] It does not appear that any attempt was made to avert the capture of Venlo, except the fool-hardy exploit of Shenck and Williams which has been alluded to at page

townes, were agreed on two monethes since to yeild to the prince, and some of them I doubt yet. I will doe my parte, being fayne for doubt[a] of some of these, to put in vj^m men of our nation; theie were quit lost ells. I trust in few day[s] you shall here some what better of vs.

I perceaue by Aty,[b] that I shall neither haue the allowance for horsage, nor for myself. I am sorry you haue such an opinion of my follie, or simplicity, that you thinke such a man as I, whose abilitie is right well knowen to you all, that you will lay a burden vpon him more then I doe beleeue v of the best of you will take in hand. Did my forwardnes to serve perswade you all that I would vtterlie vndoe myself? I pray God I maie see some others sett to the like, to see what theie will doe, or how theie would looke to be considered. Though you would seeme to be good husbands for hir majestie, yet, mythinks you should haue taken some order with the states for my entertainment there; but will you neither allow me as all generalls haue bine, nor yet provide for me at thir hands to whose service I am sent? Is it reason, that I, being sent from so great a prince as our soueraigne is, that I must come to strangers to begg my entertainment? Albeit I know it is reason theie doe allowe me, and soe I thought you had contracted with them in England, yet is it noe reason for me to stand hucking with them for myself, beside I looke for the same answere theie doe make for other principall officers serving vnder me, which you say they must pay, and theie say the queene must pay them. Yf thei are to pay me, and the rest, why is there noe remembrance made of it to them, either by her majesties letters

---

319. On the occasion of its surrender, the prince of Parma distinguished himself by two acts of generosity, which are so much at variance with the ordinary practice of this savage warfare that they deserve to be remembered. i. By his own personal interference he saved the town from being plundered by his excited and victorious soldiers. ii. Finding amongst the prisoners the wife, sister, children and household of Schenck, he furnished them with conveyances for themselves and their effects, and sent them forth attended in a most honourable manner to join his daring and vindictive enemy.

[a] hast, *in MS.*   [b] Aly, *in MS.*

or some of my lords? I am blamed for imprests, and yet you would haue men serve vnder me. If you agree with the states that theie shall pay vs, lett them be so treated withall, and I will deall for the paiment thereafter. For my parte, I knowe not what theie will allow me, but I haue had, God is my iudg! but one 1000^{li} of them from my first till this daye, and you knowe what case I was in by her majesties displeasure long continuing, all which while I remained here like a man of noe accompt; and I blame them not to haue by it[s] meanes what they could. Theie had need to allow me well, or ells I pray you I maie sitt downe with my losses already, for I can make noe more. I will abid out the brunt of this service now, and will adventure my life to settle things well; but if I be noe better considered of by nether side, I must leave all, if I liue and passe this brunt.

I heare nothinge of anie treasure, yet my lord-tresorer wrote there should haue bine xx^{m} ^{li} deliuered by exchange at Middleborrow; hit is time it were come. And for your tresorer, yf he continue, I will medle noe more, for he must haue his old instruments, or ells himself wilbe vndone, for he is caryed by them, and all the world canot make them doe well. If he cannot make his accompt without this pay, as I thinke he shall haue need to be at it, yet lett some other haue charge to disburse the treasure, for I will never deall with these men more, nor never giue them my hand, for, as I thought before, soe was I abused. He may be here well enough, and be at the pay of all men, and call for his dew all the wayes he can, and to haue that accordingly, but there shalbe other manner of examinacions, if there be some other, then either wilbe or can be, yf he be the tresorer and paymaster. I knowe what I saie, and I see how the poore souldier is handled and abused, and noe man living can devise to help it where a tresorer and his ministers are only sett vppon gaine and skraping from the souldiers. And for his bills he shewes of the captens pay,[a]

---

[a] wey, *in MS.*

there is noe one thinge in the world whereby he hath more fowly abused both hir majestie and the souldiers then in that. But I perceaue there is noe man dare speake. The auditor doth knowe it, and, I will gage my credite, at this next pay sett another to be tresorer and paymaster, and yet this man to haue all he can demand, being right, and lett him be present, and he shalbe found a third parte of these bills not payd, nor the souldier answered the tenth parte of his dew. I shewed the tresorer hir majesties order and instruccions for the pay of the souldiers, but he would not obey it, nor could bringe him to it. For one while, when he was to pay, he had thus much money, or more then he was to reckon with them, and theie were in his debt. The captens being poore, and desirous of moneie, cared not what bills theie signed, so there souldiers know not of it, but if there fall not out to much fowle matter, trust me noe more. Beside you shall see what service this is. He hath bills of the capten to serue his torne, he cares not how the souldier is payd. I will prove, that these captens he hath delt cheifly withall doe owe all their whole wages for their souldiers yet to be paid to the townes where theie lye. Sir John Norrys himself, that is best paid of all men, doth owe, in this towne alone, for his horsband and for his footmen aboue $xxij^{c}$ li sterlinge, and thus is thir owing in every towne great somes. Reason is, that, either the souldier receaue monye or his meat paid for, but I can assure you theie make their souldiers liue in garrison for iiij$d$. or iiij$d$. ob. a daye, the rest should buy them apparell. I assure you theie neither pay for their victuall nor giue them apparell, except shewes, or sometimes a paire of stockes, which theie pay truelye for. I doe shame to see them, and the oldest capten[s] keep thir men worst, I meane the capten[s] that were here before; only Lambert that came from Ireland hath his men well trimed. I doe not thinke, except such monie as I haue paid them, that ever anie souldier hath receaued at one paiment aboue ij$s$. Judge you then, what cause the poore wretches haue to complayne. I pray you, lett me find that freindshipp to make proofe of this I say. Yf I doe wronge, I will aske forgiuenes, and make amends for it.

Thus, with my heartie commendacions, praying you to haue better remembrance of me, being in this desperate thankles service, as you would haue others doe in like, I commit you to God. In much hast this xxvj. of June.

Your loving freind.

I perceaue you haue done nothing for my leaces. I assure you I forgive[a] to him that will take all extremity ij$^{m\ li}$ for the one of them, and I haue but a month now left, and one forfeited alredy, and I desire them not of guift, but to pay as my lord-tresorer and Mr. Milmay shall sett downe; though her majestie did indeed grant them me at my coming away frely. The rent of both are but lx^{li} a yere and therabout.

LETTER CXXI.

THE EARL OF LEYCESTER TO MR. SECRETARY WALSYNGHAM.

27TH JUNE, 1586. OUVRY MS. FO. 34. A COPY.

The earl requests to have Rogers and Boddyly sent to him—chamber of finances established in spite of Paul Buis— Rugolt.

Mr. secretary, I doe very heartily pray you that you will help me to Rogers that was with Shenks, not D. Rogers the lawyer; he maie doe me great pleasure, and I will see him well considered.

I would, also, most gladly haue my old servant Bodyly, whoe I suppose is idle now; he may likewise stand me in good steed. Good Mr. secretarye, procure these two with speed. I trust you shall heare well from vs dayly after x or xij dayes, that some townes be quieted and better setled.

[a] forgett *in* MS.

I haue stablished the chamber of finances against Paul Buis will, and yet hath he vnderhand shifted to let it all he could; hit is our only way of helpe, which he would not haue. I see Rugolt is a notable man.

The two men in Zeland her majestie liketh not of are, I feare, starke naught, and in a dangerous practice with the young prince pallatine; you shall heare more shortly, but keepe this. Far you well; in much hast, this 27. of June.

Your assured freind.

LETTER CXXII.

MR. SECRETARY WALSYNGHAM TO THE EARL OF LEYCESTER.

30TH JUNE, 1586. COTTON. MS. GALBA, C. IX. FOL. 280.

Rectification of former account given of the contents of the letter from the prince of Parma brought by the agents for a peace—the master of Gray discouraged—his presence useful in Scotland—anxiety as to Venlo—Mr. Bryan Fitzwilliams recommended—Seburo.

My verry good lord, wheras [in] my former [a] I dyd sygnefye unto your lordship, that sooche mynisters [as] were imployed towards the prince of Parma had used the matter so, as by the princes letter unto her majestye yt seemed, that peace had ben sowght for by them in her name: but, uppon the perusing of the letter, which before I had not seene, yt appearethe not in playn [words] that any sooche motyon hathe ben made by them, but dyd shewe [only] unto the prince that, uppon any motyon that shoold be made, eyther by him or any other fyt to deale in sooche a cause, that her majestye was not so [alyened] in good wyll from

[a] See page 321.

the king of Spayne but that she wold be content to geve eare unto the same. To this, his aunswer is, that he hathe no awthoryte, neyther in generall nor in partyculer, to deale therin, but, when he shall understande how her majesty is enclyned, he wyll not fayle, as one affected to her servyce, to imploye himselfe to the uttermost of his power in compownding the differences betwen her and the king of Spayne. To this what wyll be aunswered I knowe not. But the desyre of peace, for the easyng of charges, is so great, as I dowbt the awntswer wyll not be so honorable as were fyt, and so, consequently, wyll hynder a good peace, for lacke of countenauncyng the warre.

To the ende your lordship may see what resolucyon the master of Graye hathe taken towching the levye, I send you sooch letters as I have receyved from him. The gentleman, as yt shoold seeme, is muche dyscoraged thorrowghe the uncertayne coorse held here. The state of Scoteland, notwithstanding our leage which is now concluding, standethe but uppon dowbtfull termes. The yll usage of the noblemen and mynisters that were retyred hether hath greatly alyened the hartes of the natyon. The chefe assuraunce of the amytye dependethe uppon the king himselve, strengthened by [the] good perswatyons used by the master of Graye, and Mr. Duglass, and, therfor, yt is to be dowbted that the masters absence from thence myght doe harme.

We attend here with great devotyon the successe of Venlo, whereof there is the more dowbt conceyved for that there are no [English] troopes there. For the more savetye of the frontyer, your lordship shall doe well to place Ynglisshe garysons. The only dowbt is, that oure capteynes, being but young, knowe not what belongethe to the defence of a towne. I thinke Mr. Brian Fytswyllyams were fytt a man to be a governor in anie of the frontyer townes, being an owld sowldyer and skylfull in matters of fortyfycatyon.

I cannot yet get her majestye resolute towching Seburo. And so, for the present, having no further matter to troble your lordship withall, I most humbly take my leave. At the coorte the xxxth of June, 1586.

Your lordships to commaunde,
FRA: WALSYNGHAM.

Addressed,

To the right honourable my verie good lord, the earl of Leicester, lord lieutennant-generall of her majesties forces in the Lowe Countries.

LETTER CXXIII.

MR. SECRETARY WALSYNGHAM TO THE EARL OF LEYCESTER.

30TH JUNE, 1586. COTTON MS. GALBA, C. IX. FOL. 282. ORIG.

Burghley and Walsyngham have procured from the queen, and now forward, five letters of thanks and encouragement, to be sent by the earl to such towns in the Low Countries as he shall think fit— Mr. Kyngsmill's friends desire to ransom him.

My very good lord, upon knowledge receaved from Mr. Aty here, of a motion made by your lordship, that, in case it would please hir majestie to write some letters to certein of the townes in that countrey, it could not but in all lykelyhoode be a thinge of good consequence, and very expedient for the comforting and encouragement of the saied townes: my lord threasurer and I, acquainting hir majestie with the mater, have founde hir very well enclyned to yeeld therunto, as your lordship may perceyve by the enclosed, which is a copie of the five letters that are sent herwith, signed by hir majestie; wherin if your lordship shall thincke good to have any thinge added or altered, or any more letters to be written to the same effect, I will not faile, upon knowledge of your pleasure and desire herin, to procure the same to be dispatched with expedition. And so I humbly take my leave of your lordship. From the court at Grenewich the xxx[th][a] of June, 1586.

Your lordships to commaunde,
FRA: WALSYNGHAM.

The brethern of yong Mr. Kyngesmell being geven to understande that he shold be of late taken prysonar, have desyred me most earnestly [to represent the same] unto your lordship, that by your favorable meanes his libertye may be procured. They can be content, rather then he shoold remayn long prysoner, to paye sume reasonable ransom. It is left to your lordship to direct the letters as you shall thincke meete.

LETTER CXXIV.

THE EARL OF LEYCESTER TO MR. SECRETARY WALSYNGHAM.

1ST JULY, 1586. OUVRY MS. FOL. 34. A COPY.

The English soldiers are deserting, which is attributed to the intrigues of sir John Norris—alleged fraud practised by him in payment of his soldiers out of the treasure during the treasurer's absence—the earl entreats that Norris may be recalled.

Mr. secretary, since my last letter to you I vnderstand, from all places where our men are placed, that there be many gon to the enemye, and a mere practice, either made in England or ells by Mr. Norrys, whom [b] I haue soe vehement cause to distrust, seing his nature, as, except he be revoked, looke to heare of some

---

[a] xxxj[th], *in MS.* [b] whence, *in MS.*

mischeuous practises to scatter vs here. I see the devill worketh, and he so detesteth these worthy men here, as, vnder a marvellous dissimulacion, he intendeth some ill; for this I find, all the perswaders of our men away are [a] his old shifting souldiers, whom [b] he hath dispersed craftely almost in every band some; and, but even now knowen to me, he hath vsed another fraud to beguile all your officers and muster-masters; he hard that the tresorer was not like to come, and, because he would both be sure of full pay without correction, and to bread a mutinie among the rest, he hath, without commision, without muster, sodenly made a pay to his footmen, which are decaied greatly, and since to his horsmen; a parte that he never play before now, when his men were redye to starue, and now is it for no other end in the world but to gett his whole bands payed, being thus layd out by him, and to make our men mutine, if it be possible, in the meane time. Either gett him hence, in as good sort as you can, or ells I will surely send him to some place where he shall noe wayes comand in the feild. I beseech you doe it, if you loue the cause and my well doinge. These things be so grosse as all men see them. God keepe you. In all hast, this 1. of Julye.

Your assured.

LETTER CXXV.

MR. DAVISON TO THE EARL OF LEYCESTER.

2ND JULY, 1586. COTTON MS. GALBA, C. IX. FOL. 263. ORIG.

Excuses his long silence on account of sickness, and absence from court—now writes by his dear friend sir William Pelham, to justify himself against some persons who have accused him to the

[a] or, *in MS.* [b] whence, *in MS.*

earl of having omitted to defend his acceptance of the government of the Low Countries, and also of having been the author of the earl's recent disgrace—both accusations are solemnly declared to be untrue, and he states what he really had said and done upon the occasions referred to, appealing to the queen for the truth of his statements.

My singuler good lorde, I have so longe forborne to write unto your excellencie as may here make my duty prejudged and suspected, the rather in letting passe as well my owne [servante] lately sent over from Mr. secretary, as Mr. Aty since departed hence, without one lyne or [word] from me; but, as my syckness for the most parte of the tyme since my retorne, my absence from court and ignoraunce of the doinges there, togither with the lyttle comforte I have els had to trouble your excellencie with those thinges which I could not without greif heare, and weare otherwise to commonly brought unto you, may, on the on syde, in truth pleade for me, so may the suddennes [of my sayde servauntes dispatch, without gyvinge me so muche as one howers warninge, beinge then sycke in my bedd, and lyke departure of Mr. Atye the same nighte I came hither from my poore countrye house, meetinge late and by chance only at sir William Pelhams, on the other side, justly excuse me. Howbeyt, least my longer sylence should confirme the impression which some of my wellwyllers have, as I heare, indevored to settle in your excellencie against me, I would not omytt so fytt an opportunytie as the departure of my deare frende sir William Pelham doth offer me, to repayre my former wantes with some lyne or two. Wherin, albeyt I could have wished a more pleasinge argument then to enter into the defence of my poore doinges, against the suggestion of suche as, envyinge that lyttle interest I have had in your excellencies favoure, have laboured what they may to supplant the same; yet, because I have nothinge deerer then the preservinge of myne owne honest reputacion, which I heare is in some sorte drawn in question, I have taken the boldnes, under your correction, as well for the iustyfyenge of myne owne innocencye as the satisfyinge of your excellencie, of whose honnorable favour and good oppynion I would be lothe theire malice shoulde unjustly bereave me, to aunswer those thinges, in a woorde or two, which I heare to be specially forged and suggested unto you against me. Whereof some are only so generall as might be sufficiently aunswered with a generall deniall, others more speciall, thoughe in lyke degree of truthe or probabylitye. The generall thinges objected against me are chiefly two; one, that I shoulde deceave the trust reposed in me, in dysclayminge, as they saye, your defence; the other, that I should be author of all the disgrace and hard procedinges offered to your excellencie and the cause from hence. Which accusacions, as they appeare straunge unto myself, having so many testymonies as I have to the contrarye, so do I wonder what humor might move the reporters to bringe thinges so improbable to your eares, whose owne iudgment and informacion from hence might suffice to convince them of slaunder and untruthe.

For the first, if to iustifye the cause with the uttermost of my poore reason and hazarde of that lyttle credyt and favour I had with her majestie, a thinge apparaunte to all men; yf to confesse plainely and without difficulty myne owne consent and allowaunce thereof; if to protest, that, in case I were yet theare, being not expresslie commaunded the contrarie, I shoulde still perswade the course you had taken, as a thinge standinge with her highnes service and myne owne dutye; if to be disgraced and condempned of partialitye and faction for persistinge in this defence of your doinges, as most honnorable, safe, proffitable, and necessarye for her majesties service, warrantable by the contract, and, as I understood, iustifyable by her owne commission, beinge well considered of; yf to affirme, that without this course fortified by her majesties favoure and countenaunce she coulde attend no better fruicte of all her charge then utter undoinge to the cause, with dishonor to herself and perill to her service; yf to protest, that all the good she pretended towardes myself could no waye satisfye or grace me yf this cause, wherein consisted the good or bad success of all my laboures, were disgraced and overthrowen; yf this, I saye, were to disclayme your defence, then had myne enemies some reason. But, that I have faythfullye and confidentlie performed theis honest duties, with a thousande more, in your behaulf, howsoever I stande otherwise censured and reported of, I appeale to the testimonie of your best, yea and most partiall, frendes heere, who, of their owne knowledg, can cleare me of this sclaunder.

As for the other pointe, that I should be author of all the disgrace befalne to your excellencie and the cause theare, which I protest before God I have bene otherwise most hartely sorie for, thoughe yt be a matter so farr from likelihoode as is utterly unworthy the aunsweringe, yet would I be glad to knowe what pretext of reason my accusers have for them. Howe ready, willinge, and carefull I was, to testifie the contrarie, by all the honor and service I mighte do you for the tyme I continewed on that syde, I appeale to your excellencies owne knowledge. Yf, since my returne, I have otherwise carried myself, they should have done well to give some instance, and shewe in what particular. But how farr I am, in truthe, from the touche of this accusacion, the stormes I founde heere at my retorne, which I fayled rather in credytt then in will to appease, may aunswer for me, yf neyther thexperience of my behaviors past, both publiquely and privately, my owne interest in the present action, nor your owne triall of my dutye and respect to yourself, can satisfie; besides the testymonyes you have had from hence, alone sufficient to refute theis generalities, which therefore I pass over the more lightly.

As for the particulers alleaged against me, I finde only two worth the aunswering: the one, that I should reporte unto her majestie that I utterly misliked and disswaded the course you tooke; the other, which I learne from sir Thomas Henneage, that I should saye to her highnes, I thought you would never have accepted that charge unles you had bene assured of her allowaunce thereof.

For the first, thoughe yt may receave a sufficient disproof by that is allreadie alleaged, and to be proved of my contrarie assertion to her majestie, yet am I content to be judged herin by her highnes self, who, I am sure, neyther can or will charge me withall, howsoever myne adversaries may abuse her name for theire credittes sake.

For the other pointe, thoughe I shoulde graunte yt, yet do I not see how yt can muche prejudge me, but the woordes which happelie they ayme at are, I thinke, those I used to her majestie when, as charginge me with abusinge the trust she had reposed in me, in that I had nott sett myself against that action of youres, and threatninge upon me that I knewe her express pleasure to be suche, I asked, howe her highnes would have me understande yt, havinge neyther from herselfe nor anie person els the least inkling thereof, and leavinge her, as I dyd at my departure over, otherwise resolved, unles she woulde have me imagyne so meanly, either of her favour towardes you, beinge as you were both to her and otherwise, or of[a] your owne respect to your credytt and honour, as to come over only to succeade Mr. Norris. And what offence may be justlie gathered hereof I leave to anie indifferent construction; sure I am, and God he knoweth yt, I dyd not wittingly lett fall herein one woorde with other meaninge then to lett her majestie see howe hardlie and straunglie you were, in myne owne poore opynion, dealt withall, howsoever theis, and the rest, may be otherwise aggreaved by such as happelie seeke to grace themselves by defacinge of me.

But, as I do protest before God that I have in this action dealt uprightlie, as one tendringe both your honour, the service of her majestie, and good of the cause, wherein I have had as muche interest as some other poore man, so do I most humbly beseech

[a] yf *in MS.*

your excellencie to retayne so indifferent an oppynion of me, and to shewe that equall favour towardes me, that, howsoever my yllwillers go aboute to blemishe and deface my poore credytt with you, I may yet receave that indifferent measure that I be not, unheard, preiudged and condempned, which is the speciall and only sute I have herein to make unto your excellencie, whose greater occupacions I am lothe to interrupt with anie moe woordes in my defence. And, therfore, reposinge myselfe uppon your honorable and equall favour, and hope of your pardon, if the jealous care of preservinge my poore reputacion have made me herein forgett myself, I will ende with my most hartie and humble prayer to God for your long and happie life. At London, the seconde of July, 1586.

Your excellencies most humble, and
ever bounden to do you service,
W. Davison.

LETTER CXXVI.

MR. SECRETARY WALSYNGHAM TO THE EARL OF LEYCESTER.
8TH JULY, 1586. COTTON MS. CALIGULA, E. VII. FOL. 275. ORIG.

Walsyngham recommends to the earl Dr. Michaell, a physician, who can give him information respecting the Low Countries of great importance.

My very good lord, this bearer doctor [Michaell],[a] phisition, being lately retourned into England [is about to] repaire into those partes, about certein * * , and, bycause I knowe him to be a * * , and to cary an earnest devotion towardes [your] service there, I have the rather thought [fit to] accompany him with thease my letters of [recommendation], praying your lordship to give

---

[a] The name is gone in the MS. but it is endorsed in a contemporaneous hand, "Sir Fra. Walsyngham touching D. Michaell."

him favorable access at his repaire unto you, for that he can acquaint your lordship with some particularites of that countrey [of great] importance, and fitt to be knowen. And so [remitting your] lordship to his reporte theirin, I humbly take my leave. [From the] court at Grenewich, the viijth of July, 1586.

Your lordships to command,

FRA: WALSYNGHAM.

Addressed,

To the right honorable my very good lord, the erle of Leicester, lieutenant-generall of hir majesties forces employed in the Lowe Contries.

LETTER CXXVII.

THE EARL OF LEYCESTER TO MR. SECRETARY WALSYNGHAM.

8TH JULY, 1586.   OUVRY MS. FOL. 34 b.   A COPY.

The town of Axel taken by surprise by sir Philip Sydney and count Maurice—insufficiency of the treasure remitted—desertion of the English troops and capture of some of the deserters—the new men frightened by the appearance of the " old ragged rogues "—sad condition of the troops and danger of mutiny—evil consequences of the belief that the queen would forsake the people of the Low Countries and make peace for herself.

Yt is like you shall heare of it before this comes to you, that we haue taken Axell, a towne in Flaunders, nere Ternous, a forte of our side. Your sonne Philip with his bands had the leadinge and entringe the towne, which was notably handled, for theie caused xxx or xl to swime over the ditch, and so gett vpp the wall and opened the gate; yet, or theie could enter half their nombers, the souldiers were in armes, and came to resist our men, but they were overthrowen, and most of them slaine, being vj^c, as I heare, souldiers in that towne, beside burgers; iiij scon[c]es beside are taken. The count Morrice was there, and my lord Willoowby, and young Mr. Hatton, for his first nuselinge.[a] God send we may hold it, vittell is so hard to come by there; but all is done that can be possible.[b]

I see wee shall starue on everie side. I here now, that there is x$^{m\ li}$ sent over by exchange, and other x^m in the middest of August; you wrote vnto me that her majestie had appointed xxxij$^{m\ li}$ to come over. It is no marvell our men runn fast awaye. I am ashamed to write it, there was v^c ran away in two dayes, and a great manie to the enemye, of which sort I haue taken sixe, and Welch is taken, that went with Pigott, where the count Hollock and Robin Sidney overthrew a good cornett of horse of Camilles, beside Breda, kild and tooke 28 prisoners, and horse. This Welch was one. There is of our runagates ij^c brought againe from the coast-side. Divers I hanged before the rest, and I assure you theie could haue bine content all to haue bine hanged rather then tarry. Our old ragged roggues[c] here hath soe discouraged our new men as, I protest to you, theie looke like

[a] Noselyng, nouselyng, or nuzlyng, i. e. nursing, earliest education.

[b] The capture of Axel was one of the most gallant achievements of this campaign. After a long silent march in the dead of the night, Sydney and his band of 2000 foot reached the limits of the fortification, and, according to our previous accounts, at once scaled the walls with ladders in various places, and rushed forward to the market-place, which had been appointed as a station of rendezvous; but we learn from Leycester's report that the attacking party encountered greater difficulties than these, and that the seizure of the place was effected by a far more daring manoeuvre. The men who swam across the ditch must have carried their ladders with them, and have executed their bold attempt with admirable coolness and silence. The design was attributed to Sydney, and he is said to have rewarded the brave fellows who executed it out of his own private fortune. See Greville's Life of Sydney, p. 135. Zouch, p. 249. The " Briefe Reporte," after praising the secrecy and valour of Sydney and his soldiers, states that they " slue and put to flight foure bandes of footemen in the towne, had rich spoyle, brought away fiue ensignes of the enimies, left coronell Pyron, with eight or nine hundred souldiours in garrison, and came their way." Sig. B. 2

[c] roggues ragged *in MS.*

dead men. God once deliuer me well of this charge, and I will hange to, yf I take charge of men and not [a] be sure of better pay a forehand. I assure you it will frett me to death or longe, to see my souldiers in this case, and canot help them. I cry now, peace! peace! for neuer was there such a warr, and a cause so slenderly countenanced; but God will help vs I trust. And you must looke to yourselues there what you will doe, you see the yeare runns on apace.

I will not now hold you longer; but, Mr. secretary, I tell you, if our people shalbe noe better releiued, by the Lord, I looke for the fowlest mutiny that euer was made, both of our men and these countrey souldiers, and I am sure I can doe as much with them as ever anie man could, and I doe but wonder to see theie doe not rather kill vs all then runn away, God help vs! And I would God you were all here one moneth, to see our handling from ourselues. I doe assure you, if our paiments come thus, you must looke to heare I and theie shalbe come shortly Martin Rous and his companie, for men will not starue, and for such monie as the states owe I look verie shortlie to haue [it]. The enemie doth vse his old practice; he hath conueied above ij^c of our men by Callice, and I beseech cause good wait at Dover, and Sandwish, for such as come without my pasport, and that some example be made, or we shall never keep them here.

I haue good hope of the count Hollock. Paul Buis, a very knave, more and more.

The opinion conceaued that you will leave vs will vndoe all, and past help shortlye. Yf help doe come in sort to pull out this late deep-rooted conceat, lett me loose life, and all I haue in the world, yf these countries be not brought free of this warr within one yere, and, before the Lord I speake, I doe thinke it had bine this yere if matters had bine well followed and supplied; but, as you deall, I knowe not what to say, nor what councell to giue, but

[a] to *in* MS.

to pray to God, and looke for ruin of all here or longe, for you must thinke these conceats cause matters to alter more in a weeke then heretofore in iij monthes. And yet is there life. God be with you. In hast this 8. of July.

Your assured.

LETTER CXXVIII.

MR. SECRETARY WALSYNGHAM TO THE EARL OF LEYCESTER.

9TH JULY, 1586. COTTON MS. GALBA, C. IX. FOL. 292. ORIG.

The earl's late letters to the queen, in which he lays before her the consequences of the loss of Grave and Venlo, and urges her to assume the sovereignty of the country, and send a large army thither, have greatly perplexed her—consultation thereon between Burghley, Hatton, and Walsyngham, and their meditated advice to the queen—allusion to the discovery of Babington's conspiracy, by the " traveyl and cost " of Walsyngham.

My verry good lord, your [last] letters unto her majestye [in] which your lordship hathe layd before her the present alteratyon [in that] cuntrye, as well in the gene[ral] thorroughe the losse of Grave and Venlewe, as also in [certain] partyculer persons of * * cauling there, as the count [Maurice] and count Hollocke, for somme knowen respectes, hathe g[reatly] perplexed her, and the [more] for that she gatherethe uppon the vyewe of your lordships letter, that the only salve to cure this sore is to [make] herselve propryetarye [of] that cuntrye, and to put [in] sooche an armye into the [same] as may be able to make head to the ennemyes. The[se] two thinges being so contrarye to her majestyes dysposytyon, the one, for that yt breedethe a dowbt of a perpetuall war, the other, for that yt requireth an increas of charges, dothe merveylousely dystrackt her, and make her repent that ever she entred into the actyon.

She hathe only made the lord-thresorer and Mr. vyce-chamberlyn acquaynted, as they tell me, with parte of thos letters, and gave them order to consyder what wer fyt to be don uppon this alteratyon. To this conference by her majestyes order I was cauled. The resolutyon is not yet taken, but hangethe in susspence for that the lord-thresorer, being trobled with the gowte in his hande, canot repayre unto her. The advyce that wyll be gyven her wyll faule owt to be this; fyrst, that she must prosecute the actyon without respect of charges; secondaryly, that a gentleman of sound judgement be sent over unto your lordshyp, to confer with you howe bothe the generall and pertyculer dyscontentment reygning theare may be removed, as, also, to be informed of dyvers poynts towching the state of that cuntrye; and, lastly, that yt shall in no sorte be fyt for her majestye to take a[ny] resolutyon in the cause until sir Francis Drakes returne, at lest untyll the successe of his vyage be seene; wheruppon, in verry trothe, dependethe the lyfe and deathe of the cause according to mans judgment. She is also advysed, in the mean tyme, to make no shewe of her dyslyke, but rather to countenaunce the cause by all owtwarde meanes she may, which, contrarye to her naturall dysposytyon, she doth verry well performe, [forced thereto by mere necessytye upon the dyscoverye of some matter of importaunce in the hyest degree thorrowghe my traveyl and cost,][a] by the which yt apperethe unto her most playn, that, unles she had entred into the actyon, she had ben utterly undon, and that, yf she doe not prosecute the same, she cannot contynewe.

I have acquaynted this gentleman with the secreat to the ende he may imparte the same unto your lordshyp. [I dare make

---

[a] This and two subsequent passages in this letter printed within brackets were erased with a pen, probably by the earl. They have been made out with difficulty.

none of my servants here privy thereunto. My only feare is, that her majestye will not use the matter with that secreacye that apperteynethe, thowgh yt import yt as greatly as ever any thing dyd sythence she cam to this crown,] and suerly, yf the matter be well handeled, yt wyll breacke the necke of all dayngerowse practyces duryng her majestyes reygne. [I pray your lordship make this letter an heretyke after you have read the same.] I mean, whan the matter is growen to a full ripenes, to send some confydential person unto you, to acquaynt you fully with the matter.[a] And so, in the mean tyme, I most humbly take my leave. At the coorte, the ix[th] of Julye, 1586.

Your lordships to commaunde,
FRA: WALSYNGHAM.

LETTER CXXIX.

MR. SECRETARY WALSYNGHAM TO THE EARL OF LEYCESTER.

11TH JULY, 1586.   COTTON MS. GALBA, C. IX. FOL. 302.   ORIG.

The queen has not yet determined upon the course advised to be adopted in reference to the matters mentioned in the earl's last letter to her—probably in the end Mr. Wolly or Mr. Wylkes will be sent to the earl—she is disposed to appoint Mr. Davison to assist Walsyngham in the secretaryship—master of Gray—pioneers—levies in Ireland—the treasurer to be sent into the Low Countries, that certain charges against him may be examined there—Norris's friends anxious for his recall—want of money, and public dissatisfaction as to the war—the queen's inclination to be discontented with sir Philip Sydney—treaty with Scotland concluded.

[a] These mysterious sentences contain an allusion to Babington's conspiracy, which was discovered by Walsyngham at this time, although the persons engaged in it were not apprehended until nearly a month afterwards.

My verry good lord, by my last [letter], by sir William Pelham, I dyd let your lordship understand what advyce I thowght woold be gyven to her majestye, uppon the poyntes of your lordships last letters unto her; sythence which tyme, reporte thereof hathe ben made unto her, but she not resolved as yet, what advyce to geve unto your lordship uppon the sayd poyntes. She is lothe to sende a spetyall person to your lordship and the counsell of state there, in respect of charges; and y[et], in the ende, for that the matter is of wayght, I thinke she wyll be drawen to assent thereunto. I suppose Mr. Wolley or Mr. Wylkes wyll be used in that servyce. She seemethe to be dysposed to make Mr. Davyson my assystaunt in the place I serve. The gentleman is very muche greeved with the dyslyke he understandethe your lordship hathe of him. For my own parte, I doe not fynde but that he hathe dealt well, bothe for the cause and [also] towards your lordship, whos good opinion and favor he dothe greatly desyre.

The vth of this present captain Haggarston arryved here, whoe departed hence the daye following.

He had accesse unto her majestye, and was verry gratyousely used by her. He layd before her sondrye reasons to move her to thinke that the master of Grayes imployement in the Lowe Contreys myght yeld more proffyt to the generall cause, and furtheraunce to her servyce, by imbarquing the king his soverayn, then his contynewaunce in Scotlande. But nothing that he coold saye coold lead her majestye to be of his opinion, being perswaded that his absence from thence may breed some dayngerowse alteratyon in that realme. I fynde, bothe by the master of Graye and captain Haggerston, that, without he goe in person, he shall not be able to send over sooche nombers as your lordship desyrethe, and, therfor, I have thowght good to staye the sending of the 2000^{li}. untyll I heare from them.

Her majestye styll makes verry great dayntye to send over any of her own subjects to serve, eyther as pyoners or sowldiers. My lord-thresurer, Mr. vyce-chamberlyn and I dyd deale verry effecttually with her for the sending over of the 600 pyoners, but coold not wyn her to assent thereunto. The pyoners provyded by Mr. Rauley are nowe come to London and are readye to imbarque.

Sir William Stanley, as the lord-deputye and secretary Fenton doe advertyce me, hathe ben greatly hyndered and crossed by dyvers malytyowse and sedytyowse brutes geven owt in that realme, in the levye of the 1000 men, as thowgh ther were an intent and meaning to bryng them to the butchery. Were yt not that the deputye dothe assyst him to the uttermost of his power he shoold not, as I am informed, be able to rayse halfe the nombre. I hope the next westerly wynde wyll bryng him and his troopes unto your lordship.

What resolutyon is taken for the thresorer your lordship may perceyve by the coppye of a letter wrytten by her majestye unto yourself. By sir Thomas Shurley your lordship shall receyve the originaule letter, as also sooche matters as the sayd thresurer hathe ben charged withall, and Leyster his deputye, together with ther awntswers. And, for that ther are certeyn espetyall matters wherwith he standethe charged, and are by him denied, yt is, therfor, thowght meet, that they shoold be examyned there. I suppose he wyll himselve be a suter to be dyscharged of the place, and the rather yf coronell Norryce returne, whos frendes are verrye earnest for his revocatyon, in respect of the dyslyke your lordship hathe of him. Her majestie dothe yet oppose herselve thereunto, but I hope, in the ende, wyll be drawen to assent, which shall not lacke any furtheraunce I can yelde, for, being a person dyscontented, and not lyked of by the most part of the marshall men serving there, his contynewance in that servyce cannot but doe a great deale of harme, by maynteyning of factyon. I wyshe also bothe his brethern here, in case he leave the servyce, espetyally Edwarde, whoe I dowbt dothe advertyce but hardly of the proceadinges there.

Towchyng the 1500^{li} dysbursed by your lordship in the levyeing of the 650 horse, over and besydes the 8000^{li} alreadye receyved, I doe assure your lordship that the contrybutyon of the recusentes, and the charges, dothe not suffyce to supplye the sayd somme of 8000^{li} dysbursed by her majestye. And owr people in this realme, by the malytyowse practyces of the yll-affected, begyn to murmure at the warres, so as yt is thowght meet for a tyme to staye the makyng of any newe levyes, eyther of men or money. I doe assure your lordship there are very dangerowse humors reygnyng here amongest us, and we not dysposed to take sooche a pryncely coorse to kepe the yll-dysposed under, as the present tyme requireth.

I praye your lordship, for that her majestye dothe geve owt that the count of Hollocks dyscontentment growethe in respect he was removed from the coronellshipp of the footemen serving in Zeland, and the same bestowed uppon sir Philip Sydney, that her majestye may be satysfyed in that poynte, for that she layethe the blame uppon sir Philip, as a thing by him ambytyowsely sowght. I see her majestye verry apt uppon every lyght occasyon to fynde fault with him.

Owre treatye in Scotland was concluded the vjth of this present, and the commyssyoners dysmyssed with good contentement. Sooche advertycementes as I hav lately receyved owt of France, Flaunders, and the ennemyes camp, I send your lordship herwith. And so I most humbly take my leave. At Barnelms, the xjth of Julye, 1586.

Your lordships to commaunde,

FRA: WAL.

LETTER CXXX.

THE EARL OF LEYCESTER TO MR. SECRETARY WALSYNGHAM.

11TH JULY, 1586. OUVRY MS. FOL. 35 b. A COPY.

Arrival of sir William Pelham in the Low Countries—the prince of

Parma is besieging Nuys—the earl will not answer for any town which is not defended by Englishmen—projected pursuit of the prince if he should remove to Flanders—dismay of the new soldiers—the earl wishes to be trusted with the remainder of the queen's stipulated payments—he has never been unthrifty of the queen's money, although he has been liberal of his own—disadvantages that will arise if the master of Gray does not come himself.

I vnderstand sir William Pellam is come, and wilbe with me this night. Our late good happ in Flaunders doth much amaze and stir the enemies coller; there is not now for vs a fitter in all the countrey to anoy him. I haue giuen order for 1000 horse and 2000 footmen more to goe into those parts, and, if the prince remove his force thether, I will furnish those parts thorowly. In the meane time Sluse and Ostend are the safer. This towne of Axell is [of] very great importance; we shall haue way to get at[a] Antwerpe and Bruges by it. God send our other purpose good successe, for it is now in hand. The prince of Parma is still before Nuce, but vseth yet noe battery; some thinke he is at the mine. The capten doubteth it, and doth countermyne.

I will answere for no towne now, how stronge soeuer it be, that be furnished only with these countrey people. Berks, Gelders, Waghtenden, Arnham, Amersfort, and divers others, I haue sett some English men into them, and I doe send Mr. John Norris to haue the charge of all those places, with a nomber of footmen and horsmen beside, and if the prince remove into Flanders with his forces, then shall he follow with all such force as now I am forst to leaue behinde for garding all these parts, which is at least 7000 footmen and 800 horse, which [if] the enemie withdrawe, we maie [and] will bringe them into Flanders. I looke, also, by the 10th of August and soner, to haue 2000 royters. Theie haue receiued thir first pay a moneth agoe, soe that, by the grace

[a] Very doubtful in the MS.

of God, if we maie receaue comfort and maintenance, you shall here of good successe; but our wants hath stricken all men dead, specially our new men, who cam with gladdest minds over, and soe some tasting of want beginne to dispaire, and yet doth there appere as great courage in them as euer I saw in men. I am here onlie at Hay for getting of monie, and am not vnmindfull to see her majesties monie paid, that is disbursed, vppon the first receipt.

I beseech you lett her majestie trust me with the spending of your litle remayne, that it maie be here, that, vppon all needes, we may relieue our people. If there be not as good husbandry vsed as may be possible, lett me beare the blame. I trust that I I never vsed anie vnthriftines or prodigalitie in her majesties treasure; yf I haue bine over liberall of my none that she hath giuen me, hit was but that I meane to doe for her honor and service as far as it will stretch. Touching the master [of] Grey, I perceaue by his letter that he will send me 2000 men, and meanes not to come himself, which is the onlie thinge I did wish for, otherwise, without him, I desire not the men, for thir wilbe both more comber and more danger thereby; therefore, I pray you write soe to him. And his abode here may be the lesse while though he come.

I did write to you by Hegerston touching the monie for him, for that you wrote to me that you had staied soe much for that purpose, as, also, by another letter by another messinger for the same purpose. I haue noe liking of Balford here, he is a bad fellow, and wholy at others direccion and not mine; indeed and if the master of Greie come not, he will looke to be collonell-generall over them all, which I will no way consent to. Thus, being in hast, comits you to the Lord. In much hast this xjth of July.

Your assured freind.

What a worke I haue had here you will hardlie belieue, the alteracion and alianacion so sodenlie as I was faine to bestur me, as you shall heare shortlie.

LETTER CXXXI.

THE EARL OF LEYCESTER TO MR. SECRETARY WALSYNGHAM.

15TH JULY, 1586. OUVRY MS. FOL. 37. A COPY.

The master of Gray having expressed some disinclination to leave Scotland, the earl wishes, if money has not been sent to him, that it be retained; if it has been sent, that he be urged to fulfil his engagement—Axel victualled—the enemy is borrowing money at Cologne—letters of thanks to towns received—others needed.

Vppon the vewe of the master [of] Greys letter I fell into some doubt of some matters told me a good whyle since, though I beleeued it not, which was, that there was a plott laid to bringe manie Scotts over, by a device of some here, to make a bridle of our nacion to strengthen some other. If he haue not the monie already from you, hit may please you to stay it, and to send my letter. If the monie be paid, then I pray you write earnistly, and charge him with his promise, and my expectacion of his cominge, and you must procure a letter from her majestie to the king of Scots, or els it will not be. I had rather, as the time is, and as matters fall out, that you had the monie with you, and to hold him in his mind to stay at home; but, otherwise, make the best of it, and hasten himself awaie with his ij^m men, all you may. Soe far you well, in hast, this xvth of July.

Your assured freind.

We have vitelled Axell for iij moneths. Our enemie is begging monie at Colen. Yf her majestie hould hard, and giue yet good hope and comfort to these men here, she may sett all in tune againe; but some one of very good credite, a councellor at lest, must needs come. You are to spare there of your letters to noblemen and to the states. I thanke you for your letters to towens, but I must haue half a dozen more, but speciallie to Morris, Hollock, and Meures.

I can yet promise noe great matter for our abilitie here.

LETTER CXXXII.

THE EARL OF LEYCESTER TO THE LORDS OF THE COUNCIL.

15TH JULY, 1586. OUVRY MS. FOL. 37. A COPY.

The earl describes the panic and insecurity which prevail throughout the country in consequence of the successive losses of Grave and Venlo—progress of the siege of Nuys, the safety of which is almost despaired of by the earl—the sudden defection of the people attributed to an opinion that it is the intention of the queen to desert them, the remedy for which is to demonstrate the contrary—thanks for sending sir William Pelham—Paul Buys has been arrested by the townsmen of Utrecht without the connivance of the earl.

After my right heartie commendacions to your lordships, synce the losse of Grave and Venloe, my businesses in this troblesome rent estate of these countreys haue bine such as my leisure hath little serued me to write, or almost to thinke, of anie other thinge but how, by all the possible meanes and ways I could, to sett some stopp, such as for the time and in my want of all necessaries therefore I mought, to the violent overthrow of all, which then seemed to be presently at hand. For I assure your lordships, that, if I had not sodenlye provided, and that with effect, by Gods goodnes aboue my expectacion and hope, 14 townes moe, as good every of them for the most parte as anie of these that are lost, had bine gone at one clapp. But the Englishmen that then arrived, though vntrained and vnarmed, came in good time, whereof I haue distributed to the nomber of 4 or 5,000 in garryson, into the townes in those parts wherevnto the enemy is most like to make next approch. As into Bercke, with some Dutch, 1,500; into Gueldres, 800; into Waghtendonck, 1000; into Arnham, 1,500; into Vtreicht, which for the present, also, hath need of them, 1,200; beside some other companies here and there, in other townes and fortes. And thus haue I placed the English in places of most need, for that after the treasonable losses of Grave and Venloe, two most stronge townes and well provided of all necessaries, myself haue no confidence, neither will I putt your lordships in hope, of the keeping of anie where Englishmen are not.

Nuyse is now beseiged of the enemie. It kept out Charles the duke of Burgundy,[a] and Charles the emperor, with all their powers; yet it is now stronger than ever it was. Yt is out of my charg,[b] yet, being so nere a neighbour, and the articles of league betwene the elector and these countreys so requiring, I haue provided sufficiently for it, yf theie be men that be within it. They are 1,500 men stronge, all souldiers, few burgers or none, but noe Englishman amongst them. Theie are provided of all thinges necessary, yet can I not promise myself, nor assure your lordships, that it wilbe kept, but, by the princes manner of dealing, I am rather induced to coniecture the contrary. For, hauing lyen now a fortnight or more about it, he hath not vsed, hetherto, batterie or assault, but by semblant of mines, and other lingring showes, soe vseth the matter as it cannot be thought but that he maketh his ground vppon some partie within it.

Yf your lordships will knowe the cause of so sodaine defection of these townes, I must pray you to consider withall, that not

[a] The earl alludes to the celebrated siege in which Charles the rash met with his first reverse, and by which he was prevented joining Edward IV. in his invasion of France in 1475. Nuys withstood his power for a full year, and was ultimately relieved by the emperor.

[b] Nuys was situate in the electorate of Cologne, and at this time was held for Gebhard Truchses the deposed archbishop-elector.

onlie these townes but the whole provinces are in the same waueringe estate, yea, the principall men also, and those that haue most especiall cause to repose themselues vppon her majestie, that, to tell you the truth, I knowe not where I sett a sure foote, nor with whome of these countreis I maie confidently conferre of theis matters. And requiring of the cause, both by myselfe and with others of iudgment, I find it is not corrupcion from the prince, for he hath little to giue; not desire of the Spanish gouernment, for even the papists abhore it; not mislike of being vnder her majestie, or her officers, for theie desire nothinge more then that it will please her majestie to take the soueraigntye of them; but, indeed, the cause cannot be imagined to be anie other then a deep impression in the wiser sort, and such as looke most into the doings of things, that her majestie careth not heartily for them, and then, being left, or weaklie assisted by her, theie must fall; for which theie had rather provide in time, then by delay to expect the warr, one after an other, in ther owne doores. This conceipt tooke beginning 2 or 3 monethes since, but now bringeth forth his effects, and wanteth not politique heads to nourish it on, which, even then, layd their plotts that theie now follow. And yet, my lords, though the case be very daingerous, and such as, for duties sake and for my owne discharge, I thus lay plainlie and truelie open to you, I doe not make it desperate, but doe accept it easilie recoverable, yf remedie be vsed in time. But the remedye must be according to the nature of the disease, which, growen of the mistrust of her majesties effectuall dealing for them, must be cured, not with a showe, but by a plaine demonstracion of the contrary, by dead and presently, the meanes whereof your lordships can better consider of then it shall boote or befitt for me to prescribe. For my owne parte, what a man without money, countenaunce, or anie other sufficient meanes, in case soe broken and tottering everie waye, may doe, I promise to endeuor to doe, to the best of my poure.

As soone as I can gett anie leisure I will, by the next, aduertise your lordships of the nombers of the English that are here. Sir William Pellam is come, whoe wilbe a good aide and comfort to me. I heartilie pray your lordships from me to thanke her majestie humbly for it.

I haue not anie other news at this present to write to your lordships, saving that Mr. Paule Buyse 3 or 4 daies since is arrested prisoner by the townsmen of Vtreicht, at the verie time that I departed the towne, without my knowledge, I assure your lordships. But, indeed, being done, I am not much sorry for it, for, as he is a most odious man to those of Vtreicht, for whome he is counsailor and hath bine continuall dealor, and soe likwise to all these countreie people, [save] to a few badd followers of his owne, soe, ever since Mr. Davisons going hence, hath he bine a practiser against her majesties doings, and a crosser of all the English here. Soe was he to his good freind the prince of Orenge in the end. And so is his nature to be to all gouernment here, except he, by [being] the onlie staye of the affaires, may make his profite, as he hath greatly done alreadye. Had not these townsmen thus prevented me, I meant myself here, at the Haghe, to haue sought redresse of diuers his late badd dealings. But now I will see how the matters will goe first betwene him and these townesmen, who are indeed honest men, zealous in religion, and most devoted to her majestie.

Soe I comitt your good lordships to the Almightie. From the Haghe, the xvth of Julye, 1586.

          Your lordships loving freind.

LETTER CXXXIII.

MR. SECRETARY WALSYNGHAM TO THE EARL OF LEYCESTER.
20TH JULY, 1586. COTTON MS. TITUS, B. VII. FOL. 63. ORIG.

Letter sent by the treasurer on his return to the Low Countries, in which the earl is requested to order colonel Morgan to give the treasurer certain acquittances, without which he cannot clear his account.

My very good lord, I understand by this gentleman, her majesties thresorer there, that he cannot have coronnell Morgans acquittances to be delyverid, [as] usually unto him by all the captens and others that have chardg vppon receipt of their paye, for that yt is required that a defalcacion be made out of his enterteynement for the armour of his companyes, as hath be don to the other captens, which the coronnell refuseth to yeld unto, alleadging that he hathe sent backe the armour providid by the countrye, and furnished his companyes himself. Whereuppon the gentleman standeth chardgid with so much as the sayd paye amounteth unto, and hath nothing to shew for the same, that may dischardg him in his accomptes. I pray your lordship therfore to geve order, that Mr. Morgan maye delyver unto him his acquitaunces, as aperteyneth for his indemnitye; and, towching the matter ytself, the armour that he hath sent backe being refused by the country, I do not see howe he can be releevid unles some vent maye be found for the same, or that he will come over himself to make suite and take some order in yt. And so I most humbly take my leave. At Richmond, the xxth of July, 1586.

Your lordships to commaunde,

FRA: WALSYNGHAM.

Addressed,
To the right honorable my very good lord, thearle of Leycester, lieutenant-generall of her majesties forces in the Lowe Countryes.

LETTER CXXXIV.

LORD BURGHLEY TO THE EARL OF LEYCESTER.

21st July, 1586.   COTTON. MS. GALBA, C. IX. FOL. 313.

Proposed change of Harlingen for Brill, abandoned on the earl's advice—chamber of finances—cause of the delay of sir William Pelham—equalization of the values of English and Flemish monies—gain upon coinage—the merchant-adventurers, being alarmed by the loss of Grave and Venlo, decline making payments to the earl—treasurer's accounts—sir Thomas Shirley sent with the treasurer as overseer of his accounts—count of Emden's determined neutrality—importance of the river Ems to the Spaniards, also of Dunkirk and Nieuport, the capture of which latter is recommended to the consideration of the earl—Mr. Wilkes sent over on a special mission to encourage the states and confer with the earl—sir William Stanley has just arrived from Ireland—his levies of troops thought to have reached Flushing—state of France—master of Gray intends to send his troops to the earl.

My verie good lord, I will first beginne to awnsweare your [lordships] letter of the xviijth of June, which doth conteine your advise verie circumst[antially] geven for my sonne to have consideration of the matter that hath been [moved] to your lordship from hence, for the change of Brill for Harlingham,[a] and for that [he] was come over thither before the receipt of your [lordships] letter, I could not conferre with him theareuppon, but if I had, by the reasons alledged in your lordships letters, which are verie manie, I should have counseled him to have continued in the Brill, than to have gon so farre of as Harlingham is, being owt of the limits both of Holland and Zeland; and the rather, also, I would have advised him to have continued at the Brill, bicause I perceive by your lordships letter, you can be content

[a] Harlingen in Friesland.

that, with the Brill, he maie have the governement of the iland, which maie be very commodious for him, for the strengthening of the place; and so nowe, meaning not to trowble your lordship with this matter, I dowbt not but he himself hath commoditye to receive your lordships resolucion thearein, which I leave to himselfe to accept, and conforme himselfe to your advise.

In the postscript of your sayd letter I perceive, that by the establishing of the chamber of finances your lordship shall be more hable to make necessarie paimentes for all thinges requisite under your charge then heretofore you have been, the opinion of which lack hath most cheeflye bread dowbt in hir majestie of the good sequel of the cawse; and therefore the sooner your lordship maie make it appeare to hir majesty, that the contribucions heretofore offred by the states maie be nowe performed, which spetiallie will be best credited by hir majestie if she maie perceive, that such sommes of monie as have been paiable by the states to yourself for your enterteinement, and to satisfie the debtes due to hir majestie for hir treasure defraied to their uses, [have been paid,] the more resolute shall you find hir majestie to stand fast and firme in the prosecution of this action.

Your lordship doth in that end of the letter, also as in manie others, make mention of your desire to have sir William Pelham theare, which surelie hath not been by me omitted, nor by himself delaied, but as now he can tell your lordship, whoe I trust hath arrived theare sum fewe daies past, in whom the lett hath been, partlie for not yelding to the acquitall of his debtes, and partlie, as hir majestie did often awnsweare us, that she could not well spare such a man from the service in the office that he hath, considering both the absence of sir Philip Sidney, and the unhabilitye of my lord of Warwick, your brother, to travell. But my awnswere was theareto, that, for anie spetiall service in the field at home, in that kind of office, I thowght, as longe as you weare well occupied in thos cuntries against the common enemie, and might prosper theare, we should not have any great neade of his presence heare.

Nowe, my lord, for awnsweare of sum matters conteined in your other longe letter. Your lordship writeth, that I, in my former letter, did sett a rate of the angell and the shillinge, the one at xv^s the other at xx^d, and you did doubt wheather I ment it to be the valewe of sterling or otherwise. But I did, and doe still meane it, to have our angell, that is heare x^s, to be currant theare for xv^s Flemishe, and our sterling shilling that is heare xij^d, to be theare currant for xx^d Flemishe. And wheare the great rose-noble was theare in estimation farre above his valewe, and nowe is fallen out of that reputacion, I was ever of that minde, and shall be, that newe coine in anie cuntrie wheare knowledg is of minting, will have a higher estimacion than his ritches will yeld him, and so I think your lordship should have proved. The experience of him that offred yowe so great sommes for the coinage of the rose-nobles in that cuntrye would have tended to a fall of his great offer within one moneth or lesse; for, trewlie, it is a natural reason in all thinges, that *ex nihilo nihil fit,* and noe great gaine can ever be made to last, but wheare the cawse and grounde of the gaine shall last. We had heare the like experience for a while, of an offer made by alderman Martin, to yeld to hir majestie for the coinage of everye pownd weight of gold into rose-nobles the sum of xxx^s, wher otherwise was never paid above iiij^s, for other the best gold; and, having commission to coine the same, he was forced to leave of within the monethe, for that the estimacion of them did sodenlie decaie, and so the coinage perforce did staie, and yet, for that short time, her majestye had awnswered unto hir neare m^{li} for coinage. I perceive your lordship hath the stampes of the said rose-nobles which your offerer had provided, and, I thinke, if the matter weare renewed unto him againe, he could not mainteine any reason to yeld unto your lordship anie extraordinarie proffett by coinage of them, more then of other gold of like fines, whearein I praie your lordship cawse him to be tempted anewe, and lett me knowe his awnsweare, for if hir majestie might have the gaine thearebie, I should be right glad thereof, and would also further it, so as it might be sett downe to what quantitie the coinage should be.

And, for that I sent your lordship word of summ shillinges coined in that cuntrie, the partie that browght them unto me said, he had them from Amsterdam, as being coined theare; but, as your lordship writeth, it might be at summ other towne, as Gorcum, or such like: but this maie be held for a rule generall, that whearesoever our monies, either gold or silver, be coined in anie other cuntrie, if the same coines be in waight and fines as good as ours, theare will be noe longe continuance of coinage thereof; for the proffett of the coinage, which is the sufferantie to the prince, is so small as [it is] hard for privatt men to continue such coinage; but if, otherwise, theie be coined of lesse valewe, then, thowgh for summ time, people may be abused to receive them, yet such monies will not have longe continuance in theire estimacion.

Your lordship maketh mention of my writing that I had delt with the merchantes-adventurers to paie ther $xxx^{m\ li}$, which indeade theie weare contented to promise, at that time when I did write so, but, afterward, uppon the losse of Grave and Venlo, theie semed to have had intelligence from there factors on [that] side the seas, that the trade of merchandize began to change [and] staie, and so theie started from theire promise: and yet, after that, theie helped your lordship with $v^{m\ li}$ which was verie happelie taken upp [by] your lordship, in that it semeth, though the some weare little, the poore soldiers weare more releved with that small portion than theie had been with the paie of a great deale more before. And, trewlie, if your lordship could bring it to pass, that the poore soldiers might be paied by [the] poll, sometimes one monethes paie would doe more good in that sort, than two monethes paie to the capteine, and, in like sort, I see your lordship hath care, that theie which shall have the disposing of the treasure [may] be directed so to dispose it as it maie cum trewlie and indifferentlie to the use of the soldier.

The paiment made to the states of monie by the threasurer, whereof your lordship maketh mencion that it was paied without your warrant or assignment, hath been hard to be excused, [any] otherwise then that the threasurer saith, he made the warrant by the forme of another, written before by Mr. Atye, your lordships secretarie. I am of opinion, as your lordship is, that the states would not agree [to] make the rembursement of these thinges, if your lordships warrant had not past for the same; and one thing I find hath been greatlie forgot theare, that, according to an article of the contract, the states commissaries have not been made privie to our musters and paiements, whearebie the issue will be, respondence for repaiment to bee made [here]after to hir majesty. At this time hir majestie hath appointed sir Thomas Shurleie to cum over with the threasurer, and to be privie of all receiptes of monie that he shall have, heare or theare, and shall joine with the threasurer in all paimentes to be directed by your lordship, and not otherwise, so as it shall be in your lordships power, for this time, to see and have perfect knowledg to whome anie monie shall be paid, and how much he shall have to paie, and, uppon the paiments of this money now delivered to them both in charge, the threasurer is determined to leave the place, and so I have of long time advised him, and would have had him so to have done heare, by ending his whole accompt [on] this side, but hir majestie would have[a] him come over to make an ende of his broken paimentes theare, whereof, uppon his accompt heare, many dowbtes have been made, and he left in suspence and respect almost of xi^{m} ^{li}, though he showeth divers matters for his warrantiz to be allowed thereof, as by his peticions which at this time are sent over thither by sir Thomas Shurleie, maie appeare: which are of sundrie natures, for that he sheweth good warrantes for paiment of divers sommes, but noe perfect acquittances of the receivors,

[a] would neaver have, *in MS*.

though he saie theie be left theare on that side now to be produced, and, for sum part, he sheweth acquittances of sommes due and paied but hath not heare shewed warrantes for the same, for the which he is to receive your lordships favour, as the justice of the paimentes shall require.

Your lordship maketh mention of the sending of William Herle to Embden, from whome, at the writing of your letter, your lordship had noe awnswere. But nowe of late I have seen, in Mr. secretaries handes, the whole negotiation of William Herle, by objecting and expostulating with the comte of Embden for verie manie thinges, and of the awnsweares made thereunto; whearebie it appearethe, that manie thinges have been spread otherwise to his condemnacion than was trewe. But yet, I see the sequell will be, that, although our merchantes maie have traffique thither, yet he will keape still a newtralitie, both towardes the king of Spayne and thos provinces, for aiding and victualing of either of them. I wishe he might be otherwise recovered in favor of thos states, consideringe the benefitt that might growe to thos provinces under your government, if the river of Ems might be kept free from the trade of the Spanishe side, whoe surelie have great cawse to attaine to the possession of that river, thearebie to have sum passage open to the sea, as well to have entrance from the sea thither as to passe to the sea from thence, the lack of which commoditye is one of the principall impedimentes that impeacheth the king of Spaines actions. Having, for all his great cuntries in that part of christendome, noe commoditye to passe and repasse the seas but by Graueling, which is not worth naming, and by Dunkirke, and Newport, which two, in my opinion, weare of as [a] great moment to be wonn from him as either Gant, or Bruges, or both. And, if I knew howe to geve counsell for such an enterprise, I would preferre it before anie other in this time, for I doe conclude that the king of Spaine never can be a full master of thos cuntries without he have sum owt-gate and in-gate by the sea. And, whilest I am writing thus, I praie your lordship thinke

[a] as of, *in MS.*

howe such service might be done by your maritime forces and flie-boates theare, that are fittest to impeche thos kind of havens. Thus having been longe in trowbling your lordship, withowt anie great matter of substaunce, but uppon conclusions taken by perusing your lordships letters, and nowe, considering what thinges have hapned since the writinge of your letters, I will breefly make sum mention of thinges latelie passed.

By sum late letters written from your lordship to hir majestie, and by sum conference had with Coxe, whoe browght the same letters, hir majestye hath had sondrie ernest consultacions with Mr. vice-chamberlaine, Mr. secretarie, and me, uppon divers thinges contained in your lordships letters, and for that hir majestie perceiveth you are verie desirous to be advised and directed by hir for your governement in that place, which is accompanied with manie great difficulties at this time, thearefore, after longe debate had before hir majestie, it was thowght most necessarie to send one spetiallie from hir majestie unto your lordship, having named two or three, but in the ende, hir majesty made choise of Mr. Wilkes, the bearer of thes my letters, whoe is instructed, not onelie by sum writings, as memorialls, delivered unto him, but, also, by longe speches of hir majestie hirself, which she hath recorded in hir owne tables, and nevertheles caused him to putt the same more at length in writing, so that he commeth verie well informed of hir majesties mind, and appointed also to be informed by your lordship of manie necessarie thinges for satisfaction of hir majestie. And, besides thes, he hath letters from hir majestie for assuraunce of hir constant persisting in this common action, and, bicause your lordship shall at length understand by himself the matters committed to his charge, I doe thearefore forbeare to make any further mention thereof.

At the writinge hereof sir William Stanley was come hither, and meaneth with hast to repaire to your lordship, judging that his men are before this time at Flushing.

Mr. secretarie, I thinke, doth advertise you of the dowbtfull estate of the affaires in Fraunce, altogether in great calamitie.

And, which is most of us to be dowbted and feared, by the long delaie of the armie to cum owt of Almaign, we maie dowbt that the king of Navarre will yeld to sum peace not profitable for the religion, but yet unprofitable for the Frenche king, for that the duke of Guise and all his partye, by sum mediation of the duke of Nevers and Montmorency, offer great frendshipp to the king of Navarre, meaning to seperatt themselves both from depending uppon the Frenche king or his mother, against whome the duke of Guise professeth open hatred, as thinking himself also secretlie hated by the king. And so, by thes strange accidentes, it cannot be but France must suffer great calamities, and so as the poore flock of Christ might be safe, whilest thes great bulls of Bazan shall rage one against the other, I care not for the rest that maie followe to that wicked nation.

I understand by Mr. secretory, that the master of Gray in Scotland contynueth his purposs to send forces out of Scotland to your lordship, and myndeth to come unto England first hyther. But I dout how he shall be helped with that mony that I had purpoossly stayd, being ij$^{m\ li}$ for hym, for that, as Mr. Shyrley can tell your lordship, hir majesty was grevoussly offended with me for steying of it; and, even this daye, I moved hir majesty ageyn, that it might be stayd, or otherwise the master of Gray shuld be disapoynted therof, but in no wise she wold yeld, as Mr. secretary can advertise your lordship.

And so, with a good hart and yet an evill head, I am forced to end, besechyng God to prosper yow, and enhable yow to hold the feld, but I wish not that yow shuld hazard any fight, for, as your case is, a small loss may be a gretar to yow than the lyk to the ennemy. From Rychmont, the 21. of July, 1586.

Your lordships most assuredly,
W. Burghley.

Addressed,
  To the right honorable my verie good lord, the erle of
    Leicester, lieutennant-generall for hir majesties
    forces, and governor of the provinces united.

LETTER CXXXV.

THE EARL OF LEYCESTER TO MR. SECRETARY WALSYNGHAM.

27TH JULY, 1586.   OUVRY MS. FOL. 39.   A COPY.

Growth of dissatisfaction amongst the people of the Low Countries, and dangerous courses adopted by them—questions raised as to the earl's jurisdiction, especially over the finances—capture of Nuys by the enemy after " a great fight," in which he lost 3,000 men—difficulty of getting money from the states—Burgrave's usefulness to the earl—the earl's doubtful state—a spy taken at Utrecht—papists banished thence—Paul Buys's lamentations on the seizure of his papers, which he got back again by favour of the countess de Meurs—lord Buckhurst wished for.

Mr. secretary, I feare it be thought longe till some well-instructed come here, having giuen notice of the doubtfullnes of this state, which hath growen within these two monethes in strange sorte, and yet cannot find that their is anie intencion to receaue hastelye the Spanish, but such an absurd daingerous kind of dealinge among these we caull " states," as noe marvell though they loose more in a yere then theie will gett in three. Paul Buys hath bine a great instrument to seeke to make an alteracion, by his subtile practises in working discontentacion in the peoples minds, but he is much hated, and trewly the common people [are] better then the superiour sort.

Her majestie was offended with me for being absolute gouernour, but I feare she will shortlie find fault with my litle authoritie. Theie have incroched vppon me greatlie within this v or vj weekes, and, to be plaine with you, if theie had their former rule againe, which theie had before my cominge, I would warrant the kinge of Spain setled in the heart of Holland or Hallontide; and yet theie would it not, nor doe feare it, but, if you saw what courses theie take, you would nothing doubt it. Theie are growen now to tye me to her majesties contract with them, and would faine, by that meanes, as thinkinge it will not mislike her majestie, to draw from me all other iurisdiccion, specially the gouernment of the financs, or distribution of ther tresure, for therin consisteth all ther benefitt and aime. They haue latelie restrained the paiment of the extraordinary monie for the maintenance of the army, which should haue bine paid in March, Aprill, May, and June, and c^m· florins a moneth, but not one pennie received yet, assigning this monie, for the receipt of it, the beginning of the last moneth. Notwithstandinge theie see the force of the enemie in ther countreie, that he doth what he list, and noe resistance against him, theie are noe whitt hastened to prepare for it. I will send her majestie by Aty all I knowe.

Newce was gotten the xvjth daie [a] of this moneth; a great fight there was, from iiij a clock in the morninge till v at night, without restinge; iiij great breches was made. The prince had 45 cannons to batter it, whereof the bishopp [b] did lend him xxv; he hath lost iij^m of his souldiers, and as manie hurt. The old count Mannfild we heare to be kild thir.

I hope this day to be dispached here for some mony; how I haue delt for it, and of my determinacion, Aty shall bringe you. I knowe not what may chaunge, but, as matters presently stand, I haue little hope of anie good, but yet I stay anie iudgment till you heare againe, but never man, I thinke, hath had such a monethes toile and travell as I haue had amonge them.

I haue found one man here a most faithfull, honest, wise, servant; his name is Burgrave. I knowe not a more sufficient man among them all then he is. I could not spare him for anie good;

[a] Strada makes it the 26th, which is no doubt right.
[b] Ernest, son of the duke of Bavaria, elected to the archbishoprick of Cologne, upon the deposition of Gebhard Truchses. It was upon his solicitation that the prince of Parma undertook the seige of Nuys, which a little interfered with the prince's design of proceeding to attack the northern provinces.

he hath a brother in London called Lodovike Burgrave, I pray you, sir, shewe him your good fauor wherin he shall haue cause to vse [it], and I shall take it most kindly, for I was neuer more beholdinge to a stranger then to his brother.

I am full, and yet I dare not discharge myself; I find all things soe vncertain here of late, yet not desperate. Thus much for this time withall, to lett you knowe the advertisment her majestie sent of Vtryckt is fallen out true, for we tooke a spie this last weeke of the prince, and about him letters, a man of good behauior, and an auncient man, and appered plainelie that there is a man in Vtrickt, a potycary, whoe hath a howse vppon the wall of the towne, that hath intelligence with the enemie, to lett in as manie men as he will at anie time. This man I haue apprehended. The towne of Vtrickt haue banished a great sort of papists out of the towne, whereof some are great with Paul Buys. He is with them still, prisoner, and would needs haue cutt of his head of late. Theie be greiuously bent against him, and noe doubt he is a most ill man. The count de Meures, or rather the countis, hath done him a great fauor, for his writings, which were all taken, and seald vpp to be sent, but he soe bribed some folks as he gott his writings out; before, he lamented, saying, "O, ma papiers! O, ma papiers! The queen of England will for euer hate me." And, as farr as I can learne, it was something past betwene him and Ortell, but there was stuffe beside to haue cost him his head, and vily did that lord and his wife deall in it.

Well, sir, of all these things I referre to the next, and heare leaue you, still hopinge to heare of some person of good qualitye to come hether speedilye, yf you thinke these causes worthy regard. My Lord of Buckhurst, mythinks, would doe gret good here. I feare her majestie will thinke every man to great to serue here, in such a case, but I pray God to meane be not sent; it is for her owne self, I tell you, then, who is to good? Hast, this 27th of July.

Your assured.

LETTER CXXXVI.

THE EARL OF LEYCESTER TO MR. SECRETARY WALSYNGHAM.

29TH JULY, 1586.   OUVRY MS. FOL. 40 b.   A COPY.

Difficulty of procuring money from the states—desertions to the enemy—the earl's anxiety to be at home again—necessity for having an absolute governor—disclosures made by a discovered spy—the earl now finds the states' men to be what the queen was wont to hit them off—begs Walsyngham to further the proposal for sending some person of credit thither from her majesty—the spy confirms the treasonable surrender of Grave and Venlo—particulars of the taking of Nuys, and dreadful barbarities practised towards the governor—consequences of the want of money—Axel secure—consequences of breaking the dykes—conduct of count Hohenlohe after the surrender of Grave—fidelity of the elector Truchses, who has reconciled Hohenlohe to Leycester—Hohenlohe's position and character—and that of Truchses—number of English in the Low Countries—Emden—Dr. Barth. Clerk—Henry Killigrew.

Mr. secretarye, I must lett you knowe how daingerous a necessitie we haue bine latly drawen vnto for lack of monie for our souldiers, which the states here doth follow for theirs in such sort as noe marvell if all men were runn awaye, as I doe assure you there are to manie already gone to the enemie for very extremitye, and for that I haue layd such waite for them to goe over as I haue taken aboue iiij^c, and haue executed some for example, but not many, for that in conscience they suffer overmuche. Muse not though the enemie take townes, and doe what he list, for when we want men we are to weake, when we haue men we want money. I doe swere to you, by the living God, that if it had not bine for the monie which I borrowed and prested vnto them, now vj weeks past, we had had the fowlest and most reprochfull revolt and mutiny amonge our people that euer had bine sene, and at this daye forst[a] to feed them with faire words and promises; "To morrow, to morrowe, they shall haue"—O, Lord! whoe would thinke it possible for anie men sent as we are, and in action for that realme cheifly, and all christendome also, to be soe carelesly and overwillingly overthrowen for ordinary wants. Wishing cannot serve me to be at home, nor that I had never come here, but shame and dishonour will make me weary of my life. Lett all the world iudge here for me, and I am sure that they doe not thinke that my service and payns hath deserved soe little consideracion. What oportunityes we haue latly lost! We are ready to eate our owne flesh for anger, but that cannot helpe.

Her majestie shall now see the fruits of her displeasure, and whether there was iust cause or noe to haue absolute government. The hold was quickly taken to interrupt it, and of late very thorowly put in execucion, and the practises of Paul Buis hath greatly shaken the good trade of this government, and of a most hated man of all theis states and councellours before, he is now highly fauored for seeking to restore them to their authoritie againe. And, lett them say what theie will, theie will hardlie be brought againe to the point they were at, for as then the feare of the people, in which case theie yet stand, did much, so now the hope to pacifie them by meanes doth encourage them; for theie loue to rule wholye, and not to be gouerned, and of late theie haue exceedinglie incroched vppon me, it now apperes, for assuredlie theie will adventure to doe much to overthrow it, and speciallie findinge me so slenderlie backit.

We had a spye of the enemies taken iiij dayes past, a man of good accompt, ancient, and verie wise, little suspected to be such a man. We found many matters by letters, amonge which the confirmacion of her majesties aduertisment for the daunger of Vtryckt to be one. This man confessed to the marshall, sir Wil-

[a] first, *in MS.*

liam Pelham, and others that examined him, that the cheifest matter the prince tooke care for was, that I were not absolute governour, nor the disposer of their treasure, which the prince did tell him he thought was altered, with other more particuler declaracions touching that cause of these things, and how this state doth stand. I meane more fullie to aduertise her majestie by Aty, as soone as I can well dispach him, for there be some causes yet to staye; but all hast possible he shall make, albeit I haue not one man to doe me his service againe, but the matters be such as I cannot well sett downe in writinge. I did write to you for Bodely to be sent to me, and Rogers, for you knowe by yourself what it is to want able instruments in such service. I pray you yet help me to them; yf they be vnwillinge, to some other, such as you knowe able and honest men.

Well! I will leaue my complaynts, and referre the remedy to God and her majestie, and likwise forbeare to lett you knowe what dealing I haue bine forst to vse of late with these states men; you conceaving well enough what composicion theie are made of, as her majestie was wont most rightly to hitt of them. I find that trew all men before did. Hit ys a monstruous gouernment where so many such heads doe rule, and, except her majestie take another course, I must fall vnder this or longe. I hold out by mine owne poore creditt yet what I can, and haue won at last somewhat, but not so much as will serve at their hands. Divers honest men hold with me, as well councellors as others of the better sort; and I must say, notwithstandinge all practises and backwardnes at this present, and of late, the case is not desperate if it will please her majestie to take vppon her, and looke gratiously into hit; for only vppon her it will rest, and otherwise all wilbe lost and overthrowen, yea, soner then [by] you wilbe thought. Hit is the cause that made me so earnist and bold to write to her majestie to send some person of creditt and countenance hether, that she maie more assuredly vnderstand the state of all things than perhapps I am anie way able to doe. And I beseech you, for her service and the cause sake, further it with expedition. You maie take occasions inow, especially her majestie not being satisfied from me for ther abilitye to mainteine their charges in warr, and hearing the contracts for paiments of her people at their chardge and officers is not performed, and the doubt is hard of their countenance and holding out anie longe time, doth move her majestie, as reason is, to knowe it, being offered such offers as she hath bine for herself, and the hope she hath to doe for them if theie be in such weake estate as she heareth of, and doth feare, seeing the slowe paiments theie make, and the great hazard theie haue putt themselues of late in for lack of monie. This is a iust and a weighty cause to send to them, beside other very great and effectuall which he shall find here, to be impartid at his coming, worth the travell of a right good man, for the sure service of her majestie.

I forgott to lett you knowe, writing of the spye, how he hath flatlie confirmed the intelligence betwene the prince and Hemert for Grave, being concluded before the overthrow geven the Spaniards ther, as likewise for Venloe by the magistrates, and that the prince was sorreye Shenks was not within, as he hoped, for, at his coming thether, the prince said, that, if he had knowen of Shenks attempt with noe greater nomber, he should haue had leaue to[have] gone in, for it was promised to haue deliuered him into the princes hands, as it appered theie were able, for theie deliuered all the souldiers to him, being vj^c; he had also the like promise of Newce, and Berks, and three other places, whereof Vtrickt was one most accompted of, and myself to haue bine, as he saith, assuredlie trapt in it.

Yet hath the gouernor [a] of Newce deceaued him, for he did defend the towne very manfullye to the last, the assalts continuing from 4 in the morning till 5 at night, without intermission, and being only ij^c men left, and the others greatlie consumed, to

---

[a] Gouernment, *in MS.*

the nomber of 3000 dead in ditches, besides infinit hurt. The prince offered a parley, and made a retyre[a]; in the meane time, sodanly, a traitor ran out at the brech, told the enemy that all the souldiers were kild and hurt within, save a very fewe, and that the capten was hurt sore, as he was. Theie gaue a new furious assault, vppon this, with all the fresh men theie had left, and so the others, to weake, were overthrowen. The capten was the next daye fetch[ed] to the markett place, and was charged, not onlie with brech of promise, but with the cause of the destruccion and losse of his people, as indeed he was, and if Grave had held but half his time the prince had neuer bine able to haue held vpp his head. After he was brought to the markett-place, being sore wounded before, theie layd him vppon a table, and bound him, and nointed him with tarre all over his bodie, and half-strangling him, burnt him cruelly. This cruell death doth argue the informacion to be true that he had gevin some hope to the prince and the bushopp before, for ells theie would never have vsed a souldier in that sort, beinge noe subiect borne to the kinge nor to the bishopp. The town of Newce between the soldiers is burnt downe to the ground, not a house left.[b] Hit apperes the

[a] relyue, *in MS.*

[b] The destruction of Nuys, although one of the most terrible incidents of this dreadful war, was not quite so total as is represented by the earl, nor was the death of the governor, although one of infamous barbarity, precisely of the kind above described. A dangerous wound received by Cloet, the governor, at an early period of the siege, threw the operations of the defenders into confusion, and after the furious battery described by Leycester, led to a proposal for surrender. The prince of Parma joyfully entertained the proposal, and was in the act of conferring with the deputies for the town when his troops, determined not to be deprived of their expected plunder, as they had been in the instance of Venlo, rushed forward, in defiance of the prince's authority, and gained possession of the town. A work begun thus irregularly proceeded only from bad to worse. Crimes of every degree of atrocity were perpetrated without remorse; and after having satiated fury, avarice, and lust, the wretches completed their devilish labours by setting fire to the houses in which they had committed their crimes. A high wind favoured the conflagration, and, after a few hours, two churches, crowded with trembling fugitives, were all that remained uninjured of a populous and flourishing town. The governor was seized in his bed-chamber

losse is great, for the prince is come away to Antwerpe, and his armie is risen, and 1,500 foote with 300 horse gone toward Fresland, with Taxes, whoe is sore hurt. The rest, some saye, are marching toward Flaunders. Some say, for as yet we haue not the certenty of this, that theie remaine at Casarswart for pay, and most certen when he cam to Grave the souldiers had but a duckett a peice till now, and what is done, this night I shall heare, or to morrow. It is constantlie reported old Mansfeild is slaine, also.

The oportunity we haue lost now, for lack of our monie, you may see, for bothe the towne had bine saved, and the enemy could not but hardly escape. I had iij weeks past appointed 6000 foote, beside horse, to goe, the captens and all readye, but could not gett a pennie of the states, nor had we one groat of hir majestie, till this last weeke $x^{m\,li}$, which I darst not speake of, it was soe farr to short to helpe, without more to it, neither dare I, nor will I, make anie pay of a penny of her majesties monye to anie but to those in her owen charge. I haue bine here this xv dayes for monie, and did, at my comyng from Vtrickt, appoint another assembly to be the xx[th] of this moneth, not fearing Newce then, for, though it was besieged, yet was it not battered, nor any battery begon to it, but all had bine one, for we coold haue noe monye. I then appointed another assembly for our armie to meete, in hope of monie, not knowing neither Newce to be yet in that dainger, to be the 1st of August. It is now the xxix[th] of this moneth, and I cannot haue monye to bringe men but to the feld, soe that I am at my witts end, and sir William Pelham mervells I haue not left all, that hath found such dealinge here, and soe little comfort from home, as I haue donne; but I thanke God he

and hanged out at the window, " with some note of unsoldierlike usage," adds the writer of the Briefe Reporte (sig. C. 1.) See Strada, vol. ii. lib. viii. Stowe's (p. 734) account of this matter, which is said to have been derived from Archer, is very inaccurate. He makes the town to have been set on fire by the " lackies and boys belonging to our soldiers;" but it does not appear that there were any English troops there.

is come, I find already great comfort in him. And, albeit I haue many discomforts, I will pray to God to giue me both strength and patience to serve him and hir majestie. And one token he giueth me, of great hope, for I never had my helth better to abide travell, nor all my company more willinge to adventure their lives.

This dispersinge of the princes armie is of great imputacion, and most unhappy are we here that are soe impeched by want that we cannot direct ourselues as we should, but, noe dowts, I trust yet we shall doe well. The matter of Axell doth greiue him to the heart, and he would faine pretend some revenge in these parts, but to my vnderstandinge he will be deceaued. That place is safe enough now, and yet was there councell geven to haue burnt it and to abandon it. But I would not consent to it. The brech [a] hath wrought such effect as it hath damnified the country to the value alreadye of ij millions, in graine, grasse and cattell. There hath bine great practice vsed of late to gett Lyllo, and Lyfekinshoofe. I haue giuen my best order to withstand all, and yet all things are made light there with you. Hit is imagined that such places are impregnable, what for their scituacion and strengths theie are not to be feared, but if these that soe imagine were here, and to see not onlye the infinite practises of the enemye by gifts and rewards to corrupt men, but also the hard and streite dealings vsed towards the captens and souldiors to drive them to yt, theie would mervell more that theire is anie place at their disposition out of the enemyes hands, then why anie accompt shall be made of the holding of them. And noe prayse, or anie dew thanks, can be yeilded to these states men of the countrey for it, but onlie to the affeccion and obedience to the queens majestie, for whose sake theie doe and haue suffered much, I assure you.

I did write lately very doubtfully to hir majestie of the count

[a] This alludes to a cutting of the dykes which had been had recourse to in the neighbourhood of Axel. Stowe, 733. Holinshed, iv. 881. Briefe Report, sig. B. 2.

Hollock, whome, after the losse of Grave, I found greatly chaunged, and, where he was till that time my lieutenant-generall, he begann to make some excuses, finding some wants in himself, then lack in the states, and, lastly and cheifly, dowbt of hir majesties favour and liking of this cause. Paul Buis hath bine the onlie director of this man a good while, and was the cause, as you haue heard, of his first dealing to make a mislikeing of the capten here, which was at my first having this charge. For after Paul Buis could not place whome he would here in councell, nor rule all, he fell streit to faction, to overturne all againe, insomuch as then the count Hollock found it so playnly as he went to his howse to kill him, as the ellector Truxis told me, whoe is her majesties most faithfull servant, and I must say, is the most honest true gentleman that I found of anie since I came, yet could I never gett him thanks from her majestie, albeit, by my dewty to hir majestie, he hath deserved far great[er] consideracion, for he hath done her majestie xx^{m} ^{li} worth of good service, and the best wach over all theis men that I can finde, and in this matter of the count Hollocke hath delt most honestly and honorably. I beseech you, amonge so manie great rewards as her majestie is to giue abroad, help this gentleman to somwhat. He is exceedinge poore, and the worse for this losse of Newce, which was in controversye betwene him and the count Newenor,[a] as Berks is yet. Her majestie in her life never bestowed anie benefitt more deservedly.

He hath delt with the count Hollock soe farr as he is very well come about ageine, and hath bine these xx dayes better then ever he was, and the very cause indeed he confesseth, Paul Buis told him her majestie would quite forsake this countreie, and cared not what became of it, and as for me much lesse. This gentleman having a great minde, and having longe servid this countrey continually in warre, cannot be blamed if such a perswacion should trouble him, never hearing from her majestie but at my first comynge, nor anie comfort whereto he maie trust, yeilding himself

[a] Newces, *in MS.* See page 376, note a.

wholie to her majestie, as he did indeed; yet soe well inclyned is he to her majestie, as not onlie he will still proceed in her service vnder me, as he did, but hath secretly giuen me knowledg, but vnder exceeding great secresy, that he is greatly afferd the count Morrice is drawen to harken to some daingerous course, onlie vpon the like earnist perswasion that her majestie will forsake this countrey, at least not soe to proceed with them as may giue them hope and assurance; which practice with these is most pestilent, for these ij haue manie freinds and dependants, the one thorow the countrey for his fathers sake, the other with manie the souldiers for his authority sake, having bine manie yeres the late prince of Oranges lieutenant, and greatly esteemed by him, for doubtles he is a most valiant gentleman, and an exceeding good soldier for these countreis, and alwaies esteemed for a plaine faithfull man, where he betakes himself; and the more he is regarded in these countreys, for that it is like he shall marry the lady of Burren, the princes daughter by his first wife, and heire to all the count Burrens lands yf hir brother in Spain faile, whoe doth presently, also, enioy all those lands in theis parts.[a] I haue bine carfull to keepe this gentleman, and I trust now I haue him in good termes againe, and shall doe the better that the vile wretch Paul Buis is from him; next whom, of all men, he is most [led] by the ellecter, whome I praie God her majestie may some wayes honorably consider. I doe meane to write to her majestie touching him very shortlie. He is a gentleman she would like well as anie man I have seen com to hir being a stranger. His wisdome, his behauiour, his languages, his person, and all will like her well, and as great an affecion he beareth her as anie man, not her owne subiect, can doe. He is presentlie in great mallancholye for his towne of Newce, and for his pouertie, having a verie noble mind. I doe feare if he find not comfort the soner he wilbe lost, and

---

[a] The lady alluded to was Mary of Nassau, daughter of the prince of Orange by his first wife Anne of Egmont, countess of Buren. The "brother in Spain" was the prince's eldest son, for many years a prisoner in that country.

her majestie were better loose a c$^{m\ li}$, yf she continue this cause. He beginnes to fall toward a palsey, and yet he is but a young man; his heart is almost broken thorow want.

This day the count Hollocke and sir William Pelham are gone to certen places in Brabant; he is greatlie in love with Mr. Pellam. Theie meete me againe at our place of assemblie a Tewseday next. The count Morrice is here[a] now with me, and maketh all good shew. I haue delt already vppon verie good occacion very plainly with him; he stands vppon makinge and marringe, as he meets with good councell. The count Hollock will deall also plainely with him, yf he haue not this daye alredy. The keeping of theis men in good tune must only be hir majesties gratious vsage, spetiallie the count Hollocke and the ellector. I would to God sir Francis Drake were come with some millions, that her majestie might bestow some liberalitie vppon theis ij noblemen in time.

Touching our late nombers come over, you shall see what need we had. I assure you we are not able, of xj^m English footmen to draw out v^m men to goe to the feild, except we leaue such places vnfurnished as we are most sure as sone as our men be out theie will shutt the gates against vs; every towne doth seeke so to be at his owne libertie, that he maie deall as the world shall goe, and yet, of all men, theie covett in all places Englishmen most. And one great lacke we had, that our men came not [at] once; the most of them arrived but latelie, and at least 2,500 vnfurnished, and yet it is thought that we are able to make x^m Englishmen to the feild. Wold God without hazardinge places of great importance we maie make 6,000 English footmen strong to the feild, and, yf 12,000 haue arrived, I am sure ther is 2,000 gone and slipt awaie of our nomber.

Thus praying you to further the sending of some man of creditt hether, I bidd you, good Mr. secretary, farwell. From the Hage, this xxix. of July.

Your assured freind.

[a] nere, *in MS.*

I haue had much adoe here for the matter of Emden as ever [I] had in anie thinge in my life, and faine herein to vse authority enough. I trust I haue delt to our merchants content, and for her majesties service, but theie of Emden will not agree. I assure [you] Dr. Barthelmew Clerk doth serue exceeding honestlye and painfullie, and doth increase greatly in vnderstanding. Ha. Killegrew[a] is a quicker and stouter fellow then I tooke him for, he can deall roughly enough when it pleaseth him. Yf you doe not send the muster-master over it wilbe much to our[b] hindrance.

LETTER CXXXVII.

THE EARL OF LEYCESTER TO MR. SECRETARY WALSYNGHAM.

30TH JULY, 1586.   OUVRY MS. FO. 45.   A COPY.

Critical condition of affairs—particulars of the intrigues of Paul Buys, and of the conduct of the elector Truchses in reference to them, with a character of the latter, and suggestion that the queen should grant him a pension secretly—conduct of count Hohenlohe —the earl has taken " a little conceate " to absent himself from the council—the jealousy entertained of sir William Pelham by sir John Norris and encouraged by sir Thomas Cecill—general muster of troops about to take place—Norris's complaints—sir Francis Drake's return—treaty for the merchants as to Emden.

Sir, I haue written a letter to you by my servant Heydon, and one to her majestie, but in her majesties letter at this time noe matter, but referrs to yours, for that I meane within v or vj dayes to send Aty over; but I thought good to send this before the rest to you, being for your owne informacion onlie.

This state stands verie tickell, and only by the dowbt of her majestie, and, most assured, without some present good dealing

[a] Killigrave, *in MS.*   [b] her, *in MS.*

all wilbe lost. You knowe it stands me vppon to deall plainelie in this case. You will not beleeue what a sodaine alteracion here grew vpon this conceat of her majesties leaving them, and what deep practises were streit in hand to prevent this government. The plott [was] first layd by Paul Buys, and he began with Hollock, to discourage him; then with Morice, to advance him; thirdly with some his owen faction of the states-generall, to wrangle with me for divers points of my authority; still geuing out slanderous speeches of her majesties covetousnes, and her deceuing all men, and that he knew she ment not to reliue these countrys anie further; that my authoritie now should but vndoe them all, for that I sought onlie to make great forces of Englishmen to gett their townes vppon their pay, that thereby, whensoeuer her majestie should thinke good to treate for peace, as she was in hand with it, I should hereby be able to compell them to what end she shuld thinke good. He leyd before some of them, what charges theie must be at with me, for my particuler, and how it was looked for by her majestie, and that all theie had must now be bestowed vppon English that shall ouerrule them as they list.

Divers other particulerityes of his lewd dealinge is discouered to me by one that, but for the cause sake, and her majesties, would not doe it for x$^{m\ li}$. He is the most honest and noble gentleman that I haue meet withall in all these parts; it is the ellector Truxey. He loves her majestie with his heart, and the religion, for he professeth it truely. He wisheth altogether the prosperitye of this cause, and I haue found most true aduertisments from him of anie man, and most sound advise alwaies, for he is a very deepe wise man. He governes greatlie the count Hollocke, whoe doth imparte wholy his secrett heart to the ellector; beside Paul Buis hath made shew to depend vpon him, and is his councellor in the cause of Berks and Newce [a] between the count Meures and him, and Paul Buis hath entred as farr as he

---

[a] Berck, or Rhineberg, and Nuys, were both situate in the diocese of Cologne, but had been secured by the count de Meurs for the deposed elector. The dispute between the

durst, fearinge our freindshipp, to alienate this good gentleman both from her majestie and me, and by this man haue I knowen the whole of this practice, and, as he hath done notable offices herein to prevent Paul Buys, so hath he done it verie wisly, that he is not mistrusted. And, for to drawe the suspicion from him, I semed still to knowe Paul Buys doings by those of Vtrickt, whome I encouraged all I could still against him, whoe are exceedinglie bent against him to the vttermost, and others also hath giuen me much light of his speeches vsed at tables, but this noble gentleman hath delt most deeply to seeke out the bottome, and to withstand it. He finds for certen, that, except her majestie will declare herself to mainteine this people and countreys, theie wilbe gone. And I haue found all the manner of proceedinge true, as he did informe me, touching there meaning to revoke the authoritie giuen me by litle and litle; as well for their restraint of paiments to wery our men, as to drive them to mutinie, and soe away; to hold fast all their townes, but only froynter townes, from garisons; to shake of Gelders, Vtrickt, and Brabant, with Over Isell, by little and little, from the charge of Holland and Seland; to make their owne contribucions serve their owne turne, for defensive warr, till either theie may gett some prince able to defend them, or ells make a better end for themselues then now theie can. Particuler princes are named, as Denmark, cheifly with Paul Buys; himself told me of [this] at sir Thomas Heneage being here, but I thought him wiser then to meane it earnistlie.

These plotts, specially touchinge the count Hollock, this gentilman hath prevented well; and where the count gaue me warning, vppon the losse of Grave, he could serue noe longer as liuetenent vnder me, and prest me earnistly to receaue backe his patent, I did very earnistlie againe presse him to know the cause, he vsed other then I knewe indeed were iust causes, and he grew solemne, and withdrew himself much from me, the cause was that

elector and the count had reference to the profits which resulted from the possession of these towns. In the Briefe Report it is said that shortly after the loss of Venlo " his excellencie . . . quieted the strife betweene those two." (sig. C. 1.)

I tould you before, Paul Buys had perswaded him vtterlie from trustinge to her majestie anie more; yet by this noble gentlemans dealinge, the ellector, he hath brought the count into as good mind as euer he was, and I neuer saw him more dilligent or carefull then he is now at this present, insomuch as he hath taken vppon him to bringe Moryce to good tune[a] againe also, who is with me now here. I pray God, this gentleman cheifly may receaue some good consideracion from her majestie, in time, for he hath not a groate to liue on, and you knowe what estate he was of. I assure you that he hath had 4,000 florins in monie of me, beside other helps, and, as I am able, I will reliue him, but all I brought, and much more, is gone since; 1,000^{li} as a present from her majestie would bind him much, he hath deservid x^{mli} in respect of these matters, for, by him only, I accompt the stay of all things, but it must not be knowen, for he is vndone here then. Would to God, secretlie, he were her majesties penconer, if he had 2,000 crownes a yere, though it be to little, and a yeres rent aforehand, hit wilbe a relife to his estate that is soe poore. I meane to write of his service to her majestie, albeit I dare not write all things as I wold to her, which made me wryte soe earnistlie to haue some man of qualitie to come over, whoe shall see plainlie that all shalbe trew I write or advertise, which is, that all wilbe lost if her majestie deall not speedilie and substanciallie, and all wilbe saved and most surely established, yf she will protest yt, and yet not to be at anie great charges more then she is at. My lord of Buckhurst would be a very fitt man; I praie you furder him to it; he shall neuer liue to doe a better service.

Lett it appere as it will, I growe now a stranger in councell here. I haue taken a little conceate, but iustly, vppon great cause, to forbeare, for I find my authority is secretly shaken, which I cannot bere because it wilbe dangerous to the cause; otherwise I care not vj^d, but to giue 5,000 6^d, and 6,000 shellings, to be rid of it, and hit is not to be delt withall, this place, except I be thorowly backt by her majestie. I doe hope it shalbe found that I haue done

[a] This word is uncertain in the MS.

as much as a man with so manie wants, and being so much disgraced as I haue bine, could well doe.

I will not write anie more of Mr. John Norris backwardnes; he hath to good freinds, and soe hath all that like not me. He stomacks greatlie the marshall,[a] but I see he will not away. He is of like sett for an agent. It skills not, for he shall not doe much hurt now, I warrant you. I heare the tresorer doth come; I praie God you haue sent the muster-master also, or ells all is mard, and in all hast possible must he be sent.

Sir John Norris doth altogether [b] now follow sir Thomas Cecill; and, for that the marshall is before himself, he setts sir Thomas Cecil to take the place, which the marshall doth noe way impunge, though the other play the foole. My lord North, Audleie, yea, and Essex, doth offer the marshall the place, and will not otherwise, yet Cecill doth take it. I assure you this Norris is a most subtile daingerous man, not hauing a true word in his mouth, nor any brother. He hath factious and lyinge fellowes, I would God you could ridd vs of them; but I see theie are the better allowed for that theie are thought to mislike me. I praie you deall with ther father, but speciallie ther mother. I feare my lord-tresorer doth make his sonne fauor them. All such dealings, good Mr. secretary, you are better able to discouer and prevent then I am, and therefore I must referre the care of my poore credite to you for such matters. Sir John Norris came one day to me, and told me, that you had written to him, that you vnderstood that there was noe good agrement betweene him and me, and gaue him councell to good purpose, as he reported it. " For my parte," saith he, " I haue done all I could to haue gone into England, to haue satisfied Mr. secretary in this and other things for my accompts; but hir majestie hath flatlie denied me leaue, but will haue me continue my service here," which his manner of speech I noted, that you, hearing of our mislike, &c. yet hir majestie would not suffer him to retorne at his owne sute and his freinds. Surely

[a] The office of marshal of the field had been given to sir William Pelham.
[b] doth altogether doth, *in MS.*

her majestie doth herself, this countrey, and this whole companie, the more wronge; I will not say, myself. I am sure you doe, and will doe, what you can, and soe it must rest, and you shall see master Thomas, his patron, shall beare small rule here. I could tell you of such parts at Bryll alredy, as you would thinke much of.

This next weeke, either Tuesday or Wednesdaye, we meet all our companies, both horse and foote together, to beginn our campe, allbeit we haue but a litle monie, only so much, na, skant so much, as shall bringe vs together; our randevous shalbe at a place called Ameron, a village nere Reynye and not far from Wyke. There we will liue in hope to receaue more monie; all other things we haue geuen order for.

Mr. Norrice vseth a speech here which perhapps may come to you there, that he is now the v. officer in the feild, of late he was first. He sayth, also, all men are advanced but he; as the erle of Essex to be generall of all the horse, both English and Duch; that the marshall is also over all; that the sargant-maior is likwise ouer all; that the master of our campe is over all. In very troth he doth it onlie to bred quarrels, and to cause some mislike, for my lord of Essex is none otherwise than over the English horse, for the count de Meurs is over the rest; the sargent-maior was neuer appointed but over the English, albeit he is forst in the feild to exercise that for both, because theie haue noe man fitt for it; the marshall, indeed, is over all, for soe the whole states and countrey desires it, because of his sufficiency, and there is noe man to equall with him, neither can there be any more generall-marshalls, but our other marshalls thir may be, and more for the horse than one, as also light horses, and launces, and every nacion maie haue a generall of the horse; soe, likewise, of footmen may there be divers coronels-generall, as the nacions be; soe for the master of the campe, everie nacion maie haue one; but he seeks thwarts in everie matter: but, now I haue Pellam and Stanley, you shall se all doe well enough though my younge master would countenance him. I wilbe master whilst I remaine here, will theie nill theie. My desire is, if anie back-bitinge be vsed, I may knowe it and answere it.

Now to your good newes of sir Francis Drakes safe arrivall. I thanke God for it, and I beseech Him, that his winings be such as may supply the common cause. Your advertisment of one that came from him doth not please me much; but it cannot be that he should spoile so many places and gett noe more. He would never goe anie [a] more voyages if it be soe, but I will [hope] the best, and trust to heare shortlie from him.

I haue had dealing here for Emden. I had made a very good end, greatly to the likinge of our merchants, and now the embassadors for the count refuse it. Yf it be possible to gett another place for our men yt were a happy turne, for most certen it is, their countenance of Emden doth almost overthrow the traffique of all theis parts wholie. And yet, for her majesties sake, and to pleasure our merchants, theie offer them this, that theie shall haue frely, traffique to Emden with their clothes and all other English commodities; that they shall frelie, in their English bottoms, retorne from Emden all other commodities which theie shall either bye or barter ther, to all places whethersoeuer, only theie will, that all other strangers which shall bringe or retorne anie comodities shall pay such customes as theie doe, and haue done; but theis embassadors will not yeild, as yt yet seemes, except theie may haue the whole river free, without all interrupcion, for all persons; which, if it should be, before God this whole countrey were vtterly vndone, wherein you must haue grave and gratious consideracion.

In my other letter yt is like I haue written confusedly, for I did write also to my lord-tresorer and others with my owne hand, but I haue here written for your best informacion till Aty comes, and I haue litle leisure, and, therefore, I pray you [accept my] scribling and tedious letters. Soe far you well, and God keepe you, and send vs well to meete, either here or in heaven. From the Hage, the xxxth of July.

Your assured.

[a] have anie goe anie, *in MS*.   [b] batter, *in MS*.

Whatsoeuer it meanes, the states were never so slacke and hard to bring out monie as nowe.

LETTER CXXXVIII.

MR. SECRETARY WALSYNGHAM TO THE EARL OF LEYCESTER.

30TH JULY, 1586.   COTTON. MS. GALBA, C. IX. FOL. 326.   ORIG.

Walsyngham recommends to the favour of the earl one Brune, who had erected brewhouses and bakehouses for the supply of victual for the troops in the Low Countries, but whose dealing was sought to be interfered with under a commission from the earl.

My verie good lord, whereas my servant Brune hath, since sir John Norryces departure last out of this realme, employed himself in victualling a great part of hir majesties forces in the Lowe Countries, and for that purpose hath been at great charges, as hee advertiseth me, in erecting bruehouses and bakehowses, whereby the souldier is much better served, especiallye in drincke and bread, than otherwise hee would bee, so it is, that I am enformed, there bee some whiche intend to sue to your lordship for a commyssion to authorize them speciallye to serve in those victualling causes, whereby my sayd servant is lyke to bee undone. Wherefore, as before I have recommended my servant to your lordship, so I humblye praye you to continewe your honorable favour in suche sort towardes him as he maye not bee forbidden, but permitted still to vittall the souldiers as hee hath done; for whiche I shall thincke myself beehoulding to your lordship, and so I humblye take my leave. From the court, the xxx[th] of Julye, 1586.

Your lordships to commaund.

FRA: WALSYNGHAM.

LETTER CXXXIX.

THE EARL OF LEYCESTER TO MR. SECRETARY WALSYNGHAM.

7TH AUGUST, 1586. OUVRY MS. FOL. 48. A COPY.

The earl reiterates former requests to have Daniel Rogers and Bodely sent to him—Berck is besieged—difficulty of getting money from the states—" We must to the field, or this towne will follow the rest"—sickness amongst the garrison of Berck.

Mr. secretary, I haue written to you before now to lett you knowe the great need I haue to vse more secretaries and other ministers about me, and did earnistly pray you to procure me Daniell Rogers, and Bodely my old servant; there payns shalbe well considered, and noe charge to hir majestie. I beseech you send them to me with all speed, and I will place them both to there likinge. Yf you knew the great necessitye I am in for such you would remember me, and satisfie me. Thus, in hast, [I] bid you farwell, with hearty commendacions, this 7. of August, at Tergoad, ready to retorne to Vtrickt this daie.

Your assured freind.

Wylkes hath exceedingly wisely and wel behaued himself. Her majestie doth not know what a iewell she hath of him. I would I suffered a great payne I had such a one to ioyne withall here.

Berks is beseiged,[a] and till verie now could we gett [no] assurance of monye of the states. Assuredly there be some great traytors among them. We haue bine ready, ever since Newes was

---

[a] Berck from its situation on the Rhine was justly regarded as a place of great importance, and was garrisoned by 1200 English and " seaven or eight hundred other souldiers," under the command of Schenck and Morgan. Before the prince entered upon the siege the walls were repaired, the town victualled, and considerable preparation made for an energetic defence. Briefe Report, sig. C. 1.

beseiged, to goe to the feild, but could never gett penny from the states of that was dew, neither had we anie of hir majesties till now, for I did not medle with the merchants x^{mli} till now that the treasure[r] and the rest is come. There is noe remedie. We must to the feild, or this towne will follow the rest. I heare most of the souldiers there are very sore sicke of an infeccion fallen sodanlie; God comfort them, and send vs spedily to them, as I doubt not we shall.

LETTER CXL.

THE EARL OF LEYCESTER TO MR. SECRETARY WALSYNGHAM.

7TH AUGUST, 1586. OUVRY MS. FOL. 48. A COPY.

The earl replies to letters of her majesty in which she attributed his complaints against the treasurer, sir John Norris, and Paul Buys, to various bad feelings—Norris has become tractable—further particulars of P. Buys's misconduct, and denial of any collusion on the earl's part in procuring his arrest—the earl denies that either Hohenlohe or prince Maurice have been " lost or discouraged" through his misconduct, as the queen seems to have supposed—Wilkes's proceedings with the states—want of money—desertion of English troops—meeting of the German electors at Luneburg.

Mr. secretary, I haue receiued letters of late from her majestie greatlie to my comfort, albeit I may well perceaue, both by them and her messingers, that euery thing I doe is drawen hardly touching the tresurers cause.[a] God is my iudge, there was noe particuler cause in the world betwene him and me; and I dare appeale to yourself, whether anie man comended him more at my

[a] treasure at warrs, *in MS.*

being in England. And what hath bine the cause since? Lett the cause itself defend my doings, being for her majesties service only.

For Mr. Norris, there was neuer priuate matter yet betwene him and me; but the first mislike I am sure grew about these money and reckoning matters, which concerned hir majestie, and I, being advertised thereof by Mr. Davison, delt in that sort as he advised me; notwithstanding I loued Mr. Norris aboue all the gentlemen of this companie, my nephewes excepted, for I had great cause to wish his well doing, and to take comfort of it, being brought vpp with me, and preferred by me cheiflye, to all his former charges, specially in this countrey. Beside, there grew much mislike betwene him and divers that came over with me, whome I knowe to be both able and worthier men, and, perhapps, seeming rather to deale to indifferently then parcially, I encreased some mislike, whereby finding very slacke service to follow, and knowing what depended vpon me, that such a man should carye a misliking mind, and how much hinderance might growe to this service, hath caused me to vse verie plaine speeches of all sides, and I thinke pleased none. But not for anie one pece of matter for myself, was there euer anie ill word to him from me. And I knowe not how matters may be imagined by men at home, that looke butt to their freinds and themselues, but I am perswaded few men that had supplied my place would haue vsed more temper than I haue done; but I will harme noe man, neither loose the service of anie man whome I may thinke will doe the meanest parte of his dewtye, and for Mr. Norris I doe nothing doubt but to haue his good service hereafter, as need shalbe, whatsoeuer I haue doubtid heretofore, for I doe find great tractablenes in him, and, since sir William Pelham came, when [there were] those that would prick forward such a mind to discontentacion, he carieth himself very well, and as well as I can wish, and he shalbe assured I will never doe him but right, even to the most honor or credite that he can deserue. And, as I could not like when I saw other cause, so must I say that I find noe man more carfull or forwarder in all services now then he is, and noe doubts an able man he is, and he shall want noe incouragement at my hands. The cause I haue to note is, howsoeuer I haue had cause to mislike, the happ is to haue me blamed.[a]

Touching Paul Buis, I perceaue her majestie supposeth that I haue wronged him, and not [b] that I haue iust cause indeed to mislike him, for her owne sake. He is comended, and thought to be a worthy instrument. Well! I had need of some good spokesmen on my side; hetherto I haue had few, but this I will say, till I found to to manifest matter against him, ye, and beare to to manie faults in him, because I would wynn him, knowing the abilitie and sufficiency of the man, and spared not to tell him of some of them, onlie betwene himself and me, in freindliest manner, verie playnely, her majestie shall truelie and most assuredly vnderstand that I neuer vsed anie of these men equall to him; noe, nor in anie degree nere him; no, nor I thinke, [if] her majesties honor and the whole weale of this state had not stood vpon it, I had not yet detected him of anie fault. As soone as I was assuredly informed of his manie lewd dealings, remembring those I knew of my none knowledge before, and bare withall, I did then aduertise you, and partlie her majestie, what I hard of the man, for finding the state by his practises sodanly to decline to the present danger, yt was like I thought it high [c] time to signifie it, and send my iudgment to you what I thought he would come vnto; but, God is my iudge, as I haue written since, I noe more knewe of, nor procured, this his apprehension in Vtrickt, then you did, but theie knew and hard daily better of his lewd dealings than I, and theie hated him deadly, and did veryly thinke I would not deall with him, and if he were not thus delt [with] he would hazard them all, and the whole state, and being a vassell borne to Vtrickt, as he is indeed, and yet most contemptuously dispisinge and dissolving them, and most falsly intruding [d] himself into the councellship of

---

[a] This sentence is printed as it stands in the MS.
[b] now *in MS*.   [c] her *in MS*.   [d] intending *in MS*.

estate, made them adventure vppon his apprehension, he then going away after the other councellors, whoe were departed toward the Hage, whether also I was goinge, and did goe, the very same morning. And thus much must I add, for my owne determinacion, that I was fully bent at my repaire to the Hage to displace him out of the councell; but God, how slowlie soeuer I proceeded, provided both for her majestie and this countrey farr better, for ther was neuer a worse instrument then he was for any good to this state. His doings therein are to longe to write; her majestie shall see them all sett downe, and knowe the ground, and how he was discouered. I am sorry her majestie did thinke so hardly of me that I misliked him cheifly for the kinge of Denmarkes matter, and imputes a pece of ill nature that I should charge him with that matter that he brake with me in. Yf her majestie here truely the report I deliuered to sir Thomas Heneage, as also that I wrote, I vsed noe further that matter against him but to lett her knowe that there was like such a matter should come in question, because he dealt so farr with me therin. Hit was noe matter neither to accuse him of, nor to condemne him, for I could thinke noe lesse of him that thought her majestie would leaue these countreys but he must thinke of some other,[a] but my cause of mislike, to putt her majestie out of doubt, is for vsing ill and lewd speeches of hir and our nacion, and to seeke to sow seditiously ill conceats in peoples heads against her, as wilbe proved. Sence he came into prison he hath not stuck to speake liberally. As also he went about dangerous practises. To prevent such a lewd person, I would thinke I had deserved thanks, and anie but myself should haue had them, and, that her majestie maie thinke I had no matter for myself, she shall see or longe, in writinge, what iust cause I had for myself against him before Dauison was landed in England, imediatly after he went hence, and yet never prosecuted anie thinge against him, when he thought he had left

[a] some of other, *in MS.*

Paul Buis the onlie servant faithfull and assured to hir majestie of all others, and I thinke I wrote then to you of it, and to Mr. Davyson also, what his parte was.

There is one there now, I thinke, with you, whome you know to be honest, that can tell you somwhat, for it was Paul Buis that sett on the count Hollock first to make a kind of mutinie, and Mr. Fremyn, the gentleman I meane, was the counts interpretor to me, and lett him tell you how I vsed the count, being but a stranger here, as I was. I beseech you, aske him of it for my sake, because her majestie said, there hath lacked a Northumberland in my place; indeed I shall alwaies giue place to him, and I pray God able me for her majesties service sake to be as able to serue hir, but if I haue lost her anie thinge here, or myselfe, for lack of plaine dealinge with these men, I wilbe content to receaue a lack in hir opinion; otherwise I shalbe greaued hir majestie should conceaue that I delt weakly in her service, albeit good cause have I, yf weake maintenance and faint backing of me [be considered], to be more discouraged then yet I have shewed to be, I thanke God.

For the count Hollock, and count Morris, if anie of them, or either, [be] lost or discouraged through my default, in good faith I will take it for noe lesse then treason to me. No, Mr. secretary, hir majestie shall knowe full truely how theie were almost lost indeed, and I onlie, by my labor and meanes, haue recouered them, as I wrote in my last letters both to hir majestie and to you. Yf ever I deserued thankes at hir majesties hands I haue for the recouering of these two gentlemen: specially Hollock, and that wretch whome hir majestie is ready to doubt me for, was the onlie and cheif cause to alienate these two. Mr. Wilks and Atye both shalbe able to giue full satisfaction for these matters, and how much hir majestie is indeed beholdinge to the ellector Truxes for this matter and more, whome I praie God she maie somewhat remember for it.

Wilks hath this day deliuered his letters to the councell of estate, and hir majesties message, which was noe lesse comfortable to them then delaied for manie respects in good time. Surely he behaued himself exceedingly well, and I thinke will doe more good then anie you sent this vij yeres. I thanke God, matters ar in meetly good case presently; he can tell you, both what he finds and what it was within this moneth past. I think he will say there was cause for hir majestie to send, and that I haue not bine negligent to bringe matters to some better passe then was looked for. He shall deliuer all those himself, and, I trust, retorne with great satisfaccion to her majestie in many things.

The only fault I now find is, the slacknes and great carelesnes in the states to haue monie provided to further our armie, which we haue bine readye for a longe while, and yet cannot haue to serue the present torne; and, truely, except we haue monie, the soner both townes wilbe lost and our men will runn away. I am sorry and ashamed to tell you, the enemie hath ij or 300 of our ablest men gone to him, and I thinke it is not so much for myserie and want, though it be great, as by villanie and practice of some sett course in England, by trustinge in papists and knaves for the nonce, to cause our men to doe this, as I heare also a plott layd for the Iresh. There is one sent to a fronter towne nere vs, an Irishman borne, and a very lewd person, with a mind to corrupt others; but all that can be done shalbe, and it shall goe hard but I wilbe reuenged or longe on some of theis that be gon. Beside nombers ar stolen home, and, except you be carefull to haue your ports watched, and some example made in England, I will warrant half our men at home within this moneth, our hard paiments haue bine such, both from you there and the states here. Ys it not much for poore men in a strange land to be iiij whole moneths vnpaid, and to be ragged and torne? Well! I trust this wilbe now holpen for her majesties parte, and I will make these men afraid but I will bring them of likwise, seing we shall doe nothing but loose townes ells. What other defects be in me I know not, but well I see all things are hardlie expounded against me, but I wilbe found otherwise vppon better examinacion I doubt not, and for my fidelitie inferior to noe man.

This meeting of thes great princes at Luneburg was noe more sudden then strange to vs here. Litle we here but a flying tale that the king of Denmarke shalbe king of Romaines, a matter I thinke not possible, for want of some more ellectors, being but three onlie there. Thus, having noe more to you at this time but to desire both you, and my other good freinds, to help to keepe her majestie in such good conceate of me, as of him she hath had longe triall of to be hir trew and faithful servant, and made a stranger by hir owne commandement, both from her presence and my none countreie, subiect to many vntrue reports, but assisted with very few freinds to keep me from the hazard of it, and shall crave noe further fauor or proteccion but her majesties suspence till I be hard or tried, and soe will neuer cease to pray for her long and prosperous life, and comend you to the Almighty. At Tergowad, this vij. of August, to morrow going to Vtrickt.

Your assured freind.

LETTER CXLI.

THE EARL OF LEYCESTER TO MR. SECRETARY WALSYNGHAM.

8TH AUGUST, 1586. OUVRY MS. FOL. 51 b. A COPY.

The earl reports a quarrel between count Hohenlohe and Mr. Edward Norris, which involved the marshal and sir John Norris, and from which the earl anticipated great dissensions between the English and Dutch—a general muster of the troops for the field now in progress—the earl laments his evil hap, and wishes he were rid of his government.

This for your owne information.

Mr. secretary, since the dispach of my servant Killigrew yesterday, I haue mett with a matter at my arrivall here at Vtrickt which doth trouble me, even to my heart. There hath fallen out of late an accident of quarrell betwene the count Hollock and young Mr. Edward Norris, at a towne called Gurtrutenberge, where the count is gouernor, and had there, for an enterprize to be executed, the marshall, therll of Essex, capten Williams, and sondry others. And being newly retornid from an exploite which theie had done, my nephew Sidney, and Mr. Edward Norris in his companie, arived there also, before supper-time. Theie went all to supper, and I know not how, nor whye, but, as it is reported, yonge Norrys caried himself not all the best toward the marshall, and being full of words and speeches, the count Hollock found it was some mislike and therefore commanded Norys to silence. He, either not vnderstandinge the count or * *[a] in this matter proceeded, which soe misliked the count as he hurld a cover of a cupp at his face, and cutt him alonge the forehead as longe as half my finger. This sir John Norris taketh exceedinglie, and not only toward the count, but, by the wronge informacion of his brother, against the marshall; but this I must say, as manie as were present, except my two nephews, whoe are not here yet, doe all, vppon the examinacion of the matter, declare the greatest fault to be in Edward Norris, and that he did very arrogantly and quarelsomly vse the marshall.

I haue caused both sides to sett downe the matter, albeit I had taken present order betweene the marshall and Mr. Edward[b] Norrys in such sort as both doe promise me all quietnes, and to continue their service carefullie, for it could never haue happened in a worse time, we being now preparing our campe to the feild, and a great parte come together alredy, and these being ij of the principall men of the armye, beside the count Hollock my lieutenent-generall. There could not haue happened such a mischeif, but I

---

[a] Owremest *in the MS.* a word copied in attempted fac-simile from something in the original not understood by the transcriber.   [b] John *in MS.*

see what troble is like to growe to me. I haue giuen warninge longe agoe of this, specially of Edward Norrys, one that hath not escaped the falling out with all the captens and officers in this companye, as coronell Morgan, Roger Williams, old Read, Payton, and diuers others; and his brother by and by must be a partye, or ells he will neuer lett him be quiet. And it is strange to see soe stout and wise a man soe gouerned as he is by his rash brother.

I doe assure you I cannot but feare some marvellous mischeif to follow this. And though I can order the marshall and Mr. Norrys, yet can I not be able to stay that which may fall out yf the count Hollocke come, I see the quarrell toward him for the hurt of Edward Norrys so stomacked. The matter is by them soe giuen out amonge the English souldiers as I doe feare to haue the count come amonge them, and if he doe not, then must I looke for noe service at anie these countreymens hands at all. So that you may see my hard happ by this follie. Hit is like to bringe our quarrell from the enemie to a priuate revenge among ourselues. The count Hollock will take the matter the worse for that which he did was in respect of Edward Norrys ill-vsing the marshall, whome I think there was never a milder nor more corteous person to liue withall, and soe farr from misliking anie of them, as he most earnistly entreated me to haue good opinion of sir John Norrys, and in troth I was become againe very familiar with sir John, and he as forward and willing in service as I could wish. Euery way here may you [see] what cause of discouragment I haue, and whether it is like our matters shall goe well or noe, for I find, whatsoeuer I doe it is drawen to the worst in England, whatsoeuer others doe, or doe not, it is made the best. Lett her majestie sett downe whome she will haue serve, for I shalbe thought partiall yf I doe anie thinge. Would God I were ridd of this place! Not that I would not most willinglie abide the worst to doe anie service, but I see how it will fall out for me well enough. What man living would goe to the feild and haue his officers devyded almost into a mortall quarrell? One blow but by anie their lackis brings vs altogether by the eares. And if I goe not, or the armie, we shall loose the towne of Berks. Well! I will doe what I can; and what with this matter, being the greatest that fell to me yet, and the ouerthwart dealinge of the states, whome I find most slack, or rather over-carelesse, with other circumstances of late, which stands very tickell, and only vppon her majesties resolucion, doth not only make me wholy weary, and out of hope of anie good to be donn, but to wish good consideracion in time of this state, for there is noe way but one which I haue euer written of, that is, her majestie must take it wholy vppon her. I see into it as farr as anie other, and I see thus much that her majestie must take either a suffranty or proteccion, or ells you shall haue noe good dealinge here at all. For this longe tract of time that the enemie hath had his will to doe what he list, the people seeing and finding that neither releefe to come from England in time, nor from the states here, hath soe greatlie daunted them, as nothing but assurance of better defence at her majesties hands will satisfie. Of these matters you shall heare more by Mr. Wilks. In the meane time I pray you thinke of it, and marke what I say, for we shalbe deceaued of these men otherwise; and soe, for this time, I will leaue to trouble you, being full of troubles myself. From Vtrickt, this 8th of August.

Your assured freind.

The fruit of faction here will fall out as it hath done in England. I am not so simple but I can see how [I] am handled, and how litle reckoning is made either of my requests or advises, and how those are most cherished that anie [way] can vse me worst; but I will beare all for the cause sake, and my humble dewty to her majestie, which shall neuer be forgotten; but if matters fall not well out, remember my prophecie long since. My conscience telleth me I haue deserued better fauor and more consideracion.

I haue such encouragment as I am faine now to vse flattery to these that ought to haue sought me. Hir majesties great fauor[s] to them are so signified by letters, by messengers, and all, as either I must hazard all, or beare all, but I trust to end honorablie here and complayne neuer more.

LETTER CXLII.

THE EARL OF LEYCESTER TO MR. SECRETARY WALSYNGHAM.

10TH AUGUST, 1586. OUVRY MS. FOL. 53 b. A COPY.

Another letter of lamentation upon the subject of the quarrel between count Hohenlohe and Mr. Edward Norris—the earl complains bitterly of his hard fortune, and of the way in which his conduct is misjudged by the queen—all men have friends but himself.

Mr. secretary, after I had despatched my servant Killigrew from Tergoad, I haue heard of a matter which hath troubled me not a litle, a falling-out at Gertrudenberge betwene Edward Norris and the count Hollock, a matter of greater weight then wilbe easily conceaved, for that the marshall was a party, whome you knowe what a man he is, and, as yet it appereth, to much abused by Edward Norris. The count Hollock is my lieutenant-generall, sir John Norris my coronel-generall of the infantry, the other, sir William Pelham, the marshall of the feild. These being devided, and at the instant of my going to reliue Berkes, which is beseiged, you may iudge what my case is. I will doe what I can posible to pach it vpp among them for the time, and either it shalbe soe or he that failes I will make him smart, and yet will I examin the matter at full, and lay the fault where it is truely. You may see my happ, and what presuming boldnes groweth thorow the pampering of some, and discreditt of me.

It is well deliuered here by writinge and otherwise, how all my doings are thought of there, and taken by her majestie. God soe deliuer me in the daie of his fearefull iudgment as I haue honestlie and faithfullie serued her majestie and this state! Yf I haue wanted witt, the fault is hirs and yours amonge you for the choice, and that would not better assist me, but leaue me alone in a manner, even to my half being a stranger to all practises and all fortunes, not caring how to assist me, but rather most earnest how to deface me, which, how farr it reached, be not blind nor vnwillinge to vnderstand it. The fruit of it doth remayne to this day. And yet I must confesse the cominge of Mr. Wilks hath exceedingly stird things, I pray God not to late; for we are driuen to the last refuge, to try it by force, or all our townes wilbe gonn. Well! I must be short, (I haue made a great blert, thorow sudden dropps of rayne falling, as you may see,) and, as I will frame myself to doe all that may content her majestie, soe I beseech the Lord God she may doe that which may be best for her owne self; and soe far you well. From Vtrickt this 10th of August.

Your assured freind.

I trust I shall beare all my crosses, either to heaven by thend of life here, or by a priuate life, if God grant it longer ells, for my heart is almost broken, and more by the hard construccion I se made only of my doings against me, then for all the travells, paynes and dangers I past over beside. I see all men haue freinds but myself. I see most false suggestions help other men, and my vpright true dealinge cannot protect me. Na, my worldly protector faileth me. God for his mercie assist me!

LETTER CXLIII.

MR. SECRETARY WALSYNGHAM TO THE EARL OF LEYCESTER.

15TH AUGUST, 1586. COTTON MS. GALBA, C. IX. FOL. 363. ORIG.

The queen has consented that the master of Gray shall go into the

Low Countries, and requests that he may be well received by the earl—she also consents that £2,000 shall be advanced to him.

My very good lord, by thincloased from the master of [Gray], your lordship maye perceave howe much yt doth importe her majestyes [service] and his own credit, that the intended imployment of hym in the Lowe Countryes do take place, the consideracion whereof hath now movid hir majesty to geve hir resolut consent therunto, for that she seeth thinconveniences that are otherwise lykely to grow, yf she do not imploy him, and judgeth very necessary for her owne behoof to have his credit in Scotland and devotyon towardes her mayntayned and continued, and therfor your lordship shall do a thing very acceptable to hir majesty, to have a spetyall care that he may fynd * * of enterteynement, and receave that welcom and good * both for himself and those that accompanye him, that may satisfye his expectation and encourag him in his good disposicion. I have also movid hir majesty for an advance for him of the two thowsand poundes that he desyreth, [which she is] content to graunt a warraunt unto my lord-threasurer to disburse the same out of the next treasure that shalbe yssued for them ther, to be repayd agayn unto your lordship by the states, and * shall the somme be notwithstanding presentlye furnished to serve the masters present and necessary turne, as he desireth; and so I humbly take my leave of your lordship. At Barnelmes, xv[th] of August, 1586.

Your lordships to commaund,
FRA: WALSYNGHAM.

LETTER CXLIV.

LORD BURGHLEY TO THE EARL OF LEICESTER.

18TH AUGUST, 1586.   COTTON MS. GALBA, C. IX. FOL. 374.   ORIG.

Receipt of the earl's letter of the 29th July—the queen's old rooted opinion that all this war will be turned upon her charge now appears to be likely to turn out to be the case—intercourse with Embden—importance af keeping the field against the prince of Parma—discovery of Babington's conspiracy.

My very good lord, I have forborn to wryte to your lordship of any thyng sence Mr. Wylkes depeche, and sir Thomas Shyrley with Mr. Hudleston, and so contynued in expectation of some matter from that syde uppon their arryvall, and so we here did thynk the lack of hearyng from thence cam by contynvance of contrary wynds, and yet nevertheless yesterday cam, [in] on instant, two from your lordship, Mr. Haydon and Mr. Killigrew, and by Mr. Haydon I receaved your lordships letters of the 29th of July from the Hage, which war wrytten befor the arryvall of Mr. Wilkes and sir Thomas Shyrley, so as by those your lordships letters I cold not understand any thyng in answer to matters committed to ther severall charges, but yet by a lettre of the 6. of August from sir Thomas Shyrley at Tyrgowss, I perceaved that he had spoken with your lordship, and at that tyme he had understandyng that the prince of Parma was not at Antwerp, as before was reported, but that he was gon to besege Berk, and that, as he thought, your lordship would prepare yourself to follow with an army. And whan I consider your letter, how difficultly you bryng the states and the contrye to yeld to yow monny, accordyng to their manny promises, for mayntenance of so great an important service, tendyng to preserve themselves out of the Spanish bondage, I do truly lament your case, to be so wrapped into the cause as for hir majesties securety you may not leave it soddenly, nor yet without more redy helpe of monny can prosequut the action with that lyff as it ought to be. And no on thyng doth more hynder hir majesties forwardnes than an old rooted opinion that she hath, that all this warr will be torned uppon hir chardg, by the backwardnes in payement by the states, ageynst which I did allweys oppose in ans'veryng to comfort hir majesty, that I was assured, so as she wold contynew redy payement for hir nombres accorded, yow wold not fayle but recover such somes from the states, monthly, as they had promised your lordship shortly uppon the committyng of the government to your lordship; and so suerly I contynued my hope, although, in truth, manny privat persons did advertise it very dowtfull, and so I am sorry to se it, as I do by your own letters, very difficult to be gotten. And yet I will not leave my hope, consideryng I presume your lordship will look into [the] impedimentes, which I thynk ar not the lack of good will in the people to yeld the aydes promised, but in the maliciouss covetoosness of such as ar knytt and confederat with the states, who, I thynk, fynding ther lack of ther former gaynes, wold, if they cold, attayn to ther government ageyn, and for that purpooss seke to stopp the payment, therby to weary your lordship, and to induce yow to remitt the government, which suerly cannot be doon but with the ruyn of the whole cause, to the gretest daunger of hir majesties suerty.

Your lordship hath don very honorably and proffitably to our country in procuryng oppen passadg for our marchantes to Embden, and yet, in the end of your lordships letter, your lordship wryteth that the ambassador for Embden will not assent to the matter, except the ryver may be fre for all other marchantes besyde English, but, I thynk, if it be well stycked unto, the conte of Embden will, [for] his own proffitt, consent to our merchantes access, though others shuld not come but by permission of the Hollanders. Suerly if ther might be passadge oppen by the Rhen out of Holland, I wold less care for our trade at Embden, for than [a] our merchantes saye they wold make a great trade by Holland, but yet, with the condition that our marchandise be not burthened with great taxes, for your lordship knoweth that nothyng is so great a hyndrance to trade of merchantes as new toles and impositions, wherof our staplers of late complayned for the burden layd uppon ther wares at Midleborough. And yet, I confess, it is hard to gyve advise herin, for as resort of merchauntes to those countreys is proffitable, so how the common cause that is maynteaned by taxes may yeld a forbearance of taxes uppon marchandise, I gretly dout.

I thynk by the accompt of Englishmen of late monthes past out of this realme, ther ar besyde the queenes own army, above

---

[a] than without our, *in MS*.

vj^m footemen, so as, if your lordship may have wherwith to pay them, I would think your lordship shuld be hable so to kepe the feld as the prince of Parma shuld not be hable to contynew any sege to any town of strength, being also well-manned. And suerly, my lord, without yow shall be hable to kepe the feld, ther is no town so strong but the prynce with his battery will wyn it.

I am very glad that the town of Axell serveth to so good a purpooss. I am suer, if the prynce did not follow theise seges in Gelderland, &c. your lordship wold advance some horssmen to Sluse and Ostend to spoyle the countreys about Bruuges and Gant, which also wold make them revolt. Now, my lord, I dowt not but Mr. secretary doth at lardg acqueynt yow with the discovery of the late traytorooss conspyracies, the authors wherof, as farr furth as we do esteme, we have, savyng only ij, Thomas Salisbury and Edward Abyndon, both which ar fled, but pursued.[a] My lord-chancellor and I ar here contynuyng at London, dayly occupyed, first in procuryng ther apprehension, and now in examynyng, &c.

And so, my good lord, being urged with a weak gouty righthand to leave wryting, I pray your lordship to accept these lynes, so evill scribled, in good part.

Your lordships most assured,
W. BURGHLEY.

From my houss at Strond,
18 Aug. 1586.

LETTER CXLV.

THE EARL OF LEYCESTER TO MR. SECRETARY WALSYNGHAM.

31ST AUGUST, 1586. OUVRY MS. FOL. 54 b. A COPY.

The earl has invested Duesbourg—particulars of an alarming wound received by sir William Pelham—want of money from the states—

[a] Both were afterwards apprehended and executed. State Trials, i. 1132, 1158.

arrival of Scots—the queen is advised to be at some point with these men, and to deal plainly with them.

Mr. secretary, yesterday morning I wrote vnto you, and yet not fullie, of my determinacion touching my cominge to Dursborow, a towne that doth greatlie annoy vs, and hath garrison of horse and foot in it; and, except I doe leaue a good parte of my company behind me in sondry places, I shalbe cutt of from our victells and cariages continually, wherevppon it was thought good by all the cheif officers here to stepp suddenly to this towne,[a] and, with hope in few dayes to take it, we accordingly yesterday by 2 a clock brought all our armie hether, and presentlie invironed it. Our artillery and vittells we sent by water, which came not till this day, now are we in hand with planting our batterye, and [will] not faill to make all haste [b] possible with this towne.

[a] The siege of Berck had now continued nearly a month, but Schenck had made many sallies, and had interrupted the proceedings of the besiegers in such a variety of ways, that they had not been able to make much progress. In the meantime Leycester had been gathering his forces together with the announced intention of making a direct attack upon the prince's army. On the 14th of August Norris and Cecil, with the vanguard, passed the river Isell and advanced into Cleves; on the 17th they were joined by another division of the army under Pelham; ten days afterwards there arrived the troops under count Hohenlohe, and on the 28th Leycester himself proceeded from Utrecht to the camp, and reviewed the whole body of troops with all " the pomp and circumstance " which usually accompanied his movements. The review took place on a Sunday, and after it was concluded the English were formed into squares, " and two preachers made to them two sermons on the field, by the hill side," after which Leycester assembled the chief officers, and " fell into consultation what were fittest to be done." It was determined, that the force which had been collected together with so much parade, was insufficient for its object, and, instead of marching to give battle to the prince, it was thought better, by a sudden retrograde movement, to attack Duesburg in Guelderland, a fortified town which it was unsafe to leave in the rear of an advancing army, and which was of such importance that, if it were in danger, it was likely the prince would withdraw from Berck, and come to its succour. The writer of the Briefe Report says, that on the day of Leycester's arrival before Duesburg " himselfe in person, within arcabuze shot, tooke viewe of the wals on al the east side, and that night set pyoners and soldiers to entrenching within halfe-arcabuze shot." Briefe Report, sig. C. 2., and see Stowe's Chron. 735.

[b] hath *in MS.*

But I must tell you of a marvellous losse we were like to have had yesternight at x a clock. I being weary, and ready to go to bedd, the marshall came to me, and tould me what beastlie pioneers the Duchmen were, and having begon their trench everie shott makes them run awaye, beside their gaird was not verie good; he told me he would back againe, and take some more men with him. I, much against his will, would needs goe with him, and we, having both our gards, went towards the trench that was begon; hit was verie dark when we set out, and afterward somewhat starlight, insomuch as we found ourselves suddenly almost at the verie gate of the towne. The marshall perceiung he had mist a litle his way, he and I going before the rest vj or vij paces,[a] he stept afore me to see the right waie, with which instant a caliuer shott from the wall strake him in the belly. Thinking himself slayne, [he] turnid about, speaking verie cheerfully to me, and thanked God it was his happ to be betwene me and that blow, with very comfortable and resolute speeches to me. Soe, at his home-cominge, I had Goodrous [b] to see his wound, and hit was iij fingers iust, with the navell on the right side, and how farr the bullett entred we knowe not; but, the Lord be thanked, hit apperes now without all danger of his life, for he hath had no evill accident at all, which if he had had anie perishing of his inward parts wold streight haue shewed, both vpward and downward; beside, in this time, their would haue bine some great alteracion; but, I thanke God, he hath both slept well, and eaten that his surgeons appointid with good appetite and disgestion, beside he is in verie good temper, free from anie fever. Soe that the surgion doth fully resolue, whether the bullett be within his bodie or without, he is without danger for this blowe; for which I thanke my Lord God most humbly, for, as my earnist sute brought him over, soe his going now with me was cause of his hurt. Thus we howrelie see in these cases how some be kild, some be hurt, and some narrowlie escape; and yet men must

[a] spaces, *in* MS.   [b] See p. 174.

adventure whan the seruice doth require, and by this service to make manie able souldiers and servants hereafter, whereas there was of late few or none. And lett her majestie thinke so much monie well spent as this cause hath cost her, if it were but for so many able servants as she shall winn by it. Thus, sir, I thought good to aduertise you, least you may here some vntruth that would greiue you touchinge this noble worthie gentleman, whoe, thanks be to God, amends so well as euen now he sends me word he trusts to ridd abroad with me to morow, and assuredly he is without anie danger. It was yesternight x a clock he had his hurt, and this letter is written this next day at night, viij a clock.

We are hardlie handled by the states now for monie, yet are there Scotts arrived latly xij^c, and as many more looked for; our rutters I hope[a] shalbe with vs within viiij dayes. In the meanwhile our dealinge here is like to cause the seige at Berks to levie; we haue noe other waye, for we can haue noe vittells to put into it, yf we had gon thether; then this course is the onlye waie, to seeke some of his townes that be our frontyers, that he would be loth to loose, as I am sure he would be this towne, being a proper towne, well walled and ditched double, very strongly seated and richly; a towne of a mile and a half compasse, at lest. If God doe send it vs I will not change it for Berks, our men saved there, as I trust by this meanes theie shalbe, for, if the prince will doe anie thinge, he will seeke to releiue this towne, but it shall cost me dere but I will prevent him, and if our states deall carefullie for themselues, I doubt not but, within ij monethes, to abate the pride of the Spaniards in these parts, thorow Gods help and the goodnes of her majestie, if we may be abled to keepe our companies together so longe. But, except her majestie be at some point with these men, I see theie wilbe slacke, though theie harm themselves; but if she will deall as planelie[b] with them as there is cause, aud that the whole countrey may know whome the fault is

---

[a] I hope I *in MS*. [b] namelie *in MS*.

[with], and not wholy to lay it vpon her majestie, albeit she is not free from a parte, I will warrant, at lest ells are theie vterlie vndone, that theie will come to a better order. I will write as soone as I see the end of our seige, how things past. And thus [a] will comitt you, good Mr. secretary, to the Almightie. In much hast, from her majesties armie before Dursborgh, this Wednesday the last of August.

Your loving and assured friend.

LETTER CXLVI.

MR. SECRETARY WALSYNGHAM TO THE EARL OF LEYCESTER.

2ND SEPTEMBER, 1586. COTTON. MS. TITUS, B. VII. FOL. 61. ORIG.

The earl standeth in good terms with the queen—regret for the quarrel between Hohenlohe and Edward Norris—the lord-treasurer and Walsyngham agree as to the revoking of sir John Norris—the bearer will apprise the earl as to what is intended against the Scottish queen.

My very good lord, this gentleman hathe verry carefully and dyscretely executed the charge commytted unto him. In what good termes your lordship standethe with her majestie he can shewe you, I praye God contynewe yt, and that she may dyscerne the yll-affected from the sownde.

Sorrye I am to see your lordship trobled with the pertyculer quarrels of thos that ought to be best united. The Lord geve you wysdome to appeese them, and patyence to beare this crosse!

The lord-treasurer hathe promysed to ioyne with me in the

[a] he *in MS.*

revokyng of sir Ihon Norryce. I have imparted unto this bearer what is intended agaynst the Scottish queen. He is commanded to departe with speed, and my leysure wyll afoorde no more lynes, and therfore I most humbly take my leave. London, 2. September, 1586.

Your lordships to command,
FRA: WALSYNGHAM.

Addressed,
To the right honourable my verie good lord the erle of Leycester, lieutenant-generall of her majesties forces in the Lowe Countries.

LETTER CXLVII.

MR. SECRETARY WALSYNGHAM TO THE EARL OF LEYCESTER.

SEPTEMBER 1586. COTTON MS. GALBA, C. IX. FOL. 364. ORIG.

Walsyngham's occupation in the discovery of the accomplices in Babington's conspiracy—he trusts the queen will take advantage of it, and that the earl will use his influence with her to induce her to do so—sir John Norris—D. Rogers—Bodley—Truchses.

My very good lord, * * can wytnesse unto you [how] greatly I was busyed at the tyme of his departure in the dyscoverye of the complyces of the late conspiracye, wherof I praye God her majestye may make [more] proffyt then of lyke opportunytyes thorrowghe Gods godnes appered unto h[er]. I knowe your lordships good advyce can greatly further the matter. She dyd never make greater [speech] of her love towardes you, [or] of the trust she reposethe [in] you then at this present; therfor your lordships good cownecell will work good effects.

Your last sent by young [Gor]ge of the vijth of this present

I think meete to be communicated unto her majestye, that she may see howe hardely she dealethe with her best-affected servaunts.

I am very glad that your lordship is growen to so good a lykyng of my cosyn Jhon Norryce. I praye God he may styll carrye himself towardes your lordship in sooche [sort] as may increase your good opynion conceyved of him.

I have not been unmyndfull of your lordships request both for Danyell Rogers and your servant Bodley. Poor Rogers is forced to staye here to sollycyt the contrybution of the bishops towardes his ransom, which he fyndethe himselve bound in conscyence to see awntswered to sooche as became bounde for the same. I fynde the man well bent to serve your lordship yf this impedyment were not. Touching your servant Bodley, he hathe been owt of the towne a long whyle but is dayly looked for, at whos returne I will not fayle to deale with him.

Touchyng her majestyes goodnes to be exstende towardes the elector Truxies I wyll not fayle to sollycyt, thowghe [with] no great hoape thereof. And so I most humbly.[a]

*   *   *   *

LETTER CXLVIII.

THE EARL OF LEYCESTER TO MR. SECRETARY WALSYNGHAM.

4TH SEPTEMBER, 1586. OUVRY MS. FOL. 56. A COPY.

"*Remember Seburo*"—*Duesburg taken—sir William Pelham mends very well—sir Roger Williams wounded—count Nienar is bring-*

---

[a] The conclusion and the date of this letter are wanting, but there can be no doubt by whom it was written, and the contents indicate the time. It is evidently an answer to the earl's letters of the 7th August. See pages 383 and 384, and from its altered tone in reference to sir John Norris, it seems to have been written after letter CXLVI.

ing up reyters out of Germany—assistance offered by the king of Denmark—number of troops under the earl's command—Cassimir the palatine and the duke of Cleves—warning respecting Cæsar the physician—anxiety of the earl to know the queen's decision respecting this country—embassy from the states to her majesty—Menyn—Valck.

Good Mr. secretary, remember Seburo, my honour and creditt lieth vppon it.

The manner of our proceeding Mr. Gorge shall tell you, from our first going fourth of this iourney till he departed after the wyning of Dorsborge, which was happilie gotten,[a] being so well walled and double ditched as it was, for the prince was come as farr as Eltons with his forces to reskew it, but he came to late, for the same day we had it. Hit is the first towne wonn by the cannon for the states these ix yeres, and it is a towne as fitt for vs as can be, for Zutphin[b] can now little harme vs, for it is environed of

[a] The Briefe Report (Sig. C. 2,) and Archer's narrative printed in Stowe's Chronicle, (p. 736,) give some interesting particulars of the capture of Duesburg. Ten, or, according to Archer, nine, pieces of ordnance having been brought to bear upon the fortifications, a constant fire was kept up from break of day on the 2nd of September until two o'clock in the afternoon, and two breaches were made, which the defenders filled up, but through which it was determined to endeavour to gain an entrance. A contest arose for the honour of leading the way, which was determined by Leycester assigning one breach to count Hohenlohe and the other to sir John Norris, and, under their command, the Dutch and Scotch on the one hand, and the English and Irish on the other, were about to enter the ditch, when the town was yielded, upon condition that " the soldiers should passe away with ther lives only, the burgers should have all they had at his excellency's mercy." The usual horrors ensued. The women who passed out with the soldiers were plundered and ill-used : " it was a grievous thing to see how they were ransacked, till the earl of Essex and divers other gentlemen came downe the breach, and by smiting the souldiers made them leaue off rifling them ;" and " the captaines and souldiers that were sent to saue the towne from spoyle did to the contrary, for they made havock and most horrible spoyle, wherwith his excellency was greatly displeased."

[b] Qulphin *in MS.*

euerye side; Deventer and othir townes beneth it, and this towne and Arnham aboue it, all vppon one river.

The marshall, I thanke God, mends verie well, and shall carye a bullett in his bellie as long as he liues. God hath wonderfully delt for his saving aliue, and I escaped well, I thanke Him, the same instant. For saving me he had it, as I wrote vnto you, for I first spied the wall to be verie nere,[a] and he found he was past his marke, and stept before me, at which verie stepp he receaued the blow, which perhapps had lighted more daingerous vppon me, being higher then he, but God can defend whoe he will.

Roger Williams hath gott a blow thorow the arme, one evil fire.[b] I warned him of it, being in trench with me, and would need run vpp and downe so oft out of the trench, with a great plume of feathers in his gylt morion, as so many shott coming at him he could hardlie escape with soe little hurt. He saw ther was [some went out] of my trench to gaze and were strait hit, and on kild out-right, that were [n]euer such marks as he was, and within point-blanke of a caliver. God be thanked, all things considered, that we lost noe more. I thinke there is not xij kild since we came before the towne, and I beleeue never men lodged so nere a towne the first day as we did, and began our trench the first night, which had like to haue bine costly to some. We attend here looking for the enemie, but our stay is to strengthen the towne better, or I departe.

This day I received letters from the count Newenor who is with the rutters, and tells me theie will march further with all [speed]. He sends me worde that old Ramelius[c] was sent vnto him by the kinge of Denmarke, to will the count to send me word, that, if the rutters stay, or vse delay, that he will furnish him with ij^m of his best horse and iij^m footmen, and shalbe with him within xv dayes; and that her majestie had sent vnto him that he should help me if there were occasion, and her majestie should see he

[a] new *in MS*. [b] wilfire *in MS*. [c] Ranilso *in MS*.

was at her comandement. Though the yere be to far past now to levy those countrei horsmen, yet her majestie may see that kinges good devotion, which I pray you, sir, to remember to her majestie, that the kinge maie receaue thanks, and to keepe him in [t]his mind still; for, if her majestie doe goe forward with this cause, than his offer will serue well against the springe, for, noe doubts, against that time, the kinge of Spaine will sett vpp his rest; and truly, but for this armie of her majesties, at this time, now, the prince had prevailed this yere, to the verie townes of Holland. All these parts, Gelders, Overisell, the Vellow, Vtrickt, and Freseland, had bine gone cleane or this day, and for all the men that came over so fast, I doe assure you at Elten, our last campe, we had not 4,500 English footmen, nor xiij^c horse, English, Duch, and all, nor aboue 1,100 Scotts and Duch foote. All which [is] a small army to defend such an enemie, as is at the lest at this howre 3,000 horse, and 8,000 footmen, if not 10,000. Neuerthelesse, I trust not only to keepe all these parts safe, but, if our rutters come in time, make him seeke a new coast to dwell in. In the meane time, I am glad as he got ij townes of ours by reason, we haue gotten ij of his by force, and honorably, and, vppon my word, the states will not change these ij for iiij such as thother, theie be so fitt to annoy the enemie, as you will not beleeue the hurt Axell hath done him, and now we haue this towne, Zutphin[a] wilbe nothing, considering how it shalbe beseiged by Deventer and this towne. We haue the whole river of Isell save Zuttphin, and the prince must now gett him another place for provision then Cullen, for Cassamer hath forbidden anie vittell to passe his countrey, either to Cullen or that waye. Soe that Cullen beginns to growe weary of the prince, and so doth the duke of Cleave, albeit he and his sonne hath giuen him all the help theie can, as well in deliuering vpp their towne to him, as euerie [way] ells, but he will double smart for it, the rutters once being come.

[a] Qulphin *in MS*.

I receaued a letter from sir Edward Stafford, wherin he doth giue me warning of one Cæsar, an Italian, that is gon into England, and doth meane to come over to me for some myschief.[a] By his description it should be a surgion, for their were ij Italians, both surgions, and both their names Cæsars, and be both of Rome, and very villaines, yet found theie great fauor of me in England. Yf it be either of them, as he sayth this man confessed he serued me, it were not amisse he [and] his companion were staid there, or ells, if theie desire earnistly to come over to me, give me warninge and write your letters by them to me, and then I will handle them well enough here; in the meane time, if theie linger there, for feare of her majestie clapp them vpp, for she is their principall mark.

I trust, after Wilks be come home, I shall heare of her majesties resolucion. If she leaue of her hold that is offerd, all is gon; and except she take vppon her all, all wilbe gon, and that shortly. For my none parte, I trust not to leaue anie dishonour behind me for her majestie; and except she take the cause princly in hand, and call her parliament, and accept that hir subiects will offer her to maintayne this charge, hit will but consume her treasor and loose the countries. Yet better were it to make some secret confederacye first with Denmark, and, if I knew her pleasure onlie, I could deall by the count Hollock with the king of Denmark, quickly to knowe his mind. High time it is that her majestie did resolue one way or other, for our states growe stately, and wilbe high or low as God shall dispose of this iourney, for theie yet feare her majesties acceptacion further, and hir continuance with this charge doubtfull.[b] Theie be iumbling vnderhand, I dowbt. Theie doe send to hir majestie, as Wilks can tell you, touchinge this point. Menyn and Walke be appointed; Valk is a shrewd fellowe and a fine; Menyn is the deper man indeed, and I thinke the honester, and being well vsed the ablest man of all the states to serue her. He hath great credit as anie one man,

[a] Myf, *in MS*. [b] Doubtles, *in MS*.

Lett him be inwardly vsed; and he is but poore, which you must consider, but with great secrecy. Thus far you well; in hast, this 4th September.

Your assured freind.

I doubt not but her majestie will shewe my letter touching these causes.

LETTER CXLIX.

THE EARL OF LEYCESTER TO MR. SECRETARY WALSYNGHAM.

12TH SEPTEMBER, 1586.   OUVRY MS. FOL. 58.   A COPY.

Letter sent by sir Robert Jermyn—the queen is strongly advised to take the government of the Low Countries as the only way to save them—lord North recommended as successor to sir Thomas Cecill in the government of the Brill.

Good Mr. secretary, this good gentleman, sir Robert Jermin,[a] one that hath declared euery way his hearty zeale and loue both to religion and to her majestie, I haue thought good, euen in manner against his will, to send him home, for winter is come to vs here alreadye, and he hath a sickly bodie, yet would not forsake the feild. I haue prayed him to deliuer some matter to her majestie, which he shall imparte also to you.

There is noe other way for to saue theis countreis but for her majestie to take them wholy hirs, and that way in all reason a sound way, as she may alye and strenthen hirself, wherin I haue deliuered this berer my opinion, not doubting but Denmark and the cheife princes of Germany will ioyne themselues with her; but you must ther be more diligent and carfull then heretofore you

[a] See page 114.

haue bine, for such princes must be otherwise delt withall then by meane and comon messingers.

I vnderstand sir Thomas Cecill will giue vpp the Brill; I did once commend my lord North to her majestie for it, though I will not willingly be sene in it, for that I heare he meanes to make my lord-tresorer deall for my lord Borrowe,[a] yet I beseech you put her [majestie in] mind of my lord North, whoe hath bine verie painfull and forward in all these services from the begining, and his yeres meete for it. I pray you faill not herein to speake for him, but not willing sir Thomas or my lord-tresorer to knowe. It may appere to be hir majesties choyce. God be with you, and keepe you; 12th September.

Your assured.

LETTER CL.

LORD BURGHLEY TO THE EARL OF LEYCESTER.

15TH SEPTEMBER, 1586. COTTON. MS. GALBA, C. X. FOL. 19. ORIG.

Return of Mr. Wylkes—the occupation of the council with the proceedings connected with Babington's conspiracy and a fear of Spanish invasion prevents their considering the affairs of the Low Countries—the queen of Scots to be removed to Fotheringhay for trial on the 27th—intention of the conspirators to murder Leycester and Burghley—Seburo ready to be sent to the earl.

My very good lord, Mr. Wylkes is come wherby hir majesty falleth into consideration of the state of those countryes, which suerly requireth no small consultation, the lett wherof is, at this tyme, more than is convenient, that we of the counsell ar throghly

---

[a] Lord Burgh was appointed, but not until the 6th February 1586-7. Foed. xvi. 4.

occupyed, some at London, some here, and some abrode, to deale partly in tryall of traytors, in serching for more, in lookyng to the sea-costes, to withstand the landyng of certen Spanish shippes of warr which ar come to Brest, but as yet we know not to what end. Some thynk they cam to have bene in redynes to have landed in ayde of this late conspyracy intended, some to joyn with the French in the recovery of Rochell. Within a few dayes we shall se what they meane.

I understood your lordship did favorably stey, amongst others, my son from goyng to the assault of Dewsborogh. I do thank your lordship therfor, although I can be content that both he and I shuld spend our lyves for the queen and our countrye, but I wish it in a matter of more moment; and yet I judg the wyning of the town very necessary as the tyme was, but most of all if therby Zutphan might be gotten, which I thynk must be by perill of famyn.

The queen of Scottes is lykly to come to Fodryngham castell the 27. hereof, and I thynk a nombre of the counsellors and others of the nobilitie shall have commission, accordyng to the late statute 27º,[a] to heare and judg hir cause ther, so as in the next parlement, to begyn uppon a new summons the xv. of October, further order may be taken with that queen accordyng to part of hir desertes. Your lordship and I war very great motes in the traytors eies, for your lordship ther, and I here, shuld first, abowt on tyme, have bene killed;[b] of your lordship they thought rather of poysoning than slayeng. After us ij gon, they purposed hir majesties deth, but God our defendor hath graciously prevented ther mallyce, and I hope will contynew his favor to mak voyd the relliques of ther mallyce.

I will not fayle but remember your lordships sute for the for-

---

[a] Stat. 27 Eliz. cap. I. "An act for provision to be made for the suertie of the queenes majesties royall person, and the continuaunce of the realme in peace." Auth. ed. of Statutes, IV. 704.

[b] See State Trials, I. 1140.

fayted less of Salisbury [a] at Denbigh, being the land [of] your lordship.

I can wryte no more at this tyme, wishyng to heare some comfortable news of Berk, ether of fredom from the sege or resonable composition for our people ther.

From Wyndsor, xvth of September, 1586.

Your lordships most assuredly,
W. BURGHLEY.

Seaburo, the Spanyard, hath bene redy this month to be sent to your lordship, and so I told Mr. Dudley iij wekes past.

LETTER CLI.

THE EARL OF LEYCESTER TO MR. SECRETARY WALSYNGHAM.

27TH SEPTEMBER, 1586. OUVRY MS. FOL. 58. A COPY.

The prince has withdrawn from his attempt to relieve Zutphen—the earl has received from the surgeons a most comfortable letter of their very good hope of the recovery of sir Philip Sydney.

Good Mr. secretary, this sommers service being in a manner overpast, I haue sent you these gentlemen home againe, now that the prince hath withdrawen his forces back againe from the succour of this towne,[b] whether to meet with our ruitters by the way

---

[a] Salisbury was one of the parties to Babington's conspiracy. Upon his conviction the lease alluded to became forfeited to the crown.

[b] The stout defence of Schenck, and the diversion created by the siege of Duesburg, compelled the prince of Parma to remove from Berck and advance to the defence of his frontier towns in Guelderland. In the mean time, the earl, animated by his recent success, determined to invest Zutphen, a strong town which commanded the river Isell, in the hope of taking it before the prince could arrive to its succour. It was

cominge hitherwards, or no, we knowe not, but we keepe still our seate here before this towne, and, if he happen to returne hither againe, with anie further attempt to remove us, I doubt not but we shalbe well enough able to withstand him. Thus, for this time, I comend me heartily vnto you, and you to the blessed tuicion of thalmighty. From the campe before Zutphen, this xxvijth of September, 1586.

Your assured frend.

My greife was so great for the hurt of your sonne, my dear nephew and sonne also, as I would not encrease yours by the

a place of importance, and before the loss of Duesburg had formed, with that town, a strong defence against incursions from the northern provinces. Leycester invested Zutphen on the 13th September. Between that day and the 20th he visited Deventer, a neutral town at a distance of seven miles, from which Zutphen was supplied with provisions. On the 21st he learned, that, on the following morning, an attempt would be made by the prince to send a considerable convoy of supplies into Zutphen, which it was determined, if possible, to prevent, and for that purpose a body of English troops under the command of Norris and Stanley, and supported by a reserve, were stationed on the road which the enemy must traverse. On the morning of the 22nd there fell a great and thick mist " that you might hardly see a man ten paces off," under cover of which the enemy advanced. Suddenly the mist cleared off, and the astonished Englishmen found themselves in the very teeth of an intrenched body of 3000 of the enemy. A band of noblemen and gentlemen who were stationed in front of the English foot received instantly the fire of a body of "muskets and arcabuzes," and as instantly, apparently without a moment's consideration, rushed forward to the attack of an enemy of whose strength they were altogether ignorant, and who really were greatly superior to their own troops in numbers. The result was glorious. The enemy were driven from their position, compelled to abandon their attempt to succour Zutphen, and to retreat with great loss in killed and wounded. On the part of the English about forty were killed, " but not any of name, saue onely ser Phillip Sidney, who first hauing one horse shot under him, and mounted upon a second, was shot with a musket in the left thigh, but came home on his horse, and died the 25. day after." Briefe Report, sig. D. and see Stowe, 737, and also an interesting paper by the late Mr. Beltz in the 28th vol. of the Archæologia, p. 28, in which is printed an account of the skirmish of Zutphen written by Leycester to Burghley a day or two after it occurred, and now preserved in the State Paper Office. A letter from Leycester to sir Thomas Heneage also giving an account of the same affair is partly printed in the Sydney Papers, i. 104.

discomfort thereof; but seing this is the vjth day after his hurt, and having receaued from the surgions a most comfortable letter of their very good hope theie haue now of him, albeit yester-evening he grew heavy and into a fever, about ij a clock he fell to exceeding good rest, and after his sleep found himself very well, and fre from anie ague at all, and was dressed, and did find much more ease then at anie time since he was hurt, and his wound very fair, with the greatest amendment that is possible for the time, and with as good tokens. I doe but beg his life of God, beseeching for his mercies sake to grant it. My hope is now very good.

LETTER CLII.

THE EARL OF LEYCESTER TO MR. SECRETARY WALSYNGHAM.

28TH SEPTEMBER 1586. OUVRY MS. FOL. 58 b. A COPY.

Sir Philip Sydney still goes on favourably and hopes are entertained of his life—sir Henry Unton and sir William Hatton the bearers of the letter are praised for general bravery and forwardness, and especially for their exertions at Zutphen—narrative of the affair in which sir Philip Sydney was wounded—knights made by the earl—lord North's valour.

Mr. secretary, I was loth to trouble you to your greife with the newes which greiued me, being an eye-witnesse at the first happ of it, which it pleased God to lett fall vppon your sonne and mine, but, for that I haue receiued great comfort and hope, from time to time, speciallie this day, being the vijth day, from his surgions and phisitions, I would not forbeare anie longer time in writing to you, since the Lord geueth me good cause to hope of his mercifull dealing in granting life to our dere sonne to remaine with vs, for he hath all good accidents that maie be wished.

Now am I to recommend this honest and rare gentleman to

you, sir Harry Vmpton,[a] whoe, with his companion [b] sir William Hatton, hath not failed anie iourney since theie came over hither,[c] either a horsback or foote, and none more forward then theie were at the wininge of Axell, at the seige of Dorsborge, and in the first ranke to giue the assault. Theie haue here bin in skirmish at our first coming with the enemie, as far and as daingerously as the formost. Theie were at the last, I thinke I may saye the most notable, encounter that hath bine in our age, and will remaine to our posterity famous, the days fight, I meane, when our sonne was hurt, where these gentlemen were for hast driven to serue a foote, and sett themselues in the first rank [with] Mr. Rowland Yorke, who had the charge of that companie theie were in.

But I must retorne to that dayes service to lett you knowe, that, vpon my honor and credite, for I was the appointer myself of all that went forth, only those principall noblemen and gentlemen that staed by me in the mist (whoe was my lord of Essex, my lord Willowbye, sir William Russell, sir Phillip Sidney, sir Thomas Perrott, master, with their bands, but amonge themselues and their own servants) and ix or xij of name, in all to the nomber of l, or xl, went on till theie found sir John Norris, to whome I had comitted this service, only to haue impeached a convoy; but he, seeing these young fellowes, indeed ledd them to this charge, and all these ioined in front together, and what theie did the first charge, and after the second, doth appere by the number of men then slaine, which [is] confest by the enemy to be at lest 250, but others that haue reported of the enemies mouth theie were aboue 350, and theie were of the gallantest and best

---

[a] A valuable memoir of this gentleman, who was "the last and most distinguished member" of a worshipful Berkshire family, with a notice of his friendship for sir William Hatton, nephew and heir of sir Christopher, will be found in 'The Unton Inventories," a work edited for the Berkshire Ashmolean Society with singular care and judgment by my friend Mr. John Gough Nichols.

[b] Companies, *in MS.*   [c] Overtake, *in MS.*

sort. The odds you haue heard of, and capten George Gresier told it my none self, vppon mine honour, that theie were xv cornets of horsse and iij^m foote. There was not in the feild of ours of horse in the whole ij^c, whereof thes lords and gentlemen with their followers, to the nomber of iij^{xx} at most, did all this feate, with the helpe onlie of sir William Stanley, who had but 300 for their 3,000 foote, and he did most valiantlye himself, and his owen horsse receaued viij shott of the muskett, and yet himself not hurt. He and old Read are worth there weight in perle; theie be ij as rare [a] captens as anie prince liuing hath. Of our side we lost of horsse, as I thinke, 12 or 13, and of footmen 22; and if you saw the ground, with the nombers of the enemie, and the advantage theie had of the ground, you would mervell that euer anie one man escaped of our side, and but for the count Hollock we had had a most famous day. Beside the ouerthrow the enemie had, we tooke iij of their cornetts, whereof two I send her majestie, the other a knave cutt in peices, a present the enemie is ten times more greiued [at] then for the losse of xx captens. This hath flesht our young noblemen and gentlemen, and surely theie haue won her majestie at this day as much honour as ever so few men did their prince.

The ij gentlemen, these berers, I made knights, having well deserved it, yet had I much a doe to gett Mr. Hatton to take it. I haue not bestowed it but, you shall heare, by due deserts; others I meane to morrow to make, and not one but hath deserved it. My lord North being hurt the night before, hearinge of the encounter, which lasted an houre and a half at least, being bedde-red, rose vpp and came to the end of it, and lost some of his men. There is noe man more forward then he is, and a very sufficient gentleman assuredly, and most resolute he is. Thus pray you [her majestie,] for my sake and her owne sake, to favour and loue this honest worthy gentleman. I comit you to the Lord; in hast, this 28 Sept.

Your most assured.

[a] as of rare *in MS.*

LETTER CLIII.

THE EARL OF LEYCESTER TO LORD BURGHLEY.

29TH SEPTEMBER, 1586.   HARLEIAN MS. 6994, FOL. 37.   ORIG.

Objects for which Menin and Valck, commissioners from the states, are about to be sent to the queen—i. To know whether she will continue her favour to them, and ii. To solicit a loan—if the queen will persevere she should call a parliament and procure a contribution from her subjects—the earl will not endure such another year's service to gain as much as all these provinces are worth— he is anxious to know the queen's determination.

My lord, I wrote to you before of certain commissionours appointed to be sent to her majestie by the estates: who nowe I thinke wilbe very shortly with you. One cause of their comming wilbe, to advertise her majestie of their estate, and to be humble suytours to knowe her highness pleasure for the continewaunce of her gracious favour to them. But withall, a spetiall cause of their message wilbe, to borrow of her majestie a furder somme of monye, wherein I can saye litle. But according as her majestie shall lyke of the proceading with the cause, so must the advise be. And I do wishe, yf her majestie mynde to deale furder in this cause, and do thincke the maintenance of it to concerne the savetye of her own estate and realme, as it hathe bene allwayes so thought hitherto, that then bothe some loane of monye in this necessitye and all other effectuall courses were taken that may best furder the same. As, principallye, a parliament to be called, and that her highness do use the good willes of her subjectes to a francke contribution therto, to the which I nothing doubt but they wilbe founde moste agreeable and willinge. And no doubtes the case was never so good to deale in as nowe, and, as I trust you shall furder perceyve, yf other mayntenaunce fayle not nowe, being in good estate. But to goe on in suche sorte as it hathe hitherto bene proceaded in, is to lose all that is and shalbe spent, and, by litle and litle, to undoe the whole countrye, which the wise here see, and surely will do what they can to prevent in tyme, and it must neades be daungerous to her majesties estate, to lett it be thus weakelye dealt in on bothe sydes. For my own parte, I will not endure suche another yeares service, with so many crosses and wantes, and so litle asistaunce every waye, yf I were sure to gayne as muche as all these provinces are worthe. I hope God will put into her majesties and your lordships myndes, to do that which shalbe moste for his glorye, for the savety of her majestie, and benefite of her realme. And so, desirous to know with all spede some piece of her majesties resolucion, being hye tyme, I myselfe wilbe moste readye to performe the parte of a most duetifull servant, and obey all her commandementes. And so, with my right hartye commendacions, I do bid your good lordship farewell. At the campe before Zutphen, the 29th of September, 1586.

Your lordships very loving frende,
R. LEYCESTER.

To the right honourable my very good lord, the lord high-treasourour of Englande.

LETTER CLIV.

THE EARL OF LEYCESTER TO MR. SECRETARY WALSYNGHAM.

29TH SEPTEMBER, 1586.   OUVRY MS. FOL. 60.   A COPY.

The earl earnestly requests to be informed of her majesty's determination respecting the Low Countries—the time is at hand to draw into garrison if the English troops are to remain.

Mr. secretory, I haue written often and sent manie, desiring to knowe somwhat of her majesties resolucion for her proceeding in these countreis causes, but as yet I can receaue noe answere in that point. The time of peace now is presentlie at hand, to drawe into garrison. I would gladly be resolved whether her majestie meane that her people shall continue still here, or what elles her pleasure shalbe for them, whereof I heartily pray you that I may be advertised presently. And that you will send some speciall messenger away to me with the dispatch. And soe, with my right hearty commendacions, I bidd you farwell. At the campe before Zutphin, the 29th of September.

Your very loving freind.

LETTER CLV.

LORD BURGHLEY TO THE EARL OF LEYCESTER.

1st OCTOBER, 1586.   COTTON. MS. GALBA, C. X. FOL. 49.   ORIG.

Letter sent by Mr. Killigrew—Mr. Wylkes to return in a few days with instructions from the queen—manifest guilt of the queen of Scots—and necessity for " direct and spedy procedyng" against her—thanks for permitting sir T. Cecill to come home.

My very good lord, uppon this bearers * * Killygrews sodden departure, I cannot wryte so much as I wold; nether if he had lesur to tarry, cold I at this present wryte to myn own satisfaction. I dout not but Mr. Cavendish, whom I fynd a most ernest devoted creatur to your lordship, will, havyng lesur, wryt at length how he fyndeth her majesty disposed. For the commen causes ther under your government, Mr. Wylkes is to come from hence within these few dayes, instructed from hir majesty.

For the gretest matter here in hand, we fynd the cause so manifest ageynst the party, the party so daungerous to our quene, our countrye, and, that is of most importance, to the whole cause of Godes chirch thrugh christendom, as without a direct and spedy procedyng it had bene less daunger to have concealed then revealed this gret conspyracy. I hope that God, which hath gyven us the light to discover it, woll also give asistance to punish it, for it was intended not only ageynst hir majesties person, and yours, and myne, but utterly to have overthrown the glory of Christes chirch, and to have erected the synagog of Antychrist. I nede not to debate this argument.

My lord, for a particular plesur, I thank you for licensyng [my son] to come home, for suerly otherwise his carcass had never bene brought alyve hyther; he is yet, by the opinion of the physicians, not out of perrill, his ageu still contynuing uppon hym.

And so, my lord, forbearyng untill Mr. Wylkes coming, I take my leave of your good lordship, whom I wish so to end your jornay in the feldes, as you may retorn hyther without daunger to the commen cause ther, a thyng so nedefull, as suerly, without your presence here, I know not how hir majesty will or can resolve uppon hir manner of procedyng. From Wyndsor castle, the first of October, 1586.

Your lordships most assured,
W. Burghley.

I hope well that Cassimyre shall enter into France.

Addressed,

To the right honorable my very good lord the erle of Lecestre lieutenant-generall for the queens majesty of England in the Low Countryes.

LETTER CLVI.

THE EARL OF LEYCESTER TO MR. SECRETARY WALSYNGHAM.

2ND OCTOBER, 1586. HARLEIAN MS. 285, FOL. 253. ORIG.

The medical men report that " all the worst days be past " with sir Philip Sydney—he amends as well as is possible—Menin and

Valck sent to the queen from the states—the earl has also sent doctor Clerk and Burgrave—great commendation of the latter—advice as to the course proper to be adopted towards these countries—character of Menin—the earl's credit has been cracked ever since sir T. Heneage was sent—these people having ever been under some prince are not content to be over-ruled by their bakers, brewers, and hired advocates—character of Valck—intrigues of Paul Buys—the earl's receipts from the states, and the way in which they have delayed their payments to him.

Good Mr. secretary, I trust now you shall have longer enioying of your sonne, for all the worst days be past, as both surgeons and phisytians have informyd me, and he amends as well as ys possible in this tyme, and himselfe fyndes yt, for he slepes and restes well, and hath a good stomack to eate, without feare, or any distemper at all. I thank God for yt.

Ther be certen personns desired to be sent to hir majesty, one of the states, which ys Mening, another of the councell, which ys Valk. I have thought good to have Mr. doctor Clerk goe also, who wyll deall truly with hir majesty, and he hath byn a dilligent observer of all that hath past among them.

But I haue thought yt good for spetyall causes to send one Burgrave, and joyned him with the other, who of my knoledge ys a wyse, honest, and religious personn, and not one now amonge them that ys of better understanding of all the matters of this state than he ys, and whatsoever he doth know he wyll deall plainly with hir majesty, whome I pray you help he may haue conference with hir, and with you. You shall fynd him a substanciall wyse man. He was, in the princes tyme, one of the chife for Flanders; he hath byn also one of the prevey councell of estate, and used almost in all ther great causes. Since my coming he served first as master of requestes, after audyencer, and first secretary of the councell of estate. He ys born in Flaunders, and therefore those of Holland have byn lothe to lett him groe into to much credytt. Paul Buys could never lyke of this man, as one afrayd of him, for he ys a depe fellow; yet wold this man never speak yll of him to hurt him, and yet no man can tell more of his doinges than this man, and he can tell you whether I dyd use Paul Buis, and deservyd well at his handes, or no. This man I recomend to you, as one best able to satysfye you what courses may be best to procede for the present, yf hir majesty doe meane to deall any further in these causes, but, except you think the cause worthye to be taken thorowly and princely in hand, never pach it upp any more; rather take your owne courses betyme, and leave these to God, than to deall so as nether part shalbe the better; for most faythfully I assure you, the fear among themselves, with the dowbt of hir majesties proceding, hath almost mard the fashyon of this actyon. And yet, what hart and contentacion the shew of hir majesties favor to these countreys hath bredd doth appeare by the king of Denmarkes and other princes furtherance hereof. And, no doubtes, yf hir majesty wyll goe to the chardge but for ij yeres, she may as assuredly stablysh these countreys as she shall please, as yf ther [were] no enymye able to gaynsay yt.

Now, whether you ther conceave styll as you have done, that these countreys be of consequence for hir majesties safty and servyce, to be kept at hir devotyon, I must leave to yourselves; but yf you be, than doth now your opportunytye well serve you, both to move hir majestye and to ease hir own charges. Yf that opinione be changed, then ether must you entertein them with hope, tyll you can know whether Denmark wyll deall or no, or to make a good peace or a bad peace for hir and them. And, albeyt I wyll never councell that way which may bring but a present shew of peace for a tyme than a perfect peace in dede, yet yf others shall think and perswade that way as a necessarye way, than I say, I think hir majesty may have what peace she will at the king of Spains handes nowe. For the prince ys at his wyttes end at thys time, and a sounde and princely preparacion made for hym this wynter wold breake his backe the next yere, using such other meanes as hir majesty may with the king of Denmarke and the princes of Germany, with whome she may have the greatest reputacion of any prince in the world.

These thinges I must leave, as he that must be dyrected; and yf hir majesty doe procede with these men in the cause, you must nedes than have another manner of comission than was last, and otherwyse delt withall, both for hir majesties assurance here and a more fyrme establyshment of the government; and as these men, all but Burgrave, are sent not only for to seke relyfe, but chyfely to dyscover and understand hir majesties very full dysposytion in this cause, so ys hir majesty to consider with herself what she wyll doe, that she may use them accordinglye.

Of those ij, Mening and Valk, Meninge ys the abler man every way, and I think the better affected to hir majesty. I dyd gyve him a cheyn, one of those you sent; he was no lytle proud man to think himselfe remembered of hir majesty. For my owne parte, my credytt hath byn craked ever synce hir majesty sent sir Thomas Henege hether, as all men can tell you, for indede the government they semed they had geven from themselves to me stok in ther stomackes always, and but to have pleased hir majesty and satysfie the people, they wold never have donn yt. On the other syde, the towens and people they never could, nor yet can, well consent to be overuled by their bakers, and bruers, and hired advocattes, having byn always governed under some prince, and now spetyally under hir majesty, for so dyd they, and doe the most parte, yet take it, that they be only under hir majesties goverment and not the states, for, lett me never be trusted, yf, as sone as they shall finde that they be not under her majestyes government, that they doe not refuse to obey the states, or to lyve under the name of ther goverment iij monthes. I know they hate them, and therin Paul Buys sought to wynn his credytt wyth the people ageyn, to make that shew he dyd, as indede he dyd above all other men here, to advance hir majesties goverment, by joyning with them to press yt so uppon me, as, unless that werr donn, they wold have no goverment by the states by no meanes. Of this you hard inough, but I never found yt was well conceavyd yet, for your owne authoryty from Englond was such as gave them all good cause both to thinke hir majesty ment yt, and for them to offer yt, and confyrm yt uppon me.

Touching all these matters for these countres, I wyll referr you to Mr. Burgrave. I pray you make much of him, for he ys very religious indede, and so ar not many here. Mening ys therin better than his fellow, and one you may deall withall frely, but yet you know he ys one of the states. Valk is subtyll, and seketh wholy to content the states ever synce my authorytye cam in questyon, for, before they hard of hir majesties myslyke, they all of the councell werr sworn to me as governour. After Mr. Henege cam, they all secretly sought to the states, and tooke new patentes from them, saving ij, who plainly answered that they wer sworn to me as governour over all the provinces, and they wold no other patentes from any boddy.

The states have challenged those of Utryckt, also, for that they have contynewed themselves only obedyent to my authoryty, refusing any other comandment of ther states-generall; and herein did Paul Buys deall most badly with me, and with hir majesty also, that knowing hir good pleasure, after did always seke to make wrangling and debates among us, yet did I never any thing but by his advice, and used him above all other councellors here. I hear yt ys reportyd that he gave upp all offyces in the princes tyme for standing against Monsieur and for hir majesty, and how trew that ys all men here know, and that he had a course than in hand, nether for Monsieur nor hir majesty, but only for these countreys for the prince himselfe; and whan he was dedd wold have had him buryed as erll of Holland and Zeland, and wrought all the states of the countrey in the heyt of yt to chuse his sonne governor, which being delayed, he, being in England, was the chife cause to hasten the confyrmacion of yt, and was donn indede, as you know, and none semed to myslyke yt so much as he, and yet he chifely procured yt. His reason than was, for that he feared hir majesty wold not goe forward, and than he ment to prevent all other practyces for the French; and yet whan I cam he only sought to make a pyke between count Morris and me, and byd me take hede of him for he was only French. Indede I here that after the prince was ded, and [he] saw that his practyce that way was ended, he stoode for hir majesty before the French, for he knew the French was advertysed that he was the dealer against Monsieur; but otherwyse yf he ether lost offyce or credytt for hir majesties sake, lett my credytt be lost with you and all the frendes I have; so well have I enquyred of his doinges. But lett him and all these pass. I pray you lett spedy care be taken what course hir majesty wyll take, as a thing most nedefull, and tyme ys most precyous.

And, though I have not byn wylling to make the worst of thinges, yet wyll I not be thought so yll an husband as some I hear wold make me, that I have received of these states not only all the ordynarye allowed beforehand, but also the extraordinarye to the somme of 400,000[li] sterling. First, I wyll say, I never received the therd parte of the ordinary, and for the extraordinary, hit was 400,000 florins, and not poundes, which shuld have byn payd in March, Aprill, May, and June; but the first of that we never received before August, and of that ther ys one 100,000 dewe yet; and of the 300,0000 disbursed, yf ther hath byn paid in money 70,000 to the soldyers hit hath byn a myllion. But they doe make reckoning of all ther vyttell, of ther armour, and wepon, and of their lyke provissions, for which I dare asure yt to you, they have v, vj, viij month day for payment, and yet these provissions be of some their owen. Than judge you, what dealing this ys, or whether these sommes may be said "delivered" to us in money, or no. For the same tyme they take with the marchant for vyttell and munytion, the same might they use for the benyfyt of the soldyer; for before vj or v months come out, they myght make other money reddy for to pay the marchant, and relyve the soldyer in the meane tyme with that which they turn to their own benyfytt; but they deny all this, albeyt yt be playnly knowen.

So, praing to the Lord to dyrect all your councelles to his glory and hir majesties saftye, I comytt you to his protectyon. In hast, this 2. of October.

Your assured frend,
R. LEYCESTER.

Addressed,
To my honourable good frend sir Francis Walsingham, knight, her majesties principall secretarie.

LETTER CLVII.

THE EARL OF LEYCESTER TO MR. SECRETARY WALSYNGHAM.

6TH OCTOBER, 1586. OUVRY MS. FOL. 60. A COPY.

Capture of the Zutphen forts—extraordinary bravery of Edward Stanley—the earl wishes the queen had seen it—young Cooke, a gentleman of the earl of Warwick's, dangerously wounded—another of the forts taken by escalade in a way which no one who had not seen it would believe—" no walls of earth will hold these fellows"—sir Philip Sydney is " well amending"—Roger Williams worth his weight in gold—the earl never knew a worthier fellow than old Read.

Sir, I thanke God he hath giuen vs this day a very happy successe of the ij principall forts here. We haue taken one by a gallant and a thorow-fought assault, and for a quarter of an houre we did looke for a very furious resistance, yet so it pleased God to daunt their heartes, and to animate those worthy souldiers whoe attempted it, as hit was entred, and the enemie, as many [as] did abide, kild, the rest fledd to the other fort. There was one gentleman whome we all present did behold, that had the leading of all the rest that went to the assalt, which was Mr. Edward Stanley, lieutenent to sir William Stanley. Since I was borne I did neuer se any man to behaue himself as he did. First clime the brech, a pike-length before and aboue anie person that followed him, soe did he alone maintaine the fight, first with his pike, then with the stumpes of his pike, and afterward his sword, against at the lest ix or x, and everie man either brake his pike vppon his brest, or hit him with the shott of thir muskett, yet would he not back a foote, but kept himself in this sort without anie one man to gett vpp to him, the ground was soe false being all sandie, insomuch as we all gaue him [for] lost if he had a c lives; for I was within viij^{xx} yardes and lese myself, and v^m saw it besides, being all in yellow saving his curass.[a] When he had longe thus dealt most valientlie and worthilie, and none of his companie easily could come to him, at length theie all came so fast together as one bare vpp another even to to the topp of the brech, where that gentleman got a halberd and lept among the enemies, and then the rest with him, in so resolute manner as thei speedilie dispatched the enemye, and in the sight [b] of all the towne both placed their ainsignes and made this fight. A place theie little looked to be won so soone, and in all troth it is one of the strongest places for sure fights within, that euer I saw in all my life. But this gentleman shall I neuer forgett if I liue a c yere, for if he had fainted and tarried for his fellowes, as many one would haue done, we had bine like enough to haue made a new batterie for the rest; but even so worthilie he did by Godes goodnes, as he was the cheife cause, of mans worke, of all the honour of this day, and he shall haue parte of my living for it as longe as he liues.[c] And I would God her majestie had sene this

[a] curatts *in MS.*   [b] highst *in MS.*

[c] The bravery exhibited by Edward Stanley in this daring enterprise is highly and universally extolled, and must have been peculiarly gratifying to Leycester, whose plan of attack upon the Zutphen forts, devised " by his excellencies owneselfe," and adhered to " contrary to all and every their advises," was thus rendered successful. Leycester knighted Stanley "in the trenches, gave him fortie pounds sterling in golde, and sent him the next daie a patent of one hundred marks sterling by yeer, during the life of the said sir Edward, binding his excellencies own landes in England for the due paiment thereof." Briefe Report, sig. D. 2.

enterprise, for hit was worthy her sight to se the willingnes of her subiects, their valour in performing, and with how little losse of them it was acheiued, notwithstandinge that we had all the artillerye of the town against them on the one side, and the other fort on the other, yet was there not slayne five persons in all, nor aboue vj hurt, whereof an honest proper yong gentleman of my brother of Warwicks is one, called Cooke, whoe even at the first attempt was by the shott of a canon thwart his belly stricken soe strangly as I neuer saw; his armour broken with a hole as bigg as a bullett, himself with a piece of the armour cut alonge his bellye, ij inches deep, and yet his bowells whole, and I am in hope of his life.

This good successe God gaue vs this Thursdaie. The last Thursdaie we tooke another of the fortes, which did vs most harme before, and at nine dayes, before the enemyes face, by a flat skallader; and, if you had bine here and sene it, and that afterward a man had tould you hit had bine taken, either without ladders or a mine, you would not beleeue it, the ditch was so deepe and the ramper so high, at the lest xx foote high, and our men had not a ladder, but one climing vpp still by an other; for no walls of earth will hold these fellowes. The count Hollock was a yere and more about this fort, and had more helps then I haue, or shall haue, and as I haue already ij of the iij, soe I hope to haue the three or longe, and if I can haue that, I care not much for Zutphin, for it wilbe besett well enough, we having Deventer, Lockom, Shereberge,[a] Dotticom, and Doursborrow. I cannot see how it can be able to liue, or to be reliued, without a very great armie at euerie time hit hath need. God send it vs quicklye, for the winter is come here and foule weather alreadie, and how we be serued of our rutters I haue written to her majestie, but the king of Denmark hath deserued great thankes at her majesties hands.

Lastly, and that will not like you least, your sonne and mine is well amending as euer anie man hath done for soe short time. He feeleth noe greif now but his long lying, which he must suffer.

[a] So in the MS. but perhaps it should be Herenberg.

His wife is with him, and I to morrow am going to him for a start. But for his hurt, that Thursdaie may runn amongst anie of our Thursdaies, for there was neuer a more valiant dayes service seene this c yeres by so few men against so many, and the most of them such men as those were, lords, knights, and gentlemen, among others. In my former letters I forgott one, whoe not onlie at that day, but at everie dayes service hath bine a principall actor himself, a tall wise rare servant he is, as any I knowe, and of marvellous good gouernment and iudgment; that gentleman may take a great charge vppon him I warrant you.

The prince was here, but staied[a] onlie a night with all his forces, and brought I thinke xxx wagons of vittell with him; he doth now logg ix mile of. I sent v^c horsse this morning to vissett his campe, but there would none of his gallants come forth. Sir William Russell, Robert Sidney, Rogers Williams,[b] among them were the cheif, and that Roger Williams is worth his weight in gold, for he is noe more valiant than he is wise, and of judgment to gouerne his doings. Here wilbe manie worthie men as euer England had. Mr. Norrice is a most valiant souldier surely, and all are now perfect good freinds here. The old marshall neuer rests. Soe, good Mr. secretary, I will bidd you far well, and comit you to the Lord. Hast, this vj. of October.

Your assured freind.

I assure you I neuer knew a worthier old fellow then old Read[c] is, nor so able bodie to take pains; he hath past all men here for pains and perill.

---

[a] served *in MS*.   [b] William Rogers Williams *in MS*.
[c] Leycester knighted Reade at the same time as Edward Stanley. Stowe's Chron. p. 739.

LETTER CLVIII.

THE EARL OF LEYCESTER TO MR. SECRETARY WALSYNGHAM.

10TH OCTOBER, 1586. OUVRY MS. FOL. 61b. A COPY.

The earl urges the immediate execution of Mary queen of Scots— the great seal was sent for her execution when she was suspected of a participation in the rebellion of 1569, how much more now—the earl hopes the queen will retain Candish, the bearer of this letter, an excellent old man, but who cannot be kept out of the field.

I haue written very earnistly, both to her majestie and to my lord-tresorer, and partlie also to yourself and Mr. vice-chamberlain, for the furtherance of justice on [a] the queen of Scotts, and belieue me, if you shall deferre it, either for a parliament or a great session, you will hazard her majestie more than euer, for time to be giuen is that the traitors and enemyes to her will desire. Remember, how, vppon a lesse cause, how effectually all the councell of Enggland once delt with her majestie for justice to be done vppon that [person]; for, being suspected and informed to be consentinge with Northumberland and Westmorland in the rebellion, you knowe the great seall of England was sent then, and thought iust and meete, vppon the sudden, for her execucion. Shall now her consent and practice for the destruccion of her majesties person be vsed with more, to her, more danger than the lesse former fault? Surely I tremble at it, for I doe assure myself of a new more desperate attempt yf you shall fall to such temporisinge solemnityes, and her majestie cannot but mislike you all for it. For who can warrant these villaines from her, if that person live, or shall liue, anie time? God forbid! and be you all stout and resolute in this speedy execution, or be condemned of all the world for euer. It is most certen, if you will haue her majestie safe, hit must be done, for iustice doth craue it beside pollicye. Hit is the cause I send

[a] in *in MS.*

this poore lame man, whoe will needes be the messenger for this matter. He hath bidden such travell and paine here as you will not beleeue; a faithfull creature he is to her majestie as euer liued.

I pray you lett her reteine[a] him still now euer to saue his life, for you knowe the time of the yere is past for such a man to be in feild, yet will he needs be so, and meanes to retorne, and you must procure his stay as without my knowledge, or elles I loose him for euer. But if he come hether it is not like that he can continue. He deserues as much as anie good hart can doe. Be his good freind I pray you, and so God blesse you. Hast, written in my bedd vppon a cushion, this 10th, erely in the morning.

Your assured.

I pray you lett not Candish knowe I wrote for his stay, but yet procure it in any wise.

LETTER CLIX.

INSTRUCTIONS OF THOMAS WYLKES, ESQUIRE, SENT BY THE QUEEN TO THE STATES-GENERAL AND THE EARL OF LEYCESTER.

OCTOBER, 1586.   COTTON MS. GALBA, C. X. FOL. 79. ORIG.

The queen sends £30,000, which is to be paid to her troops serving in the Low Countries and to the garrisons of Flushing and Brill—Wylkes is to take the place of Henry Killigrew as a counsellor in the council of state, communicating to the earl of Leycester whatever passes there concerning the queen's interest, and giving notice to the queen or her secretaries of any matter relating to her service wherein he cannot obtain redress upon application to the states—a placard of the earl restraining traffic to be revoked or qualified—Ringault and Perret to be dismissed from the charge of the finances—Paul Buys either to be brought to trial or re-

---

[a] lett her not reteine *in MS.*

stored to liberty—Wylkes to urge and procure answers to letters written to the earl which have remained unanswered.

ELIZABETH R.   By the Queene.

Whereas we have appointed certaine of our treasure, amounting to the somme of 30,000 li. to be presentlie sent over into the Lowe Contries, for the payment of our forces serving in the said contries, and our garnisons in the townes of Vlissingen and Brill, parte wherof is to be made over by waye of exchaunge, and the reste to be delivered to your handes to be safelie conveyed into the said Lowe Contries, of the which we have also appointed 8,000 li to be chested here aparte, meaning that the same shalbe issued for the payment of our said garnisons at Vlissingen and Brill, to whome our pleasure is, that a full paye be made untill the twelfth of this present and if the same 8000 li shall not suffize to make unto our said garnisons [a full paye] to the xijth of Octobre aforesaid, then our will and further pleasure is, that out of the reste of our said treasure there be taken so much as may furnishe up the full paye unto the same daye. We doe, therfore, will and commaunde youe to receave and take the charge of all the said treasure, and see the same safelie transported unto the town of Midleburche in Zelande, and there lefte in the handes and custodie of the deputie of our marchantes-adventurers untill suche tyme as direction may be given to sir Thomas Shirley knight, appointed to exercise the place of our threasurer at warres, in thabsence of Richard Hudleston esquier, to repaire thither, and there to receive and make paye therof to our said garnisons, as is above specified, and that our cousin therle of Leycester, lieutenant-generall of our forces in the said contries, shall give ordre for the conveying and transporting of the reste of the treasure, made over either in spetie or by exchange, to suche other place as by him shalbe thought convenient.

And wheras, for the good opinion we doe conceave of youe, by reason of experience had of your sufficiencie and dexteritie in our former services, we have made speciall choice of youe, and thought youe fitt to be employed in our present service in the Lowe Contries, there to reside for our said services, and withall to exercise the place of our servaunt Henry Killigrew esquier, as a counseler and assistant in the counsel of state there, according to the contract heretofore passed betweene us and the states-generall of those contries. Our pleasure therfore and meaning is, that youe shall furthwith repaire thither, and there to abyde and continue until by our direction youe shalbe revoked, and besides our other services which from tyme to tyme shalbe committed unto youe, you shall lykewise give diligent attendance and be present in the said counsell of state at all tymes and uppon all occasions, as to give counsaile and advise for our service, and for the publique services of the said contries. Willing and expressly commaunding youe, that in all thinges that shall concerne us, the benefite and furtherance of our said services, and thadvauncement of thaction presently in hand for the defence and preservacion of the said contries, youe doe according to your skill and judgement, without feare or dreade of any parson or parsons whatsoever, informe and advise our said cousin therle of Leycester, to the uttermoste of your power, of all and everie suche thinges causes and matters as youe, in your knowledge and experience, shall at all tymes see to be needfull and requisite, to thende that good ordre may be had and taken in the same accordingly.

And wee doe hereby further will and commaunde youe, upon all occasions of our necessarie services, and in matters of importaunce that shall concerne us and our state, wherin there cannot or shall not be remedie and redresse had on that syde, uppon your mocions and good indevours to bee used to the states and counsell in that behalfe, that youe faile not, after youe shall have imparted the same to our said cousin, to give knowlege therof unto us, or to one of our principall secretaries, to thende the same may be weighed and considered here, and direction therin given from hence as shall apperteyne.

And wheras, by certaine articles wherewith Ortell hathe here acquainted us by ordre from the states, yt appeareth that they fynde themselfes somewhat grieved with the placard published by our said cousin in Aprill laste, in restrainte of their traffique, a matter which they thinke will greatly interesse the common cause, yf yt bee not all the sooner redressed, as well in regard of the decaye of their shipping and impoverishing of their townes, which stand altogither by sea trades, as by diminishing the proffites of their convoyes, which hathe hitherto yealded a greate parte of the meanes to defraye the charge and burthen of their warres, and must of necessitie faile yf their said traffique, a principall cause of the riches and welthe of those contries, be diverted to other partes, wherof they have already some experience by the course which the Esterlings and others have taken aboute the Orcades in conveying their commodities into Spaine and other of the south partes, which were wont to passe from the said Low Contries, where they were first stapled to the great inriching of their estate, maintenance and encreace of their navigation. Forasmuch as they have required us to have some consideration therof, and to interpose our authority with our said cousin in that behalfe, youe shall lett him understand, that as well for the greate care we have of the said contryes, as for our own particuler interest in the state therof, we thinke yt meete some suche ordre be taken for the preservacion of this said traffique, and revoking or qualifieing of the foresaid placard, as with thadvice of the states-generall, or counsell chosen by them to assiste him, shall be found moste expedient for the common good of the said countrey.

And where, also, we are infourmed of a generall myslyke conceaved by the said estates uppon the preferring of Ringault and Perret to the principall offices and charges of the finances, as well for the condicions of the men, and manifold suspicions heretofore conceaved against them upon very probable cause, as for divers bad offices they are noted to have done synce their employment by our said cousin, both in laboring to sett some difference betwixt him and others of thestates and counselers there, and in seeking to introduce newe formes of exactions under his authoritie, bothe hatefull and dangerous in regard of the tyme and present condicion of the broken and unsettled gouverment there, wherof may growe some unhappy consequence yf suche lewd instrumentes should be continued, and shrowded under his contenance and favour. Youe shall lett him knowe, that we thinke meete, as well for the better satisfyeng of the said states and people, as for preventing the hurt might otherwise growe therof, that he doe make better choice of men to occupie their roomes, or to take suche other ordre in that behalfe as with thadvice of the said estates, or counsell appointed to assiste him, shalbe thought moste agreable to the necessitie of the tyme and condition of their affaires.

And, for that we are also born in hand, that they doe fynd themselfes much greved at the proceading used against Paul Buys, bothe for the manner of his apprehension and deteyning thus longe in closse prison, without proceeding to his tryall, or bringing him to his aunsweare, contrary to the priviledges and custoumes of that countrey, youe shall tell him, we thinke yt meete that some favourable regard be also had to their contentment in this behalfe, the rather for the triall he hathe heretofore made of his loyaltie to the common cause, and particuler affection to oure state, howesoever nowe he be noted to have declined from the one or thother. And, also, to take lyke ordre that those gentlemen burgesses and others which have ben latelie banished by those of Utrecht in a populer tumulte and disordre (as we are infourmed), uppon some jalousie conceaved against them for religion sake, may by his authoritie and mediacion be either charged or restored, the rather being (as we are given to understand) suche as against whose loyalties and fidelities no just exception can be taken, as appeareth by the testimonie of th'estates themselfes, from whom their cause hathe ben earnestly recommended unto us.

And wheras, heretofore, many letters have ben written to our said cousin th'erle of Leycester, as well from us as from our privie counsell and secretary, requiring aunswere to many matters concerning our service, wherof by reason of his manifolde occupacions (as we take yt) there hathe seldome ben any aunsweare retourned, or mention of the receipte of the said letters, or matters thereby communicated unto him, for redresse wherof hereafter, even as we have appointed that notice shall be given unto youe of all suche letters as from hencefourth shall be sent thither concerning our publique services, so is yt our will and pleasure, that youe shall from tyme to tyme urge and procure aunsweare to the said letters and matters, whereof we meane to laye the charge and burthen on youe, and doe hereby will and commaunde youe, as ye will avoyde our displeasure, to take a speciall care and charge therof, and to sollicite our said cousin for aunsweare to all and everie the said letters, and matters, according to such particuler direction as youe shall receave from hence.[a]

FRA. WALSYNGHAM.

LETTER CLX.

SIR THOMAS HENEAGE TO THE EARL OF LEYCESTER.

13TH OCTOBER, 1586. COTTON. MS. GALBA, C. X. FOL. 63. ORIG.

Arrival of a messenger with tidings of the fight at Zutphen—the queen immediately sent a special messenger to sir Philip Sydney with letters of her own hand to comfort him—complaints against the earl for levying more men than he can pay and for want of accounts of the money he had received—sir Thomas suspects

---

[a] This paper is not dated, but it appears from Galba, C. x. fol. 83, that Wylkes set out from London on the 14th October, 1586, having previously received this commission.

from whom this evil grows—the queen's reception of the standards taken at Zutphen—the council are at Fotheringay—no tidings of what has been done there.

My lord, before yesterday that Martine [brought the] a newes, but very uncerten and false rumors were brought hether of your conflyct with the Spaniards, and of the great valeure b and greevous hurte [of your] noble nephewe, to whome her majesty p[resently] hath sent this bearer, both to cary her graciose letters of her highnes own hand to comforte hym, [and] to bring her word agayn how he doth as [soon] as he can.

I shewed her majesty your lordships [letter to] me, which when she had redd, she fownd [fault] anew with your callyng of moe men into [those] servyses then ether you coold pay or fende, [and] began to reherse unto me again, how your [lordship] had of the states, besydes all the money [from] hens, syns January last, above 400,000^{li}; [neither] with reason or trothe coold I allmost any thinge drawe her from so false perswasion, [nor] without sharpe wordes get her [to] heare how the states made ther own reconynges and abate[mentes out] of their own paymentes, at all tymes when [they] let your lordship have money. So still I find an injurious and prejudiciall perswasyon agaynst [you], and the cawse possesseth her majesties judgment, [that] you have had, as appeareth by your own hand, so moch money from the states and owt [of this] contrye, and can make, or hath made, no reconyng of yt, nor have paid the garrisons of her [towns]. I wrote to sir Philip Sydney of late, from whe[nce I] guessed this evell grewe, and I have ever [the] more cawse to thinke yt came from the [same] man.

Er I parted from her majesty yesterday, I left her very well pleased with the care she fownd to be in you for her servyse, and

---

a This alludes to the receipt of Leycester's letter to sir Thomas Heneage, dated 23rd September, 1586, an extract from which is printed, as before mentioned, in the Sydney Papers, i. 104.   b valewe *in MS.*

the [valour] and the victory of the noble and gentelmen [whom she doth] exceedingly commend, and after shewed to soch of her cowncell as now be hear from Fotheringay the twoe cornettes that wear taken,[a] and I delyvered to her majesty from your lordship, the one of count Hannibals,[b] and the other Martyne coold not tell me to whom yt dyd apperteyne. The Lord Jesus graunte your lordship no wurse bargen whensoever you meet agayn with the Spanyard. Your lordships letters both to my lord threasurer and Mr. secretary Walsingam I sent presently to Fotheringay[c] to them, after Martine had delyvered them. What the lordes have doonne ther I yet knowe nothing, but whatsoever they doe thear, I have great cawse to feare that the forbearyng to doo hear (that is of all the most needfull) will, er we be ware of yt, quyte undoe us all. This is both my guesse and my greefe. And now all my prayer is, that God will preserve her majesty, [and] send your lordship victory thear, with most honour, and soone and safe home. At the court, this xiij[th] of October, 1586.

  Your lordships all bownd at commandment,
             T. HENEAGE.

Addressed,
 To hys excellensye.

LETTER CLXI.

THE DEPUTY OF THE MERCHANTS-ADVENTURERS RESIDENT AT MIDDLEBURGH TO THE EARL OF LEYCESTER.

18TH OCTOBER 1586. HARL. MS. 285. FOL. 256. ORIG.

Upon the earl's letter to request them to make ready and forward him £5,000, they sent part by the bearer of his letter, and caused

---

[a] See page 417.
[b] Count Hannibal Gonzaga, "a man for nobilitie and service of speciall account amongst them." Briefe Report, sig. D. 1. He was killed at Zutphen.
[c] The commissioners for the trial of Mary queen of Scots assembled at Fotheringay on the 11th October, 1586. State Trials, i. 1168.

every brother by oath to bring in all money he could procure, and also assessed every resident brother " by the poll," but without being able to make up the sum—their governor in London having agreed with lord Burghley to furnish the treasurer for the army with £10,000 by the end of October, they will do so, but must reckon the sum wanted by the earl as so much on account.

Righte excellent our honorable good lorde, upon the receipt of your excellencies letter per your servaunt Mr. Henry Jones, we did in all readynes indebvor ourselves to make readye the fyve thousande pounde starling by your excellencie requyred, parte whereof is sent per your sayde sarvaunt, and we use all meanes possible in provydinge the rest, and, to that end, have not onlye caused every brother by othe to bringe in all sutche monies as he eyther had or coulde by any meanes receave, but also have cessed every brother that are occupiers here with us by the poll, and yet we fynde ourselves unable to furnishe the rest as yet, partlye by meanes of our slacke trade at this present, and speciallye for that our appointed shipps, which should have bin here a monethe past, are not only as yet not come, but also, by meanes of the late stormes, have receaved greate hurte, and one caste awaye, and therefor not lykelye to be here this monethe or six weekes, whereby we are altogeather unprovyded to satisfie your excellencies expectation, notwithstandinge we have sought all meanes possible, as well by interest as exchaunge.

Also, the righte honorable the lorde highe-tresorer of Englande hath delte with our gouernor at London, for the payment to sir Thomas Shurley knight [of] the some of £10,000 sterling by the last of this monethe, at xxxiij^s. iiij^d. Flemishe the pounde starling, which was yelded unto so farre fourthe as the coynes were not called doune, which some of monie, for the causes before alledged, will be very harde for us to furnishe, besyde the great losse which we shoulde susteyne by the losse of the exchange. Notwithstandinge, hopinge your excellencie will have dewe consideration thereof, we will do whatsoever possibly we maye to furnishe the sayde 10,000li as soone as we cann, so farre as the some alreadye delivered to Mr. Jones, and the rest remayninge yet in our hands unpayde, may be by sir Thomas Shurley accounted as parte of the 10,000li; otherwise, in truthe we fynde ourselves at this presente altogeather unable to furnishe the same. Thus, desyringe your excellencie favorablye to construe our good meaninges, as you have alwayes bin accustomed, we cease, prayenge to the Almightie for your good successe and longe lyffe, to the glory of God. Amen. From Midleborch this 18th of October, anno 1586.

Your excellencies at comaundment,
The deputie, assistants, and
fellowshippe of marchaunts-
adventurers of Englande
rezident *ut supra*.
ROBARTE TEYLOR deputye.

Addressed,
To the righte excellent our very honorable good lorde, the earle off Leicester, her majesties lieutenant-generall in the Lowe Cuntries, to be delivered.
At the campe.

LETTER CLXII.

DR. BARTHOLOMEW CLERK TO THE EARL OF LEYCESTER.

22ND OCTOBER, 1586.   COTTON. MS. GALBA, C. X. FOL. 73.   ORIG.

The writer has communicated to Valck and Menin, and to divers of the states, the earl's intention shortly to repair to England for a time—they all agree that it is vain for them to go before—condolence on the death of sir Philip Sydney—the states are free of speech, and have variety of judgments, but are easily persuaded by those of whom they have good opinion—a report that the queen means to take upon her the sovereignty—the states " in a maze" upon the intimation of the earl's sudden departure.

Myne humble dewtie to your excellency premised, &c. according unto your goodd pleasure I have imparted the contents of your honorable letters, not only to my colleagues in this voyage, monsieur Valke and Mr Menin, but allso to divers of the estates, signifieng unto them, that, albeit my stayenge heere is my extreeme hinderance in Englond, as indeede it is, yeat, for that your excellency, for divers weighty affaires, are shortly in person for a time to repayre thither, I thincke it vayne for us to goe beefore, for that I assure myselfe her majesty will determine nothing beefore your comminge, and that sithe shee hathe made choyse of your excellency for the mayne matter, it is lyke her highenes wille not wade farther withowte your especialle advowing and advizinge. They are heere in alle of mine opinion, and take most heavely, as wee all have cause to doe, the infortunat death of your noble nepheu, whose like, as far as I am hable to judge, for his time and years in all respects, I never fownde, nether in Englond, France, or Germany. I know I want judgement to reneue greefe by thease lines in your noble minde, but mine owne greefe wold not suffer silence.

It resteth that wee heere bee doon to undrestand of your excellencis pleasure, whether wee shalle awayte on yow at Utrecht or remayne heere, for that the estates are now fully assembled, untille your excellencis comminge. In my poore opinion it weare not amisse, in alle their assembles, to have soome of the cowncelle neere them that are gracius with them; for, allbeit they use libertye of speeche, and have great varietee of judgements, as alle popular states have, yeat I finde they are easye to bee perswaded by those of whome they have goodd opinion.

For that it is heere secretly bruted that her majesty meaneth to take uppon her the absolute goverment or soveraingnete, I have secretly fownde the meanes to gett owte of their regesters the treatise of Bowrdeaulx with the duke of Aniow, whereof I have written owte the whole negotiation. I have allso gotten the treatie with the Frenche king that now is, and have allmost copied it owte, which, under your honorable correction, wille serve us to great pourpose in England, encase her majesty shalle please to proceede eny farther in this action, for thearin shall wee not only see all the particularitees of their contry layd open, but allso how farre they went in their grawntes, and what dowbtes weare mooved uppon their articles, and how they weare answered.

And so staying myselfe uppon your excellencis farther pleasure, and wisshing alle happines to your noble desseignes, I comitt the same to the Allmighty. The Hage, the xxijth of October.

Your excellencis most bownden,
Bartholo. Clerk.

Allbeit all such of the states as I conferred withalle weare of my opinion that it weare to smalle pourpose for us to goe beefore your excellency, yeat, uppon the reading of your letters directed unto them, they finde themselves in suche a maze towching divers poyntes, especially touching your soddein departure, [the] governement in your absence, and the satisfieng of their soldiers, as I thinke they will not very speedely resolve eny thing. In my poore judgement your excellencis presence weare convenient emonge them,[a] by soome particulers to induce the generalle. In the meane time Mr Valke, Mr Menin, and myselfe, stand resolute to

---

[a] On the 31st October the earl met the council of state and announced to them his determination to return to England, producing as the cause of this sudden determination his writ of summons to attend the parliament then actually sitting at Westminster. Wilkes, who was present, says, that " the states and councell used but slender intreatie

doe nothing but according to your excellencis good plesure, which I referre to the Allmighty.

Addressed,
To his excellencye at Utrecht.

LETTER CLXIII.
MR. CHRISTOPHER BAKER TO THE EARL OF LEYCESTER.
22ND OCTOBER, 1586.   HARL. MS. 285, FOL. 258.   ORIG.

That according to the earl's order he will await his pleasure at Middleburgh with the queen's ships under his command—the earl of Essex and other gentlemen have been waiting to have passage over with the writer.

Right honorable my singler good lord, I have receved your excellences letter dated the 19. of this present, whereby I do understand your lordshipps pleasure is, that I shulde staie with her majesties barke the Charles, wherein I serve, with all the rest of the shippinge that are under my chardge, viz. the Spy, the Makeshifte, her majesties pynnace, and the Fortunate of sir Thomas Cicill, which, God willinge, I will do, till your excellences pleasure be further knowen unto me. All our victualles growe nere to an end. Beseaching your honor there maie be as much expedicion used as convenientlie maie.

Here is my lord of Essex, sir Thomas Parrot, sir Phillip Butler, sir Thomas Cooke, with divers other gentlemen, who have stayed here to have passage over with me, which are nowe to seeke, except they will staie your honours pleasure. And so I comit your excellencie to the salfe kepinge of Almightie God, with

to his excellencie for his staye and contynuance there among them, whereat his excellencie and we that were of the councell for her majestie dyd not a lyttle marvaill." Galba, C. x. fol. 83.

increase of honour unto your excellencie and all yours. From Middlebrow, this 22. daie of October, 1586.

Your excellences ever to comaunde,
Xpof^r Baker.

Addressed,
To the right excellent my very honorable good lord the earle of Leicester, her majesties lieutenant-generall in the Lowe Cuntries, hast theis.

At Utrecht. Hast. Hast.

LETTER CLXIV.

THE EARL OF LEYCESTER TO MR. SECRETARY WALSYNGHAM.

25TH OCTOBER, 1586. OUVRY MS. FOL. 62. A COPY.

The earl's grief for the death of sir Philip Sydney—his widow is with the earl much exhausted by her long care of her husband—the earl will " high him home now, leaving all as well as he can "—Deventer is secured—count Hohenlohe's treacherous character—the treasure much wanted—regrets for the delay in executing the queen of Scots.

Sir, the greif I haue taken for the losse of my dere sonne and yours [a] would not suffer me to write soner of those ill newes vnto you, specially being in so good hope soe very little time before of his good recouerie; but he is with the Lord, and his will must be done. Yf he had liued, I dowbt not but he would haue bine a comfort to vs both, and an ornament to his howse. What perfection he was growen vnto, and how able to serue her majestie and his countrey, all men here almost wondred at. For my none parte, I haue lost, beside the comfort of my life, a most principall stay and help in my seruice here, and, if I may say it, I thinke none

[a] Sir Philip Sydney died on the 17th October, 1586.

of all hath a greter losse then the queens majestie herself. Your sorrowfull daughter and mine is here with me at Vtrickt, till she may recouer some strength, for she is wonderfully overthrowen thorow hir longe care since the beginning of her husbandes hurt, and I am the more carefull that she should be in some strength or she take her iourney into England, for that she is with child, which I praye God send to be a sonne, if it be his will; but, whether sonne or daughter, theie shalbe my children to.[a] She is most ernist to be gon out of this countreie, and soe I could wish her, seeing it so against her mind, but for her weaknes yet, hir case considered.

I will high me home now, leaving all as well [as] I can. I haue assured Deuenter at length, and with much coumber,[b] wherein the marshall hath shewed himself like a man of valour, as he is indeed.[c] He is much esteemed of these countreymen. The count Hollock is, for his hurt, like to doe well, but a very dangerous man, inconstant, enuious, and hatfull, I see, to all our nacion, and, in my conscience, a very traitor to the cause, as I thinke the states begin[d] to find him now. There is noe dealing to winn him. I haue sought it, to my cost. His best freinds tell me he is not to be trusted. The tresorer is here, and sir Thomas Sherly gon, longe since, for England. The treasure is to be deliuered to the tresorer. The need is great with the souldiers. My none case[e] is not the best, but I referr that to the Lord, whoe hath sent me many crosses, which I acknowledge to deserue, with far more greater if my weaknes could beare it.

I perceiue the conclusion of all your seruice is shutt from dew

---

[a] This child was probably still-born. Two letters from the earl of Walsyngham printed in the appendix refer to an illness of lady Sidney's, perhaps a premature confinement, in December 1586.

[b] The word in the MS. is very doubtful. It looks like "counder."

[c] The garrisoning of Deventer may rank with the boldest and most successful stratagems of warfare. A valuable letter which tells the whole story in a striking manner will be found in the Appendix.

[d] begon *in MS.*   [e] care *in MS.*

execution. God be mercifull to vs, and defend her majestie, of whose desperate state I am now more affraid then euer before. My hart cannot rest for feare since I hard that your matters are deferred. All the enemyes hir majestie hath cannot worke so great a perill against herself. Well! God hath his work, and he wilbe knowen, and he will looke both to be sought and thanked for his mercies bestowed. I doe feare, if I had bine there with you, I should rather haue putt myself into her majesties place[a] then suffred this dreadfull mischeif to be prolonged for her destruccion. Thus, praying for you as for myself, will comend you to the Lords proteccion. From Vtrickt, 25 October.

Your assured freind.

LETTER CLXV.

LORD BURGHLEY AND MR. SECRETARY WALSYNGHAM TO THE EARL OF LEYCESTER.

28TH OCTOBER, 1586. COTTON. MS. GALBA, C. X. FOL. 77. ORIG.

The queen having been informed that Richard Hurlestone the treasurer was about to return home with the earl's licence, appointed sir Thomas Shirley to pay away the £30,000 sent by Wylkes, but Shirley having unexpectedly returned to England, the queen now directs that Hurlestone do issue the said treasure, and that payment be made up to a day certain.

After our hartie comendaciones unto your lordship, where her majestie by her late letters dirrected to your lordship, as also unto sir Thomas Shurley, did, uppon information geiven unto hir that

---

[a] The word in the MS. is "grace," but the sense seems to require "place." The earl apparently means, that, had he been in England, he would himself have taken upon himself the responsibility of ordering or procuring the execution of the queen of Scots, in lieu of allowing queen Elizabeth to be exposed to the great danger likely to arise to her from delay.

Rychard Hurleston esquier, nowe thresaurer there, was mynded with your lordships lycence to retourne into this realme, about certeine necessarie affaires of his owne, appointe the said sir Thomas to take charge of the treasure last sent over by Mr. Thomas Wylkes, and to issue out the same by your lordships warrante. Forasmuch as sir Thomas Shurley is nowe retourned into this realme, contrarie to her majesties expectation, and cannot returne, as he saieth, to those partes, in respect of certeine of his owne privatte causes here, with that expedition that were convenient: her majestie hath comanded us to signifie in her name unto you, that her pleasure is, the said Rychard Hurlston, nowe thresaurer, notwithstanding her former letters to your lordship, and direction gewen to the said Wylkes, shall take charge of the treasure last sent, and shall issue the same by vertue of your lordships warrant, and according to such instructions as she hath gewen to the said Wylkes, touching her pleasure for the disposing of the said treasure. And, to thend the accompte maie be the more cleere at such tyme as sir Thomas shall take charge of the treasure that is to be hereafter sent into those countries, it is also thought meete by her majestie, that this treasure might be emploied to make a full paie unto a daie certaine without issuing the same out in imprestes, which thing her majestie conceaveth maie be donne untill the 12th of this moneth of October, if it cannot be further, which her majestie referreth to your lordships good consideration, beinding the same as neare as maie be to procure unto a daie certeine a full paie under the charge of the nowe thresaurer, so as sir Thomas Shurley, or any other that shall succeede him, maie beginne uppon a cleere reckoninge. And so we comend your lordship most hartelie to the protection of Almightie God.

From the court at Rychemond, the 28th of October, 1586.
Your lordships assured loving frendes,
W. BURGHLEY.
FRA. WALSYNGHAM.

LETTER CLXVI.

LORD BURGHLEY TO THE EARL OF LEYCESTER.

4TH NOVEMBER, 1586. COTTON. MS. GALBA, C. X. FOL. 40.

The queen is willing that the earl should return home, but she wishes good order taken for the government of the country and the army during his absence—for the former she will probably send lord Grey—for the latter some suggest count Maurice—some would join lord Grey with him—the queen wishes the government were given back to the states, as before the earl went—the earl will find the queen's mislikings disappear on his return and the good answers he can make to her objections—sentence perfected against the queen of Scots.

My very good lord, this gentleman, Mr. Gorge, commeth thyther with such hast, as I have no lesur to wryte as otherwise I wold, but breffly. I have, accordyng to your lordships late lettres, moved hir majesty for your lordships licenss to retorn, wherunto hir majesty is of hirself very willyng, as well for the desyre she hath to se your lordship, as for the dout she also hath that thys wyntar season yow might fall into some sycknes; but yet herwith she also is very carefull how those countrees may be governed without harm to the public cause, and how hir own army, consistyng of hir people, might also be ruled and directed; of both which, though hir majesty hath had some kind of speches, yet she myndeth not to mak any resolution but by your lordships advise. Yet, for the government of hir army, I perceave she will laye the chardg uppon my lord Gray, who will shun it I am sure as much as he may, and yet I have perswaded hir majesty to encorradg hym with the remission of an Irish det that, in conscience, he ought not to paye.

I told Mr. Gorge by speche, that seing ther is treasur sent over, wherof your lordship had no knolledg at your late wrytyng, I wold wish your lordship to se the same, or the gretar part, issued out wher is most nede, but specially to mak full payes to some day certen.

For the government ther in your lordships absence we here cannot gyve any advise, but, consideryng your lordships great experience there, whatsoever your lordship shall declare to be mete I will assent therto, and by my advise to hir majesty furder it as reason is. Some spek of namyng the count Morrice to be governor alon in your absence, and as to have the rule under your lordship; some wish that the count Moryce shuld be joyned with the lord Graye. The queenes majesty wold that it war in the states direction ageyn as it was befor they committed it to your lordship, with the direction of the lord Graye as lieutenant of hir army; but suerly I feare greatly the success hereof, for the generall evill opinion conceaved, both by the people and the men of warr, ageynst the particular persons representyng the states, except ther might be a new election by the severall provynces of new and more upright persons to represent the states.

My lord, though presently it semeth your lordship to be greved with the sondry mislykynges of hir majesty signefyed by her privat lettres, for sondry thynges wherof your lordship hath sufficient matter to discharg yourself, yet I dowt not but uppon your lordships retorn to hir presence, she will be fully satisfyed by your lordships own good answers, for so I myself do conceave the issew will so be proved. And so, by reason of Mr. Gorges hasty departure, I am compelled to end. From Westminster, 4. November, 1586.

Yesterday all we commissioners [perfected] our sentence against the Scottish quene, with on full assent, but I feare more slackness in hir majesty than will stand ether with hir suerty or with ours. God direct hir hart to follow faythfull counsell.

Your lordships most assured to my power,

W. BURGHLEY.

LETTER CLXVII.

MR. SECRETARY DAVISON TO THE EARL OF LEYCESTER.

4TH NOVEMBER, 1586.   COTTON. MS. GALBA, C. X. FOL. 41. ORIG.

The queen was so much afflicted with sorrow for the death of sir Philip Sydney when she wrote by Mr. Gorge that she forgot some things which Davison now supplies by her direction—she wishes the earl, if his health may permit, to await the arrival of lord Grey—count Maurice's particular interest in Flushing, which has been kept in better devotion to the queen by the love and respect entertained for the late governor sir Philip Sydney, is a reason against leaving any power singly in his hands—the queen wishes the government of Flushing committed to lord Willoughby.

My singuler good lord, her majesty was so much afflicted with sorrow when she dispatched Mr. Gorge, for the loss of her deare servant, and your lordships dearest nephew, sir Philip Sidney, as she forgott to touch some thinges in those her letters which since it hath pleased her I should remember unto you.[a]

One is, the care she hath, that, before your lordships returne thence, you shold take such provident order for the settling of that government in your absence, as may be most for the suerty of the cause and her own particuler service. Wherin, bycause she dowteth how it may stand with the one or other, that the gouvernment martiall should be commytted to any one of her servantes theare, and the civill left to the disposicion of the estates, a thing bruted here, she woulde wish, notwithstanding the leave

---

[a] Davison was now in the exercise of the duties, and actually in possession of the office, of one of the queen's principal secretaries, although the warrant for his appointment was not issued until the 12th December, 1586. He is described by his new office in the commission for the trial of Mary queen of Scots, dated the 5th October, 1586. See Nicolas's Life of Davison, 33, 40.

she hath by her letters given your lordship to returne when you think good, that, if your health may permytt it, you should in any wise stay the arrivall of my lord Gray, whome her majesty promiseth very faithfully, and is resolved, to dispatch thither with all the expedition that may be, for your releasement.

The reasons that move her majesty hearin, amongst others, ar, the doubt she hath of any sound correspondence betwext these different gouvernors and gouverments, civill and martiall, in the handes of persons which perhapps may have differing respectes, endes, and affections. The emulacion and faction that may grow amongst her own servantes, if one, as sir William Pelham or sir John Norrys, be preferred before the other, and inconvenience otherwise in case they should he both conjoigned together, considering how rare a thing it is to fynd colleagues and companyons in authority soundly to agree together; though, of the two, her majesty could lyke best of the latter way if you finde it so expedient. The danger may otherwise grow to her service if the charg of thes thinges should be left to any stranger, as to the count Maurice, as well in regard of his generall pretencion and particuler interest to the towne of Flushing, as the badd disposition and offices of some ill-affected to her service which of late have wholye guided and possessed him, besides other perills may grow to the common cause [during] your absence, if things be not all the better and more seasonably provided for. Another thing, and not the least, is, her majesties particuler care of the state of Flushing, which the love and respect of your lordships deare nephew hath hitherto kept, as she confesseth, in the better devotion towards her, and bycause she feareth his loss in that behauf may bee followed with some notable dishonour and preiudice to her service, if your lordship should not take all the better order before your coming thence, her majesty hath thoght it very expedient that you comend the charg therof to the lord Willoughby, as a gentleman for his calling, valure, and fashion, agreable to the humor of that people, very fitt for yt, if you fynde no other cause to the contrary then she is yet acquainted with. And thus much her highnes pleasur is I should signify to your lordship in her name. Wherwith I will recommend your lordship to the protection of the Almighty, and so most humbly take my leave. At the court at Richemond, this iiijth of November, 1586.

Your lordships humbly at commaundment,
W. Davison.

Your lordships presence here were more then needfull for the great cause now in hand, which is feared will receave a colder proceading then may stand with the suerty of her majesty and necessity of our shaken estates.

Addressed,

For her majestes affaires.
To the right honourable the earle of Leicester, lord lieutenant-generall of her majesties forces in the Lowe Countries, &c.

LETTER CLXVIII.

MR. SECRETARY WALSYNGHAM TO THE EARL OF LEYCESTER.

5TH NOVEMBER, 1586.   COTTON. MS. TITUS, B. VII. FOL. 65b.   ORIG.

The earl is requested to assist a servant of sir Philip Sydney in recovering money paid by him to those who served under him—he has left a great number of poor creditors—Walsyngham has paid and must pay for him above £6,000.

I humbly beseeche your lordship, that this bearer may receyve your honorable assystaunce in the recovarye of sooch imprestes as have been made by his late master unto sooche as served under him. Sir Philip hathe lefte a great nombur of poore credytors; what order he hathe taken by his wyll for ther satysfactyon I knowe not. Yt is trewe, that, immedyatly after the deathe of his father, he sent me a letter of attorney for the sale of sooche portyon of lande as myght content his credytors, wherin there was nothing don before his deathe.[a] I have payde, and must paye, for him above 6,000^{li}, which I doe assure your lordship hath browght me into a most harde and desperat state, which I waighe nothing in respeact of the losse of the gentleman, whoe was my chefe worldly comporte. Sorry I am to take any occasyon to revyve the memorye of him to the renewing of your lordships grefe, for the which I praye pardon, and so I most humbly take my leave. At Barne ealmes, the vth of November, 1586.

    Your lordships to commaund,
        FRA. WALSYNGHAM.

Addressed,

To the right honourable my verie good lord the earle of Leycester, lord lieutenant-general of her majesties forces in the Lowe Countries.

LETTER CLXIX.

MR. SECRETARY DAVISON TO THE EARL OF LEYCESTER.

6TH NOVEMBER, 1586. COTTON. MS. GALBA, C. X. FOL. 43.

The queen having heard that Leycester had determined to return home immediately, and that he was expected to sail from Middleburgh on the Thursday preceding, and had ordered shipping to be prepared for him with that view, reiterates her command to him not to leave that country until the arrival of lord Grey.

My very good lord, her majesty having two or three days past receaved some advertisement of your lordships purpose to repayre home with as much speede as you could, and finding by some

[a] See p. 457.

lettres of yours to sir Thomas Henneage, that you found yourself ill-disposed for the state of your health, besides your affection for the loss of your deerest nephew, was pleased to dispatch Mr. Thomas Gorge with a few lynes of her own hand, in the which, amongst other things, she made some mention of her pleasur to license your lordship to returne when you should think good, but finding, uppon some deeper consideracion of the estate wherin you should leave both those afflicted countries and her own people, in case there were not all the better order taken before your departure, [both for] the one and other, and how daingerous the consequence might be to her own service to have them, as it were, left to themselves in such a tyme as this, it pleased her to give me order to signifie unto you the next day, that, forasmuch as she had resolved to send over the lord Gray to succeade in the charg of her lieutenaunt-generall in your lordships absence, whom she had allready commaunded to put himself in readines to that end, she thought it no way fitt, either for her honour or the suerty of the cause, that your lordship should depart thence before the said lord Grayes arryvall, as by the said lettres, sent after Mr. Gorge, your lordship shall perceave at more length. Now, hearing from Middleburgh, that your lordship should be expected theare as on Thursday last, and that you had given order to the treasurer to provide your shipping for the next day, she hath commaunded me againe to iterat her former order unto you by this bearer, for your contynuance on that syde till you heare further from her in this behaulf, and that, in the meane tyme, you take the best order you can to prepare thinges against tharryvall of my said lord Gray, whome she is resolved to hasten thitherwards with all the expedicion that may be, which is that I have presently to signifie unto your lordship, of whom I do humbly, and in haste, take my leave. At Richmond, the vj[th]. of November, 1586.

        Your lordships ever at commaundment,

                      W. DAVISON.

The consequence of your lordships so sudden departure thence, perrillous both to the common cause and her own service, is a matter doth so much move her highnes, as she would in no sort, your lordship should depart before my lord Grayes comming whome she promiseth to send away fourthwith for your redemption.

LETTER CLXX.

MR. SECRETARY WALSYNGHAM TO THE EARL OF LEYCESTER.

6TH NOVEMBER, 1586. COTTON. MS. GALBA, C. X. FOL. 44. ORIG.

The queen directs that the coming of the commissioners from the states-general should be stayed—Burgrave has arrived in London—informality of sir Philip Sydney's will, and its consequences to his creditors—his burial.

My verry good lord, even as I had gyven this bearer his dyspatche I receaved a letter from Mr. Davyson, by the which he dyd sygnefye unto me that her majesties pleasure was, that I shoold wryte unto your lordship to stay the commyng of the commyssioners, for that she is in no sort wyllyng to be pressed in a matter that she is alreadye resolved not to procead in. Thes be the verry wordes of his letter, which I refer to your lordships consideratyon. Monsieur Burgrave is alreadye come to London. I have appoynted on Mondaye next to speake with him, and wyll, for your lordships sake and the good commendatyon you gave him, use him with all the favor I may.

I have caused sir Philip Sydneys wyll to be consydered of by certeyn learned in the lawes, and I fynd the same imperfect towching the sale of his land for the satysfyeng of his poore credytors, which I doe assure your lordship doth greatly afflyct me, [that] a gentleman that hath lyved so unspotted [a] reputatyon, and had so great care to see all men satysfyed,[a] shoold be so [exposed] to the owtcrye of his creditors. His goodes wyll not suffyce to awnsware a third parte of his debtes alreadye knowen. This hard estate of this noble gentleman makethe me staye to take order for his buryall untyll your lordships returne. I doe not see howe the same can be performed with that solempnytye that apperteynethe withowt the utter undoing of his credytors, which is to be weyed [in] conscyence.[b] Sorrye I am to troble your lordship with these unplesaunt matters, but that a necessitye movethe me therto. And so hoping to see your lordship here, I most humbly take my leave. At Barne elmes the vj. of November, 1586.

Your lordships to commaund,
Fra. Walsingham.

Addressed,

For her majestyes speciall affaires.
To the right honoorable my verie good
lord the erle of Leicester, lord lieutenaunt-
generall of hir majestyes forces in the Lowe
Countries, &c.
W. Davison.

[a] Sir Philip Sydney's will contains the following clause: "I will and absolutely authorise the right honorable sir Francis Walsyngham and my brother Robert Sydney, or either of them, to sell so much of my lands lying within the countys of Lincoln Sussex or Southampton as shall pay all my debts, as well those of my father deceased as of mine own, beseeching them to hasten the same, and to pay the creditors with all possible speed, according to that letter of attorney which sir Francis Walsingham already hath, sealed and subscribed by me to that end, which letter of attorney I do hereby confirm and ratifie, so far forth as concerneth for that purpose to all effect of law." (Sydney Papers, i. 110.) The opinion of the "certeyn learned in the lawes" referred to by Walsyngham will be found printed in the appendix.

[b] Sydney's funeral was celebrated with extraordinary splendour at St. Paul's cathedral on the 16th February, 1586-7.

APPENDIX

OF

ILLUSTRATIVE PAPERS.

I. A JOURNAL OF MY LORD OF LEYCESTERS PROCEADING IN THE LOWE COUNTRIES, BY MR. STEPHEN BURROGH, ADMIRAL OF THE FLEET.

II. PROPOSED LEVY OF SAILORS IN THE LOW COUNTRIES FOR MANNING THE ENGLISH FLEET IN CASE OF AN ATTEMPTED SPANISH INVASION.

III. CORRESPONDENCE BETWEEN QUEEN ELIZABETH AND THE STATES GENERAL AND COUNCIL OF STATE IN REFERENCE TO THE APPOINTMENT OF THE EARL OF LEYCESTER AS ABSOLUTE GOVERNOR OF THE LOW COUNTRIES.

IV. HOSTILE CORRESPONDENCE BETWEEN COUNT HOHENLOHE AND SIR EDWARD NORRIS.

V. NARRATIVE OF SHENCK'S STRATAGEM FOR THE CAPTURE OF WERLE, AND OF THE EARL'S RECEPTION AT AMSTERDAM, WITH A DESCRIPTION OF THAT CITY.

VI. THE GARRISONING OF DEVENTER.

VII. LETTERS RELATING TO THE ILLNESS OF SIR PHILIP SYDNEY'S WIDOW.

VIII. QUESTIONS TOUCHING THE EXECUTION OF SIR PHILIP SIDNEY'S WILL.

APPENDIX.

I.

A Journal of my lord of Leicesters proceading in the Lowe Countries, by Mr. Stephen Burrogh, Admiral of the Fleet.

MS. HARL. 6845, FOL. 26. ORIG.

Anno 1585, December 8th. Wednsdaie beinge the 8. day of December, in the morninge, the lord of Leycester, with those righte honorable and right worshipfull that accompanied his lordship, cam from Colchester to Maningtree by land, and there tooke boates which attended theire cominge, and passed in them downe the ryver to Harwyche, where they were landed aboute 11 of the clocke in the forenoone.

The same morninge, aboute 4 of the clock, I recevid a letter from my lord, which was written in Colchester the eveninge before, wherein his lordship certified, that he was resolved not to lose the oportunytie of the wynde and weather, but wolde imbarke the nexte daie at nighte, whereupon I caused all our shipps to be caryed oute of the havon, into the rode of the rowlinge grounde, which is a myle and halfe from Harwich, from whence we mighte set saile and depart at any tyme of the tyde.

His lordship and the rest dyned that day in Harwiche, and then his lordship tolde me he wold imbarke to passe over in the Amytee, for that the lord-admyrall had advised him soe to doe, and that he wolde aboord the same shipp in the afternoone, and furder that his will and purpose was, to passe with all the fleete to the Brill, of which his lordships will and purpose I never recevid any advertisemente till then, but supposed that his lordship wold have gonne to Flushing. Notwithstandinge, because I could never receave any intelligence of his lordships meaninge in that pointe, I was carefull to be furnished of some pilott of skill, bothe for the coastes and harbroughes in Zealand, and also for the Brill, and coaste of Holland, leaste we mighte be dryven to have nede for those places, and therefore I sente my pynnes to Sandwiche the last daie of November, from whence I had brought in her a skipper who dwellithe in Midleboroughe, a man skillfull for all those places. I showed his lordship I had a man in the shipp with me of sufficient skill for that place, but there wolde be greate wante for the reste of the fleete, for that they were not easilie had; whereat his lordship seemed to be greatly offended with me, and saide it was my dutie, being admyrall, to have seene that there had bene sufficient pilottes provided for all the fleete, for any place it shoulde please his lordship to apointe to goe unto.

Heerupon the best pilottes that could be called to mynd in Ipswiche and other places theraboutes, as well Inglishe as straingers, were sent for with all spede, and apointed to be at the shipps the nexte daye in the fornoone. There was then to be rigged, victuelled, and furnished, for the passing over those of his lordships companies which could not convenyentlie be placed in those vessells under my chardge, one shipp of Harwiche called the Lyon, of burden 140 tonns, and also diverse whoyes which were to take in horses that cam that morninge with my lord, and some other that were in the towne before. Notwithstandinge the wante of pilottes, and the unredines of that shipp, and those whoies and horses, which my lord wolde have to goe over in company with himself, yet his lordship, betwene 2 and 3 of the clock in the afternoone, tooke boate, and wente aboorde the Amytie, which roade in the rolling grounde, where his lordship remayned all nighte, with diverse knightes and gentlemen of worshipp, but most of the noblemen and gentlemen lodged that night at spare in Harwiche. My lord contynued all that night a resolute mynde to goe for the Brill.

9. Thursdaie, in the morninge, those pilotes which were sent for came aborde the Amytie unto my lord, who delivered the opynion that the Brill was not a fitt harboroughe or place to carry soche a fleete unto. Notwithstandinge, my lord tolde them he wolde goe thether. They answered they wolde doe theire best to observe the will of his lordship, albeyt theire myndes and stomackes were against the going thether. After this, before noone, his lordship chainged his mynde, and determyned then to goe for Flushing, wherof all partys of every sorte were veary glad, and of this chainge I had knowledge geven me aboute noone, and thereupon made oute instructions for the fleete, to be observed in our passing over accordinglie. Betwene 1 and 2 of the clock in the afternoone, the shipp Lyon and 7 whoies with horses came oute from Harwiche, ready fitted and furnished, and anckored by us.

At 2 of the clocke I went aborde to my lord, and showed my lord the instructions that I had made for the fleet, wherof his lordship seemed to have good leekinge, and willed me to procede acordinglie in all thinges.

I apointed to way and set saile $\frac{1}{2}$ an hower past 2 of the clock, but, at the very instante when I purposed to shoote of to give warninge, his lordship sente for me and tolde me, that he had received worde that his fleete with horses and provisions that were to goe from London to the Brill, whiche he thought had bene gonne the day before, were not yet departed oute of the Theames, and therfore wolde sende my pynnes the Sygnet, into the Theames, to geve them knowledge that his lordship had altred his mynde from Brill, and would now have them to goe for Flusshinge.

I showed his lordship that both wynde and tyde was then againste her, so as shee could not possible get to Lee till the nexte day afternoone, before which tyme, the winde beinge as it was, the fleete wolde be gonne over landes end, and passe that waies to the seas, whereupon his lordship staied the sendinge of her.

It apeerethe by the reporte of Mr. Harry Churche, who was apointed by my fellow officers, sir William Winter, Mr. Hawkins, and Mr. Holstocke, to have chardge as cheefe pilot for the safe conductinge and passinge of the fleete that was to goe over from London, which were in nomber betweene 60 and 70 shipps, barckes, and whoies, that nether himself nor the saide officers, when they gave him that chardge, understood otherwise but that they were all to passe for Flushing. The saide Churche passed downe with the fleete to Gravesend, where he was sente for by one Mr. Bingham, a gentleman of my lords, who demaunded of him, whither he mente to cary the fleete, he answered, to Flushinge. Quothe the gentleman, " that shall you not doe, but you shall goe to the Brill." Churche answered, that he had recevid comission to see them safelie past over, as he thought, to Flushing, for he was not acquainted with the Brill, nor but fewe of the fleete, and therefor to goe thether he wold not. Th'other answered, he should goe. Saide Churche, " If you have aucthoritie to commaund me to goe to the Brill, let me see it and I wilbe obedient, but I will then goe as a privat man, and take noe chardge." Hereupon they brake of, and the saide Bingham the 8. December in the afternoone wente aborde the vessell he was to passe over in, and with the same and 15 barkes, whoies, and other vessells, most Hollanders, some of them men of warr, wherein divers of the states passed, set saile, and bare downe the ryver.

When Churche perceaved that so many of the flete were gonn, and that they were Hollanders, he doubted they wolde have stolen away with my lords horses and provisions, and thereupon followed downe after them in one of the shipps from Gravesend, and against Lee shot at them, whereupon they staied, and the first vessell he happened to speake to was that wherein the saide Bingham was, whom when he perceavid he was glad, and tolde him he had dealte very discourteously with him in departing with those whoies oute of his fleete in soche sorte, for he thoughte those straingers had bene stollen away with my lords horses and provisions. Bingham answered, he had warrant for that he had don, and saide, that Churche shoulde answere the disobeying of his comandment at his perill. And so, withoute further speche, they departed, and bare downe to the Cant northe the Minster, where they anckored all nighte. In the morninge the fleete followed downe from Gravesend, and came and anckored nere the saide Hollanders till the fludd, and then they all bare over the landes end and by Marget togeather. But when they set of from Marget in the eveninge, the wasters of the Hollanders, with certen other barckes and whoies to the nomber of 17, shaped their course for the Brill, and Churche with the reste of the fleete, beinge in nomber 50 saile, directed his course for Flushinge.

Nowe to retorne to our procedinges from Harwiche, a litle before 3 of the clocke in the afternoone I wayed and sett saile, so did all the fleete, beinge then in number 15 saile, the winde then at south-west, a faier gale. We bare oute at the Slade, and by shuttinge of daie lighte we were clere of the sandes, from whence we bare a small saile till 5 of the clocke the nexte morninge, and then tooke in our sailes and lay a hullinge till it was nere 7 of the clocke, at what tyme we hoised saile and bare in with the lande.

10. Fridaie, by the breake of daie, being aboute 8 of the clocke in the morninge, we had sighte of Ostend, from whence we bare longeste the coast in at the Weelinges, where we mighte see, goinge in towardes Flushinge before us, the forsaide flete that cam from London, which passed Flushinge and bare up betwene the castle Ramekins and Midleboroughe head, where they anckored.

We anckored with our shipps against the towne of Flushinge between 12 and one of the clocke afternoone. Landed in the same towne, the lord of Leycester and the reste of the lordes, knightes, and chefe gentlemen, the saide afternoone. My lord was landed betwene one and 2 of the clocke; we shot of all our ordinance at his lordships landing, and the towne shot of all the ordinance they had at the recevinge of his lordship at shore; towardes eveninge oure shippes bare up nere the castle Ramekins where they mored.

This Fridaie, aboute 5 of the clocke at nighte, the towne of Flushinge shot of all or the most parte of the ordinance that were planted at the walls, in honor of my lord, and the same nighte made score of bonfiers and fierworkes.

11. Saterdaie, ymediatlie after dinner, my lord of Leycester imbarked himselfe at Flushinge heade, in a whoy, to passe to Midlebrough; my lord of Essex imbarked in the pinnasse Signet, and the pynnes of the Amytie and some other whoie of the towne likewise toke in diverse gentlemen of my lords traine. With these 4 vessells my lord and the rest passed from Flushinge (which shot of at his departure all the ordinance of the towne) longest by 2 fly-boates of warr, our shipps, the castle Ramekyns, and the fleete that cam from London, into Midleboroughe havon, beinge saluted as he passed-by bothe of the Zelanders, our shipps, the saide castle, and the wasters of th'other fleete, &c. and landed at the steyars by the sluceheade, a litle withoute the este gate of Midleboroughe, aboute 3 of the clocke in the afternoone, where divers of the states, and majestrates of the towne recevid him. And so, very honorably accompanied and guarded, with trompetes soundinge bothe before and behinde, his lordship entred the towne

of Midleboroughe, and passed in the same unto his lodginge prepared at the friars, the same place where Mounsieur at his cominge over was lodged.

At the place of assembly of merchantes, and within the coorte of the fryeries, as likewise in diverse other places, and in the streetes, as my lord passed, the burgers of the towne, very well armed and furnished, showed themselves in the best manner they could, and dischardged their vollis of shott in veary good order. This night were made many bonfiers in the towne, and greate store of fyerworkes were showed in the courte of the abby, &c. like as when Monsieur cam in.

12. Sondaie, my lord in the forenoone was at a sermon in the Englishe churche nere the said abby. In the afternoone, one that brought lettres then oute of Holland from Utrecht to generall Norice tolde me, that 3000 Spaniardes were come over, and entred into the contrey called de Valew, 30 Englishe miles from Utrecht, of which company the cheefe leader is called Virdowgo, and that they in Holland judged he wolde goe with that company to besedge Utrecht. This day order was geven to take oute those horses that were in whoies or vessells that drewe above 8 foote water, and to shipp them in whoies that drewe lesser water, which mighte passe with them into Holland.

This daie the lord of Leycester and noblemen, &c. were invitedd by the states and burgers of the towne to dyne at their towne-house on Tewsdaie followinge.

13. Monday, my lord reposed himself in his lodginge for the dispatche of diverse affaiers; this afternoone my lord promised I shoulde be dispatched the nexte day with his lettre to my lord admerall.

14. Tewsdaie, my lord wente to the towne-house accompanied with duke Morice, the prince of Orainge his sonn, our noblemen, gentlemen, and the cheefest of the states of Zealand, &c. where met him also the widow of the prince of Orenge, and diverse ladies and gentlewomen that accompanied her. The place they dyned in was not that greate roome where Monsieur was bancqueted, but a place somwhat lesse, wherein were placed but 2 tables; one of those tables, which conteyned the whole lengthe of the house, and mighte holde 80 or 100 persons, was apointed for the lord of Leycester, lord governor-generall, and those nobles and gentills that accompanied his lordship; thother table, beinge not half so longe, was apointed for some of the states of the contrey and chief majestrates of the towne. At which seconde table my lords gentlemen at theire firste cominge-in had set themselves, before my lord himself was set, and in placinge themselfes there was soche leapinge over table, strivinge, and disorder, that diverse glasses were broken, &c. whereof my lord was informed, and thereupon gave order, that all his gentlemen shoulde goe oute of the howse, which was observed, and after that, all thinges passed in reasonable quiett order, but the roome coulde not coutain half the nomber of gentlemen that cam thither to dyne.

The fare was greate, but cheafelie the bakte meates, and after that the banckquet of sugar-workes and devises unto the highe table were most brave and sompteouse. My lordes settinge continewed from 12 till it was past 3 halfe an hower, for with the water that was brought for them to washe, came in candles.

After all was finished my lord generall and the nobles and gentlemen retyred to theire lodginges.

This dinner and banckquett, for the quantytie of it, was as sumpteous ir all pointes as that was when Monsieur was banckqueted by them.

15. Wednsdaie, by the inhabitantes of the contrey was helde for Christmas daie.

This daie the winde was westerlie with raine and fowle weather.

16. Thursdaie, diverse of the whoies with horses departed from Midleboroughe head towardes Roterdam in Hollande, where they were apointed to be landed.

This eveninge verie late I receivid of my lord his lordships letter written to my lord-admerall, and also his lordships answere for my dispatche to departe when the winde shoulde serve. This day the winde was westerly with moche rayne.

17. Fridaie, betwene 10 and 11 of the clocke in the forenoone, my lord toke a small skute at Midleboroughe, and in the same, with duke Morice, passed downe to the head, where his lordship imbarked in a whoye to passe to Dorte, where he meante to remaine one nighte, and from thence to Roterdam.

With the firste of the fludd, betwene one and 2 of the clock in the afternoone, his lordship in the saide whoie, acompanied with a greate number of other whoies that caried gentlemen, &c., passingers, as also whoies that had horses in, and 2 crompsters or wasters, to the number of 50 saile or thereaboutes, departed from the saide Midleboroughe heade towardes Hollande, beinge then calme and veary faier weather. God blisse and prosper his lordships proceedinges with good and most happie successe.

II.

PROPOSED LEVY OF SAILORS IN THE LOW COUNTRIES FOR MANNING THE ENGLISH FLEET IN CASE OF AN ATTEMPTED SPANISH INVASION.

[This proposal was mentioned to the earl of Leycester by lord Burghley by the queen's special direction on the 26th December 1585, and again on the 17th of the succeeding January, (see pages 42 and 66). The earl replied briefly on the 31st January (see page 79). The following imperfect portion of a letter, written by the earl early in the year 1586 to some one whom he styles " your honour," partly relates to the same subject. The notion, although favoured by the queen, was put an end to by the lord-admiral and the other officers of the English navy, who indignantly declared, " that they would never have any mariners, being strangers, to be matched with the English." (see page 154.)]

PART OF A LETTER OF THE EARL OF LEYCESTER.

HARL. MS. NO. 285. FOL. 156. ORIG.

. . . .

During the tyme of my sicknes my lord Wyllughby delt with the states bothe for the shippes mentioned in the treatye and also for 1000 maryners, whereof I can say nothing certeyne because I was not present when yt was moved, nor had any notice thereof from my lord, but I sent to the register of the states for the act concerning the maryners, the translate whereof I send your honour hearein, and a letter even now receaved from Mr. Vylliers, whom I fynd well inclyned to doe all good offices, and fynd yt by effect.[a]

The count of Hohenlo, as I am informed, wyll into Germany to the duk of Sax, and yt is thought he shall mary one of the countesse of Egmont, thereby to allye hemselfe with duke Casimer and his howse, whose aunt was her mother. Of coronell Skenkes jornay over and others out of Frysland, I was not acquaynted, and I think they might have ben better occupyed.

Since you have directed us this later course, my lord Wyllugbye and I are estymed to be states men, insomyche that at Utrecht they have put his company of horse out of the towne, as tho he wold have made them Hollonders agaynst ther wyll. I heare Deventer apon som letter from you of late dothe cary hemselfe som what vayne, which I am sory for, and sayth he knoweth her majesties pleasure " as well as my lord." They have yet named none to be of the counsell of state, which began to sytt on Wensday last, where I did asist before my departure, but ther wanted them of Fryse, Overisell, and Utrecht, which are looked for agaynst I retorne.[b] I have wrighten ernestly to them of Utrecht to send thers.

Yf her majestie shall resolve to have maryners hence, then must the admirall heare direct his comyssion which he wyll doe of course apon sight of thact, and men must be sent with mony to levye them and to se them transported, for which porpose I cannot comend unto you a fytter man for one than Mr. Thomas Lovell, who hathe the langage, and good credytt in the provinces.

[a] See page 73.
[b] This paper was probably written at Leyden on the 3rd or 4th January, 1585-6. (See page 49.)

III.

CORRESPONDENCE BETWEEN QUEEN ELIZABETH AND THE STATES GENERAL AND COUNCIL OF STATE IN REFERENCE TO THE APPOINTMENT OF THE EARL OF LEYCESTER AS ABSOLUTE GOVERNOR OF THE LOW COUNTRIES.

[These letters do not come within the limits prescribed to himself by the editor in the selection of papers to be inserted in the body of this work; but they are, nevertheless, so nearly connected with one of the most important events of Leycester's mission, that it is thought right to print such of them as have been found, with notes of some others the originals of which have not been discovered.]

I. THE QUEEN TO THE STATES GENERAL.

13TH FEBRUARY, 1585-6. COTTON. MS. GALBA, C. VIII. FO. 116 b. A CONTEMPORARY MINUTE.

Being advertised how that they had presented the absolut gouverment of the united provinces, she found these their proceedings verie strange, and greatlie tending to her dishonor, that to be offred unto her subject, which she had refused allreadie, and, that which is more, in a manner to constraine him to accept thereof without making her acquainted with the same, and attending her answer; as though she wanted judgement to accept or refuse what was competent, besides that it is against her protestation published to the world no further to intermeddle in these busines then to take in protection her distressed neighbour, without aspiring to any souveraignitie. Thought therefore good for these respects to command the abovesaid earle to give over all such gouverment not contained in the articles of the treatie, assuring them it not to proceede from want of affection or zeale to their cause, but onelie a meere respect to her honor, which she esteemed deerer than her life.

The like to the councell of estate.

II. THE COUNCIL OF STATE TO THE QUEEN.

18TH MARCH, 1585-6. COTTON. MS. GALBA, C. VIII. FOL. 116 b. A CONTEMPORARY MINUTE.

They are verie sorrie her majesty is offended with the election of the earle of Leicester to be absolute gouvernor. They confesse her to have just cause of displeasure, but yet hope, when her majestie is thoroughlie informed of all the matter, she will then rest better satisfied of their proceeding. The authoritie is given no otherwise then it was unto others, gouvernors hertofore; the words, although they be absolut, yet, in their use there, the meaninge is no other then to give unto the said earle full power to execute the contents of his commission, with reservation of soveraignitie and proprietie of the countrie to the people. Which commission cannot without danger be called back againe. And, therefore, they most humblie beseech her majestie to allow of their doings therein, which are agreeable to her owne advice that the multitude of heads, which bread confusion in the gouverment, should be avoyded, and some course taken for redresse of the same.

III. THE QUEEN TO THE COUNCIL OF STATE.
APRIL 1586.   COTTON. MS. GALBA, C. VIII. FOL. 117.   A CONTEMPORARY MINUTE.

In answer of their letter; wherein she declareth herselfe, that, uppon their acknowledgement of their fault, she could not but remove her dislike, yet when she looketh into the title of an absolute gouverment, and besides considereth what little proffitt the common cause hath hetherto received thereby, by yeeldinge unto the earle of Leicester rather in words a title of a kind of absolute gouvernor then anie effect of the authoritie, when he can neither be thoroughlie made acquainted with the true state of their affaires, nor yet receive the due performance of such contributions, as well ordinarie as extraordinarie, as were speciallie promised unto him both before the acceptation of the gouverment, as also manie times sithence. Therefore, unles the authoritie and title be joyned together, she is intended the title of an absolut gouvernor to be left againe. Willeth to punish such slanderous tongues as give out of a peace underhand to be made betweene her and the king of Spaine, and protesteth much of her zeale to them and to their cause.

IV. THE COUNCIL OF STATE TO THE QUEEN.
1ST MAY, 1586.   COTTON. MS. GALBA, C. IX. FOL. 215.   ORIG.

Serenissima regina, non dubitamus celeritatem nostrorum ordinum in deferenda illustrissimo comiti Leycestriæ generalis gubernationis authoritate, offensæ cujusdam speciem atque culpæ suspicionem injecisse majestati tuæ, ut quæ in longinquo consistens, extremas afflictarum provinciarum miserias, atque instantia discrimina, propius intueri non potuerit. Cum revera omnia acciderint vi magna cogente, et ad evitationem periculorum alioqui inevitabilium. Etenim compertum est, et sanctissime affirmare possumus, in prosperis adversariorum successibus, ac perturbatis rebus nostrorum ordinum, ipsum nomen gubernatoris generalis, præsentiamque prudentissimi domini comitis, cum auxiliaribus copiis majestatis tuæ, atque ex omnium provincialium voto et congratulatione delatam generalis gubernatoris authoritatem, collapsos subditorum animos mirifice erexisse et confirmasse, cum summa consternatione hostium communium. Usque adeo ut hæc authoritatis instauratio, ad egregia componendæ conservandæque reipublicæ nostræ fundamenta jacienda profuerit, et hostium ferocissimos animos imminuerit, atque potentissimi, maximisque victoriis superbientis exercitus progressus cohibuerit, commutata ex Dei beneficio belli fortuna ad prosperitatem confæderatarum provinciarum, quæ per dignitatem, virtutem, atque assiduam sollicitudinem illustrissimi comitis inter omnia aspera conservatur, et indies majora incrementa accipit. Ita ut etiam hoc nomine immortales majestati tuæ agamus gratias, quod excusationem delatæ authoritatis a nobis propositam adeo benigne clementerque acceperit, et permota commiseratione necessitatis nostræ, atque affectionis quam ordines generales vigore precedentis contractus delatione illa authoritatis erga majestatem tuam exhibere studuerunt, boni consuluerit, et nos cum ipsis ordinibus omni ulteriore criminis atque offensæ metu per legatum suum ornatissimum liberaverit, absque ulla diminutione authoritatis illustrissimo comiti attributæ, et superaddita enixa testificatione maximi favoris atque benevolentiæ in vicinas istas provincias antiquissimis fœderibus et amicitiis florentissimo tuo regno Anglicano conjunctas. Unde certissimam spem atque fiduciam concipimus, majestatem tuam nullis vel temporum intervallis, vel rumoribus atque calumniis malevolorum, commoveri posse ad deponendam aut diminuendam susceptam curam et defensionem labentis nostræ reipublicæ adversus vim et tyrannidem eorum qui arma in omnes tenent; et quorum vicinitatem prohibere, conservatis provinciis confœderatis, et prævenire periculosam invasionem, multis insidiarum generibus jamdiu patefactam, non affectati alieni principatus sed justæ defensionis esse, jura communia constituunt.

Quod vero ad ea attinet quæ intuitu tot insignium beneficiorum quæ a majestate tua accepimus, et in posterum speramus, amplissimus dominus legatus ex parte majestatis tuæ a nobis vicissim præstari desideravit. Ingenue profitemur universos ordines, nosque ipsos nihil magis in votis habere quam desiderio atque voluntati majestatis tuæ humiliter obedire, inservire, atque in omnibus satisfacere. Sed absolutæ gubernationis vocabulum (quod sine speciali ad hoc indicenda convocatione et novis conventibus provinciarum fieri nequit) immutare periculosum in hoc fragili rerum nostrarum statu existimamus, veremurque ne in ipso principio restauratæ authoritatis, ipsam authoritatem cum perturbatione reipublicæ nostræ prosternamus. Et proinde augustissimam majestatem tuam obnixe rogamus, necessitatem illam mutandi relaxare dignetur, ad avertendum periculum quod inter tot hominum suspiciones et calumnias ex variatione posset incidere, præsertim cum hactenus illustrissimus comes non nisi simpliciter generalis gubernatoris (absque ulla adjectione absolutæ potestatis) titulo, in literis, edictisque suis usus fuerit.

APPENDIX.

Illustrissimi domini comitis dignitatem atque honorem, secundum Deum, ut basim et fundamentum omnis conservationis et felicitatis nostræ sub auspiciis majestatis tuæ, merito observamus et colimus. Ipsique ordines, atque adeo omnes subditi, summam ac singularem illius prudentiam, atque laborum assiduitatem mirantur et venerantur, nullumque prætermittimus studium quod ad conservandam hanc dignitatem authoritatis et observationis pertinere possit. Agnoscunt enim omnes, post Deum atque majestatem tuam, salutem totius reipublicæ pendere a studio atque vigilantia suæ excellenciæ, quæ veræ religionis zelo, atque afflictæ fortunæ nostræ commiseratione, omnia sua, et patriam atque præsentiam suæ principis reliquit, sese in perturbata republica omnibus fortunæ incursibus objiciendo.

Reditus, census, et contributiones quales quales sunt, diligenter et sincere ex jussu et authoritate suæ excellenciæ administrari et frugaliter distribui curabimus, et in hoc totis viribus incumbemus ut ordines generales præsentem occasionem rei benegerendæ non negligant, sed subsidia belli et contributiones suas, quatenus fieri potest, adaugeant, quo belli negotia, labore, diligentia, et fortitudine illustrissimi comitis feliciter reparata, celerius securiusque peragantur, et suæ excellenciæ sua dignitas constet et conservetur.

Cumque tam arctis vinculis per longa temporum spatia vicinitas atque amicitia inter regnum Angliæ et istas ditiones conglutinata sit, et tam altas radices egerit, cumque profunda imperandi cupido et molitiones insidiarum ab Hispanis in regno Angliæ sæpe tentatæ, omnibus notæ sint, jamque majestas tua suas copias, duces, ac prudentissimum comitem et universo regno charum, ad nos delegaverit, felicitatemque et bona sua cum malis nostris pro conservandis ditionibus miscuerit, nihil formidamus rumores improborum hominum, nec dubitamus de perseverantia constantiaque majestatis tuæ, neque etiam vulgus ipsum jam re ipsa expertum summam majestatis tuæ erga se humanitatem et benevolentiam tam imperitum est, ut ullis rumoribus in sinistram aliquam suspicionem adduci se patiatur. Jam enim universis persuasum est omnia consilia majestatis tuæ cum summa prudentia conjuncta esse, nec alio spectare quam ad conservandam veterem amicitiam, ac promovendam prosperitatem harum provinciarum. Quo etiam nomine immortales gratias agentes, majestatem tuam divinæ clementiæ commendamus. Ultraiecti, Kal. Maij 1586, stilo novo. LEONINUS. v. r[a].

Majestatis tuæ,
humillimi et obsequentissimi,
consiliarii status provinciarum Belgij
confœderatarum
CHR. HUYGENS.

Serenissimæ reginæ
Angliæ, Franciæ, Hiberniæ, &c.
dominæ nostræ clementissimæ.

[a] Or 't.' The letter is doubtful in the original.

V. THE COUNCIL OF STATE TO THE QUEEN.

JUNE 11, 1586.   COTTON. MS. GALBA, C. IX. FOL. 264.   ORIG.

Serenissima regina, non leviter nos afflixit quod ornatissimus dominus Henneagius, majestatis tuæ legatus, ad nos reversus, priori postulationi suæ inherendo, instanter urserit abrogationem gubernationis generalis, non premonita majestate tua illustrissimo domino comiti Leycestriæ per ordines unitarum provinciarum attributæ. Quoniam non obtemperare requisitioni illi, serio atque iterato ex parte majestatis tuæ factæ, pro gravissima culpa atque offensa ducimus, obtemperare vero et exequi id quod postulatur absque evidenti discrimine universæ reipublicæ nostræ non possumus : omnis enim authoritatis conservatio dependet ab hoc gubernationis titulo atque officio, quod si semel nutet aut vacillet, metuimus ne in ipso principio prosperorum nostrorum successuum, qui divina clementia ac beneficio majestatis tuæ indies augentur, præcipiti ruina omnia retroferantur et corruant, cum gaudio et utilitate hostium communium, quibus formidabilis est dictæ gubernationis authoritas, conjuncta atque subserviens majestatis tuæ locumtenentiæ generali, quæ quamvis per se magna sit, et ad conservandam disciplinam in exercitu Anglicano necessaria, tamen ad compositionem totius corporis, et administrationem rerum politicarum, atque regiminis universalis, nequaquam potuit valere aut sufficere absque accessione gubernationis generalis, quæ, non nisi ex authoritate et concessione superioritatis atque imperii ordinibus relicti potest procedere, neque locumtenentiæ applicari et adjungi.

Adeo ut ordines aliter rebus suis consulere, aut intentioni majestatis tuæ secundum contractum subservire, non potuerint, nisi per usum superioritatis ordinibus relictæ, quam si majestas tua dignaretur admittere, omnia cederent dictæ locumtenentiæ, ac locumtenens majestatis tuæ omne jus, exercitiumque potestatis obtineret, quod nunc propter non admissam authoritatem in personam locumtenentis tuæ majestatis fieri nequit absque authoritate et commissione ipsorum ordinum. Quamobrem denuo obnixè humiliterque rogamus, ut majestas tua conservationem status nostri in continuatione dictæ gubernationis præferre velit, conturbationi omnium rerum quæ hoc tempore ex mutatione illa tituli sequeretur. Agnoscimus libenter, et deprecamur, culpam aliquam præcipitationis in eo commissam, quod immodico quodam benevolentiæ studio atque officio erga majestatem tuam, et reipublicæ rebus ita postulantibus, ordines de hac gubernationis delatione majestatem tuam non præmonuerint, consiliumque ejus et consensum exploraverint et obtinuerint, obsecrando ut majestas tua culpam hanc fiducia contractus cum tua majestate initi, et in præsentia domini Davidsonii legati sui contractam, necessitati temporum nostrorum et errori immodicæ devotionis atque obsequij studio condonare dignetur, commoveatque sacratissimum tuæ majestatis pectus quod non nisi solemniter convocatis ordinibus (quod longum tractum habet) et patefacto universo negotio omnibus, hæc mutatio tentari nequeat, quod propter fluctuationem animorum et hostium insidiosas suggestiones quas certissime metuimus cum summo periculo conjunctum est. Ad quod avertendum denuo supplicamus humillime, ut majestas tua pro singulari sua prudentia et affectione erga istas afflictas provincias benevole dignetur nos ab hoc onere periculosæ mutationis excusare et exonerare, saltem tantisper donec rebus magis confirmatis, et circumstantiis totius negotii plene discussis, cum majore securitate licebit cum majestate tua consilia conferre, statuere, et exequi, quod honori majestatis tuæ, et reipublicæ hujus, atque religionis conservationi, erit convenientissimum. Et si majestas tua celerius velit rem confici, oramus ut majestas tua mature perpensis omnibus, nobis præscribere non gravetur rationem et modum quo difficultatem istam commode submoveri posse arbitretur, nos paratissimi erimus quidquid a majestate tua præcipietur ordinibus proponere, persuadere, et quatenus in nobis erit ad executionem deducere, secundum ea quæ plenius majestati tuæ referre poterit ornatissimus prudentissimusque legatus suus dominus Henneagius, quem de omnibus plene informavimus. Interim omnia nostra studia obsequiumque majestati tuæ humillime offerimus, omnibus votis optando ut majestas tua longissime salutari prosperitate fruatur. Arnhemij, xj. die mensis Junii, 1586, stilo novo. LEONINUS. v. ra.

Majestati tuæ
obedientissimi
consiliarii status unitarum provinciarum,
CHR. HUYGENS.

IV.

HOSTILE CORRESPONDENCE BETWEEN COUNT HOHENLOHE AND SIR EDWARD NORRIS.

[Leycester compelled both these parties " to set down the matter " of the quarrel which he regarded so seriously (see page 391), but upon his departure the affair, which had been "patched up for the time" (page 394), broke out afresh. Hohenlohe was "remayning sicke at Delfhe of his hurte received at Zutphen," (Galba, C. x. fol. 85,) when aroused by the following hostile communication from sir Edward Norris. It is stated by Wilkes (ibid.) that the count " avowched " that Norris's cartel was sent to him " by the procurement of his excellencie." The following letters passed in November 1586, immediately after Leycester sailed for England.]

[a] Or " t." See note page 471.

Correspondence between Sir Edward Norris and Count Hohenlohe.

November 1586.   Cott. MS. Galba, C. X. Fol. 112.   Contemporary Copies.

Cartel par forme de deffiance envoyé par le sieur Edward Norrys a monsieur le conte de Hoenloe.

Monsieur le conte, il vous peult souvenir du tort et injure qu'avez faict a moy et a mon honneur, aussy de l'honnorable satisfaction que vous avez promis a feu monsieur de Sidney, de me faire avec les armes que portons, l'espée et le dague, seul a seul, en campaigne. Je vous semonce, partant icy, de vostre promesse, a laquelle ne devois faillir, tant pour l'honneur que vous fairez a vous mesmes, que aussy pour la satisfaction que vous me fairez, qui par ce moyen ne sera constrainct de cercher aultre revenge. Il vous plaira a tant en choisir deux, qui avec deux aultres que je choisiray pourront ordonner le surplus.

(Soubzscript) Cellui que vous avez faict estre
vostre ennemy,
(Signé)   Edward Nourrys.

(Superscription.)
A Monsieur
Monsieur le conte de Hoenloe.

Copie de la responce.

Monsieur Edward Nourrys, j'ay leu vostre lettre, et que vous voulez estimer, que je vous auroye offensé ou a moindre en vostre honneur, ce n'a jamais ésté mon intention, et ne le tiens encore pour tel, mais je m'esbahys, que presentement, en ma foiblesse et indisposition, vous demandez telle chose de moy. Je suis assez long temps ésté en bonne disposition, neantmoins, je vous donneray a ma premiere santé tout contentement, combien que je cognoisse mon linaige, aucthorité, et commandement que jay tousjours porté.

(Soubsigné) Philips Graff tzo Hoenloe.

(Superscription.)
A Monsieur
Monsieur Eduard Nourrys.

Replique.

Monsieur le conte, si jeusse eu le moyen de vous trouver pendant qu'estiez a Geertrudenberghe, ou que son excellence ne m'eust faict deffence et renvoyé du camp, je n'eusse tant differré d'envoyer vers vous, aussi si sa majesté d'Angleterre ne m'eust expressement commandé de me retirer vers elle, je m'eusse plus haste de vous escrire. Toutesfois acceptant vostre ohrc, j'attendray vostre meillieure disposition, vous priant, cependant, vous informer mieulx de mon linage, et touchant vostre authorité et commandement, il plaira vous souvenir, que je ne suis subject que de sa majesté d'Angleterre. A tant, me tenant fort satisfaict de vostre honorable promesse, prieray Dieu vous rendre le plus tost que se pourra vostre santé acoustumée.

(Soubzsigné) Ce de vous extremement injurié,
(Signé) EDWARD NOURRYS.

(Superscription.)
A Monsieur
Monsieur le conte de Hoenloe.

V.

NARRATIVE OF SHENCK'S STRATAGEM FOR THE CAPTURE OF WERLE, AND OF THE EARL'S RECEPTION AT AMSTERDAM, WITH A DESCRIPTION OF THAT CITY.

[The following narrative is only a fragment, but the remainder has not been found. It was written in March 1585-6, by some person who was with Leycester, a man of observation and one who possessed means of information. The earl's brief mention of the capture of Werle may be seen at pp. 139 and 167. He seems to have been mistaken in supposing that both the "town and castle" were taken.]

MARCH 1585-6. LANSD. MS. NO. 112. ART. 15.

Their is a Duche captaine called Skinck, who the last yeare servid the enymie, and being not so well rewarded as he thought he deserved, left the enymie by stealth, and since my lords coming into this cuntry hath given the enymie sundry overthrowes to great losses of them. About a month since, linge in his garryson towne called Venlo, he used a prety polycie to surprice a town therby called Workley. The tounsmen had great scarsety of sault, which he persaving, caused some of his soldiers appareled in boores garments to travill sundry times thether with sault in waggons, by which meanes he had faire accese; in fyne, he prepared so many waggons as he thought fytt to containe suche number of soldyors as he thought suffiecent for the purpose, wherin he bestowed his soldyors, being all armed, and the waggons covred, by which meanes they entred the towne at their pleasure, and being placed for their best advantage discovered themselfes, and playcing his companyes in order, charged the soldyors and the in-

habytantes in all partes of the towne, to their great slaughter. In one part
of the towne was a castle, which, hearing the alarum, shut the gattes, which
by no meanes he could surprice. Since the getting wherof the enymie
hathe twice sett one him, but to their great losse, alwaies wanting the
towne. He sawe no possabylitie to kepe the towne, preparation being maid
all this tyme to beseig him therin, wherfor spoyling and deffacinge yt all he
could, leaft the towne, and at his departure was incountred by ij thousand,
part of them soldyors part inhabytantes of the cuntrye, whearof they toock
and slew a thousand; that donne, in passing awaie he was charged by seven
ensignes of fooute that the bishop of Collyne had sent to that towne, being
in his jurisdiction, whom he overthrew and took v of his ansignes; the
report wherof came yesterdaij to his exelencye,[a] Skinkes brother beinge
sent therwith.

His exelencye at this present is one his jurney to Utrick, a place neare
the enymie. In the cetyes of his abod betwixt the Hage, the place wher
for the most part he hath and meaneth to macke his cheffe seatt, and this,
hath bene most honorably receaved and intertained, being in evry place
mett at the gattes by the governours and majestraites therof, the streattes
furnyshed with soldyors, evry corner of the streates geving their sundry
welcome, some with orations, some with interlaides, other with pagantes and
dume showes after their cuntry custome, evry one in his kind rejoycinge
at his cominge; the streates one bothe sydes from his entry into the towne
to his lodginge hunge with clothes, and allwaies 2 or 3 daies befor his de-
partur feasted by the principals of the towne in their townhousse, the chefest
nobles and ladyes therabout invited to acompany his exelency. But his re-
ceavinge heare hath fur exceded the rest. One Thursday last, being the
x[th] of this instant, in the morning, as he passed the upper gatt of Herlam
towardes this place, he was receaved by twenty gallyes furnished with
soldyors sent from this towne to gard his person. As his honor approched
the cetye, a letill distance from thence, he was receaved with sundry sortes
of great fishes, as whalls and other of great hugnesse, which so soune as
they mett his exelency toock the gard of him, inviorining his ship about
whill he came to the market place, wheare his lordshipp landed, so artificially
maid as was wonder, the rowers, and oers, and all thinges so well contrived,
that nothing could be sene but the monstros fishes swiming. At his landing he was welcomed by the majestraites, and one oration maid in Lattin,
showing the thraldom that thes Lowe Cuntries daylie indured under the
Spanish government, and that nowe they wear at the poynt to be utterly
ruinated, but that the quenes majestie, of her great mercy and for the
service of God, hath tacken the defence and protection of them, agaynst the
enemyes of his truth and people; the pety of her majestie being the more
welcom to them, in that she had maid choise of his exelency in this accion,

[a] "yesterdaij" is here repeated in the MS.

being the only man in the world most wished for and desyred of them, with many other circumstances to longe heare to recit; which donne, Docter Clark, Mr. Clarkes brother, one of the counsell heare for the statt, in his exelencyes name, maid them a breff answer, in which he declared the great care that the quenes majestye hath of them, and withall his owne willingnes to adventur his persoun in this cause, for the better advancment of Godes holy word and defence of his people, which he thinkes the better bestowd in that he findes them so joyfull of his presence. A lettell from that place was erected a stage, representing the battill betwixt the Isralytes and the Philistines, in one part wherof was placed Moyses prainge for the Isralytes, who being redy throughe contenuall prayer and faintnes tò faill, was held up by the quenes majestie, they macking themselves the Isralytes, and the Spanyards the contrary. Many other devises showing welcom, to receave evry particulere thinge would rather bread lothing then licking, I leave therfor the rest to conjecture.

This towne in the opynion of the expertest soldyors is thought imprenable; first, the towne ytself is, for the foundation, lick to Vennis, being bulded on pilles; yt is 3 mylles from the sea, the one half therin is inviorned with a great river called the Tyy, the breadthe therof, in the narrowest place, is a mylle over, in other places 2 [or] 3. One the other syde a great marice, many lettl rivers runninge through into a great diche, joyning upon the town walle, which is breadthe above three scorr foot, and of a great depnes. They are able in this town, of the townsmen, of any sodayn to mack 3 thousand men furnished for wars, which my lord toock vewe of at his hether cominge, very proper men and most bravly furnished. They kepe continually fyve hundreth men in pay for the gard of their towne. It is a place of great wealth, being the only towne for trafick in this part of Chrisendom. There belongeth to this towne a thousand ships, the least of the number of a hundreth tonne, besydes numbers of other ships and lesser vessalls. Their lyeth for the most part a thousand shipps. They travill furth of most partes to yt, being furnished in a manner for all traydes. Ther is allwaies in this towne great abundance of corne, and I think the only place for store of danty fishes in the world. I went to the heyghest steple in the town to vew yt, and in my judgment it was about the bignese of Newcastle.

Antwerp at this present is in great destres for want of victuals, and what cometh to them they pay most extream for; besides the people are devided into factions. Another city in Flaunders is lick to revolt, called Brigges, being hindred of their accustomed trafick by the meanes of Ostend, insomuche that generally they saie, unless Ostend be shortly gotten, they will yeald the towne to the stattes. Ostend is a place that greatly hindreth partes of Flaunders; Mr. William Knowlls is governor. Captain. . . . . with his company is removed thence to Flushing, and is ther chefe under sir Philipp Sydney.

VI.

THE GARRISONING OF DEVENTER.

[Henry Archer, the writer of the following letter, is the same person from whom Stowe derived his minute information respecting Leycester's proceedings in the Low Countries. In one place Stowe terms him his " good friend and neare kinsman," (page 741) and elsewhere his " cousin," (page 739.) He also states that Archer was " one of his excellencies gard," and it appears in the Cotton. MS. Galba, C. VIII. fol. 106, that he was taken into Leycester's service upon the recommendation of sir Thomas Heneage.

The following account adds a good many facts to Stowe's narrative, and is besides particularly worthy of preservation on two other accounts; first, as giving sir William Pelham's bold speeches with something of the vigour and force which, judging from the results, they must have possessed; and, secondly, as affording an illustration of the way in which our worthy old chronicler compiled his very useful and generally very accurate narrative.

Stowe says that he " received advertisements " from Archer of the actions in the Low Countries, (p. 741.) Stowe's narrative was transferred into Holinshed, and acknowledged (iv. 340) to be derived from him by the usual marginal " John Stow," but at iv. p. 660, where the account in Holinshed is brought to an end, we read, " thus far having noted out of a booke penned by Henrie Archer." I have not found any trace of such a book, either printed or in MS.]

MS. HARL. NO. 285, FOL. 264.

Right worshipfull and my singular good master, may it please your worship to knowe, that we have gotten Deventrie, which, allthoughe under his excellencies government, yet of suche disposition of religion the burgomasters weare, that they bothe in other matters besides this have shewid themeselves that in truthe they are, for by no meanes could his excellencie intreat or comand a garyson their of foote, which being senne, and further howe necessary a garyson weare theire, beinge that and Lough are the onlly places wherby the enemy passed with victalles to Suthefeild, his excellencie determyned one this followinge.

One Twsday and Weddensday last sir William Standley comandid his soldiers to get into the towne by v, x, and xv, and not above, and their beinge kep themeselves close, which was wonderfully performid, and other captayns would give theire soldiers leave, so they weare well fornished with powder and shot, to passe to ease themeselves. In the towne all thes weare not once espyed, so covertly was it handlid; and further the councell of states and Master Kyllegry and others weare theire, who kept all the burgomasters in the councell though without neede. One Thursday, the xx of this instant, came sir William Standley in and divers others with some score of troops ; in the afternonne came the lord-marshall in with a good troope. At this tyme was gotten into the townne of knowen soldiers xij hundred. The lord-marshall beinge come to his lodginge, he sent for all the burgomasters in the eveninge, tellynge theme, his excellencie was past to Utricke, for that his grefe could not suffer hyme to staie so nere where so lovid a kinsman of his dyed, elles would he have senne theme ; further, that he had sent hym thether, for that they mad some staie of takynge a garryson, to knowe their intentes, whether they ment to take in anny or not, " and," said he, " dellay not, for bothe I have matters of great importance to goe about, and further, I must send word to his excellencie to Utricke your determinations, and to morowe viij of the cloke I will attend your answer ; dellay not therfor, but let me knowe your myndes. In the even he gave sir Williame Standley comandement, that beffor vij of the cloke in the fornoonne, that all should be redy in the market-place, which is marvellos fayre. This night did the burgomasters appoynt a treble wache, for in the townne of burgers that are soldiers are nere v thousand, I meane, that watche and ward, besides a number other. The gates weare very strongly kept, the streates weare all chaynid, but in the morninge our people got all the market-place at ther appoynted tyme. The burgomasters erlly, before vj, weare in councell. About or beffor vij the lord-marshall, with a trayne of gentellmen followinge hyme, went to the states-howse, straight knoked, and was [admitted] wheare all the burgomaters weare in councell. Straight, sir William Standley with some chossen soldiers came to the dore, knockid, entrid, left his men at the dore, all beinge in and appoynt. " I ame come," said the lord-marshall, " for an answer, and tell me straight." They stod as men not fully agred, but presently one of the pryncipallist slip away, which was bothe told the lord-marshall and further his name. Quothe the lord-marshall, " There is one of youe gonne ; fetche hyme straight hether, or, by the lyvinge God before whome I stand, theire is not one of youe shall passe with youre lyves awaie from this place." They fearinge sent for hyme, and he came. " Nowe tell me," saythe he, " wherfor youe this night have chaynid your streates, mad so stronge watche, your frendes and defendors beinge in the townne. Do youe thincke," saythe he, " youe have a people that are come overe to spend theire lives, theire goodes, and leave all they have, to be thus usid of youe, as to be betrayd amongst youe ? Nay, youe shall fynd us trusty to our frendes, and as poleticke as yourselves. Well," said he, " set your hands, and give overe your government to these men here nomynated, straight, dalley not ;" which they performyd. " Nowe," said he, " let one of youe goe to the wache, dyscharge theme, let theme unarme themselves, and passe to theire lodginges," which was donne. " Nowe," said he, " fetche me the keyes of the gates, and deliver theme me, and that straight, or, befor God, youe shall all dy." This donne, he sent theme to pryson, appoynted newe offecers, and brought this stobern townne in one day to a good safty. O great was the cry of woomen, thynckynge they should have bynne sackyd, but all theire I hope is quiet. Theire is in this townne victalles for thre yeare without any relleif; for certeyn a townne, sir, (but that they are compelled for caus of the enemy to kep in theire cattaylle,) most fayre, stronge, and large; as fayre a compact townne as I have senne. My lord-marshall by the Dutcheman that brought this newes, with his lettres to his excellencie, was wonderfully praysed, " He did it," said he, " with suche wisdome and corage as was to be wondered at ;" and further he added, " his excellencie mought be happy to have suche a man about hyme." Sir Phillip Sidney one Monday dyed, to the great hevines of his excellencie and our holle people here, but he dyed so godly as all wondred, and most praysed God for it. County Hollocke was shot at the sconce throughe the cheke, a small hurt, yet is very lycke to dy. Sir, I seace, prayinge God evere to blesse your worship with my honorable lady. Utricke, this xxiijth of October, your poore and ever bond sarvant,

HENRY ARCHER.

I have sent youe divers letters of late, which I thincke, the wynd beinge contrary, will stay theare comynge.

Addressed,
    To the right worshipfull
      his singular good master
      sir Thomas Hennige, thresurer
      of her majesties chamber, thes.

VII.

LETTERS RELATING TO THE ILLNESS OF SIR PHILIP SYDNEY'S WIDOW.

[These are the letters referred to at page 446.]

THE EARL OF LEYCESTER TO MR. SECRETARY WALSYNGHAM.

22ND DECEMBER, 1586. HARL. MS. NO. 285. FOL. 266. ORIG.

I am hartyly sorry for any further vysitacion to com to that howse, for I must every way be partaker therof. But you and I must yeld to His gracious chastysment who knoweth best what ys fytt for us both.

I confes that I se what you fynde, and I fele lyke you have founde. The Lord that inflycteth us here with sharpnes can, and I know wyll, recompence us elleswhere x, xx, and xxx fold, to our everlasting joye and comfort. Wherfore I pray for you, as for myself, that the same Lord wyll contynew us in strength, and strengthen us in pacyence to receyve His blessyd wyll, as becomyth us. The lettre you sent me I wyll suspend my opinion, albeytt I fear he ys not the man we thought him. God grant us his peace, and the rest of our yeres to pass in his fear, and so to his blessyd protectyon I leave ye. Hast this 22 of December, 1586.

Yours assured,
R. LEYCESTER.

Addressed
    To my honorable frend Mr. secretarye
    Walsingham.

THE EARL OF LEYCESTER TO MR. SECRETARY WALSYNGHAM.

23RD DECEMBER, 1586. HARL. MS. NO. 285, FOL. 268. ORIG.

I cannott be quyett tyll I may know how my daughter doth amend, wyshing hir even as to my none child, which, God wylling, I shall always esteme hir to be. I wold gladly make a start to you, but to morrow king Antonio comes hether, but my hart ys ther with you, and my prayers shall goe to God for you and for yours. Ther ys a lettre com from the Scottish queen that hath wroght tears, but I trust shall doe no further harm, albeyt the delay ys so daungerous. Of all thinges that ys to be advertysed I know Mr. secretary Davyson doth wryte to you, therefore I wyll leave to trowble you, and commytt you to the Lord. From Grenwich xxiij of December.

Your assured frend,
R. LEYCESTER.

Bycause I dowbt of your spedy repayr hether I pray you send my ij leases, Mr. Secretary, to se what may be donn.

Addressed
    To the right honorable Mr. secretary Walsingham.

VIII.

QUESTIONS TOUCHING THE EXECUTION OF SIR PHILIP SIDNEYES WILL.

NOVEMBER 1586. LANSD. MS. 50, NO. 89. A CONTEMPORARY COPY.

[This is the case and opinion to which secretary Walsyngham refers in his letter printed at p. 456.]

OPINION.	CASE.
I. The will hath some difficultie in it.	I. What force the will is of for the sale of land for paiment of debtes.
Only the feesimple land.	What land may bee sould, and what

APPENDIX.

OPINION.	CASE.
The assurance is only by bargaine and sale at the comon lawe. The buyers wil hardly content themselues without collaterall assurance by statute, recognisance, or obligation.	assurance made to the contentment of the buyers.
II. As much as is entayled to the heire mayle. A full third part to be set owt by he surveyor of the wardes. She clameth dower of a third part and waueth her ioynter.	II. What land shall goe to the heire male, what to her majestie for hir thirds,[a] and what to his wife for her ioynter.
III. Only upon the feesimple lands.	III. Upon which of the portions the annuities are to be charged.
IV. Nothing done to alter his will or make void the same or hinder anie sale.	IV. If the liverie of sir Phillip haue not been sued, then what alteration it worketh in the disposing of the land.

RICHARD SHUTLWORTH.
JHON BROGRAUE.
THOMAS FARMER.
THOMAS FLEMING.
ALEXANDER FISHER.

[a] Sir Philip having survived his father only a few months, during which time he had been absent from England, the payments due to her majesty for reliefs and other incidents to lands held *in capite* had not been accounted for. Other similar payments now accrued on his own death.

NOTES AND CORRECTIONS.

Page 9, *line* 17.—For *her*, read *his*.

Page 21, *line* 8.—*Her majestie meaneth he would deceive her.* In Additional MS. No. 4105, fo. 1, is the following note of a letter written by the earl of Leycester to Walsyngham, made by Dr. Birch, from the original in the State Paper Office, in which the earl alludes to this accusation and the receipt of Letter XIII:—

" 7. December.—From Harwich to Secretary Walsingham.

" Complains that the queen should be persuaded by some persons that he had deceived her in money matters. I think I may justly say I have been the only cause of more gain to her coffers than all her chequer-men have been. But so is the hap of some, that all they do is nothing, and others that do nothing, do all, and have all the thanks. But I would this were all the grief I carry with me. But God is my comfort, and on him I cast all. There is no honesty in this world beside."

" Receives as wise a letter from lord Willoughby as ever he had read. Prays that God may open her majesty's eyes, that they may behold her present state indeed, and the wonderful means that God doth offer unto her. If she lose these opportunities who can look for other but dishonour and destruction."

" That the lord-treasurer had written him a most hearty, comfortable, letter touching this voyage, and promising his assistance in the supply of all wants."

" Complains that he has not had one penny from the queen towards all his charges."

Page 25, *line* 8.—" *This vi. of December,* 1585." The earl replied to this letter on the 7th, " from on ship-board." After thanks for Burghley's letter, the earl told him that he must trouble him often because he found "Mr. secretary utterly discouraged to deal any more in any of these causes." Addit. MS. No. 4105, fo. 2. Walsingham was such a near ally of Leycester's that the queen paid little regard to his advice in any matter affecting the earl.

Page 27, *line* 33.—For *sir*, read *St.*

Page 33, *line* 12.—For *Ruddykyrke*, read *Meddykyrke.*

Page 34, *line* 9.—" *This Sonday morning at Delph.*" On the following morning, before his departure for the Hague, the earl wrote to the lord-treasurer a letter which, judging from Birch's note of it, was nearly an echo of this to Walsyngham. Addit. MS. 4105, fo. 3.

Page 34, *Letter XVI.*—This letter has been ranged amongst those of December, 1585, but being an answer to the one which precedes it, which is dated at Delf, on the 26th December, it was, no doubt, not written until early in the following month. The draft from which it is printed is undated.

Page 44, *the last line but one.*—" *The king of Spayn maketh all the provisions that he can possible to mak a mighty navy for a great army to come by sea.*" Dr. Birch gives a note of Leycester's reply to this letter, dated the 29th January, 1585-6. It contained the following passages in allusion to the Spanish preparations for the armada :—

" No doubt but the king of Spain's preparation by sea be great, for so it standeth him upon. But I know that all that he and his friends can make are not able to match with her majesty's power by sea, if it please her to use the means that God hath given her. In this country they esteem no more of his power by sea than of six fisher-boats of Rye." Undertakes upon two months' warning to furnish the queen from the Low Countries with a navy which Spain shall not dare to encounter. (Addit. MS. No. 4105, fo. 3-4.)

Page 46, *line* 24.—For *Auchuson*, read *Anchuson.*

Page 51, *line* 1.—"*All these have lyne at Margat, in Kent, ever since to this* 12*th January.*" On the 29th January, the earl wrote that sir Thomas Cecill had arrived at the Brill. (Addit. MS. No. 4105, fo. 3.)

Page 57, *the last line but one.* "*Leoninus began an oration to me.*" In a subsequent letter the earl described Leoninus as "a very grave, wise, old man." (Addit. MS. No. 4105, fo. 5.)

Page 83, *line* 7.—*Daniel Rogers.* A letter printed at p. 326, which I had not observed when I added the note in this page, seems to render it doubtful whether some other Rogers was not here meant. The person desired by the earl was "Rogers that was with Shenks, not D. Rogers the lawyer."

Page 100, *line* 26.—*I founde her very well content I should receive anythinge from their handes whatsoever.* From the following note, by Dr. Birch, of a letter written by the earl to Walsyngham, on the evening before his departure for the Low Countries, it is clear that up to that time the queen had not released the earl from her prohibition to take any oath to the people of the Low Countries, or to procure any enlargement of his authority from them.

"1585, 3 Decem.—To Secretary Walsingham. Sends him a letter to her majesty open. "You may speak with Mr. vice-chamberlain also therein. I have not stood upon any particular matter in it. But the cause is such as truly I had as lief be dead as be in the case I shall be in if this restraint hold for taking the oath there, or give [gaining?] more authority than I see her majesty would I should. I trust ye all will hold hard for this; or else banish me England withall. I perceive by your message your peace with Spain will go fast on, but this is not the way. I go early in the morning away."—(Addit. MS. 4105. fo. 1.)

Page 129, *line* 15, *boddeleye.*—This is printed as it stands in the MS., but it should clearly be *Boddelye.* See pp. 326, 367, 383, 405.

Page 131, *line* 29.—*almost* xl. *good shippes and good cromsters.* Cromsters, as Mr. Thoms has pointed out to me, are shewn by the origin of the name to have been vessels with crooked prows. I find the word in " The actions of the Lowe Countries," written by sir Roger Williams, " Having prepared a navy of some hundred saile of ships, hoyes, and *crumsters.*"—(p. 118.)

Page 154, *line* 16.—"*Lettres sent by Mr. Davison*, 1° *Feb.*" See a note of this letter in Addit. MS. 4105, fo. 4.

Page 158, *line* 6.—" *Lettres of the* 18 *February.*" See a note of this letter in Addit. MS. 4105, fo. 5.

Page 161, *last line.*—"*Thomas Sherley.*" Leycester described Sherley as his " cousin." See a note of a letter dated " the last of February," and probably addressed to the lord-treasurer, in Addit. MS. 4105, fo. 6.

Page 177, *line* 10.—" the xvij. of Marche." The following note of an important letter, bearing this same date, and written by the earl probably to the lord-treasurer, occurs in Addit. MS. 4105, fo. 7.

" March 17.—Complains of her majesty's continuing her displeasure towards him, and refusing to hear his justification. That his acceptance of the government was of the utmost importance, and if he had not accepted it when he did, this whole state had been gone and wholly lost."

" Sir Thomas Heneage, on the 14th of that month, delivered a very sharp letter from her majesty to the council of state here beside his message, myself being present, for so was her majesty's pleasure as he said."

" That he had not heard from the court but twice in thirteen weeks."

" That he could be no fit man to serve there, his disgrace was so great. That his heart was broken. That he had Halifax law, to be condemn'd first, and inquir'd upon after."

Page 220, *line* 3.—*Haultree* is so in the MS., but it should evidently be *Daultree.* See p. 185, 237.

Page 221, *line* 16.—*Vindon.* This word is so in the MS., but it should probably be *Emden.*

Page 238, *line 2 of note.*—" *Segar the herald.*" In addition to what is stated in the note, p. 32, upon the subject of the heralds in attendance upon Leycester, I find in Addit. MS. 4105, fo. 9, the following note of a letter from the earl, dated 8th April, 1586.

"Lancaster the herald, who came over with him, deceased, his lordship desires Somerset, or some other pursuivant, may be sent over."

Page 256, *line* 13.—*Boddyby.* It is thus written in the MS., but it should probably be *Boddyly.* See pp. 326, 367, 383, 405.

Page 279, *line* 4.—*This bearer's master.* This is an allusion to Davison. See p. 332.

Page 280, *line* 12.—"*I came myself hether uppon sir Thomas Henneage letters to meet him here at Arnham.*" Leycester wrote from Arnheim, on the 23rd May, a very humble and pitiable letter of supplication to the queen. In the matter in which his " dread sovereign" " took exceptions" to his conduct, he states to her, " I do yield myself to all you will and please," appealing only to her kindly consideration, upon the ground that he had left her presence and "all, yea all that may be imagined," upon a ground which her "most wise counsellors" thought to be of greatest moment. She, on the contrary, he adds, had left him "for very little, even to the uttermost of all hard fortune." (Addit. MS. 4105, fo. 1.) A note of a subsequent letter, dated 27th May, shews what were the effects of the first alterations in sir Thomas Heneage's instructions. (Ibid.)

Page 293, *line* 20.—For *ser* read *Mr.* See p. 306. The MS. is imperfect, and what remains of the *Mr.* was mistaken.

Page 338, *note b.*—*The design was attributed to Sydney.* But erroneously; the earl says that prince Maurice suggested it, but desired that it might be kept secret from every one but sir Philip Sydney. Sir Philip stipulated that he and his band should lead the attack. (Addit. MS. 4105, fo. 8.)

Page 407, *line* 5.—For *Him* read *him.*

INDEX.

ABYNDON, Edward, 399.
Alon, 265.
Ameron, 380.
Amersford, 261, 346.
Amsterdam, 46, 296, 357; the earl's reception into, 476; description of, 477.
Anchuson, 46, 127.
Antwerp, 52, 66, 91, 262, 263, 287, 346, 379; siege of, 2; surrendered, 3; works carrying on secretly there, 45, 66.
Aquila, don John d', 245, 253.
Arnheim, 264, 265, 266, 280, 346, 350.
Ashton, sir Walter, 9.
Astell, Henry, 34.
Atye, Mr. Leycester's secretary, 37, 43, 44, 50, 51, 104, 258, 261, 269, 289, 294, 297, 313, 314, 323, 329, 332, 359, 363, 367, 375, 381, 388.
Audley, lord, 379.
Avyer, Mr. 40.
Axel, 346, 348, 371, 399, 416; capture of, 337.

Balford (Balfour?) 347.
Barber, Mr. 295.
Barker, Mr. 279.
Barkley, Edward, 304.

Basset, sir Arthur, 224.
Berck, 346, 350; besieged, 383, 393, 400, 413; relieved, 413.
Berckshoofe, 265, 270, 280.
Bergen öp Zoom, 262, 266, 320.
Berrhee, Jehan, 90.
Bettowe, the, 265, 270.
Bingham, sir Richard, 136;——463.
Bird, John, 91.
Bodenham, 319.
Bodley, 129, 256, 326, 367, 383, 405, 485, 487.
Bomell, 265, 287, 289, 315.
Borough, lord, 302, 411.
Bouillon, duke de, 53, 54, 89, 93.
Brabant, 275, 315.
Breda, 338.
Brest, 412.
Brill, the, 10, 51, 201, 205, 277, 296, 318, 354, 461—464.
Brown, Mr. 40.
Browne, sir Valentine, 273.
Bruges, 40, 315, 346, 359.
Brune, 382.
Brussels, 262, 287.
Buckhurst, lord, 161, 364, 378.
Burghley, lord, his farewell letter to Leycester, x; his interference with the queen to moderate her anger with

Leycester, xviii, xix, xxi, xxii, xxiii; general character of his letters, xxiii, xxxvii.
Burgrave, ——, 363, 422, 425, 466; Lodovick, 364.
Burrough, Stephen, 461.
Butler, sir Philip, 444.
Buys, Paul, 47, 423; Leycester's conduct to, xlii, 310, 312, 386, 425; character of, 33, 130, 291, 303, 310, 339; secret practices alleged against, 305, 311, 327, 362, 372, 376; arrested, 352, 364; the queen orders him to be brought to trial or liberated, 436.

Cæsar, an Italian surgeon, xliii, 409.
Calais, 56, 275, 317.
Candyss, Richard, 151, 160, 420.
Carey, Edmund, 256.
Carsey, captain, 218, 232.
Casimir, prince, elector palatine, 49, 52, 306, 408, 421.
Cecill, sir Thomas, appointed governor of the Brill, 10; departs for his government, 44, 45, 50, 92; has leave to return to England for his health, 183; but is to resume his government, 192; defenceless state of the Brill, 201; arrival in England, 205; sent by the queen to the states, 314; his jealousy of Pelham, 379, 380; resigns the Brill, 411; returning home, 444.
Champigny, 200, 231, 240.
Charles, (Walsyngham's man,) 289, 300.
Chartley, 9.
Chichester, sir John, 224.
Church, Harry, 463.

Clerk, Dr. Bartholomew, 16, 26, 33, 37, 58, 75, 375, 422, 477.
Colchester, 461.
Cooke, (clarencieux,) 32; sir Thomas, 444; ——, 429.
Cooman, Jehan, 90.
Cosmo, 290, 319.
Cox, 291, 305, 360.

Darcy, Mr. 283, 298.
Dautrye, Mr. 185, 237, 298, 300.
Davison, William, sent home by Leycester to explain the reasons of his acceptance of the government, xiv, 80; delay in his arrival, xvi, xvii, arrives in London, xvii, 117; his interviews with the queen, xviii, 117—126, 142; reply to Leycester's accusations, xix, 168, 206, 332—336; is appointed secretary to assist Walsyngham, 343, 451.
Delft, 31, 34, 37.
Denbigh, 413.
Denmark, king of, encourages the German princes to assist the king of Navarre, 48; answer to application for assistance to the Low Countries, 116, 128, 133, 407; his embassy to England, 259, 260; rumour of his election as king of the Romans, 390.
Dennys, Maurice, 183.
Deventer, 140; the garrisoning of, 446.
Doesburg, siege of, 400; taken, 406, 416.
Dort, 29, 30, 31, 37, 466.
Douglas, Archibald, 315, 328.
Doyly, D. 6.

Drake, sir Francis, 42, 48, 51, 173, 187, 191, 199, 223, 315, 381.
Dubaud, 309.
Duddeley, Thomas, 27, 111, 295, 413.
Dunkirk, 14, 39, 275, 359.
Dyer, Andrew, 230.
——, Edward, 230.
Dygges, Thomas, 135.

Edrington, 302.
Egmont, count, 286.
Elizabeth, queen of England, her unwillingness to assist the people of the Low Countries, vii.; she suspends the earl's proceedings, ix, 4; her anger at his acceptance of the government, xiv, 95, 96, 104, 118; she sends Heneage to him with an angry message, xvii, 105; her interviews with Davison, xviii, 118; with Sherley, xix, 171; with Vavasour, xxi, 195; qualifies Heneage's instructions, xxi, 196, 204; her displeasure with him and letter thereon, xxiii, 240, 243; she refuses to allow him to return home until he had executed her directions, xxiii; her violent language towards Leycester, xxxii, 112, 118, 151, 172, 199; general character of her conduct in reference to Leycester's proceedings, xxxiv.
Elten, 408.
Emden, 295, 302, 359, 375, 381, 398, 486; count of, 127, 129, 136, 156, 158.
Essex, earl of, 379, 380, 391, 416, 444, 464.
Exeter, gaol-fever there, 224.

Fenton, secretary, 344.
Fitzwilliams, Bryan, 304, 328.
Flowerdew, baron, 224.
Fludde, Mr. 37.
Flushing, 10, 31, 39, 262, 277, 433, 452, 461, 462, 463, 464.
Fotheringay, 412, 439.
Frankfort, 52.
Fremyn, Mr. 388.

Ghent, 315, 359.
Gertruydenburg, 391, 394.
Gilpyn, 33.
Goodrowse, ——, 174, 176.
Gorcum, 315, 357.
Gorge, Mr. 38.
——, Nicholas, 42, 293, 306.
——, Thomas, 449, 450, 451, 455.
Grafigny, Aug. 231, 246, 250, 289, 319.
Grave, attempted by the enemy, 172; besieged, 178, 189, 213; relieved by Hohenlohe and Norris, 218, 225, 245, 251; besieged by the prince of Parma, 257; assaulted, 265, 270, 280; taken, 284, 287, 291.
Graveling, 359.
Gravesend, 463.
Gray, master of, offers to levy troops for the earl in Scotland, 179, 186, 220, 223, 292, 348, 361, 396; as to an imprest for them, 233, 322; advised to forego his intention, 275, 281; the queen objects to his employment, 343.
Gresier, captain, 417.
Grey of Wilton, Arthur lord, 55, 56, 78, 259, 302, 304, 449, 450, 452, 445.

Grytry, Monsieur de, 52, 133, 139.

Haggerstone, captain, 322, 343, 347.
Hague, the, 30, 46, 347.
Hamburgh, 129.
Hamilton, Davy, 290.
Harlingham, 296, 354.
Harryngton, sir Henry, 183, 185.
Harwich, x, 461, 462, 464.
Hatton, sir Christopher, 36, 112, 113, 118, 175, 305.
——, Mr. 338; sir William, 416, 417.
Hawkins, ——, 463.
Haydon, Mr. 397.
Hemart, baron, 284, 287, 288, 303; surrenders Grave, 284; his trial, 289, 301, 302; execution, 309, 310; Leycester's conduct to, xliii, 285.
Heneage, sir Thomas, sent by the queen with an angry message to Leycester, xvii, 105, 110, 113, 118, 122, 124, 142, 152; his proceedings, xxi, 149, 189, 206, 207, 210, 211, 226; dissatisfaction of the queen with him, xxii, 241, 243; she refuses to allow him to return home until he had executed her orders, xxiii, 267; his consequent return to Arnheim and proceedings there, xxiii, 280, 473, 487; arrival in England, 307.
Herle, William, 76, 221, 359.
Herns, Grant, 76.
Heydon, ——, 375.
Hoby, Sir Edward, 11.
Hohenlohe, Count, 119, 289, 338, 349, 378; characters of, xl, 61, 74, 134, 245, 252, 339, 372, 446; relieves Grave, 218, 221; takes two forts, 234; and Berkshoof, 280; assists at the trial of Hemart, 300, 309; his regard for Pelham, 374; cause of his coolness towards Leycester, 388; quarrel with Edward Norris, 391, 394, 473; prevented full success at Zutphen, 417.
Holstocke, ——, 463.
Holy, Jacob Muys Van, 30, 115.
Huddlestone, Richard, 397, 433, 446.
Huddy, ——, 304.
Hunsdon, Lord, 11.
Hunt, the auditor, 155, 191.
Hyman, ——, 148, 187.

Irish volunteers, levy of for the Low Countries, 26, 179, 180.

Jentile, John, 213, 254.
Jermyn, sir Robert, 114, 410.
Jones, Henry, 440, 441.

Keith, sir William, 52.
Killigrew, 390, 394, 397, 420.
——, Henry, 16, 26, 32, 37, 50, 213, 375, 434.
Kingsmill, Mr. 330.
Knewstubs, 238.
Knolls, William, 51.

Lee, 463.
Leoninus, 46, 57, 58.

Leycester, countess of, 112, 144.
Leycester, Robert earl of: his intentions on going to the Low Countries, x; his preparations suspended by the queen, ix, 5; his departure, x, 21, 25, 461; landing at Flushing, xi, 464; proceeds to Middleburgh, xi, 465; to Dort, 31, 466; Rotterdam, xi, 466; Delph, 31; Amsterdam, xi, 476; the Hague, 46; rejoicings on his arrival, xi, xii, 31, 84; the government tendered to him, xiii, 57; he accepts it, xiii, 63; sends Davison home to explain his reasons to the queen, xiv, 77, 80; endeavours to divert the queen's anger towards Davison, xix, 163, 165; his complaints and Davison's reply, xix, 168; sends sir Thomas Sherley to the queen, xix, 171; his proceedings with Heneage, xxii, xxiii, 189, 226; with the states-general, xxiv; his military proceedings, xxv—xxx; general character of his letters, xxxvii; impression produced by them as to his character, xliii.
Leyden, 46, 49.
Liege, 320.
Lloyd, ——, 26.
Lope, Andreas de, 289.
Lovell, Thomas, 467.
Luneburg, 390.
Luytesforte, 265, 270.

Maestricht, 320.
Maitland of Lethington, 53.
Mallorey, 74.
Manningtree, 461.

Mansfeld, count, 288, 363, 370.
Margate, 51, 463.
Martin, alderman, 41, 155.
Martine, 438, 439.
Martino, 288.
Mary queen of Scots, removal from Tutbury to Chartley, 9; to Fotheringay, 412; warrant for her execution sealed in 1569, xliv, 431; her death urged by Leycester, 431, 447.
Maurice, prince, 14, 19, 73, 349, 376, 378, 465, 466; character of, xli, 61 119, 374; is present at the taking of Axel, 338, 487; cause of the coolness between him and Leycester, 388, 426; suggested as governor in Leycester's absence, 452.
Meddykyrke, 33, 484.
Meetkirke, 33, 74.
Mellin, 266.
Melvyn, Robert, 53.
Menin, character of, 409; objects of his mission to England, 418, 422, 424, 425, 442, 443.
Merchant-adventurers, enlargement of their privileges, 145, 146, 147; letter from their resident at Middleburgh, 439.
Meurs and Nienar, count de, 119, 140, 141, 309, 349, 372, 380, 407; countess, 217, 364.
Michaell, Dr. 336.
Middleburgh, 28, 31, 38, 271, 305, 308, 398, 441, 455, 461, 464, 465, 466.
Minster, 463.
Morgan, coronel, 302, 353, 392.
Motte, La, count, 286.
Mountjoy, lord, 143.
Munster, plantation of, 273, 315.

Nassau, William count of, 61, 79.
Navarre, king of, 48, 52, 129, 279, 361.
Nevers, duke de, 184, 220, 233.
Nieuport, 40, 359.
Nimeguen, 262, 265, 266, 270, 280.
Nixhus, 229.
Norris, sir Edward, 301, 391, 392, 394; correspondence with count Hohenlohe, 473.
———, sir John, sent into the Low Countries with an English auxiliary force, 3; departure to Utrecht with the English horse, 88; his character censured by Walsyngham, 222; relieves Grave in conjunction with Hohenlohe, 218, 225; recovers of a wound, 234; character of, xlii, 264, 301, 306, 379, 385; his conduct in reference to a quarrel between count Hohenlohe and Edward Norris, 391, 392, 394; his proposed revocation, 305, 306, 403, 404; his conduct at Zutphen, 414, 416; reconciled to the earl, 430.
North, Roger lord, 75, 114, 193, 195, 379, 411, 417.
Nuys, 266, 315; threatened to be besieged, 167; besieged, 350; taken, 363, 368, 369, 370.

Orange, prince of, his assassination, 1; his children, 14.
Ortell, 66, 130, 156, 230, 311, 312, 364, 435.
Ostend, 39, 72, 79, 167, 277, 464.
Ouvry MS. account of, i, ii, iii.

Pace, Lewis de, 137 160.
Palavicino, sir Horatio, 104, 133, 136, 139, 279, 306.
Palmer, 297.
Parma, prince of, besieges Antwerp, 1; which surrenders to him, 3; makes incursions into Zealand, 64; his disappointment on hearing of the earl's arrival in the Low Countries, 70, 71; rumours said to be given out by him, 71, 93; besieges Grave, 234, 235, 245, 257, 258; it surrenders, 284; proceeds to Venlo, 319; its gates are opened to him, 322; invests Nuys, 346; it is taken and utterly destroyed, 369; proceeds to Berck, 383; it is successfully defended by Schenck, 400, 413; the prince relinquishes the siege of Berck and succours Zutphen, 430.
Parrot, sir Thomas, 51, 416, 435?, 444.
Partridge of Kent, 40.
Payton, 392.
Pelham, sir William, the earl's anxiety to have his assistance, 28, 32, 78, 116, 128, 132, 136, 228, 250, 302, 304, 313; the queen's objections against his employment, 37, 45, 55, 125, 158, 222, 355; intended to be sent over, 238; his departure, 332, 343; arrival in the Low Countries, 346, 352; appointed marshal, 366, 388; joyfully received by the earl, 371, 374; jealousies of Norris and others, 379, 385; mixed up in a quarrel between count Hohenlohe and sir Edward Norris, 391, 394; wounded at the siege of Doesburg, 401, 407.
Perret, 435.

INDEX. 495

Pigott, 338.
Portsmouth, 51.
Powle, Henry, speaker and master of the rolls, fate of his MSS. iii.
Poyntz, Antony, 177, 198, 208.

Ralegh, sir Walter, 87, 207, 285; letter of, 193.
Ramelius, Henry, 260, 279, 407.
Rammekins, 10, 464.
Randolph, sir Thomas, 52, 179, 187, 269, 275, 315, 322.
Read, captain, 278, 302, 392, 417, 430.
Ringault, 435.
Robuckom, 309.
Rochelle, 279, 412.
Rogers, Daniel, 83, 326, 367, 383, 405, 484.
Rotterdam, 31, 37, 466.
Rous, Martin, 339.
Russell, sir William, 225, 236, 416, 330.

St. Aldegonde, 3, 27, 33, 36, 49, 73, 74, 312.
Salisbury, Ralph, 256.
Salisbury, ——, 223; Thomas, 399, 413.
Sandwich, 461.
Saxe, duke of, 48, 129, 132.
Schenck, sir Martin, 79, 141, 227, 265; takes Werle, 139, 167, 475; garrisons Nuys, 167; is knighted by Leycester, 239; his lieutenant sallies from Venlo, 244, 252; takes Mellin, 265; erects a fort at Tolhouse, 270; attempts to get into Venlo, 319, 368; defends Berck, 383, 400, 413.
Seburo, 30, 115, 156, 406, 413.
Segar (portcullis), 32.

Seguro, 32, 48, 133.
Sevilly, de, 53, 54, 89.
Sherley, sir Thomas, sent into England by Leycester, 150, 156, 158; reports his proceedings to the earl, 159, 171, 180; subsequent employment for the earl in England, 195, 197, 199; returns to the Low Countries, 204, 274, 344, 358, 361, 397; appointed temporarily as treasurer, 433, 440, 441, 447, 448.
Simeie, princess, 213, 254.
Sire, Stephen le, 157.
Sluys, 38, 39, 72, 286, 346.
Smyth, sir John, 93.
Spain, king of, (Philip II.) preparations to invade England, 41, 53, 67, 187; proceedings against the king of Navarre, 48; failure in procuring a loan, 223.
Stafford, sir Edward, 179, 314.
Stanley, Edward, 427, 428.
———, sir William, 183, 185, 219, 230, 237, 250, 257, 278, 291, 302, 344, 360, 417.
Stokes, John, 91.
Sussex, earl of, 264, 301.
Sydney, sir Philip, 8, 11, 33, 70, 142, 168, 177, 201, 275, 355, 391; out of favour with the queen, 116, 192, 345; takes Axel, 337; the contest of Zutphen, 414, 416; all danger of his wound past, 422; he is well amending, 429; the queen writes with her own hand to comfort him, 438; his death, 445; the queen's grief at his loss, 451; the state of his affairs, 453, 456, 457, 481; miscarriage of his widow, 480.
———, Robert, 338, 430.

Tergooss, 45.
Thomson, Richard, 212, 233, 316.
Tiry, captain, 186, 207.
Tolhouse, 270.
Treasurer, complaints against his accounts, 236, 264, 277, 298, 324, 353, 384.
Truchses, Gebhard, elector of Cologne, 15, 48, 129, 134; character of, xli, 372, 376; application for a pension for, 378, 388, 405.
Tutbury, 9.

Underhill, 34.
Unton, sir Henry, 307, 416, 417.
Utrecht, 46, 79, 134, 135, 140, 141, 222, 271, 289, 314, 350, 364, 368, 389, 391, 442, 445.

Valck, 33, 47; character of, 409; objects of his mission to England, 418, 422, 424, 425, 442, 443.
Vavasour, captain Thomas, 183, 187, 191, 197; letter of, 194.
Veall, captain, 80.
Venlo, 72, 319, 320, 328; captured by the prince of Parma, 323, 368.
Vyliers, 73, 74, 467.

Waghtenden, 346, 350.
Wallen, captain, 288.
Walsyngham, sir Francis : his endeavours to moderate the queen's anger towards Leycester, xv, xvii ; general character of his letters, xxxiii, xxxvi ; his conduct in reference to Sydney's debts, xlv.
Wanstead, 8.
Warde, Mr. 187.
Warwick, Ambrose earl of, 114, 183, 355; letter of, 150.
Wattes, John, 91.
Welch, 338.
Weldon, punished for libelling Leycester, 232.
Werle, taken by Schenck, 140.
Williams, sir Roger, 302, 319, 391, 392 ; wounded, 407; his conduct at Zutphen, 430.
Willoughby, lord, 116, 128, 130, 133, 338, 416, 452, 467.
Winter, sir William, 463.
Wolley, Mr. 343.
Woollen-trade, endeavour to procure a removal of the English staple in to the Low Countries, 126, 157, 160.
Wylford, Mr. 40, 79, 302.
Wylkes, Thomas, 343 ; his interview with the queen, 360 ; conduct in the Low Countries, 383, 388, 395; his return, 397 ; arrives in London, 411 ; sent again to the Low Countries, 420, 421 ; his instructions, 432, 448.

York, Rowland, 304, 416.

Zutphen, 408, 412; skirmish there, 413, 414, 416 ; capture of the forts, 427, 428.